The Blair Reader

Fifth Edition

EDITED BY

Laurie G. Kirszner
University of the Sciences in Philadelphia

Stephen R. Mandell
Drexel University

PEARSON

Prentice
Hall

Upper Saddle River, New Jersey 07458

Library of Congress Cataloging-in-Publication Data

The Blair reader / edited by Laurie G. Kirszner, Stephen R. Mandell.— 5th ed.
    p. cm.
Includes bibliographical references.
ISBN 0-13-185060-1
1. College readers.   2. English language—Rhetoric—Problems, exercises, etc.   3. Report writing—Problems, exercises, etc.   I. Kirszner, Laurie G.   II. Mandell, Stephen R.

PE1417.B54 2004
808'.0427—dc22

2004012613

Editor-in-Chief (Editorial): Leah Jewell
Editorial Assistant: Steve Kyritz
Editor-in-Chief (Development):
  Rochelle Diogenes
Developmental Editor: John Sisson
Production Liaison: Joanne Hakim
Executive Marketing Manager:
  Brandy Dawson
Marketing Assistant: Alison Peck
Senior Media Editor: Christy D. Schaack
Assistant Manufacturing Manager:
  Mary Ann Gloriande
Cover Art Director: Jayne Conte
Cover Design: Bruce Kenselaar
Cover Illustration/Photo: Deborah
  Dupont, "Ponte delle Callegheri",
  © 2004, www.DeborahDuPont.com

Director, Image Resource Center:
  Melinda Reo
Manager, Rights and Permissions: Zina
  Arabia
Manager, Visual Research: Beth Brenzel
**Manager, Cover Visual Research and
  Permissions:** Karen Sanatar
Image Permission Coordinator: Charles
  Morris
Photo Researcher: Rachel Lucas
Permissions Specialist: The Permissions
  Group
**Composition/Full-Service Project
  Management:** Karen Berry/
  Pine Tree Composition, Inc.
Printer/Binder: The Courier Companies

Credits and acknowledgments borrowed from other sources and reproduced, with permission, in this textbook appear on pages 783–790.

Pearson Education LTD., London
Pearson Education Singapore, Pte. Ltd
Pearson Education, Canada, Ltd
Pearson Education–Japan
Pearson Education Australia PTY, Limited
Pearson Education North Asia Ltd

Pearson Educación de Mexico, S.A.
  de C.V.
Pearson Education Malaysia, Pte. Ltd
Pearson Education, Upper Saddle River,
  New Jersey.

10 9 8 7 6 5 4 3 2 1
ISBN 0-13-185060-1

Contents

Topical Clusters

Note: Essays are listed in order of ascending page number.

Speeches

Note: Speeches are listed in alphabetical order.

Rhetorical Table of Contents

Note: Essays are listed alphabetically within categories.

Description

Process

Argument & Persuasion

Preface

After more than twenty-five years of teaching composition, we have come to see reading and writing are interrelated activities: if students are going to write effectively, they must also read actively and critically. In addition, we believe that writing is both a private and a public act. As a private act, it enables students to explore their feelings and reactions and to discover their ideas about a variety of subjects. As a public act, writing enables students to see how their own ideas fit into larger discourse communities, where ideas gain meaning and value. In college, we believe that students are enriched and engaged when they view the reading and writing they do as a way of participating in ongoing public discussions about subjects that matter to them. We created *The Blair Reader* to encourage students to contribute to these public discussions and to help them realize that their best ideas often take shape in response to the ideas of others.

Another reason we decided to write *The Blair Reader* was that we could not find a thematic reader that satisfied our needs as teachers. We—like you—expect compelling reading selections that involve instructors and students in spirited exchanges. We also expect readings that reflect the diversity of ideas that characterizes our society and questions that challenge students to respond critically to what they have read. In short, we expect a book that stimulates discussion and that encourages students to discover new ideas and to see familiar ideas in new ways. These expectations guided us as we initially developed *The Blair Reader* and as we worked on this fifth edition.

What's New in the Fifth Edition?

Our first goal for the fifth edition was to sharpen the focus of each thematic chapter, thereby expanding students' insight into the issue being discussed. In this process, we took into consideration the comments of the many teachers who generously shared their reactions to the fourth edition with us.

Next, we revised each chapter's Focus section, changing some questions to reflect contemporary concerns and adding new essays calculated to stimulate interest and classroom discussion. We also created two new thematic chapters, Chapter 5, "The Way We Live Now," which looks at contemporary American life, and Chapter 8, "Why We Work," which examines attitudes toward jobs and the workplace. To reflect our expanding emphasis on visual literacy, we added new images to the Focus section of each chapter. In Chapter 5, the entire Focus section now consists of a collection of visuals (followed by questions) that illustrates how men's and women's fashions have changed over the last hundred years. Finally, we refined and updated the suggestions for Internet research that appear at the end of each chapter.

As we worked on the fifth edition, we added readings designed to sharpen the focus of each chapter and to increase student interest and involvement. Among the selections that are new to this edition are Diane Ravitch's "Literature: Forgetting the Tradition," Goodwin Liu's "The Myth and Math of Affirmative Action," Christina Hoff Sommers's "For More Balance on Campuses," Louise Erdrich's "Two Languages in the Mind, but Just One in the Heart," Tim Robbins's "A Chill Wind Is Blowing in This Nation," Salmon Rushdie's "Reality TV: A Dearth of Talent and the Death of Morality," Henry Lewis Gates, Jr.'s "Delusions of Grandeur," Mona Charen's "Malpractice: By Lawyers," and Declan McCullagh's "Why Liberty Suffers in Wartime."

These and other new readings were chosen to introduce students to the enduring issues that they confront as students and as citizens. Whenever possible, we include readings that give students the historical context they need to understand a chapter's theme. For example, in Chapter 2, "Issues in Education," we include the classic essay "School Is Bad for Children" by John Holt; in Chapter 3, "The Politics of Language," we include "Learning to Read and Write" by Frederick Douglass; and in Chapter 7, "The American Dream," we include "Why the Americans Are So Restless in the Midst of Their Prosperity" by Alexis de Tocqueville. The result is a text that juxtaposes classic essays with provocative new pieces, thereby illustrating to students that ideas can continue to be exciting and relevant long after they appear in print.

The selections in this new edition of *The Blair Reader* represent a wide variety of rhetorical patterns and types of discourse as well as a variety of themes, issues, and positions. In addition to essays, *The Blair Reader* contains speeches, meditations, newspaper and magazine articles, and short stories and poems. The level of diction ranges from the relative formality of E. B. White's "Once More to the Lake" to the biting satire of Judy Brady's "Why I Want a Wife." Every effort has been made to include a wide variety of voices because we believe that students can best discover their own voices by becoming acquainted with the voices of others.

Resources for Students

We designed the apparatus in *The Blair Reader* to involve students and to encourage them to respond critically to what they read. Their responses can then become the basis for the more focused thinking that they will do when they write. In order to facilitate students' reading and writing, we have included the following features:

- **Introduction: Becoming a Critical Reader** explains and illustrates the process of reading and reacting critically to texts (including visual texts) and formulating varied and original responses.

- **Paired visuals** introduce each thematic chapter. These visuals engage students by encouraging them to find parallels and contrasts. In addition, they introduce students to the themes that they will be considering as they read the essays in the chapter.

- A brief introduction, **Preparing to Read and Write,** places each chapter's broad theme in a social or political context, enabling students to understand the issues being discussed. A list of questions at the end of these chapter introductions helps students to focus their responses to individual readings and to relate these responses to the chapter's larger issues.

- **Headnotes** that accompany each selection provide biographical information as well as insight into the writer's purpose.

- **Responding to Reading** questions that follow each selection address thematic and rhetorical considerations. By encouraging students to think critically, these questions help them to see reading as an interactive and intellectually stimulating process.

- A **Responding in Writing** prompt at the end of each selection gives students the opportunity to write an informal response to the selection.

- A **Focus** section in each chapter is introduced by a provocative question related to the chapter's theme, followed by a group of readings that take a variety of positions on the issue this question raises. The readings in this section encourage students to add their voices to the debate and demonstrate that complex issues elicit different points of view. The Focus section also includes a provocative image followed by **Responding to the Image** questions.

- A **Widening the Focus** feature lists essays in other chapters of the book that address the issues raised by the Focus question.

- **Writing** suggestions at the end of each chapter ask students to respond to the chapter's readings. In addition, an Internet research assignment, suggesting Web sites students can access to get more information about the chapter's Focus issue, follows these writing prompts.

- A **Rhetorical Table of Contents,** located at the front of the book on pages xxi–xxviii, groups the text's readings according to the way they arrange material: narration, description, process, comparison and contrast, and so on.

- **Topical Clusters,** narrowly focused thematic units (pp. viii–xx), offer students and teachers additional options for grouping readings.

Additional Resources for Instructors and Students

Instructor's Manual
(0-13-189608-3)

Because we wanted *The Blair Reader* to be a rich and comprehensive resource for instructors, a thoroughly revised and updated Instructor's Resource Manual has been developed to accompany the text. Designed to be a useful and all-inclusive tool, the manual contains teaching strategies, collaborative activities, and suggested answers for "Responding to Reading" questions. The manual includes Web and/or multimedia teaching resources for almost every reading. It also contains new questions for stimulating classroom discussions of the new chapter-opening images.

Companion Website: www.prenhall.com/kirszner

The Companion Website provides additional chapter exercises, links, and activities that reinforce and build upon the material presented in the text. It now features the Net Search, a list of topic- or chapter-specific search terms with links to search engines, and Research Navigator™.
   Website features include:

- Additional essay and short-answer questions for every reading

- Web links that provide additional contextual information

- Visual analysis questions for each chapter

- Web destinations for each essay topic

The New American Webster Handy College Dictionary
(0-13-147154-6)

FREE when packaged with the text.

Roget's College Thesaurus in Dictionary Form, The New American, Revised and Enlarged Edition
(0-13-147152-X)

FREE when packaged with the text.

iBook Express

Visit www.prenhall.com/ibx to view the NEW all-inclusive English resource. iBook Express contains basic course management tools, diagnostic tests, editing and grammar exercises, *The New York Times* Archive, a complete research guide and plagiarism tutorial, and many other useful resources. FREE when packaged with the text.

Prentice Hall Pocket Readers

These readers include essays that have withstood the test of time and teaching, making them the perfect companions for any writing course. A *Prentice Hall Pocket Reader* is the perfect way to bring additional readings to your writing classes at no additional cost to your students when packaged with this text (limit one free reader per package).

THEMES: A Prentice Hall Pocket Reader (0-13-144355-0)
ARGUMENT: A Prentice Hall Pocket Reader (0-13-189525-7)
LITERATURE: A Prentice Hall Pocket Reader (0-13-144354-2)
PATTERNS: A Prentice Hall Pocket Reader (0-13-144355-0)

Acknowledgments

The Blair Reader is the result of a fruitful collaboration between the two of us, between us and our students, between us and Prentice Hall, and between us and you—our colleagues who told us what you wanted in a reader.

At Prentice Hall we want to thank Corey Good, Senior Acquisitions Editor, and Leah Jewel, Editor-in-Chief. We also appreciate the efforts of Steve Kyritz, Editorial Assistant, as well as our copyeditor, Patricia Daly.

John Sisson, our developmental editor, spent a great deal of time and effort making this book as good as it is. His patience, professionalism, and hard work are greatly appreciated. At Pine Tree Composition, Inc., we want to thank Karen Berry, Production Editor, for seeing this book through to completion.

In preparing *The Blair Reader*, Fifth Edition, we benefited at every stage from the assistance and suggestions from colleagues from across the country: Derek Soles, Drexel University; Stephen R. Armstrong, Eastern Carolina University; Mary Williams, Midland College; Janet Eldred, University of Kentucky, Marguerite Parker, Eastern Carolina University; Pamela Howell, Midland College; Patricia Baldwin, Pitt Community College; Tara Hubschmitt, Lakeland College; and David Holper, College of the Redwoods.

We would also like to thank the following reviewers: Angie Pratt, Montgomery College; Chere Berman, College of the Canyons; Paul Northam, Johnson County Community College; Jennifer Vanags,

Johnson County Community College; CC Ryder, West L.A. College; John Lucarelli, Community College of Allegheny County; Linda A. Archer, Green River Community College; Stephen H. Wells, Community College of Allegheny County; Terry Jolliffe, Midland College; Anthony Armstrong, Richland College; Dimitri Keriotis, Modesto Junior College; Robert G. Ford, Houston Community College; Carla L. Dando, Idaho State University; Lori Ann Stephens, Richland College; Debra Shein, Idaho State University; Cara Unger, Portland Community College; Dr. Emily Dial-Driver, Rogers State University; Jesse T. Airaudi, Baylor University; Camilla Mortensen, University of Oregon; Kathryn Neal, York Technical College; K. Siobhan Wright, Carroll Community College; Rosemary Day, Ph.D., Albuquerque Community College; Jacob Agatucci, Central Oregon Community College; Peggy Cole, Ph.D., Arapahoe Community College; and James Jenkins, Mt. San Antonio College.

On the home front, we once again "round up the usual suspects" to thank—Mark, Adam, and Rebecca Kirszner and Demi, David, and Sarah Mandell. And of course, we thank each other: it really has been a "beautiful friendship."

INTRODUCTION: BECOMING
A CRITICAL READER

In his autobiographical essay "The Library Card" (p. 476), Richard Wright describes his early exposure to the world of books. He says, "The plots and stories in the novels did not interest me so much as the point of view revealed. I gave myself over to each novel without reserve, without trying to criticize it; it was enough for me to see and feel something different. Reading was like a drug."

It is a rare person today for whom reading can hold this magic or inspire this awe. Most of us take the access to books for granted. As a student, you've probably learned to be pragmatic about your reading. In fact, "reading a book" may have come to mean just reading assigned pages in a textbook. Whether the book's subject is modern American history, principles of corporate management, or quantum mechanics, you probably tend to read largely for information, expecting a book's ideas to be accessible and free of ambiguity and the book to be clearly written and logically organized.

In addition to reading textbooks, however, you also read essays and journal articles, fiction and poetry (in print or online). These present special challenges because you read them not just for information but also to discover your own ideas about what the writer is saying—what the work means to you, how you react to it, why you react as you do, and how your reactions differ from the responses of other readers. And because the writers express opinions and communicate impressions as well as facts, your role as a reader must be more active than it is when you read a textbook. Here, reading becomes not only a search for information, but also a search for meaning.

Reading and Meaning

Like many readers, you may assume that the meaning of a text is hidden somewhere between the lines and that you only have to ask the right questions or unearth the appropriate clues to discover exactly what the writer is getting at. But reading is not a game of hide-and-seek in which you search for ideas that have been hidden by the writer. As current reading theory demonstrates, meaning is created by the interaction of a reader with a text.

One way to explain this interactive process is to draw an analogy between a text—a work being read—and a word. A word is not the natural equivalent of the thing it signifies. The word *dog*, for example, does not evoke the image of a furry, four-legged animal in all parts of the world. To speakers of Spanish, the word *perro* elicits the same mental picture *dog* does in English-speaking countries. Not only does the word *dog* have meaning only in a specific cultural context, but even within that context it evokes different images in different people. Some people may picture a collie, others a poodle, and still others a particular pet.

Like a word, a text can have different meanings in different cultures—or even in different historical time periods. Each reader brings to the text associations that come from the cultural community in which he or she lives. These associations are determined by readers' experience and education as well as by their ethnic group, class, religion, gender, and many other factors that contribute to how they view the world. Each reader also brings to the text expectations, desires, and prejudices that influence how he or she reacts to and interprets it. Thus, it is entirely possible for two readers to have very different, but equally valid, interpretations of the same text. (This does not mean, of course, that a text can mean whatever any individual reader wishes it to mean. To be valid, an interpretation must be supported by what actually appears in the text.)

To get an idea of the range of possible interpretations that can be suggested by a single text, consider some of the responses different readers might have to E. B. White's classic essay "Once More to the Lake" (p. 21).

In "Once More to the Lake," White tells a story about his visit with his son to a lake in Maine in the 1940s, comparing this visit with those he made as a boy with his own father. Throughout the essay, White describes the changes that have occurred since his first visit. Memories from the past flood his consciousness, causing him to remember things that he did when he was a boy. At one point, after he and his son have been feeding worms to fish, he remembers doing the same thing with his father and has trouble separating the past from the present. As a result, White realizes that he will soon be just a memory in his son's mind—just as his father is only a memory in his.

White had specific goals in mind when he wrote this essay. His title, "Once More to the Lake," indicates that he intended to compare his childhood and adult visits to the lake. The organization of ideas in the essay, the use of flashbacks, and the choice of particular transitional phrases reinforce this purpose. In addition, descriptive details—such as the image of the tarred road that replaced the dirt road—remind readers, as well as White himself, that the years have made the lake site different from what it once was. The essay ends with White suddenly feeling the "chill of death."

Despite White's specific intentions, each person reading "Once More to the Lake" will respond to it somewhat differently. Young male readers might identify with the boy. If they have ever spent a vacation at a lake, they might have experienced the "peace and goodness and jollity" of the whole summer scene. Female readers might also want to share these experiences, but they might feel excluded because only males are described in the essay. Readers who have never been on a fishing trip might not feel the same nostalgia for the woods that White feels. To them, living in the woods away from the comforts of home might seem an unthinkably uncomfortable ordeal. Older readers might identify with White, sympathizing with his efforts as an adult to recapture the past and seeing his son as naively innocent of the challenges of life.

Thus, although each person who reads White's essay will read the same words, each will be likely to interpret it differently and to see different things as important. This is because much is left open to interpretation. All essays leave blanks or gaps—missing ideas or images—that readers have to fill in. In "Once More to the Lake," for example, readers must imagine what happened in the years that separated White's last visit to the lake and the trip he took with his son.

These gaps in the text create **ambiguities**—words, phrases, descriptions, or ideas that need to be interpreted by the reader. For instance, when you read the words "One summer, along about 1904, my father rented a camp on a lake," how do you picture the camp? White's description of the setting contains a great deal of detail, but no matter how much information he supplies, he cannot paint a complete verbal picture of the lakeside camp. He must rely on the reader's ability to visualize the setting and to supply details from his or her own experience.

Readers also bring their emotional associations to a text. For example, how readers react to White's statement above depends, in part, on their feelings about their own fathers. If White's words bring to mind a parent who is loving, strong, and protective, they will most likely respond favorably; if the essay calls up memories of a parent who is distant, bad-tempered, or even abusive, they may respond negatively.

Because each reader views the text from a slightly different angle, each may also see a different focus as central to "Once More to the Lake." Some might see nature as the primary element in the essay and believe that White's purpose is to condemn the encroachment of human beings on the environment. Others might see the passage of time as the central focus. Still others might see the initiation theme as being the most important element of the essay: each boy is brought to the wilderness by his father, and each eventually passes from childhood innocence to adulthood and to the awareness of his own mortality.

Finally, each reader may evaluate the essay differently. Some readers might think "Once More to the Lake" is boring because it has little action and deals with a subject in which they have no interest. Others might believe the essay is a brilliant meditation that makes an impact through its vivid description and imaginative figurative language. Still others might see the essay as a mixed bag—admitting, for example, that although White is an excellent stylist, he is also self-centered and self-indulgent. After all, they might argue, the experiences he describes are available only to relatively privileged members of society and are irrelevant to others.

Reading Critically

Reading critically means interacting with a text, questioning the text's assumptions and formulating and reformulating judgments about its ideas. Think of reading as a dialogue between you and the text: sometimes the author will assert himself or herself; at other times, you will dominate the conversation. Remember, though, that a critical voice is a thoughtful and responsible one, not one that shouts down the opposition. Linguist Deborah Tannen makes this distinction clear in an essay called "The Triumph of the Yell":

> In many university classrooms, "critical thinking" means reading someone's life work, then ripping it to shreds. Though critique is surely one form of critical thinking, so are integrating ideas from disparate fields and examining the context out of which they grew. Opposition does not lead to truth when we ask only "What's wrong with this argument?" and never "What can we use from this in building a new theory, a new understanding?"

In other words, being a critical reader does not necessarily mean quarreling and contradicting; more often, it means asking questions and exploring your reactions—while remaining open to new ideas.

Asking the following questions as you read will help you to become aware of the relationships between the writer's perspective and your own:

 •**What audience does the writer address?** Does the work offer clues to the writer's intended audience? For example, the title of John Holt's essay on early childhood education, "School Is Bad for Children" (p. 106), not only states his position but also suggests that he is questioning his readers' preconceived notions about the value of a traditional education.

 •**What is the writer's purpose?** Exactly what is the writer trying to accomplish in the essay? For example, is the writer attempting to explain, persuade, justify, evaluate, describe, debunk, entertain, preach, browbeat, threaten, or frighten? Or does the writer have some other purpose (or combination of purposes)? For example, is the writer trying to explain causes, as Jann S. Wenner is in "Why the Record Industry Is in Trouble" (p. 301)? To reflect on his or her life, as Sherman Alexie is in "The Unauthorized Autobiography of Me" (p. 53)? Or to move readers to action, as Shannon Brownlee is in "The Overtreated American" (p. 650)? What strategies does the writer use to achieve his or her purpose? For example, does the writer rely primarily on logic or on emotion? Does the writer appeal to the prejudices or fears of his or her readers or in any other way attempt to influence readers unfairly?

•**What voice does the writer use?** Does the writer seem to talk directly to readers? If so, does the writer's subjectivity get in the way, or does it help to involve readers? Does the writer's voice seem distant or formal? Different voices have different effects on readers. For example, an emotional tone, like the one Martin Luther King, Jr., uses in "I Have a Dream" (p. 532), can inspire; an intimate tone, like the one Lynda Barry uses in "The Sanctuary of School" (p. 103), can create reader identification and empathy; a straightforward, forthright voice, like that of Suzanne Gordon in "What Nurses Stand For" (p. 578), can make the writer's ideas seem reasonable and credible. An ironic tone can either amuse readers or alienate them; a distant, reserved tone can inspire either awe or discomfort.

•**What emotional response is the writer trying to evoke?** In "We May Be Brothers" (p. 470), Chief Seattle maintains a calm, unemotional tone even though he is describing the defeat of his people and the destruction of their land. By maintaining a dignified tone and avoiding bitterness and resentment, he succeeds in evoking sympathy and respect in his readers. Other writers may attempt to evoke other emotional responses: amusement, nostalgia, curiosity, wonder over the grandeur or mystery of the world that surrounds us, and even anger or fear.

•**What position does the writer take on the issue?** The choice of the word *war* in Christina Hoff Sommers's title "The War against Boys" (p. 453) clearly reveals her position on society's attitude toward boys; Martin Luther King, Jr., conveys his position in equally unambiguous terms when, in "Letter from Birmingham Jail" (p. 699), he asserts that people have a responsibility to disobey laws they consider unjust. Keep in mind, though, that a writer's position may not always be as obvious as it is in these two examples. As you read, look carefully for statements that suggest the writer's position on a particular subject or issue—and be sure you understand how you feel about that position, particularly if it is an unusual or controversial one. Do you agree or disagree? Can you explain your reasoning? Of course, a writer's advocacy of a position that is at odds with your own does not automatically render the work suspect or its ideas invalid. Remember, ideas that you might consider shocking or absurd may be readily accepted by many other readers. Unexpected, puzzling, or even repellent positions should encourage you to read carefully and thoughtfully, trying to understand the larger historical and cultural context of a writer's ideas.

•**How does the writer support his or her position?** What kind of support is provided? Is it convincing? Does the writer use a series of individual examples, as Alleen Pace Nilsen does in "Sexism in English: Embodiment and Language" (p. 419), or an extended example, as Austin Bunn does in "The Bittersweet Science" (p. 608)? Does the writer use statistics, as Judith Wallerstein does in "The Unexpected Legacy of Divorce" (p. 85), or does he or she rely primarily on personal experiences, as Brent Staples does in "Just Walk On By" (p. 497)? Does the writer quote experts, as Deborah Tannen does in "Marked Women" (p. 430), or present anecdotal information, as Jonathan Kozol does in "The Human Cost of an Illiterate Society" (p. 212)? Why does the writer choose a particular kind of support? Does he or she supply enough information to support the essay's points? Are the examples given relevant to the issues being discussed? Is the writer's reasoning valid, or do the arguments seem forced or unrealistic? Are any references in the work unfamiliar to you? If so, do they arouse your curiosity, or do they discourage you from reading further?

•**What beliefs, assumptions, or preconceived ideas do you have that color your responses to a work?** Does the writer challenge any ideas that you accept as "natural" or "obvious"? For example, does Garrett Hardin's controversial stand in "Lifeboat Ethics: The Case against 'Aid' That Harms" (p. 715) shock you or violate your sense of fair play? Does the fact that you oppose affirmative action prevent you from appreciating arguments presented in Goodwin Liu's essay "The Myth and Math of Affirmative Action" (p. 165)?

•**Does your background or experience give you any special insights that enable you to understand or interpret the writer's ideas?** Are the writer's experiences similar to or different from your own? Is the writer like or unlike you in terms of age, ethnic background, gender, and social class? How do the similarities and differences between you and the writer affect your reaction to the work? For example, you may be able to understand Amy Tan's "Mother Tongue" (p. 206) better than other students because you, too, speak one language at home and another in public. You may have a unique perspective on the problems Raymond Carver examines in "My Father's Life" (p. 45) because you, too, have an alcoholic parent. Or your volunteer work at a shelter may have helped you understand the plight of the homeless as described by Lars Eighner in "On Dumpster Diving" (p. 501). Any experiences you have can help you to understand a writer's ideas and shape your response to them.

Reacting to Visual Texts

Many of the written texts you read—from newspapers and magazines to textbooks like this one—include illustrations. Some of these visuals (charts, graphs, scientific diagrams, and the like) are designed primarily to present information; others (fine art, photographs, and advertisements, for example) may be designed to have an emotional effect on readers or even to persuade them.

Visuals may be analyzed, interpreted, and evaluated just as written texts are. You begin this process by looking critically at the visual, identifying its most important elements and considering the relationships of various elements to one another and to the image as a whole. Then, you try to identify the purpose for which the image was created, and you consider your own personal response to the image.

Recording Your Reactions

It is a good idea to read a work at least twice: first to get a general sense of the writer's ideas and then to react critically to these ideas. As you read critically, you interact with the text and respond in ways that will help you to interpret it. This process of coming to understand the text will prepare you to discuss the work with others and, if necessary, to write about it.

As you read and reread, record your responses; if you don't, you will forget some of your best ideas. Two activities can help you keep a record of the ideas that come to you as you read: **highlighting** (using a system of symbols and underlining to identify key ideas) and **annotating** (writing down your responses and interpretations).

When you react to what you read, don't be afraid to question or challenge the writer's ideas. As you read and make annotations, you may challenge or disagree with some of these ideas. Jot your responses down in the margin; when you have time, you can think more about what you have written. These informal responses may be the beginning of a thought process that will lead you to an original insight.

Highlighting and annotating helped a student to understand the passage on page 8, which is excerpted from Brent Staples's essay "Just Walk On By" (p. 497). As she prepared to write about the essay, the student identified and summarized the writer's key points and made a connection with another essay, Judith Ortiz Cofer's "The Myth of the Latin Woman" (p. 491). As she read, she underlined some of the passage's important words and ideas, using arrows to indicate relationships between them. She also circled a few words to remind her to look up their meaning later on, and she wrote down questions and comments as they occurred to her.

The fearsomeness mistakenly attributed to me in public places often has a perilous flavor. The most frightening of these confusions occurred in the late 1970s and early 1980s when I worked as a journalist in Chicago. One day, rushing into the office of a magazine I was writing for with a deadline story in hand, I was mistaken for a burglar. The office manager called security and, with an ad hoc posse, pursued me through the labyrinthine halls, nearly to my editor's door. I had no way of proving who I was. I could only move briskly toward the company of someone who knew me.

Another time I was on assignment for a local paper and killing time before an interview. I entered a jewelry store on the city's affluent Near North Side. The proprietor excused herself and returned with an enormous red Doberman pinscher straining at the end of a leash. She stood, the dog extended toward me, silent to my questions, her eyes bulging nearly out of her head. I took a cursory look around, nodded, and bade her good night. Relatively speaking, however, I never fared as badly as another black male journalist. He went to nearby Waukegan, Illinois, a couple of summers ago to work on a story about a murderer who was born there. Mistaking the reporter for the killer, police hauled him from his car at gunpoint and but for his press credentials would probably have tried to book him. Such episodes are not uncommon. Black men trade tales like this all the time.

Margin annotations:
Still applies — today?
(?)
(Fear creates danger)
First experience
(?)
Second experience
(?)
Compare with Ortiz Cofer's experience w/ stereotypes
*

READING TO WRITE

Much of the reading you will do as a student will be done to prepare you for writing. Writing helps you focus your ideas about various issues; in addition, the process of writing can lead you in unexpected directions, thereby enabling you to discover new insights. With this in mind, we have included in *The Blair Reader* a number of features that will help you as you read and prepare to write about its selections.

The readings in *The Blair Reader* are arranged in ten thematic chapters, each offering a variety of different vantage points from which to view the chapter's central theme. Each chapter in the book opens with a brief introduction, "Preparing to Read and Write," which provides a context for the chapter's theme and lists questions to guide your thinking as you read, thereby helping you to sharpen your critical skills and begin to apply those skills effectively. In this introduction, a pair of contrasting visual images—newspaper photographs, advertisements, Web pages, and so on—is designed to introduce you to the chapter's theme and to help you begin thinking about the issues it suggests.

Following each reading are three questions designed to encourage you to think about and respond to what you have read. These "Responding to Reading" questions ask you to think critically about the writer's ideas, perhaps focusing on a particular strategy the writer has used to achieve his or her purpose. In some cases, these questions may ask you to examine your own ideas or beliefs. Following the "Responding to Reading" questions is a "Responding in Writing" prompt that asks you to write a brief, informal response to the essay. These prompts may ask you to link the writer's experiences or ideas to your own; to do some kind of writing exercise, such as making a list, writing a summary, or drafting a letter; or to respond more critically to the writer's ideas.

Following the essays that develop aspects of each chapter's general theme is a "Focus" section that zeroes in on a specific issue related to that theme. The section's central question—for example, "How Free Should Free Speech Be?" (Chapter 3) or "Who Has It Harder, Men or Women?" (Chapter 6)—introduces a cluster of thought-provoking essays that take different positions on a single complex issue; a related visual image is also included in this Focus section. Each essay is accompanied by three "Responding to Reading" questions and one "Responding in Writing" prompt; "Responding to the Image" questions follow each visual. The Focus section ends with "Widening the Focus," which identifies related readings in other chapters of the book and provides an assignment for doing guided Internet research.

At the end of each chapter are ten suggestions for writing assignments that are longer and more formally structured than those suggested by the "Responding in Writing" prompts. These writing assignments ask you to examine some aspect of the chapter's theme by analyzing, interpreting, or evaluating ideas explored in various essays, sometimes considering parallels and contrasts with other essays in the book—or with your own life experiences.

As you read and write about the selections in this book, remember that you are learning ways of thinking about yourself and about the world. By considering and reconsidering the ideas of others, by rejecting easy answers, by considering a problem from many different angles, and by appreciating the many factors that can influence your responses, you develop critical thinking skills that you will use throughout your life. In addition, by writing about the themes discussed in this book, you participate in an ongoing conversation within the community of scholars and writers who care deeply about the issues that shape our world.

1

FAMILY
AND MEMORY

PREPARING TO READ AND WRITE

Memory preserves past events and makes them accessible to us. In this chapter, writers search their memories, trying to understand, recapture, or re-create the past, to see across the barriers imposed by time. In some cases, memories appear in sharp focus; in others, they are blurred, confused, or even partially invented. Many writers focus on themselves; others focus on their parents or other family members, struggling to close generational gaps, to replay events, to see through the eyes of others—and thus to understand their families and themselves more fully.

Family at beach at Margate, New Jersey, July 1955.

In the Focus section of this chapter, "How Has Divorce Redefined the Family?" (p. 68), three writers zero in on a painful subject: the effects of divorce on families in general and on children in particular. Looking at divorce from different perspectives, these writers consider how children's lives change (and how they stay the same) after a divorce, how divorcing adults come to terms with their decision to break up a family, and how adult children of divorce look back on their families' lives. More significantly, all three readings focus on the central questions of how *family* is defined and how divorce has changed that definition.

As you read and prepare to write about the selections in this chapter, you may consider the following questions:

- Does the writer focus on a single person, on a relationship between two people, or on larger family dynamics?

- Do you think the writer's perspective is *subjective* (shaped by his or her emotional responses or personal opinions) or *objective* (based mainly on observation and fact rather than on personal impressions)?

- Does the writer recount events from the perspective of an adult looking back at his or her childhood? If so, does the writer seem to have more insight now than when the events occurred? What has the writer learned—and how?

Family at beach, late 1990s.

- Are the memories generally happy or unhappy ones?

- Are family members presented in a favorable, unfavorable, neutral, or ambivalent light?

- Does the writer feel close to or distant from family members? Does the writer identify with a particular family member?

- Does one family member seem to have a great influence over others in the family? If so, is this influence positive or negative?

- What social, political, economic, or cultural forces influence the way the family functions?

- What is the writer's primary purpose? For example, is the writer's purpose to observe, explore, discover, explain, or persuade?

- Do you identify with the writer or with another person described in the selection? What makes you identify with that person?

- Which selections seem most similar in their views of family? How are they similar?

- Which selections seem most different in their views of family? How are they different?

THOSE WINTER SUNDAYS

Robert Hayden

1913–1980

Born in Detroit, Robert Hayden earned his MA at the University of Michigan and then taught there and at Fisk University in Nashville, Tennessee. His work includes poems about slave rebellions and the historical roots of racism as well as about more personal subjects. Hayden's first book of poetry, Heart-Shaped in the Dust, *was published in 1940. Other works include* A Ballad of Remembrance *(1962);* Words in Mourning Time *(1970);* Angle of Ascent; New and Selected Poems *(1975), in which "Those Winter Sundays" appeared;* American Journals *(1978); and* Complete Poems *(1985). To learn more about Hayden, visit the Academy of American Poets Web site, http://www.poets.org/.*

Sundays too my father got up early
and put his clothes on in the blueblack cold,
then with cracked hands that ached
from labor in the weekday weather made
5   banked fires blaze. No one ever thanked him.

I'd wake and hear the cold splintering, breaking,
When the rooms were warm, he'd call,
and slowly I would rise and dress,
fearing the chronic angers of that house,

Speaking indifferently to him,   10
who had driven out the cold
and polished my good shoes as well.
What did I know, what did I know
of love's austere and lonely offices?

Responding to Reading

1. Other than having "driven out the cold," what has the father done for his son? To what might the "chronic angers" (line 9) refer?
2. What important lessons has the speaker learned? Are these lessons primarily theoretical or practical? Explain.
3. In what respects does this poem sound like conversational prose? In what respects is it "poetic"?

Responding in Writing

What do you now know about your parents' responsibilities and sacrifices that you did not know when you were a child?

ONE LAST TIME

Gary Soto

1952–

Gary Soto was born in Fresno and grew up working along with his family as a migrant laborer in California's San Joaquin Valley. Soto often writes of the struggles of Mexican-Americans, as he does in the following autobiographical essay, in which he describes his experiences picking grapes and cotton. This essay is taken from Living Up the Street: Narrative Recollections, *for which he won the American Book Award in 1985. The author of ten poetry collections—including* New and Selected Poems, *which was a 1995 finalist for the National Book Award—Soto has also published short story collections, novels, and picture books for children. He is also involved with two organizations that work for justice for migrant workers: California Rural Legal Assistance (CRLA) and the United Farm Workers of America (UFW). To learn more about Soto, visit his Web site, http://www.garysoto.com/.*

Yesterday I saw the movie *Gandhi*[1] and recognized a few of the people—not in the theater but in the film. I saw my relatives, dusty and thin as sparrows, returning from the fields with hoes balanced on their shoulders. The workers were squinting, eyes small and veined, and were using their hands to say what there was to say to those in the audience with popcorn and Cokes. I didn't have anything, though. I sat thinking of my family and their years in the fields, beginning with Grandmother who came to the United States after the Mexican revolution to settle in Fresno where she met her husband and bore children, many of them. She worked in the fields around Fresno, picking grapes, oranges, plums, peaches, and cotton, dragging a large white sack like a sled. She worked in the packing houses, Bonner and Sun-Maid Raisin, where she stood at a conveyor belt passing her hand over streams of raisins to pluck out leaves and pebbles. For over twenty years she worked at a machine that boxed raisins until she retired at sixty-five.

Grandfather worked in the fields, as did his children. Mother also found herself out there when she separated from Father for three weeks. I remember her coming home, dusty and so tired that she had to rest on the porch before she trudged inside to wash and start dinner. I didn't understand the complaints about her ankles or the small of her back, even though I had been in the grape fields watching her work. With my brother and sister I ran in and out of the rows; we enjoyed ourselves and pretended not to hear Mother scolding us to sit down and behave ourselves. A few years later, however, I caught on when I went to pick grapes rather than play in the rows.

Mother and I got up before dawn and ate quick bowls of cereal. She drove in silence while I rambled on how everything was now solved, how I was going to make enough money to end our misery and even buy her a beautiful copper tea pot, the one I had shown her in Long's Drugs. When we arrived I was frisky and ready to go, self-consciously aware of my grape knife dangling at my wrist. I almost ran to the row the foreman had pointed out, but I returned to help Mother with the grape pans and jug of water. She told me to settle down and reminded me not to lose my knife. I walked at her side and listened to her explain how to cut grapes; bent down, hands on knees, I watched her demonstrate by cutting a few bunches into my pan. She stood over me as I tried it myself, tugging at a bunch of grapes that pulled loose like beads from a necklace. "Cut the stem all the way," she told me as last advice before she walked away, her shoes sinking in the loose dirt, to begin work on her own row.

---

[1] The 1982 film biography of the nonviolent revolutionary Mohandas Gandhi (known as Mahatma), which was set in part among the peasants of India. [Eds.]

I cut another bunch, then another, fighting the snap and whip of vines. After ten minutes of groping for grapes, my first pan brimmed with bunches. I poured them on the paper tray, which was bordered by a wooden frame that kept the grapes from rolling off, and they spilled like jewels from a pirate's chest. The tray was only half filled, so I hurried to jump under the vines and begin groping, cutting, and tugging at the grapes again. I emptied the pan, raked the grapes with my hands to make them look like they filled the tray, and jumped back under the vine on my knees. I tried to cut faster because Mother, in the next row, was slowly moving ahead. I peeked into her row and saw five trays gleaming in the early morning. I cut, pulled hard, and stopped to gather the grapes that missed the pan; already bored, I spat on a few to wash them before tossing them like popcorn into my mouth.

So it went. Two pans equaled one tray—or six cents. By lunchtime 5 I had a trail of thirty-seven trays behind me while mother had sixty or more. We met about halfway from our last trays, and I sat down with a grunt, knees wet from kneeling on dropped grapes. I washed my hands with the water from the jug, drying them on the inside of my shirt sleeve before I opened the paper bag for the first sandwich, which I gave to Mother. I dipped my hand in again to unwrap a sandwich without looking at it. I took a first bite and chewed it slowly for the tang of mustard. Eating in silence I looked straight ahead at the vines, and only when we were finished with cookies did we talk.

"Are you tired?" she asked.

"No, but I got a sliver from the frame," I told her. I showed her the web of skin between my thumb and index finger. She wrinkled her forehead but said it was nothing.

"How many trays did you do?"

I looked straight ahead, not answering at first. I recounted in my mind the whole morning of bend, cut, pour again and again, before answering a feeble "thirty-seven." No elaboration, no detail. Without looking at me she told me how she had done field work in Texas and Michigan as a child. But I had a difficult time listening to her stories. I played with my grape knife, stabbing it into the ground, but stopped when Mother reminded me that I had better not lose it. I left the knife sticking up like a small, leafless plant. She then talked about school, the junior high I would be going to that fall, and then about Rick and Debra, how sorry they would be that they hadn't come out to pick grapes because they'd have no new clothes for the school year. She stopped talking when she peeked at her watch, a bandless one she kept in her pocket. She got up with an *"Ay, Dios,"* and told me that we'd work until three, leaving me cutting figures in the sand with my knife and dreading the return to work.

10   Finally I rose and walked slowly back to where I had left off, again kneeling under the vine and fixing the pan under bunches of grapes. By that time, 11:30, the sun was over my shoulder and made me squint and think of the pool at the Y.M.C.A. where I was a summer member. I saw myself diving face first into the water and loving it. I saw myself gleaming like something new, at the edge of the pool. I had to daydream and keep my mind busy because boredom was a terror almost as awful as the work itself. My mind went dumb with stupid things, and I had to keep it moving with dreams of baseball and would-be girlfriends. I even sang, however softly, to keep my mind moving, my hands moving.

I worked less hurriedly and with less vision. I no longer saw that copper pot sitting squat on our stove or Mother waiting for it to whistle. The wardrobe that I imagined, crisp and bright in the closet, numbered only one pair of jeans and two shirts because, in half a day, six cents times thirty-seven trays was two dollars and twenty-two cents. It became clear to me. If I worked eight hours, I might make four dollars. I'd take this, even gladly, and walk downtown to look into store windows on the mall and long for the bright madras shirts from Walter Smith or Coffee's, but settling for two imitation ones from Penney's.

That first day I laid down seventy-three trays while Mother had a hundred and twenty behind her. On the back of an old envelope, she wrote out our numbers and hours. We washed at the pump behind the farm house and walked slowly to our car for the drive back to town in the afternoon heat. That evening after dinner I sat in a lawn chair listening to music from a transistor radio while Rick and David King played catch. I joined them in a game of pickle, but there was little joy in trying to avoid their tags because I couldn't get the fields out of my mind: I saw myself dropping on my knees under a vine to tug at a branch that wouldn't come off. In bed, when I closed my eyes, I saw the fields, yellow with kicked up dust, and a crooked trail of trays rotting behind me.

The next day I woke tired and started picking tired. The grapes rained into the pan, slowly filling like a belly, until I had my first tray and started my second. So it went all day, and the next, and all through the following week, so that by the end of thirteen days the foreman counted out, in tens mostly, my pay of fifty-three dollars. Mother earned one hundred and forty-eight dollars. She wrote this on her envelope, with a message I didn't bother to ask her about.

The next day I walked with my friend Scott to the downtown mall where we drooled over the clothes behind fancy windows, bought popcorn, and sat at a tier of outdoor fountains to talk about girls. Finally we went into Penney's for more popcorn, which we ate walking around, before we returned home without buying anything.

It wasn't until a few days before school that I let my fifty-three dollars slip quietly from my hands, buying a pair of pants, two shirts, and a maroon T-shirt, the kind that was in style. At home I tried them on while Rick looked on enviously; later, the day before school started, I tried them on again wondering not so much if they were worth it as who would see me first in those clothes.

Along with my brother and sister I picked grapes until I was fif- 15 teen, before giving up and saying that I'd rather wear old clothes than stoop like a Mexican. Mother thought I was being stuck-up, even stupid, because there would be no clothes for me in the fall. I told her I didn't care, but when Rick and Debra rose at five in the morning, I lay awake in bed feeling that perhaps I had made a mistake but unwilling to change my mind. That fall Mother bought me two pairs of socks, a packet of colored T-shirts, and underwear. The T-shirts would help, I thought, but who would see that I had new underwear and socks? I wore a new T-shirt on the first day of school, then an old shirt on Tuesday, then another T-shirt on Wednesday, and on Thursday an old Nehru shirt that was embarrassingly out of style. On Friday I changed into the corduroy pants my brother had handed down to me and slipped into my last new T-shirt. I worked like a magician, blinding my classmates, who were all clothes conscious and small-time social climbers, by arranging my wardrobe to make it seem larger than it really was. But by spring I had to do something—my blue jeans were almost silver and my shoes had lost their form, puddling like black ice around my feet. That spring of my sixteenth year, Rick and I decided to take a labor bus to chop cotton. In his old Volkswagen, which was more noise than power, we drove on a Saturday morning to West Fresno—or Chinatown as some call it—parked, walked slowly toward a bus, and stood gawking at the winos, toothy blacks, Okies, *Tejanos*[2] with gold teeth, whores, Mexican families, and labor contractors shouting "Cotton" or "Beets," the work of spring.

We boarded the "Cotton" bus without looking at the contractor who stood almost blocking the entrance because he didn't want winos. We boarded scared and then were more scared because two blacks in the rear were drunk and arguing loudly about what was better, a two-barrel or four-barrel Ford carburetor. We sat far from them, looking straight ahead, and only glanced briefly at the others who boarded, almost all of them broken and poorly dressed in loudly mismatched clothes. Finally when the contractor banged his palm against the side of the bus, the young man at the wheel, smiling and talking in Spanish, started the engine, idled it for a moment while he adjusted the mirrors, and started off in slow chugs. Except for the windshield there was no glass in the windows, so as soon as we were on the rural

---

[2]Descendants of early Mexican settlers in Texas. [Eds.]

roads outside Fresno, the dust and sand began to be sucked into the bus, whipping about like irate wasps as the gravel ticked about us. We closed our eyes, clotted up our mouths that wanted to open with embarrassed laughter because we couldn't believe we were on that bus with those people and the dust attacking us for no reason.

When we arrived at a field we followed the others to a pickup where we each took a hoe and marched to stand before a row. Rick and I, self-conscious and unsure, looked around at the others who leaned on their hoes or squatted in front of the rows, almost all talking in Spanish, joking, lighting cigarettes—all waiting for the foreman's whistle to begin work. Mother had explained how to chop cotton by showing us with a broom in the backyard.

"Like this," she said, her broom swishing down weeds. "Leave one plant and cut four—and cut them! Don't leave them standing or the foreman will get mad."

The foreman whistled and we started up the row stealing glances at other workers to see if we were doing it right. But after awhile we worked like we knew what we were doing, neither of us hurrying or falling behind. But slowly the clot of men, women, and kids began to spread and loosen. Even Rick pulled away. I didn't hurry, though. I cut smoothly and cleanly as I walked at a slow pace, in a sort of funeral march. My eyes measured each space of cotton plants before I cut. If I missed the plants, I swished again. I worked intently, seldom looking up, so when I did I was amazed to see the sun, like a broken orange coin, in the east. It looked blurry, unbelievable, like something not of this world. I looked around in amazement, scanning the eastern horizon that was a taut line jutted with an occasional mountain. The horizon was beautiful, like a snapshot of the moon, in the early light of morning, in the quiet of no cars and few people.

20   The foreman trudged in boots in my direction, stepping awkwardly over the plants, to inspect the work. No one around me looked up. We all worked steadily while we waited for him to leave. When he did leave, with a feeble complaint addressed to no one in particular, we looked up smiling under straw hats and bandanas.

By 11:00, our lunch time, my ankles were hurting from walking on clods the size of hardballs. My arms ached and my face was dusted by a wind that was perpetual, always busy whipping about. But the work was not bad, I thought. It was better, so much better, than picking grapes, especially with the hourly wage of a dollar twenty-five instead of piece work. Rick and I walked sorely toward the bus where we washed and drank water. Instead of eating in the bus or in the shade of the bus, we kept to ourselves by walking down to the irrigation canal that ran the length of the field, to open our lunch of sandwiches and crackers. We laughed at the crackers, which seemed like a cruel joke from our Mother, because we were working under the sun and the last thing we wanted was a salty dessert. We ate them anyway and drank more water before we returned to the field, both of us limping in exageration. Working side by side, we talked and laughed at our predicament because our Mother had warned us year after year that if we didn't get on track in school we'd have to work in the fields and then we would see. We mimicked Mother's whining voice and smirked at her smoky view of the future in which we'd be trapped by marriage and screaming kids. We'd eat beans and then we'd see.

Rick pulled slowly away to the rhythm of his hoe falling faster and smoother. It was better that way, to work alone. I could hum made-up songs or songs from the radio and think to myself about school and friends. At the time I was doing badly in my classes, mainly because of a difficult stepfather, but also because I didn't care anymore. All through junior high and into my first year of high school there were those who said I would never do anything, be any-one. They said I'd work like a donkey and marry the first Mexican girl that came along. I was reminded so often, verbally and in the way I was treated at home, that I began to believe that chopping cotton might be a lifetime job for me. If not chopping cotton, then I might get lucky and find myself in a car wash or restaurant or junkyard. But it was clear; I'd work, and work hard.

I cleared my mind by humming and looking about. The sun was directly above with a few soft blades of clouds against a sky that seemed bluer and more beautiful than our sky in the city. Occasionally the breeze flurried and picked up dust so that I had to cover my eyes and screw up my face. The workers were hunched, brown as the clods under our feet, and spread across the field that ran without end—fields that were owned by corporations, not families.

I hoed trying to keep my mind busy with scenes from school and pretend girlfriends until finally my brain turned off and my thinking went fuzzy with boredom. I looked about, no longer mesmerized by the beauty of the landscape, no longer wondering if the winos in the fields could hold out for eight hours, no longer dreaming of the clothes I'd buy with my pay. My eyes followed my chopping as the plants, thin as their shadows, fell with each strike. I worked slowly with ankles and arms hurting, neck stiff, and eyes stinging from the dust and the sun that glanced off the field like a mirror.

By quitting time, 3:00, there was such an excruciating pain in my [25] ankles that I walked as if I were wearing snowshoes. Rick laughed at me and I laughed too, embarrassed that most of the men were walk-ing normally and I was among the first timers who had to get used to this work. "And what about you, wino," I came back at Rick. His eyes were meshed red and his long hippie hair was flecked with dust and gnats and bits of leaves. We placed our hoes in the back of a pickup and stood in line for our pay, which was twelve fifty. I was amazed at the pay, which was the most I had ever earned in one day, and thought that I'd come back the next day, Sunday. This was too good.

Instead of joining the others in the labor bus, we jumped in the back of a pickup when the driver said we'd get to town sooner and were welcome to join him. We scrambled into the truck bed to be joined by a heavy-set and laughing *Tejano* whose head was shaped like an egg, particularly so because the bandana he wore ended in a point on the top of his head. He laughed almost demonically as the pickup roared up the dirt path, a gray cape of dust rising behind us. On the highway, with the wind in our faces, we squinted at the fields as if we were looking for someone. The *Tejano* had quit laughing but was smiling broadly, occasionally chortling tunes he never finished. I was scared of him, though Rick, two years older and five inches taller, wasn't. If the *Tejano* looked at him, Rick stared back for a second or two before he looked away to the fields.

I felt like a soldier coming home from war when we rattled into Chinatown. People leaning against car hoods stared, their necks following us, owl-like; prostitutes chewed gum more ferociously and showed us their teeth; Chinese grocers stopped brooming their storefronts to raise their cadaverous faces at us. We stopped in front of the Chi Chi Club where Mexican music blared from the juke box and cue balls cracked like dull ice. The *Tejano*, who was dirty as we were, stepped awkwardly over the side rail, dusted himself off with his bandana, and sauntered into the club.

Rick and I jumped from the back, thanked the driver who said *de nada* and popped his clutch, so that the pickup jerked and coughed blue smoke. We returned smiling to our car, happy with the money we had made and pleased that we had, in a small way, proved ourselves to be tough; that we worked as well as other men and earned the same pay.

We returned the next day and the next week until the season was over and there was nothing to do. I told myself that I wouldn't pick grapes that summer, saying all through June and July that it was for Mexicans, not me. When August came around and I still had not found a summer job, I ate my words, sharpened my knife, and joined Mother, Rick, and Debra for one last time.

Responding to Reading

1. In paragraph 1, Soto says he recognizes his relatives in the characters he sees in the film *Gandhi*. What does he mean?
2. Why would Soto at age fifteen "rather wear old clothes than stoop like a Mexican" (15)? Does the adult Soto understand the reasons for this senti-

ment? What does this comment reveal about the society in which Soto grew up?

3. What does Soto learn from the events he describes? What more do you think he still has to learn?

Responding in Writing

Is there a film or TV show in whose characters you recognize your own family members as Soto recognizes his relatives in *Gandhi*? How are your relatives like those you see on the screen?

Once More to the Lake

E. B. White

1899–1985

Well known for his children's stories, Elwyn Brooks White was also a talented essayist and a witty observer of contemporary society. His expansion of Will Strunk's The Elements of Style *remains one of the most popular and concise grammar and style texts in use today. White grew up in Mt. Vernon, New York, and graduated from Cornell University in 1921. He wrote for the* New Yorker *and* Harper's Magazine, *and his essays are collected in* Essays of E. B. White *(1977). In 1939, White moved to a farm in North Brooklin, Maine, where he wrote the children's classics* Stuart Little *(1945) and* Charlotte's Web *(1952). As a youth, White vacationed with his family on a lake in Maine. It is to this lake that he returned with his son, and he describes his experience in the following essay. To learn more about White, visit the official Web site, http://www.ebwhitebooks.com/.*

One summer, along about 1904, my father rented a camp on a lake in Maine and took us all there for the month of August. We all got ringworm from some kittens and had to rub Pond's Extract on our arms and legs night and morning, and my father rolled over in a canoe with all his clothes on; but outside of that the vacation was a success and from then on none of us ever thought there was any place in the world like that lake in Maine. We returned summer after summer—always on August 1st for one month. I have since become a salt-water man, but sometimes in summer there are days when the restlessness of the tides and the fearful cold of the sea water and the incessant wind which blows across the afternoon and into the evening make me wish for the placidity of a lake in the woods. A few weeks ago this feeling got so strong I bought myself a couple of bass hooks and a spinner and returned to the lake where we used to go, for a week's fishing and to revisit old haunts.

I took along my son, who had never had any fresh water up his nose and who had seen lily pads only from train windows. On the journey over to the lake I began to wonder what it would be like. I wondered how time would have marred this unique, this holy spot— the coves and streams, the hills that the sun set behind, the camps and the paths behind the camps. I was sure the tarred road would have found it out and I wondered in what other ways it would be desolated. It is strange how much you can remember about places like that once you allow your mind to return into the grooves which lead back. You remember one thing, and that suddenly reminds you of another thing. I guess I remembered clearest of all the early mornings, when the lake was cool and motionless, remembered how the bedroom smelled of the lumber it was made of and of the wet woods whose scent entered through the screen. The partitions in the camp were thin and did not extend clear to the top of the rooms, and as I was always the first up I would dress softly so as not to wake the others, and sneak out into the sweet outdoors and start out in the canoe, keeping close along the shore in the long shadows of the pines. I remembered being very careful never to rub my paddle against the gunwale for fear of disturbing the stillness of the cathedral.

The lake had never been what you would call a wild lake. There were cottages sprinkled around the shores, and it was in farming country although the shores of the lake were quite heavily wooded. Some of the cottages were owned by nearby farmers, and you would live at the shore and eat your meals at the farmhouse. That's what our family did. But although it wasn't wild, it was a fairly large and undisturbed lake and there were places in it which, to a child at least, seemed infinitely remote and primeval.

I was right about the tar: it led to within half a mile of the shore. But when I got back there, with my boy, and we settled into a camp near a farmhouse and into the kind of summertime I had known, I could tell that it was going to be pretty much the same as it had been before—I knew it, lying in bed the first morning, smelling the bedroom, and hearing the boy sneak quietly out and go off along the shore in a boat. I began to sustain the illusion that he was I, and therefore, by simple transposition, that I was my father. This sensation persisted, kept cropping up all the time we were there. It was not an entirely new feeling, but in this setting it grew much stronger. I seemed to be living a dual existence. I would be in the middle of some simple act, I would be picking up a bait box or laying down a table fork, or I would be saying something, and suddenly it would be not I but my father who was saying the words or making the gesture. It gave me a creepy sensation.

5   We went fishing the first morning. I felt the same damp moss covering the worms in the bait can, and saw the dragonfly alight on the

tip of my rod as it hovered a few inches from the surface of the water. It was the arrival of this fly that convinced me beyond any doubt that everything was as it always had been, that the years were a mirage and there had been no years. The small waves were the same, chucking the rowboat under the chin as we fished at anchor, and the boat was the same boat, the same color green and the ribs broken in the same places, and under the floor-boards the same freshwater leavings and débris—the dead helgramite,[1] the wisps of moss, the rusty discarded fishhook, the dried blood from yesterday's catch. We stared silently at the tips of our rods, at the dragonflies that came and went. I lowered the tip of mine into the water, tentatively, pensively dislodging the fly, which darted two feet away, poised, darted two feet back, and came to rest again a little farther up the rod. There had been no years between the ducking of this dragonfly and the other one—the one that was part of memory. I looked at the boy, who was silently watching his fly, and it was my hands that held his rod, my eyes watching. I felt dizzy and didn't know which rod I was at the end of.

We caught two bass, hauling them in briskly as though they were mackerel, pulling them over the side of the boat in a businesslike manner without any landing net, and stunning them with a blow on the back of the head. When we got back for a swim before lunch, the lake was exactly where we had left it, the same number of inches from the dock, and there was only the merest suggestion of a breeze. This seemed an utterly enchanted sea, this lake you could leave to its own devices for a few hours and come back to, and find that it had not stirred, this constant and trustworthy body of water. In the shallows, the dark, water-soaked sticks and twigs, smooth and old, were undulating in clusters on the bottom against the clean ribbed sand, and the track of the mussel was plain. A school of minnows swam by, each minnow with its small individual shadow, doubling the attendance, so clear and sharp in the sunlight. Some of the other campers were in swimming, along the shore, one of them with a cake of soap, and the water felt thin and clear and unsubstantial. Over the years there had been this person with the cake of soap, this cultist, and here he was. There had been no years.

Up to the farmhouse to dinner through the teeming, dusty field, the road under our sneakers was only a two-track road. The middle track was missing, the one with the marks of the hooves and the splotches of dried, flaky manure. There had always been three tracks to choose from in choosing which track to walk in; now the choice was narrowed down to two. For a moment I missed terribly the middle alternative. But the way led past the tennis court, and something about the way it lay there in the sun reassured me; the tape had

---

[1]The nymph of the May-fly, used as bait. [Eds.]

loosened along the backline, the alleys were green with plantains and other weeds, and the net (installed in June and removed in September) sagged in the dry noon, and the whole place steamed with mid-day heat and hunger and emptiness. There was a choice of pie for dessert, and one was blueberry and one was apple, and the waitresses were the same country girls, there having been no passage of time, only the illusion of it as in a dropped curtain—the waitresses were still fifteen; their hair had been washed, that was the only difference—they had been to the movies and seen the pretty girls with the clean hair.

Summertime, oh summertime, pattern of life indelible, the fade-proof lake, the woods unshatterable, the pasture with the sweetfern and the juniper forever and ever, summer without end; this was the background, and the life along the shore was the design, the cottagers with their innocent and tranquil design, their tiny docks with the flag-pole and the American flag floating against the white clouds in the blue sky, the little paths over the roots of the trees leading from camp to camp and the paths leading back to the outhouses and the can of lime for sprinkling, and at the souvenir counters at the store the miniature birch-bark canoes and the post cards that showed things looking a little better than they looked. This was the American family at play, escaping the city heat, wondering whether the newcomers in the camp at the head of the cove were "common" or "nice," wondering whether it was true that the people who drove up for Sunday dinner at the farmhouse were turned away because there wasn't enough chicken.

It seemed to me, as I kept remembering all this, that those times and those summers had been infinitely precious and worth saving. There had been jollity and peace and goodness. The arriving (at the beginning of August) had been so big a business in itself, at the railway station the farm wagon drawn up, the first smell of the pine-laden air, the first glimpse of the smiling farmer, and the great importance of the trunks and your father's enormous authority in such matters, and the feel of the wagon under you for the long ten-mile haul, and at the top of the last long hill catching the first view of the lake after eleven months of not seeing this cherished body of water. The shouts and cries of the other campers when they saw you, and the trunks to be unpacked, to give up their rich burden. (Arriving was less exciting nowadays, when you sneaked up in your car and parked it under a tree near the camp and took out the bags and in five minutes it was all over, no fuss, no loud wonderful fuss about trunks.)

10   Peace and goodness and jollity. The only thing that was wrong now, really, was the sound of the place, an unfamiliar nervous sound of the outboard motors. This was the note that jarred, the one thing that would sometimes break the illusion and set the years moving. In

those other summertimes all motors were inboard; and when they were at a little distance, the noise they made was a sedative, an ingredient of summer sleep. They were one-cylinder and two-cylinder engines, and some were make-and-break and some were jump-spark,[2] but they all made a sleepy sound across the lake. The one-lungers throbbed and fluttered, and the twin-cylinder ones purred and purred, and that was a quiet sound too. But now the campers all had outboards. In the daytime, in the hot mornings, these motors made a petulant, irritable sound; at night, in the still evening when the afterglow lit the water, they whined about one's ears like mosquitoes. My boy loved our rented outboard, and his great desire was to achieve singlehanded mastery over it, and authority, and he soon learned the trick of choking it a little (but not too much), and the adjustment of the needle valve. Watching him I would remember the things you could do with the old one-cylinder engine with the heavy flywheel, how you could have it eating out of your hand if you got really close to it spiritually. Motor boats in those days didn't have clutches, and you would make a landing by shutting off the motor at the proper time and coasting in with a dead rudder. But there was a way of reversing them, if you learned the trick, by cutting the switch and putting it on again exactly on the final dying revolution of the flywheel, so that it would kick back against compression and begin reversing. Approaching a dock in a strong following breeze, it was difficult to slow up sufficiently by the ordinary coasting method, and if a boy felt he had complete mastery over his motor, he was tempted to keep it running beyond its time and then reverse it a few feet from the dock. It took a cool nerve, because if you threw the switch a twentieth of a second too soon you would catch the flywheel when it still had speed enough to go up past center, and the boat would leap ahead, charging bull-fashion at the dock.

We had a good week at the camp. The bass were biting well and the sun shone endlessly, day after day. We would be tired at night and lie down in the accumulated heat of the little bedrooms after the long hot day and the breeze would stir almost imperceptibly outside and the smell of the swamp drift in through the rusty screens. Sleep would come easily and in the morning the red squirrel would be on the roof, tapping out his gay routine. I kept remembering everything, lying in bed in the mornings—the small steamboat that had a long rounded stern like the lip of a Ubangi, and how quietly she ran on the moonlight sails, when the older boys played their mandolins and the girls sang and we ate doughnuts dipped in sugar, and how sweet the music was on the water in the shining night, and what it had felt like to think about girls then. After breakfast we would go up

---

[2]Methods of ignition timing. [Eds.]

to the store and the things were in the same place—the minnows in a bottle, the plugs and spinners disarranged and pawed over by the youngsters from the boys' camp, the fig newtons and the Beeman's gum. Outside, the road was tarred and cars stood in front of the store. Inside, all was just as it had always been, except there was more Coca-Cola and not so much Moxie and root beer and birch beer and sarsaparilla. We would walk out with a bottle of pop apiece and sometimes the pop would backfire up our noses and hurt. We explored the streams, quietly, where the turtles slid off the sunny logs and dug their way into the soft bottom; and we lay on the town wharf and fed worms to the tame bass. Everywhere we went I had trouble making out which was I, the one walking at my side, the one walking in my pants.

One afternoon while we were there at that lake a thunderstorm came up. It was like the revival of an old melodrama that I had seen long ago with childish awe. The second-act climax of the drama of the electrical disturbance over a lake in America had not changed in any important respect. This was the big scene, still the big scene. The whole thing was so familiar, the first feeling of oppression and heat and a general air around camp of not wanting to go very far away. In midafternoon (it was all the same) a curious darkening of the sky, and a lull in everything that had made life tick; and then the way the boats suddenly swung the other way at their moorings with the coming of a breeze out of the new quarter, and the premonitory rumble. Then the kettle drum, then the snare, then the bass drum and cymbals, then crackling light against the dark, and the gods grinning and licking their chops in the hills. Afterward the calm, the rain steadily rustling in the calm lake, the return of light and hope and spirits, and the campers running out in joy and relief to go swimming in the rain, their bright cries perpetuating the deathless joke about how they were getting simply drenched, and the children screaming with delight at the new sensation of bathing in the rain, and the joke about getting drenched linking the generations in a strong indestructible chain. And the comedian who waded in carrying an umbrella.

When the others went swimming my son said he was going in too. He pulled his dripping trunks from the line where they had hung all through the shower, and wrung them out. Languidly, and with no thought of going in, I watched him, his hard little body, skinny and bare, saw him wince slightly as he pulled up around his vitals the small, soggy, icy garment. As he buckled the swollen belt suddenly my groin felt the chill of death.

Responding to Reading

1. How is White's "holy spot" different when he visits it with his son from how it was when he visited it with his father?

2. Is this essay primarily about a time, a place, or a relationship? Explain.
3. Why does White feel "the chill of death" (13) as he watches his son? Do you identify more with White the father or White the child? Explain.

Responding in Writing

Write two short paragraphs about a place that was important to you as a child: one from the point of view of your adult self, and one from the point of view of your childhood self. How are the two paragraphs different?

NO NAME WOMAN

Maxine Hong Kingston

1940–

Maxine Hong Kingston was born in Stockton, California, the daughter of Chinese immigrants who ran a gambling house and, later, a laundry where she and her five siblings worked. She attended public schools, where she was an excellent student, receiving multiple scholarships and eventually graduating from the University of California, Berkeley. Since her first book, The Woman Warrior: Memoirs of a Girlhood Among Ghosts *(1976), was published, Kingston has been acclaimed as a writer of fiction and nonfiction. Her most recent novel is* The Fifth Book of Peace *(2003). In the following autobiographical essay from* The Woman Warrior, *Kingston speculates about the life and death of a family member she has never met. To read more about Kingston, visit the Voices from the Gaps Web site at the University of Minnesota, http://voices.cla.umn.edu/.*

"You must not tell anyone," my mother said, "what I am about to tell you. In China your father had a sister who killed herself. She jumped into the family well. We say that your father has all brothers because it is as if she had never been born.

"In 1924 just a few days after our village celebrated seventeen hurry-up weddings—to make sure that every young man who went 'out on the road' would responsibly come home—your father and his brothers and your grandfather and his brothers and your aunt's new husband sailed for America, the Gold Mountain. It was your grandfather's last trip. Those lucky enough to get contracts waved good-bye from the decks. They fed and guarded the stowaways and helped them off in Cuba, New York, Bali, Hawaii. 'We'll meet in California next year,' they said. All of them sent money home.

"I remember looking at your aunt one day when she and I were dressing; I had not noticed before that she had such a protruding melon of a stomach. But I did not think, 'She's pregnant,' until she began to look like other pregnant women, her shirt pulling and the white tops of her black pants showing. She could not have been pregnant, you see, because her husband had been gone for years. No one said anything. We did not discuss it. In early summer she was ready to have the child, long after the time when it could have been possible.

"The village had also been counting. On the night the baby was to be born the villagers raided our house. Some were crying. Like a great saw, teeth strung with lights, files of people walked zigzag across our land, tearing the rice. Their lanterns doubled in the disturbed black water, which drained away through the broken bunds. As the villagers closed in, we could see that some of them, probably men and women we knew well, wore white masks. The people with long hair hung it over their faces. Women with short hair made it stand up on end. Some had tied white bands around their foreheads, arms, and legs.

5   "At first they threw mud and rocks at the house. Then they threw eggs and began slaughtering our stock. We could hear the animals scream their deaths—the roosters, the pigs, a last great roar from the ox. Familiar wild heads flared in our night windows; the villagers encircled us. Some of the faces stopped to peer at us, their eyes rushing like searchlights. The hands flattened against the panes, framed heads, and left red prints.

"The villagers broke in the front and the back doors at the same time, even though we had not locked the doors against them. Their knives dripped with the blood of our animals. They smeared blood on the doors and walls. One woman swung a chicken, whose throat she had slit, splattering blood in red arcs about her. We stood together in the middle of our house, in the family hall with the pictures and tables of the ancestors around us, and looked straight ahead.

"At the time the house had only two wings. When the men came back, we would build two more to enclose our courtyard and a third one to begin a second courtyard. The villagers pushed through both wings, even your grandparents' rooms, to find your aunt's, which was also mine until the men returned. From this room a new wing for one of the younger families would grow. They ripped up her clothes and shoes and broke her combs, grinding them underfoot. They tore her work from the loom. They scattered the cooking fire and rolled the new weaving in it. We could hear them in the kitchen breaking our bowls and banging the pots. They overturned the great waist-high earthenware jugs; duck eggs, pickled fruits, vegetables burst out and mixed in acrid torrents. The old woman from the next field swept a broom through the air and loosed the spirits-of-the-broom over our heads. 'Pig.' 'Ghost.' 'Pig,' they sobbed and scolded while they ruined our house.

"When they left, they took sugar and oranges to bless themselves. They cut pieces from the dead animals. Some of them took bowls that were not broken and clothes that were not torn. Afterward we swept up the rice and sewed it back up into sacks. But the smells from the spilled preserves lasted. Your aunt gave birth in the pigsty that night. The next morning when I went for the water, I found her and the baby plugging up the family well.

"Don't let your father know that I told you. He denies her. Now that you have started to menstruate, what happened to her could happen to you. Don't humiliate us. You wouldn't like to be forgotten as if you had never been born. The villagers are watchful."

Whenever she had to warn us about life, my mother told stories 10 that ran like this one, a story to grow up on. She tested our strength to establish realities. Those in the emigrant generations who could not reassert brute survival died young and far from home. Those of us in the first American generations have had to figure out how the invisible world the emigrants built around our childhoods fit in solid America.

The emigrants confused the gods by diverting their curses, misleading them with crooked streets and false names. They must try to confuse their offspring as well, who, I suppose, threaten them in similar ways—always trying to get things straight, always trying to name the unspeakable. The Chinese I know hide their names; sojourners take new names when their lives change and guard their real names with silence.

Chinese-Americans, when you try to understand what things in you are Chinese, how do you separate what is peculiar to childhood, to poverty, insanities, one family, your mother who marked your growing with stories, from what is Chinese? What is Chinese tradition and what is the movies?

If I want to learn what clothes my aunt wore, whether flashy or ordinary, I would have to begin, "Remember Father's drowned-in-the-well sister?" I cannot ask that. My mother has told me once and for all the useful parts. She will add nothing unless powered by Necessity, a riverbank that guides her life. She plants vegetable gardens rather than lawns; she carries the odd-shaped tomatoes home from the fields and eats food left for the gods.

Whenever we did frivolous things, we used up energy; we flew high kites. We children came up off the ground over the melting cones our parents brought home from work and the American movie on New Year's Day—*Oh, You Beautiful Doll* with Betty Grable one year, and *She Wore a Yellow Ribbon* with John Wayne another year. After the one carnival ride each, we paid in guilt; our tired father counted his change on the dark walk home.

Adultery is extravagance. Could people who hatch their own 15 chicks and eat the embryos and the heads for delicacies and boil the feet in vinegar for party food, leaving only the gravel, eating even the gizzard lining—could such people engender a prodigal aunt? To be a woman, to have a daughter in starvation time was a waste enough. My aunt could not have been the lone romantic who gave up everything for sex. Women in the old China did not choose. Some man had commanded her to lie with him and be his secret evil. I wonder whether he masked himself when he joined the raid on her family.

Perhaps she encountered him in the fields or on the mountain where the daughters-in-law collected fuel. Or perhaps he first noticed her in the marketplace. He was not a stranger because the village housed no strangers. She had to have dealings with him other than sex. Perhaps he worked an adjoining field, or he sold her the cloth for the dress she sewed and wore. His demand must have surprised, then terrified her. She obeyed him; she always did as she was told.

When the family found a young man in the next village to be her husband, she stood tractably beside the best rooster, his proxy, and promised before they met that she would be his forever. She was lucky that he was her age and she would be the first wife, an advantage secure now. The night she first saw him, he had sex with her. Then he left for America. She had almost forgotten what he looked like. When she tried to envision him, she only saw the black and white face in the group photograph the men had had taken before leaving.

The other man was not, after all, much different from her husband. They both gave orders: she followed. "If you tell your family, I'll beat you. I'll kill you. Be here again next week." No one talked sex, ever. And she might have separated the rapes from the rest of living if only she did not have to buy her oil from him or gather wood in the same forest. I want her fear to have lasted just as long as rape lasted so that the fear could have been contained. No drawn-out fear. But women at sex hazarded birth and hence lifetimes. The fear did not stop but permeated everywhere. She told the man, "I think I'm pregnant." He organized the raid against her.

On nights when my mother and father talked about their life back home, sometimes they mentioned an "outcast table" whose business they still seemed to be settling, their voices tight. In a commensal[1] tradition, where food is precious, the powerful older people made wrongdoers eat alone. Instead of letting them start separate new lives like the Japanese, who could become samurais and geishas, the Chinese family, faces averted but eyes glowering sideways, hung on to the offenders and fed them leftovers. My aunt must have lived in the same house as my parents and eaten at an outcast table. My mother spoke about the raid as if she had seen it, when she and my aunt, a

---

[1]Eating at the same table; sharing meals as table companions. [Eds.]

daughter-in-law to a different household, should not have been living together at all. Daughters-in-law lived with their husbands' parents, not their own; a synonym for marriage in Chinese is "taking a daughter-in-law." Her husband's parents could have sold her, mortgaged her, stoned her. But they had sent her back to her own mother and father, a mysterious act hinting at disgraces not told me. Perhaps they had thrown her out to deflect the avengers.

She was the only daughter; her four brothers went with her father, husband, and uncles "out on the road" and for some years became western men. When the goods were divided among the family, three of the brothers took land, and the youngest, my father, chose an education. After my grandparents gave their daughter away to her husband's family, they had dispensed all the adventure and all the property. They expected her alone to keep the traditional ways, which her brothers, now among the barbarians, could fumble without detection. The heavy, deep-rooted women were to maintain the past against the flood, safe for returning. But the rare urge west had fixed upon our family, and so my aunt crossed boundaries not delineated in space. 20

The work of preservation demands that the feelings playing about in one's guts not be turned into action. Just watch their passing like cherry blossoms. But perhaps my aunt, my forerunner, caught in a slow life, let dreams grow and fade and after some months or years went toward what persisted. Fear at the enormities of the forbidden kept her desires delicate, wire and bone. She looked at a man because she liked the way the hair was tucked behind his ears, or she liked the question-mark line of a long torso curving at the shoulder and straight at the hip. For warm eyes or a soft voice or a slow walk— that's all—a few hairs, a line, a brightness, a sound, a pace, she gave up family. She offered us up for a charm that vanished with tiredness, a pigtail that didn't toss when the wind died. Why, the wrong lighting could erase the dearest thing about him.

It could very well have been, however, that my aunt did not take subtle enjoyment of her friend, but, a wild woman, kept rollicking company. Imagining her free with sex doesn't fit, though. I don't know any women like that, or men either. Unless I see her life branching into mine, she gives me no ancestral help.

To sustain her being in love, she often worked at herself in the mirror, guessing at the colors and shapes that would interest him, changing them frequently in order to hit on the right combination. She wanted him to look back.

On a farm near the sea, a woman who tended her appearance reaped a reputation for eccentricity. All the married women blunt-cut their hair in flaps about their ears or pulled it back in tight buns. No nonsense. Neither style blew easily into heart-catching tangles. And at their weddings they displayed themselves in their long hair for the last time. "It brushed the backs of my knees," my mother tells me. "It was braided, and even so, it brushed the backs of my knees."

25   At the mirror my aunt combed individuality into her bob. A bun could have been contrived to escape into black streamers blowing in the wind or in quiet wisps about her face, but only the older women in our picture album wear buns. She brushed her hair back from her forehead, tucking the flaps behind her ears. She looped a piece of thread, knotted into a circle between her index fingers and thumbs, and ran the double strand across her forehead. When she closed her fingers as if she were making a pair of shadow geese bite, the string twisted together catching the little hairs. Then she pulled the thread away from her skin, ripping the hairs out neatly, her eyes watering from the needles of pain. Opening her fingers, she cleaned the thread, then rolled it along her hairline and the tops of her eyebrows. My mother did the same to me and my sisters and herself. I used to believe that the expression "caught by the short hairs" meant a captive held with a depilatory string. It especially hurt at the temples, but my mother said we were lucky we didn't have to have our feet bound when we were seven. Sisters used to sit on their beds and cry together, she said, as their mothers or their slave removed the bandages for a few minutes each night and let the blood gush back into their veins. I hope that the man my aunt loved appreciated a smooth brow, that he wasn't just a tits-and-ass man.

Once my aunt found a freckle on her chin, at a spot that the almanac said predestined her for unhappiness. She dug it out with a hot needle and washed the wound with peroxide.

More attention to her looks than these pullings of hairs and pickings at spots would have caused gossip among the villagers. They owned work clothes and good clothes, and they wore good clothes for feasting the new seasons. But since a woman combing her hair hexes beginnings, my aunt rarely found an occasion to look her best. Women looked like great sea snails—the corded wood, babies, and laundry they carried were the whorls on their backs. The Chinese did not admire a bent back; goddesses and warriors stood straight. Still there must have been a marvelous freeing of beauty when a worker laid down her burden and stretched and arched.

Such commonplace loveliness, however, was not enough for my aunt. She dreamed of a lover for the fifteen days of New Year's, the time for families to exchange visits, money, and food. She plied her secret comb. And sure enough she cursed the year, the family, the village, and herself.

Even as her hair lured her imminent lover, many other men looked at her. Uncles, cousins, nephews, brothers would have looked, too, had they been home between journeys. Perhaps they had already been restraining their curiosity, and they left, fearful that their glances, like a field of nesting birds, might be startled and caught. Poverty hurt, and that was their first reason for leaving. But another, final reason for leaving the crowded house was the never-said.

She may have been unusually beloved, the precious only daugh- 30 ter, spoiled and mirror gazing because of the affection the family lavished on her. When her husband left, they welcomed the chance to take her back from the in-laws; she could live like the little daughter for just a while longer. There are stories that my grandfather was different from other people, "crazy ever since the little Jap bayoneted him in the head." He used to put his naked penis on the dinner table, laughing. And one day he brought home a baby girl, wrapped up inside his brown western-style greatcoat. He had traded one of his sons, probably my father, the youngest, for her. My grandmother made him trade back. When he finally got a daughter of his own, he doted on her. They must have all loved her, except perhaps my father, the only brother who never went back to China, having once been traded for a girl.

Brothers and sisters, newly men and women, had to efface their sexual color and present plain miens.[2] Disturbing hair and eyes, a smile like no other, threatened the ideal of five generations living under one roof. To focus blurs, people shouted face to face and yelled from room to room. The immigrants I know have loud voices, unmodulated to American tones even after years away from the village where they called their friendships out across the fields. I have not been able to stop my mother's screams in public libraries or over telephones. Walking erect (knees straight, toes pointed forward, not pigeon-toed, which is Chinese-feminine) and speaking in an inaudible voice, I have tried to turn myself American-feminine. Chinese communication was loud, public. Only sick people had to whisper. But at the dinner table, where the family members came nearest one another, no one could talk, not the outcasts nor any eaters. Every word that falls from the mouth is a coin lost. Silently they gave and accepted food with both hands. A preoccupied child who took his bowl with one hand got a sideways glare. A complete moment of total attention is due everyone alike. Children and lovers have no singularity here, but my aunt used a secret voice, a separate attentiveness.

She kept the man's name to herself throughout her labor and dying; she did not accuse him that he be punished with her. To save her inseminator's name she gave silent birth.

He may have been somebody in her own household, but intercourse with a man outside the family would have been no less abhorrent. All the village were kinsmen, and the titles shouted in loud

---

[2]Appearances. [Eds.]

country voices never let kinship be forgotten. Any man within visiting distance would have been neutralized as a lover—"brother," "younger brother," "older brother"—one hundred and fifteen relationship titles. Parents researched birth charts probably not so much to assure good fortune as to circumvent incest in a population that has but one hundred surnames. Everybody has eight million relatives. How useless then sexual mannerisms, how dangerous.

As if it came from an atavism[3] deeper than fear, I used to add "brother" silently to boys' names. It hexed the boys, who would or would not ask me to dance, and made them less scary and as familiar and deserving of benevolence as girls.

35   But, of course, I hexed myself also—no dates. I should have stood up, both arms waving, and shouted out across libraries, "Hey, you! Love me back." I had no idea, though, how to make attraction selective, how to control its direction and magnitude. If I made myself American-pretty so that the five or six Chinese boys in the class fell in love with me, everyone else—the Caucasian, Negro, and Japanese boys—would too. Sisterliness, dignified and honorable, made much more sense.

Attraction eludes control so stubbornly that whole societies designed to organize relationships among people cannot keep order, not even when they bind people to one another from childhood and raise them together. Among the very poor and the wealthy, brothers married their adopted sisters, like doves. Our family allowed some romance, paying adult brides' prices and providing dowries so that their sons and daughters could marry strangers. Marriage promises to turn strangers into friendly relatives—a nation of siblings.

In the village structure, spirits shimmered among the live creatures, balanced and held in equilibrium by time and land. But one human being flaring up into violence could open up a black hole, a maelstrom that pulled in the sky. The frightened villagers, who depended on one another to maintain the real, went to my aunt to show her a personal, physical representation of the break she had made in the "roundness." Misallying couples snapped off the future, which was to be embodied in true offspring. The villagers punished her for acting as if she could have a private life, secret and apart from them.

If my aunt had betrayed the family at a time of large grain yields and peace, when many boys were born, and wings were being built on many houses, perhaps she might have escaped such severe punishment. But the men—hungry, greedy, tired of planting in dry soil, cuckolded—had had to leave the village in order to send food-money home. There were ghost plagues, bandit plagues, wars with the Japanese, floods. My Chinese brother and sister had died of an un-

---

[3]The reappearance of a characteristic after a long absence. [Eds.]

known sickness. Adultery, perhaps only a mistake during good times, became a crime when the village needed food.

The round moon cakes and round doorways, the round tables of graduated size that fit one roundness inside another, round windows and rice bowls—these talismans had lost their power to warn this family of the law: a family must be whole, faithfully keeping the descent line by having sons to feed the old and the dead, who in turn look after the family. The villagers came to show my aunt and her lover-in-hiding a broken house. The villagers were speeding up the circling of events because she was too shortsighted to see that her infidelity had already harmed the village, that waves of consequences would return unpredictably, sometimes in disguise, as now, to hurt her. This roundness had to be made coin-sized so that she would see its circumference: punish her at the birth of her baby. Awaken her to the inexorable. People who refused fatalism because they could invent small resources insisted on culpability. Deny accidents and wrest fault from the stars.

After the villagers left, their lanterns now scattering in various di- 40 rections toward home, the family broke their silence and cursed her. "Aiaa, we're going to die. Death is coming. Death is coming. Look what you've done. You've killed us. Ghost! Dead ghost! Ghost! You've never been born." She ran out into the fields, far enough from the house so that she could no longer hear their voices, and pressed herself against the earth, her own land no more. When she felt the birth coming, she thought that she had been hurt. Her body seized together. "They've hurt me too much," she thought. "This is gall, and it will kill me." With forehead and knees against the earth, her body convulsed and then relaxed. She turned on her back, lay on the ground. The black well of sky and stars went out and out and out forever; her body and her complexity seemed to disappear. She was one of the stars, a bright dot in blackness, without home, without a companion, in eternal cold and silence. And agoraphobia[4] rose in her, speeding higher and higher, bigger and bigger; she would not be able to contain it; there would be no end to fear.

Flayed, unprotected against space, she felt pain return, focusing her body. This pain chilled her—a cold, steady kind of surface pain. Inside, spasmodically, the other pain, the pain of the child, heated her. For hours she lay on the ground, alternately body and space. Sometimes a vision of normal comfort obliterated reality: she saw the family in the evening gambling at the dinner table, the young people massaging their elders' backs. She saw them congratulating one

---

[4]Pathological fear of being helpless or embarrassed in a pubic situation, characterized by avoidance of public places. [Eds.]

another, high joy on the mornings the rice shoots came up. When these pictures burst, the stars drew yet further apart. Black space opened.

She got to her feet to fight better and remembered that old-fashioned women gave birth in their pigsties to fool the jealous, pain-dealing gods, who do not snatch piglets. Before the next spasms could stop her, she ran to the pigsty, each step a rushing out into emptiness. She climbed over the fence and knelt in the dirt. It was good to have a fence enclosing her, a tribal person alone.

Laboring, this woman who had carried her child as a foreign growth that sickened her every day, expelled it at last. She reached down to touch the hot, wet, moving mass, surely smaller than anything human, and could feel that it was human after all—fingers, toes, nails, nose. She pulled it up on to her belly, and it lay curled there, butt in the air, feet precisely tucked one under the other. She opened her loose shirt and buttoned the child inside. After resting, it squirmed and thrashed and she pushed it up to her breast. It turned its head this way and that until it found her nipple. There, it made little snuffling noises. She clenched her teeth at its preciousness, lovely as a young calf, a piglet, a little dog.

She may have gone to the pigsty as a last act of responsibility: she would protect this child as she had protected its father. It would look after her soul, leaving supplies on her grave. But how would this tiny child without family find her grave when there would be no marker for her anywhere, neither in the earth nor the family hall? No one would give her a family hall name. She had taken the child with her into the wastes. At its birth the two of them had felt the same raw pain of separation, a wound that only the family pressing tight could close. A child with no descent line would not soften her life but only trail after her, ghost-like, begging her to give it purpose. At dawn the villagers on their way to the fields would stand around the fence and look.

45 Full of milk, the little ghost slept. When it awoke, she hardened her breasts against the milk that crying loosens. Toward morning she picked up the baby and walked to the well.

Carrying the baby to the well shows loving. Otherwise abandon it. Turn its face into the mud. Mothers who love their children take them along. It was probably a girl; there is some hope of forgiveness for boys.

"Don't tell anyone you had an aunt. Your father does not want to hear her name. She has never been born." I have believed that sex was unspeakable and words so strong and fathers so frail that "aunt" would do my father mysterious harm. I have thought that my family, having settled among immigrants who had also been their neighbors in the ancestral land, needed to clean their name, and a wrong word

would incite the kinspeople even here. But there is more to this silence: they want me to participate in her punishment. And I have.

In the twenty years since I heard this story I have not asked for
details nor said my aunt's name; I do not know it. People who can
comfort the dead can also chase after them to hurt them further—a reverse ancestor worship. The real punishment was not the raid swiftly
inflicted by the villagers, but the family's deliberately forgetting her.
Her betrayal so maddened them, they saw to it that she would suffer
forever, even after death. Always hungry, always needing, she would
have to beg food from other ghosts, snatch and steal it from those
whose living descendants give them gifts. She would have to fight the
ghosts massed at crossroads for the buns a few thoughtful citizens
leave to decoy her away from village and home so that the ancestral
spirits could feast unharassed. At peace, they could act like gods, not
ghosts, their descent lines providing them with paper suits and
dresses, spirit money, paper houses, paper automobiles, chicken,
meat, and rice into eternity—essences delivered up in smoke and
flames, steam and incense rising from each rice bowl. In an attempt to
make the Chinese care for people outside the family, Chairman Mao[5]
encourages us now to give our paper replicas to the spirits of outstanding soldiers and workers, no matter whose ancestors they may
be. My aunt remains forever hungry. Goods are not distributed evenly
among the dead.

My aunt haunts me—her ghost drawn to me because now, after
fifty years of neglect, I alone devote pages of paper to her, though not
origamied into houses and clothes. I do not think she always means
me well. I am telling on her, and she was a spite suicide, drowning
herself in the drinking water. The Chinese are always very frightened
of the drowned one, whose weeping ghost, wet hair hanging and skin
bloated, waits silently by the water to pull down a substitute.

Responding to Reading

1. How accurate do you imagine Kingston's "facts" are? Do you think strict
   accuracy is important in this essay? Why or why not?
2. Kingston never met her aunt; in fact, she doesn't even know her name.
   Even so, in what sense is this essay about her relationship with her aunt
   (and with other family members, both known and unknown)?
3. In paragraph 49, Kingston says, "My aunt haunts me—" Why do you think
   Kingston is "haunted" by her aunt's story?

---

[5]Mao Zedong (1893–1976), founder and leader of the communist People's Republic of China from
1949 until his death. [Eds.]

Responding in Writing

Write a one-paragraph biographical sketch of a family member—or a short obituary of a deceased relative.

BEAUTY: WHEN THE OTHER DANCER IS THE SELF

Alice Walker

1944–

Alice Walker, best known for her award-winning novel The Color Purple *(1982), is recognized as one of the leading voices among African-American women writers. Born in Georgia, the daughter of sharecroppers, Walker received scholarships to Spelman College in Atlanta and Sarah Lawrence College in Bronxville, New York. Walker's work, which often focuses on racism and sexism, includes poetry, novels, short stories, essays, criticism, a biography of Langston Hughes, and an edition of Zora Neale Hurston's collection* I Love Myself When I Am Laughing *(1979). Walker's recent works include* Sent by Earth: A Message from the Grandmother Spirit after the Bombing of the World Trade Center and the Pentagon *(2001) and* A Poem Traveled Down My Arm: Poems and Drawings *(2003). Like much of her writing, the following essay moves from pain and despair to self-celebration. To read more about Walker, visit this "featured author" Web site maintained by the* New York Times, *http://www.nytimes.com/books/ 98/10/04/specials/ walker.html/.*

It is a bright summer day in 1947. My father, a fat, funny man with beautiful eyes and a subversive wit, is trying to decide which of his eight children he will take with him to the county fair. My mother, of course, will not go. She is knocked out from getting most of us ready: I hold my neck stiff against the pressure of her knuckles as she hastily completes the braiding and then beribboning of my hair.

My father is the driver for the rich old white lady up the road. Her name is Miss Mey. She owns all the land for miles around, as well as the house in which we live. All I remember about her is that she once offered to pay my mother thirty-five cents for cleaning her house, raking up piles of her magnolia leaves, and washing her family's clothes, and that my mother—she of no money, eight children, and a chronic earache—refused it. But I do not think of this in 1947. I am two and a half years old. I want to go everywhere my daddy goes. I am excited at the prospect of riding in a car. Someone has told me fairs are fun. That there is room in the car for only three of us doesn't faze me at all. Whirling happily in my starchy frock, showing off my biscuit-polished patent-leather shoes and lavender socks, tossing my head in a way that makes my ribbons bounce, I stand, hands on hips, before my father. "Take me, Daddy," I say with assurance; "I'm the prettiest!"

Later, it does not surprise me to find myself in Miss Mey's shiny black car, sharing the back seat with the other lucky ones. Does not surprise me that I thoroughly enjoy the fair. At home that night I tell the unlucky ones all I can remember about the merry-go-round, the man who eats live chickens, and the teddy bears, until they say: that's enough, baby Alice. Shut up now, and go to sleep.

It is Easter Sunday, 1950. I am dressed in a green, flocked, scalloped-hem dress (handmade by my adoring sister, Ruth) that has its own smooth satin petticoat and tiny hot-pink roses tucked into each scallop. My shoes, new T-strap patent leather, again highly biscuit-polished. I am six years old and have learned one of the longest Easter speeches to be heard that day, totally unlike the speech I said when I was two: "Easter lilies/pure and white/blossom in/the morning light." When I rise to give my speech I do so on a great wave of love and pride and expectation. People in the church stop rustling their new crinolines. They seem to hold their breath. I can tell they admire my dress, but it is my spirit, bordering on sassiness (womanishness), they secretly applaud.

"That girl's a little *mess*," they whisper to each other, pleased.   5

Naturally I say my speech without stammer or pause, unlike those who stutter, stammer, or, worst of all, forget. This is before the word "beautiful" exists in people's vocabulary, but "Oh, isn't she the *cutest* thing!" frequently floats my way. "And got so much sense!" they gratefully add . . . for which thoughtful addition I thank them to this day.

It was great fun being cute. But then, one day, it ended.

I am eight years old and a tomboy. I have a cowboy hat, cowboy boots, checkered shirt and pants, all red. My playmates are my brothers, two and four years older than I. Their colors are black and green, the only difference in the way we are dressed. On Saturday nights we all go to the picture show, even my mother; Westerns are her favorite kind of movie. Back home, "on the ranch," we pretend we are Tom Mix, Hopalong Cassidy, Lash LaRue (we've even named one of our dogs Lash LaRue); we chase each other for hours rustling cattle, being outlaws, delivering damsels from distress. Then my parents decide to buy my brothers guns. These are not "real" guns. They shoot "BBs," copper pellets my brothers say will kill birds. Because I am a girl, I do not get a gun. Instantly I am relegated to the position of Indian. Now there appears a great distance between us. They shoot and shoot at everything with their new guns. I try to keep up with my bow and arrows.

One day while I am standing on top of our makeshift "garage"—pieces of tin nailed across some poles—holding my bow and arrow and looking out toward the fields, I feel an incredible blow in my right eye. I look down just in time to see my brother lower his gun.

10   Both brothers rush to my side. My eye stings, and I cover it with my hand. "If you tell," they say, "we will get a whipping. You don't want that to happen, do you?" I do not. "Here is a piece of wire," says the older brother, picking it up from the roof; "say you stepped on one end of it and the other flew up and hit you." The pain is beginning to start. "Yes," I say, "Yes, I will say that is what happened." If I do not say this is what happened, I know my brothers will find ways to make me wish I had. But now I will say anything that gets me to my mother.

Confronted by our parents we stick to the lie agreed upon. They place me on a bench on the porch and I close my left eye while they examine the right. There is a tree growing from underneath the porch that climbs past the railing to the roof. It is the last thing my right eye sees. I watch as its trunk, its branches, and then its leaves are blotted out by the rising blood.

I am in shock. First there is intense fever, which my father tries to break using lily leaves bound around my head. Then there are chills: my mother tries to get me to eat soup. Eventually, I do not know how, my parents learn what has happened. A week after the "accident" they take me to see a doctor. "Why did you wait so long to come?" he asks, looking into my eye and shaking his head. "Eyes are sympathetic," he says. "If one is blind, the other will likely become blind too."

This comment of the doctor's terrifies me. But it is really how I look that bothers me most. Where the BB pellet struck there is a glob of whitish scar tissue, a hideous cataract, on my eye. Now when I stare at people—a favorite pastime, up to now—they will stare back. Not at the "cute" little girl, but at her scar. For six years I do not stare at anyone, because I do not raise my head.

Years later, in the throes of a mid-life crisis, I ask my mother and sister whether I changed after the "accident." "No," they say, puzzled. "What do you mean?"

15   *What do I mean?*

I am eight, and, for the first time, doing poorly in school, where I have been something of a whiz since I was four. We have just moved to the place where the "accident" occurred. We do not know any of the people around us because this is a different county. The only time I see the friends I knew is when we go back to our old church. The new school is the former state penitentiary. It is a large stone building, cold and drafty, crammed to overflowing with boisterous, ill-disciplined children. On the third floor there is a huge circular imprint of some partition that has been torn out.

"What used to be here?" I ask a sullen girl next to me on our way past it to lunch.

"The electric chair," says she.

At night I have nightmares about the electric chair, and about all the people reputedly "fried" in it. I am afraid of the school, where all the students seem to be budding criminals.

"What's the matter with your eye?" they ask, critically.   20

When I don't answer (I cannot decide whether it was an "accident" or not), they shove me, insist on a fight.

My brother, the one who created the story about the wire, comes to my rescue. But then brags so much about "protecting" me, I become sick.

After months of torture at the school, my parents decide to send me back to our old community, to my old school. I live with my grandparents and the teacher they board. But there is no room for Phoebe, my cat. By the time my grandparents decide there *is* room, and I ask for my cat, she cannot be found. Miss Yarborough, the boarding teacher, takes me under her wing, and begins to teach me to play the piano. But soon she marries an African—a "prince," she says—and is whisked away to his continent.

At my old school there is at least one teacher who loves me. She is the teacher who "knew me before I was born" and bought my first baby clothes. It is she who makes life bearable. It is her presence that finally helps me turn on the one child at the school who continually calls me "one-eyed bitch." One day I simply grab him by his coat and beat him until I am satisfied. It is my teacher who tells me my mother is ill.

My mother is lying in bed in the middle of the day, something I   25 have never seen. She is in too much pain to speak. She has an abscess in her ear. I stand looking down on her, knowing that if she dies, I cannot live. She is being treated with warm oils and hot bricks held against her cheek. Finally a doctor comes. But I must go back to my grandparents' house. The weeks pass but I am hardly aware of it. All I know is that my mother might die, my father is not so jolly, my brothers still have their guns, and I am the one sent away from home.

"You did not change," they say.

Did I imagine the anguish of never looking up?

I am twelve. When relatives come to visit I hide in my room. My cousin Brenda, just my age, whose father works in the post office and whose mother is a nurse, comes to find me. "Hello," she says. And then she asks, looking at my recent school picture, which I did not want taken, and on which the "glob," as I think of it, is clearly visible, "You still can't see out of that eye?"

"No," I say, and flop back on the bed over my book.

30   That night, as I do almost every night, I abuse my eye. I rant and rave at it, in front of the mirror. I plead with it to clear up before morning. I tell it I hate and despise it. I do not pray for sight. I pray for beauty.

"You did not change," they say.

I am fourteen and baby-sitting for my brother Bill, who lives in Boston. He is my favorite brother and there is a strong bond between us. Understanding my feelings of shame and ugliness he and his wife take me to a local hospital, where the "glob" is removed by a doctor named O. Henry. There is still a small bluish crater where the scar tissue was, but the ugly white stuff is gone. Almost immediately I become a different person from the girl who does not raise her head. Or so I think. Now that I've raised my head I win the boyfriend of my dreams. Now that I've raised my head I have plenty of friends. Now that I've raised my head classwork comes from my lips as faultlessly as Easter speeches did, and I leave high school as valedictorian, most popular student, and *queen*, hardly believing my luck. Ironically, the girl who was voted most beautiful in our class (and was) was later shot twice through the chest by a male companion, using a "real" gun, while she was pregnant. But that's another story in itself. Or is it?

"You did not change," they say.

It is now thirty years since the "accident." A beautiful journalist comes to visit and to interview me. She is going to write a cover story for her magazine that focuses on my latest book. "Decide how you want to look on the cover," she says. "Glamorous, or whatever."

35   Never mind "glamorous," it is the "whatever" that I hear. Suddenly all I can think of is whether I will get enough sleep the night before the photography session: if I don't, my eye will be tired and wander, as blind eyes will.

At night in bed with my lover I think up reasons why I should not appear on the cover of a magazine. "My meanest critics will say I've sold out," I say. "My family will now realize I write scandalous books."

"But what's the real reason you don't want to do this?" he asks.

"Because in all probability," I say in a rush, "my eye won't be straight."

"It will be straight enough," he says. Then, "Besides, I thought you'd made your peace with that."

And I suddenly remember that I have.   40

I remember:

I am talking to my brother Jimmy, asking if he remembers anything unusual about the day I was shot. He does not know I consider that day the last time my father, with his sweet home remedy of cool lily leaves, chose me, and that I suffered and raged inside because of this. "Well," he says, "all I remember is standing by the side of the highway with Daddy, trying to flag down a car. A white man stopped, but when Daddy said he needed somebody to take his little girl to the doctor, he drove off."

I remember:

I am in the desert for the first time. I fall totally in love with it. I am so overwhelmed by its beauty, I confront for the first time, consciously, the meaning of the doctor's words years ago: "Eyes are sympathetic. If one is blind, the other will likely become blind too." I realize I have dashed about the world madly, looking at this, looking at that, storing up images against the fading of the light. *But I might have missed seeing the desert!* The shock of that possibility—and gratitude for over twenty-five years of sight—sends me literally to my knees. Poem after poem comes—which is perhaps how poets pray.

On Sight

I am so thankful I have seen
The Desert
And the creatures in the desert
And the desert Itself.

The desert has its own moon
Which I have seen
With my own eye.
There is no flag on it.

Trees of the desert have arms
All of which are always up
That is because the moon is up
The sun is up
Also the sky
The stars
Clouds
None with flags.

If there were flags, I doubt
the trees would point.
Would you?

But mostly, I remember this:

I am twenty-seven, and my baby daughter is almost three. Since her birth I have worried about her discovery that her mother's eyes are different from other people's. Will she be embarrassed? I think. What will she say? Every day she watches a television program called "Big Blue Marble." It begins with a picture of the earth as it appears from the moon. It is bluish, a little battered-looking, but full of light, with whitish clouds swirling around it. Every time I see it I weep with love, as if it is a picture of Grandma's house. One day when I am putting Rebecca down for her nap, she suddenly focuses on my eye. Something inside me cringes, gets ready to try to protect myself. All children are cruel about physical differences, I know from experience, and that they don't always mean to be is another matter. I assume Rebecca will be the same.

But no-o-o-o. She studies my face intently as we stand, her inside and me outside her crib. She even holds my face maternally between her dimpled little hands. Then, looking every bit as serious and lawyerlike as her father, she says, as if it may just possibly have slipped my attention: "Mommy, there's a *world* in your eye." (As in, "Don't be alarmed, or do anything crazy.") And then, gently, but with great interest: "Mommy, where did you get that world in your eye?"

For the most part, the pain left then. (So what, if my brothers grew up to buy even more powerful pellet guns for their sons and to carry real guns themselves. So what, if a young "Morehouse man"[1] once nearly fell off the steps of Trevor Arnett Library because he thought my eyes were blue.) Crying and laughing I ran to the bathroom, while Rebecca mumbled and sang herself off to sleep. Yes indeed, I realized, looking into the mirror. There was a world in my eye. And I saw that it was possible to love it: that in fact, for all it had taught me of shame and anger and inner vision, I *did* love it. Even to see it drifting out of orbit in boredom, or rolling up out of fatigue, not to mention floating back at attention in excitement (bearing witness, a friend has called it), deeply suitable to my personality, and even characteristic of me.

That night I dream I am dancing to Stevie Wonder's song "Always" (the name of the song is really "As," but I hear it as "Always"). As I dance, whirling and joyous, happier than I've ever been in my life, another bright-faced dancer joins me. We dance and kiss each other and hold each other through the night. The other dancer has obviously come through all right, as I have done. She is beautiful, whole and free. And she is also me.

---

[1]A student at Morehouse College, a historically black college in Atlanta, Georgia. [Eds.]

Responding to Reading

1. Although she is remembering past events, Walker uses present tense ("It is a bright summer day in 1947") to tell her story. Why do you think she does this? Is the present tense more effective than the past tense ("It *was* a bright summer day in 1947") would be? Explain.
2. At several points in the essay, Walker repeats the words her relatives used to reassure her: "You did not change." Why does she repeat this phrase? Were her relatives correct?
3. What circumstances or individuals does Walker blame for the childhood problems she describes? Who do you think is responsible for her misery? Would you be as forgiving as Walker seems to be?

Responding in Writing

Using present tense, write a paragraph or two about a painful incident from your childhood. Begin with a sentence that tells how old you are ("I am _____.").

MY FATHER'S LIFE

Raymond Carver

(1938–1988)

Raymond Carver was born in Clatskanie, Oregon, and grew up in the Pacific Northwest in a working-class family. In the following essay, Carver examines the life of his father, an alcoholic who suffered from depression, and writes about his father's influences on his own personal life as well as on his fiction and poetry. Admired as a talented short story writer, Carver, like his father, led a troubled life. He earned an AB degree from Humboldt State College in northern California and received a scholarship to the prestigious Iowa Writer's Workshop, but he had to leave in order to support his young family. Throughout his adult life, Carver struggled with alcoholism and marital problems, but he remained sober and productive during the last ten years of his life. His story collections include Will You Please Be Quiet, Please? *(1976);* What We Talk About When We Talk About Love *(1981);* Cathedral *(1984); and* Short Cuts *(1984), which was adapted to the screen by director Robert Altman in 1993. To read more about Carver, visit the pages about him on The Art and Culture Network's Web site, http://www.artandculture.com/.*

My dad's name was Clevie Raymond Carver. His family called him Raymond and friends called him C. R. I was named Raymond Clevie Carver Jr. I hated the "Junior" part. When I was little my dad called me Frog, which was okay. But later, like everybody else in the family, he began calling me Junior. He went on calling me this until I was thirteen or fourteen and announced that I wouldn't answer to that name any longer. So he began calling me Doc. From then until his death, on June 17, 1967, he called me Doc, or else Son.

When he died, my mother telephoned my wife with the news. I was away from my family at the time, between lives, trying to enroll in the School of Library Science at the University of Iowa. When my wife answered the phone, my mother blurted out. "Raymond's dead!" For a moment, my wife thought my mother was telling her that I was dead. Then my mother made it clear *which* Raymond she was talking about and my wife said, "Thank God. I thought you meant *my* Raymond."

My dad walked, hitched rides, and rode in empty boxcars when he went from Arkansas to Washington State in 1934, looking for work. I don't know whether he was pursuing a dream when he went out to Washington. I doubt it. I don't think he dreamed much. I believe he was simply looking for steady work at decent pay. Steady work was meaningful work. He picked apples for a time and then landed a construction laborer's job on the Grand Coulee Dam.[1] After he'd put aside a little money, he bought a car and drove back to Arkansas to help his folks, my grandparents, pack up for the move west. He said later that they were about to starve down there, and this wasn't meant as a figure of speech. It was during that short while in Arkansas, in a town called Leola, that my mother met my dad on the sidewalk as he came out of a tavern.

"He was drunk," she said. "I don't know why I let him talk to me. His eyes were glittery. I wish I'd had a crystal ball." They'd met once, a year or so before, at a dance. He'd had girlfriends before her, my mother told me. "Your dad always had a girlfriend, even after we married. He was my first and last. I never had another man. But I didn't miss anything."

5   They were married by a justice of the peace on the day they left for Washington, this big, tall country girl and a farmhand-turned construction worker. My mother spent her wedding night with my dad and his folks, all of them camped beside the road in Arkansas.

In Omak, Washington, my dad and mother lived in a little place not much bigger than a cabin. My grandparents lived next door. My dad was still working on the dam, and later, with the huge turbines producing electricity and the water backed up for a hundred miles into Canada, he stood in the crowd and heard Franklin D. Roosevelt when he spoke at the construction site. "He never mentioned those guys who died building that dam," my dad said. Some of his friends had died there, men from Arkansas, Oklahoma, and Missouri.

---

[1]On the Columbia River, northwest of Spokane, Washington. [Eds.]

He then took a job in a sawmill in Clatskanie, Oregon, a little town alongside the Columbia River. I was born there, and my mother has a picture of my dad standing in front of the gate to the mill, proudly holding me up to face the camera. My bonnet is on crooked and about to come untied. His hat is pushed back on his forehead, and he's wearing a big grin. Was he going in to work or just finishing his shift? It doesn't matter. In either case, he had a job and a family. These were his salad days.

In 1941 we moved to Yakima, Washington, where my dad went to work as a saw filer, a skilled trade he'd learned in Clatskanie. When war broke out, he was given a deferment because his work was considered necessary to the war effort. Finished lumber was in demand by the armed services, and he kept his saws so sharp they could shave the hair off your arm.

After my dad had moved us to Yakima, he moved his folks into the same neighborhood. By the mid-1940s the rest of my dad's family—his brother, his sister, and her husband, as well as uncles, cousins, nephews, and most of their extended family and friends—had come out from Arkansas. All because my dad came out first. The men went to work at Boise Cascade, where my dad worked, and the women packed apples in the canneries. And in just a little while, it seemed—according to my mother—everybody was better off than my dad. "Your dad couldn't keep money," my mother said. "Money burned a hole in his pocket. He was always doing for others."

The first house I clearly remember living in, at 1515 South Fif- 10 teenth Street, in Yakima, had an outdoor toilet. On Halloween night, or just any night, for the hell of it, neighbor kids, kids in their early teens, would carry our toilet away and leave it next to the road. My dad would have to get somebody to help him bring it home. Or these kids would take the toilet and stand it in somebody else's backyard. Once they actually set it on fire. But ours wasn't the only house that had an outdoor toilet. When I was old enough to know what I was doing, I threw rocks at the other toilets when I'd see someone go inside. This was called bombing the toilets. After a while, though, everyone went to indoor plumbing until, suddenly, our toilet was the last outdoor one in the neighborhood. I remember the shame I felt when my third-grade teacher, Mr. Wise, drove me home from school one day. I asked him to stop at the house just before ours, claiming I lived there.

I can recall what happened one night when my dad came home late to find that my mother had locked all the doors on him from the inside. He was drunk, and we could feel the house shudder as he rattled the door. When he'd managed to force open a window, she hit him between the eyes with a colander and knocked him out. We could see him down there on the grass. For years afterward, I used to pick up this colander—it was as heavy as a rolling pin—and imagine what it would feel like to be hit in the head with something like that.

It was during this period that I remember my dad taking me into the bedroom, sitting me down on the bed, and telling me that I might have to go live with my Aunt La Von for a while. I couldn't understand what I'd done that meant I'd have to go away from home to live. But this, too—whatever prompted it—must have blown over, more or less, anyway, because we stayed together, and I didn't have to go live with her or anyone else.

I remember my mother pouring his whiskey down the sink. Sometimes she'd pour it all out and sometimes, if she was afraid of getting caught, she'd only pour half of it out and then add water to the rest. I tasted some of his whiskey once myself. It was terrible stuff, and I don't see how anybody could drink it.

After a long time without one, we finally got a car, in 1949 or 1950, a 1938 Ford. But it threw a rod the first week we had it, and my dad had to have the motor rebuilt.

15   "We drove the oldest car in town," my mother said. "We could have had a Cadillac for all he spent on car repairs." One time she found someone else's tube of lipstick on the floorboard, along with a lacy handkerchief. "See this?" she said to me. "Some floozy left this in the car."

Once I saw her take a pan of warm water into the bedroom where my dad was sleeping. She took his hand from under the covers and held it in the water. I stood in the doorway and watched. I wanted to know what was going on. This would make him talk in his sleep, she told me. There were things she needed to know, things she was sure he was keeping from her.

Every year or so, when I was little, we would take the North Coast Limited across the Cascade Range from Yakima to Seattle and stay in the Vance Hotel and eat, I remember, at a place called the Dinner Bell Cafe. Once we went to Ivar's Acres of Clams and drank glasses of warm clam broth.

In 1956, the year I was to graduate from high school, my dad quit his job at the mill in Yakima and took a job in Chester, a little sawmill town in northern California. The reasons given at the time for his taking the job had to do with a higher hourly wage and the vague promise that he might, in a few years' time, succeed to the job of head filer in this new mill. But I think, in the main, that my dad had grown restless and simply wanted to try his luck elsewhere. Things had gotten a little too predictable for him in Yakima. Also, the year before, there had been the deaths, within six months of each other, of both his parents.

But just a few days after graduation, when my mother and I were packed to move to Chester, my dad penciled a letter to say he'd been sick for a while. He didn't want us to worry, he said, but he'd cut himself on a saw. Maybe he'd got a tiny sliver of steel in his blood. Anyway, something had happened and he'd had to miss work, he said. In the same mail was an unsigned postcard from somebody down there telling my mother that my dad was about to die and that he was drinking "raw whiskey."

When we arrived in Chester, my dad was living in a trailer that 20 belonged to the company. I didn't recognize him immediately. I guess for a moment I didn't want to recognize him. He was skinny and pale and looked bewildered. His pants wouldn't stay up. He didn't look like my dad. My mother began to cry. My dad put his arm around her and patted her shoulder vaguely, like he didn't know what this was all about, either. The three of us took up life together in the trailer, and we looked after him as best we could. But my dad was sick, and he couldn't get any better. I worked with him in the mill that summer and part of the fall. We'd get up in the mornings and eat eggs and toast while we listened to the radio, and then go out the door with our lunch pails. We'd pass through the gate together at eight in the morning, and I wouldn't see him again until quitting time. In November I went back to Yakima to be closer to my girlfriend, the girl I'd made up my mind I was going to marry.

He worked at the mill in Chester until the following February, when he collapsed on the job and was taken to the hospital. My mother asked if I would come down there and help. I caught a bus from Yakima to Chester, intending to drive them back to Yakima. But now, in addition to being physically sick, my dad was in the midst of a nervous breakdown, though none of us knew to call it that at the time. During the entire trip back to Yakima, he didn't speak, not even when asked a direct question. ("How do you feel, Raymond?" "You okay, Dad?") He'd communicate if he communicated at all, by moving his head or by turning his palms up as if to say he didn't know or care. The only time he said anything on the trip, and for nearly a month afterward, was when I was speeding down a gravel road in Oregon and the car muffler came loose. "You were going too fast," he said.

Back in Yakima a doctor saw to it that my dad went to a psychiatrist. My mother and dad had to go on relief,[2] as it was called, and the county paid for the psychiatrist. The psychiatrist asked my dad. "Who is the President?" He'd had a question put to him that he could answer. "Ike," my dad said. Nevertheless, they put him on the fifth floor of Valley Memorial Hospital and began giving him electroshock treatments. I was married by then and about to start my own family. My dad was still locked up when my wife went into this same

---

[2]What would today be called "public assistance" or "welfare." [Eds.]

hospital, just one floor down, to have our first baby. After she had delivered, I went upstairs to give my dad the news. They let me in through a steel door and showed me where I could find him. He was sitting on a couch with a blanket over his lap. *Hey*, I thought. *What in hell is happening to my dad?* I sat down next to him and told him he was a grandfather. He waited a minute and then he said, "I feel like a grandfather." That's all he said. He didn't smile or move. He was in a big room with a lot of other people. Then I hugged him, and he began to cry.

Somehow he got out of there. But now came the years when he couldn't work and just sat around the house trying to figure what next and what he'd done wrong in his life that he'd wound up like this. My mother went from job to crummy job. Much later she referred to that time he was in the hospital, and those years just afterward, as "when Raymond was sick." The word *sick* was never the same for me again.

In 1964, through the help of a friend, he was lucky enough to be hired on at a mill in Klamath, California. He moved down there by himself to see if he could hack it. He lived not far from the mill, in a one-room cabin not much different from the place he and my mother had started out living in when they went west. He scrawled letters to my mother, and if I called she'd read them aloud to me over the phone. In the letters, he said it was touch and go. Every day that he went to work, he felt like it was the most important day of his life. But every day, he told her, made the next day that much easier. He said for her to tell me he said hello. If he couldn't sleep at night, he said, he thought about me and the good times we used to have. Finally, after a couple of months, he regained some of his confidence. He could do the work and didn't think he had to worry that he'd let anybody down ever again. When he was sure, he sent for my mother.

25   He'd been off from work for six years and had lost everything in that time—home, car, furniture, and appliances, including the big freezer that had been my mother's pride and joy. He'd lost his good name too—Raymond Carver was someone who couldn't pay his bills—and his self-respect was gone. He'd even lost his virility. My mother told my wife, "All during that time Raymond was sick we slept together in the same bed, but we didn't have relations. He wanted to a few times, but nothing happened. I didn't miss it, but I think he wanted to, you know."

During those years I was trying to raise my own family and earn a living. But, one thing and another, we found ourselves having to move a lot. I couldn't keep track of what was going down in my dad's life. But I did have a chance one Christmas to tell him I wanted to be a writer. I might as well have told him I wanted to become a plastic surgeon. "What are you going to write about?" he wanted to know.

Then, as if to help me out, he said, "Write about stuff you know about. Write about some of those fishing trips we took." I said I would, but I knew I wouldn't. "Send me what you write," he said. I said I'd do that, but then I didn't. I wasn't writing anything about fishing, and I didn't think he'd particularly care about, or even necessarily understand, what I was writing in those days. Besides, he wasn't a reader. Not the sort, anyway, I imagined I was writing for.

Then he died. I was a long way off, in Iowa City, with things still to say to him. I didn't have the chance to tell him goodbye, or that I thought he was doing great at his new job. That I was proud of him for making a comeback.

My mother said he came in from work that night and ate a big supper. Then he sat at the table by himself and finished what was left of a bottle of whiskey, a bottle she found hidden in the bottom of the garbage under some coffee grounds a day or so later. Then he got up and went to bed, where my mother joined him a little later. But in the night she had to get up and make a bed for herself on the couch. "He was snoring so loud I couldn't sleep," she said. The next morning when she looked in on him, he was on his back with his mouth open, his cheeks caved in. *Graylooking,* she said. She knew he was dead— she didn't need a doctor to tell her that. But she called one anyway, and then she called my wife.

Among the pictures my mother kept of my dad and herself during those early days in Washington was a photograph of him standing in front of a car, holding a beer and a stringer of fish. In the photograph he is wearing his hat back on his forehead and has this awkward grin on his face. I asked her for it and she gave it to me, along with some others. I put it up on my wall, and each time we moved, I took the picture along and put it up on another wall. I looked at it carefully from time to time, trying to figure out some things about my dad, and maybe myself in the process. But I couldn't. My dad just kept moving further and further away from me and back into time. Finally, in the course of another move, I lost the photograph. It was then that I tried to recall it, and at the same time make an attempt to say something about my dad, and how I thought that in some important ways we might be alike. I wrote the poem when I was living in an apartment house in an urban area south of San Francisco, at a time when I found myself, like my dad, having trouble with alcohol. The poem was a way of trying to connect up with him.

Photograph of My Father in His Twenty-Second Year

October. Here in this dank, unfamiliar kitchen
I study my father's embarrassed young man's face.

Sheepish grin, he holds in one hand a string
of spiny yellow perch, in the other
a bottle of Carlsberg beer.

In jeans and flannel shirt, he leans
against the front fender of a 1934 Ford.
He would like to pose brave and hearty for his posterity,
wear his old hat cocked over his ear.
All his life my father wanted to be bold.

But the eyes give him away, and the hands
that limply offer the string of dead perch
and the bottle of beer. Father, I love you,
yet how can I say thank you, I who can't hold my liquor either
and don't even know the places to fish.

30   The poem is true in its particulars, except that my dad died in June and not October, as the first word of the poem says. I wanted a word with more than one syllable to it to make it linger a little. But more than that, I wanted a month appropriate to what I felt at the time I wrote the poem—a month of short days and failing light, smoke in the air, things perishing. June was summer nights and days, graduations, my wedding anniversary, the birthday of one of my children. June wasn't a month your father died in.

After the service at the funeral home, after we had moved outside, a woman I didn't know came over to me and said, "He's happier where he is now." I stared at this woman until she moved away. I still remember the little knob of a hat she was wearing. Then one of my dad's cousins—I didn't know the man's name—reached out and took my hand, "We all miss him," he said, and I knew he wasn't saying it just to be polite.

I began to weep for the first time since receiving the news. I hadn't been able to before. I hadn't had the time, for one thing. Now, suddenly, I couldn't stop. I held my wife and wept while she said and did what she could do to comfort me there in the middle of that summer afternoon.

I listened to people say consoling things to my mother, and I was glad that my dad's family had turned up, had come to where he was. I thought I'd remember everything that was said and done that day and maybe find a way to tell it sometime. But I didn't. I forgot it all, or nearly. What I do remember is that I heard our name used a lot that afternoon, my dad's name and mine. But I knew they were talking about my dad. *Raymond*, these people kept saying in their beautiful voices out of my childhood. *Raymond*.

Responding to Reading

1. Why does Carver include details about his father's work history? His drinking? His mental illness? The photograph? Do you think all these details are necessary? Explain.
2. What information is provided by the poem that follows paragraph 29 that is not provided by the essay itself? Could Carver have conveyed this information as effectively in prose?
3. What does Carver finally come to realize about his father, and about himself?

Responding in Writing

Draw a family tree that includes as many family members as you can identify. Then, draw lines to connect your name to the names of those relatives you think you most resemble in terms of character traits. Write a paragraph or two explaining the similarities you observe.

THE UNAUTHORIZED AUTOBIOGRAPHY OF ME

Sherman J. Alexie, Jr.

1966–

Sherman Alexie, who grew up on an Indian reservation in Wellpinit, Washington, about 50 miles northwest of Spokane, is a Spokane/Coeur d'Alene Indian whose works focus on tribal connections and draw upon the oral and religious traditions of his heritage. In his writings, Alexie often seems to be constructing a Native American web of life, weaving together elements of the personal, mythical, historical, and modern. Alexie received a BA from Washington State University in Pullman in 1991. Although he began his writing career as a poet, Alexie has also written stories and novels. A story from his first collection, The Lone Ranger and Tonto Fistfight in Heaven *(1993), became the basis for the screenplay and film* Smoke Signals *(1998). Alexie has published 14 books, most recently a short story collection,* The Toughest Indian in the World *(2000), and a collection of poems,* One Stick Song *(1999). To read more about Alexie, visit his Web site, http://www.fallsapart.com/.*

Late summer night on the Spokane Indian Reservation. Ten Indians are playing basketball on a court barely illuminated by the streetlight above them. They will play until the brown, leather ball is invisible in the dark. They will play until an errant pass jams a finger, knocks a pair of glasses off a face, smashes a nose and draws blood. They will play until the ball bounces off the court and disappears into the shadows.

Sometimes, I think this is all you need to know about Native American literature.

Thesis: I have never met a Native American. Thesis reiterated: I have met thousands of Indians.

PEN American panel in Manhattan, November 1994, on Indian Literature. N. Scott Momaday, James Welch, Gloria Miguel, Joy Harjo, and myself. Two or three hundred people in the audience. Mostly non-Indians; an Indian or three. Questions and answers.

5   "Why do you insist on calling yourselves Indian?" asked a white woman in a nice hat. "It's so demeaning."

"Listen," I said. "The word belongs to us now. We are Indians. That has nothing to do with Indians from India. We are not American Indians. We are Indians, pronounced In-din. It belongs to us. We own it and we're not going to give it back."

So much has been taken from us that we hold on to the smallest things with all the strength we have left.

Winter on the Spokane Indian Reservation, 1976. My two cousins, S and G, have enough money for gloves. They buy them at Irene's Grocery Store. Irene is a white woman who has lived on our reservation since the beginning of time. I have no money for gloves. My hands are bare.

We build snow fortresses on the football field. Since we are Indian boys playing, there must be a war. We stockpile snowballs. S and G build their fortress on the fifty-yard line. I build mine on the thirty-yard line. We begin our little war. My hands are bare.

10   My cousins are good warriors. They throw snowballs with precision. I am bombarded, under siege, defeated quickly. My cousins bury me in the snow. My grave is shallow. If my cousins knew how to dance, they might have danced on my grave. But they know how to laugh, so they laugh. They are my cousins, meaning we are related in the Indian way. My father drank beers with their father for most of two decades, and that is enough to make us relatives. Indians gather relatives like firewood, protection against the cold. I am buried in the snow, cold, without protection. My hands are bare.

After a short celebration, my cousins exhume me. I am too cold to fight. Shivering, I walk for home, anxious for warmth. I know my mother is home. She is probably sewing a quilt. She is always sewing quilts. If she sells a quilt, we have dinner. If she fails to sell a quilt, we go hungry. My mother has never failed to sell a quilt. But the threat of hunger is always there.

When I step into the house, my mother is sewing yet another quilt. She is singing a song under her breath. You might assume she is singing a highly traditional Spokane Indian song. She is singing Donna Fargo's "The Happiest Girl in the Whole USA." Improbably, this is a highly traditional Spokane Indian song. The living room is dark in the late afternoon. The house is cold. My mother is wearing her coat and shoes.

"Why don't you turn up the heat?" I ask my mother.

"No electricity," she says.

"Power went out?" I ask.   15

"Didn't pay the bill," she says.

I am colder. I inhale, exhale, my breath visible inside the house. I can hear a car sliding on the icy road outside. My mother is making a quilt. This quilt will pay for the electricity. Her fingers are stiff and painful from the cold. She is sewing as fast as she can.

On the jukebox in the bar: Hank Williams, Patsy Cline, Johnny Cash, Charlie Rich, Freddy Fender, Donna Fargo.

On the radio in the car: Creedence Clearwater Revival, Three Dog Night, Blood, Sweat and Tears, Janis Joplin, early Stones, earlier Beatles.

On the stereo in the house: Glen Campbell, Roy Orbison, Johnny 20 Horton, Loretta Lynn, "The Ballad of the Green Beret."

The fourth-grade music teacher, Mr. Manley, set a row of musical instruments in front of us. From left to right, a flute, clarinet, French horn, trombone, trumpet, tuba, drum. We had our first chance to play that kind of music.

"Now," he explained, "I want all of you to line up behind the instrument you want to learn how to play."

Dawn, Loretta, and Karen lined up behind the flute. Melissa and Michelle behind the clarinet. Lori and Willette behind the French horn. All ten Indian boys lined up behind the drum.

My sister, Mary, was beautiful. She was fourteen years older than me. She wore short skirts and nylons because she was supposed to wear short skirts and nylons. It was expected. Her black hair combed long and straight. 1970. Often, she sat in her favorite chair, the fake leather lounger we rescued from the dump. Holding a hand mirror, she combed her hair, applied her makeup. Much lipstick and eyeshadow, no foundation. She was always leaving the house. I do not remember where she went. I do remember sitting at her feet, rubbing my cheek against her nyloned calf, while she waited for her ride.

25   She died in an early morning fire in Montana in 1981. At the time,
I was sleeping at a friend's house in Washington. I was not dreaming
of my sister.

"Sherman," asks the critic, "how does your work apply to the oral
tradition?"
      "Well," I say, as I hold my latest book close to me, "it doesn't
apply at all because I type this. And I'm really, really quiet when I'm
typing it."

Summer 1977. Steve and I want to attend the KISS concert in Spokane.
KISS is very popular on my reservation. Gene Simmons, the bass
player. Paul Stanley, lead singer and rhythm guitarist. Ace Frehley, lead
guitar. Peter Criss, drummer. All four hide their faces behind elaborate
makeup. Simmons the devil, Stanley the lover, Frehley the space man,
Criss the cat.
      The songs: "Do You Love Me," "Calling Dr. Love," "Love Gun,"
"Makin' Love," "C'mon and Love Me."

30   Steve and I are too young to go on our own. His uncle and aunt,
born-again Christians, decide to chaperon us. Inside the Spokane Coliseum, the four of us find seats far from the stage and the enormous
speakers. Uncle and Aunt wanted to avoid the bulk of the crowd, but
have landed us in the unofficial pot smoking section. We are overwhelmed by the sweet smoke. Steve and I cover our mouths and
noses with Styrofoam cups and try to breathe normally.
      KISS opens their show with staged explosions, flashing red lights,
a prolonged guitar solo by Frehley. Simmons spits fire. The crowd
rushes the stage. All the pot smokers in our section hold lighters, tiny
flames flickering, high above their heads. The songs are so familiar.
We know all the words. The audience sings along.
      The songs: "Let Me Go, Rock 'n Roll," "Detroit Rock City," "Rock
and Roll All Nite."
      The decibel level is tremendous. Steve and I can feel the sound
waves crashing against the Styrofoam cups we hold over our faces.
Aunt and Uncle are panicked, finally assured that the devil plays a
mean guitar. This is too much for them. It is too much for Steve and
me, but we pretend to be disappointed when Aunt and Uncle drag us
out of the coliseum.
      During the drive home, Aunt and Uncle play Christian music on
the radio. Loudly and badly, they sing along. Steve and I are in the
back of the Pacer, looking up through the strangely curved rear window. There is a meteor shower, the largest in a decade. Steve and I
smell like pot smoke. We smile at this. Our ears ring. We make wishes
on the shooting stars, though both of us know that a shooting star is
not a star. It's just a sliver of stone.

I made a very conscious decision to marry an Indian woman, who 35 made a very conscious decision to marry me.

Our hope: to give birth to and raise Indian children who love themselves. That is the most revolutionary act possible.

1982. I am the only Indian student at Reardan High, an all-white school in a small farm town just outside my reservation. I am in the pizza parlor, sharing a deluxe with my white friends. We are talking and laughing. A drunk Indian walks into the parlor. He staggers to the counter and orders a beer. The waiter ignores him. Our table is silent.

At our table, S is shaking her head. She leans toward the table as if to share a secret. We all lean toward her.

"Man," she says, "I hate Indians."

I am curious about the Indian writers who identify themselves as 40 mixed-blood. It must be difficult for them, trying to decide into which container they should place their nouns and verbs. Yet, it must be good to be invisible, as a blond, Aryan-featured Jew might have known in Germany during World War II. Then again, I think of the horror stories that a pale Jew might tell about his life during the Holocaust.

An Incomplete List of People Whom I Wish Were Indian

1. Martin Luther King, Jr.
2. Robert Johnson
3. Meryl Streep
4. Helen Keller
5. Walt Whitman
6. Emily Dickinson
7. Superman
8. Adam
9. Eve
10. Muhammad Ali
11. Billie Jean King
12. John Lennon
13. Jimmy Carter
14. Rosa Parks
15. Shakespeare
16. John Steinbeck
17. Billy the Kid
18. Voltaire
19. Harriet Tubman
20. Flannery O'Connor

21. Pablo Neruda
22. Amelia Earhart
23. Sappho
24. Mary Magdalene
25. Robert DeNiro
26. Susan B. Anthony
27. Kareem Abdul-Jabbar
28. Wilma Rudolph
29. Isadora Duncan
30. Bruce Springsteen
31. Dian Fossey
32. Patsy Cline
33. Jesus Christ

Summer 1995. Seattle, Washington. I am idling at a red light when a car filled with white boys pulls up beside me. The white boy in the front passenger seat leans out his window.

"I hate you Indian motherfuckers," he screams.

I quietly wait for the green light.

1978. David, Randy, Steve, and I decide to form a reservation doo-wop group, like the Temptations. During recess, we practice behind the old tribal school. Steve, a falsetto, is the best singer. I am the worst singer, but have the deepest voice, and am therefore an asset.

45   "What songs do you want to sing?" asks David.

"'Tracks of My Tears,'" says Steve, who always decides these kind of things.

We sing, desperately trying to remember the lyrics to that song. We try to remember other songs. We remember the chorus to most, the first verse of a few, and only one in its entirety. For some unknown reason, we all know the lyrics of "Monster Mash," a novelty hit from the fifties. However, I'm the only one who can manage to sing with the pseudo-Transylvanian accent that "Monster Mash" requires. This dubious skill makes me the lead singer, despite Steve's protests.

"We need a name for our group," says Randy.

"How about The Warriors?" I ask.

50   Everybody agrees. We watch westerns.

We sing "Monster Mash" over and over. We want to be famous. We want all the little Indian girls to shout our names. Finally, after days of practice, we are ready for our debut. Walking in a row like soldiers, the four of us parade around the playground. We sing "Monster Mash." I am in front, followed by Steve, David, then Randy, who is the shortest, but the toughest fighter our reservation has ever known. We sing. We are The Warriors. All the other Indian boys and girls line up behind us as we march. We are heroes. We are loved. I sing with everything I have inside of me: pain, happiness, anger, depression, heart, soul, small intestine. I sing and am rewarded with people who listen.

This is why I am a poet.

I remember watching Richard Nixon, during the whole Watergate affair, as he held a press conference and told the entire world that he was not a liar.

For the first time, I understood that storytellers could be bad people.

Poetry = Anger • Imagination

Every time I venture into the bookstore, I find another book about Indi- 55 ans. There are hundreds of books about Indians published every year, yet so few are written by Indians. I gather all the books written about Indians. I discover:

1. A book written by a person who identifies herself as mixed-blood will sell more copies than a book written by a person who identifies herself as strictly Indian.
2. A book written by a non-Indian will sell more copies than a book written by a mixed-blood or Indian writer.
3. A book about Indian life in the pre-twentieth century, whether written by a non-Indian, mixed-blood, or Indian, will sell more copies than a book about twentieth-century Indian life.
4. If you are a non-Indian writing about Indians, it is almost guaranteed that Tony Hillerman will write something positive about you.
5. Reservation Indian writers are rarely published in any form.
6. Every Indian woman writer will be compared with Louise Erdrich. Every Indian man writer will be compared with Michael Dorris.
7. A very small percentage of the readers of Indian literature have heard of Simon J. Ortiz. This is a crime.
8. Books about the Sioux sell more copies than all of the books written about other tribes combined.
9. Mixed-blood writers often write about any tribe that interests them, whether or not the writer is descended from that tribe.
10. Most of the writers who use obviously Indian names, such as Eagle Woman and Pretty Shield, are usually non-Indian.
11. Non-Indian writers usually say "Great Spirit," "Mother Earth," "Two-Legged, Four-Legged, and Winged." Mixed-

blood writers usually say "Creator," "Mother Earth," "Two-Legged, Four-Legged, and Winged." Indian writers usually say "God," "Earth," "Human Being, Dog, and Bird."

12. If an Indian book contains no dogs, then the book is written by a non-Indian or mixed-blood writer.

13. If there are winged animals who aren't supposed to have wings on the cover of the book, then it is written by a non-Indian.

14. Successful non-Indian writers are thought to be learned experts on Indian life. Successful mixed-blood writers are thought to be wonderful translators of Indian life. Successful Indian writers are thought to be traditional storytellers of Indian life.

15. Very few Indian and mixed-blood writers speak their tribal languages. Even fewer non-Indian writers speak their tribal languages.

16. Mixed-bloods often write exclusively about Indians, even if they grew up in non-Indian communities.

17. Indians often write exclusively about reservation life, even if they never lived on a reservation.

18. Non-Indian writers always write about reservation life.

19. Nobody has written the great urban Indian novel yet.

20. Most non-Indians who write about Indians are fiction writers. They write fiction about Indians because it sells.

Have you stood in a crowded room where nobody looks like you? If you are white, have you stood in a room full of black people? Are you an Irish man who has strolled through the streets of Compton? If you are black, have you stood in a room full of white people? Are you an African man who has been playing the back nine at the local country club? If you are a woman, have you stood in a room full of men? Are you Sandra Day O'Connor or Ruth Ginsburg?

Since I left the reservation, almost every room I enter is filled with people who do not look like me. There are only two million Indians in this country. We could all fit into one medium-sized city. We should look into it.

Often, I am most alone in bookstores where I am reading from my work. I look up from the page at a sea of white faces. This is frightening.

There was an apple tree outside my grandmother's house on the reservation. The apples were green; my grandmother's house was green. This was the game. My siblings and I would try to sneak apples from the tree. Sometimes, our friends would join our raiding expeditions. My grandmother believed green apples were poison and was simply trying to protect us from sickness. There is nothing biblical about this story.

The game had rules. We always had to raid the tree during day- 60 light. My grandmother had bad eyes and it would have been unfair to challenge her during the dark. We all had to approach the tree at the same time. Arnold, my older brother, Kim and Arlene, my younger twin sisters. We had to climb the tree to steal apples, ignoring the fruit that hung low to the ground.

Arnold, of course, was the best apple thief on the reservation. He was chubby but quick. He was fearless in the tree, climbing to the top for the plumpest apples. He'd hang from a branch with one arm, reach for apples with the other, and fill his pockets with his booty. I loved him like crazy. My sisters were more conservative. They often grabbed one apple and are it quickly while they sat on a sturdy branch. I always wanted the green apples that contained a hint of red. While we were busy raiding the tree, we'd also keep an eye on my grandmother's house. She was a big woman, nearly six feet tall. At the age of seventy, she could still outrun any ten-year-old.

Arnold, of course, was always the first kid out of the tree. He'd hang from a branch, drop to the ground, and scream loudly, announcing our presence to our grandmother. He'd run away, leaving my sisters and me stuck in the tree. We'd scramble to the ground and try to escape. If our grandmother said our name, we were automatically captured.

"Junior," she'd shout and I'd freeze. It was the rule. A dozen Indian kids were sometimes in that tree, scattering in random directions when our grandmother burst out of the house. If our grandmother remembered your name, you were a prisoner of war. And, believe me, no matter how many kids were running away, my grandmother always remembered my name.

"Junior," she'd shout and I would close my eyes in disgust. Captured again! I'd wait as she walked up to me. She'd hold out her hand and I'd give her any stolen apples. Then she'd smack me gently on the top of my head. I was free to run then, pretending she'd never caught me in the first place. I'd try to catch up with my siblings and friends. I would shout their names as I ran through the trees surrounding my grandmother's house.

My grandmother died when I was fourteen years old. I miss her. I 65 miss everybody.

So many people claim to be Indian, speaking of an Indian grandmother, a warrior grandfather. Let's say the United States government announced that every Indian had to return to their reservation. How many people would shove their Indian ancestor back into the closet?

My mother still makes quilts. My wife and I sleep beneath one. My brother works for our tribal casino. One sister works for our bingo hall, while the other works in the tribal finance department. Our adopted little brother, James, who is actually our second cousin, is a freshman at Reardan High School. He can run the mile in five minutes.

My father used to leave us for weeks at a time to drink with his friends and cousins. I missed him so much I'd cry myself sick. Every time he left, I ended up in the emergency room. But I always got well and he always came back. He'd walk in the door without warning. We'd forgive him.

I could always tell when he was going to leave. He would be tense, quiet, unable to concentrate. He'd flip through magazines and television channels. He'd open the refrigerator door, study its contents, shut the door, and walk away. Five minutes later, he'd be back at the fridge, rearranging items on the shelves. I would follow him from place to place, trying to prevent his escape.

70   Once, he went into the bathroom, which had no windows, while I sat outside the only door and waited for him. I could not hear him inside. I knocked on the thin wood. I was five years old.

"Are you there?" I asked. "Are you still there?"

Years later, I am giving a reading at a bookstore in Spokane, Washington. There is a large crowd. I read a story about an Indian father who leaves his family for good. He moves to a city a thousand miles away. Then he dies. It is a sad story. When I finish, a woman in the front row breaks into tears.

"What's wrong?" I ask her.

"I'm so sorry about your father," she says.

75   "Thank you," I say. "But that's my father sitting right next to you."

Responding to Reading

1. Why does Alexie call his memoir an "unauthorized autobiography"?
2. What is Alexie's attitude toward his Indian heritage? Is his attitude consistent, or does he seem to have mixed feelings about his heritage?
3. What do you think Alexie is saying in this essay about the difference between fiction and nonfiction? Between storytelling and lying?

Responding in Writing

Alexie mentions many musicians and many songs in his "unauthorized autobiography." What do you think these references add to his memoir?

THE KEY TO MY FATHER

Harlan Coben

1962–

After graduating from Amherst College as political science major and work-
ing in the travel industry, Harlan Coben became a well-known writer of
mystery novels set in the glamorous worlds of the media and professional
sports. Since 1990, Coben has published twelve popular mystery novels, in-
cluding No Second Chance *(2003) and* Tell No One *(2001), which is*
being made into a film. In the following short story, which appeared in the
New York Times *on June 15, 2003—Father's Day—Coben considers how*
much and how little a son can know about his own father. To learn more
about Coben, visit his Web site, http://www.harlancoben.com/.

Let's get something straight right away: my father was hopelessly
unhip. He was the corporeal embodiment of an Air Supply eight-
track. He'd come home from work, shed the powder-blue suit with
reversible vest, the tie so polyester it would melt during heat waves,
the V-neck Hanes undershirt of startling white, the gray socks bought
by the dozen at Burlington Coat Factory. He'd don a logo T-shirt that
was compulsorily a size too snug, if you know what I mean, and
shorts that were, uh, short, like something John McEnroe wore at
Wimbledon in 1979.

His sunglasses were big, too big. They might have worked on
Sophia Loren but on Dad they looked like manhole covers.

He had thin legs. My mom teased him about this, this 6-foot-2
man with the barrel chest and olive skin, teetering on spindly legs.
His hair, as described by my mother, was "tired," wispy and flyaway.
He had big arms. To his children, they looked like oak branches. The
biceps would grow spongy with the years. But they never had time to
fully atrophy.

He would play ball with us, but he was a terrible athlete.

I remember going to that Little League coaches' softball game, the   5
one they have at the end of every season, and watching my father—
this man who had taught me to keep my elbow up and back foot
planted—take to the plate and ground out weakly to third. Three
times in a row. To his credit, he never made excuses. "You," he'd tell
me. "You're an athlete. Me, I'm a spaz."

His after-shave was Old Spice. There had been a radical period
when he tried an eau called Royal Copenhagen—someone had given
him a gift set and damned if he was going to let it go to waste—but he
veered back onto his Old Spice route. That is still my strongest bar
mitzvah recollection—that smell.

No, I can't tell you what part of the haphtara I recited from the pulpit of B'nai Jeshurun. Something from Ezekiel, I think. But there's that part in the ceremony where the father blesses the son. My father bent down and whispered in my ear. He said something about loving me and being proud—much as I want to, I can't remember the exact words—and then he kissed me on the cheek. I remember the feel of his cheek on mine, the catcher's-glove hand cupping my head, and the smell of Old Spice.

On Saturday mornings, we went to Seymour's luncheonette on Livingston Avenue for a milkshake and maybe a pack of baseball cards. I'd sit on a stool at the counter and twirl. He'd stand next to me, always, as if that was what a man did.

He'd lean against the counter and eat—too quickly, I think. He was never fat but he was always on the wrong side of the weight curve. He was uneven about physical activity. He'd discover a work-out program, do it for three months, go idle for about six, find something new. Rinse, repeat. Like with shampoo.

10   He hated his job.

He never told me this. He dutifully went to work every day. But I knew. He didn't have a lot of friends either, but that was by choice. He could have been a popular man. People liked him. He could feign charm and warmth, but there was a coldness there. He cared only about his family and he cared with a ferocity that both frightened and exhilarated. You know those stories about someone lifting a car to save a trapped loved one? It took little to imagine him performing such a feat. The world was his family—the rest of the planet's inhabitants no more than the periphery, deep background, scenery.

The night was his domain. He slept lightly, too lightly. I wonder if that is to blame, the way he'd startle awake. I would try my hardest to tiptoe past his door, but no matter how great my stealth, he would jerk upright in his bed as if I'd dropped a Popsicle on his stomach. Every night the same thing:

"Marc?" he'd shout.

"Yes, Dad."

15   "Something wrong?"

"Just going to the bathroom," I'd say. "I've been going by myself since I was 14."

During my freshman year at college, after a particularly debauched frat party, I was struck by a strange realization: this was the first time I'd woken up sick without my father present. His hand was not on my forehead. He was not speaking softly or rubbing my back.

I was alone.

I blame myself for what happened.

20   Three days before my college graduation, I dropped my father off at the airport.

We were late. He ran to catch his flight. That is the image I can't shake all these years later. My father, hopelessly unhip and out of shape, running for that stupid flight so he could be at a meeting that meant nothing to anybody.

Six hours later, he called from the Comfort Suite in Tampa.

"Let me speak to your mother."

I handed her the phone.

I watched her listen. I saw her face turn white.   25

"What?" I asked.

"He's having chest pains, but he says he's fine."

And I knew.

And she knew. I called the front desk. I told them to send an ambulance. I called my father back. "I told the front desk to send someone up," and then my father said the most frightening thing of all: "O.K."

No argument, no brave front, no I'm fine.   30

"But I have to find the room key first," he added.

"What?"

"They'll be here soon. I have to go. I have to find the key."

"Forget the key."

"You might need it."   35

"For what?"

But he hung up. And again I knew. He had never been ill, but I knew. With my father's strength, you somehow still sensed the fragile.

My mother and I rushed to the airport. I called the hotel from a pay phone. They just wheeled him out the lobby, I was told.

Wheeled him out. I pictured the oxygen mask on his face. I imagined him as I had never seen him: afraid.

He liked building things, my father, but he was bad with his 40 hands. He gardened on weekends, but our shrubs never looked right, not like the shrubs that belonged to the Bauers, who lived next door. Their lawn looked as if it'd been trimmed for a P.G.A. event.

Ours had dandelions tall enough to go on the adult rides at Six Flags.

My father fought in the Korean War but never talked about it.

I didn't even know he'd been in the military until I explored his junk drawer when I was 8 and found a bunch of medals in the bottom. They were loose in the drawer, mingling with spare change.

Our plane had a stopover at the Atlanta airport, the epicenter of the stopover. I called the hospital. The nurse assured me that my father was fine.

But I didn't believe her. She transferred me to the doctor. I told 45 the doctor I was calling about my father, that I was his son. The doctor did that calm voice thing and asked me my name. He told me,

Marc—using my name so often it became like an annoying tick—that my father was in serious condition, Marc, that they are going to operate in a few minutes. I felt my legs go. He's awake and comfortable, the doctor told me. He understands what is happening. I asked to speak to him. "The phone cord won't reach, Marc," the doctor said.

"Tell him we're on our way," I insisted.

"I will." But I didn't believe him.

My father always longed for a Cadillac. He got one when he turned 52.

He listened only to AM radio. Every once in a while a certain song would come on and he'd turn it up. His face would change. The lines would soften. He'd lean back and steer with his wrists and whistle.

50   By the time we arrived at the hospital, night had fallen. I sat in the waiting room. He was still in surgery. My mother did not speak, something that is usually accompanied by a parting sea or burning bush.

I began to make deals with whatever higher power would listen, you know the kind, about what I'd do, what I'd risk, what I'd trade, if only it could be morning again and we could leave for that damn plane a few minutes earlier and if he hadn't run to catch that flight, if he'd just walked instead, if he didn't devour his food, if he kept up with an exercise program, if I'd been an easier son.

At 4 a.m., that awful hospital beeping sound echoed down the still corridor, then a rush that stole our breath. The air was suddenly gone. And so, too, was my father.

We bury him on Father's Day.

The weather is, of course, spectacular, mocking my gloom. The men his age come up to me and tell me all about their own heart problems, about their close calls, about how lucky they've been. I look through them, wondering why they are the ones who get to stand before me, happily breathing. I wish them ill. I call his former boss, the one who sold the company and made my father stuff envelopes with his resume at the age of 56. I tell him that if he shows up at the funeral, I'll punch him in the face. He, too, is to blame.

55   I wonder if my father was scared near the end or if he went into surgery thinking it would be all be O.K. Don't know, of course.

There is a lot I don't know. I don't know what my father wanted out of life. I don't know what he wanted to be when he was a young man, before I came around and changed everything. He never expressed any of that to me. And I never asked.

A week after the funeral, I call his doctor down in Tampa.

"He died alone," I say.

"He knew you were there."

60   "You didn't tell him."

"I did."

"What did he say?"

The doctor takes a second.

"He said for you to check his pocket."

"What?"   65

"You'd need a place to stay overnight. He said to check his pocket."

Cradling the phone, I go to the closet where his belongings, still in the plastic hospital bag the nurse handed me, are hanging. I break the seal. The Old Spice scent is faint but there. I dig past the Hanes V-Neck and find his pants.

"What else?" I ask.

"Pardon?"

"What else did he say?"   70

"That's it."

"Those were his final words? Check his pocket?"

His voice is suddenly soft.

"Yes."

My fingers slip into the pocket of his pants and hit something   75
metallic. I pull it out.

The hotel key. He'd found it after all. He put it in his pocket. His last words, his last act, for us.

I still have the key.

I keep it in a drawer with his medals.

Responding to Reading

1. Why does the narrator blame himself for his father's death? Who (or what) else does he blame? What, specifically, do you think the narrator regrets?

2. What does the key in his father's pocket represent to the narrator? In what sense is it, as the story's title claims, "the key to [his] father"?

3. Paragraph 10 begins with the sentence, "He hated his job." Paragraph 11 ends with the sentence, "The world was his family—the rest of the planet's inhabitants no more than the periphery, deep background, scenery." What is the significance of these two sentences in the story?

Responding in Writing

Coben uses many small physical details—for example, his gray socks and his aftershave—to characterize his father. List as many of these details as you can. Then, create a similar list of the physical details that characterize one of your own parents.

--- FOCUS ---

How Has Divorce Redefined the Family?

Responding to the Image

1. How do you interpret this image? Do you think that most people involved in a divorce want to separate themselves from memories of the past?
2. Who do you suppose might have torn this picture in half? Under what circumstances?

PUTTING DIVORCE IN PERSPECTIVE
Stephanie Coontz
1944–

Born in Seattle, Stephanie Coontz attended the University of California, Berkeley, where she earned a BA degree (1966). She received an MA degree from the University of Washington, Seattle (1970) and has taught family studies at The Evergreen State College since 1975. Her articles have appeared in the Wall Street Journal, *the* Washington Post, Vogue, *and many other publications. She has published six books on family history, gender roles, and family issues, including* The Way We Never Were: American Families and the Nostalgia Trap *(1992) and* The Way We Really Are: Coming to Terms with America's Changing Families *(1997), from which the following essay is taken. To learn more about Coontz, visit her Web site, http://academic.evergreen.edu/c/coontzs/home.htm/.*

We have already accepted the fact that aging Americans are increasingly unlikely to live out their lives in "traditional" nuclear families, where they can be supported and cared for entirely by a spouse or a child. We can no longer assume that a high enough proportion of kids grow up with both biological parents that society can continue to ignore the "exceptions" that were there all along. Nor can our school schedules, work policies, and even emotional expectations of family life continue to presume that every household has a husband to earn the income and a wife to take care of family needs.

The social and personal readjustments required by these changes can seem awfully daunting. Here's what a spokesman for the Institute for American Values told me during a tape-recorded debate over whether it was possible to revive male breadwinning and restore permanent marriage to its former monopoly over personal life: "The strongest point in your argument is that the toothpaste is out of the tube. There's no longer the subordinate status of women to the extent there was in earlier eras—there is simply too much freedom and money sloshing around. We may be heading into what some sociologists call a 'postmarriage society,' where women will raise the children and men will not be there in any stable, institutional way. If so, we'd better build more prisons, even faster than we're building 'em now."[1]

I don't think the consequences of facing reality are quite so bleak. As my grandmother used to say, sometimes problems are opportunities in work clothes. Changes in gender roles, for example, may be hard to adjust to, yet they hold out the possibility of constructing far more honest and satisfying relationships between men and women, parents and children, than in the past. But this doesn't mean that every change is for the better, or that we don't pay a price for some of the new freedoms that have opened up. Divorce is a case in point. While divorce has rescued some adults and children from destructive marriages, it has thrown others into economic and psychological turmoil.

For the family values crusaders, this is where the discussion of how to help families begins and ends. "Let's face it," one "new consensus" proponent told me privately, "the interests of adults and children are often different, and there are too many options today for parents to pursue personal fulfillment at the expense of their children's needs. Sure there are other issues. But unless we keep the heat on about the dangers of divorce, parents will be tempted to put their own selfish concerns above the needs of their children." Fighting the "divorce culture" has to be the top priority, he argued, because "it's the one thing we can affect" by making parents realize what disastrous consequences divorce has for the future of their kids.

5   I have met only a tiny handful of divorced parents who didn't worry long and hard about the effects of divorce on their children (almost a third of divorced women, for example, attempted a reconciliation between the time of initial separation and the final divorce, according to data from 1987–1988).[2] And while it's true that a few pop psychologists have made irresponsible claims that divorce is just a "growth experience," I don't believe we are really a culture that "celebrates" divorce, even if well-meaning people sometimes issue overly rosy reassurances to those who have undergone this trauma.

But for the record, let me be clear. Ending a marriage is an agonizing process that can seriously wound everyone involved, especially the children. Divorce can interfere with effective parenting and deprive children of parental resources. Remarriage solves some of the economic problems associated with divorce but introduces a new set of tensions that sometimes, at least temporarily, make things even more difficult.

Surely, however, it's permissible to put the risks in perspective without being accused of glorifying single parenthood or attempting, in Barbara Dafoe Whitehead's words, "to discredit the two-parent family." And the truth is that there has been a lot of irresponsible doom-saying about "disrupted" families. In a widely distributed article in the *Atlantic Monthly*, for example, Whitehead spends eight pages explaining why kids from divorced families face almost insurmountable deficits. Then, when she's convinced the average single mom to run out immediately to find a father for her child, she lowers the boom: Children in stepfamilies turn out even worse.[3]

While it is true that children in divorced and remarried families are more likely to drop out of school, exhibit emotional distress, get in trouble with the law, and abuse drugs or alcohol than children who grow up with both biological parents, most kids, from *every* kind of family, avoid these perils. And to understand what the increased risk entails for individual families, we need to be clear about what sociologists mean when they talk about such children having more behavior problems or lower academic achievement. What they really mean to say is *not* that children in divorced families have more problems but that *more* children of divorced parents have problems.

It's an important distinction, especially if you are a divorced or divorcing parent. It doesn't mean that all kids from divorced families will have more problems. There will be outstanding kids and kids with severe problems in both groups, but there will be a slightly higher proportion of kids from never-disrupted families in the outstanding group and a slightly lower proportion of them in the group with severe problems.

As family researcher Paul Amato notes, in measures of both achievement and adjustment, "a large proportion of children in the divorced group score *higher* than the average score of children in the nondivorced group. Similarly, a large proportion of children in the nondivorced group score *lower* than the average score of children in the divorced group." Comparing the average outcomes of children in various types of families obscures the fact that there is "more variability in the adjustment of children in divorced and remarried families than in nondivorced families." So knowing there are more divorced kids who do poorly is not really helpful. The question is how many more children from divorced and never-married parents are doing poorly, and what accounts for this, since some divorced children do exceptionally well and most are within normal range.[4]

Researchers who use clinical samples, drawn from people already in therapy because their problems are severe enough that they have sought outside help, tend to come up with the highest estimates of how many children are damaged by divorce. In 1989, for example, Judith Wallerstein published a long-term study of middle-class children from divorced families, arguing that almost half experienced long-term pain, worry, and insecurity that adversely affected their love and work relationships. Her work was the basis for Whitehead's claim in the *Atlantic Monthly* that "the evidence is in: Dan Quayle was right." But this supposedly definitive study, based on a self-selected sample of only sixty couples, did not compare the children of divorced couples with those of nondivorced ones to determine whether some of their problems might have stemmed from other factors, such as work pressures, general social insecurities, or community fragmentation. Moreover, the sample was drawn from families already experiencing difficulty and referred to the clinic for therapy. Only a third of the families were judged to be functioning adequately *prior* to the divorce.[5]

Research based on more representative samples yields much lower estimates of the risks. Paul Amato and Bruce Keith recently reviewed nearly every single quantitative study that has been done on divorce. Although they found clear associations with lower levels of child well-

10

being, these were, on average, "not large." And the more carefully controlled the studies were, the smaller were the differences reported. The
"large majority" of children of divorce, wrote eleven family researchers
in response to Whitehead's misuse of their data, do not experience severe or long-term problems: *Most* do not drop out of school, get arrested, abuse drugs, or suffer long-term emotional distress. "Examining
a nationally representative sample of children and adolescents living in
four diverse family structures," write researchers Alan Acock and
David Demo, "we find few statistically significant differences across
family types on measures of socioemotional adjustment and well-
being."[6]

Sara McLanahan, often cited by family values crusaders for her research on the risks of divorce, points out that divorce does not account
for the majority of such social problems as high school dropout
rates and unwed teen motherhood. "Outlawing divorce would raise
the national high school graduation rate from about 86 percent to 88
percent. . . . It would reduce the risk of a premarital birth among young
black women from about 45 percent to 39 percent."[7]

To be sure I'm not minimizing the risks, let's take a comparatively
high estimate of divorce-related problems, based on the research of
Mavis Hetherington, one of the most respected authorities in the field.
She argues that "20 to 25 percent of kids from divorced families have
behavior problems—about twice as many as the 10 percent from nondivorced families. You can say, 'Wow, that's terrible,'" she remarks,
"but it means that 75 to 80 percent of kids from divorced families *aren't*
having problems, that the vast majority are doing perfectly well."[8]

15   The fact that twice as many children of divorce have problems as
children in continuously married families should certainly be of concern to parents. But it's important to remember that the doubling of
risk is not evenly distributed among all families who divorce. Some of
the families who contribute to these averages have had several divorces
and remarriages. A study of boys who had been involved in divorce
and remarriage found that those who had experienced many transitions, such as two or more divorces and remarriages, "showed the
poorest adjustment." But even here the causal relationship involved
more than divorce alone. It was "antisocial mothers" who were most
likely *both* to experience many marital transitions and to engage in
unskilled parenting practices that in turn placed their sons at risk for
maladjustment.[9]

Many of the problems seen in children of divorced parents are
caused not by divorce alone but by other frequently coexisting yet ana-
lytically separate factors such as poverty, financial loss, school relocation, or a prior history of severe marital conflict. When Rand Institute
researchers investigated the relation between children's test scores and
residence in a female-headed family, for example, the gross scores they

obtained showed a significant deficit, but the disadvantage of children in mother-headed families was reduced to "essentially zero" when they controlled for other factors. "Apparently," they concluded, "a lot of the gross difference is . . . due to income, low maternal education, and other factors that frequently characterize single-parent families, rather than family structure itself."[10]

Income differences account for almost 50 percent of the disadvantage faced by children in single-parent homes. The tendency of less-educated women to have higher rates of divorce and unwed motherhood also skews the statistics. In fact, a mother's educational background has more impact on her child's welfare than her marital status. Other research suggests that the amount of television kids watch affects aggressive behavior whether or not their parents are divorced; one survey found that eating meals together was associated with a bigger advantage in school performance than was having two parents.[11]

Researchers who managed to disentangle the effects of divorce itself from the effects of a change in residence found that relocation and loss of peer support were more likely to interfere with school completion than parental separation. McLanahan's research with Gary Sandefur suggests that up to 40 percent of the increased risk of dropping out of school for children in single-parent families is attributable to moving after the divorce. A 1996 study found that the impact of family structure on schooling is "reduced substantially" when the number of school changes is controlled.[12]

Obviously, divorce often triggers financial loss, withdrawal of parental attention, and change of residence or schools. In this sense it is fair to say that divorce causes many childhood problems by creating these other conditions. But it makes more sense to adopt policies to minimize income loss or school and residence changes than to prohibit divorce across the board, for there are no hard and fast links between family structure, parental behaviors, and children's outcomes. One pair of leading researchers in the field conclude that there is "*no clear, consistent, or convincing evidence that alterations in family structure per se are detrimental to children's development.*"[13]

The worst problems for children stem from parental conflict, before, during, and after divorce—*or within marriage.* In fact, children in "intact" families that are marked by high levels of conflict tend to do worse than children in divorced and never-married families. Two researchers who compared family types and child outcomes over a period of five years found that children who remained in highly conflicted marriages had more severe behavior problems than children in any other kind of family. They "were more depressed, impulsive, and hyperactive" than children from either low-conflict marriages or divorced families.[14]

In the first two years after a divorce, says Hetherington, children of divorce "look worse off than kids from intact families, even bad intact families." But after two or three years, "the kids who lived in one-parent households, with a competent mother, were doing better—with half as many behavioral problems—than the kids in the conflict-ridden homes."[15]

Furthermore, the problems found in children of divorced parents were often there months, or even years, *prior* to the parental separation. Eight to twelve years before a family breakup, researchers have found, parents who would eventually divorce were already reporting significantly more problems with their children than parents who ended up staying together. This finding suggests that "the association between divorce and poor parent–child relationships may be spurious; the low quality of the parents' marriage may be a cause of both." Alternatively, severely troubled children may help to precipitate a divorce, further distorting the averages.[16]

Some behaviors that make kids look worse off in the first few years after divorce may actually be the first steps toward recovery from damaging family patterns. For example, psychologist Richard Weissbourd cites the case of Ann, a 10-year-old girl who had become the family caretaker to cope with her father's alcoholism and her mother's long work hours. This role gave her many satisfactions and a strong sense of importance within the family, but it cut her off from friends and schoolmates. After the divorce, Ann's mother recovered from her own stress, spent more time at home, and resumed her parental role. Ann resented her "demotion" in the family and began to throw temper tantrums that landed her in a therapist's office. Yet her turmoil, far from being evidence of the destructive effects of divorce, was probably a necessary stage in the move to healthier relations with both parents and peers.[17]

One long-term study found that divorce produced extremes of *either* negative or positive behavior in children. At one end of the spectrum were children who were aggressive and insecure. These children were likely to have been exposed to a disengaged or inconsistently harsh parenting style. A significant number of these children were boys who had been temperamentally difficult early in life and whose behavior problems were made worse by family conflict or divorce.

25   At the other extreme were caring, competent children who were exceptionally popular, self-confident, well behaved, and academically adept. These children had the most stable peer friendships and solid relations with adults. And a high proportion—more than half—of the girls in this group came from divorced, female-headed families. Their mothers were typically warm, but not always available, and most of these girls had had to assume some caretaking responsibility for siblings, grandparents, or even their mothers at a young age. "Experiences

in a one-parent, mother-headed family seemed to have a positive effect for these girls."[18]

As Mavis Hetherington sums up the research, most family members go through a period of difficulty after a divorce but recover within two to three years. Some exhibit immediate and long-term problems, while others adapt well in the early stages but have problems that emerge later. "Finally, a substantial minority of adults and children . . . emerge as psychologically enhanced and exceptionally competent and fulfilled individuals."[19] It should be reassuring for divorced parents to realize that such enhancement is possible, and that we also know a lot about how to avoid the *worst* outcomes for children.

When Divorce Has Long-Term Effects, and How to Minimize Them

I don't want to trivialize the consequences of divorce. Transitions of any kind are stressful for kids, mostly because they are stressful for parents and therefore disrupt parental functioning. But it is important to point out the variability in the outcomes of divorce. Divorce is only one part of a much larger group of factors affecting parental functioning and child well-being. In many cases, the conditions imperiling children existed in the family prior to the divorce and would not be solved by convincing the parents to get back together. In other cases, divorce does create new problems but parents can minimize the disruptions if they set their minds to it. For these reasons, researchers have begun to emphasize that divorce is an ongoing process beginning long before physical separation and continuing long after the divorce is finalized. It is the *process*, not the divorce itself, that "is most significant in shaping subsequent family dynamics and individual adjustment."[20]

A critical factor in children's adjustment to divorce is how effectively the custodial parent functions. Usually this means the mother. The main problem for children of divorce is when depression, anger, or economic pressures distract their mothers' attention. A recent study of 200 single-parent families in Iowa found that somewhere between 20 and 25 percent of mothers became preoccupied in the aftermath of divorce, paying less attention to what their children were doing or focusing too much on negative behavior and responding to it harshly. A large part of their reactions stemmed from economic stress. But many of these distracted mothers had always been more self-centered, impatient, disorganized, and insensitive than the other mothers, traits that may have triggered their divorces in the first place. Only a small amount of dysfunctional parenting seemed to be associated with family structure alone, yet there were enough incidences for researchers to conclude that divorce does make it harder for many mothers to parent well, even when they are stable individuals who are not overwhelmed by economic stress.[21]

The main danger for children is conflict between parents during and after divorce. Few marriages disintegrate overnight; the last few months or years are often marked by severe strife. More than half of divorced couples in one national survey reported frequent fighting prior to separation. More than a third of those who fought said that the fights sometimes became physical. And children were often present during these incidents.[22]

30   Divorce may allow parents to back off, but sometimes it produces continuing or even escalating conflict over finances and custody. And post-divorce marital conflict, especially around issues connected with the children, is the largest single factor associated with poor adjustment in youngsters whose parents have divorced. A study of more than 1,000 divorcing families in California found that children in disputed custody cases (about 10 percent of the sample) seemed the most disturbed. They were two to four times more likely than the national average to develop emotional and behavioral problems, with boys generally displaying more symptoms than girls.[23]

Parents certainly should be educated about the potential problems associated with divorce and with raising children alone. But outlawing divorce or making it harder to get would not prevent parents from fighting or separating, and could easily prolong the kinds of conflict and disrupted parenting that raise the risks for children. While people who are simply discontented or bored with their relationship should be encouraged to try and work things out, campaigns to scare parents into staying married for the sake of the kids are simply out of touch with the real complexities and variability in people's lives. As psychologist Weissbourd writes, "divorce typically has complex costs and benefits" for children. They may be more vulnerable in some ways after the divorce and more protected in other ways.[24]

Studies show that fathers in unhappy marriages tend to treat their daughters negatively, especially when the daughters are young. These girls may benefit by getting away from this negative spillover, even if their brothers go through a hard period. Women who are dissatisfied with their marriage are at high risk of developing a drinking problem. Divorce or separation lowers such women's stress and tends to reduce their alcohol dependence. Getting sober may improve their parenting enough to counteract the negative effects of divorce on their children.[25]

As such examples reveal, open conflict is not the only process that harms children in a bad marriage. One recent study of adolescent self-image found the *lowest* self-esteem in teens of two-parent families where fathers showed little interest in their children. Such youngsters, lacking even the excuse of the father's absence to explain his lack of interest, were more likely than kids in divorced families to internalize the problem in self-blame.[26]

Given these kinds of trade-offs, it is not enough to just reiterate the risks of divorce. We also need to tell people what they can do to minimize these risks. The most important thing is to contain conflict with the former spouse and to refrain from "bad mouthing" the other parent to the children. Divorcing parents must not involve their children in the hostilities between them or demand that the child choose sides. They should not ask children to report on the other's activities, or to keep secrets about what's going on in one household.[27]

Leaders of the "new consensus" crusade are fond of saying that trying to teach people how to divorce with less trauma is like offering low-tar cigarettes to people instead of helping them quit smoking. But this is a sound bite, not a sound argument. Yes, there are clearly people who could save their marriages, or at least postpone their divorces, and should be encouraged to do so by friends, colleagues, or professionals who know their situation. But there are others whose marriages are in the long run more damaging to themselves and their children than any problems associated with divorce. In between there are many more people for whom it's a close call. Yet since "most divorced mothers are as effective as their married counterparts once the parenting boundaries are renegotiated," and since most families recover from divorce within a few years, it is neither accurate nor helpful to compare divorce to a carcinogenic substance.[28]

Is it possible for divorced parents to behave civilly? A national sample of parents who divorced in 1978 and were interviewed one, three, and five years later found that half of the couples were able to coparent effectively. The other half, unfortunately, were unable "to confine their anger to their marital differences; it infused all the relationships in the family" and made cooperative or even civil coparenting extremely rare. A more recent California study found that three to four years after separation, only a quarter of divorced parents were engaged in such "conflicted coparenting," marked by high discord and low communication. Twenty-nine percent were engaging in cooperative coparenting, characterized by high communication and low dissension, while 41 percent were engaging in a kind of parallel parenting, where there was low communication between parents but also low conflict.[29]

Time helps. In one study of couples splitting up, "strong negative feelings among women dropped from 43 to 19 percent in the two years following separation, while for men they declined from 22 to 10 percent." There are encouraging signs that more immediate results can be obtained when parents are shown how their behavior affects their children. A recent study found that simply having children fill out a questionnaire and then sending that information to their divorced parents was enough to effect "significant change in the behavior of the parents." Specialists in divorce research recommend early intervention strategies to encourage parents to think of themselves as a "binuclear" family and separate their ongoing parenting commitments from any leftover marital disagreements.[30]

We know that people can learn to manage anger, and this seems to be the key to successful coparenting. It is not necessary for parents to like each other or even to "make up." The difference between divorced parents who were and were not able to coparent effectively, writes researcher Constance Ahrons, "was that the more cooperative group *managed* their anger better. They accepted it and diverted it, and it diminished over time." Establishing boundaries between the parents' relationship with each other and their relationships with their children is critical. For instance, it helps if parents have a friend to whom they can vent about all the crazy or terrible things they think their former partner has done. This is not something that should be discussed with the children. Most parents know this in the abstract, but they often need a friend, colleague, or professional to help them prevent their feelings about the partner from spilling over into interactions with their children.[31]

What about the problem of father absence? Surveys at the beginning of the 1980s found that more than 50 percent of children living with divorced mothers had not seen their fathers within the preceding year, while only 17 percent reported visiting their fathers weekly. But more recent studies show higher levels of paternal contact. A 1988 sample found that 25 percent of previously married fathers saw their children at least once a week, and only 18 percent had not visited their children during the past year. This may mean that as divorce has become more common, fathers have begun to realize that they must work out better ways of remaining in touch with their children, while mothers may be more willing to encourage such involvement.[32]

40   One of the puzzling findings of much divorce research is how little impact frequent visitation with fathers has on children's adjustment after divorce. But one recent study found evidence that while divorce weakened the significance of fathers for children's overall psychological well-being, a close relationship to a father, even when contact was minimal, seemed to have a strong association with a child's happiness. Other research shows that nonresidential fathers help their children best when they continue to behave as parents, "monitoring academic progress, emphasizing moral principles, discussing problems, providing advice, and supporting the parenting decisions of the custodial mother," rather than behaving as a friendly uncle who shows up to have fun with the children for a day.[33]

People need to know this kind of information, and a truly pro-family social movement would spend much more time publicizing such findings than making sweeping pronouncements about what's good and bad for children in the abstract. Again, it's a matter of coming to terms with reality. Historically speaking, the rise of alternatives to marriage is a done deal. Right here, right now, 50 percent of children are growing up in a home with someone other than two married, biological parents. It is not a pro-child act to deny divorced parents the information they need to help them function better or to try so hard to prevent divorce that we suppress research allowing parents to weigh their options, both pro and con.

Of course we should help parents stay together where possible, but the evidence suggests that we will save more marriages by developing new family values and support systems than by exhorting people to revive traditional commitments. And the fact remains that we will never again live in a world where people are compelled to stay married "until death do us part." Some couples will not be willing to go through the hard work of renegotiating traditional gender roles and expectations. Some individuals will choose personal autonomy over family commitments. Some marriages will fail for other reasons, such as abuse, personal betrayals, or chronic conflict—and often it is in no one's interest that such marriages be saved.

That is why, shocking though it may sound to the family values think tanks, we need, as researcher William Goode suggests, to "institutionalize" divorce in the same way that marriage remains institutionalized—to surround it with clear obligations and rights, supported by law, customs, and social expectations. To institutionalize divorce is not the same as advocating it. It simply means society recognizes that divorce will continue to occur, whether we like it or not. Reducing the ambiguity, closing the loopholes, and getting rid of the idea that every divorce case is a new contest in which there are no accepted ground rules will *minimize* the temptation for individuals to use divorce to escape obligations to children. Setting up clear expectations about what is civilized behavior will cut back on the adversarial battles that bankrupt adults and escalate the bitterness to which children are exposed.[34]

As one divorce lawyer writes, "I see couples every day who never lay a hand on one another but are experts in using children as instruments of psychological torture." Such children are not served well, she argues, by a high-minded refusal to sanction divorce or a rear-guard battle to slow it down. As the president of the Family and Divorce Mediation Council of Greater New York puts it: "Blaming children's problems on a megalith called 'Divorce' is a bit like stating that cancer is caused by chemotherapy. Neither divorce nor chemotherapy is a step people hope to have to take in their lives, but each may be the healthiest option in a given situation." He suggests that mediation "can restore parents' and children's sense of well-being" better than attempts to keep people locked in unhappy marriages where pent-up frustrations eventually make postdivorce cooperation even harder to obtain.[35]

45   Similarly, we need to institutionalize remarriage. Experts on step-families argue that clearer norms and expectations for stepparents would facilitate easier adjustments and more enduring relationships. At the legal level, we must recognize and support the commitments that stepparents make, rather than excluding them from rights and obligations to their stepchildren. In one court case, for example, a boy named Danny was raised by his stepfather from the age of one, after his mother died. The biological father did not ask for custody until Danny was seven. Although a lower court ruled that Danny should be allowed to stay with his stepparent, who had been the primary parent for six of Danny's seven years, a higher court overruled this decision, calling the stepfather "a third party" whose claims should not be allowed to interfere with the rights of the biological parent.[36]

While we must adjust our laws to validate ties between stepparents and stepchildren, we also need to develop flexible models of various ways to achieve a "good" relationship. The worst problems facing step-families, experts on remarriage now believe, are produced by unrealistic fantasies about re-creating an exclusive nuclear family unit in a situation where this is impossible because the child has at least one parent who lives outside the home. The best way to succeed, researchers in the field agree, is to reject the nuclear family model and to develop a new set of expectations and behaviors.[37]

What it all comes down to is this. Today's diversity in family forms, parenting arrangements, and sex roles constitutes a tremendous sea change in family relations. We will not reverse the tide by planting our chair in the sand like King Canute and crying, "Go back! Go back!" There are things we can do to prevent the global tide of changing work situations and gender roles from eroding as many marriages as it presently does, but our primary task is to find new and firmer ground on which to relocate family life.

Notes

1. David Blankenhorn, "Can We Talk? The Marriage Strategy," *Mirabella*, March 1995, p. 91.
2. Howard Wineberg and James McCarthy, "Separation and Reconciliation in American Marriages," *Journal of Divorce and Remarriage* 20 (1993).
3. Barbara Dafoe Whitehead, "Dan Quayle Was Right," *Atlantic Monthly*, April 1993, p. 55.
4. Paul R. Amato, "Life-Span Adjustment of Children to Their Parents' Divorce," *The Future of Children* 4, no. 1 (Spring 1994), p. 147; E. Mavis Hetherington, "An Overview of the Virginia Longitudinal Study of Divorce and Remarriage with a Focus on Early Adolescence," *Journal of Family Psychology* 7, no. 1 (June 1, 1993), p. 53.
5. Judith Wallerstein and Sandra Blakeslee, *Second Chances: Men, Women and Children a Decade After Divorce* (New York: Ticknor & Fields, 1989); Frank

Furstenberg, Jr., and Andrew Cherlin, *Divided Families: What Happens to Children When Parents Part* (Cambridge, Mass.: Harvard University Press, 1991), p. 68; Andrew Cherlin and Frank Furstenberg, "Divorce Doesn't Always Hurt the Kids," *Washington Post*, March 19, 1989 (emphasis added). Wallerstein and Kelly suggested that there was a "sleeper effect" for young women, where problems caused by divorce were not evident until years later. But a ten-year Australian study found "no convincing evidence" for such an effect. Rosemary Dunlop and Ailsa Burns, "The Sleeper Effect—Myth or Reality?" *Journal of Marriage and the Family* 58 (May 1995), p. 375. It is possible that the young women who reported such effects to Wallerstein were engaging in an after-the-fact attempt to explain why they were having troubles.

6. Paul Amato, "Children's Adjustment to Divorce," *Journal of Marriage and the Family* 55 (1993); Paul Amato and Bruce Keith, "Parental Divorce and the Well-Being of Children: A Meta-Analysis," *Psychological Bulletin* 110 (1991); Arlene Skolnick and Stacey Rosencrantz, "The New Crusade for the Old Family," *American Prospect*, Summer 1994, p. 62; Rex Forehand, Bryan Neighbors, Danielle Devine, and Lisa Armistead, "Interparental Conflict and Parental Divorce: The Individual, Relative, and Interactive Effects on Adolescents Across Four Years," *Family Relations* 43 (1994), p. 387; Bonnie Thornton Dill, Maxine Baca Zinn, and Sandra Patton, "Feminism, Race, and the Politics of Family Values," *Report from the Institute for Philosophy and Public Policy* 13 (1993), p. 17; Alan C. Acock and David H. Demo, *Family Diversity and Well-Being* (Thousand Oaks, Calif.: Sage, 1994), p. 213; P. Lindsay Chase-Lansdale, Andrew Cherlin, and Kathleen Kiernan, "The Long-Term Effects of Parental Divorce on the Mental Health of Young Adults: A Developmental Perspective," *Child Development* 66 (1995).

7. Sara S. McLanahan, "The Two Faces of Divorce: Women's and Children's Interests," *Macro-Micro Linkages in Sociology* (Newbury Park, Calif.: Sage, 1991), p. 202. She notes that these "estimates assume that all of the negative impact of family disruption is due to the disruption itself as opposed to preexisting characteristics of the parents."

8. Kathryn Robinson, "The Divorce Debate: Which Side Are You On?" *Family Therapy Networker* (May/June 1994), p. 20.

9. D. M. Capaldi and G. R. Patterson, "Relation of Parental Transitions to Boy's Adjustment Problems: I. A Linear Hypothesis. II. Mothers at Risk for Transitions and Unskilled Parenting," *Developmental Psychology* 27, no. 3 (1991), p. 489; William S. Aquilino, "The Life Course of Children Born to Unmarried Mothers: Childhood Living Arrangements and Young Adult Outcomes," *Journal of Marriage and the Family* 58 (May 1996), p. 306.

10. David Grissmer, Sheila Nataraj Kirby, Mark Berends, and Stephanie Williamson, *Student Achievement and the Changing American Family* (Santa Monica, Calif.: Rand Institute on Education and Training, 1994), p. 66; Doris R. Entwisle and Karl L. Alexander, "A Parent's Economic Shadow: Family Structure Versus Family Resources as Influences on Early School Achievement," *Journal of Marriage and the Family* 57 (May 1995), p. 399.

11. Sara McLanahan and Gary Sandefur, *Growing Up with a Single Parent: What Hurts, What Helps?* (Cambridge, Mass.: Harvard University Press, 1995), pp. 2–3; Elizabeth Kolbert, "Television Gets a Closer Look as a Factor in Real

Violence," *New York Times*, December 14, 1994; Rachel Wildavsky, "What's Behind Success in School?" *Reader's Digest*, October 1994, p. 52.

12. Sameera Teja and Arnold L. Stolberg, "Peer Support, Divorce, and Children's Adjustment," *Journal of Divorce and Remarriage* 20, no. 3/4 (1993); Robert Haveman, Barbara Wolfe, and James Spaulding, "The Relation of Educational Attainment to Childhood Events and Circumstances," *Institute for Research on Poverty Discussion Paper No. 908–90*, Madison, Wisconsin, 1990, p. 28; David Demo and Alan Acock, "The Impact of Divorce on Children," in Alan Booth, ed., *Contemporary Families: Looking Forward, Looking Back* (Minneapolis: National Council on Family Relations, 1991), p. 185; Maxine Baca Zinn and Stanley D. Eitzen, *Diversity in American Families* (New York: Harper and Row, 1987), p. 317; "Frequent Moving Harmful, Study Says," *Olympian*, July 24, 1996, p. A3; Jay Teachman, Kathleen Paasch, and Karen Carver, "Social Capital and Dropping Out of School Early," *Journal of Marriage and the Family* 58 (1996), p. 782.

13. Adele Eskeles Gottfried and Allen W. Gottfried, eds., *Redefining Families: Implications for Children's Development* (New York: Plenum, 1994), p. 224.

14. Furstenberg and Cherlin, *Divided Families*, p. 70; Amato and Keith, "Parental Divorce and the Well-Being of Children," p. 40; Andrew Cherlin, "Longitudinal Studies of Effects of Divorce on Children in Great Britain and the United States," *Science*, June 7, 1991, pp. 1386–1389; Joan Kelly, "Longer-Term Adjustment in Children of Divorce," *Journal of Family Psychology* 2 (1988); Larry Lettich, "When Baby Makes Three," *Family Therapy Networker* (January/February 1993), p. 66; Forehand et al., "Interparental Conflict and Parental Divorce," p. 387; Stacy R. Markland and Eileen S. Nelson, "The Relationship Between Familial Conflict and the Identity of Young Adults," *Journal of Divorce and Remarriage* 20, no. 3/4 (1993), p. 204.

15. Hetherington quoted in Robinson, "The Divorce Debate," pp. 27–28.

16. Furstenberg and Cherlin, *Divided Families*, p. 64; Paul R. Amato and Alan Booth, "A Prospective Study of Divorce and Parent–Child Relationships," *Journal of Marriage and the Family* 58 (May 1996), pp. 356–357; Robert E. Emery and Michele Tuer, "Parenting and the Marital Relationship," in Tom Luster and Lynn Okagaki, eds., *Parenting: An Ecological Perspective* (Hillsdale, N.J.: Lawrence Erlbaum, 1993), p. 135.

17. Richard Weissbourd, "Divided Families, Whole Children," *American Prospect* (Summer 1994), p. 69.

18. E. Mavis Hetherington, "Coping with Family Transitions: Winners, Losers, and Survivors," in *Annual Progress in Child Psychiatry and Child Development* (New York: Brunner/Mazel, 1990), pp. 237–239.

19. Hetherington, "Coping with Family Transitions," p. 221.

20. Marilyn Coleman and Lawrence H. Ganong, "Family Reconfiguring Following Divorce," in Steve Duck and Julia T. Wood, eds., *Confronting Relationship Challenges*, vol. 5 (Thousand Oaks, Calif.: Sage, 1995), pp. 81–85. See also: Acock and Demo, *Family Diversity and Well-Being*, p. 224; Paul R. Amato, Laura Spencer Loomis, and Alan Booth, "Parental Divorce, Marital Conflict, and Offspring Well-being During Early Adulthood," *Social Forces* 73, no. 3 (March 1995), p. 895; Nan Marie Astone and Sara S. McLanahan, "Family Structure, Parental Practice and High School Completion,"

American Sociological Review 56 (June 1991), p. 318; Forehand et al., "Interparental Conflict and Parental Divorce," p. 392.

21. Furstenberg and Cherlin, *Divided Families*, p. 71. Ronald L. Simons and Associates, *Understanding Differences Between Divorced and Intact Families: Stress, Interaction, and Child Outcome* (Thousand Oaks, Calif.: Sage, 1996), pp. 208, 210, 222. For an argument that it is almost entirely family processes rather than divorce per se that cause poor outcomes, see Teresa M. Cooney and Jane Kurz, "Mental Health Outcomes Following Recent Parental Divorce: The Case of Young Adult Offspring," *Journal of Family Issues: The Changing Circumstances of Children's Lives* 17, no. 4 (July 1996), p. 510.

22. Furstenberg and Cherlin, *Divided Families*, p. 21.

23. Janet Johnston, "Family Transitions and Children's Functioning," in Philip Cowan et al., eds., *Family, Self, and Society: Toward a New Agenda for Family Research* (Hillsdale, N.J.: Lawrence Erlbaum, 1993); Amato, "Life-Span Adjustment of Children to Their Parents' Divorce," p. 175; James Bray and Sandra Berger, "Noncustodial Father and Paternal Grandparent Relationships in Stepfamilies," *Family Relations* 39 (1990), p. 419.

24. Weissbourd, "Divided Families, Whole Children," p. 68.

25. Philip A. Cowan, Carolyn Pape Cowan, and Patricia Kerig, "Mothers, Fathers, Sons, and Daughters: Gender Differences in Family Formation and Parenting Style," in Cowan et al., eds., *Family, Self, and Society*, p. 186; Sharon Wilsnack, Albert Klasson, and Brett Schurr, "Predicting Onset and Pernicity of Women's Problem Drinking: A Five-Year Longitudinal Analysis," *American Journal of Public Health* 81 (1991), pp. 305–318.

26. Jennifer Clark and Bonnie Barber, "Adolescents in Postdivorce and Always-Married Families: Self-Esteem and Perceptions of Fathers' Interest," *Journal of Marriage and the Family* 56 (1994), p. 609.

27. Susan Gano-Phillips and Frank D. Fincham, "Family Conflict, Divorce, and Children's Adjustment," in Mary Anne Fitzpatrick and Anita L. Vangelisti, eds., *Explaining Family Interactions* (Thousand Oaks, Calif.: Sage, 1995), p. 207.

28. Emery and Tuer, "Parenting and the Marital Relationship," pp. 138–139.

29. Constance Ahrons, *The Good Divorce: Keeping Your Family Together When Your Marriage Comes Apart* (New York: Harper Perennial, 1994), p. 6; Amato, "Life-Span Adjustment of Children to Their Parents' Divorce," p. 167.

30. Joyce A. Arditti and Michaelena Kelly, "Fathers' Perspectives of Their Co-Parental Relationships Postdivorce: Implications for Family Practice and Legal Reform," *Family Relations* 43 (January 1994), p. 65; Furstenberg and Cherlin, *Divided Families*, pp. 26–27; Kevin P. Kurkowski, Donald A. Gordon, and Jack Arbuthnot, "Children Caught in the Middle: A Brief Educational Intervention for Divorced Parents," *Journal of Divorce and Remarriage* 20, no. 3/4 (1993), p. 149; Constance Ahrons and R. B. Miller, "The Effect of Postdivorce Relationship on Paternal Involvement: A Longitudinal Analysis," *American Journal of Orthopsychiatry* 63 (1993).

31. Ahrons, *The Good Divorce*, p. 82; Emery and Tuer, "Parenting and the Marital Relationship," p. 145. See also Melinda Blau, *Families Apart: Ten Keys to Successful Co-parenting* (New York: G. P. Putnam's Sons, 1993).

32. James H. Bray and Charlene E. Depner, "Perspectives on Nonresidential Parenting," in Charles E. Depner and James H. Bray, eds., *Nonresidential Parenting: New Vistas in Family Living* (Newbury Park, Calif.: Sage, 1993), pp. 6–7.

33. Paul R. Amato, "Father–Child Relations, Mother–Child Relations, and Off-spring Psychological Well-Being in Early Adulthood," *Journal of Marriage and the Family* 56 (November 1994), p. 1039; Susan Chollar, "Happy Families: Who Says They All Have to Be Alike?" *American Health* (July/August 1993); Simons and Associates, *Understanding Differences Between Divorced and Intact Families*, p. 224; Bonnie L. Barber, "Support and Advice from Married and Divorced Fathers: Linkages and Adolescent Adjustment," *Family Relations* 43 (1994), p. 433.

34. William Goode, *World Changes in Divorce Patterns* (New Haven, Conn.: Yale University Press, 1993), pp. 330, 345; Robert Emory, "Divorce Mediation: Negotiating Agreements and Renegotiating Relationships," *Family Relations* 44 (1995); Cheryl Buehler and Jean Gerard, "Divorce Law in the United States: A Focus on Child Custody," *Family Relations* 44 (1995).

35. "Letters to the Editor," *New York Times*, December 31, 1995.

36. Andrew Cherlin, "Remarriage as an Incomplete Institution," *American Journal of Sociology* 84 (1978); Mark A. Fine, "A Social Science Perspective on Step-family Law: Suggestions for Legal Reform," *Family Relations* 38 (1989); Andrew Schwebel, Mark Fine, and Maureena Renner, "A Study of Perceptions of the Stepparent Role," *Journal of Family Issues* 12 (1991); Mark A. Fine and David R. Fine, "Recent Changes in Laws Affecting Stepfamilies: Suggestions for Legal Reform," *Family Relations* 41 (1992); Andrew Cherlin and Frank Furstenberg, "Stepfamilies in the United States: A Reconsideration," *American Review of Sociology* 20 (1994), p. 378.

37. Virginia Rutter, "Lessons from Stepfamilies," *Psychology Today* (May/June 1994), pp. 66–67; Lynn White, "Growing Up with Single Parents and Step-parents: Long-Term Effects on Family Solidarity," *Journal of Marriage and the Family* 56 (1994), p. 946.

Responding to Reading

1. Writing three years before Judith Wallerstein (p. 85) published her landmark study of the effects of divorce, Coontz begins by acknowledging the negative effects of divorce. What negative effects does she identify? Does she anticipate all the negative effects Wallerstein discusses? Does she identify others?

2. In what sense is Coontz "putting divorce in perspective" in this essay? How does she use the expert testimony of researchers to help her achieve her goal? (Note that Coontz, unlike Wallerstein and Smiley [p. 94], includes extensive documentation.)

3. Do you think that, despite her denial in paragraph 14, Coontz is "minimizing the risks" of divorce on the family? Would Wallerstein think so?

Responding in Writing

Using paragraph 16's topic sentence, write a paragraph that uses examples from your own experience to support Coontz's statement that "Many of the problems seen in children of divorced parents are caused not by divorce alone but by other . . . factors[,] such as poverty, financial loss, school relocation, or a prior history of severe marital conflict."

THE UNEXPECTED LEGACY OF DIVORCE

Judith Wallerstein

1922–

Judith Wallerstein, considered one of the foremost authorities on the effects of divorce on children and adults, was born in New York City. She received a BA degree from Hunter College (1943), a master's degree from Columbia University (1946), and a PhD from Lund University in Sweden. From 1966 to 1992, Wallerstein was on the faculty of the University of California, Berkeley, where in 1971 she founded the California Study of Children of Divorce. In 1980, she founded the Judith Wallerstein Center for the Family in Transition. Wallerstein has published the results of her work in Second Chances: Men, Women, and Children: A Decade after Divorce *(1989) and* The Good Marriage *(1995), both coauthored with Sandra Blakeslee. The following essay is taken from the conclusion of* The Unexpected Legacy of Divorce: A 25 Year Study *(2000), coauthored with Blakeslee and Julia M. Lewis. Wallerstein's most recent book, also coauthored with Blakeslee, is* What About the Kids? Raising Your Children Before, During, and After Divorce *(2003).*

Having spent the last thirty years of my life traveling here and abroad talking to professional, legal, and mental health groups plus working with thousands of parents and children in divorced families, it's clear that we've created a new kind of society never before seen in human culture. Silently and unconsciously, we have created a culture of divorce. It's hard to grasp what it means when we say that first marriages stand a 45 percent chance of breaking up and that second marriages have a 60 percent chance of ending in divorce. What are the consequences for all of us when 25 percent of people today between the ages of eighteen and forty-four have parents who divorced? What does it mean to a society when people wonder aloud if the family is about to disappear? What can we do when we learn that married couples with children represent a mere 26 percent of households in the 1990s and that the most common living arrangement nowadays is a household of unmarried people with no children? These numbers are terrifying. But like all massive social change, what's happening is affecting us in ways that we have yet to understand.

For people like me who work with divorcing families all the time, these abstract numbers have real faces. . . . I can relate to the millions of children and adults who suffer with loneliness and to all the teenagers who say, "I don't want a life like either of my parents." I can empathize with the countless young men and women who despair of ever finding a lasting relationship and who, with a brave toss of the head, say, "Hey, if you don't get married then you can't get divorced." It's only later, or sometimes when they think I'm not listening, that they add softly, "but I don't want to grow old alone." I am especially worried about how our divorce culture has changed childhood itself. A million new children a year are added to our march of marital failure. As they explain so eloquently, they lose the carefree play of childhood as well as the comforting arms and lap of a loving parent who is always rushing off because life in the postdivorce family is so incredibly difficult to manage. We must take very seriously the complaint of children like Karen who declare, "The day my parents divorced is the day my childhood ended."

Many years ago the psychoanalyst Erik Erikson taught us that childhood and society are vitally connected. But we have not yet come to terms with the changes ushered in by our divorce culture. Childhood is different, adolescence is different, and adulthood is different. Without our noticing, we have created a new class of young children who take care of themselves, along with a whole generation of overburdened parents who have no time to enjoy the pleasures of parenting. So much has happened so fast, we cannot hold it all in our minds. It's simply overwhelming.

But we must not forget a very important other side to all these changes. Because of our divorce culture, adults today have a greater sense of freedom. The importance of sex and play in adult life is widely accepted. We are not locked into our early mistakes and forced to stay in wretched, lifelong relationships. The change in women—their very identity and freer role in society—is part of our divorce culture. Indeed, two-thirds of divorces are initiated by women despite the high price they pay in economic and parenting burdens afterward. People want and expect a lot more out of marriage than did earlier generations. Although the divorce rate in second and third marriages is sky-high, many second marriages are much happier than the ones left behind. Children and adults are able to escape violence, abuse, and misery to create a better life. Clearly there is no road back.

5   The sobering truth is that we have created a new kind of society that offers greater freedom and more opportunities for many adults, but this welcome change carries a serious hidden cost. Many people, adults and children alike, are in fact not better off. We have created new kinds of families in which relationships are fragile and often unreliable. Children today receive far less nurturance, protection, and parenting than was their lot a few decades ago. Long-term marriages come apart at still surprising rates. And many in the older generation who started the divorce revolution find themselves estranged from their adult children. Is this the price we must pay for needed change? Can't we do better?

I'd like to say that we're at a crossroads but I'm afraid I can't be that optimistic. We can choose a new route only if we agree on where we are and where we want to be in the future. The outlook is cloudy.

For every person who wants to sound an alarm, there's another who says don't worry. For everyone concerned about the economic and emotional deprivations inherited by children of divorce there are those who argue that those kids were "in trouble before" and that divorce is irrelevant, no big deal. People want to feel good about their choices. Doubtless many do. In actual fact, after most divorces, one member of the former couple feels much better while the other feels no better or even worse. Yet at any dinner party you will still hear the same myths: Divorce is a temporary crisis. So many children have experienced their parents' divorce that kids nowadays don't worry so much. It's easier. They almost expect it. It's a rite of passage. If I feel better, so will my children. And so on. As always, children are voiceless or unheard.

But family scholars who have not always seen eye to eye are converging on a number of findings that fly in the face of our cherished myths. We agree that the effects of divorce are long-term. We know that the family is in trouble. We have a consensus that children raised in divorced or remarried families are less well adjusted as adults than those raised in intact families.

The life histories of this first generation to grow up in a divorce culture tells us truths we dare not ignore. Their message is poignant, clear, and contrary to what so many want to believe. They have taught me the following:

From the viewpoint of the children, and counter to what happens to their parents, divorce is a cumulative experience. Its impact increases over time and rises to a crescendo in adulthood. At each developmental stage divorce is experienced anew in different ways. In adulthood it affects personality, the ability to trust, expectations about relationships, and ability to cope with change.

The first upheaval occurs at the breakup. Children are frightened 10 and angry, terrified of being abandoned by both parents, and they feel responsible for the divorce. Most children are taken by surprise; few are relieved. As adults, they remember with sorrow and anger how little support they got from their parents when it happened. They recall how they were expected to adjust overnight to a terrifying number of changes that confounded them. Even children who had seen or heard violence at home made no connection between that violence and the decision to divorce. The children concluded early on, silently and sadly, that family relationships are fragile and that the tie between a man and woman can break capriciously, without warning. They worried ever after that parent-child relationships are also unreliable and can break at any time. These early experiences colored their later expectations.

As the postdivorce family took shape, their world increasingly resembled what they feared most. Home was a lonely place. The household was in disarray for years. Many children were forced to move, leaving behind familiar schools, close friends, and other supports. What they remember vividly as adults is the loss of the intact family and the safety net it provided, the difficulty of having two parents in two homes, and how going back and forth cut badly into playtime and friendships. Parents were busy with work, preoccupied with rebuilding their social lives. Both moms and dads had a lot less time to spend with their children and were less responsive to their children's needs or wishes. Little children especially felt that they had lost both parents and were unable to care for themselves. Children soon learned that the divorced family has porous walls that include new lovers, live-in partners, and stepparents. Not one of these relationships was easy for anyone. The mother's parenting was often cut into by the very heavy burdens of single parenthood and then by the demands of remarriage and stepchildren.

Relationships with fathers were heavily influenced by live-in lovers or stepmothers in second and third marriages. Some second wives were interested in the children while others wanted no part of them. Some fathers were able to maintain their love and interest in their children but few had time for two or sometimes three families. In some families both parents gradually stabilized their lives within happy remarriages or well-functioning, emotionally gratifying single parenthood. But these people were never a majority in any of my work.

Meanwhile, children who were able to draw support from school, sports teams, parents, stepparents, grandparents, teachers, or their own inner strengths, interests, and talents did better than those who could not muster such resources. By necessity, many of these so-called resilient children forfeited their own childhoods as they took responsibility for themselves; their troubled, overworked parents; and their siblings. Children who needed more than minimal parenting because they were little or had special vulnerabilities and problems with change were soon overwhelmed with sorrow and anger at their parents. Years later, when contemplating having their own children, most children in this study said hotly, "I never want a child of mine to experience a childhood like I had."

As the children told us, adolescence begins early in divorced homes and, compared with that of youngsters raised in intact families, is more likely to include more early sexual experiences for girls and higher alcohol and drug use for girls and boys. Adolescence is more prolonged in divorced families and extends well into the years of early adulthood. Throughout these years children of divorce worry about following in their parents' footsteps and struggle with a sinking sense that they, too, will fail in their relationships.

15   But it's in adulthood that children of divorce suffer the most. The impact of divorce hits them most cruelly as they go in search of love, sexual intimacy, and commitment. Their lack of inner images of a man and a woman in a stable relationship and their memories of their parents' failure to sustain the marriage badly hobbles their search, leading them to heartbreak and even despair. They cried, "No one taught me."

They complain bitterly that they feel unprepared for adult relationships and that they have never seen a "man and woman on the same beam," that they have no good models on which to build their hopes. And indeed they have a very hard time formulating even simple ideas about the kind of person they're looking for. Many end up with unsuitable or very troubled partners in relationships that were doomed from the start.

The contrast between them and children from good intact homes, as both go in search of love and commitment, is striking. . . . Adults in their twenties from reasonably good or even moderately unhappy intact families had a fine understanding of the demands and sacrifices required in a close relationship. They had memories of how their parents struggled and overcame differences, how they cooperated in a crisis. They developed a general idea about the kind of person they wanted to marry. Most important, they did not expect to fail. The two groups differed after marriage as well. Those from intact families found the example of their parent's enduring marriage very reassuring when they inevitably ran into marital problems. But in coping with the normal stresses in a marriage, adults from divorced families were at a grave disadvantage. Anxiety about relationships was at the bedrock of their personalities and endured even in very happy marriages. Their fears of disaster and sudden loss rose when they felt content. And their fear of abandonment, betrayal, and rejection mounted when they found themselves having to disagree with someone they loved. After all, marriage is a slippery slope and their parents fell off it. All had trouble dealing with differences or even moderate conflict in their close relationships. Typically their first response was panic, often followed by flight. They had a lot to undo and a lot to learn in a very short time.

Those who had two parents who rebuilt happy lives after divorce and included children in their orbits had a much easier time as adults. Those who had committed single parents also benefited from that parent's attention and responsiveness. But the more frequent response in adulthood was continuing anger at parents, more often at fathers, whom the children regarded as having been selfish and faithless.

Others felt deep compassion and pity toward mothers or fathers who failed to rebuild their lives after divorce. The ties between daughters and their mothers were especially close but at a cost. Some young women found it very difficult to separate from their moms and to lead their own lives. With some notable exceptions, fathers in divorced families were less likely to enjoy close bonds with their adult children, especially their sons. This stood in marked contrast to fathers and sons from intact families, who tended to grow closer as the years went by.

Fortunately for many children of divorce, their fears of loss and betrayal can be conquered by the time they reach their late twenties and thirties. But what a struggle that takes, what courage and persistence.

Those who succeed overcome their difficulties the hard way—by learning from their own failed relationships and gradually rejecting the models they were raised with to create what they want from a love relationship. Those lucky enough to have found a loving partner are able to interrupt their self-destructive course with a lasting love affair or marriage.

20   In other realms of adult life—financial and security, for instance—some children were able to overcome difficulties through unexpected help from fathers who had vanished long before. Still others benefit from the constancy of parents or grandparents. Many men and women raised in divorced families establish successful careers. Their workplace performance is largely unaffected by the divorce. But no matter what their success in the world, they retain some serious residues—fear of loss, fear of change, and fear that disaster will strike, especially when things are going well. They're still terrified by the mundane differences and inevitable conflicts found in every close relationship.

I'm heartened by the hard-won success of these adults. But at the same time, I can't forget those who've failed to straighten out their lives. I'm especially troubled by how many divorced or remained in wretched marriages. Of those who have children and who are now divorced, many, to my dismay, are not protecting their children in ways we might expect. They go on to repeat the same mistakes their own parents made, perpetuating problems that have plagued them all their lives. I'm also concerned about many who, by their mid- and late thirties, are neither married nor cohabiting and who are leading lonely lives. They're afraid of getting involved in a relationship they they think is doomed to fail. After a divorce or breakup, they're afraid to try again. And I'm struck by continuing anger at parents and flat-out statements by many of these young adults that they have no intention of helping their moms and especially their dads or stepparents in old age. This may change. But if it doesn't, we'll be facing another unanticipated consequence of our divorce culture. Who will take care of an older generation estranged from its children?

What We Can and Cannot Do

Our efforts to improve our divorce culture have been spotty and the resources committed to the task are pitifully small. The courts have given the lion's share of attention to the 10 to 15 percent of families that continue to fight bitterly. Caught between upholding the rights of parents and protecting the interests of children, they have tilted heavily toward parents. Such parents allegedly speak in the name of the child just as those who fight bloody holy wars allegedly speak in the name of religion. Thus, as I explained to the judge with whom I began this chapter, our court system has unintentionally contributed to the suffering of children. At the same time, most parents receive little guidance. Some courts offer educational lectures to families at the time of the breakup, but the emphasis is on preventing further litigation. Such courses are typically evaluated according to how much they reduce subsequent litigation and not on how they might improve parenting. Curricula to educate teachers, school personnel, pediatricians, and other professionals about child and parenting issues in divorce are rare. Few university or medical school programs in psychiatry, psychology, social work, or law include courses on how to understand or help children and parents after separation, divorce, and remarriage. This lack of training persists despite the fact that a disproportionate number of children and adolescents from divorced homes are admitted as patients for psychological treatment at clinics and family agencies. In many social agencies, close to three-quarters of the children in treatment are from divorced families. Some school districts have organized groups for children whose parents are divorcing. And some communities have established groups to help divorcing parents talk about their children's problems. A few centers such as ours have developed programs to help families cope with high conflict and domestic violence. But such efforts are not widespread. As a society, we have not set up services to help people relieve the stresses of divorce. We continue to foster the myth that divorce is a transient crisis and that as soon as adults restabilize their lives, the children will recover fully. When will the truth sink in?

Let's suppose for a moment that we had a consensus in our society. Suppose we could agree that we want to maintain the advantages of divorce but that we need to protect our children and help parents mute the long-term effects of divorce on future generations. Imagine we were willing to roll up our sleeves and really commit the enormous resources of our society toward supplementing the knowledge we have. Suppose we gave as much time, energy, and resources to protecting children as we give to protecting the environment. What might we try?

I would begin with an effort to strengthen marriage. Obviously, restoring confidence in marriage won't work if we naively call for a return to marriage as it used to be. To improve marriage, we need to fully understand the nature of contemporary man-woman relationships. We need to appreciate the difficulties modern couples confront in balancing work and family, separateness and togetherness, conflict and cooperation. It's no accident that 80 percent of divorces occur in the first nine years of marriage. These new families should be our target.

What threats to marriage can we change? First, there's a serious imbalance between the demands of the workplace and the needs of family life. The corporate world rarely considers the impact of its policies on parents and children. Some companies recognize that parents need time to spend with their children but they don't understand that the workplace exerts a major influence on the quality and stability of marriage. 25

Heavy work schedules and job insecurity erode married life. Families with young children especially postpone intimate talk, sex, and friendship. These are the ties that replenish a marriage. When the boss calls, we go to the office. When the baby cries, we pick up the child. But when a marriage is starving, we expect it to bumble along. Most Western European countries provide paid family leave. What about us? Why do we persist in offering unpaid leave and pretend that it addresses the young family's problem? One additional solution might be social security and tax benefits for a parent who wants to stay home and care for young children. That alone would lighten the burden on many marriages. Other suggestions for reducing the stresses on young families include more flex time, greater opportunities for part-time work, assurances that people who take family leave will not lose their place on the corporate ladder, tax advantages for families, and many other ideas that have been on the table for years. Public policy cannot create good marriages. But it can buffer some of the stresses people face, especially in those early, vulnerable years when couples need time to establish intimacy, a satisfying sex life, and a friendship that will hold them together through the inevitable challenges that lie ahead. Ultimately, if we're really interested in improving marriage so that people have time for each other and their children, we need to realign our priorities away from the business world and toward family life.

We might also try to help the legions of young adults who complain bitterly that they're unprepared for marriage. Having been raised in divorced or very troubled homes, they have no idea how to choose a partner or what to do to build the relationship. They regard their parents' divorce as a terrible failure and worry that they're doomed to follow in the same footsteps. Many adults stay in unhappy marriages just to avoid divorce. We don't know if we can help them with educational methods because we haven't tried. Our experience is too limited and our experience models nonexistent. But when so many young people have never seen a good marriage, we have a moral obligation to try to intervene preventively. Most programs that give marital advice are aimed at engaged couples who belong to churches and synagogues. These are very good beginnings that should be expanded. But many offer too little and arrive too late to bring about changes in any individual's values or knowledge. Nor is the excitement that precedes a wedding the best time for reflection on how to choose a lifetime partner or what makes a marriage work. Academic courses on marriage mostly look at families from the lofty perch of the family scholar and not from the perspective of children of divorce who feel "no one ever taught me."

In my opinion, a better time to begin helping these youngsters is during mid-adolescence, when attitudes toward oneself and relationships with the opposite sex are beginning to gel. Adolescence is the time when worries about sex, love, betrayal, and morality take center stage. Education for and about relationships should begin at that time, since if we do it right, we'll have their full attention. It could be based in the health centers that have been established in many schools throughout the country. Churches and synagogues and social agencies might provide another launching place. Ideally, adolescents in a well-functioning society should have the opportunity to think and talk about a wide range of relationships, issues, and conflicts confronting them. As an opening gambit, think about asking the deceptively simple question: "How do you choose a friend?" A group of teenagers considering this problem could be drawn to the important question of how to choose a lover and life partner—and even more important, how not to choose one. Specific topics such as differences between boys and girls, cultural subgroups, and how people resolve tensions would follow based on the teenagers' interests and their willingness to discuss real issues. Colleges could also offer continuing and advanced courses on an expanded range of subjects, including many problems that young men and women now struggle with alone.

We are on the threshold of learning what we can and cannot do for these young people. Still one wonders, can an educational intervention replace the learning that occurs naturally over many years within the family? How do we create a corps of teachers who are qualified to lead meaningful courses on relationships? By this I mean courses that are true to life, honest, and respectful of students. I worry about the adult tendency to lecture or sermonize. In a society where the family has become a political issue, I'm concerned about attacks from the left and the right, about the many people who would attack such interventions the way they've attacked the Harry Potter books. Mostly I'm concerned about finding a constituency of adults who would rally behind an idea that has so many pitfalls. But I'm also convinced that doing nothing—leaving young people alone in their struggles—is more dangerous. We should not give up without a try.

Responding to Reading

1. In paragraph 1, Wallerstein states, "Silently and unconsciously, we have created a culture of divorce." She goes on in this paragraph to pose some disturbing questions. How do you believe Stephanie Coontz (p. 69) or Jane Smiley (p. 94) might respond to this statement and to the related questions Wallerstein raises?
2. In summing up the findings of a twenty-five-year study of the effects of divorce on children, Wallerstein enumerates many results, mostly negative, of the "divorce culture" she defines. What *positive* results does she identify? Can you think of others?
3. Wallerstein does not condemn divorce, but she does find it responsible for some very harmful long-term problems. She believes, for example, that because of divorce, "the family is in trouble" and that "children raised in

divorced or remarried families are less well adjusted as adults than those raised in intact families" (7). What does Wallerstein believe ought to be done to "improve our divorce culture" (22)? Do you see her suggestions as realistic? Do you see them as necessary?

Responding in Writing

Write a one-paragraph summary of the key ideas Wallerstein presents. Do not include your own opinions or evaluate her ideas.

THERE THEY GO, BAD-MOUTHING DIVORCE AGAIN

Jane Smiley

1949–

Born in Los Angeles, Jane Smiley grew up in St. Louis and graduated from Vassar (1971), later earning her MA, MFA, and PhD from the University of Iowa (1975, 1976, and 1978). The child of divorced parents, she herself has been married three times and divorced twice. A novelist who taught creative writing at the University of Iowa, Smiley is best known for A Thousand Acres *(1991), a Pulitzer Prize–winning novel made into a film, and* Moo *(1995), an academic satire. Her most recent works are the novel* Good Faith *(2003) and the nonfiction book* A Year at the Races: Reflections on Horses, Humans, Love, Money, and Luck *(2004).*

Several years ago at a party, I asked a woman I had just met how her Christmas had been. She said, "First good Christmas in 25 years."

"Why was that?"

"Oh, my father died."

"And that made it good?"

5   "Well, every year for 25 years, he would gather us all around the Christmas tree and tell us how terrible his life was and how disappointed he was in everyone."

"How did your mother feel, though?"

"Oh, she was relieved. He'd been telling her for 60 years that she wasn't pretty or smart enough for him. Now she's planning to do some of the things she's wanted to do all along."

I thought this was an excellent example of a thank-God-for-divorce tale. Here's another one: When the grandfather of a friend of mine died many years ago, his last words to his wife of 50 years were, "I'm sorry I married you."

I admit that I am susceptible to such tales. I am the poster child for the recent study by Judith Wallerstein et al. of the long-term effects of divorce on children—the child of parents who parted before I was a year old and divorced uncountable times (well, three).

Bad habits? Bad choices? Perhaps it is time to subject myself to 10 Wallersteinian analysis. But when I do my own little survey, and come up with the marital histories of my 32 closest friends and relatives, the picture grows more complex. All of the 32 are baby boomers or a bit older—oldest, 58, youngest, 40. Twenty-six are the offspring of long-term first marriages that ended in the death of one spouse or the other; six of them come from divorced families.

Of the 26 whose parents had long-term marriages, 17 have been divorced at least once.

What does my mini-survey tell me? It tells me the same thing that any cursory review of the last 50 years of married life in America tells us—most baby boomers were born into intact families. On the surface nearly all adhered to the ideal. Dad earned enough money so that Mom could stay home and take care of the 3.2 children and the house. Marital roles were divided by gender, and Mom was regularly advised by Ann Landers and Abigail Van Buren, not to mention everyone else, to cater to Dad's sense of privileged masculinity: Should she iron his shorts? If he didn't give her any money of her own, was it permissible to take it out of his pockets while he was sleeping? If, when she was doing the laundry, she found lipstick on his collar, should she mention it?

And most baby boomers, learning how to be married, as Ms. Wallerstein suggests, by witnessing the examples of marriage that they grew up with, voted with their feet when the time came to endure or not in their own.

Twenty-six boomers from 26 intact marriages. Seventeen divorced. That's about 65 percent.

The fact is, the goals of marriage have changed. In the first half of 15 the century people married to survive, reproduce, join properties, become a part of the mainstream community of adults. Individual happiness might have been foreseen and desired, but if as the marriage wore on happiness came to seem elusive, other goals dominated. Some marriages did work on both levels: several of my divorced peers had parents whose marriages I know to have been happy, compatible and peaceful.

Whatever the reasons for their parents' marital longevity, though, the children in my group did not learn from their example how to choose their own partners wisely or how to stick with it, as Ms. Wallerstein would have expected. Some who were divorced chose to try again, and have found happiness. Others in second or third marriages have not. The person I know whose parents had the longest, happiest marriage recently wrote me: "We plug along." A thank-God-for-divorce tale, midlife version.

Americans born since mid-century marry for the same reason they do anything else—to be happy. Yet literature of all periods tells us that marrying to be happy is at best an iffy proposition. Historians of domestic life have suggested that marriages in the premodern period were usually short—death did the work of divorce.

Marrying with the overriding goal of being happy for all your adult life with a single other (since survival, reproduction, property joining and being part of a community of adults can be achieved now without marriage) is a new experiment. Divorce is its corollary. This is an experiment that our children will engage in, whatever models we give them.

Divorce is a right that took many generations to gain. It is no more a guarantor of happiness than marriage, but also no less. The rate of divorce in our country tells us very little other than that our culture is in transition to new ways of organizing itself. Given the social and technological changes of the past century, this can hardly be surprising.

20   Personally, in spite of the testaments of the Wallersteinians, I'm glad my parents divorced, and I have been since I first began to actually think about it. I can't speak for my children, but I do hope they try more than one way of being happy, rather than turning around at 84 and saying, "Free at last."

Responding to Reading

1. Responding to Wallerstein's study of divorce (p. 85), Smiley, who calls herself the "poster child" (9) for the study, conducts her own informal survey of friends and family. What does she conclude? What does she see as the significance of her conclusions? Do you find the informal evidence she presents convincing?

2. In paragraph 15, Smiley states, "[T]he goals of marriage have changed." Do you see this change as largely positive or negative? Do you think it is in any way responsible for creating what Wallerstein calls our "divorce culture"? Explain.

3. In paragraph 19, Smiley states that divorce is "no more a guarantor of happiness than marriage, but also no less." Do you agree? Do you find this statement in any way disturbing?

Responding in Writing

Unlike Wallerstein, Smiley bases her conclusions not on twenty-five years of research but on her own experiences with divorce and on the "mini-survey" she describes in paragraphs 10–12. In a paragraph presenting the results of your own informal "mini-survey," summarize your conclusions about the effects of divorce on families you know.

WIDENING THE FOCUS

The following readings can suggest additional perspectives for thinking and writing about the subject of divorce and the family. You may also want to do further research about this subject on the Internet.

- Lynda Barry, "The Sanctuary of School" (p. 103)

- Marie Winn, "Television: The Plug-in Drug" (p. 270)

- Arlie Hochschild, "The Second Shift" (p. 554)

For Internet Research: As the readings in the Focus section suggest, the rising number of divorces in the past four decades has changed society's perception of marriage as an institution. What are your thoughts on marriage? Is it growing stronger or weaker? How has it changed in your lifetime? Visit *The Marriage Project* <http://marriage.rutgers.edu/>, and read its annual report, "The State of Our Unions." Also go to the *Alternative to Marriage Project*, <http://www.unmarried.org/>, and click on the Library link to read essays with contrasting viewpoints on marriage as an institution. Choose either the *Marriage Project*'s annual report or one of the other online readings, and write an essay in which you evaluate the arguments and evidence it presents.

---------------------- WRITING ----------------------

Family and Memory

1. What exactly is a family? Is it a group of people bound together by love? By marriage? By blood? By history? By shared memories? By economic dependency? By habit? What unites family members, and what divides them? Does *family* denote only a traditional nuclear family or also a family broken by divorce and blended by remarriage? Define *family* as it is presented in several of the readings in this chapter.

2. Leo Tolstoy's classic Russian novel *Anna Karenina* opens with the sentence, "Happy families are all alike; every unhappy family is unhappy in its own way." Write an essay in which you concur with or challenge this statement, supporting your position with references to several of the readings in this chapter.

3. In a sense, memories are like snapshots, a series of disconnected candid pictures, sometimes unflattering, often out of focus, eventually fading. Writers of autobiographical memoirs often explore this idea; for example, Alice Walker (p. 38) sees her painful childhood as a series of snapshots, and Raymond Carver calls the poem that appears in his essay "Photograph of My Father in His Twenty-Second Year" (p. 51). Using information from your own family life as well as from your reading, discuss the relationship between memories and photographs. If you like, you may describe and discuss some of your own family photographs. (You may also want to examine the two photos that open this chapter.)

4. Several of the writers represented in this chapter—for example, Kingston (p. 27) and Carver (p. 45)—present fairly detailed biographical sketches of a family member. Using these essays as guides, write a detailed biographical essay about a member of your family. Prepare for this assignment by interviewing several family members.

5. In "The Unauthorized Autobiography of Me" (p. 53), Sherman Alexie uses song titles and names of musicians and groups to re-create a sense of the background music of his life. List the songs and musical artists that have been central to various stages of your own life. Then, write a musical autobiography that gives readers a sense of who you were at different times of your life. Using the music as the "sound track of your life," try to help readers understand the times you grew up in and the person you were (and became).

6. How do your parents' notions of success and failure affect you? Do you think your parents tend to expect too much of you? Too little? Explore these ideas in an essay, referring to essays in this chapter and in Chapter 7, "The American Dream."

7. Gary Soto comes to understand his parents better by seeing them in the role of workers (p. 13). Discuss his changing attitude toward his parents' work, comparing his views with ideas expressed by Scott Russell Sanders in "The Men We Carry in Our Minds" (p. 408) in Chapter 5 and by one or more essays in Chapter 8. (You may also discuss how your experience as a worker has helped you to understand or appreciate your own parents.)

8. Read the poem "Photograph of My Father in His Twenty-Second Year," which follows paragraph 29 of Raymond Carver's essay. Then, write an essay in which you compare and contrast this poem with Robert Hayden's poem "Those Winter Sundays" (p. 12) or with Harlan Coben's short story "The Key to My Father" (p. 63).

9. What traits, habits, and values (positive or negative) have you inherited from your parents? What qualities do you think you will pass on to your children? Write a letter to your parents in which you answer these two questions, incorporating the ideas of several of the writers in this chapter.

10. After reading the selections in the Focus section, write an essay in which you answer the question "How has divorce redefined the family?" In gathering support for your essay, you should consider information from the readings in the Focus section (Stephanie Coontz's "Putting Divorce in Perspective," p. 69, Judith Wallerstein's "The Unexpected Legacy of Divorce," p. 85, and Jane Smiley's "There They Go, Bad-Mouthing Divorce Again," p. 94), but you may also wish to include information from your own personal experience or from the experience of friends or relatives.

2

ISSUES
IN EDUCATION

──────── PREPARING TO READ AND WRITE ────────

In the nineteenth century, most people had little difficulty defining the purpose of education: they assumed that it was the school's job to prepare students for the roles they would play in the adult world. To accomplish this end, public school administrators made sure that the elementary school curriculum gave students a good dose of the basics: arithmetic, grammar, spelling, reading, composition, and penmanship. High school students studied literature, history, geography, and civics.

Elementary school children in traditional classroom.

At the more elite private schools, students learned physics, rhetoric, and elocution—as well as Latin and Greek so that they could read the classics in the original.

Today, educators seem to have a great deal of difficulty agreeing on what purpose schools are supposed to serve. No longer can a group of school administrators simply proscribe a curriculum. Parents, students, politicians, academics, special interest groups, and religious leaders all attempt to influence what is taught. The result, according to some educators, is an environment in which it is almost impossible for any real education to take place. In fact, in many of today's schools, more emphasis seems to be placed on increasing self-esteem and avoiding controversy than on challenging students to discover new ways of thinking about the world. In this milieu, classic books are censored or rewritten to eliminate offending passages, ideas are presented as if they all have equal value, and the curriculum is revised so that all groups are represented equally. The result is an educational environment that has all the intellectual appeal of elevator music. Many people—educators included—seem to have forgotten that ideas must be unsettling if they are to make us think. After all, what is education but a process that encourages us to think critically about our world and develop a healthy skepticism—to question, evaluate, and reach conclusions about ideas and events?

The Focus section of this chapter (p. 157) addresses one issue in education, considering the question, "Do we still need affirmative

Children being home schooled.

action?" as well as other questions that this one raises. For example, what is the real purpose of affirmative action? Do affirmative action admissions policies really promote educational diversity, or do they simply give some minorities unfair advantages over other groups? Can affirmative action help us as a nation to achieve the color-blind society that Dr. Martin Luther King, Jr. envisioned in this "I Have a Dream" speech (p. 532), or will it do just the opposite?

As you read and prepare to write about the selections in this chapter, you may consider the following questions:

- How does the writer define education? Is this definition consistent with yours?

- What does the writer think the main goals of education should be? Do you agree?

- Which does the writer believe is more important, formal or informal education?

- On what aspect or aspects of education does the writer focus?

- Who does the writer believe bears primary responsibility for a student's education? The student? The family? The school? The community? The government?

- Does the writer use personal experience to support his or her position? Does he or she use facts and statistics or expert opinion as support? Do you find the writer's ideas convincing?

- What changes in the educational system does the writer recommend? Do you agree with these recommendations?

- Are the writer's educational experiences similar to or different from yours? How do these similarities or differences affect your response to the essay?

- In what way is the essay you are reading similar to or different from other essays in this chapter?

The Sanctuary of School
Lynda Barry
1956–

Born in Richland Center, Wisconsin, Lynda Barry grew up in Seattle, Washington, as part of an extended Filipino family (her mother was Filipino, her father an alcoholic Norwegian-Irishman). She majored in art at Evergreen State College—the first member of her family to pursue higher education—and began her career as a cartoonist shortly after graduation. Barry is known as a chronicler of adolescent angst both in her syndicated comic strip Ernie Pook's Comeek *and in collections like* My Perfect Life *(1992),* The Freddie Stories *(1997), and* Cruddy *(2000). Barry has also written a novel,* The Good Times Are Killing Me *(1988), which was turned into a successful musical. In the following essay, Barry remembers her Seattle grade school in a racially mixed neighborhood as a nurturing safe haven from her difficult family life.*

I was 7 years old the first time I snuck out of the house in the dark. It was winter and my parents had been fighting all night. They were short on money and long on relatives who kept "temporarily" moving into our house because they had nowhere else to go.

My brother and I were used to giving up our bedroom. We slept on the couch, something we actually liked because it put us that much closer to the light of our lives, our television.

At night when everyone was asleep, we lay on our pillows watching it with the sound off. We watched Steve Allen's mouth moving. We watched Johnny Carson's mouth moving. We watched movies filled with gangsters shooting machine guns into packed rooms, dying soldiers hurling a last grenade and beautiful women crying at windows. Then the sign-off finally came and we tried to sleep.

The morning I snuck out, I woke up filled with a panic about needing to get to school. The sun wasn't quite up yet but my anxiety was so fierce that I just got dressed, walked quietly across the kitchen and let myself out the back door.

It was quiet outside. Stars were still out. Nothing moved and no one was in the street. It was as if someone had turned the sound off on the world.

I walked the alley, breaking thin ice over the puddles with my shoes. I didn't know why I was walking to school in the dark. I didn't think about it. All I knew was a feeling of panic, like the panic that strikes kids when they realize they are lost.

That feeling eased the moment I turned the corner and saw the dark outline of my school at the top of the hill. My school was made up of about 15 nondescript portable classrooms set down on a fenced concrete lot in a rundown Seattle neighborhood, but it had the most beautiful view of the Cascade Mountains. You could see them from anywhere on the playfield and you could see them from the windows of my classroom—Room 2.

I walked over to the monkey bars and hooked my arms around the cold metal. I stood for a long time just looking across Rainier Valley. The sky was beginning to whiten and I could hear a few birds.

In a perfect world my absence at home would not have gone unnoticed. I would have had two parents in a panic to locate me, instead of two parents in a panic to locate an answer to the hard question of survival during a deep financial and emotional crisis.

10   But in an overcrowded and unhappy home, it's incredibly easy for any child to slip away. The high levels of frustration, depression and anger in my house made my brother and me invisible. We were children with the sound turned off. And for us, as for the steadily increasing number of neglected children in this country, the only place where we could count on being noticed was at school.

"Hey there, young lady. Did you forget to go home last night?" It was Mr. Gunderson, our janitor, whom we all loved. He was nice and he was funny and he was old with white hair, thick glasses and an unbelievable number of keys. I could hear them jingling as he walked across the playfield. I felt incredibly happy to see him.

He let me push his wheeled garbage can between the different portables as he unlocked each room. He let me turn on the lights and raise the window shades and I saw my school slowly come to life. I saw Mrs. Holman, our school secretary, walk into the office without her orange lipstick on yet. She waved.

I saw the fifth-grade teacher Mr. Cunningham, walking under the breezeway eating a hard roll. He waved.

And I saw my teacher, Mrs. Claire LeSane, walking toward us in a red coat and calling my name in a very happy and surprised way, and suddenly my throat got tight and my eyes stung and I ran toward her crying. It was something that surprised us both.

15   It's only thinking about it now, 28 years later, that I realize I was crying from relief. I was with my teacher, and in a while I was going to sit at my desk, with my crayons and pencils and books and classmates all around me, and for the next six hours I was going to enjoy a thoroughly secure, warm and stable world. It was a world I absolutely relied on. Without it, I don't know where I would have gone that morning.

Mrs. LeSane asked me what was wrong and when I said "Nothing," she seemingly left it at that. But she asked me if I would carry her purse for her, an honor above all honors, and she asked if I wanted to come into Room 2 early and paint.

She believed in the natural healing power of painting and draw-ing for troubled children. In the back of her room there was always a drawing table and an easel with plenty of supplies, and sometimes during the day she would come up to you for what seemed like no good reason and quietly ask if you wanted to go to the back table and "make some pictures for Mrs. LeSane." We all had a chance at it—to sit apart from the class for a while to paint, draw and silently work out impossible problems on 11 × 17 sheets of newsprint.

Drawing came to mean everything to me. At the back table in Room 2, I learned to build myself a life preserver that I could carry into my home.

We all know that a good education system saves lives, but the people of this country are still told that cutting the budget for public schools is necessary, that poor salaries for teachers are all we can man-age and that art, music and all creative activities must be the first to go when times are lean.

Before- and after-school programs are cut and we are told that 20 public schools are not made for baby-sitting children. If parents are neglectful temporarily or permanently, for whatever reason, it's cer-tainly sad, but their unlucky children must fend for themselves. Or slip through the cracks. Or wander in a dark night alone.

We are told in a thousand ways that not only are public schools not important, but that the children who attend them, the children who need them most, are not important either. We leave them to learn from the blind eye of a television, or to the mercy of "a thousand points of light"[1] that can be as far away as stars.

I was lucky. I had Mrs. LeSane. I had Mr. Gunderson. I had an abundance of art supplies. And I had a particular brand of neglect in my home that allowed me to slip away and get to them. But what about the rest of the kids who weren't as lucky? What happened to them?

By the time the bell rang that morning I had finished my drawing and Mrs. LeSane pinned it up on the special bulletin board she re-served for drawings from the back table. It was the same picture I al-ways drew—a sun in the corner of a blue sky over a nice house with flowers all around it.

Mrs. LeSane asked us to please stand, face the flag, place our right hands over our hearts and say the Pledge of Allegiance. Children across the country do it faithfully. I wonder now when the country will face its children and say a pledge right back.

---

[1]Catchphrase for the first president George Bush's plan to substitute volunteerism for government programs. [Eds.]

Responding to Reading

1. Was Barry's school like the one you attended? What kind of information does she not provide? How can you explain these omissions?
2. In paragraph 22, Barry asks two questions. Why doesn't she answer them? What do you think the answers to these questions might be?
3. Barry's essay ends on a somewhat cynical note. How effective is this conclusion? What does Barry gain or lose with this concluding strategy?

Responding in Writing

Has school been a sanctuary for you as it was for Barry? Write a paragraph or two in which you answer this question.

School Is Bad for Children

John Holt

1923–1985

John Holt, a teacher and education theorist, believed that traditional schooling suppresses children's natural curiosity and love of life. In his writings about education, Holt suggests that there should be more than one path for learning and that students should be allowed to pursue what interests them. Born in New York City, Holt received a BS degree in industrial engineering from Yale College (1943) and then joined the US Navy and served on a submarine in the Pacific Ocean during World War II. Returning to civilian life, Holt worked for an international peace group, traveled in Europe, and then worked at the private Colorado Rocky Mountain School in Carbondale, Colorado, where he taught high school English, French, and mathematics and coached soccer and baseball. His many books include How Children Fail *(1964),* How Children Learn *(1967),* Instead of Education *(1976), and* Learning All the Time *(1989). In the following essay, first published in the* Saturday Evening Post *in 1969, Holt makes a plea to free children from the classroom, a "dull and ugly place, where nobody ever says anything very truthful," and to "give them a chance to learn about the world at first hand." Holt was also a major educational figure in the Home Schooling movement.*

Almost every child, on the first day he sets foot in a school building, is smarter, more curious, less afraid of what he doesn't know, better at finding and figuring things out, more confident, resourceful, persistent and independent than he will ever be again in his schooling—or, unless he is very unusual and very lucky, for the rest of his life. Already, by paying close attention to and interacting with the world and people around him, and without any school-type formal instruction, he has done a task far more difficult, complicated and abstract than anything he will be asked to do in school, or than any of his teachers has done for years. He has solved the mystery of language. He has discovered it—babies don't even know that language exists—and he has found out how it works and learned to use it. He has done it by exploring, by experimenting, by developing his own model of the grammar of language, by trying it out and seeing whether it works, by gradually changing it and refining it until it does work. And while he has been doing this, he has been learning other things as well, including many of the "concepts" that the schools think only they can teach him, and many that are more complicated than the ones they do try to teach him.

In he comes, this curious, patient, determined, energetic, skillful learner. We sit him down at a desk, and what do we teach him? Many things. First, that learning is separate from living. "You come to school to learn," we tell him, as if the child hadn't been learning before, as if living were out there and learning were in here, and there were no connection between the two. Secondly, that he cannot be trusted to learn and is no good at it. Everything we teach about reading, a task far simpler than many that the child has already mastered, says to him, "If we don't make you read, you won't, and if you don't do it exactly the way we tell you, you can't." In short, he comes to feel that learning is a passive process, something that someone else does *to* you, instead of something you do for yourself.

In a great many other ways he learns that he is worthless, untrustworthy, fit only to take other people's orders, a blank sheet for other people to write on. Oh, we make a lot of nice noises in school about respect for the child and individual differences, and the like. But our acts, as opposed to our talk, say to the child, "Your experience, your concerns, your curiosities, your needs, what you know, what you want, what you wonder about, what you hope for, what you fear, what you like and dislike, what you are good at or not so good at—all this is of not the slightest importance, it counts for nothing. What counts here, and the only thing that counts, is what we know, what we think is important, what we want you to do, think and be." The child soon learns not to ask questions—the teacher isn't there to satisfy his curiosity. Having learned to hide his curiosity, he later learns to be ashamed of it. Given no chance to find out who he is—and to develop that person, whoever it is—he soon comes to accept the adults' evaluation of him.

He learns many other things. He learns that to be wrong, uncertain, confused, is a crime. Right Answers are what the school wants, and he learns countless strategies for prying these answers out of the teacher, for conning her into thinking he knows what he doesn't know. He learns to dodge, bluff, fake, cheat. He learns to be lazy.

Before he came to school, he would work for hours on end, on his own, with no thought of reward, at the business of making sense of the world and gaining competence in it. In school he learns, like every buck private, how to goldbrick, how not to work when the sergeant isn't looking, how to know when he is looking, how to make him think you are working even when he is looking. He learns that in real life you don't do anything unless you are bribed, bullied or conned into doing it, that nothing is worth doing for its own sake, or that if it is, you can't do it in school. He learns to be bored, to work with a small part of his mind, to escape from the reality around him into daydreams and fantasies—but not like the fantasies of his preschool years, in which he played a very active part.

5   The child comes to school curious about other people, particularly other children, and the school teaches him to be indifferent. The most interesting thing in the classroom—often the only interesting thing in it—is the other children, but he has to act as if these other children, all about him, only a few feet away, are not really there. He cannot interact with them, talk with them, smile at them. In many schools he can't talk to other children in the halls between classes; in more than a few, and some of these in stylish suburbs, he can't even talk to them at lunch. Splendid training for a world in which, when you're not studying the other person to figure out how to do him in, you pay no attention to him.

In fact, he learns how to live without paying attention to anything going on around him. You might say that school is a long lesson in how to turn yourself off, which may be one reason why so many young people, seeking the awareness of the world and responsiveness to it they had when they were little, think they can only find it in drugs. Aside from being boring, the school is almost always ugly, cold, inhuman—even the most stylish, glass-windowed, $20-a-square-foot schools.

And so, in this dull and ugly place, where nobody ever says anything very truthful, where everybody is playing a kind of role, as in a charade, where the teachers are no more free to respond honestly to the students than the students are free to respond to the teachers or each other, where the air practically vibrates with suspicion and anxiety, the child learns to live in a daze, saving his energies for those small parts of his life that are too trivial for the adults to bother with, and thus remain his. It is a rare child who can come through his schooling with much left of his curiosity, his independence or his sense of his own dignity, competence and worth.

So much for criticism. What do we need to do? Many things. Some are easy—we can do them right away. Some are hard, and may take some time. Take a hard one first. We should abolish compulsory school attendance. At the very least we should modify it, perhaps by giving children every year a large number of authorized absences. Our compulsory school-attendance laws once served a humane and useful purpose. They protected children's right to some schooling, against those adults who would otherwise have denied it to them in order to exploit their labor, in farm, store, mine or factory. Today the laws help nobody, not the schools, not the teachers, not the children. To keep kids in school who would rather not be there costs the schools an enormous amount of time and trouble—to say nothing of what it costs to repair the damage that these angry and resentful prisoners do every time they get a chance. Every teacher knows that any kid in class who, for whatever reason, would rather not be there not only doesn't learn anything himself but makes it a great deal tougher for anyone else. As for protecting the children from exploitation, the chief and indeed only exploiters of children these days *are* the schools. Kids caught in the college rush more often than not work 70 hours or more a week, most of it on paper busywork. For kids who aren't going to college, school is just a useless time waster, preventing them from earning some money or doing some useful work, or even doing some true learning.

Objections. "If kids didn't have to go to school, they'd all be out in the streets." No, they wouldn't. In the first place, even if schools stayed just the way they are, children would spend at least some time there because that's where they'd be likely to find friends; it's a natural meeting place for children. In the second place, schools wouldn't stay the way they are, they'd get better, because we would have to start making them what they ought to be right now—places where children would *want* to be. In the third place, those children who did not want to go to school could find, particularly if we stirred up our brains and gave them a little help, other things to do—the things many children now do during their summers and holidays.

There's something easier we could do. We need to get kids out of 10 the school buildings, give them a chance to learn about the world at first hand. It is a very recent idea, and a crazy one, that the way to teach our young people about the world they live in is to take them out of it and shut them up in brick boxes. Fortunately, educators are beginning to realize this. In Philadelphia and Portland, Oreg., to pick only two places I happen to have heard about, plans are being drawn up for public schools that won't have any school buildings at all, that will take the students out into the city and help them to use it and its people as a learning resource. In other words, students, perhaps in groups, perhaps independently, will go to libraries, museums, exhibits, court rooms, legislatures, radio and TV stations, meetings, businesses and laboratories to learn about their world and society at first hand. A small private school in Washington is already doing this. It makes sense. We need more of it.

As we help children get out into the world, to do their learning there, we get more of the world into the schools. Aside from their parents, most children never have any close contact with any adults except people whose sole business is children. No wonder they have no idea what adult life or work is like. We need to bring a lot more people who are *not* full-time teachers into the schools and into contact with the children. In New York City, under the Teachers and Writers Collaborative, real writers, working writers—novelists, poets, playwrights—come into the schools, read their work, and talk to the children about the problems of their craft. The children eat it up. In another school I know of, a practicing attorney from a nearby city comes in every month or so and talks to several classes about the law. Not the law as it is in books but as he sees it and encounters it in his cases, his problems, his work. And the children love it. It is real, grown-up, true, not *My Weekly Reader*, not "social studies," not lies and baloney.

Something easier yet. Let children work together, help each other, learn from each other and each other's mistakes. We now know, from the experience of many schools, both rich-suburban and poor-city, that children are often the best teachers of other children. What is more important, we know that when a fifth- or sixth-grader who has been having trouble with reading starts helping a first-grader, his own reading sharply improves. A number of schools are beginning to use what some call Paired Learning. This means that you let children form partnerships with other children, do their work, even including their tests, together, and share whatever marks or results this work gets—just like grownups in the real world. It seems to work.

Let the children learn to judge their own work. A child learning to talk does not learn by being corrected all the time—if corrected too much, he will stop talking. *He* compares, a thousand times a day, the difference between language as he uses it and as those around him use it. Bit by bit, he makes the necessary changes to make his language like other people's. In the same way, kids learning to do all the other things they learn without adult teachers—to walk, run, climb, whistle, ride a bike, skate, play games, jump rope—compare their own performance with what more skilled people do, and slowly make the needed changes. But in school we never give a child a chance to detect his mistakes, let alone correct them. We do it all for him. We act as if we thought he would never notice a mistake unless it was pointed out to him, or correct it unless he was made to. Soon he becomes dependent on the expert. We should let him do it himself. Let him figure out, with the help of other children if he wants it, what this word says, what is the answer to that problem, whether this is a good way of saying or doing this or that. If right answers are involved, as in some math or science, give him the answer book, let him correct his own papers. Why should we teachers waste time on such donkey work? Our job should be to help the kid when he tells us that he can't find a way to get the right answer. Let's get rid of all this nonsense of grades, exams, marks. We don't know now, and we never will know, how to measure what another person knows or understands. We certainly can't find out by asking him questions. All we find out is what he doesn't know—which is what most tests are for, anyway. Throw it all out, and let the child learn what every educated person must someday learn, how to measure his own understanding, how to know what he knows or does not know.

We could also abolish the fixed, required curriculum. People remember only what is interesting and useful to them, what helps them make sense of the world, or helps them get along in it. All else they quickly forget, if they ever learn it at all. The idea of a "body of knowledge," to be picked up in school and used for the rest of one's life, is nonsense in a world as complicated and rapidly changing as ours. Anyway, the most important questions and problems of our time are not *in* the curriculum, not even in the hotshot universities, let alone the schools.

Children want, more than they want anything else, and even after 15 years of miseducation, to make sense of the world, themselves, and other human beings. Let them get at this job, with our help if they ask for it, in the way that makes most sense to them.

Responding to Reading

1. In what ways does Holt believe schools fail children?
2. According to Holt, what should schools do to correct their shortcomings? Are his suggestions realistic or unrealistic?
3. In paragraph 13, Holt says, "Let's get rid of all this nonsense of grades, exams, marks." Do you agree? What would be the advantages and disadvantages of this course of action?

Responding in Writing

What would your ideal elementary school be like? How would it be like the schools you attended? How would it be different?

SCHOOL'S OUT
Daniel H. Pink
1964–

Daniel Pink received a BA in linguistics from Northwestern University and a law degree from Yale University Law School. He worked from 1995 to 1997 as chief speechwriter to Vice President Al Gore. Pink writes mainly about business, work, and economic transformation. His articles and essays have appeared in Wired, *the* New York Times, *the* New Republic, Slate, *and other publications. Currently, he is a contributing editor to* Wired *magazine. The following essay is taken from Pink's book* Free Agent Nation: How America's New Independent Workers Are Transforming the Way We Live *(2001). To read more about this author, visit his Web site,* http://www.freeagentnation.com.

Here's a riddle of the New Economy: Whenever students around the world take those tests that measure which country's children know the most, American kids invariably score near the bottom. No matter the subject, when the international rankings come out, European and Asian nations finish first while the U.S. pulls up the rear. This, we all know, isn't good. Yet by almost every measure, the American economy outperforms those very same nations of Asia and Europe. We create greater wealth, deliver more and better goods and services, and positively kick butt on innovation. This, we all know, *is* good.

Now the riddle: If we're so dumb, how come we're so rich? How can we fare so poorly on international measures of education yet perform so well in an economy that depends on brainpower? The answer is complex, but within it are clues about the future of education—and how "free agency" may rock the school house as profoundly as it has upended the business organization.

We are living in the founding of what I call "free agent nation." Over the past decade, in nearly every industry and region, work has been undergoing perhaps its most significant transformation since Americans left the farm for the factory a century ago. Legions of Americans, and increasingly citizens of other countries as well, are abandoning one of the Industrial Revolution's most enduring legacies—the "job"—and forging new ways to work. They're becoming self-employed knowledge workers, proprietors of home-based businesses, temps and permatemps, freelancers and e-lancers, independent contractors and independent professionals, micropreneurs and infopreneurs, part-time consultants, interim executives, on-call troubleshooters, and full-time soloists.

In the U.S. today, more than 30 million workers—nearly one-fourth of the American workforce—are free agents. And many others who hold what are still nominally "jobs" are doing so under terms closer in spirit to free agency than to traditional employment. They're telecommuting. They're hopping from company to company. They're forming ventures that are legally their employers', but whose prospects depend largely on their own individual efforts.

In boom times, many free agents—fed up with bad bosses and 5 dysfunctional workplaces and yearning for freedom—leapt into this new world. In leaner times, other people—clobbered by layoffs, mergers, and downturns—have been pushed. But these new independent workers are transforming the nation's social and economic future. Soon they will transform the nation's education system as well.

The Homogenizing Hopper

Whenever I walk into a public school, I'm nearly toppled by a wave of nostalgia. Most schools I've visited in the 21st century look and feel exactly like the public schools I attended in the 1970s. The classrooms are the same size. The desks stand in those same rows. Bulletin boards preview the next national holiday. The hallways even *smell* the same. Sure, some classrooms might have a computer or two. But in most respects, the schools American children attend today seem indistinguishable from the ones their parents and grandparents attended.

At first, such déjà vu warmed my soul. But then I thought about it. How many other places look and feel exactly as they did 20, 30, or 40 years ago? Banks don't. Hospitals don't. Grocery stores don't. Maybe the sweet nostalgia I sniffed on those classroom visits was really the odor of stagnation. Since most other institutions in American society have changed dramatically in the past half-century, the stasis of schools is strange. And it's doubly peculiar because school itself is a modern invention, not something we inherited from antiquity.

Through most of history, people learned from tutors or their close relatives. In 19th-century America, says education historian David Tyack, "the school was a voluntary and incidental institution." Not until the early 20th century did public schools as we know them—places where students segregated by age learn from government-certified professionals—become widespread. And not until the 1920s did attending one become compulsory. Think about that last fact a moment. Compared with much of the world, America is a remarkably hands-off land. We don't force people to vote, or to work, or to serve in the military. But we do compel parents to relinquish their kids to this institution for a dozen years, and threaten to jail those who resist.

Compulsory mass schooling is an aberration in both history and modern society. Yet it was the ideal preparation for the Organization Man economy, a highly structured world dominated by large, bureaucratic corporations that routinized the workplace. Compulsory mass schooling equipped generations of future factory workers and middle managers with the basic skills and knowledge they needed on the job. The broader lessons it conveyed were equally crucial. Kids learned how to obey rules, follow orders, and respect authority—and the penalties that came with refusal.

10   This was just the sort of training the old economy demanded. Schools had bells; factories had whistles. Schools had report card grades; offices had pay grades. Pleasing your teacher prepared you for pleasing your boss. And in either place, if you achieved a minimal level of performance, you were promoted. Taylorism—the management philosophy, named for efficiency expert Frederick Winslow Taylor, that there was One Best Way of doing things that could and should be applied in all circumstances—didn't spend all its time on the job. It also went to class. In the school, as in the workplace, the reigning theory was One Best Way. Kids learned the same things at the same time in the same manner in the same place. Marshall McLuhan once described schools as "the homogenizing hopper into which we toss our integral tots for processing." And schools made factory-style processing practically a religion—through standardized testing, standardized curricula, and standardized clusters of children. (Question: When was the last time *you* spent all day in a room filled exclusively with people almost exactly your own age?)

So when we step into the typical school today, we're stepping into the past—a place whose architect is Frederick Winslow Taylor and whose tenant is the Organization Man. The one American institution that has least accommodated itself to the free agent economy is the one Americans claim they value most. But it's hard to imagine that this arrangement can last much longer—a One Size Fits All education system cranking out workers for a My Size Fits Me economy. Maybe the answer to the riddle I posed at the beginning is that we're succeeding *in spite of* our education system. But how long can that continue? And imagine how we'd prosper if we began educating our children more like we earn our livings. Nearly 20 years ago, a landmark government report, *A Nation at Risk*, declared that American education was "being eroded by a rising tide of mediocrity." That may no longer be true. Instead, American schools are awash in a rising tide of irrelevance.

Don't get me wrong. In innumerable ways, mass public schooling has been a stirring success. Like Taylorism, it has accomplished some remarkable things—teaching immigrants both English and the American way, expanding literacy, equipping many Americans to succeed beyond their parents' imaginings. In a very large sense, America's schools have been a breathtaking democratic achievement.

But that doesn't mean they ought to be the same as they were when we were kids. Parents and politicians have sensed the need for reform, and have pushed education to the top of the national agenda. Unfortunately, few of the conventional remedies—standardized testing, character training, recertifying teachers—will do much to cure what ails American schools, and may even make things worse. Free agency, though, will force the necessary changes. Look for free agency to accelerate and deepen three incipient movements in education— home schooling, alternatives to traditional high school, and new approaches to adult learning. These changes will prove as pathbreaking as mass public schooling was a century ago.

The Home-Schooling Revolution

"School is like starting life with a 12-year jail sentence in which bad habits are the only curriculum truly learned." Those are the words of John Taylor Gatto, who was named New York state's Teacher of the Year in 1991. Today he is one of the most forceful voices for one of the most powerful movements in American education—home schooling. In home schooling, kids opt out of traditional school to take control of their own education and to learn with the help of parents, tutors, and peers. Home schooling is free agency for the under-18 set. And it's about to break through the surface of our national life.

As recently as 1980, home schooling was illegal in most states. In the early 1980s, no more than 15,000 students learned this way. But Christian conservatives, unhappy with schools they considered Godfree zones and eager to teach their kids themselves, pressed for changes. Laws fell, and home schooling surged. By 1990, there were as many as 300,000 American home-schoolers. By 1993, home schooling was legal in all 50 states. Since then, home schooling has swum into the mainstream—paddled there by secular parents dissatisfied with low-quality, and even dangerous, schools. In the first half of the 1990s, the home-schooling population more than doubled. Today some 1.7 million children are home-schoolers, their ranks growing as much as 15 percent each year. Factor in turnover, and one in 10 American kids under 18 has gotten part of his or her schooling at home.

Home schooling has become perhaps the largest and most successful education reform movement of the last two decades:

- While barely 3 percent of American schoolchildren are now home-schoolers, that represents a surprisingly large dent in the public school monopoly—especially compared with private schools. For every four kids in private school, there's one youngster learning at home. The home-schooling population is roughly equal to all the school-age children in Pennsylvania.

- According to *The Wall Street Journal,* "Evidence is mounting that home-schooling, once confined to the political and religious fringe, has achieved results not only on par with public education, but in some ways surpassing it." Home-schooled children consistently score higher than traditional students on standardized achievement tests, placing on average in the 80th percentile in all subjects.

- Home-schooled children also perform extremely well on nearly all measures of socialization. One of the great misconceptions about home schooling is that it turns kids into isolated loners. In fact, these children spend more time with adults, more time in their community, and more time with children of varying ages than their traditional-school counterparts. Says one researcher, "The conventionally schooled tended to be considerably more aggressive, loud, and competitive than the home educated."

"Home schooling," though, is a bit of a misnomer. Parents don't re-create the classroom in the living room any more than free agents re-create the cubicle in their basement offices. Instead, home schooling makes it easier for children to pursue their own interests in their own way—a My Size Fits Me approach to learning. In part for this reason, some adherents—particularly those who have opted out of traditional schools for reasons other than religion—prefer the term "unschooling."

The similarities to free agency—having an "unjob"—are many. Free agents are independent workers; home-schoolers are independent learners. Free agents maintain robust networks and tight connections through informal groups and professional associations; home-schoolers have assembled powerful groups—like the 3,000-family Family Unschoolers Network—to share teaching strategies and materials and to offer advice and support. Free agents often challenge the idea of separating work and family; home-schoolers take the same approach to the boundary between school and family.

Perhaps most important, home schooling is almost perfectly consonant with the four animating values of free agency: having freedom, being authentic, putting yourself on the line, and defining your own success. Take freedom. In the typical school, children often aren't permitted to move unless a bell rings or an adult grants them permission. And except for a limited menu of offerings in high school, they generally can't choose what to study or when to study it. Home-schoolers have far greater freedom. They learn more like, well, children. We don't teach little kids how to talk or walk or understand the world. We simply put them in nurturing situations and let them learn on their own. Sure, we impose certain restrictions. ("Don't walk in the middle of the street.") But we don't go crazy. ("Please practice talking for 45 minutes until a bell rings.") It's the same for home-schoolers. Kids can become agents of their own education rather than merely recipients of someone else's noble intentions.

Imagine a 5-year-old child whose current passion is building with 20 Legos. Every day she spends up to an hour, maybe more, absorbed in complex construction projects, creating farms, zoos, airplanes, spaceships. Often her friends come over and they work together. No one assigns her this project. No one tells her when and how to do it. And no one will give her creation a grade. Is she learning? Of course. This is how many home-schoolers explore their subjects.

Now suppose some well-intentioned adults step in to teach the child a thing or two about Lego building. Let's say they assign her a daily 45-minute Lego period, give her a grade at the end of each session, maybe even offer a reward for an A+ building. And why not bring in some more 5-year-olds to teach them the same things about Legos? Why not have them all build their own 45-minute Lego buildings at the same time, then give them each a letter grade, with a prize for the best one? My guess: Pretty soon our 5-year-old Lego lover would lose her passion. Her buildings would likely become less creative, her learning curve flatter. This is how many conventional schools work—or, I guess, *don't work.*

The well-meaning adults have squelched the child's freedom to play and learn and discover on her own. She's no longer in control. She's no longer having fun. Countless studies, particularly those by University of Rochester psychologist Edward L. Deci, have shown that kids and adults alike—in school, at work, at home—lose the intrinsic motivation and the pure joy derived from learning and working when somebody takes away their sense of autonomy and instead imposes some external system of reward and punishment. Freedom isn't a detour from learning. It's the best pathway toward it.

Stay with our Lego lass a moment and think about authenticity— the basic desire people have to be who they are rather than conform to someone else's standard. Our young builder has lost the sense that she is acting according to her own true self. Instead, she has gotten the message. You build Legos for the same reason your traditionally employed father does his work assignments: because an authority figure tells you to.

Or take accountability. The child is no longer fully accountable for her own Lego creating. Whatever she has produced is by assignment. Her creations are no longer truly hers. And what about those Lego grades? That A+ may motivate our girl to keep building, but not on her own terms. Maybe she liked the B− building better than the A+ creation. Oh well. Now she'll probably bury that feeling and work to measure up—to someone else's standards. Should she take a chance—try building that space shuttle she's been dreaming about? Probably not. Why take that risk when, chances are, it won't make the grade? Self-defined success has no place in this regime. But for many home-schoolers, success is something they can define themselves. (This is true even though, as I mentioned, home-schoolers score off the charts on conventional measures of success—standardized tests in academic subjects.)

25   To be sure, some things most kids should learn are not intrinsically fun. There are times in life when we must eat our Brussels sprouts. For those subjects, the punishment-and-reward approach of traditional schooling may be in order. But too often, the sheer thrill of learning a new fact or mastering a tough equation is muted when schools take away a student's sense of control. In home schooling, kids have greater freedom to pursue their passions, less pressure to conform to the wishes of teachers and peers—and can put themselves on the line, take risks, and define success on their own terms. As more parents realize that the underlying ethic of home schooling closely resembles the animating values of free agency, home schooling will continue to soar in popularity.

Free Agent Teaching

Several other forces will combine to power home schooling into greater prominence. One is simply the movement's initial prominence. As more families choose this option, they will make it more socially acceptable—thereby encouraging other families to take this once-unconventional route. The home-schooling population has already begun to look like the rest of America. While some 90 percent of home-schoolers are white, the population is becoming more diverse, and may be growing fastest among African Americans. And the median income for a home-school family is roughly equal to the median income for the rest of the country; about 87 percent have annual household incomes under $75,000.

Recent policy changes—in state legislatures and principals' offices—will further clear the way. Not only is home schooling now legal in every state, but many public schools have begun letting home-schoolers take certain classes or play on school teams. About two-thirds of American colleges now accept transcripts prepared by parents, or portfolios assembled by students, in lieu of an accredited diploma.

Another force is free agency itself. Thanks to flexible schedules and personal control, it's easier for free agents than for traditional employees to home-school their children. Free agents will also become the professionals in this new world of learning. A carpenter might hire herself out to teach carpentry skills to home-schoolers. A writer might become a tutor or editor to several home-schoolers interested in producing their own literary journal. What's more, the huge cadre of teachers hired to teach the baby boom will soon hit retirement age. However, perhaps instead of fully retiring, many will hire themselves out as itinerant tutors to home-schoolers—and begin part-time careers as free agent educators. For many parents, of course, the responsibility and time commitment of home schooling will be daunting. But the wide availability of teachers and tutors might help some parents overcome the concern that they won't be able to handle this awesome undertaking by themselves.

The Internet makes home schooling easier, too. Indeed, home-schoolers figured out the Internet well before most Americans. For example, my first Internet connection was a DOS-based Compuserve account I acquired in 1993. Before the wide acceptance of the Internet and the advent of the World Wide Web, the most active discussion groups on Compuserve were those devoted to home schooling. Using the Web, home-schoolers can do research and find tutors anywhere in the world. There are now even online ventures—for instance, the Christa McAuliffe Academy (www.cmacademy.org) in Washington state and ChildU.com in Florida—that sell online courses and provide e-teachers for home-schoolers. Physical infrastructure might also accelerate this trend. Almost three-fourths of America's public school buildings were built before 1969. School administrations might be more likely to encourage some amount of home schooling if that means less strain on their crowded classrooms and creaky buildings.

I don't want to overstate the case. Home schooling, like free 30 agency, won't be for everyone. Many parents won't have the time or the desire for this approach. And home schooling won't be for all time. Many students will spend a few years in a conventional school and a few years learning at home—just as some workers will migrate between being a free agent and holding a job. But home schooling is perhaps the most robust expression of the free agent way outside the workplace, making its continued rise inevitable.

The End of High School

One other consequence of the move toward home schooling will be something many of us wished for as teenagers: the demise of high school. It wasn't until the 1920s that high school replaced work as the thing most Americans did in their teens. "American high school is obsolete," says Bard College president Leon Botstein, one of the first to call for its end. He says today's adolescents would be better off pursuing a college degree, jumping directly into the job market, engaging in public service, or taking on a vocational apprenticeship. Even the

National Association of Secondary School Principals, which has blasted home schooling, concedes that "high schools continue to go about their business in ways that sometimes bear startling resemblance to the flawed practices of the past."

In the future, expect teens and their families to force an end to high school as we know it. Look for some of these changes to replace and augment traditional high schools with free-agent-style learning—and to unschool the American teenager:

- *A renaissance of apprenticeships.* For centuries, young people learned a craft or profession under the guidance of an experienced master. This method will revive and expand to include skills like computer programming and graphic design. Imagine a 14-year-old taking two or three academic courses each week, and spending the rest of her time apprenticing as a commercial artist. Traditional high schools tend to separate learning and doing. Free agency makes them indistinguishable.

- *A flowering of teenage entrepreneurship.* Young people may become free agents even before they get their driver's licenses—and teen entrepreneurs will become more common. Indeed, most teens have the two crucial traits of a successful entrepreneur: a fresh way of looking at the world and a passionate intensity for what they do. In San Diego County, 8 percent of high school students already run their own online business. That will increasingly become the norm and perhaps even become a teenage rite of passage.

- *A greater diversity of academic courses.* Only 16 states offer basic economics in high school. That's hardly a sound foundation for the free agent workplace. Expect a surge of new kinds of "home economics" courses that teach numeracy, accounting, and basic business.

- *A boom in national service.* Some teenagers will seek greater direction than others and may want to spend a few years serving in the military or participating in a domestic service program. Today, many young people don't consider these choices because of the pressure to go directly to college. Getting people out of high school earlier might get them into service sooner.

- *A backlash against standards.* A high school diploma was once the gold standard of American education. No more. Yet politicians seem determined to make the diploma meaningful again by erecting all sorts of hurdles kids must leap to attain one—standardized subjects each student must study, standardized tests each student must pass. In some schools, students are already staging sit-ins to protest these tests. This could be American youth's new cause célèbre. ("Hey hey, ho ho. Standardized testing's got to go.")

Most politicians think the answer to the problems of high schools is to exert more control. But the real answer is *less* control. In the free agent future, our teens will learn by less schooling and more doing.

The Unschooling of Adults

For much of the 20th century, the U.S. depended on what I call the Thanksgiving turkey model of education. We placed kids in the oven of formal education for 12 years, and then served them up to employers. (A select minority got a final, four-year basting at a place called college.) But this model doesn't work in a world of accelerated cycle times, shrinking company half-lives, and the rapid obsolescence of knowledge and skills. In a free agent economy, our education system must allow people to learn throughout their lives.

Home schooling and alternatives to high school will create a na- 35 tion of self-educators, free agent learners, if you will. Adults who were home-schooled youths will know how to learn and expect to continue the habit throughout their lives.

For example, how did anybody learn the Web? In 1993, it barely existed. By 1995, it was the foundation of dozens of new industries and an explosion of wealth. There weren't any college classes in Web programming, HTML coding, or Web page design in those early years. Yet somehow hundreds of thousands of people managed to learn. How? They taught themselves—working with colleagues, trying new things, and making mistakes. That was the secret to the Web's success. The Web flourished almost entirely through the ethic and practice of self-teaching. This is not a radical concept. Until the first part of this century, most Americans learned on their own—by reading. Literacy and access to books were an individual's ticket to knowledge. Even today, according to my own online survey of 1,143 independent workers, "reading" was the most prevalent way free agents said they stay up-to-date in their field.

In the twenty-first century, access to the Internet and to a network of smart colleagues will be the ticket to adult learning. Expect more of us to punch those tickets throughout our lives. Look for these early signs:

- *The devaluation of degrees.* As the shelf life of a degree shortens, more students will go to college to acquire particular skills than to bring home a sheepskin. People's need for knowledge doesn't respect semesters. They'll want higher education just in time—and if that means leaving the classroom before earning a degree, so be it. Remember: Larry Ellison, Steve Jobs, and Steven Spielberg never finished college.

- *Older students.* Forty percent of college students are now older than 25. According to *The Wall Street Journal*, "By some projections, the number of students age 35 and older will exceed those 18 and 19 within a few years." Young adults who do forgo a diploma in their early 20s may find a need and desire for college courses in their 40s.

- *Free agent teaching.* Distance learning (private ventures like the University of Phoenix, Unext, Ninth House Network, and Hungry Minds University) will help along this self-teaching trend. Today, some 5,000 companies are in the online education business. Their $2 billion of revenues is expected to hit $11 billion by 2003. And nontraditional teaching arrangements will abound. One lament of independent scholars—genre-straddling writers like Judith Rich Harris and Anne Hollander—is that they don't have students. Here's a ready supply. More free agent teachers and more free agent students will create tremendous liquidity in the learning market—with the Internet serving as the matchmaker for this new marketplace of learning.

- *Big trouble for elite colleges.* All this means big trouble in Ivy City. Attending a fancy college serves three purposes in contemporary life: to prolong adolescence, to award a credential that's modestly useful early in one's working life, and to give people a network of friends. Elite colleges have moved slowly to keep up with the emerging free agent economy. In 1998, 78 percent of public four-year colleges offered distance-learning programs, compared with only 19 percent of private schools. Private college costs have soared, faster even than health care costs, for the past 20 years. But have these colleges improved at the same rate? Have they improved at all? What's more, the students who make it to elite colleges are generally those who've proved most adroit at conventional (read: outdated) schooling. That could become a liability rather than an advantage. In his bestseller, *The Millionaire Mind*, Thomas J. Stanley found a disproportionately large number of millionaires were free agents—but that the higher somebody's SAT scores, the *less* likely he or she was to be a financial risk-taker and therefore to become a free agent.

- *Learning groupies.* The conference industry, already hot, will continue to catch fire as more people seek gatherings of like-minded souls to make new connections and learn new things. Conferences allow attendees to become part of a sort of Socratic institution. They can choose the mentor they will pay attention to for an hour, or two hours, or a day—whatever. In addition, many independent workers have formed small groups that meet regularly and allow members to exchange business advice and offer personal support. These Free Agent Nation Clubs, as I call them, also provide an important staging ground for self-education. At F.A.N.

Club meetings, members discuss books and articles and share their particular expertise with the others. This type of learning— similarly alive in book clubs and Bible study groups—represents a rich American tradition. One of the earliest self-organized clusters of free agents was Benjamin Franklin's Junto, formed in 1727, which created a subscription library for its members, which in turn became the first public library in America.

The next few decades will be a fascinating, and perhaps revolutionary, time for learning in America. The specifics will surprise us and may defy even my soundest predictions. But the bottom line of the future of education in Free Agent Nation is glaringly clear: School's out.

Responding to Reading

1. What is a "free agent nation" (3)? In what way is work in the United States undergoing a transformation? Why is this transformation the "most significant transformation since Americans left the farm for the factory" (3)?
2. According to Pink, how are traditional public schools not meeting the challenges of the new economy? In what way does home schooling better prepare students for the new realities of free agency?
3. Do you think Pink is correct when he says that one of the consequences of home schooling will be "the demise of high school" (31)? What other changes does Pink see occurring in education?

Responding in Writing

List three advantages and three disadvantages of home schooling, and then write a paragraph in which you argue for or against it.

GRADUATION

Maya Angelou

1928–

Maya Angelou was born in St. Louis, where her mother lived, but was raised in Arkansas by her grandmother, who ran a general store. She began a theatrical career when she toured with Porgy and Bess *in 1954–1955. Angelou is now a poet, writer, lecturer, and teacher. She read her poem "On the Pulse of Morning" at the 1993 presidential inauguration of Bill Clinton. A critic in* Southern Humanities Review *has said that "her genius as a writer is in her ability to recapture the texture of the way of life in the texture of its idioms, its idiosyncrasies, and especially its process of image-making." Angelou's many books include* Oh Pray My Wings Are Gonna Fit Me Well *(poetry, 1975) and* I Know Why the Caged Bird Sings *(autobiography, 1969); her most recent is an autobiographical volume,* A Song Flying Up to Heaven *(2002). In "Graduation," Angelou remembers the anger and pride of graduation day at her segregated school in Stamps, Arkansas. To learn more about Angelou, visit her Web site, http://www.mayaangelou.com.*

The children in Stamps trembled visibly with anticipation. Some adults were excited too, but to be certain the whole young population had come down with graduation epidemic. Large classes were graduating from both the grammar school and the high school. Even those who were years removed from their own day of glorious release were anxious to help with preparations as a kind of dry run. The junior students who were moving into the vacating classes' chairs were tradition-bound to show their talents for leadership and management. They strutted through the school and around the campus exerting pressure on the lower grades. Their authority was so new that occasionally if they pressed a little too hard it had to be overlooked. After all, next term was coming, and it never hurt a sixth grader to have a play sister in the eighth grade, or a tenth-year student to be able to call a twelfth grader Bubba. So all was endured in a spirit of shared understanding. But the graduating classes themselves were the nobility. Like travelers with exotic destinations on their minds, the graduates were remarkably forgetful. They came to school without their books, or tablets or even pencils. Volunteers fell over themselves to secure replacements for the missing equipment. When accepted, the willing workers might or might not be thanked, and it was of no importance to the pregraduation rites. Even teachers were respectful of the now quiet and aging seniors, and tended to speak to them, if not as equals, as beings only slightly lower than themselves. After tests were returned and grades given, the student body, which acted like an extended family, knew who did well, who excelled, and what piteous ones had failed.

Unlike the white high school, Lafayette County Training School distinguished itself by having neither lawn, nor hedges, nor tennis court, nor climbing ivy. Its two buildings (main classrooms, the grade school and home economics) were set on a dirt hill with no fence to limit either its boundaries or those of bordering farms. There was a large expanse to the left of the school which was used alternately as a baseball diamond or basketball court. Rusty hoops on swaying poles represented the permanent recreational equipment, although bats and balls could be borrowed from the P.E. teacher if the borrower was qualified and if the diamond wasn't occupied.

Over this rocky area relieved by a few shady tall persimmon trees the graduating class walked. The girls often held hands and no longer bothered to speak to the lower students. There was a sadness about them, as if this old world was not their home and they were bound for higher ground. The boys, on the other hand, had become more friendly, more outgoing. A decided change from the closed attitude they projected while studying for finals. Now they seemed not ready to give up the old school, the familiar paths and classrooms. Only a small percentage would be continuing on to college—one of the South's A & M (agricultural and mechanical) schools, which trained Negro youths to be carpenters, farmers, handymen, masons, maids, cooks and baby nurses. Their future rode heavily on their shoulders, and blinded them to the collective joy that had pervaded the lives of the boys and girls in the grammar school graduating class.

Parents who could afford it had ordered new shoes and ready-made clothes for themselves from Sears and Roebuck or Montgomery Ward. They also engaged the best seamstresses to make the floating graduating dresses and to cut down secondhand pants which would be pressed to a military slickness for the important event.

Oh, it was important, all right. Whitefolks would attend the cere- 5 mony, and two or three would speak of God and home, and the Southern way of life, and Mrs. Parsons, the principal's wife, would play the graduation march while the lower-grade graduates paraded down the aisles and took their seats below the platform. The high school seniors would wait in empty classrooms to make their dramatic entrance.

In the Store I was the person of the moment. The birthday girl. The center. Bailey[1] had graduated the year before, although to do so he had had to forfeit all pleasures to make up for his time lost in Baton Rouge.

My class was wearing butter-yellow piqué dresses, and Momma launched out on mine. She smocked the yoke into tiny crisscrossing puckers, then shirred the rest of the bodice. Her dark fingers ducked in and out of the lemony cloth as she embroidered raised daisies around the hem. Before she considered herself finished she had added a crocheted cuff on the puff sleeves, and a pointy crocheted collar.

I was going to be lovely. A walking model of all the various styles of fine hand sewing and it didn't worry me that I was only twelve years old and merely graduating from the eighth grade. Besides, many teachers in Arkansas Negro schools had only that diploma and were licensed to impart wisdom.

---

[1]Angelou's brother. The Store was run by Angelou's grandmother, whom she called Momma, and Momma's son, Uncle Willie. [Eds.]

The days had become longer and more noticeable. The faded beige of former times had been replaced with strong and sure colors. I began to see my classmates' clothes, their skin tones, and the dust that waved off pussy willows. Clouds that lazed across the sky were objects of great concern to me. Their shiftier shapes might have held a message that in my new happiness and with a little bit of time I'd soon decipher. During that period I looked at the arch of heaven so religiously my neck kept a steady ache. I had taken to smiling more often, and my jaws hurt from the unaccustomed activity. Between the two physical sore spots, I suppose I could have been uncomfortable, but that was not the case. As a member of the winning team (the graduating class of 1940) I had outdistanced unpleasant sensations by miles. I was headed for the freedom of open fields.

10   Youth and social approval allied themselves with me and we trammeled memories of slights and insults. The wind of our swift passage remodeled my features. Lost tears were pounded to mud and then to dust. Years of withdrawal were brushed aside and left behind, as hanging ropes of parasitic moss.

My work alone had awarded me a top place and I was going to be one of the first called in the graduating ceremonies. On the classroom blackboard, as well as on the bulletin board in the auditorium, there were blue stars and white stars and red stars. No absences, no tardinesses, and my academic work was among the best of the year. I could say the preamble to the Constitution even faster than Bailey. We timed ourselves often: "WethepeopleoftheUnitedStatesinordertoformamoreperfectunion . . ." I had memorized the Presidents of the United States from Washington to Roosevelt in chronological as well as alphabetical order.

My hair pleased me too. Gradually the black mass had lengthened and thickened, so that it kept at last to its braided pattern, and I didn't have to yank my scalp off when I tried to comb it.

Louise and I had rehearsed the exercises until we tired out ourselves. Henry Reed was class valedictorian. He was a small, very black boy with hooded eyes, a long, broad nose and an oddly shaped head. I had admired him for years because each term he and I vied for the best grades in our class. Most often he bested me, but instead of being disappointed I was pleased that we shared top places between us. Like many Southern Black children, he lived with his grandmother, who was as strict as Momma and as kind as she knew how to be. He was courteous, respectful and soft-spoken to elders, but on the playground he chose to play the roughest games. I admired him. Anyone, I reckoned, sufficiently afraid or sufficiently dull could be polite. But to be able to operate at a top level with both adults and children was admirable.

His valedictory speech was entitled "To Be or Not to Be." The rigid tenth-grade teacher had helped him write it. He'd been working on the dramatic stresses for months.

The weeks until graduation were filled with heady activities. A 15 group of small children were to be presented in a play about butter-cups and daisies and bunny rabbits. They could be heard throughout the building practicing their hops and their little songs that sounded like silver bells. The older girls (nongraduates, of course) were as-signed the task of making refreshments for the night's festivities. A tangy scent of ginger, cinnamon, nutmeg and chocolate wafted around the home economics building as the budding cooks made samples for themselves and their teachers.

In every corner of the workshop, axes and saws split fresh timber as the woodshop boys made sets and stage scenery. Only the gradu-ates were left out of the general bustle. We were free to sit in the li-brary at the back of the building or look in quite detachedly, naturally, on the measures being taken for our event.

Even the minister preached on graduation the Sunday before. His subject was, "Let your light so shine that men will see your good works and praise your Father, Who is in Heaven." Although the ser-mon was purported to be addressed to us, he used the occasion to speak to backsliders, gamblers and general ne'er-do-wells. But since he had called our names at the beginning of the service we were mollified.

Among Negroes the tradition was to give presents to children going only from one grade to another. How much more important this was when the person was graduating at the top of the class. Uncle Willie and Momma had sent away for a Mickey Mouse watch like Bailey's. Louise gave me four embroidered handkerchiefs. (I gave her crocheted doilies.) Mrs. Sneed, the minister's wife, made me an undershirt to wear for graduation, and nearly every customer gave me a nickel or maybe even a dime with the instruction "Keep on mov-ing to higher ground," or some such encouragement.

Amazingly the great day finally dawned and I was out of bed before I knew it. I threw open the back door to see it more clearly, but Momma said, "Sister, come away from that door and put your robe on."

I hoped the memory of that morning would never leave me. Sun- 20 light was itself young, and the day had none of the insistence matu-rity would bring it in a few hours. In my robe and barefoot in the backyard, under cover of going to see about my new beans, I gave myself up to the gentle warmth and thanked God that no matter what evil I had done in my life He had allowed me to live to see this day. Somewhere in my fatalism I had expected to die, accidentally, and never have the chance to walk up the stairs in the auditorium and gracefully receive my hard-earned diploma. Out of God's merciful bosom I had won reprieve.

Bailey came out in his robe and gave me a box wrapped in Christmas paper. He said he had saved his money for months to pay for it. It felt like a box of chocolates, but I knew Bailey wouldn't save money to buy candy when we had all we could want under our noses.

He was as proud of the gift as I. It was a soft-leather-bound copy of a collection of poems by Edgar Allan Poe, or, as Bailey and I called him, "Eap." I turned to "Annabel Lee" and we walked up and down the garden rows, the cool dirt between our toes, reciting the beautifully sad lines.

Momma made a Sunday breakfast although it was only Friday. After we finished the blessing, I opened my eyes to find the watch on my plate. It was a dream of a day. Everything went smoothly and to my credit. I didn't have to be reminded or scolded for anything. Near evening I was too jittery to attend to chores, so Bailey volunteered to do all before his bath.

Days before, we had made a sign for the Store, and as we turned out the lights Momma hung the cardboard over the doorknob. It read clearly: CLOSED. GRADUATION.

25   My dress fitted perfectly and everyone said that I looked like a sunbeam in it. On the hill, going toward the school, Bailey walked behind with Uncle Willie, who muttered, "Go on, Ju." He wanted him to walk ahead with us because it embarrassed him to have to walk so slowly. Bailey said he'd let the ladies walk together, and the men would bring up the rear. We all laughed, nicely.

Little children dashed by out of the dark like fireflies. Their crepe-paper dresses and butterfly wings were not made for running and we heard more than one rip, dryly, and the regretful "uh uh" that followed.

The school blazed without gaiety. The windows seemed cold and unfriendly from the lower hill. A sense of ill-fated timing crept over me, and if Momma hadn't reached for my hand I would have drifted back to Bailey and Uncle Willie, and possibly beyond. She made a few slow jokes about my feet getting cold, and tugged me along to the now-strange building.

Around the front steps, assurance came back. There were my fellow "greats," the graduating class. Hair brushed back, legs oiled, new dresses and pressed pleats, fresh pocket handkerchiefs and little handbags, all homesewn. Oh, we were up to snuff, all right. I joined my comrades and didn't even see my family go in to find seats in the crowded auditorium.

The school band struck up a march and all classes filed in as had been rehearsed. We stood in front of our seats, as assigned, and on a signal from the choir director, we sat. No sooner had this been accomplished than the band started to play the national anthem. We rose again and sang the song, after which we recited the pledge of allegiance. We remained standing for a brief minute before the choir director and the principal signaled to us, rather desperately I thought, to take our seats. The command was so unusual that our carefully rehearsed and smooth-running machine was thrown off. For a full minute we fumbled for our chairs and bumped into each other awkwardly. Habits change or solidify under pressure, so in our state of nervous tension we had been ready to follow our usual assembly pattern: the American national anthem, then the pledge of allegiance, then the song every Black person I knew called the Negro National Anthem. All done in the same key, with the same passion and most often standing on the same foot.

Finding my seat at last, I was overcome with a presentiment of 30 worse things to come. Something unrehearsed, unplanned, was going to happen, and we were going to be made to look bad. I distinctly remember being explicit in the choice of pronoun. It was "we," the graduating class, the unit, that concerned me then.

The principal welcomed "parents and friends" and asked the Baptist minister to lead us in prayer. His invocation was brief and punchy, and for a second I thought we were getting on the high road to right action. When the principal came back to the dais, however, his voice had changed. Sounds always affected me profoundly and the principal's voice was one of my favorites. During assembly it melted and lowed weakly into the audience. It had not been in my plan to listen to him, but my curiosity was piqued and I straightened up to give him my attention.

He was talking about Booker T. Washington, our "late great leader," who said we can be as close as the fingers on the hand, etc. . . . Then he said a few vague things about friendship and the friendship of kindly people to those less fortunate than themselves. With that his voice nearly faded, thin, away. Like a river diminishing to a stream and then to a trickle. But he cleared his throat and said, "Our speaker tonight, who is also our friend, came from Texarkana to deliver the commencement address, but due to the irregularity of the train schedule, he's going to, as they say, 'speak and run.'" He said that we understood and wanted the man to know that we were most grateful for the time he was able to give us and then something about how we were willing always to adjust to another's program, and without more ado—"I give you Mr. Edward Donleavy."

Not one but two white men came through the door off-stage. The shorter one walked to the speaker's platform, and the tall one moved to the center seat and sat down. But that was our principal's seat, and already occupied. The dislodged gentleman bounced around for a long breath or two before the Baptist minister gave him his chair, then with more dignity than the situation deserved, the minister walked off the stage.

Donleavy looked at the audience once (on reflection, I'm sure that he wanted only to reassure himself that we were really there), adjusted his glasses and began to read from a sheaf of papers.

35   He was glad "to be here and to see the work going on just as it was in the other schools."

At the first "Amen" from the audience I willed the offender to immediate death by choking on the word. But Amens and Yes, sir's began to fall around the room like rain through a ragged umbrella.

He told us of the wonderful changes we children in Stamps had in store. The Central School (naturally, the white school was Central) had already been granted improvements that would be in use in the fall. A well-known artist was coming from Little Rock to teach art to them. They were going to have the newest microscopes and chemistry equipment for their laboratory. Mr. Donleavy didn't leave us long in the dark over who made these improvements available to Central High. Nor were we to be ignored in the general betterment scheme he had in mind.

He said that he had pointed out to people at a very high level that one of the first-line football tacklers at Arkansas Agricultural and Mechanical College had graduated from good old Lafayette County Training School. Here fewer Amen's were heard. Those few that did break through lay dully in the air with the heaviness of habit.

He went on to praise us. He went on to say how he had bragged that "one of the best basketball players at Fisk[2] sank his first ball right here at Lafayette County Training School."

40   The white kids were going to have a chance to become Galileos and Madame Curies and Edisons and Gauguins,[3] and our boys (the girls weren't even in on it) would try to be Jesse Owenses and Joe Louises.[4]

Owens and the Brown Bomber were great heroes in our world, but what school official in the white-goddom of Little Rock had the right to decide that those two men must be our only heroes? Who decided that for Henry Reed to become a scientist he had to work like George Washington Carver, as a bootblack, to buy a lousy microscope? Bailey was obviously always going to be too small to be an athlete, so which concrete angel glued to what country seat had decided that if my brother wanted to become a lawyer he had to first pay penance for his skin by picking cotton and hoeing corn and studying correspondence books at night for twenty years?

---

[2]Highly regarded, predominantly black university in Nashville. [Eds.]

[3]Inventors, scientists, and artists. [Eds.]

[4]The black track star and Olympic gold medalist, and the longtime world heavyweight boxing champion known as the "Brown Bomber." [Eds.]

The man's dead words fell like bricks around the auditorium and too many settled in my belly. Constrained by hard-learned manners I couldn't look behind me, but to my left and right the proud graduating class of 1940 had dropped their heads. Every girl in my row had found something new to do with her handkerchief. Some folded the tiny squares into love knots, some into triangles, but most were wadding them, then pressing them flat on their yellow laps.

On the dais, the ancient tragedy was being replayed. Professor Parsons sat, a sculptor's reject, rigid. His large, heavy body seemed devoid of will or willingness, and his eyes said he was no longer with us. The other teachers examined the flag (which was draped stage right) or their notes, or the windows which opened on our now-famous playing diamond.

Graduation, the hush-hush magic time of frills and gifts and congratulations and diplomas, was finished for me before my name was called. The accomplishment was nothing. The meticulous maps, drawn in three colors of ink, learning and spelling decasyllabic words, memorizing the whole of *The Rape of Lucrece*[5]—it was for nothing. Donleavy had exposed us.

We were maids and farmers, handymen and washerwomen, and anything higher that we aspired to was farcical and presumptuous. 45

Then I wished that Gabriel Prosser and Nat Turner[6] had killed all whitefolks in their beds and that Abraham Lincoln had been assassinated before the signing of the Emancipation Proclamation, and that Harriet Tubman[7] had been killed by that blow on her head and Christopher Columbus had drowned in the *Santa Maria*.

It was awful to be a Negro and have no control over my life. It was brutal to be young and already trained to sit quietly and listen to charges brought against my color with no chance of defense. We should all be dead. I thought I should like to see us all dead, one on top of the other. A pyramid of flesh with the whitefolks on the bottom, as the broad base, then the Indians with their silly tomahawks and teepees and wigwams and treaties, the Negroes with their mops and recipes and cotton sacks and spirituals sticking out of their mouths. The Dutch children should all stumble in their wooden shoes and break their necks. The French should choke to death on the Louisiana Purchase (1803) while silkworms ate all the Chinese with their stupid pigtails. As a species, we were an abomination. All of us.

Donleavy was running for election, and assured our parents that if he won we could count on having the only colored paved playing

---

[5]*The Rape of Lucrece* is a long narrative poem by Shakespeare. [Eds.]

[6]Prosser and Turner both led slave rebellions. [Eds.]

[7]Harriet Tubman (1820–1913) was an African-American abolitionist who became one of the most successful guides on the Underground Railroad. [Eds.]

field in that part of Arkansas. Also—he never looked up to acknowledge the grunts of acceptance—also, we were bound to get some new
equipment for the home economics building and the workshop.

He finished, and since there was no need to give any more than
the most perfunctory thank-you's, he nodded to the men on the stage,
and the tall white man who was never introduced joined him at the
door. They left with the attitude that now they were off to something
really important. (The graduation ceremonies at Lafayette County
Training School had been a mere preliminary.)

50   The ugliness they left was palpable. An uninvited guest who
wouldn't leave. The choir was summoned and sang a modern
arrangement of "Onward, Christian Soldiers," with new words per-
taining to graduates seeking their place in the world. But it didn't
work. Elouise, the daughter of the Baptist minister, recited "Invictus,"[8]
and I could have cried at the impertinence of "I am the master of my
fate, I am the captain of my soul."

My name had lost its ring of familiarity and I had to be nudged to
go and receive my diploma. All my preparations had fled. I neither
marched up to the stage like a conquering Amazon, nor did I look in
the audience for Bailey's nod of approval. Marguerite Johnson,[9] I heard
the name again, my honors were read, there were noises in the audience of appreciation, and I took my place on the stage as rehearsed.

I thought about colors I hated: ecru, puce, lavender, beige and
black.

There was shuffling and rustling around me, then Henry Reed
was giving his valedictory address, "To Be or Not to Be." Hadn't he
heard the whitefolks? We couldn't *be,* so the question was a waste of
time. Henry's voice came out clear and strong. I feared to look at him.
Hadn't he got the message? There was no "nobler in the mind" for
Negroes because the world didn't think we had minds, and they let
us know it. "Outrageous fortune"? Now, that was a joke. When the
ceremony was over I had to tell Henry Reed some things. That is, if I
still cared. Not "rub," Henry, "erase." "Ah, there's the erase." Us.

Henry had been a good student in elocution. His voice rose on
tides of promise and fell on waves of warnings. The English teacher
had helped him to create a sermon winging through Hamlet's solilo-
quy. To be a man, a doer, a builder, a leader, or to be a tool, an un-
funny joke, a crusher of funky toadstools. I marveled that Henry
could go through with the speech as if we had a choice.

55   I had been listening and silently rebutting each sentence with my
eyes closed; then there was a hush, which in an audience warns that

---

[8]An inspirational poem written in 1875 by William Ernest Henley (1849–1903). Its defiant and stoic
sentiments made it extremely popular with nineteenth-century readers. [Eds.]
[9]Angelou's given name. [Eds.]

something unplanned is happening. I looked up and saw Henry Reed, the conservative, the proper, the A student, turn his back to the audience and turn to us (the proud graduating class of 1940) and sing, nearly speaking,

> "Lift ev'ry voice and sing
> Till earth and heaven ring
> Ring with the harmonies of Liberty . . ."

It was the poem written by James Weldon Johnson. It was the music composed by J. Rosamond Johnson. It was the Negro national anthem. Out of habit we were singing it.

Our mothers and fathers stood in the dark hall and joined the hymn of encouragement. A kindergarten teacher led the small children onto the stage and the buttercups and daisies and bunny rabbits marked time and tried to follow:

> "Stony the road we trod
> Bitter the chastening rod
> Felt in the days when hope, unborn, had died.
> Yet with a steady beat
> Have not our weary feet   5
> Come to the place for which our fathers sighed?"

Each child I knew had learned that song with his ABC's and along with "Jesus Loves Me This I Know." But I personally had never heard it before. Never heard the words, despite the thousands of times I had sung them. Never thought they had anything to do with me.

On the other hand, the words of Patrick Henry had made such an impression on me that I had been able to stretch myself tall and trembling and say, "I know not what course others may take, but as for me, give me liberty or give me death."

And now I heard, really for the first time: 60

> "We have come over a way that with tears
> has been watered,
> We have come, treading our path through
> the blood of the slaughtered."

While echoes of the song shivered in the air, Henry Reed bowed his head, said "Thank you," and returned to his place in the line. The tears that slipped down many faces were not wiped away in shame.

We were on top again. As always, again. We survived. The depths had been icy and dark, but now a bright sun spoke to our souls. I was no longer simply a member of the proud graduating class of 1940; I was a proud member of the wonderful, beautiful Negro race.

Oh, Black known and unknown poets, how often have your auctioned pains sustained us? Who will compute the lonely nights made less lonely by your songs, or the empty pots made less tragic by your tales?

If we were a people much given to revealing secrets, we might raise monuments and sacrifice to the memories of our poets, but slavery cured us of that weakness. It may be enough, however, to have it said that we survive in exact relationship to the dedication of our poets (include preachers, musicians and blues singers).

Responding to Reading

1. Angelou's graduation took place in 1940. What expectations did educators have for Angelou and her classmates? In what ways were these expectations different from the expectations Angelou and her fellow students had?
2. In what way did Mr. Donleavy's speech "educate" the graduates? How did Angelou's thinking change as she listened to him?
3. In paragraph 62, Angelou says, "We were on top again." In what way were she and the graduates "on top"? Do you think Angelou was being overly optimistic in light of what she had just experienced?

Responding in Writing

In the 1954 *Brown v. Board of Education* decision, the Supreme Court of the United States ruled that the "separate but equal" education that Angelou experienced was unconstitutional. How do you suppose her education would have been different had she attended high school in 1960 instead of in 1940?

THE WAR AGAINST TESTING

David W. Murray

David W. Murray is the former director of the Washington-based Statistical Assessment Service, a nonpartisan organization that examines the use of quantitative research by the media. In the following article, which appeared in Commentary Magazine *(September 1998), he examines the criticisms that opponents of standard testing level at the SATs and offers his own view on the subject.*

It is safe to say that Thomas Jefferson never took a standardized test, and would probably consider them hopelessly inadequate as measures of what an educated person should know. Yet Jefferson, in

his way, was the inspiration behind our present vast apparatus for assessing academic aptitude and achievement. Looking toward America's future, he imagined an educational system that would seek
young people from "every condition of life," students of "virtue and
talents" who would someday form a "natural aristocracy" to replace
the old-fashioned kind based on wealth and family background.

The U.S. of course has never fully achieved this ideal. But particularly in the period after World War II, as ever larger numbers of Americans entered colleges and universities, Jefferson's educational vision did
begin to appear closer than ever to being realized. To an extent unimaginable a few generations earlier, access to American universities, and especially the elite ones, became based on considerations of merit. The
chief instrument of this transformation was the standardized test—
mass-administered, machine-scored, and utterly indifferent to every
characteristic of a student save his ability to get the answers right.

And yet, for all its obvious benefits in helping to identify Jefferson's "natural aristocracy," and for all its widespread acceptance—
this year, the Educational Testing Service (ETS), the organization that
does the bulk of such evaluation, will administer its tests to some nine
million students—the enterprise of testing has never been free from
criticism. Today, in fact, its critics are more numerous and more vocif-
erous than ever.

Indignant over the recent drop in minority enrollment at some
state universities as a result of bans on affirmative action, the foes
of standardized assessment argue with bitterness that America's
vaunted meritocracy has never served all its citizens equally well. As
they see it, moreover, the real issue is not the abilities of the test-
takers, minority or otherwise. Rather, it is the tests themselves, and
the unreasonable emphasis placed on them by the gatekeepers of
American higher education.

The oldest and most familiar accusation against standardized 5
tests is that they are discriminatory. As the advocacy group FairTest
puts it, a seemingly objective act, namely, "filling in little bubbles"
with a No. 2 pencil, conceals a process that is "racially, culturally, and
sexually biased."

The prime evidence for this charge is the test results themselves.
For many years now, the median score for blacks on the Scholastic Assessment Test (SAT) has fallen 200 points short of that for whites (on a
scale of 400 to 1600, divided equally between math and verbal skills).
Less dramatic, but no less upsetting to groups like the Center for
Women's Policy Studies, has been the persistent 35-point gender gap
in scores on the math section of the SAT.

The SAT produces such disparate results, say critics, because its
very substance favors certain kinds of students over others. Thus,

fully comprehending a reading selection might depend on background knowledge naturally available to an upper-middle-class white student (by virtue, say, of foreign travel or exposure to the performing arts) but just as naturally unavailable to a lower-class black student from the ghetto. The education writer Peter Sacks calls this the "Volvo effect," and has offered for proof an ETS study according to which, within certain income brackets, the difference between the test scores of white and black students disappears.

At the same time, women are said to be put at a disadvantage by the multiple-choice format itself. Singled out for blame are math questions that emphasize abstract reasoning and verbal exercises based on selecting antonyms, both of which supposedly favor masculine modes of thought. "[F]emales process and express knowledge differently, and more subtly," explains FairTest's Robert Schaeffer. "They look for nuances, shades of gray, different angles."

In fact, so biased are the tests, according to their opponents, that they fail to perform even the limited function claimed for them: forecasting future grades. The SAT, says Peter Sacks, consistently "underpredicts" the college marks of both women and minorities, which hardly inspires confidence in its ability to measure the skills it purports to identify. As for the Graduate Record Exam (GRE), required by most academic graduate programs, a recent study of 5,000 students found that their scores told us almost nothing, beyond what we might already know from their grades, about how they would perform in graduate school.

10   Another line of attack against the tests grants their accuracy in measuring certain academic skills but challenges the notion that these are the skills most worth having. High test scores, opponents insist, reveal little more than a talent for—taking tests. According to a 1994 study by the National Association of School Psychologists, students who do well on the SAT tend to think by "rote" and to favor a "surface approach" to schoolwork. Low scorers, by contrast, are more likely to delve into material, valuing "learning for its own sake."

It is likewise contended that no mere standardized test can capture the qualities that translate into real-world achievement. Thus, when it emerged last year that American children ranked dead last among the major industrial nations in the Third International Mathematics and Science Study, the Harvard education expert Howard Gardner declared himself unconcerned. The tests, after all, "don't measure whether students can think," just their exposure to "the lowest common denominator of facts and skills." Besides, Gardner observed, at a time when America enjoys unrivaled prosperity, what could be more obvious than that "high scores on these tests . . . aren't crucial to our economic success"?

In a similar vein, the social commentator Nicholas Lemann has called for a reassessment of what we mean by meritocracy. Our current view of it, he argued recently in the New York Times, is "badly warped." If universities are to regain the "moral and public dimensions" that once connected them to the wider society, instead of being mere instruments for "distributing money and prestige," they should begin to select not those students who excel on standardized tests but those with the skills necessary to lead "a good, decent life."

This varied chorus of critics has already won some significant concessions from the current testing regime. For one thing, ETS, faced with both adverse publicity and threats of legal action by activists and the U.S. Department of Education, has tried to remedy differences in group performance. On the Preliminary Scholastic Assessment Test (PSAT), which is used for choosing National Merit Scholars, a new method of scoring was recently introduced in the hope that more women might garner the prestigious award. The old formula, which assigned equal weight to the math and verbal sections of the test, was replaced by an index in which the verbal score, usually the higher one for female test-takers, was doubled. The point, as a prominent testing official put it, was "to help girls catch up."

More widely publicized was the massive "recentering" of SAT scores that went into effect with the 1996 results. Though the declared aim of ETS was a technical one—to create a better distribution of scores clustered around the test's numerical midpoint—the practical effect was a windfall for students in almost every range. A test-taker who previously would have received an excellent score of 730 out of 800 on the verbal section, for example, is now granted a "perfect" 800, while the average scores for groups like blacks and Hispanics have received a considerable boost.

But since neither "recentering" nor any other such device has succeeded in eliminating disparities in scores, opponents of tests have had to look elsewhere. At universities themselves, affirmative action has long been the tool of choice for remedying the alleged biases of tests. With racial preferences now under siege, economic disadvantage is being talked about as a new compensating factor that may help shore up the numbers of minority students. The law school at the University of California at Berkeley, for instance, has introduced a selection system that will consider a "coefficient of social disadvantage" in ranking applicants.

Some schools go farther, hoping simply to do away with standardized tests altogether. There are, they insist, other, less problematic indicators of student merit. High-school grades are a starting point, but no less important are essays, interviews, and work portfolios that offer a window into personal traits no standardized test can reveal.

Bates College in Maine, like several other small liberal-arts schools, has already stopped requiring applicants to take the SAT. According to the college's vice president, William Hiss, standardized scores are far less meaningful than "evidence of real intelligence, real drive, real creative abilities, real cultural sensitivities." These qualities, moreover, are said to be especially prominent in the applications of minority students, whose numbers at the school have indeed shot upward since the change in policy.

Taken as a whole, the campaign currently being mounted against standardized testing constitutes a formidable challenge to what was once seen as the fairest means of identifying and ranking scholastic merit. Since that campaign shows every sign of intensifying in the years ahead, it may be relevant to point out that every major premise on which it rests is false.

In the first place, the SAT and GRE are hardly the meaningless academic snapshots described by their critics. Results from these tests have been shown to correspond with those on a whole range of other measures and outcomes, including IQ tests, the National Assessment of Educational Progress, and the National Educational Longitudinal Study. Though each of these uses a different format and has a somewhat different aim, a high degree of correlation obtains among all of them.

20   This holds true for racial and ethnic groups as well. Far from being idiosyncratic, the scoring patterns of whites, blacks, Hispanics, and Asians on the SAT and GRE are replicated on other tests as well. It was in light of just such facts that the National Academy of Science concluded in the 1980's that the most commonly used standardized tests display no evidence whatsoever of cultural bias.

Nor do the tests fail to predict how minority students will ultimately perform in the classroom. If, indeed, the purported bias in the tests were real, such students would earn better grades in college than what is suggested by their SAT scores; but that is not the case. As Keith Widaman, a psychologist at the University of California, showed in a recent study, the SAT actually overestimates the first-year grades of blacks and Hispanics in the UC system.

Foes of testing are a bit closer to the mark when they claim that women end up doing better in college than their scores would indicate. But the "underprediction" is very slight—a tenth of a grade point on the four-point scale—and only applies to less demanding schools. For more selective institutions, the SAT predicts the grades of both sexes quite accurately.

As for the claim that test scores depend heavily on income, the facts again tell us otherwise. Though one can always point to exceptions, students who are not of the same race but whose families earn alike tend, on average, to perform very differently. A California study found, for example, that even among families with annual incomes over $70,000, blacks still fell short in median SAT scores, trailing Hispanics by 79 points, whites by 148 points, and Asians by 193 points.

This suggests that universities turning to economic disadvantage as a surrogate for racial preferences will be disappointed with the results. And this has already proved to be the case. When the University of Texas medical school mounted such an effort, it found that most of its minority applicants did not qualify for admission, coming as they did from fairly comfortable circumstances but still failing to match the academic credentials of less-well-off whites and others. In fact, as a University of California task force concluded last year, so-called economic affirmative action, by opening the door to poor but relatively high-scoring whites and Asians, might actually hurt the prospects of middle-class blacks and Hispanics.

What about relying less on tests and more on other measuring 25 rods like high-school grades? Unfortunately, as everyone knows, high schools across the country vary considerably, not only in their resources but in the demands they make of students. An A− from suburban Virginia's elite Thomas Jefferson High School of Science and Technology cannot be ranked with an A− from a school in rural Idaho or inner-city Newark, especially at a time of rampant grade inflation aimed at bolstering "self-esteem." It was precisely to address this problem that a single nationwide test was introduced in the first place.

Nor is it even clear that relying more exclusively on grades would bump up the enrollment numbers of blacks and Hispanics, as many seem to think. While it is true that more minority students would thereby become eligible for admission, so would other students whose grade-point averages (GPA's) outstripped their test scores. A state commission in California, considering the adoption of such a scheme, discovered that in order to pick students from this larger pool for the limited number of places in the state university system, the schools would have to raise their GPA cut-off point. As a result, the percentage of eligible Hispanics would have remained the same, and black eligibility actually would have dropped.

In Texas, vast disparities in preparation have already damped enthusiasm for a much-publicized "top-10-percent" plan under which the highest-ranking tenth of graduates from any Texas high school win automatic admission to the state campus of their choice, regardless of their test scores. Passed in the wake of the 1996 Hopwood case (1996), which scuttled the state university's affirmative-action program, the plan has forced many high schools to discourage their students from getting in over their heads when choosing a college. As one guidance counselor quoted in the *Chronicle of Higher Education* warned her top seniors, "You may be sitting in a classroom where the majority of students have demonstrated . . . higher-order thinking skills that are beyond what you have. You'll have to struggle."

Grades aside, what of the various less measurable signs of student potential? Should not a sterling character or artistic sensitivity count for something? What of special obstacles overcome?

Certainly, such things should count, and always have counted—more so today than ever, to judge by the sorts of questions most schools currently ask of applicants. But gaining a fuller picture of a particular student's promise is a difficult business, especially in an admissions process that very often involves sorting through thousands of individuals. Moreover, it can only go so far before it ceases to have anything to do with education. What a student is like outside the classroom is surely significant, but until we are prepared to say outright that the heart of the matter is something other than fitness for academic work, a crucial gauge of whether a student is going to be able to pass a biology final or write a political-science research paper will remain that old, much-maligned SAT score.

30   There are, to be fair, social commentators who acknowledge this ineluctable fact, and who therefore urge us to direct all our remedial efforts toward improving the test scores of American blacks.* But for the true opponents of testing, such efforts—the work of generations—are clearly beside the point. Basically, what these critics are hoping to do is to achieve the ends of affirmative action by other, more politic means.

Hence the search for supposedly more "nuanced" measures of scholastic merit like "creativity" and "leadership," tacitly understood as stand-ins for skin color. But there is no reason to think that minority students possess these qualities in greater abundance than do their peers. The attempt to substitute them for test scores will thus only perpetuate the corrupt logic of affirmative action by piling deception upon deception.

Whatever the euphemism used to describe it, only counting by race and gender can produce the result that will satisfy the most determined critics of standardized testing. If they have their way, and such testing wholly or partly disappears, we will have forfeited our best and most objective means of knowing how our schools are doing, as well as any clear set of standards by which students themselves can judge their own progress. On that day, America's astonishingly successful experiment in educational meritocracy will have come to an end. How this will benefit the poor and disadvantaged among us, or help them get ahead, is anybody's guess.

---

*See "America's Next Achievement Test" by Christopher Jencks and Meredith Phillips in the September–October *American Prospect*.

Responding to Reading

1. According to Murray, what is the relationship between today's standard-ized tests and Jefferson's dream of a "'natural aristocracy'" (1)? Why do critics oppose these tests?
2. What arguments do the foes of standardized testing make? What is Mur-ray's opinion of these arguments? What specific points does Murray make in refuting each of the arguments against standardized testing?
3. How have supporters of standardized testing responded to their critics? How effective have these responses been? According to Murray, what will satisfy the most extreme critics of standardized testing? Why does he be-lieve the end of testing will be the end of "America's astonishingly success-ful experiment in educational meritocracy" (32)?

Responding in Writing

In your case, were the SATs an accurate or inaccurate indicator of your perfor-mance in college?

WHO CARES ABOUT THE RENAISSANCE?

Leslie S. P. Brown

1957–

Leslie S. P. Brown, a native of Columbus, Ohio, wrote the essay "Who Cares about the Renaissance?" when she was an Annenberg graduate fellow at the University of Pennsylvania studying for a PhD in Renaissance art history. In the essay, which was published in the "My Turn" column of Newsweek Magazine *in 1983, Brown argues in favor of scholarship and the worthiness of intellectual pursuits.*

Last September, with the aid of an unusually generous fellow-ship, I enrolled in a doctoral program in Italian Renaissance art his-tory. Although I had selected this particular career path as a college freshman and had never seriously considered any alternatives, I expe-rienced severe doubts as I packed my bags and prepared to re-enter the academic life after a year away. For although my return to school elicited a few wistful wishes for happiness, and success, it primarily provoked a chorus of lugubrious warnings about the "lack of rele-vance" of my chosen field and the uncertainty of my professional and financial future.

I coped easily with the tired jokes about Ph.D.'s driving cabs from the lawyers, doctors and M.B.A.'s of my acquaintance. But when a professor who had encouraged me to apply for graduate study sat me down and described in lurid detail his 20 years of frustration and comparative poverty as an academic, I began to be disturbed. And it was something of a shock to hear him say, as he leafed through the pages of his latest book, "I spent 10 years of my life on this thing, and what do I get? A thousand bucks and a pat on the back from a couple of colleagues. Sometimes I think it isn't worth it anymore."

Escapists: Not surprisingly, there aren't many of us left, we young scholars of the past. Out of a total of 25 art-history majors at the college I attended, the vast majority went to law school. In these days of frantic attempts to gain admission to the best professional schools, the decision to pursue an advanced degree in literature, history, music or art is often viewed as a symptom of rapidly advancing lunacy—or, at least, as a sign of total disregard for the practical concerns of life. Media articles relentlessly describe the abysmal condition of the job market for Ph.D.'s in the humanities and the worry of department chairmen at universities where students are avoiding Chaucer and baroque music in favor of technical courses. Friends and family consider those of us who have chosen this course as aberrations. Some of us have been accused of being escapists, of refusing to face the constant changes of a technological society, of shutting ourselves up in ivory towers out of fear of competing with our pragmatic and computer-literate peers. In short, we hopeful scholars have had to accept the fact that we are considered anachronisms.

Why do we do it, then? Why have we, highly educated and raised, for the most part, by ambitious and upwardly mobile parents, turned our backs on the 20th century in order to bury our noses in dusty books and write articles that only our colleagues will read?

5   Well, in part we do it for love. Despite the gibes and jeers of our friends (and I might note that I have never once accused any of my lawyer friends of rampant materialism), we *are* realists. We are forced to be. We live in tiny, inexpensive apartments, take public transportation (or, more often, walk) and eat cheaply between long hours at the library. Many of us will be paying back huge educational loans for years and may never own a house or buy a new car. It is not a soft life, and sometimes we do complain. But usually we glory in it. We admire our contemporaries who are now making salaries that we only dream about, but we are secure in the knowledge that we have chosen to do what we love best. We have not relegated our joy in literature and art to the status of hobbies, and we can only hope that our passions will help us survive the lean years, the frustration and the occasional intellectual exhaustion.

Nor are we less competent or socially aware than our friends in more practical professions. Several of my teachers and classmates have verbal and analytical abilities that would make them gifted lawyers or product managers; a small contingent is making fascinating discoveries about medieval architecture by performing astounding arithmetical gymnastics—with the aid of a computer. Many of us love science—several of my most enjoyable hours have been spent with a telescope in a freezing observatory—and we pay close attention to political developments. And many of us are enthusiastic sports fans. In other words, we are not social cripples or intellectual snobs with no interests beyond our own esoteric and rarefied disciplines. We have chosen to endure the raised eyebrows and the despair of our families because we hope that, with hard work and dedication, we will never have to mourn a lost love of Botticelli or Bach while working in jobs that fail to touch our souls or feed our human hunger for beauty.

Not long ago, a bright 16-year-old girl—a mathematics prodigy—asked me who Michelangelo was. When I told her that he was one of the greatest artists who had ever lived, she asked me why she had never heard of him. Unfortunately, she is not alone. Universities today are wondering where they will find scholars of the humanities for new generations of students; perhaps it will be necessary to tell future freshmen that they cannot study literature, art, music or foreign languages because there is nobody to teach them.

Elegance: So there is yet another—perhaps less selfish—reason that we persist. We are the men and women who prepare the museum exhibitions and keep the classics alive. We hold up the lessons of history before the world and try to ensure that they will not be forgotten, even if they go unlearned. We scramble for the funding and the grants—increasingly difficult to obtain these days—to save the deteriorating art works, to publish new editions and translations of the great books, to give recitals of the loveliest music. In short, we fight to maintain the pockets of warmth and elegance that provide some relief to others who are tired and harried in a sometimes sterile and technological society. I am not a particularly altruistic person, but my studies have made me deeply sensitive to the alienation and coldness of our times. While I occasionally wish that I had a time machine to deposit me in the 16th century, where I would never have to worry about a bank card or a failed transmission, I believe that I can perform a certain service here and now. My work may go largely unappreciated by many, but a few will be grateful. And that is enough.

Responding to Reading

1. Brown claims that she is a realist. Do her arguments in favor of getting a PhD in Italian Renaissance art history support this claim?
2. What preconceived ideas does Brown assume readers have about people who get PhD's in the humanities? How effectively does she address these stereotypes?

3. How does Brown characterize those outside academia? Do you think that her assertion that we live in a "sterile and technological society" (8) still holds true today? Do you think it is possible for lawyers, doctors, or MBA's to feel as passionately about their fields as Brown feels about hers?

Responding in Writing

In choosing a major, do you think you will be influenced primarily by love of your subject or by your need to find employment?

LITERATURE: FORGETTING THE TRADITION

Diane Ravitch

1938–

Born in Houston, Texas, Diane Ravitch received a BA from Wellesley College (1960) and a PhD in history from Columbia University (1975). She taught at Teachers College of Columbia University from 1975 until 1991, when she served two years as Assistant Secretary of Education. Today, Ravitch is a research professor of education at New York University and a senior fellow of the Brookings Institution in Washington, DC, where she edits the Brookings Papers on Education Policy. *Her recent books include* Left Back: A Century of Failed School Reforms *(2000) and* The Language Police: How Pressure Groups Restrict What Students Learn *(2003), from which the following selection was taken. To read more of Ravitch's work, visit the Brookings Institution Web site, http://www.brook.edu/, and look under the heading "Research Topics: Education."*

Today's literature textbooks reflect the state of the field of English language arts: large, beautifully packaged, and incoherent. They are incoherent in the sense that they lack any unity of principle; they are not logically or aesthetically organized. They are a potpourri of fiction, nonfiction, social commentary, graphics, special features, and pedagogical aids. Even when the selections are good, the texts are almost painful to read because of their visual clutter and sensory overload. They make no attempt to teach children about the time-honored tradition of literature shared by English-speaking peoples, nor do they recognize and honor the great writers of the American literary tradition. To the contrary, today's textbooks strain to obscure any sense of literary tradition; they pretend that there is no such tradition. Nor do they attempt to teach students how to make judgments among literary works. They instead indiscriminately mix pieces by writers who are great, ordinary, and undistinguished.

The literature textbooks for middle school and high school from the major publishers are compilations of odds and ends. They have no overarching ends. The books are littered with nonliterary features, such as an essay about homelessness or air pollution. One teaches students how to read a weather map, a time line, and a telephone book. Another contains features about careers. All include some excellent literature, some mediocre selections, and lots of advice about how to think, to read, to write, to summarize, to take tests, to find the main idea, or to read a classified ad. Some include social studies articles, science articles, and other miscellany.

None of the textbooks is designed to build a foundation of cultural knowledge; none encourages students to discern why some pieces of writing are considered classic. Writing is writing; text is text. Everything is treated as literature, just because it happens to be printed. No effort is expended to teach students the differences among writing that is banal, good, better, or best. The stories of Edgar Allan Poe, Mark Twain, and O. Henry are mixed haphazardly with student essays, study skills, and never-heard-of, soon-to-be-forgotten pieces by little-known writers. One book, published by Prentice Hall (with the subtitle "Timeless Voices, Timeless Themes") has an excerpt from a script of the once-popular television program *Xena: Warrior Princess*. This script would not qualify as "literature" by any standard other than one in which absolutely everything in print is "literature."

The literature textbooks for these grades (5–10) contain from 650 to 1,200 pages. Often the selections are accompanied by photographs and biographies of authors so that students are made aware of their gender and ethnic background. Every textbook has a representation of well-known authors, but they are mainly seasoning in a very big and varied stew. The textbooks include selections by recognized writers, such as O. Henry, Edgar Allan Poe, Robert W. Service, Henry Wadsworth Longfellow, John Greenleaf Whittier, Ray Bradbury, Walt Whitman, Emily Dickinson, John Ciardi, Lewis Carroll, Christina Rossetti, Robert Frost, Jack London, Robert Louis Stevenson, Isaac Bashevis Singer, Arthur Miller, Sara Teasdale, E. B. White, Shakespeare, Carl Sandburg, Doris Lessing, and Mark Twain. But one will not find too many of them in any single volume. Nor will one find many traditional American tall tales or legends in the reading books. The student is more likely to encounter folktales from Japan, China, Africa, or India than to read one from the American past.

There is a new canon in today's literature textbooks. Certain 5 writers appear again and again. They are Sandra Cisneros, Nikki Giovanni, Toni Cade Bambara, Jane Yolen, Gary Soto, Lawrence Yep, Pat Mora, Julia Alvarez, Walter Dean Myers, Naomi Shihab Nye, and Rudolfo A. Anaya. Most of them are not well known to the general public, but their stories, essays, and poems are omnipresent in the textbook world. Students may never encounter Herman Melville, Ralph Waldo Emerson, Joseph Conrad, or Nathaniel Hawthorne, but they will certainly know the work of Cisneros; there is hardly a literary textbook at any grade level, regardless of publisher, that does not include her writing.

Even McDougal Littell's senior high school textbook, ostensibly devoted to a chronological treatment of major American literature, cannot resist the temptation to trivialize that tradition by randomly adding to it without regard to chronology. In a section allegedly devoted to American works written from "2000 B.C. to A.D. 1620," the editors insert a short story written in 1969 by a Native American writer, a 1982 travelogue by another Native American writer, and an excerpt from Maya Angelou's autobiography. The section covering the era from 1620 to 1800 offers such writers as Jonathan Edwards, Benjamin Franklin, and Thomas Jefferson, but also includes Martin Luther King Jr., Malcolm X, and a Chicano poet.

Today's literature textbooks are motivated by a spirit of miscellany. None of them consists only of text and pictures, like a real book; that would be way too simple. Even when the entries are well chosen and enjoyable, the textbook pokes the reader in the eye with pedagogical strategies. The reason that the books are so large is that they are puffed up with instructions and activities that belong in the teachers' edition. The people who prepare these textbooks don't seem to have much faith in teachers. The books strive to be "teacher-proof." They leave nothing to the teacher's initiative or ingenuity. They lay out in minute detail precisely what the teacher should ask and do, which is incredibly distracting to the reader. Despite the fact that the NCTE-IRA national standards say that teachers and administrators should make their own selections of literature, many of the professional leaders of the NCTE and IRA edited the textbooks that make the selections for teachers and tell them exactly what to say when they are teaching.

The National Council of Teachers of English was not always opposed to reading lists. In 1935, for example, the NCTE's curriculum commission compiled an extensive list of readings that began with traditional nursery tales and fairy tales in kindergarten (such as *Peter Rabbit* and "Jack and the Beanstalk"), and advanced in complexity through high school, with selections from Whitman, Riis, Tennyson, Dickens, Eliot, Twain, Cooper, Thackeray, the Brontës, Hawthorne, Longfellow, Alcott, Defoe, Ferber, and Shakespeare. The commission said, "Like the fight for health, the struggle for culture must be systematic and persistent.[1]

We have come a long way since then, and so has the NCTE. It opposes any list of recommended readings for fear that it will become a dreaded canon. In 1997, the NCTE elected a new president, Sheridan

Blau of the University of California at Santa Barbara, who suggested that the organization might consider constructing a reading list, because "in a nation as diverse as ours we must count on schools to provide the materials for building a common culture beyond that created by commercial TV and popular music." He noted that there were already many lists in circulation and that the profession should take control of decisions about what to teach away from the textbook publishers. Some NCTE members reacted with horror, fearful that a list would represent only the politically powerful, that it would exclude the voices of the powerless, that the people of the United States do not have a common culture, that they should not have a common culture, and that only middle-class whites would be part of a national culture. Faced with overwhelmingly negative responses from professors of education in the NCTE (not the teachers!), Blau's proposal was tabled by the organization's executive committee. The NCTE chose to leave control of what to teach in the hands of the textbook industry by default.[2]

The NCTE's opposition to a reading list has many sources, but 10 some deserve special attention.

One is the rise of young adult fiction since the late 1960s, popular novels written for adolescents by an author who writes in the voice of an adolescent. Such novels, like those of Robert Cormier, S. E. Hinton, and Judy Blume, deal with adolescent problems about self-esteem and issues like drugs, alcohol, sexuality, peer pressure, and relationships with parents. Some of these books are engaging, and some are utterly banal. Defenders of this genre fear that it would be excluded from any list of great American literature. It might be. Some teachers are not sure that teen fiction deserves class time. Carol Jago, a California teacher who is a leader in the NCTE, maintains that students read two kinds of books, what she calls "mirror books" and "window books." The mirror books reflect their experiences with peers, parents, school, drugs, and sex; the window books offer "access to other worlds, other times, other cultures." Teenagers, she says, don't need help reading mirror books, but they need teachers to guide them through the unfamiliar language and references of window books. "If students can read a book on their own," she writes, "it probably isn't the best choice for classroom study. Classroom texts should pose intellectual challenges to young readers."[3]

A second, and related, reason for rejecting a reading list is the conviction, supported by the NCTE-IRA standards, that whatever is taught in school must be relevant to today's teens. The story must "include" them. It must be about them, not about adults in another era and culture. It must connect to their personal life experience, and it must be interpreted through the lens of their personal response. If students can't "relate" personally to *Lord Jim* or *Madame Bovary* or *Emma*, there is no point expecting them to read the book. This assumption encourages the narcissism of adolescence. Students are taught to look for themselves in the stories they read, rather than activate their imagination to enter other lives and other worlds.

A third, and related, source of opposition to a reading list is the assumption that students can comprehend only the literature written by and about people who share their racial, ethnic, or gender identity (embedded in this assumption is the belief that people have a single identity rather than multiple, intertwined identities). Girls must read stories about girls, which will then boost their self-esteem, and African American students must read stories by and about people who are also African American, for the same reason. Forgotten is W. E. B. Du Bois's statement about how his reading of classic literature liberated him and allowed him to break through "the veil" that white racists used to keep black people subjugated. He wrote: "I sit with Shakespeare, and he winces not. Across the color line I move arm in arm with Balzac and Dumas, where smiling men and welcoming women glide in gilded halls. From out the caves of evening that swing between the strong-limbed earth and the tracery of the stars, I summon Aristotle and Aurelius and what soul I will, and they come all graciously with no scorn nor condescension. So, wed with Truth, I dwell above the Veil." Certainly American schools must teach the nation's rich heritage of African American literature, which is a vital part of the American literary tradition, but it is wrong to exile the classic literature that inspired writers such as Du Bois, Ralph Ellison, Langston Hughes, Zora Neale Hurston, and Richard Wright.

Is reading a tool for social change? Those who are familiar with the sensational impact of Harriet Beecher Stowe's *Uncle Tom's Cabin* or James Baldwin's *The Fire Next Time* or Rachel Carson's *Silent Spring* would insist that it is. Is reading a tool for personal transformation? Those who have fallen in love with a poem and learned it "by heart" would argue that it is. But so long as curriculum experts continue to believe that young people should read only about themselves and should not be expected to reach beyond their own experiences, then the literature prized by generations of Americans of all races and conditions does not stand a chance.

Notes

1. W. Wilbur Hatfield, *An Experience Curriculum in English: A Report of the Curriculum Commission of the National Council of Teachers of English* (Appleton-Century, 1935), pp. 25–77.
2. "Should We Create an Authorized National Literary Canon?" *California English,* Fall 1997, pp. 6–8.
3. Carol Jago, "Something There Is That Doesn't Love a List," *American Educator,* Winter 2001, p. 36.

Responding to Reading

1. What does Ravitch mean when she says, "everything in print is 'literature'" (3)? According to her, why is this a problem—especially in literature textbooks?
2. According to Ravitch, which writers appear over and over in contemporary literature textbooks? Why does Ravitch call this collection of writers the "new canon" (5)? What writers are almost never included in the new canon?
3. Why does the National Council of Teachers of English (NCTE) oppose reading lists? What are the implications of their opposition?

Responding in Writing

Ravitch says that literature is a tool for personal change. What do you think she means? What piece of literature has led to a "personal transformation" (14) in you?

FOR MORE BALANCE ON CAMPUSES

Christina Hoff Sommers

1956–

Christina Hoff Sommers received her BA degree from New York University and a PhD in philosophy from Brandeis University. She has taught at the University of Massachusetts at Boston and at Clark University, and she currently works as a fellow at the American Enterprise Institute. Sommers is the author of essays in a wide variety of periodicals and has published several books but is best known for Who Stole Feminism?: How Women Have Betrayed Women *(1994) and* The War against Boys: How Misguided Feminism Is Harming Our Young Men *(2000). She frequently appears on television as a commentator. The following essay is the introduction to a longer essay that appeared in the* Atlantic Monthly. *To read more of this author's work, visit the American Enterprise Institution Web site, http://www.aei.org/, and look for Sommers under the heading "Scholars & Fellows."*

Washington—In a recent talk at Haverford College, I questioned the standard women's studies teaching that the United States is a patriarchal society that oppresses women.

For many in the audience, this was their first encounter with a dissident scholar. One student was horrified when I said that the free market had advanced the cause of women by affording them unprecedented economic opportunities. "How can anyone say that capitalism has helped women?" she asked.

Nor did I win converts when I said that the male heroism of special forces soldiers and the firefighters at ground zero should persuade gender scholars to acknowledge that "stereotypical masculinity" had some merit. Later an embarrassed and apologetic student said to me, "Haverford is just not ready for you."

After my talk, the young woman who invited me told me there was little intellectual diversity at Haverford and that she had hoped I would spark debate. In fact, many in the audience were quietly delighted by the exchanges. But two angry students accused her of providing "a forum for hate speech."

5   As the 2000 election made plain, the United States is pretty evenly divided between conservatives and liberals. Yet conservative scholars have effectively been marginalized, silenced, and rendered invisible on most campuses. This problem began in the late '80s and has become much worse in recent years. Most students can now go through four years of college without encountering a scholar of pronounced conservative views.

Few conservatives make it past the gantlet of faculty hiring in political-science, history, or English departments. In 1998, when a reporter from Denver's Rocky Mountain News surveyed the humanities and social sciences at the University of Colorado, Boulder, he found that of 190 professors with party affiliations, 184 were Democrats.

There wasn't a single Republican in the English, psychology, journalism, or philosophy departments. A 1999 survey of history departments found 22 Democrats and 2 Republicans at Stanford. At Cornell and Dartmouth there were 29 and 10 Democrats, respectively, and no Republicans.

The dearth of conservatives in psychology departments is so striking, that one (politically liberal) professor has proposed affirmative-action outreach. Richard Redding, a professor of psychology at Villanova University, writing in a recent issue of American Psychologist, notes that of the 31 social-policy articles that appeared in the journal between 1990 and 1999, 30 could be classified as liberal, one as conservative.

The key issue, Professor Redding says, is not the preponderance of Democrats, but the liberal practice of systematically excluding conservatives. Redding cites an experiment in which several graduate departments received mock applications from two candidates nearly identical, except that one "applicant" said he was a conservative Christian. The professors judged the nonconservative to be the significantly better candidate.

10   Redding asks, rhetorically: "Do we want a professional world where our liberal world view prevents us from considering valuable strengths of conservative approaches to social problems . . . where conservatives are reluctant to enter the profession and we tacitly discriminate against them if they do? That, in fact, is the academic world we now have. . . ."

Campus talks by "politically incorrect" speakers happen rarely; visits are resisted and almost never internally funded. When Dinesh D'Souza, Andrew Sullivan, David Horowitz, or Linda Chavez do appear at a college, they are routinely heckled and sometimes threatened. The academy is now so inhospitable to free expression that conservatives buy advertisements in student newspapers. But most school newspapers won't print them. And papers that do are sometimes vandalized and the editors threatened.

The classical liberalism articulated by John Stuart Mill in his book "On Liberty" is no longer alive on campuses, having died of the very disease Mr. Mill warned of when he pointed out that ideas not freely and openly debated become "dead dogmas." Mill insisted that the intellectually free person must put himself in the "mental position of those who think differently" adding that dissident ideas are best understood "by hear[ing] them from persons who actually believe them."

Several groups are working to bring some balance to campus. The Intercollegiate Studies Institute, Young America's Foundation, Clare Boothe Luce Policy Institute, and Accuracy in Academia sponsor lectures by leading conservatives and libertarians. Students can ask these groups for funds to sponsor speakers.

More good news is that David Horowitz's Center for the Study of Popular Culture has launched a "Campaign for Fairness and Inclusion in Higher Education." It calls for university officials to:

1. Establish a zero-tolerance policy for vandalizing newspapers or heckling speakers.
2. Conduct an inquiry into political bias in the allocation of student program funds, including speakers' fees, and seek ways to promote underrepresented perspectives.
3. Conduct an inquiry into political bias in the hiring process of faculty and administrators and seek ways to promote fairness toward—and inclusion of—underrepresented perspectives.

Were even one high-profile institution like the University of Colorado to adopt a firm policy of intellectual inclusiveness, that practice would quickly spread, and benighted students everywhere would soon see daylight. 15

Responding to Reading

1. Why does Sommers call herself a "dissident scholar" (2)? What generally accepted beliefs does she question? During her talk at Haverford College, why do her remarks cause such uneasiness?

2. According to Sommers, conservatives have been marginalized on most American college campuses. What does she mean? How has this occurred? What evidence does Sommers present to support her claim? Is her evidence persuasive?

3. In Sommers's view, what is the effect of excluding conservatives from the intellectual life of a college or university? What does Sommers say is being done "to bring some balance to campus" (13)?

Responding in Writing

Sommers says that students almost never hear campus talks by "'politically incorrect' speakers" (11). What does the term *politically incorrect* mean? Do you agree with Sommers, or do you believe that at your college or university you are exposed to a cross section of ideas?

THE FIRST DAY

Edward P. Jones

1950–

Edward P. Jones attended the College of the Holy Cross in Worcester, Massachusetts, and studied writing at the University of Virginia. His book Lost in the City *(1992), is a collection of stories set in the hometown of his childhood, Washington, DC, a city of working-class black men and women who struggle heroically in their daily lives. The book was nominated for the National Book Award and lauded by critics both for addressing racial issues and for transcending them. His first novel,* The Known World, *published in 2003, was chosen as one of the year's nine best books (and four best novels) by the editors of the* New York Times Book Review. The Known World *also won the fiction prize of the National Book Critics Circle and the 2004 Pulitzer Prize for fiction. The short story that follows is from* Lost in the City.*

In an otherwise unremarkable September morning, long before I learned to be ashamed of my mother, she takes my hand and we set off down New Jersey Avenue to begin my very first day of school. I am wearing a checkeredlike blue-and-green cotton dress, and scattered about these colors are bits of yellow and white and brown. My mother has uncharacteristically spent nearly an hour on my hair that morning, plaiting and replaiting so that now my scalp tingles. Whenever I turn my head quickly, my nose fills with the faint smell of Dixie Peach hair grease. The smell is somehow a soothing one now and I will reach for it time and time again before the morning ends. All the plaits, each with a blue barrette near the tip and each twisted into an uncommon sturdiness, will last until I go to bed that night, something that has never happened before. My stomach is full of milk and oatmeal sweetened with brown sugar. Like everything else I have on, my pale green slip and underwear are new, the underwear having come three to a plastic package with a little girl on the front who appears to be dancing. Behind my ears, my mother, to stop my whining, has dabbed the stingiest bit of her gardenia perfume, the last present my father gave her before he disappeared into memory. Because I cannot smell it, I have only her word that the perfume is there. I am also wearing yellow socks trimmed with thin lines of black and white around the tops. My shoes are my greatest joy, black patent-leather miracles, and when one is nicked at the toe later that morning in class, my heart will break.

I am carrying a pencil, a pencil sharpener, and a small ten-cent tablet with a black-and-white speckled cover. My mother does not believe that a girl in kindergarten needs such things, so I am taking them only because of my insistent whining and because they are presents from our neighbors, Mary Keith and Blondelle Harris. Miss Mary and Miss Blondelle are watching my two younger sisters until my mother returns. The women are as precious to me as my mother and sisters. Out playing one day, I have overheard an older child, speaking to another child, call Miss Mary and Miss Blondelle a word that is brand new to me. This is my mother: When I say the word in fun to one of my sisters, my mother slaps me across the mouth and the word is lost for years and years.

All the way down New Jersey Avenue, the sidewalks are teeming with children. In my neighborhood, I have many friends, but I see none of them as my mother and I walk. We cross New York Avenue, we cross Pierce Street, and we cross L and K, and still I see no one who knows my name. At I Street, between New Jersey Avenue and Third Street, we enter Seaton Elementary School, a timeworn, sad-faced building across the street from my mother's church, Mt. Carmel Baptist.

Just inside the front door, women out of the advertisements in *Ebony* are greeting other parents and children. The woman who greets us has pearls thick as jumbo marbles that come down almost to her navel, and she acts as if she had known me all my life, touching my shoulder, cupping her hand under my chin. She is enveloped in a perfume that I only know is not gardenia. When, in answer to her question, my mother tells her that we live at 1227 New Jersey Avenue, the woman first seems to be picturing in her head where we live. Then she shakes her head and says that we are at the wrong school, that we should be at Walker-Jones.

My mother shakes her head vigorously. "I want her to go here," my mother says. "If I'da wanted her someplace else, I'da took her there." The woman continues to act as if she has known me all my life, but she tells my mother that we live beyond the area that Seaton 5 serves. My mother is not convinced and for several more minutes she questions the woman about why I cannot attend Seaton. For as many Sundays as I can remember, perhaps even Sundays when I was in her womb, my mother has pointed across I Street to Seaton as we come and go to Mt. Carmel. "You gonna go there and learn about the whole world." But one of the guardians of that place is saying no, and no again. I am learning this about my mother: The higher up on the scale of respectability a person is—and teachers are rather high up in her eyes—the less she is liable to let them push her around. But finally, I see in her eyes the closing gate, and she takes my hand and we leave the building. On the steps, she stops as people move past us on either side.

"Mama, I can't go to school?"

She says nothing at first, then takes my hand again and we are down the steps quickly and nearing New Jersey Avenue before I can blink. This is my mother: She says, "One monkey don't stop no show."

Walker-Jones is a larger, newer school and I immediately like it because of that. But it is not across the street from my mother's church, her rock, one of her connections to God, and I sense her doubts as she absently rubs her thumb over the back of her hand. We find our way to the crowded auditorium where gray metal chairs are set up in the middle of the room. Along the wall to the left are tables and other chairs. Every chair seems occupied by a child or adult. Somewhere in the room a child is crying, a cry that rises above the buzz-talk of so many people. Strewn about the floor are dozens and dozens of pieces of white paper, and people are walking over them without any thought of picking them up. And seeing this lack of concern, I am all of a sudden afraid.

"Is this where they register for school?" my mother asks a woman at one of the tables.

10   The woman looks up slowly as if she has heard this question once too often. She nods. She is tiny, almost as small as the girl standing beside her. The woman's hair is set in a mass of curlers and all of those curlers are made of paper money, here a dollar bill, there a five-dollar bill. The girl's hair is arrayed in curls, but some of them are beginning to droop and this makes me happy. On the table beside the woman's pocketbook is a large notebook, worthy of someone in high school, and looking at me looking at the notebook, the girl places her hand possessively on it. In her other hand she holds several pencils with thick crowns of additional erasers.

"These the forms you gotta use?" my mother asks the woman, picking up a few pieces of the paper from the table. "Is this what you have to fill out?"

The woman tells her yes, but that she need fill out only one.

"I see," my mother says, looking about the room. Then: "Would you help me with this form? That is, if you don't mind."

The woman asks my mother what she means.

"This form. Would you mind helpin me fill it out?"   15

The woman still seems not to understand.

"I can't read it. I don't know how to read or write, and I'm askin you to help me." My mother looks at me, then looks away. I know almost all of her looks, but this one is brand new to me. "Would you help me, then?"

The woman says Why sure, and suddenly she appears happier, so much more satisfied with everything. She finishes the form for her daughter and my mother and I step aside to wait for her. We find two chairs nearby and sit. My mother is now diseased, according to the girl's eyes, and until the moment her mother takes her and the form to the front of the auditorium, the girl never stops looking at my mother. I stare back at her. "Don't stare," my mother says to me. "You know better than that."

Another woman out of the *Ebony* ads takes the woman's child away. Now, the woman says upon returning, let's see what we can do for you two.

My mother answers the questions the woman reads off the form.   20 They start with my last name, and then on to the first and middle names. This is school, I think. This is going to school. My mother slowly enunciates each word of my name. This is my mother: As the questions go on, she takes from her pocketbook document after document, as if they will support my right to attend school, as if she has been saving them up for just this moment. Indeed, she takes out more papers than I have ever seen her do in other places: my birth certificate, my baptismal record, a doctor's letter concerning my bout with chicken pox, rent receipts, records of immunization, a letter about our public assistance payments, even her marriage license—every single paper that has anything even remotely to do with my five-year-old life. Few of the papers are needed here, but it does not matter and my mother continues to pull out the documents with the purposefulness of a magician pulling out a long string of scarves. She has learned that money is the beginning and end of everything in this world, and when the woman finishes, my mother offers her fifty cents, and the woman accepts it without hesitation. My mother and I are just about the last parent and child in the room.

My mother presents the form to a woman sitting in front of the stage, and the woman looks at it and writes something on a white card, which she gives to my mother. Before long, the woman who has taken the girl with the drooping curls appears from behind us, speaks to the sitting woman, and introduces herself to my mother and me. She's to be my teacher, she tells my mother. My mother stares.

We go into the hall, where my mother kneels down to me. Her lips are quivering. "I'll be back to pick you up at twelve o'clock. I don't want you to go nowhere. You just wait right here. And listen to every word she say." I touch her lips and press them together. It is an old, old game between us. She puts my hand down at my side, which is not part of the game. She stands and looks a second at the teacher, then she turns and walks away. I see where she has darned one of her socks the night before. Her shoes make loud sounds in the hall. She passes through the doors and I can still hear the loud sounds of her shoes. And even when the teacher turns me toward the classrooms and I hear what must be the singing and talking of all the children in the world, I can still hear my mother's footsteps above it all.

Responding to Reading

1. Why does the narrator's mother want to enroll her in Seaton Elementary School? Why is she unable to? What does the mother's reaction to this situation tell you about her?
2. What are the mother's limitations? What are her strengths? What do you think the mother wants the school to do for her daughter?
3. Do you think that this story is primarily about the mother or her daughter? How do you explain the mother's reaction as she leaves her daughter? Why does the daughter still remember this reaction years later as she is telling this story? Why do you think the story ends with the mother's footsteps?

Responding in Writing

Write a paragraph describing your earliest memory of school.

---------------------------------- Focus ----------------------------------

Do We Still Need Affirmative Action?

Civil rights activist James Meredith, escorted by federal marshals, entering all-white University of Mississippi, 1962.

Responding to the Image

1. The photograph above, taken in 1962, depicts James Meredith, the first African American admitted to University of Mississippi, being escorted to class by federal marshals to protect him from threats of being lynched. Why do you think Meredith, an undergraduate student, is dressed so formally?
2. What does the number of people accompanying Meredith tell you about his situation? What do their reactions suggest?

REMEMBERING THE NEGATIVE SIDE
OF AFFIRMATIVE ACTION

Linda Chavez

1947–

Born in Albuquerque, New Mexico, Linda Chavez received a BA from the University of Colorado and did graduate work at the University of California at Los Angeles (1970–1972). An author, activist, and commentator, Chavez is the president of the Center for Equal Opportunity, a nonprofit public policy research organization in Washington, DC. She writes a weekly syndicated column and works as a political analyst for FOX News Channel. Her most recent book is An Unlikely Conservative: The Transformation of an Ex-Liberal, or, How I Became the Most Hated Hispanic in America *(2002). In the following essay, which appeared in the* Chronicle of Higher Education, *Chavez writes of her personal experiences with affirmative action. To learn more about Chavez, visit her Web site, http://www .lindachavez.org/.*

I grew up in a working-class home, the daughter of a Mexican-American house painter, believing that disadvantaged students deserved a chance at a college education even if their grades and test scores didn't measure up to the usual admissions standards. When I entered the University of Colorado in 1965, there were no affirmative-action programs to assist me, but by the time I was a graduate student at the University of California in Los Angeles in 1970, such programs had proliferated. Initially, I thought that affirmative action would extend a helping hand to those who might not otherwise learn about available opportunities and might lack the skills to be able to compete for them.

I would soon learn, however, that affirmative action could be a double-edged sword, even for its intended beneficiaries. My experiences as a grad student at UCLA would profoundly influence not just my personal life but the role I would play in public policy in years to come.

About a week before my classes at the university were to begin, I received a telegram from the university asking me to contact the "High Potential Program" immediately. In addition to the regular affirmative-action program on the campus, UCLA had set up a special program for young black and brown men coming out of prison, admitting dozens of felons as students. I was assigned to teach two classes: a composition class made up of Chicano men in the ex-offender program, and another class that was essentially a reading discussion group made up of regular HPP students.

There were eight men in the composition class, most of whom were a good deal older than I. Their spelling and grammar were atrocious, and they had great fun at my expense. They took every chance to embarrass me, and I soon found out that open-ended writing assignments usually turned into fantasies of what they would like to do to me if they could get me alone sometime. Not quite knowing how to handle the situation, I decided to correct the spelling and syntax and return the papers with a note suggesting the writers ought to learn how to spell the sex acts they described. I also decided to forgo the short skirts and hip-hugger slacks then in fashion in favor of more conservative dress, but I often felt vulnerable when the classroom door closed and I faced the group of sometimes leering young men.

The students in my reading class were less provocative but no less ₅ challenging to teach. I had students of all races in the class, including one or two Anglo kids from poor, rural backgrounds; a middle-aged American Indian couple; and several Mexican-American and black students. The Indian couple was heartbreaking. They were the most serious and devoted of any of the students, but they read at a grade-school level. I have often wondered what happened to them, if they made it through four years at one of the best colleges in the country, and if so, whether that said more about the university's indifference to standards than it did about their power to overcome disadvantages.

The text we used in the class, Mixed Bag: Artifacts from the Contemporary Culture, was typical of the era: hip, multicultural, and interdisciplinary. But I soon found that not only were the selections in the text (everything from Sophocles to Lenny Bruce) way over the heads of most of the kids, but the topics themselves (race, violence, religion, family, and death) provoked anger and hostility among the students. Classroom discussions quickly degenerated into name-calling between groups of students. With no sense of irony and lots of racial grievances, real and perceived, most of the students found it impossible to empathize with characters and situations beyond their own racial experience.

For example, when one student called me a "honky," the Chicano kids in the class seemed to think the remark was particularly funny. Many came from the barrios of East L.A. and viewed me as an outsider. I talked funny—"like a gabacho," as one student pointed out, which meant I spoke standard English without an accent. I also used my married name, Gersten, and I didn't speak Spanish—unlike many of my students who were first- and second-generation Americans.

But perhaps their reaction had less to do with me personally than it did with the shift taking place in the organized Chicano movement, especially in California, which had become increasingly radicalized as Mexican-American groups joined the antiwar movement and mixed with violent black groups like the Black Panthers for national attention.

On August 29, 1970, Mexican-Americans rioted in East Los Angeles. The riot erupted during the Chicano Moratorium, a march of more than 20,000 through the streets to protest U.S. involvement in Vietnam. It began when police responded to complaints from neighborhood merchants that protesters were stealing from them. The police wielded clubs and set off tear gas into the crowds gathered to hear moratorium speakers. They also shot tear gas into a building where an armed robber had supposedly hidden, and the tear-gas projectile hit a local TV reporter, Ruben Salazar, in the head, killing him instantly. Salazar soon became a martyr to many in the Chicano movement who believed he'd been murdered by the LAPD.

10   The university's administrators, worried by the unrest in the Mexican-American community, were anxious to demonstrate their sensitivity and good will. In response to student demands, they created courses in Chicano studies in the political-science, history, and sociology departments. They also established a Chicano library, run by a graduate student from Chile. Finally, the English department decided it would offer a sophomore-level "Chicano Literature" course—but had little idea about what would be taught or who would teach it.

In 1970 there weren't enough novels, short stories, poems, or essays published by Mexican-American authors to fill a syllabus for a 12-week course. Nor was there anyone on the faculty to teach the course—especially since MEChA, the Chicano student association, insisted that all of the new Chicano-studies courses had to be taught by Mexican-Americans. The English department approached me, since I was the only Mexican-American in their Ph.D. program. Despite my total unfamiliarity with the field, I would be paid as a regular faculty member at the lecturer level—nearly twice as much as I earned in the High Potential Program for teaching just half as many hours. Plus it would give me another teaching credential, which would make it easier to secure a faculty job once I completed my doctorate.

I accepted the offer but soon discovered that I had struck no bargain. Nothing I had encountered in my teaching assignments to that point had prepared me for the problems I would face in the classroom that spring.

I had no real idea what I was doing, and there were few academic resources to draw on. Although a huge body of excellent Latin American literature existed in English translation, the Chicano students wanted a course devoted exclusively to works written by Mexican-American authors. I chose two contemporary novels, City of Night, by John Rechy, and Chicano, by Richard F. Vasquez. Rechy, whose mother was Mexican, was a talented writer, but only the first chapter of his memoir touched on his ethnic background. Though more traditional in its subject matter, Chicano was a second-rate novel in which the heroes were hard-working Mexicans and the villains, hard-hearted Anglos. The plot and characters were better suited to an afternoon soap opera than a college literature class, but it was one of the few novels published by a Mexican-American author at the time. I also assigned Corky Gonzales's poem "I Am

Joaquin," an epic about a Mexican "Everyman." In addition, I chose several short stories from a new publication called El Grito. I supplemented the readings with analysis—such as there was—of Chicano culture, including books written by non-Mexican-American authors.

Despite my efforts to give students an authentic Chicano literary experience, the class got off to a bad start and quickly went downhill. When I tried to organize classroom discussions, it became clear that most of the students hadn't bothered to look at the assignments at all. One group of students sat sullenly as I lectured or audibly talked to each other as if I wasn't there. Finally, the ringleader of the dissident group, Richard, spoke up.

"I don't need to read Chicano literature. I live Chicano literature," he said. "And you—you don't even know how to say 'Chicano,' Mrs. Gersteeeen," he said, drawing out the last syllable in case anyone in the class had failed to notice it was a Jewish name.

With that the class erupted in hoots and hollers, slapping their desks and stomping their feet.

I could feel my face turn crimson. "You may not like the way I pronounce 'Chicano,'" I said, in the nasal tones that characterized my students' barrio pronunciation, "but at least I know something about Chicano literature because I've actually read it."

"She got you, man," another of the boys chimed, drawing appreciative assents from the others.

For the moment, I'd taken back control of the classroom. But not for long. The students sensed they could intimidate me, and I felt shaky and frightened, despite my bravado. A week later, I encountered more trouble when I wrote a list of reference books on the chalkboard. Among the books was a short work on the Pachuco dialect, a hybrid Spanish and English slang spoken originally by "zoot-suiters" in the 1930s, which had become very popular once again among young Chicanos throughout the Southwest. The book traced the origin of the dialect to first-generation Mexican immigrants of the Depression era. Naively, I thought students might actually enjoy learning the etymology of words like cholo, pocho, ese, even Chicano, which they regularly sprinkled through their conversation. I was wrong.

The dust from the chalk had barely settled on the board when Richard jumped up.

"I ain't reading no gabacho books. They got nothin' to teach me." And with that he turned his back to me, still standing. One by one, other students stood up, and in almost drill-like precision, turned on their heels to present a phalanx of backs to me. Only a half-dozen students remained in their seats, but I decided to try to teach the class anyway.

"The point of a college education," I lectured, "is to acquaint ourselves with ideas and people unfamiliar to us. Just because someone has a different background from you doesn't mean he doesn't have something important to teach you." I kept my voice low and steady. "The book is the only thing written on the Pachuco dialect. Maybe someday one of you will write a better book, but not by refusing to read everything that has already been written on the subject, no matter who wrote it."

Any hopes I had of using reason to deflect the students' anger vanished as the standing students began stamping their feet in unison, creating a clamor that resounded throughout the building. Within minutes, puzzled professors were peering through the small window of my classroom door.

"What are you teaching in here, a flamenco class?" one befuddled man asked me when I went out to tell them what was going on. As I was explaining that I had a class protest on my hands, the stomping students began marching out in military formation, leaving us standing in the hall shaking our heads.

25 I reported the incident to the English department but got no sympathy or help. The message came down loud and clear: "You're on your own. Handle it." At 23 years of age, younger than many of my students and clearly less wise in the ways of protest politics or the streets, I was ill prepared to manage the situation. A few of the protesters trickled back into class over the next few weeks, but most never returned. I began to dread teaching the class, whose subject matter held no particular interest for me in the first place. The books, stories, and poems I was using were clearly inferior to anything I had ever studied in a college classroom, and I thought it was a waste of everyone's time to create a Chicano literature course when the literary output didn't even exist.

I managed to finish the class, but with no enthusiasm. Only one student in the class made any real effort to do the assigned work. And by the last week, barely a half-dozen kids bothered to show up. I knew that I was going to have to flunk about half the class, especially since most of the protesters hadn't bothered to formally drop the course. I posted notices offering students the opportunity to drop the class, even though the usual period to do so had elapsed. I gave the High Potential Program office a list of students who had never shown up for a test or handed in any papers, warning them that unless the students dropped the course, they would receive F's, but only a few students took me up on the offer. I ended up flunking a dozen students. I was surprised that I received no complaints when grades were posted, but I surmised that many of the students may have dropped out altogether or had gone home for the summer without knowing their grades.

When fall came, the HPP students began drifting back to campus, and with them came more trouble for me.

The English department had hired a talented young professor from Texas, Ray Paredes, to teach Chicano literature, so I was back to teaching composition, a subject I was far more comfortable with. But one morning, I went out to my car with my 2-year-old son in tow. As we approached the vehicle, I noticed a swarm of flies hovering around the open window on the driver's side. Picking my son up in my arms to put him in his car seat, I opened the car door.

"Mommy, somebody pooped in our car," he yelled out in excitement. I pulled back in horror. Indeed, someone had ripped open the seat on the driver's side and dumped a hideous liquid mixture of excrement and water in the gash in the upholstery. Then, within days of the attack on my car, I started getting threatening phone calls warning me that if I didn't watch out, I'd find a bomb in my car.

And the harassment didn't stop with my car. I came home one 30 evening to find that my electricity had been shut off. When I called to find out what the problem was, the utility company told me that service had been terminated at my request. Someone posing as me had told the electric company that I was moving and requested that service be stopped. Then pizzas started coming—by the dozens, company after company showing up at my door day after day until the delivery boys finally wised up to the pranks.

And when I went to sleep at night, I was often awakened by the sound of sticks being dragged across my apartment windows. I borrowed a six-foot-long African spear from a friend who had served in the Peace Corps. At the first sound of sticks against glass, I raced out of the apartment in my nightgown, spear in hand, screaming every foul epithet I could think of as the car sped down the alley. It's a wonder my neighbors didn't have me arrested or sent off to a mental institution.

I had no idea who was harassing me. It was hard to imagine what I had done to engender such hatred, but I was fairly certain it was one of the students I had flunked the previous spring. I couldn't imagine that any of them would have reacted the same way toward an Anglo teacher. Their anger toward me was more visceral. I suppose in their eyes I was a traitor. I had married an Anglo, adopted Anglo values, and was accepted in the Anglo world, which they claimed to reject, but which many of them, no doubt, feared would never accept them.

No one in the English department or the High Potential Program was interested in helping track down the perpetrators, so I turned to MEChA, the Chicano student group on campus. Luis Ortiz, a fellow HPP instructor and native of Mexico, suggested that I approach the MEChA leadership and ask for their help. Unlike the American-born Chicanos, the Mexican students harbored fewer racial grievances. They were, on average, better prepared academically than their American counterparts and less self-conscious about their ethnicity. Luis got an agreement from the head of MEChA to handle the issue at the next meeting. I later learned that the message was delivered unambiguously: "If we find out who's doing this, we're going to beat the crap out of them." The incidents stopped immediately. I was deeply grateful for the intervention.

As the end of the quarter approached, I decided that I did not want to stay in Los Angeles. Having worked on affirmative-action programs for two and a half years, I knew that I could not continue teaching in an environment that rewarded ignorance, made students the arbiters of what would be taught and who would teach it, and was better suited to political indoctrination than genuine learning. More and more, I felt alienated from my students, my fellow teachers in the affirmative-action programs, and the university itself.

35   I had started out hoping to inspire underachievers like myself to reach beyond the world they grew up in. For me, college had changed everything—it had opened up new vistas for me. For the first time, I realized that I didn't have to settle for what opportunities came my way; I could go out and create them for myself. I also discovered that the harder I worked, the more I could achieve. I wanted my students to see those same possibilities.

Instead I found myself confronted with kids who sincerely believed that the world was out to defeat them. They blamed racism for all their problems and would never consider that their own behavior might be partly to blame for their failures.

Affirmative action began with the premise that black students and, later, Mexican-American, Puerto Rican, and other disadvantaged minorities deserved a helping hand. Years of officially sanctioned discrimination had created an uneven playing field in which not everyone had the same opportunity to succeed. But most affirmative-action programs, like those in place in major colleges and universities by the early 1970s, tried to level that playing field by ignoring the huge skills gap that existed between disadvantaged minority students, on the one hand, and middle-class whites, on the other.

Such programs were doomed from the start. If anything, they enhanced racial and ethnic tensions and animosity and reinforced stereotypes. I had witnessed firsthand the devastating impact those programs had on academic standards, on race relations, and on the intended beneficiaries as well. The kids came into school with huge handicaps, but instead of recognizing their academic deficiencies and trying to do whatever it took to improve them, many of the affirmative-action students I taught preferred to wallow in self-pity. Their attitude—as much as their social, economic, and educational disadvantages—would make life difficult and success elusive.

Responding to Reading

1. What were Chavez's ideas about disadvantaged students as she was growing up? What did she believe about affirmative action programs? How did her experiences as a graduate teaching assistant at UCLA change her ideas? Would Richard Harwood (p. 170) agree with her assessment of her students' chances of graduating?

2. Why was Chavez asked to teach a Chicano studies class? What difficulties did she have with her class?
3. What lessons about life did college teach Chavez? How were these lessons different from the ones her underachieving students had learned? Why, in her opinion, did affirmative action programs in the 1970s not help students overcome their difficulties? According to Chavez, what effect did these programs have?

Responding in Writing

What kind of affirmative action program could have helped the students Chavez taught? How receptive do you think her students would have been to such a program?

THE MYTH AND MATH
OF AFFIRMATIVE ACTION

Goodwin Liu

1970–

Goodwin Liu received his undergraduate degree from Stanford University, was a Rhodes Scholar at Oxford University in England, and then earned his law degree from Yale University Law School. He served as a law clerk to US Supreme Court Justice Ruth Bader Ginsberg, worked as an attorney, and has written several law review articles on education-related topics. The following essay, which appeared in the Washington Post, *was quoted in the federal appeals court decision upholding the University of Michigan Law School affirmative action policy. Liu teaches at the University of California at Berkeley.*

With the arrival of spring, thousands of high school and college seniors have been anxiously checking the mail for word from the nation's most prestigious universities. Although some envelopes are thick with good news, most are thin and disappointing. For many white applicants, the disappointment will become bitterness if they suspect the reason for their rejection was affirmative action. But such suspicions, in all likelihood, are misplaced.

Affirmative action is widely thought to be unfair because it benefits minority applicants at the expense of more deserving whites. Yet this perception tends to inflate the cost beyond its real proportions. While it is true that affirmative action gives minority applicants a significant boost in selective admissions, it is not true that most white applicants would fare better if elite schools eliminated the practice. Understanding why is crucial to separating fact from fiction in the national debate over affirmative action.

Any day now,[1] a federal appeals court in Cincinnati will issue a decision in a major test lawsuit challenging the use of race as a factor in selective admissions.[2] In that case, the University of Michigan denied admission in 1995 to a white undergraduate applicant named Jennifer Gratz. Charging reverse discrimination, Gratz said, "I knew of people accepted to Ann Arbor who were less qualified, and my first reaction when I was rejected was, 'Let's sue.'"

The Michigan case will likely end up at the Supreme Court. If it does, Gratz will try to follow in the footsteps of Allan Bakke, a rejected white applicant who won admission in 1978 to the University of California at Davis's medical school after convincing the high court that the school's policy of reserving 16 of 100 seats each year for minority students was unconstitutional. For many Americans, the success of Bakke's lawsuit has long highlighted what is unfair about affirmative action: Giving minority applicants a significant advantage causes deserving white applicants to lose out. But to draw such an inference in Bakke's case—or in the case of the vast majority of rejected white applicants—is to indulge in what I call "the causation fallacy."

5   There's no doubt, based on test scores and grades, that Bakke was a highly qualified applicant. Justice Lewis Powell, who authored the decisive opinion in the case, observed that Bakke's Medical College Admission Test (MCAT) scores placed him in the top tier of test-takers, whereas the average scores of the quota beneficiaries in 1974 placed them in the bottom third. Likewise, his science grade point average was 3.44 on a 4.0 scale, compared with a 2.42 average for the special admittees, and his overall GPA was similarly superior. Given these numbers, the only reason for Bakke's rejection was the school's need to make room for less qualified minority applicants, right?

Wrong. Although Justice Powell pointed out that minority applicants were admitted with grades and test scores much lower than Bakke's, he did not discuss what I found to be the most striking data that appeared in his opinion: Bakke's grades and scores were significantly higher than the average for the regular admittees. In other words, his academic qualifica-

---

[1]On June 23, 2003, in the case of *Gratz et al v. Bollinger et al*, the US Supreme Court ruled 6-3 against the University of Michigan's points system that benefited minorities in the undergraduate admissions process. However, on the same day, in *Grutter v. Bollinger et al*, the court ruled 5-4 in favor of the University of Michigan's Law School use of race in considering admissions. The nation's highest court appeared to be saying that limited use of race as a factor in the admissions process may be constitutional. The complete texts of both rulings are available on the court's Web site, <http://www.supremecourtus.gov/opinions/>. [Eds.]

[2]According to the US Commission on Civil Rights, a student's high school grade point average is the most widely used factor in admissions decisions, followed closely by standardized test scores, such as the SAT and ACT. Controversy often arises when admissions practices include race as a factor. Such selective practices may be at odds with the 14th Amendment, which guarantees "equal protection under the law" for all US citizens, and the Civil Rights Act of 1964, which prohibits programs that receive federal funding from discriminating based on race. To read more about race and admissions practices, see the staff report "Beyond Percentage Plans: The Challenge of Equal Opportunity in Higher Education" on the commission's Web site, <http://www.usccr.gov/pubs/percent2/main.htm>. [Eds.]

tions were better than those of the majority of applicants admitted outside the racial quota. So why didn't he earn one of the 84 regular places?

It is clear that the medical school admitted students not only on the basis of grades and test scores, but on other factors relevant to the study and practice of medicine, such as compassion, communication skills and commitment to research. Justice Powell's opinion does not tell us exactly what qualities the regular admittees had that Bakke lacked. But it notes that the head of the admissions committee, who interviewed Bakke, found him "rather limited in his approach" to medical problems and thought he had "very definite opinions which were based more on his personal viewpoints than upon a study of the total problem."

Whatever Bakke's weaknesses were, there were several reasons, apart from affirmative action, that might have led the medical school to reject his application. Grades and test scores do not tell us the whole story.

Of course, affirmative action did lower Bakke's chance of admission. But by how much? One way to answer this question is to compare Bakke's chance of admission had he competed for all 100 seats in the class with his chance of admission competing for the 84 seats outside of the racial quota. To simplify, let's assume none of the special applicants would have been admitted ahead of any regular candidate.

In 1974, Bakke was one of 3,109 regular applicants to the medical   10
school. With the racial quota, the average likelihood of admission for regular applicants was 2.7 percent (84 divided by 3,109). With no racial quota, the average likelihood of admission would have been 3.2 percent (100 divided by 3,109). So the quota increased the average likelihood of rejection from 96.8 percent to 97.3 percent.

To be sure, Bakke was not an average applicant. Only one-sixth of regular applicants (roughly 520) received an interview. But even among these highly qualified applicants, eliminating the racial quota would have increased the average rate of admission from 16 percent (84 divided by 520) to only 19 percent (100 divided by 520). Certainly a few more regular applicants would have been admitted were it not for affirmative action. But Bakke, upon receiving his rejection letter, had no reason to believe he would have been among the lucky few.

In fact, Bakke applied in both 1973 and 1974 and, according to evidence in the lawsuit, he did not even make the waiting list in either year.

The statistical pattern in Bakke's case is not an anomaly. It occurs in any selection process in which the applicants who do not benefit from affirmative action greatly outnumber those who do.

Recent research confirms this point. Using 1989 data from a representative sample of selective schools, former university presidents William Bowen and Derek Bok showed in their 1998 book, "The Shape of the River," that eliminating racial preferences would have increased the likelihood of admission for white undergraduate applicants from 25 percent to only 26.5 percent.

15   The Mellon Foundation, which sponsored the study, provided me with additional data to calculate admission rates by SAT score. If the schools in the Bowen/Bok sample had admitted applicants with similar SAT scores at the same rate regardless of race, the chance of admission for white applicants would have increased by one percentage point or less at scores 1300 and above, by three to four percentage points at scores from 1150 to 1299, and by four to seven percentage points at scores below 1150.

It is true that black applicants were admitted at much higher rates than white applicants with similar grades and test scores. But that fact does not prove that affirmative action imposes a substantial disadvantage on white applicants. The extent of the disadvantage depends on the number of blacks and whites in the applicant pool. Because the number of black applicants to selective institutions is relatively small, admitting them at higher rates does not significantly lower the chance of admission for the average individual in the relatively large sea of white applicants.

In the Bowen/Bok study, for example, 60 percent of black applicants scoring 1200–1249 on the SAT were admitted, compared with 19 percent of whites. In the 1250–1299 range, 74 percent of blacks were admitted, compared with 23 percent of whites. These data indicate—more so than proponents of affirmative action typically acknowledge—that racial preferences give minority applicants a substantial advantage. But eliminating affirmative action would have increased the admission rate for whites from 19 percent to only 21 percent in the 1200–1249 range, and from 23 percent to only 24 percent in the 1250–1299 range.

These figures show that rejected white applicants have every reason not to blame their misfortune on affirmative action. In selective admissions, the competition is so intense that even without affirmative action, the overwhelming majority of rejected white applicants still wouldn't get in.

Still, isn't it true that minority applicants are admitted at rates up to three times higher than white applicants with similar SAT scores? Isn't that unfair?

20   To answer that question, it's important to observe that racial preferences are not the only preferences that cause different groups of applicants with similar test scores to be admitted at different rates. Geographic, athletic and alumni preferences also weigh heavily, to the detriment of applicants such as Jennifer Gratz at Michigan. Gratz hailed from a Detroit suburb, not from a rural area or the inner city. She was not a star athlete. And her working-class parents were high school graduates, not University of Michigan alumni.

Yet preferences for athletes, though occasionally criticized, have never galvanized the kind of outrage often directed at affirmative action. Similarly, there is no organized legal campaign against geographic preferences, even though where one grows up is as much an accident of circumstance as one's skin color. And neither Gratz nor her lawyers at the

Washington-based Center for Individual Rights have publicly denounced alumni preferences, much less launched a moral crusade against them.

Such preferences reflect institutional interests that are unrelated to an applicant's grades or test scores. But the same is true of affirmative action when it is used to enhance educational diversity. The question, then, is not whether unequal treatment is unfair as a general rule, but whether unequal treatment based on race should be singled out for special condemnation.

As the Supreme Court said in 1954, unequal treatment based on race can inflict on members of a disfavored race "a feeling of inferiority as to their status in the community that may affect their hearts and minds in a way unlikely ever to be undone." But social stigma is not the complaint pressed by white applicants such as Bakke or Gratz. Despite 30 years of affirmative action, white students continue to dominate most of the nation's best colleges and all of the top law and medical schools. Against this backdrop, not even the most ardent foe of affirmative action would say that it stamps white applicants with a badge of racial inferiority. Indeed, just as athletic and geographic preferences do not denigrate applicants who are uncoordinated or suburban, affirmative action is not a policy of racial prejudice.

For white applicants, the unfairness of affirmative action lies not in its potential to displace or stigmatize, but in its potential to stereotype. Minority applicants are not the only ones who contribute to educational diversity. Were a school to use race as its sole "plus" factor in admissions, then white applicants could legitimately complain that the school failed to take into account non-racial attributes essential to genuine educational diversity.

Putting the complaint in these terms is an important first step toward rethinking the conventional view that a race-conscious admissions policy pits whites against minorities in a zero-sum game. Instead of attacking affirmative action, white applicants such as Jennifer Gratz might do better to urge top schools committed to educational diversity to place a higher premium on first-generation college attendance or growing up in a blue-collar home. Ironically, the stories of affirmative action's "victims" could spur America's colleges to further widen the elite circles of educational opportunity. And that would be a result students of any color could applaud.

Responding to Reading

1. According to Liu, what do most people believe about affirmative action? Why are they wrong? Why does Liu use the Bakke case to support his argument?

2. According to Liu, how much does affirmative action hurt white applicants? What facts does Liu supply to support his position?

3. What other admission preferences exist? Why, according to Liu, don't people seem to be bothered by them while racial preferences are singled out

for condemnation? What suggestion does Liu have for rethinking an admissions policy that, he says, "pits whites against minorities" (25)?

Responding in Writing

Before reading this essay, what was your position on affirmative action? Has Liu's essay changed your opinion? Explain.

DEBATING WITHOUT FACTS

Richard Harwood

1925–2001

Richard Harwood was a nationally renowned journalist whose career spanned five decades. He was born in Wisconsin, where his father was a missionary to the Menominee Indian Tribe, but grew up in Nebraska, Oklahoma, and Tennessee. In 1942, after graduating from high school in Nashville, he joined the US Marine Corps and served three years in the Pacific during World War II. Harwood returned to Nashville in 1947 and began working for the Nashville Tennessean *while attending Vanderbilt University. He received a bachelor's degree in 1950 and made newspaper journalism his career. He joined the* Washington Post *in 1966 and, during the next 22 years, worked as a reporter, national correspondent, national editor, assistant managing editor, deputy managing editor, and ombudsman. After retiring from the newspaper, he continued working as an editorial columnist. Harwood was known as an exacting journalist and an unflinching critic of the news business.*

The White House–sponsored dialogue on race has been a flop up to now in large part because too many people, black and white, don't know what they're talking about.

That includes the media, especially in our treatment of affirmative action. We have created the impression that without "preferences" blacks would be shut out of the higher education system. And we have created the corollary impression that "minority preferences" are rampant, imperiling the educational future of far too many whites.

But in all of the uproar and despite countless words written and broadcast on the issue, the information offered the public on affirmative action is limited. How many people are affected? Who benefits? Who is hurt?

The truth is that with or without affirmative action almost any high school graduate who can read, write and do the multiplication tables— and a lot who can do none of those things well—can go to college today. It's a buyer's market. Schools bid against one another for students, using financial incentives and other inducements. Many institutions admit almost everyone who applies. Others, including such well-regarded schools as Michigan, Tulane, Wisconsin, Auburn, Ohio State, Purdue and American University in Washington, admit 70 percent to 90 percent of applicants.

Of course, it's a lot easier to get into college than to stay there. Only 45 percent of the students who graduated from high school in 1982 and earned at least 10 college credits had received a bachelor's degree by the time they were 30 years old. Dropout rates at many institutions are 70 percent to 90 percent. At Fisk University in Nashville, for years one of the most prestigious of the historically black colleges, the graduation rate is 2 percent, according to U.S. News and World Report. These dropout rates tell us that tens of thousands of students not cut out for college work are being drawn into the higher education system.

Such statistics are rarely or inadequately reported. The press instead focuses on affirmative action "problems" at "highly selective" schools such as Harvard and Yale. And even in our obsessive scrutiny of matters involving those celebrated citadels of learning, the reporting is often murky and misleading. In part that is because of the failure of the U.S. Department of Education and other government agencies to publish the kind of information that would clarify the issues. Some colleges and universities involved in "affirmative action" controversies also complicate the problem by withholding information, for example, on the nature of "preferential" admissions.

The Journal of Blacks in Higher Education, however, has been able to assemble much of the relevant information. So have some academicians. We learn from the journal that 292,855 students applied to the 24 most prestigious universities in America for admission to the freshman class of 1996. About 5 percent of these applicants—13,801—were black. The schools offered admission to 96,369 students (33 percent of all the students who applied). They offered admission to 35 percent of the black applicants—5,563 students—but only 2,305 accepted (41 percent). They represented a small percentage of the new freshmen that year—from fewer than one percent at CalTech to 12 percent at the University of Virginia.

How many of these black students were academically "unqualified" for the schools that admitted them? The journal obtained SAT scores from a number of these leading schools. The midpoint score for white students in all the schools was higher than the midpoint scores of black students. The gap ranged from 288 points at the Berkeley campus of the University of California to 150 points at Princeton, Johns Hopkins and other schools. Those numbers quantify the "racial preference" involved in some of these admissions. But in every case, the black students in these elite schools had higher average SAT scores—in some cases as much as 200 points higher—than the national average (946) for whites. The explanation is simple. SAT scores at these "elite" schools are astronomical in terms of what the average high school graduate achieves on the test. At Harvard, for example, the midpoint SAT score for blacks in the freshman class in 1992 (I have not found more recent numbers) was 1,305, a score that would get these students into any university in the world, a score so close to the white midpoint score that it was described by an affirmative action critic as not "statistically meaningful."

This doesn't resolve the larger issues raised by affirmative action and racial preference in college admissions: Some high-scoring whites and probably Asians too are being passed over for black applicants with lower test scores. But the numbers are small, and the evidence refutes the common argument that blacks admitted to these highly selective schools are necessarily "unqualified" to be there. But this gets lost in the debate.

10 Affirmative action has other problems. It began as a way to get women, blacks and other specified minorities into jobs and schools formerly unavailable to them. Women may no longer qualify, and if they do get preferences in college admissions, they shouldn't, now being in the majority (more than 55 percent nationally) on campuses all over the country. Asian Americans also may no longer qualify—and shouldn't—in many jurisdictions because they have the highest level of educational attainment in the country and the highest incomes as well.

Hispanics are often shortchanged under affirmative action. They outnumber blacks in California by more than 3 to 1 but, according to Stephan Thernstrom of Harvard, they have been receiving no more places than blacks in the state's college set-asides for "underrepresented" minorities.

Another question is whether the beneficiaries of affirmative action are not disproportionately drawn from the middle and upper class. Few black kids from the inner cities are lining up outside Ivy League institutions. We would know more about that subject if the government and the universities released more information about who gets what.

That's a job for the president's advisory board for the initiative on race. Until the issues are better understood, we can stage dialogues and talk till we're blue in the face without achieving anything.

Responding to Reading

1. Why does Harwood think that the White House-sponsored discussion of race was unsuccessful? According to him, what is the "truth" about affirmative action?
2. What do high dropout rates at many of the nation's colleges and universities indicate? Why does Harwood think the press does not report these statistics?
3. What questions does Harwood raise about affirmative action as it applies to Asians, women, and Hispanics? According to Harwood, why is any conversation about race doomed until we know the answers to these questions? How do Harwood's facts support or challenge the facts Liu mentions in his essay?

Responding in Writing

Do you think Harwood supports affirmative action and racial preferences in college admissions?

--------------- WIDENING THE FOCUS ---------------

The following readings can suggest additional perspectives for thinking and writing about affirmative action. You may also want to do further research about this subject on the Internet.

- Richard Rodriguez, "Aria" (p. 179)

- Christina Hoff Sommers, "The War against Boys" (p. 453)

- Richard Wright, "The Library Card" (p. 476)

For Internet Research: Throughout US history, people have been the victims of prejudice based on religious, ethnic, gender, or other differences. *The Affirmative Action and Diversity Project: A Web Page for Research,* http://aad.english.ucsb.edu/pages/discrim.html, presents various opinions regarding affirmative action topics, such as institutional discrimination, reverse discrimination, and "glass ceilings." Read through some of the selections on this Web site, and choose one essay to evaluate. Your evaluation of the essay should answer the following questions: How does the essay define discrimination? What is the main point of the essay? How does the author's tone strengthen (or weaken) his case? Does the essay cover the topic thoroughly? How could the essay be strengthened?

If you would like to read a brief overview of the 30-year history of Affirmative Action, consult *The Stanford Encyclopedia of Philosophy,* http://plato.stanford.edu/entries/affirmative-action/.

─────────── **WRITING** ───────────

Issues in Education

1. Both Lynda Barry (p. 103) and Maya Angelou (p. 122) describe personal experiences related to their education. Write an essay in which you describe a positive or negative experience you have had with your education. Be specific, and make sure you include plenty of vivid descriptive details.

2. Many of the essays in this chapter discuss the role of education in society. In the process, they try to define exactly what constitutes a "good" education. Write an essay in which you define a good education. Explain your view with specific references to essays in this chapter by Holt (p. 106), Pink (p. 112), and Brown (p. 141) as well as with examples from your own experience.

3. According to Diane Ravich (p. 144), those who publish literature textbooks are more interested in being inclusive and relevant than in exposing students to great literature. Christina Hoff Sommers (p. 149) asserts that instructors with conservative political views are being systematically excluded from many American colleges and universities. Select one of these essays, and write a letter to the author in which you agree or disagree with her contentions. Make sure that you address the writer's specific points and that you use examples from both the essay and your own experience to support your position.

4. In his essay "The War against Testing" (p. 134), David W. Murray attempts to refute the arguments made by critics of standardized testing. His major argument is that standardized tests, such as the SATs, are the best method we have of determining how much students have actually learned. Write an essay in which you discuss how John Holt would respond to Murray's ideas. Use specific examples from both essays to support your points.

5. In "School's Out" (p. 112), Daniel H. Pink quotes John Taylor Gatto, New York State's Teacher of the Year. According to Gatto, "School is like starting life with a 12-year jail sentence in which bad habits are the only curriculum truly learned" (14). Write an editorial for your school newspaper in which you agree or disagree with Gatto's observation—at least as it applies to the schools you have attended. Use your own experience as well as references to the essays in this chapter by Daniel H. Pink (p. 112) and John Holt (p. 106).

6. Leslie Brown (p. 141) justifies her pursuit of a career in Renaissance art history despite its "'lack of relevance'" (1). Assume that you have decided to choose a similar course of action. Select a major

that would prepare you for this career, and then write a letter to your parents in which you try to convince them that your plans deserve their support.

7. Define your educational philosophy. Then, choose one grade level, and design a curriculum that reflects your philosophy. Finally, write a proposal in which you present your ideal curriculum, referring to the ideas of at least one of the writers in this chapter.

8. All the writers in this chapter believe in the power of education to change a person. For many people, this process begins with a teacher who has a profound influence on them. Write an essay in which you discuss such a teacher. What, in your opinion, made this teacher so effective? In what ways did contact with this teacher change you?

9. Write an essay in which you develop a definition of good teaching. As you write, consider the relationship of the teacher to the class, the standards teachers should use to evaluate students, and what students should gain from their educational experience. Make sure you refer to the ideas of John Holt (p. 106) and Daniel H. Pink (p. 112) in your essay.

10. Write an essay in which you answer the Focus question, "Do we still need affirmative action?" In your essay, refer to the ideas in Linda Chavez's "Remembering the Negative Side of Affirmative Action" (p. 158), Goodwin Liu's "The Myth and Math of Affirmative Action" (p. 165), and Richard Harwood's "Debating without Facts" (p. 170).

3

THE POLITICS
OF LANGUAGE

PREPARING TO READ AND WRITE

During the years he spent in prison, political activist Malcolm X became increasingly frustrated by his inability to express himself in writing, so he began the tedious and often frustrating task of copying words from the dictionary—page by page. The eventual result was that for the first time, he could pick up a book and read it with under-standing: "Anyone who has read a great deal," he says, "can imagine the new world that opened." In addition, by becoming a serious

Abortion-rights demonstrators outside a Buffalo, NY, clinic.

reader, Malcolm X was able to develop the ideas about race, politics, and economics that he presented so forcefully after he was released from prison.

In our society, language is constantly manipulated for political ends. This fact should come as no surprise if we consider the potential power of words. Often, the power of a word comes not from its dictionary definition, or *denotation,* but from its *connotations,* the associations that surround it. Often these connotations are subtle, giving language the power to confuse and even to harm. For example, whether a doctor who performs an abortion is "terminating a pregnancy" or "murdering a preborn child" is not just a matter of semantics. It is also a political issue, one that has provoked not only debate but also violence. This potential for misunderstanding, disagreement, deception, and possibly danger, makes careful word choice very important.

The Focus section of this chapter (p. 239) addresses the question "How Free Should Free Speech Be?" As the essays in this section illustrate, the answer to this question is by no means simple. In "The Free-Speech Follies," Stanley Fish makes the point that the First Amendment is often misused and misinterpreted by those who seek to invoke it. In "A Chill Wind Is Blowing," Tim Robbins implies that his constitutional rights were taken away after he spoke out against the war in Iraq. And finally, in "It's Time to Junk the Double Standard on Free Speech," Stuart Taylor, Jr. accuses the media of having a double standard when it comes to making the case for freedom of speech.

Anti-abortion demonstrators outside a Buffalo, NY, clinic.

As you read and prepare to write about the essays in this chapter, you may consider the following questions:

- Does the selection deal primarily with written or spoken language?

- Does the writer place more emphasis on the denotations or the connotations of words?

- Does the writer make any distinctions between language applied to males and language applied to females? Do you consider such distinctions valid?

- Does the writer discuss language in the context of a particular culture? Does he or she see language as a unifying or a divisive factor?

- In what ways would the writer like to change or reshape language? What do you see as the possible advantages or disadvantages of such change?

- Does the writer believe that people are shaped by language or that language is shaped by people?

- Does the writer see language as having a particular social or political function? In what sense?

- Does the writer see language as empowering?

- Does the writer make assumptions about people's status on the basis of their use of language? Do these assumptions seem justified?

- Does the writer make a convincing case for the importance of language?

- Is the writer's focus primarily on language's ability to help or its power to harm?

- In what ways are your ideas about the power of words similar to or different from the writer's?

- How is the essay like and unlike other essays in this chapter?

ARIA[1]

Richard Rodriguez

1944–

Born in San Francisco, the son of Mexican-American immigrants, Richard Rodriguez earned a PhD in Renaissance literature from the University of California at Berkeley (1975). In his first book, Hunger of Memory: The Education of Richard Rodriguez *(1982), from which the following selection is taken, the author writes about the experience of growing up in a Spanish-speaking home and adapting to the English-speaking community around him. His most recent books include* Days of Obligation: An Argument with My Mexican Father *(1992) and* Brown: The Last Discovery of America *(2002). Currently a journalist and author, Rodriguez is a frequent contributor to National Public Radio and an editor for the Pacific News Service (PNS), a nonprofit media organization that provides an alternative source of news and analysis. To read some of his current articles, search the PNS Web site http://news.pacificnews.org/.*

Supporters of bilingual education today imply that students like me miss a great deal by not being taught in their family's language. What they seem not to recognize is that, as a socially disadvantaged child. I considered Spanish to be a private language. What I needed to learn in school was that I had the right—and the obligation—to speak the public language of *los gringos*.[2] The odd truth is that my first-grade classmates could have become bilingual, in the conventional sense of that word, more easily than I. Had they been taught (as upper-middle-class children are often taught early) a second language like Spanish or French, they could have regarded it simply as that: another public language. In my case such bilingualism could not have been so quickly achieved. What I did not believe was that I could speak a single public language.

Without question, it would have pleased me to hear my teachers address me in Spanish when I entered the classroom. I would have felt much less afraid. I would have trusted them and responded with ease. But I would have delayed—for how long postponed?—having to learn the language of public society, I would have evaded—and for how long could I have afforded to delay?—learning the great lesson of school, that I had a public identity.

Fortunately, my teachers were unsentimental about their responsibility. What they understood was that I needed to speak a public language. So their voices would search me out, asking me questions.

---

[1]Solo vocal piece with instrumental accompaniment or melody. [Eds.]
[2]Foreigners, especially Americans. [Eds.]

Each time I'd hear them, I'd look up in surprise to see a nun's face frowning at me. I'd mumble, not really meaning to answer. The nun would persist, "Richard, stand up. Don't look at the floor. Speak up. Speak to the entire class, not just to me!" But I couldn't believe that the English language was mine to use. (In part, I did not want to believe it.) I continued to mumble. I resisted the teacher's demands. (Did I somehow suspect that once I learned public language my pleasing family life would be changed?) Silent, waiting for the bell to sound, I remained dazed, diffident, afraid.

Because I wrongly imagined that English was intrinsically a public language and Spanish an intrinsically private one, I easily noted the difference between classroom language and the language of home. At school, words were directed to a general audience of listeners. ("Boys and girls.") Words were meaningfully ordered. And the point was not self-expression alone but to make oneself understood by many others. The teacher quizzed: "Boys and girls, why do we use that word in this sentence? Could we think of a better word to use there? Would the sentence change its meaning if the words were differently arranged? And wasn't there a better way of saying much the same thing?" (I couldn't say. I wouldn't try to say.)

5   Three months. Five. Half a year passed. Unsmiling, ever watchful, my teachers noted my silence. They began to connect my behavior with the difficult progress my older sister and brother were making. Until one Saturday morning three nuns arrived at the house to talk to our parents. Stiffly, they sat on the blue living room sofa. From the doorway of another room, spying the visitors, I noted the incongruity—the clash of two worlds, the faces and voices of school intruding upon the familiar setting of home. I overheard one voice gently wondering, "Do your children speak only Spanish at home, Mrs. Rodriguez?" While another voice added, "That Richard especially seems so timid and shy."

That Rich-heard!

With great tact the visitors continued, "Is it possible for you and your husband to encourage your children to practice their English when they are home?" Of course, my parents complied. What would they not do for their children's well-being? And how could they have questioned the Church's authority which those women represented? In an instant, they agreed to give up the language (the sounds) that had revealed and accentuated our family's closeness. The moment after the visitors left, the change was observed, "*Ahora*, speak to us *en inglés*,[3] my father and mother united to tell us.

At first, it seemed a kind of game. After dinner each night, the family gathered to practice "our" English. (It was still then *inglés*, a

---

[3]"Now, speak to us in English." [Eds.]

language foreign to us, so we felt drawn as strangers to it.) Laughing, we would try to define words we could not pronounce. We played with strange English sounds, often overanglicizing our pronunciations. And we filled the smiling gaps of our sentences with familiar Spanish sounds. But that was cheating, somebody shouted. Everyone laughed. In school, meanwhile, like my brother and sister, I was required to attend a daily tutoring session. I needed a full year of special attention. I also needed my teachers to keep my attention from straying in class by calling out, *Rich-heard*—their English voices slowly prying loose my ties to my other name, its three notes, *Ri-car-do*. Most of all I needed to hear my mother and father speak to me in a moment of seriousness in broken—suddenly heartbreaking—English. The scene was inevitable: One Saturday morning I entered the kitchen where my parents were talking in Spanish. I did not realize that they were talking in Spanish however until, at the moment they saw me, I heard their voices change to speak English. Those *gringo* sounds they uttered startled me. Pushed me away. In that moment of trivial misunderstanding and profound insight, I felt my throat twisted by unsounded grief. I turned away quickly and left the room. But I had no place to escape to with Spanish. (The spell was broken.) My brother and sisters were speaking English in another part of the house.

Again and again in the days following, increasingly angry, I was obliged to hear my mother and father: "Speak to us *en inglés*" (*Speak.*) Only then did I determine to learn classroom English. Weeks after, it happened: One day in school I raised my hand to volunteer an answer. I spoke out in a loud voice. And I did not think it remarkable when the entire class understood. That day, I moved very far from the disadvantaged child I had been only days earlier. The belief, that calming assurance that I belonged in public, had at last taken hold.

Shortly after, I stopped hearing the high and loud sounds of *los* 10
gringos. A more and more confident speaker of English, I didn't trouble to listen to *how* strangers sounded, speaking to me. And there simply were too many English-speaking people in my day for me to hear American accents anymore. Conversations quickened. Listening to persons who sounded eccentrically pitched voices, I usually noted their sounds for an initial few seconds before I concentrated on *what* they were saying. Conversations became content-full. Transparent. Hearing someone's *tone* of voice—angry or questioning or sarcastic or happy or sad—I didn't distinguish it from the words it expressed. Sound and word were thus tightly wedded. At the end of a day, I was often bemused, always relieved, to realized how "silent," though crowded with words, my day in public had been. (This public silence measured and quickened the change in my life.)

At last, seven years old, I came to believe what had been technically true since my birth; I was an American citizen.

But the special feeling of closeness at home was diminished by then. Gone was the desperate, urgent, intense feeling of being at home, rare was the experience of feeling myself individualized by family intimates. We remained a loving family, but one greatly changed. No longer so close; no longer bound tight by the pleasing and troubling knowledge of our public separateness. Neither my older brother nor sister rushed home after school anymore. Nor did I. When I arrived home there would often be neighborhood kids in the house. Or the house would be empty of sounds.

Following the dramatic Americanization of their children, even my parents grew more publicly confident. Especially my mother. She learned the names of all the people on our block. And she decided we needed to have a telephone installed in the house. My father continued to use the word *gringo*. But it was no longer charged with the old bitterness of distrust. (Stripped of any emotional content, the word simply became a name for those Americans not of Hispanic descent.) Hearing him, sometimes, I wasn't sure if he was pronouncing the Spanish word *gringo* or saying gringo in English.

Matching the silence I started hearing in public was a new quiet at home. The family's quiet was partly due to the fact that, as we children learned more and more English, we shared fewer and fewer words with our parents. Sentences needed to be spoken slowly when a child addressed his mother or father. (Often the parent wouldn't understand.) The child would need to repeat himself. (Still the parent misunderstood.) The young voice, frustrated, would end up saying, "Never mind"—the subject was closed. Dinners would be noisy with the clinking of knives and forks against dishes. My mother would smile softly between her remarks; my father at the other end of the table would chew and chew at his food, while he stared over the heads of his children.

15 My *mother!* My *father!* After English became my primary language, I no longer knew what words to use in addressing my parents. The old Spanish words (those tender accents of sound) I had used earlier—*mamá* and *papá*—I couldn't use anymore. They would have been too painful reminders of how much had changed in my life. On the other hand, the words I heard neighborhood kids call their parents seemed equally unsatisfactory. *Mother* and *Father; Ma, Papa, Pa, Dad, Pop* (how I hated the all American sound of that last word especially)—all these terms I felt were unsuitable, not really terms of address for my parents. As a result, I never used them at home. Whenever I'd speak to my parents, I would try to get their attention with eye contact alone. In public conversations, I'd refer to "my parents" or "my mother and father."

My mother and father, for their part, responded differently, as their children spoke to them less. She grew restless, seemed troubled and anxious at the scarcity of words exchanged in the house. It was she who would question me about my day when I came home from school. She smiled at small talk. She pried at the edges of my sentences to get me to say something more. (What?) She'd join conversations she overheard, but her intrusions often stopped her children's talking. By contrast, my father seemed reconciled to the new quiet. Though his English improved somewhat, he retired into silence. At dinner he spoke very little. One night his children and even his wife helplessly giggled at his garbled English pronunciation of the Catholic Grace before Meals. Thereafter he made his wife recite the prayer at the start of each meal, even on formal occasions, when there were guests in the house. Hers became the public voice of the family. On official business, it was she, not my father, one would usually hear on the phone or in stores, talking to strangers. His children grew so accustomed to his silence that, years later, they would speak routinely of his shyness. (My mother would often try to explain: Both his parents died when he was eight. He was raised by an uncle who treated him like little more than a menial servant. He was never encouraged to speak. He grew up alone. A man of few words.) But my father was not shy, I realized, when I'd watch him speaking Spanish with relatives. Using Spanish, he was quickly effusive. Especially when talking with other men, his voice would spark, flicker, flare alive with sounds. In Spanish, he expressed ideas and feelings he rarely revealed in English. With firm Spanish sounds, he conveyed confidence and authority English would never allow him.

The silence at home, however, was finally more than a literal silence. Fewer words passed between parent and child, but more profound was the silence that resulted from my inattention to sounds. At about the time I no longer bothered to listen with care to the sounds of English in public, I grew careless about listening to the sounds family members made when they spoke. Most of the time I heard someone speaking at home and didn't distinguish his sounds from the words people uttered in public. I didn't even pay much attention to my parents' accented and ungrammatical speech. At least not at home. Only when I was with them in public would I grow alert to their accents. Though, even then, their sounds caused me less and less concern. For I was increasingly confident of my own public identity.

I would have been happier about my public success had I not sometimes recalled what it had been like earlier, when my family had conveyed its intimacy through a set of conveniently private sounds. Sometimes in public, hearing a stranger, I'd hark back to my past. A Mexican farmworker approached me downtown to ask directions to somewhere, "*¿Hijito . . .?*"[4] he said. And his voice summoned deep

---

[4]"Little boy . . . ?" [Eds.]

longing. Another time, standing beside my mother in the visiting room of a Carmelite convent, before the dense screen which rendered the nuns shadowy figures, I heard several Spanish-speaking nuns—their busy, singsong overlapping voices—assure us that yes, yes, we were remembered, all our family was remembered in their prayers. (Their voices echoed faraway family sounds.) Another day, a dark-faced old woman—her hand light on my shoulder—steadied herself against me as she boarded a bus. She murmured something I couldn't quite comprehend. Her Spanish voice came near, like the face of a never-before-seen relative in the instant before I was kissed. Her voice, like so many of the Spanish voices I'd hear in public, recalled the golden age of my youth. Hearing Spanish then, I continued to be a careful, if sad, listener to sounds. Hearing a Spanish-speaking family walking behind me, I turned to look. I smiled for an instant, before my glance found the Hispanic-looking faces of strangers in the crowd going by.

Today I hear bilingual educators say that children lose a degree of "individuality" by becoming assimilated into public society. (Bilingual schooling was popularized in the seventies, that decade when middle-class ethnics began to resist the process of assimilation—the American melting pot). But the bilingualists simplistically scorn the value and necessity of assimilation. They do not seem to realize that there are *two* ways a person is individualized. So they do not realize that while one suffers a diminished sense of *private* individuality by becoming assimilated into public society, such assimilation makes possible the achievement of *public* individuality.

20   The bilingualists insist that a student should be reminded of his difference from others in mass society, his heritage. But they equate mere separateness with individuality. The fact is that only in private—with intimates—is separateness from the crowd a prerequisite for individuality. (An intimate draws me apart, tells me that I am unique, unlike all others.) In public, by contrast, full individuality is achieved, paradoxically, by those who are able to consider themselves members of the crowd. Thus it happened for me: Only when I was able to think of myself as an American, no longer an alien in *gringo* society, could I seek the rights and opportunities necessary for full public individuality. The social and political advantages I enjoy as a man result from the day that I came to believe that my name, indeed, is *Rich-heard Road-ree-guess*. It is true that my public society today is often impersonal. (My public society is usually mass society). Yet despite the anonymity of the crowd and despite the fact that the individuality I achieve in public is often tenuous—because it depends on my being one in a crowd—I celebrate the day I acquired my new name. Those middle-class ethnics who scorn assimilation seem to me filled with decadent self-pity, obsessed by the burden of public life. Danger-

ously, they romanticize public separateness and they trivialize the dilemma of the socially disadvantaged.

My awkward childhood does not prove the necessity of bilingual education. My story discloses instead an essential myth of child-hood—inevitable pain. If I rehearse here the changes in my private life after my Americanization, it is finally to emphasize the public gain. The loss implies the gain: The house I returned to each after-noon was quiet. Intimate sounds no longer rushed to the door to greet me. There were other noises inside. The telephone rang. Neighbor-hood kids ran past the door of the bedroom where I was reading my school-books—covered with shopping-bag paper. Once I learned public language, it would never again be easy for me to hear intimate family voices. More and more of my day was spent hearing words. But that may only be a way of saying that the day I raised my hand in class and spoke loudly to an entire roomful of faces, my childhood started to end.

Responding to Reading

1. What distinction does Rodriguez make between public and private lan-guage? What larger point does this distinction help him make?
2. What does Rodriguez say he gains by speaking English? What does he say he loses? Do you agree with his assessment?
3. What is Rodriguez's main argument against those who support bilingual education? What evidence does he use to support his argument? How con-vincing is he?

Responding in Writing

Do you agree with Rodriguez's opposition to bilingual education, or do you think that children who do not speak English should be taught in their na-tive language?

Two Languages in Mind, But Just One in the Heart

Louise Erdrich

1954–

Of German and Chippewa descent, Louise Erdrich was born in Little Falls, Minnesota. She grew up in Wahpeton, North Dakota, on the Minnesota bor-der, where her parents taught at the Bureau of Indian Affairs school. In 1972, Erdrich was among the first women admitted to Dartmouth College, where she majored in English and creative writing and took courses in Native

American Studies. In 1979, she earned an MFA degree in writing from Johns Hopkins University. Erdrich's first collection of stories, published as the novel Love Medicine *(1979), won a National Book Critics Circle Award. Recent works include* The Birchbark House *(1999), a children's book;* The Last Report on the Miracles at Little No Horse *(2001); and* The Master Butchers Singing Club *(2003). Known for her moving and often humorous portrayals of Chippewa life, Erdrich writes poetry and prose that draw on her heritage to portray the endurance of women and Native Americans.*

For years now I have been in love with a language other than the English in which I write, and it is a rough affair. Every day I try to learn a little more Ojibwe. I have taken to carrying verb conjugation charts in my purse, along with the tiny notebook I've always kept for jotting down book ideas, overheard conversations, language detritus, phrases that pop into my head. Now that little notebook includes an increasing volume of Ojibwe words. My English is jealous, my Ojibwe elusive. Like a besieged unfaithful lover, I'm trying to appease them both.

Ojibwemowin, or Anishinabemowin, the Chippewa language, was last spoken in our family by Patrick Gourneau, my maternal grandfather, a Turtle Mountain Ojibwe who used it mainly in his prayers. Growing up off reservation, I thought Ojibwemowin mainly was a language for prayers, like Latin in the Catholic liturgy. I was unaware for many years that Ojibwemowin was spoken in Canada, Minnesota and Wisconsin, though by a dwindling number of people. By the time I began to study the language, I was living in New Hampshire, so for the first few years I used language tapes.

I never learned more than a few polite phrases that way, but the sound of the language in the author Basil Johnson's calm and dignified Anishinabe voice sustained me through bouts of homesickness. I spoke basic Ojibwe in the isolation of my car traveling here and there on twisting New England roads. Back then, as now, I carried my tapes everywhere.

The language bit deep into my heart, but it was an unfulfilled longing. I had nobody to speak it with, nobody who remembered my grandfather's standing with his sacred pipe in the woods next to a box elder tree, talking to the spirits. Not until I moved back to the Midwest and settled in Minneapolis did I find a fellow Ojibweg to learn with, and a teacher.

5   Mille Lac's Ojibwe elder Jim Clark—Naawi-giizis, or Center of the Day—is a magnetically pleasant, sunny, crew-cut World War II veteran with a mysterious kindliness that shows in his slightest gesture. When he laughs, everything about him laughs; and when he is serious, his eyes round like a boy's.

Naawi-giizis introduced me to the deep intelligence of the language and forever set me on a quest to speak it for one reason: I want to get the jokes. I also want to understand the prayers and the adis-ookaanug, the sacred stories, but the irresistible part of language for me is the explosion of hilarity that attends every other minute of an Ojibwe visit. As most speakers are now bilingual, the language is spiked with puns on both English and Ojibwe, most playing on the oddness of gichi-mookomaan, that is, big knife or American, habits and behavior.

This desire to deepen my alternate language puts me in an odd relationship to my first love, English. It is, after all, the language stuffed into my mother's ancestors' mouths. English is the reason she didn't speak her native language and the reason I can barely limp along in mine. English is an all-devouring language that has moved across North America like the fabulous plagues of locusts that darkened the sky and devoured even the handles of rakes and hoes. Yet the omnivorous nature of a colonial language is a writer's gift. Raised in the English language, I partake of a mongrel feast.

A hundred years ago most Ojibwe people spoke Ojibwemowin, but the Bureau of Indian Affairs and religious boarding schools punished and humiliated children who spoke native languages. The program worked, and there are now almost no fluent speakers of Ojibwe in the United States under the age of 30. Speakers like Naawi-giizis value the language partly because it has been physically beaten out of so many people. Fluent speakers have had to fight for the language with their own flesh, have endured ridicule, have resisted shame and stubbornly pledged themselves to keep on talking the talk.

My relationship is of course very different. How do you go back to a language you never had? Why should a writer who loves her first language find it necessary and essential to complicate her life with another? Simple reasons, personal and impersonal. In the past few years I've found that I can talk to God only in this language, that somehow my grandfather's use of the language penetrated. The sound comforts me.

What the Ojibwe call the Gizhe Manidoo, the great and kind spirit 10 residing in all that lives, what the Lakota call the Great Mystery, is associated for me with the flow of Ojibwemowin. My Catholic training touched me intellectually and symbolically but apparently never engaged my heart.

There is also this: Ojibwemowin is one of the few surviving languages that evolved to the present here in North America. The intelligence of this language is adapted as no other to the philosophy bound up in northern land, lakes, rivers, forests, arid plains; to the animals and their particular habits; to the shades of meaning in the very placement of stones. As a North American writer it is essential to me that I try to understand our human relationship to place in the deepest way possible, using my favorite tool, language.

There are place names in Ojibwe and Dakota for every physical feature of Minnesota, including recent additions like city parks and dredged lakes. Ojibwemowin is not static, not confined to describing the world of some out-of-reach and sacred past. There are words for e-mail, computers, Internet, fax. For exotic animals in zoos. Anaamibiig gookoosh, the underwater pig, is a hippopotamus. Nandookomeshiinh, the the lice hunter, is the monkey.

There are words for the serenity prayer used in 12-step programs and translations of nursery rhymes. The varieties of people other than Ojibwe or Anishinabe are also named: Aiibiishaabookewininiwag, the tea people, are Asians. Agongosininiwag, the chipmunk people, are Scandinavians. I'm still trying to find out why.

For years I saw only the surface of Ojibwemowin. With any study at all one looks deep into a stunning complex of verbs. Ojibwemowin is a language of verbs. All action. Two-thirds of the words are verbs, and for each verb there are as many as 6,000 forms. The storm of verb forms makes it a wildly adaptive and powerfully precise language. Changite-ige describes the way a duck tips itself up in the water butt first. There is a word for what would happen if a man fell off a motorcycle with a pipe in his mouth and the stem of it went through the back of his head. There can be a verb for anything.

15   When it comes to nouns, there is some relief. There aren't many objects. With a modest if inadvertent political correctness, there are no designations of gender in Ojibwemowin. There are no feminine or masculine possessives or articles.

Nouns are mainly designated as alive or dead, animate or inanimate. The word for stone, asin, is animate. Stones are called grandfathers and grandmothers and are extremely important in Ojibwe philosophy. Once I began to think of stones as animate, I started to wonder whether I was picking up a stone or it was putting itself into my hand. Stones are not the same as they were to me in English. I can't write about a stone without considering it in Ojibwe and acknowledging that the Anishinabe universe began with a conversation between stones.

Ojibwemowin is also a language of emotions; shades of feeling can be mixed like paints. There is a word for what occurs when your heart is silently shedding tears. Ojibwe is especially good at describing intellectual states and the fine points of moral responsibility.

Ozozamenimaa pertains to a misuse of one's talents getting out of control. Ozozamichige implies you can still set things right. There are many more kinds of love than there are in English. There are myriad shades of emotional meaning to designate various family and clan members. It is a language that also recognizes the humanity of a creaturely God, and the absurd and wondrous sexuality of even the most deeply religious beings.

Slowly the language has crept into my writing, replacing a word here, a concept there, beginning to carry weight. I've thought of course of writing stories in Ojibwe, like a reverse Nabokov. With my Ojibwe at the level of a dreamy 4-year-old child's, I probably won't.

Though it was not originally a written language, people simply adapted the English alphabet and wrote phonetically. During the Second World War, Naawi-giizis wrote Ojibwe letters to his uncle from Europe. He spoke freely about his movements, as no censor could understand his writing. Ojibwe orthography has recently been standardized. Even so, it is an all-day task for me to write even one paragraph using verbs in their correct arcane forms. And even then, there are so many dialects of Ojibwe that, for many speakers, I'll still have gotten it wrong. 20

As awful as my own Ojibwe must sound to a fluent speaker, I have never, ever, been greeted with a moment of impatience or laughter. Perhaps people wait until I've left the room. But more likely, I think, there is an urgency about attempting to speak the language. To Ojibwe speakers the language is a deeply loved entity. There is a spirit or an originating genius belonging to each word.

Before attempting to speak this language, a learner must acknowledge these spirits with gifts of tobacco and food. Anyone who attempts Ojibwemowin is engaged in something more than learning tongue twisters. However awkward my nouns, unstable my verbs, however stumbling my delivery, to engage in the language is to engage the spirit. Perhaps that is what my teachers know, and what my English will forgive.

Responding to Reading

1. Why did Erdrich want to learn Ojibwe? What difficulties did she have with this language? How did she overcome these difficulties?
2. Why did the Bureau of Indian Affairs and religious boarding schools punish and humiliate "children who spoke native languages" (8)?
3. What advantages does Ojibwe have over English? What effect has learning Ojibwe had on Erdrich? What does she mean when she says, "to engage in the language is to engage the spirit" (22)?

Responding in Writing

Does your family speak a language other than English? What emotional ties, if any, do you have to this language?

LEARNING TO READ AND WRITE

Frederick Douglass

1817?–1895

Frederick Douglass was born a slave in rural Talbot County, Maryland, and later served a family in Baltimore. In the city, he had opportunities for personal improvement—and the luck to escape to the North in 1838. He settled in Bedford, Massachusetts, where he became active in the abolitionist movement. He recounts these experiences in his most famous work, Narrative of the Life of Frederick Douglass *(1845). After spending almost two years in England and Europe on a lecture tour, Douglass returned to the United States and purchased his freedom. In 1847, he launched the antislavery newspaper* The North Star *and became a vocal supporter of both Abraham Lincoln and the Civil War. As a result of his support of the Republican Party, Douglass was rewarded with appointments to prestigious political offices: federal marshal and recorder of deeds for the District of Columbia, president of the Freedman's Bureau, counsul to Haiti, and chargé d'affaires for the Dominican Republic. Throughout his life, Douglass believed that the United States Constitution, if interpreted correctly, would enable African Americans to become full participants in the economic, social, and intellectual life of America. In the following excerpt from his* Narrative, *Douglass writes of outwitting his owners to become literate, thereby finding "the pathway from slavery to freedom."*

I lived in Master Hugh's family about seven years. During this time, I succeeded in learning to read and write. In accomplishing this, I was compelled to resort to various stratagems. I had no regular teacher. My mistress, who had kindly commenced to instruct me, had, in compliance with the advice and direction of her husband, not only ceased to instruct, but had set her face against my being instructed by any one else. It is due, however, to my mistress to say of her, that she did not adopt this course of treatment immediately. She at first lacked the depravity indispensable to shutting me up in mental darkness. It was at least necessary for her to have some training in the exercise of irresponsible power, to make her equal to the task of treating me as though I were a brute.

My mistress was, as I have said, a kind and tender-hearted woman; and in the simplicity of her soul she commenced, when I first went to live with her, to treat me as she supposed one human being ought to treat another. In entering upon the duties of a slaveholder, she did not seem to perceive that I sustained to her the relation of a mere chattel,[1] and that for her to treat me as a human being was not only wrong, but dangerously so. Slavery proved as injurious to her as

---

[1]Property. [Eds.]

it did to me. When I went there, she was a pious, warm, and tender-hearted woman. There was no sorrow or suffering for which she had not a tear. She had bread for the hungry, clothes for the naked, and comfort for every mourner that came within her reach. Slavery soon proved its ability to divest her of these heavenly qualities. Under its influence, the tender heart became stone, and the lamblike disposition gave way to one of tigerlike fierceness. The first step in her downward course was in her ceasing to instruct me. She now commenced to practice her husband's precepts. She finally became even more violent in her opposition than her husband himself. She was not satisfied with simply doing as well as he had commanded; she seemed anxious to do better. Nothing seemed to make her more angry than to see me with a newspaper. She seemed to think that here lay the danger. I have had her rush at me with a face made all up of fury, and snatch from me a newspaper, in a manner that fully revealed her apprehension. She was an apt woman; and a little experience soon demonstrated, to her satisfaction, that education and slavery were incompatible with each other.

From this time I was most narrowly watched. If I was in a separate room any considerable length of time, I was sure to be suspected of having a book, and was at once called to give an account of myself. All this, however, was too late. The first step had been taken. Mistress, in teaching me the alphabet, had given me the *inch*, and no precaution could prevent me from taking the *ell*.

The plan which I adopted, and the one by which I was most successful, was that of making friends of all the little white boys whom I met in the street. As many of these as I could, I converted into teachers. With their kindly aid, obtained at different times and in different places, I finally succeeded in learning to read. When I was sent on errands, I always took my book with me, and by going one part of my errand quickly, I found time to get a lesson before my return. I used also to carry bread with me, enough of which was always in the house, and to which I was always welcome; for I was much better off in this regard than many of the poor white children in our neighborhood. This bread I used to bestow upon the hungry little urchins, who, in return, would give me that more valuable bread of knowledge. I am strongly tempted to give the names of two or three of those little boys, as a testimonial of the gratitude and affection I bear them; but prudence forbids;—not that it would injure me, but it might embarrass them; for it is almost an unpardonable offense to teach slaves to read in this Christian country. It is enough to say of the dear little fellows, that they lived on Philpot Street, very near Durgin and Bailey's ship-yard. I used to talk this matter of slavery over with them. I would sometimes say to them, I wished I could be as free as they would be when they got to be men. "You will be free as soon as you are twenty-one, *but I am a slave for life!* Have not I as good a right to be free as you have?" These words used to trouble them; they would express for me the liveliest sympathy, and console me with the hope that something would occur by which I might be free.

5   I was now about twelve years old, and the thought of being *a slave for life* began to bear heavily upon my heart. Just about this time, I got hold of a book entitled "The Columbian Orator."[2] Every opportunity I got, I used to read this book. Among much of other interesting matter, I found in it a dialogue between a master and his slave. The slave was represented as having run away from his master three times. The dialogue represented the conversation which took place between them, when the slave was retaken the third time. In this dialogue, the whole argument in behalf of slavery was brought forward by the master, all of which was disposed of by the slave. The slave was made to say some very smart as well as impressive things in reply to his master—things which had the desired though unexpected effect; for the conversation resulted in the voluntary emancipation of the slave on the part of the master.

In the same book, I met with one of Sheridan's might speeches on and in behalf of Catholic emancipation.[3] These were choice documents to me. I read them over and over again with unabated interest. They gave tongue to interesting thoughts of my own soul, which had frequently flashed through my mind, and died away for want of utterance. The moral which I gained from the dialogue was the power of truth over the conscience of even a slaveholder. What I got from Sheridan was a bold denunciation of slavery, and a powerful vindication of human rights. The reading of these documents enabled me to utter my thoughts, and to meet the arguments brought forward to sustain slavery; but while they relieved me of one difficulty, they brought on another even more painful than the one of which I was relieved. The more I read, the more I was led to abhor and detest my enslavers. I could regard them in no other light than a band of successful robbers, who had left their homes, and gone to Africa, and stolen us from our homes, and in a strange land reduced us to slavery. I loathed them as being the meanest as well as the most wicked of men. As I read and contemplated the subject, behold! that very discontentment which Master Hugh had predicted would follow my learning to read had already come, to torment and sting my soul to unutterable anguish. As I writhed under it, I would at times feel that learning to read had been a curse rather than a blessing. It had given me a view of my wretched condition, without the remedy. It opened

---

[2] A popular textbook that taught the principles of effective public speaking. [Eds.]

[3] Richard Brinsley Sheridan (1751–1816), British playwright and statesman who made speeches supporting the right of English Catholics to vote. Full emancipation was not granted to Catholics until 1829. [Eds.]

my eyes to the horrible pit, but to no ladder upon which to get out. In moments of agony, I envied my fellow-slaves for their stupidity. I have often wished myself a beast. I preferred the condition of the meanest reptile to my own. Any thing, no matter what, to get rid of thinking! It was the everlasting thinking of my condition that tormented me. There was no getting rid of it. It was pressed upon me by every object within sight or hearing, animate or inanimate. The silver trump of freedom had roused my soul to eternal wakefulness. Freedom now appeared, to disappear no more forever. It was heard in every sound, and seen in every thing. It was ever present to torment me with a sense of my wretched condition. I saw nothing without seeing it, I heard nothing without hearing it, and felt nothing without feeling it. It looked from every star, it smiled in every calm, breathed in every wind, and moved in every storm.

I often found myself regretting my own existence, and wishing myself dead; and but for the hope of being free, I have no doubt but that I should have killed myself, or done something for which I should have been killed. While in this state of mind, I was eager to hear any one speak of slavery. I was a ready listener. Every little while, I could hear something about the abolitionists. It was some time before I found what the word meant. It was always used in such connections as to make it an interesting word to me. If a slave ran away and succeeded in getting clear, or if a slave killed his master, set fire to a barn, or did any thing very wrong in the mind of a slaveholder, it was spoken of as the fruit of *abolition*. Hearing the word in this connection very often, I set about learning what it meant. The dictionary afforded me little or no help. I found it was "the act of abolishing"; but then I did not know what was to be abolished. Here I was perplexed. I did not dare to ask any one about its meaning, for I was satisfied that it was something they wanted me to know very little about. After a patient waiting, I got one of our city papers, containing an account of the number of petitions from the north, praying for the abolition of slavery in the District of Columbia, and of the slave trade between the States. From this time I understood the words *abolition* and *abolitionist*, and always drew near when that word was spoken, expecting to hear something of importance to myself and fellow-slaves. The light broke in upon me by degrees. I went one day down on the wharf of Mr. Waters; and seeing two Irishmen unloading a scow of stone, I went, unasked, and helped them. When we had finished, one of them came to me and asked me if I were a slave. I told him I was. He asked, "Are ye a slave for life?" I told him that I was. The good Irishman seemed to be deeply affected by the statement. He said to the other that it was a pity so fine a little fellow as myself should be a slave for life. He said it was a shame to hold me. They both advised me to run away to the north; that I should find friends there, and that I should be free. I pretended not to be interested in what they said, and treated them as if I did not understand them; for I feared they might be treacherous. White men have been known to encourage slaves to escape, and then, to get the reward, catch them and return them to their masters. I was afraid that these seemingly good men might use me so; but I nevertheless remembered their advice, and from that time I resolved to run away. I looked forward to a time at which it would be safe for me to escape. I was too young to think of doing so immediately; besides, I wished to learn how to write, as I might have occasion to write my own pass. I consoled myself with the hope that I should one day find a good chance. Meanwhile, I would learn to write.

The idea as to how I might learn to write was suggested to me by being in Durgin and Bailey's ship-yard, and frequently seeing the ship carpenters, after hewing, and getting a piece of timber ready for use, write on the timber the name of that part of the ship for which it was intended. When a piece of timber was intended for the larboard side, it would be marked thus—"L." When a piece was for the starboard side, it would be marked thus—"S." A piece for the larboard side forward, would be marked thus—"L. F." When a piece was for starboard side forward, it would be marked thus—"S. F." For larboard aft, it would be marked thus—"L. A." For starboard aft, it would be marked thus—"S. A." I soon learned the names of these letters, and for what they were intended when placed upon a piece of timber in the shipyard. I immediately commenced copying them, and in a short time was able to make the four letters named. After that, when I met with any boy who I knew could write, I would tell him I could write as well as he. The next word would be, "I don't believe you. Let me see you try it." I would then make the letters which I had been so fortunate as to learn, and ask him to beat that. In this way I got a good many lessons in writing, which it is quite possible I should never have gotten in any other way. During this time, my copy-book was the board fence, brick wall, and pavement; my pen and ink was a lump of chalk. With these, I learned mainly how to write. I then commenced and continued copying the Italics in Webster's Spelling Book, until I could make them all without looking on the book. By this time, my little Master Thomas had gone to school, and learned how to write, and had written over a number of copy-books. These had been brought home, and shown to some of our near neighbors, and then laid aside. My mistress used to go to class meeting at the Wilk Street meetinghouse every Monday afternoon, and leave me to take care of the house. When left thus, I used to spend the time in writing in the spaces left in Master Thomas's copy-book, copying what he had written. I continued to do this until I could write a hand very similar to that of Master Thomas. Thus, after a long, tedious effort for years, I finally succeeded in learning how to write.

Responding to Reading

1. What does Douglass mean in paragraph 2 when he says that slavery proved as injurious to his mistress as it did to him? In spite of his owners' actions, what strategies did Douglass use to learn to read?
2. Douglass escaped from slavery in 1838 and became a leading figure in the antislavery movement. How did reading and writing help him develop his ideas about slavery? In what way did language empower him?
3. What comment do you think Douglass's essay makes on the conditions of African Americans in the mid-nineteenth century?

Responding in Writing

Does this essay, written over 150 years ago, have relevance today? Explain.

A HOMEMADE EDUCATION

Malcolm X

1925–1965

Malcolm X was born Malcolm Little in Omaha, Nebraska, the son of a Baptist minister who was threatened by the Ku Klux Klan and forced to move several times. Eventually, his father died under mysterious circumstances, and his mother was committed to a mental institution. Little quit high school, preferring the street world of criminals and drug addicts. While serving time in prison from 1946 to 1952, he became a follower of the Black Muslim religion and took the name Malcolm X. After his release from prison, he eventually took over the leadership of the Harlem mosque and became a controversial political figure and an articulate advocate of black separatism. In 1964, after visiting Africa, Europe, and Mecca, Malcolm X softened his radical views. He returned to New York to advocate cooperation with other organizations seeking civil and political rights for African Americans. As a result of his defection, he was murdered in 1965. Some of his works are The Autobiography of Malcolm X *(dictated to Alex Haley and published in 1965) and* Malcolm X on Afro-American Unity *(1970). "A Homemade Education," from Malcolm X's autobiography, describes his program of self-education. To learn more about this writer, visit the official Web site of Malcolm X, http://www.cmgww.com/historic/malcolm/.*

It was because of my letters that I happened to stumble upon starting to acquire some kind of a homemade education.

I became increasingly frustrated at not being able to express what I wanted to convey in letters that I wrote, especially those to Mr. Elijah Muhammad. In the street, I had been the most articulate hustler out there—I had commanded attention when I said something. But now, trying to write simple English, I not only wasn't articulate, I wasn't even functional. How would I sound writing in slang, the way I would *say* it, something such as, "Look, daddy, let me pull your coat about a cat, Elijah Muhammad—"

Many who today hear me somewhere in person, or on television, or those who read something I've said, will think I went to school far beyond the eighth grade. This impression is due entirely to my prison studies.

It had really begun back in the Charlestown Prison, when Bimbi[1] first made me feel envy of his stock of knowledge. Bimbi had always taken charge of any conversations he was in, and I had tried to emulate him. But every book I picked up had few sentences which didn't contain anywhere from one to nearly all of the words that might as well have been in Chinese. When I just skipped those words, of course, I really ended up with little idea of what the book said. So I had come to the Norfolk Prison Colony still going through only book-reading motions. Pretty soon, I would have quit even these motions, unless I had received the motivation that I did.

5   I saw that the best thing I could do was get hold of a dictionary—to study, to learn some words. I was lucky enough to reason also that I should try to improve my penmanship. It was sad. I couldn't even write in a straight line. It was both ideas together that moved me to request a dictionary along with some tablets and pencils from the Norfolk Prison Colony school.

I spent two days just riffling uncertainly through the dictionary's pages. I'd never realized so many words existed! I didn't know *which* words I needed to learn. Finally, just to start some kind of action, I began copying.

In my slow, painstaking, ragged handwriting, I copied into my tablet everything printed on that first page, down to the punctuation marks.

I believe it took me a day. Then, aloud, I read back, to myself, everything I'd written on the tablet. Over and over, aloud, to myself, I read my own handwriting.

I woke up the next morning, thinking about those words—immensely proud to realize that not only had I written so much at one time, but I'd written words that I never knew were in the world. Moreover, with a little effort, I also could remember what many of these words meant. I reviewed the words whose meanings I didn't remember. Funny thing, from the dictionary first page right now, that "aardvark" springs to my mind. The dictionary had a picture of it, a long-tailed, long-eared, burrowing African mammal, which lives off termites caught by sticking out its tongue as an anteater does for ants.

10   I was so fascinated that I went on—I copied the dictionary's next page. And the same experience came when I studied that. With every succeeding page, I also learned of people and places and events from

---

[1]A fellow inmate. [Eds.]

history. Actually the dictionary is like a miniature encyclopedia. Finally the dictionary's A section had filled a whole tablet—and I went on into the B's. That was the way I started copying what eventually became the entire dictionary. It went a lot faster after so much practice helped me to pick up handwriting speed. Between what I wrote in my tablet, and writing letters, during the rest of my time in prison I would guess I wrote a million words.

I suppose it was inevitable that as my word-base broadened, I could for the first time pick up a book and read and now begin to understand what the book was saying. Anyone who has read a great deal can imagine the new world that opened. Let me tell you something: from then until I left that prison, in every free moment I had, if I was not reading in the library, I was reading on my bunk. You couldn't have gotten me out of books with a wedge. Between Mr. Muhammad's teachings, my correspondence, my visitors—usually Ella and Reginald[2]—and my reading of books, months passed without my even thinking about being imprisoned. In fact, up to then, I never had been so truly free in my life.

The Norfolk Prison Colony's library was in the school building. A variety of classes was taught there by instructors who came from such places as Harvard and Boston universities. The weekly debates between inmate teams were also held in the school building. You would be astonished to know how worked up convict debaters and audiences would get over subjects like "Should Babies Be Fed Milk?"

Available on the prison library's shelves were books on just about every general subject. Much of the big private collection that Parkhurst[3] had willed to the prison was still in crates and boxes in the back of the library—thousands of old books. Some of them looked ancient: covers faded; old-time parchment-looking binding. Parkhurst, I've mentioned, seemed to have been principally interested in history and religion. He had the money and the special interest to have a lot of books that you wouldn't have in general circulation. Any college library would have been lucky to get that collection.

As you can imagine, especially in a prison where there was heavy emphasis on rehabilitation, an inmate was smiled upon if he demonstrated an unusually intense interest in books. There was a sizable number of well-read inmates, especially the popular debaters. Some were said by many to be practically walking encyclopedias. They were almost celebrities. No university would ask any student to devour literature as I did when this new world opened to me, of being able to read and *understand*.

I read more in my room than in the library itself. An inmate who 15 was known to read a lot could check out more than the permitted

---

[2]Ella was Malcolm's half sister, and Reginald was his brother. [Eds.]
[3]A philanthropist. [Eds.]

maximum number of books. I preferred reading in the total isolation of my own room.

When I had progressed to really serious reading, every night at about ten P.M. I would be outraged with the "lights out." It always seemed to catch me right in the middle of something engrossing.

Fortunately, right outside my door was a corridor light that cast a glow into my room. The glow was enough to read by, once my eyes adjusted to it. So when "lights out" came, I would sit on the floor where I could continue reading in that glow.

At one-hour intervals the night guards paced past every room. Each time I heard the approaching footsteps, I jumped into bed and feigned sleep. And as soon as the guard passed, I got back out of bed onto the floor area of that light-glow, where I would read for another fifty-eight minutes—until the guard approached again. That went on until three or four every morning. Three or four hours of sleep a night was enough for me. Often in the years in the streets I had slept less than that.

The teachings of Mr. Muhammad stressed how history had been "whitened"—when white men had written history books, the black man simply had been left out. Mr. Muhammad couldn't have said anything that would have struck me much harder. I had never forgotten how when my class, me and all of those whites, had studied seventh-grade United States history back in Mason,[4] the history of the Negro had been covered in one paragraph, and the teacher had gotten a big laugh with his joke, "Negroes' feet are so big that when they walk, they leave a hole in the ground."

20   This is one reason why Mr. Muhammad's teachings spread so swiftly all over the United States, among *all* Negroes, whether or not they became followers of Mr. Muhammad. The teachings ring true—to every Negro. You can hardly show me a black adult in America—or a white one, for that matter—who knows from the history books anything like the truth about the black man's role. In my own case, once I heard of the "glorious history of the black man," I took special pains to hunt in the library for books that would inform me on details about black history.

I can remember accurately the very first set of books that really impressed me. I have since bought that set of books and I have it at home for my children to read as they grow up. It's called *Wonders of the World*. It's full of pictures of archeological finds, statues that depict, usually, non-European people.

I found books like Will Durant's *Story of Civilization*. I read H. G. Wells' *Outline of History*. *Souls of Black Folk* by W. E. B. Du Bois gave me a glimpse into the black people's history before they came to this

---

[4]The junior high school that Malcolm X attended. [Eds.]

country. Carter G. Woodson's *Negro History* opened my eyes about black empires before the black slave was brought to the United States, and the early Negro struggles for freedom.

J. A. Rogers' three volumes of *Sex and Race* told about race-mixing before Christ's time; about Aesop being a black man who told fables; about Egypt's Pharaohs; about the great Coptic Christian Empires; about Ethiopia, the earth's oldest continuous black civilization, as China is the oldest continuous civilization.

Mr. Muhammad's teaching about how the white man had been created led me to *Findings in Genetics* by Gregor Mendel.[5] (The dictionary's G section was where I had learned what "genetics" meant.) I really studied this book by the Austrian monk. Reading it over and over, especially certain sections, helped me to understand that if you started with a black man, a white man could be produced; but starting with a white man, you never could produce a black man—because the white chromosome is recessive. And since no one disputes that there was but one Original Man, the conclusion is clear.

During the last year or so, in the *New York Times*, Arnold Toynbee[6] 25 used the word "bleached" in describing the white man. (His words were: "White [i.e. bleached] human beings of North European origin. . . .") Toynbee also referred to the European geographic area as only a peninsula of Asia. He said there is no such thing as Europe. And if you look at the globe, you will see for yourself that America is only an extension of Asia. (But at the same time Toynbee is among those who have helped to bleach history. He has written that Africa was the only continent that produced no history. He won't write that again. Every day now, the truth is coming to light.)

I never will forget how shocked I was when I began reading about slavery's total horror. It made such an impact upon me that it later became one of my favorite subjects when I became a minister of Mr. Muhammad's. The world's most monstrous crime, the sin and the blood on the white man's hands, are almost impossible to believe. Books like the one by Frederick Olmstead[7] opened my eyes to the horrors suffered when the slave was landed in the United States. The European woman, Fannie Kimball, who had married a Southern white slaveowner, described how human beings were degraded. Of course I read *Uncle Tom's Cabin*. In fact, I believe that's the only novel I have ever read since I started serious reading.

Parkhurst's collection also contained some bound pamphlets of the Abolitionist Anti-Slavery Society of New England. I read descriptions of atrocities, saw those illustrations of black slave women tied

---

[5]Austrian monk (1822–1884) acknowledged as the father of modern genetics. [Eds.]

[6]English historian (1889–1975). [Eds.]

[7]American landscape architect and writer (1822–1903) who first achieved fame for his accounts of the South in the early 1850s. [Eds.]

up and flogged with whips; of black mothers watching their babies being dragged off, never to be seen by their mothers again; of dogs after slaves, and of the fugitive slave catchers, evil white men with whips and clubs and chains and guns. I read about the slave preacher Nat Turner, who put the fear of God into the white slavemaster. Nat Turner wasn't going around preaching pie-in-the-sky and "nonviolent" freedom for the black man. There in Virginia one night in 1831, Nat and seven other slaves started out at his master's home and through the night they went from one plantation "big house" to the next, killing, until by the next morning 57 white people were dead and Nat had about 70 slaves following him. White people, terrified for their lives, fled from their homes, locked themselves up in public buildings, hid in the woods, and some even left the state. A small army of soldiers took two months to catch and hang Nat Turner. Somewhere I have read where Nat Turner's example is said to have inspired John Brown to invade Virginia and attack Harper's Ferry nearly thirty years later, with thirteen white men and five Negroes.

I read Herodotus, "the father of History," or, rather, I read about him. And I read the histories of various nations, which opened my eyes gradually, then wider and wider, to how the whole world's white men had indeed acted like devils, pillaging and raping and bleeding and draining the whole world's non-white people. I remember, for instance, books such as Will Durant's *The Story of Oriental Civilization*, and Mahatma Gandhi's accounts of the struggle to drive the British out of India.

Book after book showed me how the white man had brought upon the world's black, brown, red, and yellow peoples every variety of the sufferings of exploitation. I saw how since the sixteenth century, the so-called "Christian trader" white man began to ply the seas in his lust for Asian and African empires, and plunder, and power. I read, I saw, how the white man never has gone among the non-white peoples bearing the Cross in the true manner and spirit of Christ's teachings—meek, humble, and Christlike.

30   I perceived, as I read, how the collective white man had been actually nothing but a piratical opportunist who used Faustian machinations to make his own Christianity his initial wedge in criminal conquests. First, always "religiously," he branded "heathen" and "pagan" labels upon ancient non-white cultures and civilizations. The stage thus set, he then turned upon his non-white victims his weapons of war.

I read how, entering India—half a *billion* deeply religious brown people—the British white man, by 1759, through promises, trickery and manipulations, controlled much of India through Great Britain's East India Company. The parasitical British administration kept tentacling out to half of the subcontinent. In 1857, some of the desperate people of India finally mutinied—and, excepting the African slave trade, nowhere has history recorded any more unnecessary bestial and ruthless human carnage than the British suppression of the non-white Indian people.

Over 115 million African blacks—close to the 1930s population of the United States—were murdered or enslaved during the slave trade. And I read how when the slave market was glutted, the cannibalistic white powers of Europe next carved up, as their colonies, the richest areas of the black continent. And Europe's chancelleries for the next century played a chess game of naked exploitation and power from Cape Horn to Cairo.

Ten guards and the warden couldn't have torn me out of those books. Not even Elijah Muhammad could have been more eloquent than those books were in providing indisputable proof that the collective white man had acted like a devil in virtually every contact he had with the world's collective non-white man. I listen today to the radio, and watch television, and read the headlines about the collective white man's fear and tension concerning China. When the white man professes ignorance about why the Chinese hate him so, my mind can't help flashing back to what I read, there in prison, about how the blood forebears of this same white man raped China at a time when China was trusting and helpless. Those original white "Christian traders" sent into China millions of pounds of opium. By 1839, so many of the Chinese were addicts that China's desperate government destroyed twenty thousand chests of opium. The first Opium War was promptly declared by the white man. Imagine! Declaring war upon someone who objects to being narcotized! The Chinese were severely beaten, with Chinese-invented gunpowder.

The Treaty of Nanking made China pay the British white man for the destroyed opium: forced open China's major ports to British trade; forced China to abandon Hong Kong; fixed China's import tariffs so low that cheap British articles soon flooded in, maiming China's industrial development.

After a second Opium War, the Tientsin Treaties legalized the rav- 35 aging opium trade, legalized a British-French-American control of China's customs. China tried delaying that Treaty's ratification; Peking was looted and burned

"Kill the foreign white devils" was the 1901 Chinese war cry in the Boxer Rebellion. Losing again, this time the Chinese were driven from Peking's choicest areas. The vicious, arrogant white man put up the famous signs, "Chinese and dogs not allowed."

Red China after World War II closed its doors to the Western white world. Massive Chinese agricultural, scientific, and industrial efforts are described in a book that *Life* magazine recently published. Some observers inside Red China have reported that the world never has known such a hate-white campaign as is now going on in this nonwhite country where, present birthrates continuing, in fifty more years Chinese will be half the earth's population. And it seems that some Chinese chickens will soon come home to roost, with China's recent successful nuclear tests.

Let us face reality. We can see in the United Nations a new world order being shaped, along color lines—an alliance among the nonwhite nations. America's U.N. Ambassador Adlai Stevenson complained not long ago that in the United Nations "a skin game" was being played. He was right. He was facing reality. A "skin game" *is* being played. But Ambassador Stevenson sounded like Jesse James accusing the marshal of carrying a gun. Because who in the world's history ever has played a worse "skin game" than the white man?

Mr. Muhammad, to whom I was writing daily, had no idea of what a new world had opened up to me through my efforts to document his teachings in books.

40   When I discovered philosophy, I tried to touch all the landmarks of philosophical development. Gradually, I read most of the old philosophers, Occidental and Oriental. The Oriental philosophers were the ones I came to prefer; finally, my impression was that most Occidental philosophy had largely been borrowed from the Oriental thinkers. Socrates, for instance, traveled in Egypt. Some sources even say that Socrates was initiated into some of the Egyptian mysteries. Obviously Socrates got some of his wisdom among the East's wise men.

I have often reflected upon the new vistas that reading opened to me. I knew right there in prison that reading had changed forever the course of my life. As I see it today, the ability to read awoke inside me some long dormant craving to be mentally alive. I certainly wasn't seeking any degree, the way a college confers a status symbol upon its students. My homemade education gave me, with every additional book that I read, a little bit more sensitivity to the deafness, dumbness, and blindness that was afflicting the black race in America. Not long ago, an English writer telephoned me from London, asking questions. One was, "What's your alma mater?" I told him, "Books." You will never catch me with a free fifteen minutes in which I'm not studying something I feel might be able to help the black man.

Yesterday I spoke in London, and both ways on the plane across the Atlantic I was studying a document about how the United Nations proposes to insure the human rights of the oppressed minorities of the world. The American black man is the world's most shameful case of minority oppression. What makes the black man think of himself as only an internal United States issue is just a catch-phrase, two words, "civil rights." How is the black man going to get "civil rights" before first he wins his *human* rights? If the American black man will start thinking about his *human* rights, and then start thinking of himself as part of one of the world's great peoples, he will see he has a case for the United Nations.

I can't think of a better case! Four hundred years of black blood and sweat invested here in America, and the white man still has the black man begging for what every immigrant fresh off the ship can take for granted the minute he walks down the gangplank.

But I'm digressing. I told the Englishman that my alma mater was books, a good library. Every time I catch a plane, I have with me a book that I want to read—and that's a lot of books these days. If I weren't out here every day battling the white man, I could spend the rest of my life reading, just satisfying my curiosity—because you can hardly mention anything I'm not curious about. I don't think anybody ever got more out of going to prison than I did. In fact, prison enabled me to study far more intensively than I would have if my life had gone differently and I had attended some college. I imagine that one of the biggest troubles with colleges is there are too many distractions, too much panty-raiding, fraternities, and boola-boola and all of that. Where else but in a prison could I have attacked my ignorance by being able to study intensely sometimes as much as fifteen hours a day?

Responding to Reading

1. What were Malcolm X's reasons for wanting to increase his skill in reading and writing? What did his "homemade" education give him?
2. Why didn't prison officials encourage Malcolm X to learn to read?
3. In what ways are Frederick Douglass's (p. 190) and Malcolm X's methods for learning to read similar? In what ways are they different? What message do you think Malcom X's essay has for contemporary readers?

Responding in Writing

Select a page at random from your college dictionary. How many words on the page are unfamiliar to you? How might knowing these words help you become a better reader or writer?

FOUR-LETTER WORDS CAN HURT YOU

Barbara Lawrence

Born in Hanover, New Hampshire, Barbara Lawrence earned a Bachelor's degree from Connecticut College and a Master's degree from New York University. She has served on the faculty of the State University of New York at Old Westbury and has also worked as a magazine editor for Redbook *and* Harper's Bazaar, *among others. The following essay, which appeared in the* New York Times, *takes a serious look at the derivation of taboo words and considers the harm they do.*

Why should any words be called obscene? Don't they all describe natural human functions? Am I trying to tell them, my students demand, that the "strong, earthy, gut-honest"—or, if they are fans of Norman Mailer, the "rich, liberating, existential"—language they use to describe sexual activity isn't preferable to "phony-sounding, middle-class words like 'intercourse' and 'copulate'?" "Cop You Late!" they say with fancy and gagging grimaces. "Now, what is *that* supposed to mean?"

Well, what is it supposed to mean? And why indeed should one group of words describing human functions and human organs be acceptable in ordinary conversation and another, describing presumably the same organs and functions, be tabooed—so much so, in fact, that some of these words still cannot appear in print in many parts of the English-speaking world?

The argument that these taboos exist only because of "sexual hang-ups (middle-class, middle-age, feminist), or even that they are a result of class oppression (the contempt of the Norman conquerors for the language of their Anglo-Saxon serfs), ignores a much more likely explanation, it seems to me, and that is the sources and functions of the words themselves.

The best known of the tabooed sexual verbs, for example, comes from the German *ficken*, meaning "to strike"; combined, according to Partridge's etymological dictionary *Origins*, with the Latin sexual verb *futuere*; associated in turn with the Latin *fustis*, "a staff or cudgel"; the Celtic *buc*, "a point, hence to pierce"; the Irish *bot*, "the male member"; the Latin *battuere*, "to beat"; the Gaelic *batair*, "a cudgeller"; the Early Irish *bualaim*, "I strike"; and so forth. It is one of what etymologists sometimes call "the sadistic group of words for the man's part in copulation."

5　　The brutality of this word, then, and its equivalents ("screw," "bang," etc.), is not an illusion of the middle class or a crotchet of Women's Liberation. In their origins and imagery these words carry undeniably painful, if not sadistic, implications, the object of which is almost always female. Consider, for example, what a "screw" actually does to the wood it penetrates; what a painful, even mutilating, activity this kind of analogy suggests. "Screw" is particularly interesting in this context, since the noun, according to Partridge comes from words meaning "groove," "nut," "ditch," "breeding sow" "scrofula" and "swelling," while the verb, besides its explicit imagery, has antecedent associations to "write on," "scratch," "scarify," and so forth—a revealing fusion of a mechanical or painful action with an obviously denigrated object.

Not all obscene words, of course, are as implicitly sadistic or denigrating to women as these, but all that I know seem to serve a similar purpose: to reduce the human organism (especially the female organism) and human functions (especially sexual and procreative) to their least organic, most mechanical dimension; to substitute a trivializing deforming resemblance for the complex human reality of what is being described.

Tabooed male descriptives, when they are not openly denigrating to women, often serve to divorce a male organ or function from any significant interaction with the female. Take the word "testes," for example, suggesting "witnesses" (from the Latin *testis*) to the sexual and procreative strengths of the male organ; and the obscene counterpart of this word, which suggests little more than a mechanical shape. Or compare almost any of the "rich," "liberating" sexual verbs, so fashionable today among male writers, with that much-derided Latin word "copulate" ("to bind or join together") or even that Anglo-Saxon phrase (which seems to have had no trouble surviving the Norman Conquest) "make love."

How arrogantly self-involved the tabooed words seem in comparison to either of the other terms, and how contemptuous of the female partner. Understandably so, of course, if she is only a "skirt," a "broad," a "chick," a "pussycat" or a "piece." If she is, in other words, no more than her skirt, or what her skirt conceals; no more than a breeder, or the broadest part of her; no more than a piece of a human being or a "piece of tail."

The most severely tabooed of all the female descriptives, incidentally, are those like a "piece of tail," which suggest (either explicitly or through antecedents) that there is no significant difference between the female channel through which we are all conceived and born and the anal outlet common to both sexes—a distinction that pornographers have always enjoyed obscuring.

This effort to deny women their biological identity, their individuality, their humanness, is such an important aspect of obscene language that one can only marvel at how seldom, in an era preoccupied with definitions of obscenity, this fact is brought to our attention. One problem, of course, is that many of the people in the best position to do this (critics, teachers, writers) are so reluctant today to admit that they are angered or shocked by obscenity. Bored, maybe, unimpressed, aesthetically, displeased, but—no matter how brutal or denigrating the material—never angered, never shocked.

And yet how eloquently angered, how piously shocked many of these same people become if denigrating language is used about any minority group other than women; if the obscenities are racial or ethnic, that is, rather than sexual. Words like "coon," "kike," "spic," "wop," after all, deform identity, deny individuality and humanness in almost exactly the same way that sexual vulgarisms and obscenities do.

No one that I know, least of all my students, would fail to question the values of a society whose literature and entertainment rested heavily on racial or ethnic pejoratives. Are the values of a society whose literature and entertainment rest as heavily as ours on sexual pejoratives any less questionable?

Responding to Reading

1. Lawrence begins her essay with a series of questions. Is this an effective strategy? Does she answer all these questions in her essay?
2. Lawrence's title sums up the main point of her essay. Does she succeed in convincing you that "four-letter words" can, indeed, hurt you?
3. Do you agree with Lawrence when she says the use of obscene sexual references is as hurtful to women as the use of racial or ethnic epithets is to minorities?

Responding in Writing

Can you think of any other kinds of words that could be as harmful as the ones Lawrence discusses in her essay? In what ways are they harmful? What alternatives are there for these words?

MOTHER TONGUE

Amy Tan

1952–

Amy Tan was born in Oakland, California, to parents who had emigrated from China only a few years earlier. (Her given name is actually An-mei, which means "blessing from America.") After receiving degrees from San Francisco State University (including a master's degree in linguistics), she became a business writer, composing speeches for corporate executives. A workaholic, Tan began writing stories as a means of personal therapy, and these stories eventually became the highly successful The Joy Luck Club *(1987), a novel about Chinese-born mothers and their American-born daughters that was later made into a widely praised film. Tan's other books include three more novels—*The Kitchen God's Wife *(1991),* The Hundred Secret Senses *(1995), and* The Bonesetter's Daughter *(2001)—and two illustrated children's books,* The Moon Lady *(1992) and* The Chinese Siamese Cat *(1994). In the following essay, which was originally delivered as a speech, Tan considers her relationship with her own mother, concentrating on the different "Englishes" they use to communicate with each other and with the world.*

I am not a scholar of English or literature. I cannot give you much more than personal opinions on the English language and its variations in this country or others.

I am a writer. And by that definition, I am someone who has always loved language. I am fascinated by language in daily life. I spend a great deal of my time thinking about the power of language—the way it can evoke an emotion, a visual image, a complex idea, or a simple truth. Language is the tool of my trade. And I use them all—all the Englishes I grew up with.

Recently, I was made keenly aware of the different Englishes I do use. I was giving a talk to a large group of people, the same talk I had already given to half a dozen other groups. The nature of the talk was about my writing, my life, and my book, *The Joy Luck Club*. The talk was going along well enough, until I remembered one major difference that made the whole talk sound wrong. My mother was in the room. And it was perhaps the first time she had heard me give a lengthy speech, using the kind of English I have never used with her. I was saying things like, "The intersection of memory upon imagination" and "There is an aspect of my fiction that relates to thus-and-thus"—a speech filled with carefully wrought grammatical phrases, burdened, it suddenly seemed to me, with nominalized forms, past perfect tenses, conditional phrases, all the forms of standard English that I had learned in school and through books, the forms of English I did not use at home with my mother.

Just last week, I was walking down the street with my mother, and I again found myself conscious of the English I was using, and the English I do use with her. We were talking about the price of new and used furniture and I heard myself saying this: "Not waste money that way." My husband was with us as well, and he didn't notice any switch in my English. And then I realized why. It's because over the twenty years we've been together I've often used that same kind of English with him, and sometimes he even uses it with me. It has become our language of intimacy, a different sort of English that relates to family talk, the language I grew up with.

So you'll have some idea of what this family talk I heard sounds ⁵ like, I'll quote what my mother said during a recent conversation which I videotaped and then transcribed. During this conversation, my mother was talking about a political gangster in Shanghai who had the same last name as her family's, Du, and how the gangster in his early years wanted to be adopted by her family, which was rich by comparison. Later, the gangster became more powerful, far richer than my mother's family, and one day showed up at my mother's wedding to pay his respects. Here's what she said in part:

"Du Yusong having business like fruit stand. Like off the street kind. He is Du like Du Zong—but not Tsung-ming Island people. The local people call putong, the river east side, he belong to that side local people. The man want to ask Du Zong father take him in like become own family. Du Zong father wasn't look down on him, but didn't take seriously, until that man big like become a mafia. Now important person, very hard to inviting him. Chinese way, came only to show respect, don't stay for dinner. Respect for making big celebration, he shows up. Mean gives lots of respect. Chinese custom. Chinese social life that way. If too important won't have to stay too long. He come to my wedding. I didn't see, I heard it. I gone to boy's side, they have YMCA dinner. Chinese age I was nineteen."

You should know that my mother's expressive command of English belies how much she actually understands. She reads the Forbes report, listens to *Wall Street Week*, converses daily with her stockbroker, reads all of Shirley MacLaine's[1] books with ease—all kinds of things I can't begin to understand. Yet some of my friends tell me they understand 50 percent of what my mother says. Some say they understand 80 to 90 percent. Some say they understand none of it, as if she were speaking pure Chinese. But to me, my mother's English is perfectly clear, perfectly natural. It's my mother tongue. Her language, as I hear it, is vivid, direct, full of observation and imagery. That was the language that helped shape the way I saw things, expressed things, made sense of the world.

Lately, I've been giving more thought to the kind of English my mother speaks. Like others, I have described it to people as "broken" or "fractured" English. But I wince when I say that. It has always bothered me that I can think of no way to describe it other than "broken," as if it were damaged and needed to be fixed, as if it lacked a certain wholeness and soundness. I've heard other terms used, "limited English," for example. But they seem just as bad, as if everything is limited, including people's perceptions of the limited English speaker.

I know this for a fact, because when I was growing up, my mother's "limited" English limited *my* perception of her. I was ashamed of her English. I believed that her English reflected the quality of what she had to say. That is, because she expressed them imperfectly her thoughts were imperfect. And I had plenty of empirical evidence to support me: the fact that people in department stores, at banks, and at restaurants did not take her seriously, did not give her good service, pretended not to understand her, or even acted as if they did not hear her.

10   My mother has long realized the limitations of her English as well. When I was fifteen, she used to have me call people on the phone to pretend I was she. In this guise, I was forced to ask for information or even to complain and yell at people who had been rude to her. One time it was a call to her stockbroker in New York. She had

---

[1]Actress known for her autobiographical books, in which she traces her many past lives. [Eds.]

cashed out her small portfolio and it just so happened we were going to go to New York the next week, our very first trip outside California. I had to get on the phone and say in an adolescent voice that was not very convincing, "This is Mrs. Tan."

And my mother was standing in the back whispering loudly, "Why he don't send me check, already two weeks late. So mad he lie to me, losing me money."

And then I said in perfect English, "Yes, I'm getting rather concerned. You had agreed to send the check two weeks ago, but it hasn't arrived."

Then she began to talk more loudly. "What he want, I come to New York tell him front of his boss, you cheating me?" And I was trying to calm her down, make her be quiet, while telling the stockbroker, "I can't tolerate any more excuses. If I don't receive the check immediately, I am going to have to speak to your manager when I'm in New York next week." And sure enough, the following week there we were in front of this astonished stockbroker, and I was sitting there red-faced and quiet, and my mother, the real Mrs. Tan, was shouting at his boss in her impeccable broken English.

We used a similar routine just five days ago, for a situation that was far less humorous. My mother had gone to the hospital for an appointment, to find out about a benign brain tumor a CAT scan had revealed a month ago. She said she had spoken very good English, her best English, no mistakes. Still, she said, the hospital did not apologize when they said they had lost the CAT scan and she had come for nothing. She said they did not seem to have any sympathy when she told them she was anxious to know the exact diagnosis, since her husband and son had both died of brain tumors. She said they would not give her any more information until the next time and she would have to make another appointment for that. So she said she would not leave until the doctor called her daughter. She wouldn't budge. And when the doctor finally called her daughter, me, who spoke in perfect English—lo and behold—we had assurances the CAT scan would be found, promises that a conference call on Monday would be held, and apologies for any suffering my mother had gone through for a most regrettable mistake.

I think my mother's English almost had an effect on limiting my 15 possibilities in life as well. Sociologists and linguists probably will tell you that a person's developing language skills are more influenced by peers. But I do think that the language spoken in the family, especially in immigrant families which are more insular, plays a large role in shaping the language of the child. And I believe that it affected my results on achievement tests, IQ tests, and the SAT. While my English skills were never judged as poor, compared to math, English could not be considered my strong suit. In grade school I did moderately well, getting perhaps B's, sometimes B-pluses, in English and scoring perhaps in the sixtieth or seventieth percentile on achievement tests. But those scores were not good enough to override the opinion that my true abilities lay in math and science, because in those areas I achieved A's and scored in the ninetieth percentile or higher.

This was understandable. Math is precise; there is only one correct answer. Whereas, for me at least, the answers on English tests were always a judgment call, a matter of opinion and personal experience. Those tests were constructed around items like fill-in-the-blank sentence completion, such as, "Even though Tom was , Mary thought he was ." And the correct answer always seemed to be the most bland combinations of thoughts, for example, "Even though Tom was shy, Mary thought he was charming," with the grammatical structure "even though" limiting the correct answer to some sort of semantic opposites, so you wouldn't get answers like, "Even though Tom was foolish, Mary thought he was ridiculous." Well, according to my mother, there were very few limitations as to what Tom could have been and what Mary might have thought of him. So I never did well on tests like that.

The same was true with word analogies, pairs of words in which you were supposed to find some sort of logical, semantic relationship—for example, "*Sunset* is to *nightfall* as is to ." And here you would be presented with a list of four possible pairs, one of which showed the same kind of relationship: *red* is to s*toplight, bus* is to *arrival, chills* is to *fever, yawn* is to *boring.* Well, I could never think that way. I knew what the tests were asking, but I could not block out of my mind the images already created by the first pair, "*sunset* is to *nightfall*"—and I would see a burst of colors against a darkening sky, the moon rising, the lowering of a curtain of stars. And all the other pairs of words—red, bus, stoplight, boring—just threw up a mass of confusing images, making it impossible for me to sort out something as logical as saying: "A sunset precedes nightfall" is the same as "a chill precedes a fever." The only way I would have gotten that answer right would have been to imagine an associative situation, for example, my being disobedient and staying out past sunset, catching a chill at night, which turns into feverish pneumonia as punishment, which indeed did happen to me.

I have been thinking about all this lately, about my mother's English, about achievement tests. Because lately I've been asked, as a writer, why there are not more Asian Americans represented in American literature. Why are there few Asian Americans enrolled in creative writing programs? Why do so many Chinese students go into engineering? Well, these are broad sociological questions I can't begin to answer. But I have noticed in surveys—in fact, just last week—that Asian students, as a whole, always do significantly better on math achievement tests than in English. And this makes me think that there are other Asian-American students whose English spoken in the home might also be described as "broken" or "limited." And perhaps they also have teachers who are steering them away from writing and into math and science, which is what happened to me.

Fortunately, I happen to be rebellious in nature and enjoy the challenge of disproving assumptions made about me. I became an English major my first year in college, after being enrolled as pre-med. I started writing nonfiction as a freelancer the week after I was told by my former boss that writing was my worst skill and I should hone my talents toward account management.

But it wasn't until 1985 that I finally began to write fiction. And at 20 first I wrote using what I thought to be wittily crafted sentences, sentences that would finally prove I had mastery over the English language. Here's an example from the first draft of a story that later made its way into *The Joy Luck Club,* but without this line: "That was my mental quandary in its nascent state." A terrible line, which I can barely pronounce.

Fortunately, for reasons I won't get into today, I later decided I should envision a reader for the stories I would write. And the reader I decided upon was my mother, because these were stories about mothers. So with this reader in mind—and in fact she did read my early drafts—I began to write stories using all the Englishes I grew up with: the English I spoke to my mother, which for lack of a better term might be described as "simple"; the English she used with me, which for lack of a better term might be described as "broken"; my translation of her Chinese, which could certainly be described as "watered down"; and what I imagined to be her translation of her Chinese if she could speak in perfect English, her internal language, and for that I sought to preserve the essence, but neither an English nor a Chinese structure. I wanted to capture what language ability tests can never reveal: her intent, her passion, her imagery, the rhythms of her speech and the nature of her thoughts.

Apart from what any critic had to say about my writing, I knew I had succeeded where it counted when my mother finished reading my book and gave me her verdict: "So easy to read."

Responding to Reading

1. Why does Tan begin her essay with the disclaimer "I am not a scholar of English or literature. I cannot give you much more than personal opinions" (1)? Do these opening statements add to her credibility or detract from it? Explain.

2. Tan implies that some languages are more expressive than others. Do you agree? Are there some ideas you can express in one language that are difficult or impossible to express in another? Give examples if you can.
3. Do you agree with Tan's statement in paragraph 15 that the kind of English spoken at home can have an effect on a student's performance on IQ tests and the SAT?

Responding in Writing

Do you think the English you speak at home has had a positive or a negative effect on your performance in school?

THE HUMAN COST
OF AN ILLITERATE SOCIETY
Jonathan Kozol
1936–

Born in Boston into a "privileged" family, Jonathan Kozol received his BA in literature from Harvard University (1958). Returning to Boston in 1964 and inspired by the civil rights movement, Kozol took a teaching job in the Boston Public Schools System. In 1967, he published his first book, Death at an Early Age: The Destruction of the Hearts and Minds of Negro Children in the Boston Public Schools. *Based on his experiences as a fourth-grade teacher in an inner-city school, a position from which he was fired for "curriculum deviation," this book won the National Book Award in 1968 and led to a number of specific reforms. Since then, Kozol has divided his time between teaching and social activism. His books include* Illiterate America *(1985);* Rachel and Her Children *(1988), a study of homeless families;* Savage Inequalities *(1991);* Amazing Grace *(1995); and* Ordinary Resurrections *(2000). In the following essay, a chapter of* Illiterate America, *Kozol exposes the problems facing the sixty million Americans who are unable to read and argues that their plight has important implications for the nation as a whole.*

PRECAUTIONS. READ BEFORE USING.
Poison: Contains sodium hydroxide (caustic soda-lye).
Corrosive: Causes severe eye and skin damage, may cause blindness.
Harmful or fatal if swallowed.
If swallowed, give large quantities of milk or water.
Do not induce vomiting.
Important: Keep water out of can at all times to prevent contents from violently erupting . . .

—warning on a can of Drano

Questions of literacy, in Socrates' belief, must at length be judged as matters of morality. Socrates could not have had in mind the moral compromise peculiar to a nation like our own. Some of our Founding Fathers did, however, have this question in their minds. One of the wisest of those Founding Fathers (one who may not have been most compassionate but surely was more prescient than some of his peers) recognized the special dangers that illiteracy would pose to basic equity in the political construction that he helped to shape.

"A people who mean to be their own governors," James Madison wrote, "must arm themselves with the power knowledge gives. A popular government without popular information or the means of acquiring it, is but a prologue to a farce or a tragedy, or perhaps both."

Tragedy looms larger than farce in the United States today. Illiterate citizens seldom vote. Those who do are forced to cast a vote of questionable worth. They cannot make informed decisions based on serious print information. Sometimes they can be alerted to their interests by aggressive voter education. More frequently, they vote for a face, a smile, or a style, not for a mind or character or body of beliefs.

The number of illiterate adults exceeds by 16 million the entire vote cast for the winner in the 1980 presidential contest. If even one third of all illiterates could vote, and read enough and do sufficient math to vote in their self-interest, Ronald Reagan would not likely have been chosen president. There is, of course, no way to know for sure. We do know this: Democracy is a mendacious[1] term when used by those who are prepared to countenance the forced exclusion of one third of our electorate. So long as 60 million people are denied significant participation, the government is neither of, nor for, nor by, the people. It is a government, at best, of those two thirds whose wealth, skin color, or parental privilege allows them opportunity to profit from the provocation and instruction of the written word.

The undermining of democracy in the United States is one "expense" that sensitive Americans can easily deplore because it represents a contradiction that endangers citizens of all political positions. The human price is not so obvious at first.   5

Since I first immersed myself within this work I have often had the following dream: I find that I am in a railroad station or a large department store within a city that is utterly unknown to me and where I cannot understand the printed words. None of the signs or symbols is familiar. Everything looks strange: like mirror writing of some kind. Gradually I understand that I am in the Soviet Union. All the letters on the walls around me are Cyrillic. I look for my pocket dictionary but I find that it has been mislaid. Where have I left it? Then I recall that I forgot to bring it with me when I packed my bags

---

[1]Basely dishonest. [Eds.]

in Boston. I struggle to remember the name of my hotel. I try to ask somebody for directions. One person stops and looks at me in a peculiar way. I lose the nerve to ask. At last I reach into my wallet for an ID card. The card is missing. Have I lost it? Then I remember that my card was confiscated for some reason, many years before. Around this point, I wake up in a panic.

This panic is not so different from the misery that millions of adult illiterates experience each day within the course of their routine existence in the U.S.A.

Illiterates cannot read the menu in a restaurant.

They cannot read the cost of items on the menu in the *window* of the restaurant before they enter.

10   Illiterates cannot read the letters that their children bring home from their teachers. They cannot study school department circulars that tell them of the courses that their children must be taking if they hope to pass the SAT exams. They cannot help with homework. They cannot write a letter to the teacher. They are afraid to visit in the classroom. They do not want to humiliate their child or themselves.

Illiterates cannot read instructions on a bottle of prescription medicine. They cannot find out when a medicine is past the year of safe consumption; nor can they read of allergenic risks, warnings to diabetics, or the potential sedative effect of certain kinds of nonprescription pills. They cannot observe preventive health care admonitions. They cannot read about "the seven warning signs of cancer" or the indications of blood-sugar fluctuations or the risks of eating certain foods that aggravate the likelihood of cardiac arrest.

Illiterates live, in more than literal ways, an uninsured existence. They cannot understand the written details on a health insurance form. They cannot read the waivers that they sign preceding surgical procedures. Several women I have known in Boston have entered a slum hospital with the intention of obtaining a tubal ligation and have emerged a few days later after having been subjected to a hysterectomy.[2] Unaware of their rights, incognizant of jargon, intimidated by the unfamiliar air of fear and atmosphere of ether that so many of us find oppressive in the confines even of the most attractive and expensive medical facilities, they have signed their names to documents they could not read and which nobody, in the hectic situation that prevails so often in those overcrowded hospitals that serve the urban poor, had even bothered to explain.

Childbirth might seem to be the last inalienable right of any female citizen within a civilized society. Illiterate mothers, as we shall see, already have been cheated of the power to protect their progeny

---

[2]A hysterectomy, the removal of the uterus, is a much more radical procedure than a tubal ligation, a method of sterilization that is a common form of birth control. [Eds.]

against the likelihood of demolition in deficient public schools and, as a result, against the verbal servitude within which they themselves exist. Surgical denial of the right to bear that child in the first place represents an ultimate denial, an unspeakable metaphor, a final darkness that denies even the twilight gleamings of our own humanity. What greater violation of our biological, our biblical, our spiritual humanity could possibly exist than that which takes place nightly, perhaps hourly these days, within such over-burdened and benighted institutions as the Boston City Hospital? Illiteracy has many costs; few are so irreversible as this.

Even the roof above one's head, the gas or other fuel for heating that protects the residents of northern city slums against the threat of illness in the winter months become uncertain guarantees. Illiterates cannot read the lease that they must sign to live in an apartment which, too often, they cannot afford. They cannot manage check accounts and therefore seldom pay for anything by mail. Hours and entire days of difficult travel (and the cost of bus or other public transit) must be added to the real cost of whatever they consume. Loss of interest on the check accounts they do not have, and could not manage if they did, must be regarded as another of the excess costs paid by the citizen who is excluded from the common instruments of commerce in a numerate society.

"I couldn't understand the bills," a woman in Washington, D.C., 15 reports, "and then I couldn't write the checks to pay them. We signed things we didn't know what they were."

Illiterates cannot read the notices that they receive from welfare offices or from the IRS. They must depend on word-of-mouth instruction from the welfare worker—or from other persons whom they have good reason to mistrust. They do not know what rights they have, what deadlines and requirements they face, what options they might choose to exercise. They are half-citizens. Their rights exist in print but not in fact.

Illiterates cannot look up numbers in a telephone directory. Even if they can find the names of friends, few possess the sorting skills to make use of the yellow pages; categories are bewildering and trade names are beyond decoding capabilities for millions of nonreaders. Even the emergency numbers listed on the first page of the phone book—"Ambulance," "Police," and "Fire"—are too frequently beyond the recognition of nonreaders.

Many illiterates cannot read the admonition on a pack of cigarettes. Neither the Surgeon General's warning nor its reproduction on the package can alert them to the risks. Although most people learn by word of mouth that smoking is related to a number of grave physical disorders, they do not get the chance to read the detailed stories which can document this danger with the vividness that turns concern into determination to resist. They can see the handsome cowboy or the slim Virginia lady lighting up a filter cigarette; they cannot heed the words that tell them that this product is (not "may be") dangerous to their health. Sixty million men and women are condemned to be the unalerted, high-risk candidates for cancer.

Illiterates do not buy "no-name" products in the supermarkets. They must depend on photographs or the familiar logos that are printed on the packages of brand-name groceries. The poorest people, therefore, are denied the benefits of the least costly products.

20   Illiterates depend almost entirely upon label recognition. Many labels, however, are not easy to distinguish. Dozens of different kinds of Campbell's soup appear identical to the nonreader. The purchaser who cannot read and does not dare to ask for help, out of the fear of being stigmatized (a fear which is unfortunately realistic), frequently comes home with something which she never wanted and her family never tasted.

Illiterates cannot read instructions on a pack of frozen food. Packages sometimes provide an illustration to explain the cooking preparations; but illustrations are of little help to someone who must "boil water, drop the food—*within* its plastic wrapper—in the boiling water, wait for it to simmer, instantly remove."

Even when labels are seemingly clear, they may be easily mistaken. A woman in Detroit brought home a gallon of Crisco for her children's dinner. She thought that she had bought the chicken that was pictured on the label. She had enough Crisco now to last a year—but no more money to go back and buy the food for dinner.

Recipes provided on the packages of certain staples sometimes tempt a semiliterate person to prepare a meal her children have not tasted. The longing to vary the uniform and often starchy content of low-budget meals provided to the family that relies on food stamps commonly leads to ruinous results. Scarce funds have been wasted and the food must be thrown out. The same applies to distribution of food-surplus produce in emergency conditions. Government inducements to poor people to "explore the ways" in which to make a tasty meal from tasteless noodles, surplus cheese, and powdered milk are useless to nonreaders. Intended as benevolent advice, such recommendations mock reality and foster deeper feelings of resentment and of inability to cope. (Those, on the other hand, who cautiously refrain from "innovative" recipes in preparation of their children's meals must suffer the opprobrium of "laziness," "lack of imagination. . . .")

Illiterates cannot travel freely. When they attempt to do so, they encounter risks that few of us can dream of. They cannot read traffic signs and, while they often learn to recognize and to decipher symbols, they cannot manage street names which they haven't seen before. The same is true for bus and subway stops. While ingenuity can sometimes help a man or woman to discern directions from familiar landmarks, buildings, cemeteries, churches, and the like, most illiterates are virtually immobilized. They seldom wander past the streets and neighborhoods they know. Geographical paralysis becomes a bitter metaphor for their entire existence. They are immobilized in almost every sense we can imagine. They can't move up. They can't move out. They cannot see beyond. Illiterates may take an oral test for drivers' permits in most sections of America. It is a questionable concession. Where will they go? How will they get there? How will they get home? Could it be that some of us might like it better if they stayed where they belong?

Travel is only one of many instances of circumscribed existence. 25 Choice, in almost all its facets, is diminished in the life of an illiterate adult. Even the printed TV schedule, which provides most people with the luxury of preselection, does not belong within the arsenal of options in illiterate existence. One consequence is that the viewer watches only what appears at moments when he happens to have time to turn the switch. Another consequence, a lot more common, is that the TV set remains in operation night and day. Whatever the program offered at the hour when he walks into the room will be the nutriment that he accepts and swallows. Thus, to passivity, is added frequency— indeed, almost uninterrupted continuity. Freedom to select is no more possible here than in the choice of home or surgery or food.

"You don't choose," said one illiterate woman. "You take your wishes from somebody else." Whether in perusal of a menu, selection of highways, purchase of groceries, or determination of affordable enjoyment, illiterate Americans must trust somebody else: a friend, a relative, a stranger on the street, a grocery clerk, a TV copywriter.

"All of our mail we get, it's hard for her to read. Settin' down and writing a letter, she can't do it. Like if we get a bill . . . we take it over to my sister-in-law . . . My sister-in-law reads it."

Billing agencies harass poor people for the payment of the bills for purchases that might have taken place six months before. Utility companies offer an agreement for a staggered payment schedule on a bill past due. "You have to trust them," one man said. Precisely for this reason, you end up by trusting no one and suspecting everyone of possible deceit. A submerged sense of distrust becomes the corollary to a constant need to trust. "They are cheating me . . . I have been tricked . . . I do not know . . ."

Not knowing: This is a familiar theme. Not knowing the right word for the right thing at the right time is one form of subjugation. Not knowing the world that lies concealed behind those words is a more terrifying feeling. The longitude and latitude of one's existence are beyond all easy apprehension. Even the hard, cold stars within the firmament above one's head begin to mock the possibilities for self-location. Where am I? Where did I come from? Where will I go?

30   "I've lost a lot of jobs," one man explains. "Today, even if you're a janitor, there's still reading and writing . . . They leave a note saying, 'Go to room so-and-so . . .' You can't do it. You can't read it. You don't know."

"The hardest thing about it is that I've been places where I didn't know where I was. You don't know where you are . . . You're lost."

"Like I said: I have two kids. What do I do if one of my kids starts choking? I go running to the phone . . . I can't look up the hospital phone number. That's if we're at home. Out on the street, I can't read the sign. I get to a pay phone. 'Okay, tell us where you are. We'll send an ambulance.' I look at the street sign. Right there, I can't tell you what it says. I'd have to spell it out, letter for letter. By that time, one of my kids would be dead . . . These are the kinds of fears you go with, every single day . . ."

"Reading directions, I suffer with. I work with chemicals . . . That's scary to begin with . . ."

"You sit down. They throw the menu in front of you. Where do you go from there? Nine times out of ten you say, 'Go ahead. Pick out something for the both of us.' I've eaten some weird things, let me tell you!"

35   Menus. Chemicals. A child choking while his mother searches for a word she does not know to find assistance that will come too late. Another mother speaks about the inability to help her kids to read: "I can't read to them. Of course that's leaving them out of something they should have. Oh, it matters. You *believe* it matters! I ordered all these books. The kids belong to a book club. Donny wanted me to read a book to him. I told Donny: 'I can't read,' He said: 'Mommy, you sit down. I'll read it to you.' I tried it one day, reading from the pictures. Donny looked at me. He said, 'Mommy, that's not right.' He's only five. He knew I couldn't read . . ."

A landlord tells a woman that her lease allows him to evict her if her baby cries and causes inconvenience to her neighbors. The consequence of challenging his words conveys a danger which appears, unlikely as it seems, even more alarming than the danger of eviction. Once she admits that she can't read, in the desire to maneuver for the time in which to call a friend, she will have defined herself in terms of an explicit impotence that she cannot endure. Capitulation in this case is preferable to self-humiliation. Resisting the definition of oneself in terms of what one cannot do, what others take for granted, represents a need so great that other imperatives (even one so urgent as the need to keep one's home in winter's cold) evaporate and fall away in face of fear. Even the loss of home and shelter, in this case, is not so terrifying as the loss of self.

"I come out of school. I was sixteen. They had their meetings. The directors meet. They said that I was wasting their school paper. I was wasting pencils . . ."

Another illiterate, looking back, believes she was not worthy of her teacher's time. She believes that it was wrong of her to take up space within her school. She believes that it was right to leave in order that somebody more deserving could receive her place.

Children choke. Their mother chokes another way: on more than chicken bones.

People eat what others order, know what others tell them, strug- 40 gle not to see themselves as they believe the world perceives them. A man in California speaks about his own loss of identity, of self-location, definition:

"I stood at the bottom of the ramp. My car had broke down on the freeway. There was a phone. I asked for the police. They was nice. They said to tell them where I was. I looked up at the signs. There was one that I had seen before. I read it to them: ONE WAY STREET. They thought it was a joke. I told them I couldn't read. There was other signs above the ramp. They told me to try. I looked around for somebody to help. All the cars was going by real fast. I couldn't make them understand that I was lost. The cop was nice. He told me: 'Try once more.' I did my best. I couldn't read. I only knew the sign above my head. The cop was trying to be nice. He knew that I was trapped. 'I can't send out a car to you if you can't tell me where you are.' I felt afraid. I nearly cried. I'm forty-eight years old. I only said: 'I'm on a one-way street . . .' "

The legal problems and the courtroom complications that confront illiterate adults have been discussed above. The anguish that may underlie such matters was brought home to me this year while I was working on this book. I have spoken, in the introduction, of a sudden phone call from one of my former students, now in prison for a criminal offense. Stephen is not a boy today. He is twenty-eight years old. He called to ask me to assist him in his trial, which comes up next fall. He will be on trial for murder. He has just knifed and killed a man who first enticed him to his home, then cheated him, and then insulted him—as "an illiterate subhuman."

Stephen now faces twenty years to life. Stephen's mother was illiterate. His grandparents were illiterate as well. What parental curse did not destroy was killed off finally by the schools. Silent violence is repaid with interest. It will cost us $25,000 yearly to maintain this broken soul in prison. But what is the price that has been paid by Stephen's victim? What is the price that will be paid by Stephen?

Perhaps we might slow down a moment here and look at the realities described above. This is the nation that we live in. This is a society that most of us did not create but which our President and other leaders have been willing to sustain by virtue of malign neglect. Do we possess the character and courage to address a problem which so many nations, poorer than our own, have found it natural to correct?

45   The answers to these questions represent a reasonable test of our belief in the democracy to which we have been asked in public school to swear allegiance.

Responding to Reading

1. According to Kozol, how does illiteracy undermine democracy in the United States? Do you agree with him?
2. Do you think Kozol accurately describes the difficulties illiterates face in their daily lives, or does he seem to be exaggerating? If you think he is exaggerating, what motive might he have?
3. Kozol concludes his essay by asking whether we as a nation have "the character and the courage to address" illiteracy (44). He does not, however, offer any concrete suggestions for doing so. Can you offer any suggestions?

Responding in Writing

Keep a log of your activities for a day. Then, write a few paragraphs discussing which of these activities you could and could not perform if you were illiterate.

PROPAGANDA UNDER A DICTATORSHIP

Aldous Huxley

1894–1963

Aldous Huxley was born in Surrey, England, and educated at Eton and Balliol College, Oxford. Despite a serious eye disease that forced him to read with a magnifying glass, Huxley graduated in 1915 with honors in English literature. Joining the staff of the Atheneum, *he wrote brilliant social and political satires and essays on architecture, science, music, history, philosophy, and religion. He came to the United States in the late 1930s and settled in California.* Brave New World *(1932), his best-known work, describes a sinister Utopia that depends on scientific breeding and conditioned happiness. Huxley's other books include* Eyeless in Gaza *(1936),* After Many a Summer *(1939),* Time Must Have a Stop *(1944),* Ape and Essence *(1948),* The Doors of Perception *(1954),* Heaven and Hell, *and* Island *(1962). In the following essay, from* Brave New World Revisited *(1958), Huxley shows how the manipulation of language in the propaganda of Nazi Germany conditioned the thoughts and behavior of the masses. To learn more about this author, visit some of the Huxley-inspired Web sites, such as http://www.huxley.net/ or http://somaweb.org/.*

At his trial after the Second World War, Hitler's Minister for Armaments, Albert Speer, delivered a long speech in which, with remarkable acuteness, he described the Nazi tyranny and analyzed its methods. "Hitler's dictatorship," he said, "differed in one fundamental point from all its predecessors in history. It was the first dictatorship in the present period of modern technical development, a dictatorship which made complete use of all technical means for the domination of its own country. Through technical devices like the radio and the loud-speaker, eighty million people were deprived of independent thought. It was thereby possible to subject them to the will of one man. . . . Earlier dictators needed highly qualified assistants even at the lowest level—men who could think and act independently. The totalitarian system in the period of modern technical development can dispense with such men; thanks to modern methods of communication, it is possible to mechanize the lower leadership. As a result of this there has arisen the new type of the uncritical recipient of orders."

In the Brave New World of my prophetic fable technology had advanced far beyond the point it had reached in Hitler's day; consequently the recipients of orders were far less critical than their Nazi counterparts, far more obedient to the order-giving elite. Moreover, they had been genetically standardized and postnatally conditioned to perform their subordinate functions, and could therefore be depended upon to behave almost as predictably as machines. . . . This conditioning of "the lower leadership" is already going on under the Communist dictatorships. The Chinese and the Russians are not relying merely on the indirect effects of advancing technology; they are working directly on the psychophysical organisms of their lower leaders, subjecting minds and bodies to a system of ruthless and, from all accounts, highly effective conditioning. "Many a man," said Speer, "has been haunted by the nightmare that one day nations might be dominated by technical means. That nightmare was almost realized in Hitler's totalitarian system." Almost, but not quite. The Nazis did not have time—and perhaps did not have the intelligence and the necessary knowledge—to brainwash and condition their lower leadership. This, it may be, is one of the reasons why they failed.

Since Hitler's day the armory of technical devices at the disposal of the would-be dictator has been considerably enlarged. As well as the radio, the loud-speaker, the moving picture camera and the rotary press, the contemporary propagandist can make use of television to broadcast the image as well as the voice of his client, and can record both image and voice on spools of magnetic tape. Thanks to technological progress, Big Brother can now be almost as omnipresent as God. Nor is it only on the technical front that the hand of the would-be dictator has been strengthened. Since Hitler's day a great deal of work has been carried out in those fields of applied psychology and neurology which are the special province of the propagandist, the indoctrinator and the brainwasher. In the past these specialists in the art of changing people's minds were empiricists. By a method of trial and error they had worked out a number of techniques and procedures, which they used very effectively without, however, knowing precisely why they were effective. Today the art of mind-control is in process of becoming a science. The practitioners of this science know what they are doing and why. They are guided in their work by theories and hypotheses solidly established on a massive foundation of experimental evidence. Thanks to the new insights and the new techniques made possible by these insights, the nightmare that was "all but realized in Hitler's totalitarian system" may soon be completely realizable.

But before we discuss these new insights and techniques let us take a look at the nightmare that so nearly came true in Nazi Germany. What were the methods used by Hitler and Goebbels[1] for "depriving eighty million people of independent thought and subjecting them to the will of one man"? And what was the theory of human nature upon which those terrifyingly successful methods were based? These questions can be answered, for the most part, in Hitler's own words. And what remarkably clear and astute words they are! When he writes about such vast abstractions as Race and History and Providence, Hitler is strictly unreadable. But when he writes about the German masses and the methods he used for dominating and directing them, his style changes. Nonsense gives place to sense, bombast to a hard-boiled and cynical lucidity. In his philosophical lucubrations Hitler was either cloudily daydreaming or reproducing other people's half-baked notions. In his comments on crowds and propaganda he was writing of things he knew by firsthand experience. In the words of his ablest biographer, Mr. Alan Bullock, "Hitler was the greatest demagogue in history." Those who add "only a demagogue," fail to appreciate the nature of political power in an age of mass politics. As he himself said, "To be a leader means to be able to move the masses." Hitler's aim was first to move the masses and then, having pried them loose from their traditional loyalties and moralities, to impose upon them (with the hypnotized consent of the majority) a new authoritarian order of his own devising. "Hitler," wrote Hermann Rauschning in 1939, "has a deep respect for the Catholic church and the Jesuit order; not because of their Christian doctrine, but because of the 'machinery' they have elaborated and controlled, their hierarchical system, their extremely clever tactics, their knowledge of

---

[1]*Joseph Paul Goebbels (1897–1945)*, the propaganda minister under Hitler. [Eds.]

human nature and their wise use of human weaknesses in ruling over believers." Ecclesiasticism without Christianity, the discipline of a monastic rule, not for God's sake or in order to achieve personal salvation, but for the sake of the State and for the greater glory and power of the demagogue turned Leader—this was the goal toward which the systematic moving of the masses was to lead.

Let us see what Hitler thought of the masses he moved and how he did the moving. The first principle from which he started was a value judgment: the masses are utterly contemptible. They are incapable of abstract thinking and uninterested in any fact outside the circle of their immediate experience. Their behavior is determined, not by knowledge and reason, but by feelings and unconscious drives. It is in these drives and feelings that "the roots of their positive as well as their negative attitudes are implanted." To be successful a propagandist must learn how to manipulate these instincts and emotions. "The driving force which has brought about the most tremendous revolutions on this earth has never been a body of scientific teaching which has gained power over the masses, but always a devotion which has inspired them, and often a kind of hysteria which has urged them into action. Whoever wishes to win over the masses must know the key that will open the door of their hearts." . . . In post-Freudian jargon, of their unconscious.

Hitler made his strongest appeal to those members of the lower middle classes who had been ruined by the inflation of 1923, and then ruined all over again by the depression of 1929 and the following years. "The masses" of whom he speaks were these bewildered, frustrated and chronically anxious millions. To make them more masslike, more homogeneously subhuman, he assembled them, by the thousands and the tens of thousands, in vast halls and arenas, where individuals could lose their personal identity, even their elementary humanity, and be merged with the crowd. A man or woman makes direct contact with society in two ways: as a member of some familial, professional or religious group, or as a member of a crowd. Groups are capable of being as moral and intelligent as the individuals who form them; a crowd is chaotic, has no purpose of its own and is capable of anything except intelligent action and realistic thinking. Assembled in a crowd, people lose their powers of reasoning and their capacity for moral choice. Their suggestibility is increased to the point where they cease to have any judgment or will of their own. They become very excitable, they lose all sense of individual or collective responsibility, they are subject to sudden accesses of rage, enthusiasm and panic. In a word, a man in a crowd behaves as though he had swallowed a large dose of some powerful intoxicant. He is a victim of what I have called "herd-poisoning." Like alcohol, herd-poison is an active, extraverted drug. The crowd-intoxicated individual escapes from responsibility, intelligence and morality into a kind of frantic, animal mindlessness.

During his long career as an agitator, Hitler had studied the effects of herd-poison and had learned how to exploit them for his own purposes. He had discovered that the orator can appeal to those "hidden forces" which motivate men's actions, much more effectively than can the writer. Reading is a private, not a collective activity. The writer speaks only to individuals, sitting by themselves in a state of normal sobriety. The orator speaks to masses of individuals, already well primed with herd-poison. They are at his mercy and, if he knows his business, he can do what he likes with them. As an orator, Hitler knew his business supremely well. He was able, in his own words, "to follow the lead of the great mass in such a way that from the living emotion to his hearers the apt word which he needed would be suggested to him and in its turn this would go straight to the heart of his hearers." Otto Strasser called him a "loud-speaker, proclaiming the most secret desires, the least admissible instincts, the sufferings and personal revolts of a whole nation." Twenty years before Madison Avenue embarked upon "Motivational Research," Hitler was systematically exploring and exploiting the secret fears and hopes, the cravings, anxieties and frustrations of the German masses. It is by manipulating "hidden forces" that the advertising experts induce us to buy their wares—a toothpaste, a brand of cigarettes, a political candidate. And it is by appealing to the same hidden forces—and to others too dangerous for Madison Avenue to meddle with—that Hitler induced the German masses to buy themselves a Fuehrer, an insane philosophy and the Second World War.

Unlike the masses, intellectuals have a taste for rationality and an interest in facts. Their critical habit of mind makes them resistant to the kind of propaganda that works so well on the majority. Among the masses "instinct is supreme, and from instinct comes faith. . . . While the healthy common folk instinctively close their ranks to form a community of the people" (under a Leader, it goes without saying) "intellectuals run this way and that, like hens in a poultry yard. With them one cannot make history; they cannot be used as elements composing a community." Intellectuals are the kind of people who demand evidence and are shocked by logical inconsistencies and fallacies. They regard oversimplification as the original sin of the mind and have no use for the slogans, the unqualified assertions and sweeping generalizations which are the propagandist's stock in trade. "All effective propaganda," Hitler wrote, "must be confined to a few bare necessities and then must be expressed in a few stereotyped formulas." These stereotyped formulas must be constantly repeated, for "only constant repetition will finally succeed in imprinting an idea upon the memory of a crowd." Philosophy teaches us to feel uncertain about the things that seem to us self-evident. Propaganda, on the other hand, teaches us to accept as self-evident matters about which it would be reasonable to suspend our judgment or to feel doubt. The aim of the demagogue is to create social coherence under his own leadership. But, as Bertrand Russell has pointed out, "systems of dogma without empirical foundations, such as scholasticism, Marxism and fascism, have the advantage of producing a great deal of social coherence among their disciples." The demagogic propagandist must therefore be consistently dogmatic. All his statements are made without qualification. There are no grays in his picture of the world; everything is either diabolically black or celestially white. In Hitler's words, the propagandist should adopt "a systematically one-sided attitude towards every problem that has to be dealt with." He must never admit that he might be wrong or that people with a different point of view might be even partially right. Opponents should not be argued with; they should be attacked, shouted down, or, if they become too much of a nuisance, liquidated. The morally squeamish intellectual may be shocked by this kind of thing. But the masses are always convinced that "right is on the side of the active aggressor."

Such, then, was Hitler's opinion of humanity in the mass. It was a very low opinion. Was it also an incorrect opinion? The tree is known by its fruits, and a theory of human nature which inspired the kind of techniques that proved so horribly effective must contain at least an element of truth. Virtue and intelligence belong to human beings as individuals freely associating with other individuals in small groups. So do sin—and stupidity. But the subhuman mindlessness to which the demagogue makes his appeal, the moral imbecility on which he relies when he goads his victims into action, are characteristic not of men and women as individuals, but of men and women in masses. Mindlessness and moral idiocy are not characteristically human attributes; they are symptoms of herd-poisoning. In all the world's higher religions, salvation and enlightenment are for individuals. The kingdom of heaven is within the mind of a person, not within the collective mindlessness of a crowd. Christ promised to be present where two or three are gathered together. He did not say anything about being present where thousands are intoxicating one another with herd-poison. Under the Nazis enormous numbers of people were compelled to spend an enormous amount of time marching in serried ranks from point A to point B and back again to point A. "This keeping of the whole population on the march seemed to be a senseless waste of time and energy. Only much later," adds Hermann Rauschning, "was there revealed in it a subtle intention based on a well-judged adjustment of ends and means. Marching diverts men's thoughts. Marching kills thought. Marching makes an end of individuality. Marching is the indispensable magic stroke performed in order to accustom the people to a mechanical, quasi-ritualistic activity until it becomes second nature."

10   From his point of view and at the level where he had chosen to do his dreadful work, Hitler was perfectly correct in his estimate of human nature. To those of us who look at men and women as individuals rather than as members of crowds, or of regimented collectives, he seems hideously wrong. In an age of accelerating over-population, of accelerating over-organization and even more efficient means of mass communication, how can we preserve the integrity and reassert the value of the human individual? This is a question that can still be asked and perhaps effectively answered. A generation from now it may be too late to find an answer and perhaps impossible, in the stifling collective climate of that future time, even to ask the question.

Responding to Reading

1. According to Huxley, why was Hitler's dictatorship different from its predecessors? What techniques did Hitler use to manipulate the German people? Why do you think he was so successful?
2. What was Hitler's opinion of the masses? Does Huxley agree with this evaluation?
3. In paragraph 3, Huxley says, "Since Hitler's day the armory of technical devices at the disposal of the would-be dictator has been considerably enlarged." What are some of these devices, and how have they made a dictator's job easier?

Responding in Writing

Do you think the existence of the Internet makes it easier or more difficult for a dictator to control the masses?

POLITICS AND THE ENGLISH LANGUAGE

George Orwell

1903–1950

George Orwell was born Eric Arthur Blair in Bengal, India, the son of a British colonial civil servant, and attended school in England, graduating from Eton College (1921). He joined the Indian Imperial Police in Burma, where he came to question the British methods of colonialism. (See "Shooting an Elephant" in Chapter 10.) An enemy of totalitarianism in any form and a spokesperson for the oppressed, Orwell criticized totalitarian regimes in his bitterly satirical novels Animal Farm *(1945) and* 1984 *(1949). He wrote many literary essays and is much admired for his lucid prose style. Much of his nonfiction prose is collected in the four-volume* Collected Essays, Journalism and Letters of George Orwell *(1968). The following essay was written during the period between the publication of* Animal Farm *and* 1984, *at the end of World War II, when jingoistic praise for "our democratic institutions" and blindly passionate defenses of Marxist ideology were the two common extremes of public political discourse. Orwell's plea for clear thinking and writing at a time when "political language . . . [was] designed to make lies sound truthful and murder respectable, and to give an appearance of solidity to pure wind" is as relevant today as it was when it was written. To learn more about this writer, visit some of the Orwell-inspired Web sites, such as http://www.k-1.com/Orwell/ and http://www.resort.com/~prime8/Orwell/.*

Most people who bother with the matter at all would admit that the English language is in a bad way, but it is generally assumed that we cannot by conscious action do anything about it. Our civilization is decadent and our language—so the argument runs—must inevitably share in the general collapse. It follows that any struggle against the abuse of language is a sentimental archaism, like preferring candles to electric light or hansom cabs to airplanes. Underneath this lies the half-conscious belief that language is a natural growth and not an instrument which we shape for our own purposes.

Now, it is clear that the decline of a language must ultimately have political and economic causes: it is not due simply to the bad influence of this or that individual writer. But an effect can become a cause, reinforcing the original cause and producing the same effect in an intensified form, and so on indefinitely. A man may take to drink because he feels himself to be a failure, and then fail all the more completely because he drinks. It is rather the same thing that is happening to the English language. It becomes ugly and inaccurate because our thoughts are foolish, but the slovenliness of our language makes it easier for us to have foolish thoughts. The point is that the process is reversible. Modern English, especially written English, is full of bad habits which spread by imitation and which can be avoided if one is willing to take the necessary trouble. If one gets rid of these habits one can think more clearly, and to think clearly is a necessary first step towards political regeneration: so that the fight against bad English is not frivolous and is not the exclusive concern of professional writers. I will come back to this presently, and I hope that by that time the meaning of what I have said here will have become clearer. Meanwhile, here are five specimens of the English language as it is now habitually written.

These five passages have not been picked out because they are especially bad—I could have quoted far worse if I had chosen—but because they illustrate various of the mental vices from which we now suffer.

They are a little below the average, but are fairly representative samples. I number them so that I can refer back to them when necessary:

"(1) I am not, indeed, sure whether it is not true to say that the Milton who once seemed not unlike a seventeenth-century Shelley had not become, out of an experience ever more bitter in each year, more alien (*sic*) to the founder of that Jesuit sect which nothing could induce him to tolerate."

Professor Harold Laski (Essay in *Freedom of Expression*).

"(2) Above all, we cannot play ducks and drakes with a native battery of idioms which prescribes such egregious collocations of vocables as the Basic *put up with* for *tolerate* or *put at a loss* for *bewilder*."

Professor Lancelot Hogben (*Interglossa*).

"(3) On the one side we have the free personality: by definition it is not neurotic, for it has neither conflict nor dream. Its desires, such as they are, are transparent, for they are just what institutional approval keeps in the forefront of consciousness; another institutional pattern would alter their number and intensity; there is little in them that is natural, irreducible, or culturally dangerous. But *on the other side*, the social bond itself is nothing but the mutual reflection of these self-secure integrities. Recall the definition of love. Is not this the very picture of a small academic? Where is there a place in this hall of mirrors for either personality or fraternity?"

Essay on psychology in *Politics* (New York).

"(4) All the 'best people' from the gentlemen's clubs, and all the frantic fascist captains, united in common hatred of Socialism and bestial horror of the rising tide of the mass revolutionary movement, have turned to acts of provocation, to foul incendiarism, to medieval legends of poisoned wells, to legalize their own destruction of proletarian organizations, and rouse the agitated petty-bourgeoisie to chauvinistic fervor on behalf of the fight against the revolutionary way out of the crisis."

Communist pamphlet.

"(5) If a new spirit *is* to be infused into this old country, there is one thorny and contentious reform which must be tackled, and that is the humanization and galvanization of the B.B.C. Timidity here will bespeak cancer and atrophy of the soul. The heart of Britain may be sound and of strong beat, for instance, but the British lion's roar at present is like that of Bottom in Shakespeare's *Midsummer Night's Dream*—as gentle as any sucking dove. A virile new Britain cannot continue indefinitely to be traduced in the eyes, or rather ears, of the world by the effete languors of Langham Place, brazenly masquerading as 'standard English.' When the Voice of Britain is heard at nine o'clock, better far and infinitely less ludicrous to hear aitches honestly dropped than the present priggish, inflated, inhibited, school-ma'amish arch braying of blameless bashful mewing maidens!"

Letter in Tribune.

Each of these passages has faults of its own, but, quite apart from avoidable ugliness, two qualities are common to all of them. The first is staleness of imagery: the other is lack of precision. The writer either has a meaning and cannot express it, or he inadvertently says something else, or he is almost indifferent as to whether his words mean anything or not. This mixture of vagueness and sheer incompetence is the most marked characteristic of modern English prose, and especially of any kind of political writing. As soon as certain topics are raised, the concrete melts into the abstract and no one seems able to think of turns of speech that are not hackneyed: prose consists less and less of *words* chosen for the sake of their meaning, and more and more of *phrases* tacked together like the sections of a prefabricated henhouse. I list below, with notes and examples, various of the tricks by means of which the work of prose-construction is habitually dodged:

Dying Metaphors

A newly invented metaphor assists thought by evoking a visual image, while on the other hand a metaphor which is technically "dead" (e.g. *iron resolution*) has in effect reverted to being an ordinary word and can generally be used without loss of vividness. But in between these two classes there is a huge dump of worn-out metaphors which have lost all evocative power and are merely used because they save people the trouble of inventing phrases for themselves. Examples are: *Ring the changes on, take up the cudgels for, toe the line, ride roughshod over, stand shoulder to shoulder with, play into the hands of, no axe to grind, grist to the mill, fishing in troubled waters, on the order of the day, Achilles' heel, swan song, hotbed.* Many of these are used without knowledge of their meaning (what is a "rift,"[1] for instance?), and incompatible metaphors are frequently mixed, a sure sign that the writer is not interested in what he is saying. Some metaphors now current have been twisted out of their original meaning without those who use them even being aware of the fact. For example, *toe the line* is sometimes written *tow the line*. Another example is the *hammer and the anvil*, now always used with the implication that the anvil gets the worst of it. In real life it is always the anvil that breaks the hammer, never the other way about: a writer who stopped to think what he was saying would be aware of this, and would avoid perverting the original phrase.

---

[1]Originally *rift* referred to a geological fault or fissure. Now it is commonly used to indicate a breach or estrangement. [Eds.]

Operators or Verbal False Limbs

These save the trouble of picking out appropriate verbs and nouns, and at the same time pad each sentence with extra syllables which give it an appearance of symmetry. Characteristic phrases are: *render inoperative, militate against, make contact with, be subjected to, give rise to, give grounds for, have the effect of, play a leading part (role) in, make itself felt, take effect, exhibit a tendency to, serve the purpose of, etc., etc.* The keynote is the elimination of simple verbs. Instead of being a single word, such as *break, stop, spoil, mend, kill,* a verb becomes a *phrase,* made up of a noun or adjective tacked on to some general-purposes verb such as *prove, serve, form, play, render.* In addition, the passive voice is wherever possible used in preference to the active, and noun constructions are used instead of gerunds (*by examination of* instead of *by examining*). The range of verbs is further cut down by means of the *-ize* and *de-* formation, and the banal statements are given an appearance of profundity by means of the *not un-* formation. Simple conjunctions and prepositions are replaced by such phrases as *with respect to, having regard to, the fact that, by dint of, in view of, in the interests of, on the hypothesis that;* and the ends of sentences are saved from anticlimax by such resounding commonplaces as *greatly to be desired, cannot be left out of account, a development to be expected in the near future, deserving of serious consideration, brought to a satisfactory conclusion,* and so on and so forth.

Pretentious Diction

Words like *phenomenon, element, individual* (as noun), *objective, categorical, effective, virtual, basic, primary, promote, constitute, exhibit, exploit, utilize, eliminate, liquidate,* are used to dress up simple statements and give an air of scientific impartiality to biased judgments. Adjectives like *epoch-making, epic, historic, unforgettable, triumphant, age-old, inevitable, inexorable, veritable,* are used to dignify the sordid processes of international politics, while writing that aims at glorifying war usually takes on an archaic color, its characteristic words being: *realm, throne, chariot, mailed fist, trident, sword, shield, buckler, banner, jackboot, clarion.* Foreign words and expressions such as *cul de sac, ancien régime, deus ex machina, mutatis mutandis, status quo, gleichschaltung, weltanschauung,* are used to give an air of culture and elegance. Except for the useful abbreviations *i.e., e.g.,* and *etc.,* there is no real need for any of the hundreds of foreign phrases now current in English. Bad writers, and especially scientific, political and sociological writers, are nearly always haunted by the notion that Latin or Greek words are grander than Saxon ones, and unnecessary words like *expedite, ameliorate, predict, extraneous, deracinated, clandestine, subaqueous* and hundreds of others constantly gain ground from their Anglo-Saxon opposite numbers.[2] The jargon peculiar to Marxist writing (*hyena, hangman, cannibal, petty bourgeois, these gentry, lacquey, flunkey, mad dog, White Guard*, etc.) consists largely of words and phrases translated from Russian, German or French; but the normal way of coining a new word is to use a Latin or Greek root with the appropriate affix and, where necessary, the *-ize* formation. It is often easier to make up words of this kind (*deregionalize, impermissible, extra-marital, nonfragmentatory* and so forth) than to think up the English words that will cover one's meaning. The result, in general, is an increase in slovenliness and vagueness.

Meaningless Words

In certain kinds of writing, particularly in art criticism and literary criticism, it is normal to come across long passages which are almost completely lacking in meaning.[3] Words like *romantic, plastic, values, human, dead, sentimental, natural, vitality*, as used in art criticism, are strictly meaningless in the sense that they not only do not point to any discoverable object, but are hardly ever expected to do so by the reader. When one critic writes, "The outstanding feature of Mr. X's work is its living quality," while another writes, "The immediately striking thing about Mr. X's work is its peculiar deadness," the reader accepts this as a simple difference of opinion. If words like *black* and *white* were involved, instead of the jargon words *dead* and *living*, he would see at once that language was being used in an improper way. Many political words are similarly abused. The word *Fascism* has now no meaning except in so far as it signifies "something not desirable." The words *democracy, socialism, freedom, patriotic, realistic, justice*, have each of them several different meanings which cannot be reconciled with one another. In the case of a word like *democracy*, not only is there no agreed definition, but the attempt to make one is resisted from all sides. It is almost universally felt that when we call a country democratic we are praising it: consequently the defenders of every kind of regime claim that it is a democracy, and fear that they might have to stop using the word if it were tied down to any one meaning.

---

[2]An interesting illustration of this is the way in which the English flower names which were in use till very recently are being ousted by Greek ones, *snapdragon* becoming *antirrhinum, forget-me-not* becoming *myosotis*, etc. It is hard to see any practical reason for this change in fashion: it is probably due to an instinctive turning-away from the more homely word and a vague feeling that the Greek word is scientific.

[3]Example: "Comfort's catholicity of perception and image, strangely Whitmanesque in range, almost the exact opposite in aesthetic compulsion, continues to evoke that trembling atmospheric accumulative hinting at a cruel, an inexorably serene timelessness. . . . Wrey Gardiner scores by aiming at simple bull's-eyes with precision. Only they are not so simple, and through this contended sadness—runs more than the surface bittersweet of resignation" (*Poetry Quarterly*).

Words of this kind are often used in a consciously dishonest way. That is, the person who uses them has his own private definition, but allows his hearer to think he means something quite different. Statements like *Marshal Pétain was a true patriot, The Soviet Press is the freest in the world, The Catholic Church is opposed to persecution,* are almost always made with intent to deceive. Other words used in variable meanings, in most cases more or less dishonestly, are: *class, totalitarian, science, progressive, reactionary, bourgeois, equality.*

Now that I have made this catalogue of swindles and perversions, let me give another example of the kind of writing that they lead to. This time it must of its nature be an imaginary one. I am going to translate a passage of good English into modern English of the worst sort. Here is a well-known verse from *Ecclesiastes:*

> "I returned and saw under the sun, that the race is not to the swift, nor the battle to the strong, neither yet bread to the wise, nor yet riches to men of understanding, nor yet favor to men of skill; but time and chance happeneth to them all."

10   Here it is in modern English:

> "Objective consideration of contemporary phenomena compels the conclusion that success or failure in competitive activities exhibits no tendency to be commensurate with innate capacity, but that a considerable element of the unpredictable must invariably be taken into account."

This is a parody, but not a very gross one. Exhibit (3), above, for instance, contains several patches of the same kind of English. It will be seen that I have not made a full translation. The beginning and ending of the sentence follow the original meaning fairly closely, but in the middle the concrete illustrations—race, battle, bread—dissolve into the vague phrase "success or failure in competitive activities." This had to be so, because no modern writer of the kind I am discussing—no one capable of using phrases like "objective consideration of contemporary phenomena"—would ever tabulate his thoughts in that precise and detailed way. The whole tendency of modern prose is away from concreteness. Now analyze these two sentences a little more closely. The first contains forty-nine words but only sixty syllables, and all its words are those of everyday life. The second contains thirty-eight words of ninety syllables: eighteen of its words are from Latin roots, and one from Greek. The first sentence contains six vivid images, and only one phrase ("time and chance") that could be called vague. The second contains not a single fresh, arresting phrase, and in spite of its ninety syllables it gives only a shortened version of the meaning contained in the first. Yet without a doubt it is the second kind of sentence that is gaining ground in modern English. I do not want to exaggerate. This kind of writing is not yet universal, and outcrops of simplicity will occur here and there in the worst-written page. Still, if you or I were told to write a few lines on the uncertainty of human fortunes, we should probably come much nearer to my imaginary sentence than to the one from *Ecclesiastes*.

As I have tried to show, modern writing at its worst does not consist in picking out words for the sake of their meaning and inventing images in order to make the meaning clearer. It consists in gumming together long strips of words which have already been set in order by someone else, and making the results presentable by sheer humbug. The attraction of this way of writing is that it is easy. It is easier—even quicker, once you have the habit—to say *In my opinion it is a not unjustifiable assumption that* than to say *I think*. If you use ready-made phrases, you not only don't have to hunt about for words; you also don't have to bother with the rhythms of your sentences, since these phrases are generally so arranged as to be more or less euphonious. When you are composing in a hurry—when you are dictating to a stenographer, for instance, or making a public speech—it is natural to fall into a pretentious, Latinized style. Tags like *a consideration which we should do well to bear in mind* or *a conclusion to which all of us would readily assent* will save many a sentence from coming down with a bump. By using stale metaphors, similes and idioms, you save much mental effort, at the cost of leaving your meaning vague, not only for your reader but for yourself. This is the significance of mixed metaphors. The sole aim of a metaphor is to call up a visual image. When these images clash—as in *The Fascist octopus has sung its swan song, the jackboot is thrown into the melting pot*—it can be taken as certain that the writer is not seeing a mental image of the objects he is naming; in other words he is not really thinking. Look again at the examples I gave at the beginning of this essay. Professor Laski (1) uses five negatives in fifty-three words. One of these is superfluous, making nonsense of the whole passage, and in addition there is the slip *alien* for *akin*, making further nonsense, and several avoidable pieces of clumsiness which increase the general vagueness. Professor Hogben (2) plays ducks and drakes with a battery which is able to write prescriptions, and, while disapproving of the everyday phrase *put up with*, is unwilling to look *egregious* up in the dictionary and see what it means. (3), if one takes an uncharitable attitude towards it, is simply meaningless: probably one could work out its intended meaning by reading the whole of the article in which it occurs. In (4), the writer knows more or less what he wants to say, but an accumulation of stale phrases chokes him like tea leaves blocking a sink. In (5), words and meaning have almost parted company. People who write in this manner usually have a general emotional meaning—they dislike one thing and want to express solidarity with another—but they are not interested in the detail of what they are saying. A scrupulous writer, in every sentence that he writes, will ask himself at least four questions, thus: What am I trying to say? What words will express it? What image or idiom will make it clearer? Is this image fresh enough to have an effect? And he will probably ask himself two more: Could I put it more shortly? Have I said anything that is avoidably ugly? But you are not obliged to go to all this trouble. You can shirk it by simply throwing your mind open and letting the ready-made phrases come crowding in. They will construct your sentences for you—even think your thoughts for you, to a certain extent—and at need they will perform the important service of partially concealing your meaning even from yourself. It is at this point that the special connection between politics and the debasement of language becomes clear.

In our time it is broadly true that political writing is bad writing. Where it is not true, it will generally be found that the writer is some kind of rebel, expressing his private opinions and not a "party line." Orthodoxy, of whatever color, seems to demand a lifeless, imitative style. The political dialects to be found in pamphlets, leading articles, manifestos, White Papers and the speeches of under-secretaries do, of course, vary from party to party, but they are all alike in that one almost never finds in them a fresh, vivid, home-made turn of speech. When one watches some tired hack on the platform mechanically repeating the familiar phrases—*bestial atrocities, iron heel, bloodstained tyranny, free peoples of the world, stand shoulder to shoulder*—one often has a curious feeling that one is not watching a live human being but some kind of dummy: a feeling which suddenly becomes stronger at moments when the light catches the speaker's spectacles and turns them into blank discs which seem to have no eyes behind them. And this is not altogether fanciful. A speaker who uses that kind of phraseology has gone some distance towards turning himself into a machine. The appropriate noises are coming out of his larynx, but his brain is not involved as it would be if he were choosing his words for himself. If the speech he is making is one that he is accustomed to make over and over again, he may be almost unconscious of what he is saying, as one is when one utters the responses in church. And this reduced state of consciousness, if not indispensable, is at any rate favorable to political conformity.

In our time, political speech and writing are largely the defense of the indefensible. Things like the continuance of British rule in India, the Russian purges and deportations, the dropping of the atom bombs on Japan, can indeed be defended, but only by arguments which are too brutal for most people to face, and which do not square with the professed aims of political parties. Thus political language has to consist largely of euphemism, question-begging and sheer cloudy vagueness. Defenseless villages are bombarded from the air, the inhabitants driven out into the countryside, the cattle machine-gunned, the huts set on fire with incendiary bullets: this is called *pacification*. Millions of peasants are robbed of their farms and sent trudging along the roads with no more than they can carry: this is called *transfer of population* or *rectification of frontiers*. People are imprisoned for years without trial, or shot in the back of the neck or sent to die of scurvy in Arctic lumber camps: this is called *elimination of unreliable elements*. Such phraseology is needed if one wants to name things without calling up mental pictures of them. Consider for instance some comfortable English professor defending Russian totalitarianism. He cannot say outright, "I believe in killing off your opponents when you can get good results by doing so." Probably, therefore, he will say something like this:

"While freely conceding that the Soviet régime exhibits certain features which the humanitarian may be inclined to deplore, we must, I think, agree that a certain curtailment of the right to political opposition is an unavoidable concomitant of transitional periods, and that the rigors which the Russian people have been called upon to undergo have been amply justified in the sphere of concrete achievement." 15

The inflated style is itself a kind of euphemism. A mass of Latin words falls upon the facts like soft snow, blurring the outlines and covering up all the details. The great enemy of clear language is insincerity. When there is a gap between one's real and one's declared aims, one turns as it were instinctively to long words and exhausted idioms, like a cuttlefish squirting out ink. In our age there is no such thing as "keeping out of politics." All issues are political issues, and politics itself is a mass of lies, evasions, folly, hatred and schizophrenia. When the general atmosphere is bad, language must suffer. I should expect to find—this is a guess which I have not sufficient knowledge to verify—that the German, Russian and Italian languages have all deteriorated in the last ten to fifteen years, as a result of dictatorship.

But if thought corrupts language, language can also corrupt thought. A bad usage can spread by tradition and imitation, even among people who should and do know better. The debased language that I have been discussing is in some ways very convenient. Phrases like *a not unjustifiable assumption, leaves much to be desired, would serve no good purpose, a consideration which we should do well to bear in mind*, are a continuous temptation, a packet of aspirins always at one's elbow. Look back through this essay, and for certain you will find that I have again and again committed the very faults I am protesting against. By this morning's post I have received a pamphlet dealing with conditions in Germany. The author tells me that he "felt impelled" to write it. I open it at random, and here is almost the first sentence that I see:

"(The Allies) have an opportunity not only of achieving a radical transformation of Germany's social and political structure in such a way as to avoid a nationalistic reaction in Germany itself, but at the same time of laying the foundations of a cooperative and unified Europe." You see, he "feels impelled" to write—feels, presumably, that he has something new to say—and yet his words, like cavalry horses answering the bugle, group themselves automatically into the familiar dreary pattern. This invasion of one's mind by ready-made phrases (*lay the foundations, achieve a radical transformation*) can only be prevented if one is constantly on guard against them, and every such phrase anesthetizes a portion of one's brain.

I said earlier that the decadence of our language is probably curable. Those who deny this would argue, if they produced an argument at all, that language merely reflects existing social conditions, and that we cannot influence its development by any direct tinkering with words and constructions. So far as the general tone or spirit of a language goes, this may be true, but it is not true in detail. Silly words and expressions have often disappeared, not through any evolutionary process but owing to the conscious action of a minority. Two recent examples were *explore every avenue* and *leave no stone unturned*, which were killed by the jeers of a few journalists. There is a long list of flyblown metaphors which could similarly be got rid of if enough people would interest themselves in the job; and it should also be possible to laugh the *not un-* formation out of existence,[4] to reduce the amount of Latin and Greek in the average sentence, to drive out foreign phrases and strayed scientific words, and, in general, to make pretentiousness unfashionable. But all these are minor points. The defense of the English language implies more than this, and perhaps it is best to start by saying what it does *not* imply.

To begin with it has nothing to do with archaism, with the salvaging of obsolete words and turns of speech, or with the setting up of a "standard English" which must never be departed from. On the contrary, it is especially concerned with the scrapping of every word or idiom which has outworn its usefulness. It has nothing to do with correct grammar and syntax, which are of no importance so long as one makes one's meaning clear, or with the avoidance of Americanisms, or with having what is called a "good prose style." On the other hand it is not concerned with fake simplicity and the attempt to make written English colloquial. Nor does it even imply in every case preferring the Saxon word to the Latin one, though it does imply using the fewest and shortest words that will cover one's meaning. What is above all needed is to let the meaning choose the word and not the

---

[4]One can cure oneself of the *not un-* formation by memorizing this sentence: *A not unblack dog was chasing a not unsmall rabbit across a not ungreen field.*

other way about. In prose, the worst thing one can do with words is to surrender to them. When you think of a concrete object, you think wordlessly, and then, if you want to describe the thing you have been visualizing you probably hunt about till you find the exact words that seem to fit. When you think of something abstract you are more inclined to use words from the start, and unless you make a conscious effort to prevent it, the existing dialect will come rushing in and do the job for you, at the expense of blurring or even changing your meaning. Probably it is better to put off using words as long as possible and get one's meaning as clear as one can through pictures or sensations. Afterwards one can choose—not simply accept—the phrases that will best cover the meaning, and then switch round and decide what impression one's words are likely to make on another person. This last effort of the mind cuts out all stale or mixed images, all prefabricated phrases, needless repetitions, and humbug and vagueness generally. But one can often be in doubt about the effect of a word or a phrase, and one needs rules that one can rely on when instinct fails. I think the following rules will cover most cases:

(i)   Never use a metaphor, simile or other figure of speech which you are used to seeing in print.

(ii) Never use a long word where a short one will do.

(iii) If it is possible to cut a word out, always cut it out.

(iv) Never use the passive where you can use the active.

(v)   Never use a foreign phrase, a scientific word, or a jargon word if you can think of an everyday English equivalent.

(vi) Break any of these rules sooner than say anything outright barbarous.

These rules sound elementary, and so they are, but they demand a 20 deep change of attitude in anyone who has grown used to writing in the style now fashionable. One could keep all of them and still write bad English, but one could not write the kind of stuff that I quoted in those five specimens at the beginning of this article.

I have not here been considering the literary use of language, but merely language as an instrument for expressing and not for concealing or preventing thought. Stuart Chase[5] and others have come near to claiming that all abstract words are meaningless, and have used this as a pretext for advocating a kind of political quietism. Since you don't know what Fascism is, how can you struggle against Fascism? One need not swallow such absurdities as this, but one ought to recognize that the present political chaos is connected with the decay of language, and that one can probably bring about some improvement

---

[5] Author known for his advocacy of clear writing and clear thinking. [Eds.]

by starting at the verbal end. If you simplify your English, you are freed from the worst follies of orthodoxy. You cannot speak any of the necessary dialects, and when you make a stupid remark its stupidity will be obvious, even to yourself. Political language—and with variations this is true of all political parties, from Conservatives to Anarchists—is designed to make lies sound truthful and murder respectable, and to give an appearance of solidity to pure wind. One cannot change this all in a moment, but one can at least change one's own habits, and from time to time one can even, if one jeers loudly enough, send some worn-out and useless phrase, some *jackboot, Achilles' heel, hotbed, melting pot, acid test, veritable inferno* or other lump of verbal refuse—into the dustbin where it belongs.

Responding to Reading

1. According to Orwell, what is the relationship between politics and the English language?
2. What does Orwell mean in paragraph 14 when he says, "In our time, political speech and writing are largely the defense of the indefensible"? Do you believe his statement applies to current political speech and writing as well?
3. Locate some examples of dying metaphors used in the popular press. Do you agree with Orwell that they undermine clear thought and expression? Why or why not?

Responding in Writing

As you listen to the local news on TV, write down several sentences that contain words and phrases that are vague, repetitious, or meaningless. Then, substitute your own clearer, more explicit words for the ones you identified.

Focus

How Free Should Free Speech Be?

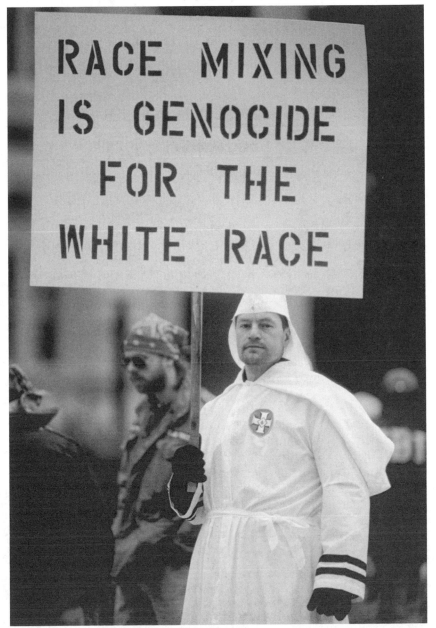

Ku Klux Klan member carrying sign outside Capitol building, Washington, DC.

Responding to the Image

1. The image on page 239 depicts a Ku Klux Klan member in full regalia, looking directly at the camera. Which do you find more disturbing, the man or the sign he is holding? Explain.

2. The Supreme Court has repeatedly affirmed the right of groups such as the Ku Klux Klan to express their views in public—for example, in protest marches or in parades. Do you agree with this position? Given the nature of their message, what limitations (if any) do you think should be placed on such hate groups?

THE FREE-SPEECH FOLLIES

Stanley Fish

1939–

Born in Providence, Rhode Island, Stanley Fish is a scholar known for his writings about the relationship between the reader and a literary text. Fish, who received a BA degree from the University of Pennsylvania (1959) and a PhD in English literature from Yale (1962), has taught at the University of California at Berkeley, Johns Hopkins University, and Duke University. Since 1999, Fish has been a college dean at the University of Illinois at Chicago. He is known as a provocative and original thinker, with expertise in English literature, law, and literary theory. His books include There's No Such Thing as Free Speech, and It's a Good Thing, Too *(1994),* Professional Correctness: Literary Studies and Political Change *(1995),* The Stanley Fish Reader *(1999), and* How Milton Works *(2001). To read more essays by and about Fish, visit the Web site of Kyösti Niemelä at the University of Helsinki, http://www.mv.helsinki.fi/home/kniemela/ fish.htm.*

The modern American version of crying wolf is crying First Amendment. If you want to burn a cross on a black family's lawn or buy an election by contributing millions to a candidate or vilify Jerry Falwell and his mother in a scurrilous "parody," and someone or some government agency tries to stop you, just yell "First Amendment rights" and you will stand a good chance of getting to do what you want to do.

In the academy, the case is even worse: Not only is the First Amendment pressed into service at the drop of a hat (especially whenever anyone is disciplined for anything), it is invoked ritually when there are no First Amendment issues in sight.

Take the case of the editors of college newspapers who will always cry First Amendment when something they've published turns out to be the cause of outrage and controversy. These days the of-fending piece or editorial or advertisement usually involves (what is at least perceived to be) an attack on Jews. In January of this year, the *Daily Illini*, a student newspaper at the University of Illinois at Urbana-Champaign, printed a letter from a resident of Seattle with no university affiliation. The letter ran under the headline "Jews Ma-nipulate America" and argued that because their true allegiance is to the state of Israel, the president should "separate Jews from all gov-ernment advisory positions"; otherwise, the writer warned, "the Jews might face another Holocaust."

When the predictable firestorm of outrage erupted, the newspa-per's editor responded by declaring, first, that "we are committed to giving all people a voice"; second, that, given this commitment, "we print the opinions of others with whom we do not agree"; third, that to do otherwise would involve the newspaper in the dangerous acts of "silencing" and "self-censorship"; and, fourth, that "what is hate speech to one member of a society is free speech to another."

Wrong four times.   5

I'll bet the *Daily Illini* is not committed to giving all people a voice—the KKK? man-boy love? advocates of slavery? would-be Un-abombers? Nor do I believe that the editors sift through submissions looking for the ones they disagree with and then print those. No doubt they apply some principles of selection, asking questions like, Is it rele-vant, or Is it timely, or Does it get the facts right, or Does it present a co-herent argument?

That is, they exercise judgment, which is quite a different thing from silencing or self-censorship. No one is silenced because a single outlet declines to publish him; silencing occurs when that outlet (or any other) is forbidden by the state to publish him on pain of legal action; and that is also what censorship is.

As for self-censoring, if it is anything, it is what we all do whenever we decide it would be better not to say something or cut a sentence that went just a little bit too far or leave a manuscript in the bottom drawer because it is not yet ready. Self-censorship, in short, is not a crime or a moral failing; it is a responsibility.

And, finally, whatever the merits of the argument by which all as-sertions are relativised—your hate speech is my free speech—this inci-dent has nothing to do with either hate speech or free speech and everything to do with whether the editors are discharging or defaulting on their obligations when they foist them off on an inapplicable doc-trine, saying in effect, "The First Amendment made us do it."

More recently, the same scenario played itself out at Santa Rosa 10
Junior College. This time it was a student who wrote the offending article. Titled "Is Anti-Semitism Ever the Result of Jewish Behavior?"

it answered the question in the affirmative, creating an uproar that included death threats, an avalanche of hate mail, and demands for just about everyone's resignation. The faculty adviser who had approved the piece said, "The First Amendment isn't there to protect agreeable stories."

He was alluding to the old saw that the First Amendment protects unpopular as well as popular speech. But what it protects unpopular speech *from* is abridgment by the government of its free expression; it does not protect unpopular speech from being rejected by a newspaper, and it confers no positive obligation to give your pages over to unpopular speech, or popular speech, or any speech.

Once again, there is no First Amendment issue here, just an issue of editorial judgment and the consequences of exercising it. (You can print anything you like; but if the heat comes, it's yours, not the Constitution's.)

In these controversies, student editors are sometimes portrayed, or portray themselves, as First Amendment heroes who bravely risk criticism and censure in order to uphold a cherished American value. But they are not heroes; they are merely confused and, in terms of their understanding of the doctrine they invoke, rather hapless.

Not as hapless, however, as the Harvard English department, which made a collective fool of itself three times when it invited, disinvited and then reinvited poet Tom Paulin to be the Morris Gray lecturer. Again the flash point was anti-Semitism. In his poetry and in public comments, Paulin had said that Israel had no right to exist, that settlers on the West Bank "should be shot dead," and that Israeli police and military forces were the equivalent of the Nazi SS. When these and other statements came to light shortly before Paulin was to give his lecture, the department voted to rescind the invitation. When the inevitable cry of "censorship, censorship" was heard in the land, the department flip-flopped again, and a professor-spokesman declared, "This was a clear affirmation that the department stood strongly by the First Amendment."

15   It was of course nothing of the kind; it was a transparent effort of a bunch that had already put its foot in its mouth twice to wriggle out of trouble and regain the moral high ground by striking the pose of First Amendment defender. But, in fact, the department and its members were not First Amendment defenders (a religion they converted to a little late), but serial bunglers.

What should they have done? Well, it depends on what they wanted to do. If they wanted to invite this particular poet because they admired his poetry, they had a perfect right to do so. If they were aware ahead of time of Paulin's public pronouncements, they could have chosen either to say something by way of explanation or to remain silent and let the event speak for itself; either course of action would have been at once defensible and productive of risk. If they knew nothing of Paulin's anti-Israel sentiments (difficult to believe of a gang of world-class researchers) but found out about them after the fact, they might have said, "Oops, never mind" or toughed it out—again alternatives not without risk. But at each stage, whatever they did or didn't do would have had no relationship whatsoever to any First Amendment right—Paulin had no right to be invited—or obligation—there was no obligation either to invite or disinvite him, and certainly no obligation to reinvite him, unless you count the obligations imposed on yourself by a succession of ill-thought-through decisions. Whatever the successes or failures here, they were once again failures of judgment, not doctrine.

In another case, it looked for a moment that judgment of an appropriate kind was in fact being exercised. The University of California at Berkeley houses the Emma Goldman Papers Project, and each year the director sends out a fund-raising mailer that always features quotations from Goldman's work. But this January an associate vice chancellor edited the mailer and removed two quotations that in context read as a criticism of the Bush administration's plans for a war in Iraq. He explained that the quotations were not randomly chosen and were clearly intended to make a "political point, and that is inappropriate in an official university situation."

The project director (who acknowledged that the quotes were selected for their contemporary relevance) objected to what she saw as an act of censorship and a particularly egregious one given Goldman's strong advocacy of free expression.

But no one's expression was being censored. The Goldman quotations are readily available and had they appeared in the project's literature in a setting that did not mark them as political, no concerns would have been raised. It is just, said the associate vice chancellor, that they are inappropriate in this context, and, he added, "It is not a matter of the First Amendment."

Right, it's a matter of whether or not there is even the appearance 20 of the university's taking sides on a partisan issue; that is, it is an empirical matter that requires just the exercise of judgment that associate vice chancellors are paid to perform. Of course he was pilloried by members of the Berkeley faculty and others who saw First Amendment violations everywhere.

But there were none. Goldman still speaks freely through her words. The project director can still make her political opinions known by writing letters to the editor or to everyone in the country, even if she cannot use the vehicle of a university flier to do so. Everyone's integrity is preserved. The project goes on unimpeded, and the university goes about its proper academic business. Or so it would have been had the administration stayed firm. But it folded and countermanded the associate vice chancellor's decision.

At least the chancellor had sense enough to acknowledge that no one's speech had been abridged. It was just, he said, an "error in judgment." Aren't they all?

Are there then no free-speech issues on campuses? Sure there are; there just aren't very many. When Toni Smith, a basketball player at Manhattanville College, turned her back to the flag during the playing of the national anthem in protest against her government's policies, she was truly exercising her First Amendment rights, rights that ensure that she cannot be compelled to an affirmation she does not endorse (see *West Virginia v. Barnette*). And as she stood by her principles in the face of hostility, she truly was (and is) a First Amendment hero, as the college newspaper editors, the members of the Harvard English department, and the head of the Emma Goldman Project are not. The category is a real one, and it would be good if it were occupied only by those who belong in it.

Responding to Reading

1. What does Fish mean when he says, "The modern American version of crying wolf is crying First Amendment" (1)?
2. According to Fish, what constitutes a "First Amendment issue" (12)? In what way is a First Amendment issue different from an issue of "editorial judgment"?
3. How convincing are the examples Fish presents to support his argument? For example, why is the case of Toni Smith a free speech issue? Why does Fish think that she is "a First Amendment hero" and that "the college newspaper editors, the members of the Harvard English department, and the head of the Emma Goldman Project are not" (23)?

Responding in Writing

Do you believe that all viewpoints should be allowed to reach an audience? Or, do you believe that some ideas are so repugnant or dangerous that they should be censored? Explain.

A CHILL WIND IS BLOWING IN THIS NATION

Tim Robbins

1958–

*Actor, director, screenwriter, producer—and husband of actress Susan Saran-don—Tim Robbins was born in West Covina, California, grew up in New York City and began acting at age twelve. He received an undergraduate degree in drama from the University of California, Los Angeles (1981). Robbins has di-rected and appeared in many films and is best known for his roles that depict individuals wronged by the system (*The Shawshank Redemption, 1994)*; in-dividuals who abuse power (*Bob Roberts, 1992)*; and individuals caught up in a system gone awry (*The Hudsucker Proxy, 1994)*. Robbins wrote and di-rected* Dead Man Walking *(1995), for which he received an Oscar nomina-tion, and he won the best supporting actor award for his role in the 2003 film* Mystic River. *Robbins gave the following speech at the National Press Club in Washington, DC, on April 15, 2003, just after his invitation to speak at The Baseball Hall of Fame had been withdrawn because of his outspoken opposition to the war in Iraq.*

I can't tell you how moved I have been at the overwhelming sup-port I have received from newspapers throughout the country in these past few days. I hold no illusions that all of these journalists agree with me on my views against the war. While the journalists' outrage at the cancellation of our appearance in Cooperstown is not about my views, it is about my right to express these views. I am extremely grateful that there are those of you out there still with a fierce belief in constitution-ally guaranteed rights. We need you, the press, now more than ever. This is a crucial moment for all of us.

For all of the ugliness and tragedy of 9/11, there was a brief period afterward where I held a great hope, in the midst of the tears and shocked faces of New Yorkers, in the midst of the lethal air we breathed as we worked at Ground Zero, in the midst of my children's terror at being so close to this crime against humanity, in the midst of all this, I held on to a glimmer of hope in the naive assumption that something good could come out of it.

I imagined our leaders seizing upon this moment of unity in Amer-ica, this moment when no one wanted to talk about Democrat versus Republican, white versus black, or any of the other ridiculous divisions that dominate our public discourse. I imagined our leaders going on television telling the citizens that although we all want to be at Ground Zero, we can't, but there is work that is needed to be done all over America. Our help is needed at community centers to tutor children, to teach them to read. Our work is needed at old-age homes to visit the lonely and infirmed; in gutted neighborhoods to rebuild housing and clean up parks, and convert abandoned lots to baseball fields. I imagined leadership that would take this incredible energy, this generosity of spirit and create a new unity in America born out of the chaos and tragedy of 9/11, a new unity that would send a message to terrorists everywhere: If you attack us, we will become stronger, cleaner, better educated, and more unified. You will strengthen our commitment to justice and democracy by your inhumane attacks on us. Like a Phoenix out of the fire, we will be reborn.

And then came the speech: You are either with us or against us. And the bombing began. And the old paradigm was restored as our leader encouraged us to show our patriotism by shopping and by volunteering to join groups that would turn in their neighbor for any suspicious behavior.

5   In the 19 months since 9/11, we have seen our democracy compromised by fear and hatred. Basic inalienable rights, due process, the sanctity of the home have been quickly compromised in a climate of fear. A unified American public has grown bitterly divided, and a world population that had profound sympathy and support for us has grown contemptuous and distrustful, viewing us as we once viewed the Soviet Union, as a rogue state.

This past weekend, Susan and I and the three kids went to Florida for a family reunion of sorts. Amidst the alcohol and the dancing, sugar-rushing children, there was, of course, talk of the war. And the most frightening thing about the weekend was the amount of times we were thanked for speaking out against the war because that individual speaking thought it unsafe to do so in their own community, in their own life. Keep talking, they said; I haven't been able to open my mouth.

A relative tells me that a history teacher tells his 11-year-old son, my nephew, that Susan Sarandon is endangering the troops by her opposition to the war. Another teacher in a different school asks our niece if we are coming to the school play. They're not welcome here, said the molder of young minds.

Another relative tells me of a school board decision to cancel a civics event that was proposing to have a moment of silence for those who have died in the war because the students were including dead Iraqi civilians in their silent prayer.

A teacher in another nephew's school is fired for wearing a T-shirt with a peace sign on it. And a friend of the family tells of listening to the radio down South as the talk radio host calls for the murder of a prominent anti-war activist. Death threats have appeared on other prominent anti-war activists' doorsteps for their views. Relatives of ours have received threatening e-mails and phone calls. And my 13-year-old boy, who has done nothing to anybody, has recently been embarrassed and humiliated by a sadistic creep who writes—or, rather, scratches his column with his fingernails in dirt.

Susan and I have been listed as traitors, as supporters of Saddam,   10 and various other epithets by the Aussie gossip rags masquerading as newspapers, and by their fair and balanced electronic media cousins, 19th Century Fox. (Laughter.) Apologies to Gore Vidal. (Applause.)

Two weeks ago, the United Way canceled Susan's appearance at a conference on women's leadership. And both of us last week were told that both we and the First Amendment were not welcome at the Baseball Hall of Fame.

A famous middle-aged rock-and-roller called me last week to thank me for speaking out against the war, only to go on to tell me that he could not speak himself because he fears repercussions from Clear Channel. "They promote our concert appearances," he said. "They own most of the stations that play our music. I can't come out against this war."

And here in Washington, Helen Thomas finds herself banished to the back of the room and uncalled on after asking Ari Fleischer whether our showing prisoners of war at Guantanamo Bay on television violated the Geneva Convention.

A chill wind is blowing in this nation. A message is being sent through the White House and its allies in talk radio and Clear Channel and Cooperstown. If you oppose this administration, there can and will be ramifications.

Every day, the air waves are filled with warnings, veiled and un-   15 veiled threats, spewed invective and hatred directed at any voice of dissent. And the public, like so many relatives and friends that I saw this weekend, sit in mute opposition and fear.

I am sick of hearing about Hollywood being against this war. Hollywood's heavy hitters, the real power brokers and cover-of-the-magazine stars, have been largely silent on this issue. But Hollywood, the concept, has always been a popular target.

I remember when the Columbine High School shootings happened. President Clinton criticized Hollywood for contributing to this terrible tragedy—this, as we were dropping bombs over Kosovo. Could the violent actions of our leaders contribute somewhat to the violent fantasies of our teenagers? Or is it all just Hollywood and rock and roll?

I remember reading at the time that one of the shooters had tried to enlist to fight the real war a week before he acted out his war in real life at Columbine. I talked about this in the press at the time. And curiously, no one accused me of being unpatriotic for criticizing Clinton. In fact, the same radio patriots that call us traitors today engaged in daily personal attacks on their president during the war in Kosovo.

Today, prominent politicians who have decried violence in movies—the "Blame Hollywooders," if you will—recently voted to give our current president the power to unleash real violence in our current war. They want us to stop the fictional violence but are okay with the real kind.

20   And these same people that tolerate the real violence of war don't want to see the result of it on the nightly news. Unlike the rest of the world, our news coverage of this war remains sanitized, without a glimpse of the blood and gore inflicted upon our soldiers or the women and children in Iraq. Violence as a concept, an abstraction—it's very strange.

As we applaud the hard-edged realism of the opening battle scene of "Saving Private Ryan," we cringe at the thought of seeing the same on the nightly news. We are told it would be pornographic. We want no part of reality in real life. We demand that war be painstakingly realized on the screen, but that war remain imagined and conceptualized in real life.

And in the midst of all this madness, where is the political opposition? Where have all the Democrats gone? Long time passing, long time ago. (Applause.) With apologies to Robert Byrd, I have to say it is pretty embarrassing to live in a country where a five-foot-one comedian has more guts than most politicians. (Applause.) We need leaders, not pragmatists that cower before the spin zones of former entertainment journalists. We need leaders who can understand the Constitution, congressman who don't in a moment of fear abdicate their most important power, the right to declare war to the executive branch. And, please, can we please stop the congressional sing-a-longs? (Laughter.)

In this time when a citizenry applauds the liberation of a country as it lives in fear of its own freedom, when an administration official releases an attack ad questioning the patriotism of a legless Vietnam veteran running for Congress, when people all over the country fear reprisal if they use their right to free speech, it is time to get angry. It is time to get fierce. And it doesn't take much to shift the tide. My 11-year-old nephew, mentioned earlier, a shy kid who never talks in class, stood up to his history teacher who was questioning Susan's patriotism. "That's my aunt you're talking about. Stop it." And the stunned teacher backtracks and began stammering compliments in embarrassment.

Sportswriters across the country reacted with such overwhelming fury at the Hall of Fame that the president of the Hall admitted he made a mistake and Major League Baseball disavowed any connection to the actions of the Hall's president. A bully can be stopped, and so can a mob. It takes one person with the courage and a resolute voice.

25   The journalists in this country can battle back at those who would rewrite our Constitution in Patriot Act II, or "Patriot, The Sequel," as

we would call it in Hollywood. We are counting on you to star in that movie. Journalists can insist that they not be used as publicists by this administration. (Applause.) The next White House correspondent to be called on by Ari Fleischer should defer their question to the back of the room, to the banished journalist du jour. (Applause.) And any instance of intimidation to free speech should be battled against. Any acquiescence or intimidation at this point will only lead to more intimidation. You have, whether you like it or not, an awesome responsibility and an awesome power: the fate of discourse, the health of this republic is in your hands, whether you write on the left or the right. This is your time, and the destiny you have chosen.

We lay the continuance of our democracy on your desks, and count on your pens to be mightier. Millions are watching and waiting in mute frustration and hope—hoping for someone to defend the spirit and letter of our Constitution, and to defy the intimidation that is visited upon us daily in the name of national security and warped notions of patriotism.

Our ability to disagree, and our inherent right to question our leaders and criticize their actions define who we are. To allow those rights to be taken away out of fear, to punish people for their beliefs, to limit access in the news media to differing opinions is to acknowledge our democracy's defeat. These are challenging times. There is a wave of hate that seeks to divide us—right and left, pro-war and anti-war. In the name of my 11-year-old nephew, and all the other unreported victims of this hostile and unproductive environment of fear, let us try to find our common ground as a nation. Let us celebrate this grand and glorious experiment that has survived for 227 years. To do so we must honor and fight vigilantly for the things that unite us—like freedom, the First Amendment and, yes, baseball. (Applause.)

Responding to Reading

1. What does Robbins believe America's public leaders should have done after the 9/11 attacks? Do you agree with him that his suggestions would have created "a new unity" that would have said to terrorists, "If you attack us, we will become stronger, cleaner, better educated, and more unified" (3)?

2. What does Robbins mean when he says, "A chill wind is blowing in this nation" (14)? What evidence does he give to support this assertion? What does Robbins think should be done "to shift the tide" (23)?

3. In paragraph 1, Robbins implies that his constitutional rights were taken away when his scheduled appearance at the Baseball Hall of Fame in Cooperstown was cancelled because of his opposition to the war in Iraq. Would Stanley Fish (p. 240) agree that this action deprived Robbins of his "constitutionally guaranteed" right (1) to express his views?

Responding in Writing

Do you believe that the government should be able to suspend or limit citizens' constitutional rights of privacy and free speech in time of war? How far should such limitations go?

IT'S TIME TO JUNK
THE DOUBLE STANDARD
ON FREE SPEECH

Stuart Taylor Jr.

1948–

Stuart Taylor, Jr., is a senior writer and weekly opinion columnist for the National Journal *and a contributing editor at* Newsweek. *His writing focuses on national legal, political, and policy issues. Taylor earned an AB degree from Princeton University (1970) and a JD from Harvard Law School (1977). He practiced law and then worked as a legal affairs reporter and Supreme Court reporter for the Washington Bureau of the* New York Times. *He lives in Washington, DC.*

It made news when hecklers booed *Sacramento Bee* publisher Janis Besler Heaphy so loudly and long—for suggesting that the government had gone too far in curbing civil liberties since September 11—that she could not finish her December 15 commencement speech at California State University (Sacramento). "Many interpret it as a troubling example of rising intolerance for public discourse that questions the nation's response to the September 11 terror attacks," reported the *Los Angeles Times. The New York Times* and other major newspapers weighed in with similar articles. ABC News' *Nightline* did a special report.

Another burst of publicity—and more worries about threats to First Amendment rights—attended the University of New Mexico's reprimand of professor Richard Berthold for opening his September 11 history class with what he later admitted to be a "stupid" remark: "Anyone who can blow up the Pentagon gets my vote." Berthold also received death threats.

It's nice to see the media showing some concern for the freedom of speech. But where have they been during the past two decades of efforts coming from the politically correct Left—and especially from devotees of identity politics, racial preferences, and the male-bashing brand of feminism—to suppress unwelcome speech on our campuses and elsewhere? Examples:

- Ward Connerly, the black California businessman who has campaigned across the nation to outlaw racial preferences, has been shouted down and drowned out so abusively as to cut short his remarks on at least five campuses since 1996, he recalls, including Atlanta's Emory University in 1998 and the University of Texas School of Law in 1999. The consequence, he says, is that "it totally throws you off your stride. Freedom of speech is not just being able to complete your speech, it's being able to speak without fear of personal harm being done to you. . . . I am not free to speak openly and honestly." College administrators, Connerly adds, "almost go out of their way to make me out as a monster, which incites the audience all the more." Taunts of "Uncle Tom" are routine and, more than once, Connerly notes, hecklers have threatened violence or announced menacingly, "We know where you live."

- Linda Chavez, another leading critic of racial preferences, says: "I have been disinvited, harassed, shouted down, threatened, and [on one occasion] physically assaulted at campuses around the country," including the University of Northern Colorado and the University of Illinois (Urbana-Champaign). Chavez says that while the most-menacing hecklers appeared to be "street thugs" brought in from outside the campuses, students who join in "are being primed by the professors, being told that I'm the devil incarnate, that I want to do terrible things to Hispanics."

- Christina Hoff Sommers, a trenchant critic of liberal feminism, was speaking as an invited panelist at a November 1 conference on preventing substance abuse, organized by the Health and Human Services Department, when some officials, academics, and others took offense at her doubts about a program called "Girl Power." A department official named Linda Bass interrupted and angrily ordered Sommers to stop talking about Girl Power. Later, Sommers said, Fordham University psychology professor (and paid department consultant) Jay Wade told Sommers, "Shut the f— up, bitch," amid mocking laughter from the crowd. Sommers, effectively silenced, left. "As Stanley Kurtz pointed out in *National Review*," Sommers notes, "if Catharine MacKinnon or Carol Gilligan had been treated that way in a government meeting, it would have been reported." Very widely.

But none of these efforts to silence Connerly, Chavez, and Sommers by heckler's veto has ever been reported in any national newspaper, as far as I can find, excepting some coverage in the conservative *Washington Times*, a few opinion columns, *Wall Street Journal* editorials, and a passing mention of Connerly's complaint deep in *The New York Times*. Nor have the national media paid much attention to the pervasive use of speech codes to chill politically incorrect expression on campus. They have likewise ignored the long-running epidemic of thefts of campus newspapers for carrying politically incorrect commentary or advertisements.

5   "University PR and spin has led too many of the media into a terrible double standard" in dealing with such heckler's vetoes and other forms of censorship, says Thor L. Halvorssen, executive director of the Foundation for Individual Rights in Education Inc. (FIRE). "When it's a conservative [being shouted down], the university will downplay this as a free speech protest, and the media will agree."

The Philadelphia-based FIRE was created two years ago by Boston civil liberties lawyer Harvey Silverglate and University of Pennsylvania professor Alan Charles Kors to protect free speech and other liberties on the nation's campuses. And Halvorssen seethes with the same passionate indignation in denouncing censorial efforts coming from the political Right as those from the Left. But before September 11, he says, the campus censorship came mostly from the Left. And the big media were not interested.

"Close to three-quarters of the colleges and universities, private and public, have speech codes," Halvorssen stresses. "They are applied selectively, with a double standard depending on your blood and culture. I've never heard of a case of anyone being suspended or fired or expelled for insulting a born-again Christian. On a college campus, Andres Serrano's photograph of a crucifix in urine, titled *Piss Christ*, is a work of art. Immerse a photograph of Martin Luther King Jr. in urine, and the sky would fall and the entire school would be put through sensitivity training. There is also a ferocious assault on due process and fairness on campus."

Administrators mete out discipline for offending remarks, for other alleged "harassment," and even for disputed charges of date rape with no semblance of a fair hearing. "We hear a lot of people talking about military tribunals," Halvorssen notes. "We have the equivalent on campus. . . . I see this stuff on a daily basis, and it is a real struggle to get it into the media. Speech codes, thought reform, due process—where have these folks been?"

Since September 11, with leftist critics of the war against terrorism complaining of efforts to intimidate and punish them both on campus and elsewhere, the media have paid a bit more attention—although, Halvorssen says, "it's the equivalent of reporting on how many people are getting into the boats rather than reporting that the *Titanic* is sinking." The coverage has also been more balanced, if only because it would be hard to chronicle the punitive measures against anti-war leftists and Islamists without noticing that, on the campuses, efforts to silence forcefully hawkish statements deemed offensive by Muslims seem about as common.

The reporting on the Berthold "blow up the Pentagon" case, for ex- 10 ample, has been paralleled by extensive coverage of a case at Orange Coast College in California in which Professor Kenneth Hearlson was suspended for 11 weeks without a hearing and threatened with dismissal after four Muslim students complained that he had called them terrorists and murderers in class. When other students produced tape-recordings proving this charge to be false, the college reprimanded Hearlson anyway, for accusing Muslims in general of condoning terrorism against Israel.

Meanwhile, the University of South Florida is seeking to fire Sami Al-Arian—a tenured Palestinian professor of computer science who is suspected (but not formally accused) of links to Islamic extremists— for courting publicity (amid dozens of death threats) about his views and controversial past. On the other end of the spectrum, a library assistant at UCLA was suspended for a week without pay for calling Israel an "apartheid state" in an e-mail. An Ethiopian student at San Diego State University was warned that he could be suspended or expelled for "harassment" after he had confronted and criticized a group of Saudi students for celebrating the destruction of the World Trade Center. And so on.

Many campus administrators, notes Halvorssen, bend according to "where the political winds are blowing." And now that some of the winds are blowing against the Left, even on a lot of campuses, the left-liberal *Nation* sees the danger. "The last generation's wave of campus speech codes and anti-harassment policies," wrote David Glenn in December, "may have done more to suppress freedom than to remedy injustice in any meaningful way—and it may be only now, after September 11, that the full costs will become apparent."

The rediscovery, by some in the media and the Left, of the case for free speech makes FIRE's Halvorssen optimistic about the future. But will politically powerful conservatives—some of whom have become First Amendment stalwarts while seeing their own oxes gored by campus censors—prove equally selective in their devotion to free speech? "We have to be careful," says Christina Hoff Sommers, "not to play by the rules written by the intolerant Left."

Responding to Reading

1. According to Taylor, the media is concerned about freedom of speech only when someone on the left cannot express his or her views. What examples does he present to support this contention? Do you think he presents enough examples to establish his case?
2. What examples of censorship on college campuses does Taylor give? How does Taylor think things have changed since September 11? Would Tim Robbins (p. 245) agree with Taylor's assessment?

3. Do you think Taylor presents a balanced view of his subject, or do you think he favors one group over another?

Responding in Writing

Do you think your college or university encourages all ideas, or do you think it favors one political or social viewpoint over another?

———————— WIDENING THE FOCUS ————————

The following readings can suggest additional perspectives for thinking and writing about freedom of speech. You may also want to do further research about this subject on the Internet.

- Christina Hoff Sommers, "For More Balance on Campuses" (p. 149)

- James Fallows, "Who Shot Mohammed al-Dura?" (p. 303)

- Warren Farrell, "Man Bashing" (p. 458)

For Internet Research: Should the US have an official language policy? According to *Ethnolog*, http://www.ethnologue.com/, more than 176 languages are spoken in the US. How should the federal government respond to this situation? Do minority languages threaten our national interest and democratic traditions? Should the Congress introduce a constitutional amendment that makes English the official language of the United States? Or, do you see language diversity as a national asset? Should the government encourage speakers of other languages while providing them with ample opportunities to learn English? Write an essay in which you outline a national language policy, basing your argument on information from one of the following Web pages:

- "Bilingual Education: a Critique," an essay published by the Hoover Institution, http://www-hoover.stanford.edu/publications/he/22/22a.html

- James Crawford's Language Policy Web site, http://ourworld.compuserve.com/homepages/jwcrawford/langpol.htm

- The "Analysis and Information" pages of the Web site run by English for the Children, a group lobbying to end bilingual education nationwide, http://onenation.org/

——————————— **WRITING** ———————————

The Politics of Language

1. Both Malcolm X (p. 195) and Frederick Douglass (p. 190) discuss how they undertook a program of self-education. Write an essay in which you discuss how their efforts were similar and different. Make certain you discuss what they learned about themselves and about their respective societies by learning to read and write.

2. Assume that you are the editor of your school newspaper and that you have received an editorial taking the position that to make up for past injustices, minorities and women should have points added to their test scores. Several days after rejecting the article, you receive a letter from the author, who accuses you of depriving him of his First Amendment right to freedom of expression. Write a response to this letter. You can either justify your previous position or reconsider your position and accept the article for publication. When formulating your answer, be sure to refer to at least one of the essays in the Focus section of this chapter.

3. In "Mother Tongue" (p. 206), Amy Tan distinguishes between the English she speaks to her mother and the English she speaks to the rest of the world. Write an essay in which you describe the various types of English you speak—at home, at school, at work, to your friends, and so on. In what ways are these Englishes alike, and in what ways are they different? What ideas are you able to express best with each type of English?

4. Over fifty years ago, both Aldous Huxley and George Orwell wrote essays in which they discussed how governments use language to control their citizens. Write an essay in which you discuss how today's governments do this. Do you think such control is easier or more difficult to achieve than it was fifty years ago? In your essay, be sure you refer specifically to "Propaganda under a Dictatorship" (p. 220) and "Politics and the English Language" (p. 226).

5. Both Amy Tan in "Mother Tongue" (p. 206) and Richard Rodriguez in "Aria" (p. 179) talk about how education can change one's use of language. Write an essay discussing the effect education has had on your own spoken and written language. What do you think you have gained and lost as your language has changed?

6. Which of your daily activities would you be unable to carry out if, like the people Jonathan Kozol describes in "The Human Cost of an Illiterate Society" (p. 212), you could neither read nor write? Write an article for your local newspaper in which you report on a typical day, being sure to identify specific tasks you could not do. In addi-

tion, explain some strategies you would use to hide the fact that you couldn't read or write.

7. In paragraph 21 of "Politics and the English Language" (p. 226), Orwell says, "Political language . . . is designed to make lies sound truthful and murder respectable, and to give an appearance of solidity to pure wind." Write an essay in which you agree or disagree with this statement. Support your position with examples you find in newspapers and magazines, on TV, or on the Internet.

8. Write a letter to Barbara Lawrence (p. 203) in which you agree or disagree with her contention that sexual vulgarisms about women are as bad as racial or ethnic obscenities. In addition to Lawrence's essay, refer to Alleen Pace Nilsen's essay "Sexism in English: Embodiment and Language" (p. 419) as well as to your own experience.

9. Recently, there has been a great deal of debate about the benefits and drawbacks of a multilingual society. Supporters say that a multilingual society allows people to preserve their own cultures and thus fosters pride. Detractors say that a multilingual society reinforces differences and ultimately tears a country apart. What do you see as the benefits and drawbacks of a multilingual society? As a country, what would we gain if we encouraged multilingualism? What would we lose? Refer to the essays in this chapter by Rodriguez (p. 179), Erdrich (p. 185), and Tan (p. 206) to support your position.

10. Write an essay in which you answer the Focus question, "How free should free speech be?" In your essay, refer to the ideas in Stanley Fish's "The Free-Speech Follies" (p. 240), Tim Robbins's "A Chill Wind Is Blowing in This Nation" (p. 245), and Stuart Taylor, Jr.'s "It's Time to Junk the Double Standard on Free Speech" (p. 250).

4

MEDIA
AND SOCIETY

PREPARING TO READ AND WRITE

The popular media—newspapers and magazines, radio, television, and film—have been around for a long time, but in recent years, they have come to have a particularly powerful and significant impact on our lives. Cable television has brought us literally hundreds of stations—along with sitcom reruns that endlessly recycle our childhoods (and our parents' childhoods). Satellites have brought immediacy: The Vietnam War was the first televised war, but we had to wait for the evening

Fifteenth-century illuminated manuscript depicting the angel Gabriel speaking to Mary.

news to see it; during the 2003 Iraq war, journalists were actually "embedded" with military units, bringing us events in real time on 24-hour cable news programs. Other innovations have also appeared: film special effects that have the power to mystify or terrify, newspapers that seem to have more color and graphics than words; and, on television, tabloid journalism, home shopping, reality TV, infomercials, and music videos. And, of course, the Internet has made available a world of information—and the ability to communicate this information almost instantly to millions of people all over the planet.

The increasing power and scope of the media have helped to turn the world into what Canadian cultural critic Marshall McLuhan called a "global village," a world of nations that are more and more interconnected and interdependent. This is seen by many as a positive development. Ideally, as citizens of the global village, we should be able to understand one another as we increasingly come to share a common culture, with access to the same music, films, Web sites, and television programs. But the power of the media has also brought problems. The tool that can unite, inform, instruct, entertain, and inspire can also deceive, stereotype, and brainwash—and, perhaps, even incite violence.

As the Focus section of this chapter, "Does Media Violence Hurt?" (p. 319), suggests, some people believe that the violent images in films, TV shows, and video games may play a significant role in encouraging violent behavior as well as promoting fear, paranoia, and alienation

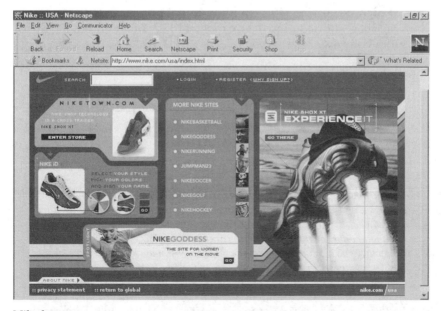

Nike home page.

from mainstream society. Whether or not we accept that there is a direct causal connection between media violence and the violence we see in our society, our awareness of the possible negative effects of the all-pervasive media has tempered our enthusiasm and made us embrace its virtues with caution.

As you read and prepare to write about the essays in this chapter, you may consider the following questions:

- Does the essay focus on one particular medium or on the media in general?

- Does the writer see the media as a positive, negative, or neutral force? Why?

- If the writer sees negative effects, where does he or she place blame? Do you agree?

- Does the writer make any recommendations for change? Do these recommendations seem reasonable?

- Is the writer focusing on the media's effects on individuals or on society?

- Does the writer discuss personal observations or experiences? If so, are they similar to or different from your own?

- When was the essay written? Has the situation the writer describes changed since then?

- Which writers' positions on the impact of the media (or on the media's shortcomings) are most alike? Most different? Most like your own?

INFORMING OURSELVES TO DEATH

Neil Postman

1931–2003

Neil Postman, who held an EdD from Columbia University, was a professor of education and until 2002 served as chair of the Culture and Communication Department at New York University, where he taught for nearly 40 years. Postman wrote many books about education, media, communication, and technology. Critical of the effects of media, Postman voiced concern about those who only see the positive aspects of technology. Although Postman delivered "Informing Ourselves to Death" as a speech to a meeting of information specialists sponsored by IBM in 1990, it continues to be relevant today. Postman's books include Amusing Ourselves to Death: Public Discourse in the Age of Show Business *(1985),* Technopoly: The Surrender of Cul-*

ture to Technology *(1992),* The End of Education: Redefining the Value of School *(1995), and* Building a Bridge to the Eighteenth Century: How the Past Can Improve Our Future *(1999). Visit the "edtechNOT" Web site http://www.edtechnot.com to find online readings by this writer.*

The great English playwright and social philosopher George Bernard Shaw once remarked that all professions are conspiracies against the common folk. He meant that those who belong to elite trades—physicians, lawyers, teachers, and scientists—protect their special status by creating vocabularies that are incomprehensible to the general public. This process prevents outsiders from understanding what the profession is doing and why—and protects the insiders from close examination and criticism. Professions, in other words, build forbidding walls of technical gobbledygook over which the prying and alien eye cannot see.

Unlike George Bernard Shaw, I raise no complaint against this, for I consider myself a professional teacher and appreciate technical gobbledygook as much as anyone. But I do not object if occasionally someone who does not know the secrets of my trade is allowed entry to the inner halls to express an untutored point of view. Such a person may sometimes give a refreshing opinion or, even better, see something in a way that the professionals have overlooked. I believe I have been invited to speak at this conference for just such a purpose.

I do not know very much more about computer technology than the average person—which isn't very much. I have little understanding of what excites a computer programmer or scientist, and in examining the descriptions of the presentations at this conference, I found each one more mysterious than the next. So, I clearly qualify as an outsider.

But I think that what you want here is not merely an outsider but an outsider who has a point of view that might be useful to the insiders. And that is why I accepted the invitation to speak. I believe I know something about what technologies do to culture, and I know even more about what technologies undo in a culture. In fact, I might say, at the start, that what a technology undoes is a subject that computer experts apparently know very little about. I have heard many experts in computer technology speak about the advantages that computers will bring. With one exception—namely, Joseph—I have never heard anyone speak seriously and comprehensively about the disadvantages of computer technology, which strikes me as odd, and makes me wonder if the profession is hiding something important. That is to say, what seems to be lacking among computer experts is a sense of technological modesty.

After all, anyone who has studied the history of technology knows [5] that technological change is always a Faustian bargain[1]: Technology

---

[1] A bargain made by Faust, a character in German legend who sells his soul to the devil in exchange for knowledge and power. [Eds.]

giveth and technology taketh away, and not always in equal measure. A new technology sometimes creates more than it destroys. Sometimes, it destroys more than it creates. But it is never one-sided.

The invention of the printing press is an excellent example. Printing fostered the modern idea of individuality but it destroyed the medieval sense of community and social integration. Printing created prose but made poetry into an exotic and elitist form of expression. Printing made modern science possible but transformed religious sensibility into an exercise in superstition. Printing assisted in the growth of the nation-state but, in so doing, made patriotism into a sordid if not a murderous emotion.

Another way of saying this is that a new technology tends to favor some groups of people and harms other groups. School teachers, for example, will, in the long run, probably be made obsolete by television, as blacksmiths were made obsolete by the automobile, as balladeers were made obsolete by the printing press. Technological change, in other words, always results in winners and losers.

In the case of computer technology, there can be no disputing that the computer has increased the power of large-scale organizations like military establishments or airline companies or banks or tax collecting agencies. And it is equally clear that the computer is now indispensable to high-level researchers in physics and other natural sciences. But to what extent has computer technology been an advantage to the masses of people? To steel workers, vegetable store owners, teachers, automobile mechanics, musicians, bakers, brick layers, dentists and most of the rest into whose lives the computer now intrudes? These people have had their private matters made more accessible to powerful institutions. They are more easily tracked and controlled; they are subjected to more examinations, and are increasingly mystified by the decisions made about them. They are more often reduced to mere numerical objects. They are being buried by junk mail. They are easy targets for advertising agencies and political organizations. The schools teach their children to operate computerized systems instead of teaching things that are more valuable to children. In a word, almost nothing happens to the losers that they need, which is why they are losers.

It is to be expected that the winners—for example, most of the speakers at this conference—will encourage the losers to be enthusiastic about computer technology. That is the way of winners, and so they sometimes tell the losers that with personal computers the average person can balance a checkbook more neatly, keep better track of recipes, and make more logical shopping lists. They also tell them that they can vote at home, shop at home, get all the information they wish at home, and thus make community life unnecessary. They tell them that their lives will be conducted more efficiently, discreetly neglecting to say from whose point of view or what might be the costs of such efficiency.

Should the losers grow skeptical, the winners dazzle them with 10
the wondrous feats of computers, many of which have only marginal
relevance to the quality of the losers' lives but which are nonetheless
impressive. Eventually, the losers succumb, in part because they believe that the specialized knowledge of the masters of a computer
technology is a form of wisdom. The masters, of course, come to believe this as well. The result is that certain questions do not arise, such
as, to whom will the computer give greater power and freedom, and
whose power and freedom will be reduced?

Now, I have perhaps made all of this sound like a well planned
conspiracy, as if the winners know all too well what is being won and
what lost. But this is not quite how it happens, for the winners do not
always know what they are doing, and where it will all lead. The
Benedictine monks who invented the mechanical clock in the 12th
and 13th centuries believed that such a clock would provide a precise
regularity to the seven periods of devotion they were required to observe during the course of the day. As a matter of fact, it did. But what
the monks did not realize is that the clock is not merely a means of
keeping track of the hours but also of synchronizing and controlling
the actions of men. And so, by the middle of the 14th century, the
clock had moved outside the walls of the monastery, and brought a
new and precise regularity to the life of the workman and the mer-
chant. The mechanical clock made possible the idea of regular production, regular working hours, and a standardized product. Without
the clock, capitalism would have been quite impossible. And so, here
is a great paradox: the clock was invented by men who wanted to devote themselves more rigorously to God; and it ended as the technology of greatest use to men who wished to devote themselves to the
accumulation of money. Technology always has unforeseen consequences, and it is not always clear, at the beginning, who or what will
win, and who or what will lose.

I might add, by way of another historical example, that Johann
Gutenberg was by all accounts a devoted Christian who would have
been horrified to hear Martin Luther, the accursed heretic, declare that
printing is "God's highest act of grace, whereby the business of the
Gospel is driven forward." Gutenberg thought his invention would advance the cause of the Holy Roman See, whereas in fact, it turned out
to bring a revolution which destroyed the monopoly of the Church.

We may well ask ourselves, then, is there something that the masters of computer technology think they are doing for us which they
and we may have reason to regret? I believe there is, and it is suggested by the title of my talk, "Informing Ourselves to Death." In the
time remaining, I will try to explain what is dangerous about the computer, and why. And I trust you will be open enough to consider what
I have to say. Now, I think I can begin to get at this by telling you of
a small experiment I have been conducting, on and off, for the past

several years. There are some people who describe the experiment as an exercise in deceit and exploitation but I will rely on your sense of humor to pull me through.

Here's how it works: It is best done in the morning when I see a colleague who appears not to be in possession of a copy of *The New York Times*. "Did you read *The Times* this morning?," I ask. If the colleague says yes, there is no experiment that day. But if the answer is no, the experiment can proceed. "You ought to look at Page 23, I say. "There's a fascinating article about a study done at Harvard University." "Really? What's it about?" is the usual reply. My choices at this point are limited only by my imagination. But I might say something like this: "Well, they did this study to find out what foods are best to eat for losing weight, and it turns out that a normal diet supplemented by chocolate eclairs, eaten six times a day, is the best approach. It seems that there's some special nutrient in the eclairs—economical dioxin—that actually uses up calories at an incredible rate."

15   Another possibility, which I like to use with colleagues who are known to be health conscious is this one: "I think you'll want to know about this," I say. "The neuro-physiologists at the University of Stuttgart have uncovered a connection between jogging and reduced intelligence. They tested more than 1200 people over a period of five years, and found that as the number of hours people jogging increased, there was a corresponding decrease in their intelligence. They don't know exactly why but there it is."

I'm sure, by now, you understand what my role is in the experiment: to report something that is quite ridiculous—one might say, beyond belief. Let me tell you, then, some of my results: Unless this is the second or third time I've tried this on the same person, most people will believe or at least not disbelieve what I have told them. Sometimes they say: "Really? Is that possible?" Sometimes they do a double-take, and reply, "Where'd you say that study was done?" And sometimes they say, "You know, I've heard something like that."

Now, there are several conclusions that might be drawn from these results, one of which was expressed by H.L. Mencken fifty years ago when he said, there is no idea so stupid that you can't find a professor who will believe it. This is more of an accusation than an explanation but in any case I have tried this experiment on non-professors and get roughly the same results. Another possible conclusion is one expressed by George Orwell—also about fifty years ago—when he remarked that the average person today is about as naive as was the average person in the Middle Ages. In the Middle Ages people believed in the authority of their religion, no matter what. Today, we believe in the authority of our science, no matter what.

But I think there is still another and more important conclusion to be drawn, related to Orwell's point but rather off at a right angle to it. I am referring to the fact that the world in which we live is very nearly incomprehensible to most of us. There is almost no fact—whether actual or imagined—that will surprise us for very long, since we have no comprehensive and consistent picture of the world which would make the fact appear as an unacceptable contradiction. We believe because there is no reason not to believe. No social, political, historical, metaphysical, logical or spiritual reason. We live in a world that, for the most part, makes no sense to us. Not even technical sense. I don't mean to try my experiment on this audience, especially after having told you about it, but if I informed you that the seats you are presently occupying were actually made by a special process which uses the skin of a Bismark herring, on what grounds would you dispute me? For all you know—indeed, for all I know—the skin of a Bismark herring could have made the seats on which you sit. And if I could get an industrial chemist to confirm this fact by describing some incomprehensible process by which it was done, you would probably tell someone tomorrow that you spent the evening sitting on a Bismark herring.

Perhaps I can get a bit closer to the point I wish to make with analogy: If you opened a brand-new deck of cards, and started turning the cards over, one by one you would have a pretty good idea of what their order is. After you had gone from the ace of spades through the nine of spades, you would expect a ten of spades to come up next. And if a three of diamonds showed up instead, you would be surprised and wonder what kind of deck of cards this is. But if I gave you a deck that had been shuffled twenty times, and then asked you to turn the cards over, you would not expect any card in particular—a three of diamonds would be just as likely as a ten of spades. Having no basis for assuming a given order, you would have no reason to react with disbelief or even surprise to whatever card turns up.

The point is that, in a world without spiritual or intellectual order, 20 nothing is unbelievable; nothing is predictable, and therefore, nothing comes as a particular surprise.

In fact, George Orwell was more than a little unfair to the average person in the Middle Ages. The belief system of the Middle Ages was rather like my brand-new deck of cards. There existed an ordered, comprehensible world-view, beginning with the idea that all knowledge and goodness come from God. What the priests had to say about the world was derived from the logic of their theology. There was nothing arbitrary about the things people were asked to believe, including the fact that the world itself was created at 9 A.M. on October 23 in the year 4004 B.C. That could be explained, and was, quite lucidity, to the satisfaction of anyone. So could the fact that 10,000 angels could dance on the head of a pin. It made quite good sense, if you believed that the Bible is the revealed word of God and that the universe is populated with angels. The medieval world was, to be sure, mysterious and filled with wonder, but it was not without a sense of order.

Ordinary men and women might not clearly grasp how the harsh realities of their lives fit into the grand and benevolent design, but they had no doubt that there was such a design, and their priests were well able, by deduction from a handful of principles, to make it, if not rational, at least coherent.

The situation we are presently in is much different. And I should say, sadder and more confusing and certainly more mysterious. It is rather like the shuffled deck of cards I referred to. There is no consistent, integrated conception of the world which serves as the foundation on which our edifice of belief rests. And therefore, in a sense, we are more naive than those of the Middle Ages, and more frightened, for we can be made to believe almost anything. The skin of a Bismark herring makes about as much sense as a vinyl alloy or encomial dioxin.

Now, in a way, none of this is our fault. If I may turn the wisdom of Cassius on its head: the fault is not in ourselves but almost literally in the stars. When Galileo turned his telescope toward the heavens, and allowed Kepler to look as well, they found no enchantment or authorization in the stars, only geometric patterns and equations. God, it seemed, was less of a moral philosopher than a master mathematician. This discovery helped to give impetus to the development of physics but did nothing but harm to theology. Before Galileo and Kepler, it was possible to believe that the Earth was the stable center of the universe, and that God took a special interest in our affairs. Afterward, the Earth became a lonely wanderer in an obscure galaxy in a hidden corner of the universe, and we were left to wonder if God had any interest in us at all. The ordered, comprehensible world of the Middle Ages began to unravel because people no longer saw in the stars the face of a friend.

And something else, which once was our friend, turned against us, as well. I refer to information. There was a time when information was a source that helped human beings to solve specific and urgent problems of their environment. It is true enough that in the Middle Ages, there was a scarcity of information but its very scarcity made it both important and usable. This began to change, as everyone knows, in the late 15th century when a goldsmith named Gutenberg, from Mainz, converted an old wine press into a printing machine, and in so doing, created what we now call an information explosion. Forty years after the invention of the press, there were printing machines in 110 different countries; 50 years after, more than eight million books had been printed, almost all of them filled with information that had previously not been available to the average person.

25   Nothing could be more misleading than the idea that computer technology introduced the age of information. The printing press began that age, and we have not been free of it since. But what started out as a liberating stream has turned into a deluge of chaos. If I may take my

own country as an example, here is what we are faced with: In America, there are 260,000 billboards; 11,520 newspapers; 11,556 periodicals; 27,000 video outlets for renting tapes; 362 million TV sets; and over 400 million radios. There are 40,000 new book titles published every year (300,000 world-wide) and every day in America 41 million photographs are taken, and just for the record, over 60 billion pieces of advertising junkmail come into our mail boxes every year. Everything from telegraphy and photography in the nineteenth century to the silicon chip in the twentieth has amplified the din of information, until matters have reached such proportions today that for the average person, information no longer has any relation to the solution of problems.

The tie between information and action has been severed. Information is now a commodity that can be sought and sold, or used as a form of entertainment, or worn like a garment to enhance one's status. It comes indiscriminately, directed at no one in particular, disconnected from usefulness; we are glutted with information, drowning in information, have no control over it, don't know what to do with it. And there are two reasons we do not know what to do with it. First, as I have said, we no longer have a coherent conception of ourselves, and our universe, and our relation to one another and our world. We no longer know, as the Middle Ages did, where we come from, and where we are going, or why. That is, we don't know what information is relevant, and what information is irrelevant to our lives. Second, we have directed all of our energies and intelligence to inventing machinery that does nothing but increase the supply of information. As a consequence, our defenses against information glut have broken down; our information immune system is inoperable. We don't know how to filter it out, we don't know how to reduce it; we don't know to use it. We suffer from a kind of cultural AIDS.

Now, into this situation comes the computer. The computer, as we know, has a quality of universality, not only because its uses are almost infinitely various but also because computers are commonly integrated into the structure of other machines. Therefore it would be fatuous of me to warn against every conceivable use of a computer. But there is no denying that the most prominent uses of computers have to do with information. When people talk about "information sciences," they are talking about computers—how to store information, how to retrieve information, how to organize information. The computer is an answer to the questions, How can I get more information, faster, and in a more usable form? These would appear to be reasonable questions. But now I should like to put some other questions to you that seem to me more reasonable. Did Iraq invade Kuwait because of a lack of information? If a hideous war should ensue between Iraq and the U.S., will it happen because of a lack of information? If children die of starvation in Ethiopia, does it occur because of a lack of information? Does racism in South Africa exist because of a lack of information? If criminals roam the streets of New York City, do they do so because of a lack of information?

Or, let us come down to a more personal level: If you and your spouse are unhappy together, and end your marriage in divorce, will it happen because of a lack of information? If your children misbehave and bring shame to your family, does it happen because of a lack of information? If someone in your family has a mental breakdown, will it happen because of a lack of information?

I believe you will have to concede that what ails us, what causes us the most misery and pain—at both cultural and personal levels—has nothing to do with the sort of information made accessible by computers. The computer and its information cannot answer any of the fundamental questions we need to address to make our lives more meaningful and humane. The computer cannot provide an organizing moral framework. It cannot tell us what questions are worth asking. It cannot provide a means of understanding why we are here or why we fight each other or why decency eludes us so often, especially when we need it the most. The computer is, in a sense, a magnificent toy that distracts us from facing what we most needed to confront—spiritual emptiness, knowledge of ourselves, usable conceptions of the past and future. Does one blame the computer for this? Of course not. It is, after all, only a machine. But it is presented to us, with trumpets blaring, as at this conference, as a technological messiah.

30   Through the computer, the heralds say, we will make education better, religion better, politics better, our minds better—best of all, ourselves better. This is, of course, nonsense, and only the young or the ignorant or the foolish could believe it. I said a moment ago that computers are not to blame for this. And that is true, at least in the sense that we do not blame an elephant for its huge appetite or a stone for being hard or a cloud for hiding the Sun. That is their nature, and we expect nothing different from them. But the computer has a nature, as well. True, it is only a machine but a machine designed to manipulate and generate information. That is what computers do, and therefore they have an agenda and an unmistakable message. The message is that through more and more information, more conveniently packaged, more swiftly delivered, we will find solutions to our problems. And so all the brilliant young men and women, believing this, create ingenious things for the computer to do, hoping that in this way, we will become wiser and more decent and more noble. And who can blame them? By becoming masters of this wondrous technology, they will acquire prestige and power and some will even become famous.

In a world populated by people who believe that through more and more information, paradise is attainable, the computer scientist is king. But I maintain that all of this is a monumental and dangerous waste of human talent and energy. Imagine what might be accomplished if this talent and energy were turned to philosophy, to theology, to the arts, to imaginative literature or to education? Who knows what we could learn from such people—perhaps why there are wars, and hunger, and homelessness and mental illness and danger. As things stand now, the geniuses of computer technology will give us Star Wars, and tell us that is the answer to nuclear war. They will give us artificial intelligence, and tell us that this is the way to self-knowledge. They will give us instantaneous global communication, and tell us this is the way to mutual understanding. They will give us Virtual Reality and tell us this is the answer to spiritual poverty. But that is only the way of the technician, the fact-mongerer, the information junkie, and the technological idiot.

Here is what Henry David Thoreau told us: "All our inventions are but improved means to an unimproved end." Here is what Goethe told us: "One should, each day, try to hear a little song read a good poem, see a fine picture, and, if it is possible, speak a few reasonable words." And here is what Socrates told us: "The unexamined life is not worth living." And here is what the prophet Micah told us: "What does the Lord require of thee but to do justly, and to love mercy and to walk humbly with thy God?" And I can tell you—if I had the time (although you all know it well enough)—what Confucius, Isaiah, Jesus, Mohammed, the Buddha, Spinoza and Shakespeare told us. It is all the same: There is no escaping from ourselves. The human dilemma is as it has always been, and we solve nothing fundamental by cloaking ourselves in technological glory. Even the humblest cartoon character knows this, and I shall close by quoting the wise old possum named Pogo, created by the cartoonist, Walt Kelley. I commend his words to all the technological utopians and messiahs present. "We have met the enemy," Pogo said, "and he is us."

Responding to Reading

1. In paragraph 7, Postman observes that "a new technology tends to favor some groups of people and harms other groups." What examples does he present to support this statement? Do his characterizations of "winners" and "losers" still make as much sense today as they did when he delivered this speech in 1990?

2. Postman believes that information, "which once was our friend," has "turned against us" (24). What does he mean? Do you think he might have had a different opinion today?

3. In paragraph 29, Postman says, "The computer and its information cannot answer any of the fundamental questions we need to address to make our lives more meaningful and humane." For this reason, he sees the quest for information as "a monumental and dangerous waste of human talent and energy" (31). Do you think he is overstating his case, or do you think he has a point?

Responding in Writing

List five useful pieces of information and five useless pieces of information that you have found on the Internet. Then, write two short paragraphs, one arguing that the Internet is a valuable resource, and another arguing that it is mostly a waste of time. Which paragraph is more convincing? Combine the information in the two paragraphs into a third paragraph that expresses your opinion on this issue.

TELEVISION: THE PLUG-IN DRUG

Marie Winn

1936–

Born in Prague, Marie Winn immigrated to the United States with her family in 1939. A graduate of Radcliffe College and Columbia University, she has written on a variety of subjects, but she is probably best known for her three critiques of television's effects on children and families: The Plug-In Drug: Television, Children and Family *(1977, revised 2002), from which the following selection was taken;* Children Without Childhood *(1983); and* Unplugging the Plug-In Drug *(1987). Winn, who writes a column on nature and bird watching for the* Wall Street Journal, *has also published* Red-Tails in Love: A Wildlife Drama in Central Park *(1998).*

Not much more than fifty years after the introduction of television into American society, the medium has become so deeply ingrained in daily life that in many states the TV set has attained the rank of a legal necessity, safe from repossession in case of debt along with clothes and cooking utensils. Only in the early years after television's introduction did writers and commentators have sufficient perspective to separate the activity of watching television from the actual content it offers the viewer. In those days writers frequently discussed the effects of television on family life. However, a curious myopia afflicted those first observers: almost without exception they regarded television as a favorable, beneficial, indeed, wondrous influence upon the family.

"Television is going to be a real asset in every home where there are children," predicted a writer in 1949.

"Television will take over your way of living and change your children's habits, but this change can be a wonderful improvement," claimed another commentator.

"No survey's needed, of course, to establish that television has brought the family together in one room," wrote the *New York Times*'s television critic in 1949.

5   The early articles about television were almost invariably accompanied by a photograph or illustration showing a family cozily sitting

together before the television set, Sis on Mom's lap, Buddy perched on the arm of Dad's chair, Dad with his arm around Mom's shoulder. Who could have guessed that twenty or so years later Mom would be watching a drama in the kitchen, the kids would be looking at cartoons in their room, while Dad would be taking in the ball game in the living room?

Of course television sets were enormously expensive when they first came on the market. The idea that by the year 2000 more than three quarters of all American families would own two or more sets would have seemed preposterous. The splintering of the multiple-set family was something the early writers did not foresee. Nor did anyone imagine the number of hours children would eventually devote to television, the changes television would effect upon child-rearing methods, the increasing domination of family schedules by children's viewing requirements—in short, the power of television to dominate family life.

As children's consumption of the new medium increased together with parental concern about the possible effects of so much television viewing, a steady refrain helped soothe and reassure anxious parents. "Television always enters a pattern of influences that already exist: the home, the peer group, the school, the church and culture generally," wrote the authors of an early and influential study of television's effects on children. In other words, if the child's home life is all right, parents need not worry about the effects of too much television watching.

But television did not merely influence the child; it deeply influenced that "pattern of influences" everyone hoped would ameliorate the new medium's effects. Home and family life have changed in important ways since the advent of television. The peer group has become television-oriented, and much of the time children spend together is occupied by television viewing. Culture generally has been transformed by television. Participation in church and community activities has diminished, with television a primary cause of this change. Therefore it is improper to assign to television the subsidiary role its many apologists insist it plays. Television is not merely one of a number of important influences upon today's child. Through the changes it has made in family life, television emerges as *the* important influence in children's lives today.

The Quality of Life

Television's contribution to family life has been an equivocal one. For while it has, indeed, kept the members of the family from dispersing, it has not served to bring them together. By its domination of the time families spend together, it destroys the special quality that distinguishes one family from another, a quality that depends to a great extent on what a family does, what special rituals, games, recurrent jokes, familiar songs, and shared activities it accumulates.

10   Yet parents have accepted a television-dominated family life so completely that they cannot see how the medium is involved in whatever problems they might be having. A first-grade teacher reports:

> I have one child in the group who's an only child. I wanted to find out more about her family life because this little girl was quite isolated from the group, didn't make friends, so I talked to her mother. Well, they don't have time to do anything in the evening, the mother said. The parents come home after picking up the child at the baby-sitter's. Then the mother fixes dinner while the child watches TV. Then they have dinner and the child goes to bed. I said to this mother. "Well, couldn't she help you fix dinner? That would be a nice time for the two of you to talk," and the mother said, "Oh, but I'd hate to have her miss *Zoom*. It's such a good program!"

Several decades ago a writer and mother of two boys aged three and seven described her family's television schedule in a newspaper article. Though some of the programs her kids watched then have changed, the situation she describes remains the same for great numbers of families today:

> We were in the midst of a full-scale War. Every day was a new battle and every program was a major skirmish. We agreed it was a bad scene all around and were ready to enter diplomatic negotiations. . . . In principle we have agreed on 2½ hours of TV a day, *Sesame Street, Electric Company* (with dinner gobbled up in between) and two half-hour shows between 7 and 8:30, which enables the grown-ups to eat in peace and prevents the two boys from destroying one another. Their pre-bedtime choice is dreadful, because, as Josh recently admitted, "There's nothing much on I really like." So . . . it's *What's My Line* or *To Tell the Truth.* . . . Clearly there is a need for first-rate children's shows at this time. . . .

Consider the "family life" described here: Presumably the father comes home from work during the *Sesame Street–Electric Company* stint. The children are either watching television, gobbling their dinner, or both. While the parents eat their dinner in peaceful privacy, the children watch another hour of television. Then there is only a half-hour left before bedtime, just enough time for baths, getting pajamas on, brushing teeth, and so on. The children's evening is regimented with an almost military precision. They watch their favorite programs, and when there is "nothing much on I really like," they watch whatever else is on—because *watching* is the important thing. Their mother does not see anything amiss with watching programs just for the sake of watching; she only wishes there were some first-rate children's shows on at those times.

Without conjuring up fantasies of bygone eras with family games and long, leisurely meals, the question arises: isn't there a better family life available than this dismal, mechanized arrangement of children watching television for however long is allowed them, evening after evening?

Of course, families today still do things together at times: go camping in the summer, go to the zoo on a nice Sunday, take various trips and expeditions. But their ordinary daily life together is diminished—those hours of sitting around at the dinner table, the spontaneous taking up of an activity, the little games invented by children on the spur of the moment when there is nothing else to do, the scribbling, the chatting, and even the quarreling, all the things that form the fabric of a family, that define a childhood. Instead, the children have their regular schedule of television programs and bedtime, and the parents have their peaceful dinner together.

The author of the quoted newspaper article notes that "keeping a 15 family sane means mediating between the needs of both children and adults." But surely the needs of the adults in that family were being better met than the needs of the children. The kids were effectively shunted away and rendered untroublesome, while their parents enjoyed a life as undemanding as that of any childless couple. In reality, it is those very demands that young children make upon a family that lead to growth, and it is the way parents respond to those demands that builds the relationships upon which the future of the family depends. If the family does not accumulate its backlog of shared experiences, shared everyday experiences that occur and recur and change and develop, then it is not likely to survive as anything other than a caretaking institution.

Family Rituals

Ritual is defined by sociologists as "that part of family life that the family likes about itself, is proud of and wants formally to continue." Another text notes that "the development of a ritual by a family is an index of the common interest of its members in the family as a group."

What has happened to family rituals, those regular, dependable, recurrent happenings that gave members of a family a feeling of belonging to a home rather than living in it merely for the sake of convenience, those experiences that act as the adhesive of family unity far more than any material advantages?

Mealtime rituals, going-to-bed rituals, illness rituals, holiday rituals—how many of these have survived the inroads of the television set?

A young woman who grew up near Chicago reminisces about her childhood and gives an idea of the effects of television upon family rituals:

> As a child I had millions of relatives around—my parents both come from relatively large families. My father had nine brothers and sisters. And so every holiday there was this great swoop-down of aunts, uncles, and millions of cousins. I just remember how wonderful it used to be. These thousands of cousins would come and everyone would play and ultimately, after dinner, all the women would be in the front of the house, drinking coffee and talking, all the men would be in the back of the house, drinking and smoking, and all the kids would be all over the place, playing hide and seek. Christmas time was particularly nice because everyone always brought all their toys and games. Our house had a couple of rooms with go-through closets, so there were always kids running in a great circle route. I remember it was just wonderful.
>
> And then all of a sudden one year I remember becoming suddenly aware of how different everything had become. The kids were no longer playing Monopoly or Clue or the other games we used to play together. It was because we had a television set which had been turned on for a football game. All of that socializing that had gone on previously had ended. Now everyone was sitting in front of the television set, on a holiday, at a family party! I remember being stunned by how awful that was. Somehow the television had become more attractive.

20   As families have come to spend more and more of their time together engaged in the single activity of television watching, those rituals and pastimes that once gave family life its special quality have become more and more uncommon. Not since prehistoric times, when cave families hunted, gathered, ate, and slept, with little time remaining to accumulate a culture of any significance, have families been reduced to such a sameness.

Real People

The relationships of family members to each other are affected by television's powerful competition in both obvious and subtle ways. For surely the hours that children spend in a one-way relationship with television people, an involvement that allows for no communication or interaction, must have some effect on their relationships with real-life people.

Studies show the importance of eye-to-eye contact, for instance, in real-life relationships, and indicate that the nature of one's eye-contact patterns, whether one looks another squarely in the eye or looks to the side or shifts one's gaze from side to side, may play a significant role in one's success or failure in human relationships. But no eye contact is possible in the child-television relationship, although in certain children's programs people purport to speak directly to the child and the camera fosters this illusion by focusing directly upon the person being filmed. How might such a distortion affect a child's development of trust, of openness, of an ability to relate well to *real* people? Bruno Bettelheim suggested an answer:

> Children who have been taught, or conditioned, to listen passively most of the day to the warm verbal communications coming from the TV screen, to the deep emotional appeal of the so-called TV personality, are often unable to respond to real persons because they arouse so much less feeling than the skilled actor. Worse, they lose the ability to learn from reality because life experiences are much more complicated than the ones they see on the screen. . ..

A teacher makes a similar observation about her personal viewing experiences:

> I have trouble mobilizing myself and dealing with real people after watching a few hours of television. It's just hard to make that transition from watching television to a real relationship. I suppose it's because there was no effort necessary while I was watching, and dealing with real people always requires a bit of effort. Imagine, then, how much harder it might be to do the same thing for a small child, particularly one who watches a lot of television every day.

But more obviously damaging to family relationships is the elimi- 25
nation of opportunities to talk and converse, or to argue, to air grievances between parents and children and brothers and sisters. Families frequently use television to avoid confronting their problems, problems that will not go away if they are ignored but will only fester and become less easily resolvable as time goes on.

A mother reports:

> I find myself, with three children, wanting to turn on the TV set when they're fighting. I really have to struggle not to do it because I feel that's telling them this is the solution to the quarrel—but it's so tempting that I often do it.

A family therapist discusses the use of television as an avoidance mechanism:

> In a family I know the father comes home from work and turns on the television set. The children come and watch with him and the wife serves them their meal in front of the set. He then goes and takes a

shower, or works on the car or something. She then goes and has her own dinner in front of the television set. It's a symptom of a deeper-rooted problem, sure. But it would help them all to get rid of the set. It would be far easier to work on what the symptom really means without the television. The television simply encourages a double avoidance of each other. They'd find out more quickly what was going on if they weren't able to hide behind the TV. Things wouldn't necessarily be better, of course, but they wouldn't be anesthetized.

A number of research studies done when television was a relatively new medium demonstrated that television interfered with family activities and the formation of family relationships. One survey showed that 78 percent of the respondents indicated no conversation taking place during viewing except at specified times such as commercials. The study noted: "The television atmosphere in most households is one of quiet absorption on the part of family members who are present. The nature of the family social life during a program could be described as 'parallel' rather than interactive, and the set does seem to dominate family life when it is on." Thirty-six percent of the respondents in another study indicated that television viewing was the only family activity participated in during the week.

The situation has only worsened during the intervening decades. When the studies were made, the great majority of American families had only one television set. Though the family may have spent more time watching TV in those early days, at least they were all together while they watched. Today the vast majority of all families have two or more sets, and nearly a third of all children live in homes with four or more TVs. The most telling statistic: almost 60 percent of all families watch television during meals, and not necessarily at the same TV set. When do they talk about what they did that day? When do they make plans, exchange views, share jokes, tell about their triumphs or little disasters? When do they get to be a real family?

Undermining the Family

30 Of course television has not been the only factor in the decline of family life in America. The steadily rising divorce rate, the increase in the number of working mothers, the trends towards people moving far away from home, the breakdown of neighborhoods and communities—all these have seriously affected the family.

Obviously the sources of family breakdown do not necessarily come from the family itself, but from the circumstances in which the family finds itself and the way of life imposed upon it by those circumstances. As Urie Bronfenbrenner has suggested:

When those circumstances and the way of life they generate undermine relationships of trust and emotional security between family
members, when they make it difficult for parents to care for, educate,
and enjoy their children, when there is no support or recognition
from the outside world for one's role as a parent, and when time
spent with one's family means frustration of career, personal fulfillment, and peace of mind, then the development of the child is adversely affected.

Certainly television is not the single destroyer of American family
life. But the medium's dominant role in the family serves to anesthetize parents into accepting their family's diminished state and prevents them from struggling to regain some of the richness the family
once possessed.

One research study alone seems to contradict the idea that television has a negative impact on family life. In their important book
Television and the Quality of Life, sociologists Robert Kubey and Mihaly
Csikszentmihalyi observe that the heaviest viewers of TV among their
subjects were "no less likely to spend time with their families" than
the lightest viewers. Moreover, those heavy viewers reported feeling
happier, more relaxed, and satisfied when watching TV with their
families than light viewers did. Based on these reports, the researchers reached the conclusion that "television viewing harmonizes
with family life."

Using the same data, however, the researchers made another observation about the heavy and light viewers: ". . . families that spend
substantial portions of their time together watching television are
likely to experience greater percentages of their family time feeling
relatively passive and unchallenged compared with families who
spend small proportions of their time watching TV."

At first glance the two observations seem at odds: the heavier 35
viewers feel happy and satisfied, yet their family time is more passive
and unchallenging—less satisfying in reality. But when one considers
the nature of the television experience, the contradiction vanishes.
Surely it stands to reason that the television experience is instrumental in preventing viewers from recognizing its dulling effects, much as
a mind-altering drug might do.

In spite of everything, the American family muddles on, dimly
aware that something is amiss but distracted from an understanding
of its plight by an endless stream of television images. As family ties
grow weaker and vaguer, as children's lives become more separate
from their parents', as parents' educational role in their children's
lives is taken over by the media, the school, and the peer group, family life becomes increasingly more unsatisfying for both parents and
children. All that seems to be left is love, an abstraction that family
members know is necessary but find great difficulty giving to each

other since the traditional opportunities for expressing it within the family have been reduced or eliminated.

Responding to Reading

1. Winn says, "Home and family life have changed in important ways since the advent of television" (8). How, according to Winn, has family life changed? What kind of support does she offer for this conclusion? Is it enough?
2. Do you agree with Winn that television is an evil, addictive drug that has destroyed cherished family rituals, undermined family relationships, and "[anesthetized] parents into accepting their family's diminished state and [prevented] them from struggling to regain some of the richness the family once possessed" (32)? Or, do you think she is exaggerating the dangers of TV?
3. Although it was updated in 2002, Winn's essay was written more than twenty-five years ago. In light of how much time has passed, do you think she needs to change any of her examples or add new information?

Responding in Writing

Do you consider any other item—for example, your cell phone or your computer—to be a "plug-in drug" for you? Do you see any danger in your dependence on this object, or do you consider it just a routine part of your life?

TESTIFYING: TELEVISION
Wendy Kaminer
1950–

Cultural critic Wendy Kaminer received a Bachelor's degree from Smith College and a law degree from Boston University Law School. She practiced law in New York City from 1977 to 1984, working both for the Legal Aid Society and for the Office of the Mayor, and later taught English at Tufts University. A fellow at Radcliffe College, Kaminer is a senior correspondent for the American Prospect *and a contributing editor to the* Atlantic Monthly. *Her articles and reviews have also appeared in many national publications, and her commentaries have aired on National Public Radio. The following essay is taken from her book* I'm Dysfunctional, You're Dysfunctional: The Recovery Movement and Other Self-Help Fashions *(1992), in which she evaluates and criticizes the various self-help movements. Kaminer's recent books include* Sleeping with Extra-Terrestrials: The Rise of Irrationalism and Perils of Piety *(1999) and* Free For All: Defending Liberty in America Today *(2002).*

Recovering substance abuser Kitty Dukakis once called a press conference to announce her descent into alcoholism and request respect for her privacy. It was shortly after her husband's defeat in the 1988 presidential race, when she was less newsworthy than the pearls adorning Barbara Bush's neck. I marveled only briefly at the spectacle of a woman seeking privacy in a press conference and public confession of an addiction. Some people, especially famous and formerly famous ones, seem to enjoy their privacy only in public. Now You Know, Kitty Dukakis called her book, in case you cared.

Still, millions of readers who don't care about Dukakis and all the other recovering personalities who write books are curious, I guess. Confessional autobiographies by second-string celebrities are publishing staples (and where would the talk shows be without them?). Ali MacGraw exposes her sex addiction and the lurid details of her marriage to Steve McQueen. Suzanne Somers chronicles her life as an ACOA [Adult Child of an Alcoholic]. Former first children Michael Reagan and Patti Davis reveal their histories of abuse.

"I truly hope my book will help others to heal," the celebrity diarists are likely to say. Or they assure us that writing their books was therapeutic (and if they pay me to read them, I will). But the celebrities don't really have to explain the decision to go public. In our culture of recovery we take their confessions for granted. Talking about yourself is "part of the process." Suggesting to someone that she is talking too much about herself is a form of abuse. If you can't feign interest in someone else's story, you're supposed to maintain respectful or, better yet, stunned silence. In recovery, where everyone gets to claim that she's survived some holocaust of family life, everyone gets to testify.

The tradition of testifying in court, church, or the marketplace for justice, God, or the public good is a venerable one that I would not impugn. But it is also a tradition I'd rather not debase by confusing testifying with advertisements for yourself or simple plays for sympathy and attention. The recovery movement combines the testimonial tradition that serves a greater good, like justice, with the therapeutic tradition in which talking about yourself is its own reward. It also borrows liberally from the revivalist tradition of testifying to save your soul and maybe others: in recovery, even the most trivial testimony is sanctified.

I'm not impugning therapy or religion either, but I wish that people would keep them off the streets. Religion has, of course, a complicated, controversial history of public uses and abuses, which are beyond the scope of this [essay]. But therapy was conceived as a private transaction between doctors and patients (experts and clients) or between groups of patients, clients, seekers of psychic well-being. Testimony was public. By blurring the distinction between confession and testimony, recovery transforms therapy into a public process too. People even do it on TV.

Most of us do love to talk about ourselves, although I've always regarded it as a slightly illicit pleasure or one you pay for by the hour. Etiquette books dating back over a century gently admonish readers to cultivate the art of listening, assuming that, unmannered in their natural states, most people are braggarts and bores. Success primers have always stressed that listening skills will help you get ahead: Listen raptly to someone in power who loves talking about himself in order to impress him with your perspicacity. Listening is a useful form of flattery, Dale Carnegie[1] advised, sharing with men what women have always known. Flirting is a way of listening. (Feminism is women talking.)

For women who were socialized to listen, uncritically, talking too much about themselves may feel like an act of rebellion. Maybe Kitty Dukakis felt liberated by her book. Personal development passes for politics, and what might once have been called whining is now exalted as a process of asserting selfhood; self-absorption is regarded as a form of self-expression, as if creative acts involved no interactions with the world. Feminists did say that the personal was political, but they meant that private relations between the sexes reflected public divisions of power, that putatively private events, like wife beating, were public concerns. They didn't mean that getting to know yourself was sufficient political action. Consciousness raising was supposed to inspire activism. Feminism is women talking, but it is not women only talking and not women talking only about themselves.

Talk shows and the elevation of gossip to intellectual discourse are, after all, postfeminist, postmodern phenomena. In academia, where gossip is now text, poststructural scholars scour history for the private, particular experiences of ordinary "unempowered" people; and like denizens of daytime TV, they also talk a lot about themselves, deconstructing their own class, racial, or ethnic biases in perverse assertions of solidarity with what are presumed to be other entirely subjective selves. On talk shows, ordinary people, subject of tomorrow's scholars, find their voice. Men and mostly women distinguished only by various and weird infidelities or histories of drug abuse and overeating get equal time with movie actors, soap stars, and the occasional hair stylist. Now everyone can hope for sixty minutes of fame, minus some time for commercials.

I never really wonder anymore why people want to talk about themselves for nearly an hour in front of millions of strangers. They find it "affirming"; like trees that fall in the forest, they're not sure that they exist when no one's watching. I've accepted that as post-

---

[1]Author of one of the first successful series of self-improvement books [Eds.]

modern human nature. I do wonder at the eagerness and pride with which they reveal, on national television, what I can't help thinking of as intimacies—sexual and digestive disorders; personal conflicts with parents, children, spouses, lovers, bosses, and best friends. I wonder even more at the intensity with which the audience listens.

Why aren't they bored? It may be that listening is simply the price 10 they pay for their turn to grab the mike and have their say, offering criticism or advice, just like the experts. But they seem genuinely intrigued by the essentially unremarkable details of other people's lives and other people's feelings. Something in us likes soap operas, I know, but watching the talks is not like watching "Dallas" or "Days of Our Lives." The guests aren't particularly articulate, except on "Geraldo" sometimes, where they seem to be well coached; they rarely finish their sentences, which trail off in vague colloquialisms, you know what I mean? Most guests aren't witty or perceptive or even telegenic. They aren't artful. They are the people you'd ignore if you saw them on line at the supermarket instead of on TV.

I'm not sure how we got to the point of finding anyone else's confessions, obsessions, or advertisements for herself entertaining. I'm not sure why watching other people's home movies became fun; the appeal of "America's Funniest Home Videos" eludes me. But it's clear that the popularity of "real people" television—talk shows and home videos—has little to do with compassion and the desire to connect. If an average person on the subway turns to you, like the ancient mariner, and starts telling you her tale, you turn away or nod and hope she stops, not just because you fear she might be crazy. If she tells her tale on camera, you might listen. Watching strangers on television, even responding to them from a studio audience, we're disengaged—voyeurs collaborating with exhibitionists in rituals of sham community. Never have so many known so much about people for whom they cared so little.

A woman appears on "Oprah Winfrey" to tell the nation that she hates herself for being ugly. Oprah and the expert talk to her about self-esteem and the woman basks, I think, in their attention. The spectacle is painful and pathetic, and watching it, I feel diminished.

Oprah, I suspect, regards her show as a kind of public service. The self-proclaimed ugly woman is appearing on a segment about our obsession with good looks. We live in a society that values pretty people over plain, Oprah explains; and maybe she is exploring a legitimate public issue, by exploiting a private pathology.

Daytime TV, however, is proudly pathological. On "Geraldo" a recovering sex addict shares a story of incest—she was raped by her father and stepfather; her husband and children are seated next to her on the stage. This is family therapy. (The family that reveals together congeals together.) Her daughter talks about being a lesbian. Two sex addiction experts—a man and a woman, "professional and personal partners"—explain and offer commentary on sex and love addictions. "It's not a matter of frequency," they say in response to questions about how often sex addicts have sex. Anonymous addicts call in with their own tales, boring and lurid: "I do specifically use sex to make myself feel better," one caller confesses. Who doesn't?

15   Geraldo, his experts, and the members of his audience address the problem of promiscuity with the gravity of network anchors discussing a sub-Saharan famine. If I were a recovering person, I might say that they're addicted to melodrama. In fact, Geraldo does a show on people "addicted to excitement—drama, danger, and self destruction"—people who create crises for themselves. He offers us a self-evaluation tool—eleven questions "to determine whether you're a soap opera queen." Do you get mad at other drivers on the road? Do you talk about your problems with a lot of other people? Questions like these make addicts of us all, as experts must hope. Labeling impatience in traffic a symptom of disease creates a market for the cure; and Joy Davidson, the expert author who identified the "soap opera syndrome" for us is here on "Geraldo," peddling her book.

The audience is intrigued. People stand up to testify to their own experiences with drama and excitement addictions. With the concern of any patient describing her symptoms, one woman says that she often disagrees with her husband for no good reason. Someone else confesses to being a worrier.

No one suggests to Davidson that calling the mundane concerns and frustrations of daily life symptoms of the disease of overdramatizing is, well, overdramatizing. In the language of recovery, we might say that Davidson is an enabler, encouraging her readers to indulge in their melodrama addictions, or we might say that she too is a practicing melodrama addict. One man does point out that there are "people in the ghetto" who don't have to fabricate their crises. But if Davidson gets the point, she successfully eludes it. Yes, she admits, the crises in the ghetto are real, but what matters is the way you deal with them. As Norman Vincent Peale[2] might say, people in crisis have only to develop a happiness habit.

Meanwhile, on daytime TV, middle-class Americans are busy practicing their worry habits, swapping stories of disease and controversial eccentricities. Here is a sampling of "Oprah": Apart from the usual assortment of guests who eat, drink, shop, worry, or have sex too much, there are fathers who sleep with their sons' girlfriends (or try to), sisters who sleep with their sisters' boyfriends, women who

---

[2]Minister, lecuturer, and writer (1898–1993), whose best-selling series of books, beginning with *The Power of Positive Thinking* (1952), made him one of the first self-help authors. [Eds.]

sleep with their best friends' sons, women who sleep with their husbands' bosses (to help their husbands get ahead), men who hire only pretty women, and men and women who date only interracially. Estranged couples share their grievances while an expert provides on-air counseling: "Why are you so afraid to let your anger out at her?" he asks a husband. "Why don't you let him speak for himself," he chides the wife. Couples glare at each other, sometimes the women cry, and the expert keeps advising them to get in touch with their feelings and build up their self-esteem. The chance to sit in on someone else's therapy session is part of the appeal of daytime TV. When Donahue[3] interviews the children of prostitutes, he has an expert on hand to tell them how they feel.

The number of viewers who are helped by these shows is impossible to know, but it's clear that they're a boon to several industries— publishing, therapy, and, of course, recovery. Commercials often tie in to the shows. A segment on food addiction is sponsored by weight-loss programs: "It's not what you're eating. It's what's eating you," the ads assure anxious overeaters. Shows on drug and alcohol abuse are sponsored by treatment centers, set in sylvan glades. Standing by lakes, leaning on trees, the pitchmen are soft and just a little somber— elegiac; they might be selling funeral plots instead of a recovery lifestyle and enhanced self-esteem.

On almost every show, someone is bound to get around to self esteem; most forms of misconduct are said to be indicative of low self-esteem. On every other show, someone talks about addiction. The audiences usually speak fluent recovery. You can talk about your inner child or your grief work on "Oprah" and no one will ask you what you mean. "I follow a twelve-step program that helps me deal with the disease concept, the addiction [to overeating]," a man in the audience announces, and people nod. No one asks, "What's a twelve-step program?" or "What do you mean by addiction?" Oprah testifies too: "I'm still addicted [to food]. I'll never be free." 20

On stage, a panel of recovering food addicts, all women, is vowing never to diet again. "We have to allow ourselves to love ourselves," they say, and Oprah agrees. "I'm never going to weigh another piece of chicken." Tired of "seeking control," these women want to accept their weight, not constantly struggle to lose it, and I wish them luck. Beauty may lack moral value, but it's useful, and what has been labeled beastly—obesity or really bad skin—is a painful liability, as the women on "Oprah" make clear. They've apparently spent much of their lives embarrassed by their bodies; now, in recovery, they talk about the "shame" of fatness. They find some

---

[3]Among the first to host a day-time talk show focusing on the personal problems of "average" people, Phil Donahue was on the air from 1967 to 1996. [Eds.]

self-esteem in victimhood. They aren't gluttons but "victims of a dis-ease process." Being fat is not their fault. Recovering from obesity "is not about self-control," one woman says, voicing the ethos of recovery that dispenses with will. "It's about self-love."

But the next day, when Oprah does a show on troubled marriages, some sort of therapist, Dr. Ron, advises a woman who is self-conscious about her small breasts to have implants. He berates her unfaithful husband for not supporting her in this quest for a better body, for her own good, for the sake of her self-esteem, and to help save their marriage: her poor self-image was one of the reasons he strayed. That a woman with small breasts can't be expected to improve her self-esteem without implants is apparently evident to Dr. Ron and everyone else on the show. No one questions his wisdom, not even learning-to-love-herself Oprah, recovering dieter.

I digress, but so do Geraldo, Donahue, and Oprah. Talking about these shows, I find it hard to be entirely coherent, and coherence would not do justice to the kaleidoscope of complaints, opinions, prejudices, revelations, and celebrations they comprise: Geraldo discusses celibacy with a panel of virgins and Helen Gurley Brown. "There are no medical risks associated with virginity," a doctor assures us. Adopted children and their biological parents as well as siblings separated from birth for over twenty years meet, for the first time, on "Geraldo" ("Reunions of the Heart: Finding a Lost Love," the show is called). "Welcome long-lost brother Brian," Geraldo commands, to wild applause, as Brian emerges from backstage, and in a TV minute people are hugging and sobbing on camera as they did years ago on "This Is Your Life." I want someone in the audience to ask them why they're not having their reunions in private, but I already know the answer. "We want to share the love and joy of this moment," they'd say. "We want to inspire other people from broken families not to give up the search." I suspect that the audience knows these answers too. Clapping and crying (even Geraldo is teary), reached for and touched, they offer support and validation: "It's a real blessing to see how you've all been healed of your hurts," one woman in the audience declares. Geraldo makes a plea for open adoption, grappling with an issue, I guess.

Occasionally, I admit, the shows are instructive in ways they intend, not just as portraits of popular culture. Donahue's segment on grandparents who are raising the children of their drug-addicted children manages to be dignified and sad. He talks to obese children without overdramatizing their struggles or exploiting them. (Donahue is good with kids.) Oprah seems likable and shrewd in the midst of her silliest shows, and, once in a while, the testimony illuminates an issue: date rape or racially segregated proms.

25   This is the new journalism—issues packaged in anecdotes that may or may not be true. As an occasional, alternative approach to news

and analysis, it is affecting; as the predominant approach, it is not just trite but stupefying. If all issues are personalized, we lose our capacity to entertain ideas, to generalize from our own or someone else's experiences, to think abstractly. We substitute sentimentality for thought.

TV talk shows certainly didn't invent the new journalism and are hardly the only abusers of it. But they are emblematic of the widespread preference for feelings over ideas that is celebrated by recovery and other personal development movements. It is no coincidence that the two trends—talk shows and recovery—have fueled each other. The shows often seem like orchestrated support groups; the groups seem like rehearsals for the shows.

Accusing talk shows of not providing critical analysis of issues is, I know, like accusing *"Ozzie and Harriet"*[4] of idealizing the nuclear family. "He wrestles with the obvious," a friend once said of an especially boring pundit, and I don't mean to wrestle with TV. I just wanna testify too.

Once, I appeared on the "Oprah Winfrey" show. I was one of six alleged experts participating in what was billed as a "debate" on codependency. Joining me onstage were two against-codependency allies and three for-codependency opponents. (The two sides were driven in separate limousines and kept in separate rooms before the show.) Oprah was more or less pro-codependency too—someone said she had just returned from one of John Bradshaw's retreats—and the audience seemed filled with evangelical twelve steppers.

"Just jump in. Don't wait to be called on," one of Oprah's people told us when she prepped us for the show. "You mean you want us to interrupt each other?" I asked; the woman nodded. "You want us to be really rude and step on each other's lines?" She nodded again. "You want us to act as if we're at a large, unruly family dinner on Thanksgiving?" She smiled and said, "You got it!"

I had a good time on "Oprah." Being chauffeured around in a   30
limo and housed in a first-class hotel, I felt like Cinderella, especially when I got home. I liked being on national television, almost as much as my mother liked watching me. I also like unruly family dinners, but I'd never call what goes on over the turkey a debate.

The trouble with talk shows is that they claim to do so much more than entertain; they claim to inform and explain. They dominate the mass marketplace and help make it one that is inimical to ideas.

That's probably not a startling revelation, but appearing on a talk show, you are hit hard with the truth of it. Being on "Oprah" was still a shock, although not a surprise. I watch a fair amount of talk shows and understand the importance of speaking in sound bites, although I don't always succeed in doing so. I know that talk show "debates" are

---

[4]Quitessential 1950s familiy sitcom. [Eds.]

not usually coherent; they don't usually follow any pattern of statement and response. They don't make sense. The host is less a moderator than a traffic cop. People don't talk to each other; they don't even talk at each other. They talk at the camera. So I wasn't surprised when Oprah's assistant told us to "just jump in." I expected the show to be chaotic (the experience exceeded the expectation). What I did not expect, and should have, was the audience's utter lack of interest in argument; they wanted only to exchange testimony.

I had nothing to say to the studio audience—and talked at the camera too—because I had no personal experience with addiction and recovery to convey. The most popular "expert" on our panel was the most melodramatic: Lois, a recovering codependent from Texas, declared repeatedly, in response to nothing in particular, "Mah parents died of this disease!" ("What disease?" we asked, in vain.) "Recovery saved mah life!" Once or twice she added cryptically, "Ah was not supposed to be born! Ah was a mistake!" as the audience applauded.

On daytime talk shows a "debate" generally consists of a parade of people onstage or in the audience stating strong personal preferences with frequent references to some searing personal experience. "Does too!" "Does not!" people say, debating whether the recovery movement helps us. "I'm a recovering person and I just want to say that this movement saved my life," members of the audience on "Oprah" declared. "I would be dead today if it weren't for this movement!"

35   You can't argue with a testimonial. You can only counter it with a testimonial of your own. ("Does too!" "Does not!") Testimony has no value as argument. You can't even be sure of its value as testimony. Is it true? What do people mean when they say that they are addicted? Addicted to what, at what cost? What do people mean when they say they've been abused? Are they talking about emotional or physical abuse? Was it real or imagined? Were they beaten by their parents or ignored? "What are you all recovering from?" one man in the back row of Oprah's audience asked repeatedly and in vain as self-proclaimed recovering persons testified.

But if you can't evaluate or argue with testimony, you can say that it's beside the point. How one hundred people in a studio audience feel about codependency doesn't tell us very much about its impact on the culture, or even its general success and failure rate with individuals. Testimony often precludes analysis. What was striking to me about the audience on "Oprah" was its collective inability or unwillingness to think about recovery in any terms other than the way it made them feel. To the extent that they commented on it as a cultural phenomenon at all, they simply universalized their own experiences: "It worked for me. So it will work for everyone else."

Testifying, as a substitute for thinking, is contagious. You even find it in the halls of academe. Teaching college freshmen, I quickly discovered that my students were interested only in issues that were dramatized—in fiction, memoirs, or popular journalism. Raised on "Donahue" and docudramas, they found mere discussions of ideas "too dry and academic." You can't even be academic in academia anymore. Instead of theory, they sought testimony.

Among graduate students and professors too, subjectivity has been in fashion for several years. The diversification of student populations and concern for multiculturalism have made respect for subjective experiences and points of view political imperatives. Fashions in literary and legal theory and historical research focus on knowledge as a matter of perspective, disdaining the "pretense" of objectivity. Scholars get to talk about themselves. Theory is nothing but testimony.

I'm not suggesting that the dead white males who once held sway and set standards had The Answer or that a multiplicity of perspectives in matters of politics and theory isn't welcome. Nor am I suggesting that analysis should somehow be divorced from experience. I'm only suggesting the obvious—that analysis and experience need to be balanced. There are degrees of objectivity worth trying to acquire.

It should be needless to say that individual preferences are not al- 40 ways the best measures of what is generally good. A tax provision that saves you money may still be generally unfair. Of course, the recovery movement is not analogous to the tax code. It is not imposed on us. It is not a public policy that demands deliberation and debate. I don't want to gloss over the difference between public acts and private experiments with personality development. Indeed, I want to highlight it.

A self-referential evaluation of a self-help movement is probably inevitable and, to some extent, appropriate. A self-referential evaluation of public policies can be disastrous. What is disturbing about watching the talk shows is recognizing in discussions of private problems a solipsism that carries over into discussions of public issues. What you see on "Oprah" is what you see in the political arena. We choose our elected officials and formulate policies on the basis of how they make us feel about ourselves. (Jimmy Carter's biggest mistake was in depressing us.) We even evaluate wars according to their effect on our self-esteem: Vietnam was a downer. The Persian Gulf War, like a good self-help program, cured us of our "Vietnam syndrome" and "gave us back our pride," as General Motors hopes to do with Chevrolets. Norman Schwarzkopf and Colin Powell satisfied our need for heroes, everyone said. The networks stroked us with video montages of handsome young soldiers, leaning on tanks, staring off into the desert, wanting to "get the job done" and go home. By conservative estimates, 150,000 people were killed outright in the war; the number who will die from disease, deprivation, and environmental damage may be incalculable. Whether or not the war was necessary, whether or not the victory was real, we should consider it a great success because it gave us parades and a proud Fourth of July. The culture of recovery is insidious: now the moral measure of a war is how it makes us feel about ourselves.

"Try and put aside your own experiences in recovery and the way it makes you feel," I suggested to the audience on "Oprah." "Think about what the fascination with addiction means to us as a culture. Think about the political implications of advising people to surrender their will and submit to a higher power." People in the audience looked at me blankly. Later, in the limo, one of my copanelists (against codependency) shook his head at me and smiled and said, "That was a PBS comment."

Some two months later I showed my "Oprah" tape to a group of college friends, over a bottle of wine. None of them is involved in the recovery movement or familiar with its programs or jargon. Listening to six panelists and a studio audience compete for air time, in eight-minute segments between commercials, none of them thought the "Oprah" show made any sense. Like the man in the audience who asked, "What are you all recovering from?" they didn't have a clue. "You have to think with your hearts and not your heads," a for-codependency expert exhorted us at the end of the show, as the credits rolled.

Responding to Reading

1. According to Kaminer, what is the difference between "confessing" and "testifying"? What danger does she see in "blurring the distinction between confession and testimony" (5)?

2. In paragraph 11, Kaminer says, "Never have so many known so much about people for whom they cared so little." Why do you suppose so many people are willing "to talk about themselves for nearly an hour in front of millions of strangers" (9)? Why do you think so many viewers of talk shows find them so compelling?

3. "The trouble with talk shows," Kaminer says, "is that they claim to do so much more than entertain; they claim to inform and explain" (31). In paragraph 24, she concedes that talk shows are sometimes "instructive"; for the most part, though, she is highly critical of these programs, saying, among other things, that they encourage viewers to "substitute sentimentality for thought" (25). Do you think Kaminer is being too hard on talk shows? Do you think she is taking them too seriously? Explain your views.

Responding in Writing

Watch 15 minutes of a television talk show, and then write a paragraph explaining how the program you watched is or is not consistent with Kaminer's characterization of talk shows. Be very specific in identifying any differences you observe.

REALITY TV: A DEARTH OF TALENT AND THE DEATH OF MORALITY

Salman Rushdie

1947–

Born in Bombay, India, Salman Rushdie earned an MA in history from King's College in Cambridge, England (1968). Before his first novel was published in 1975, he wrote for and acted in theater for several years and worked as a freelance advertising copywriter. Rushdie is perhaps best known for his novel The Satanic Verses *(1988), which infuriated Muslims around the world. The book was banned in a dozen countries, caused riots in several, and led to a multimillion-dollar bounty being offered for Rushdie's assassination. In 1998, the* fatwa *(death sentence) was lifted by the Iranian government (although some fundamentalist Muslim groups increased the reward for killing him). Rushdie lives in seclusion and continues to publish articles, essays, and books, including* The Ground beneath Her Feet *(1999),* Fury *(2001), and* Step Across This Line: Collected Nonfiction 1992–2002 *(2002). The following selection appeared in* The Guardian *in 2001. To read more about this author, visit the Salman Rushdie–inspired Web site, http:// www.subir.com/rushdie.html/.*

I've managed to miss out on reality TV until now. In spite of all the talk in Britain about nasty Nick and flighty Mel, and in America about the fat, naked bastard Richard manipulating his way to desert-island victory, I have somehow preserved my purity. I wouldn't recognise Nick or Mel if I passed them in the street, or Richard if he was standing in front of me unclothed.

Ask me where the Big Brother house is, or how to reach Temptation Island, and I have no answer. I do remember the American *Survivor* contestant who managed to fry his own hand so that the skin peeled away until his fingers looked like burst sausages, but that's because he got on to the main evening news. Otherwise, search me. Who won? Who lost? Who cares?

The subject of reality TV shows, however, has been impossible to avoid. Their success is the media story of the (new) century, along with the ratings triumph of the big-money game shows such as *Who Wants to Be a Millionaire?* Success on this scale insists on being examined, because it tells us things about ourselves; or ought to.

And what tawdry narcissism is here revealed! The television set, once so idealistically thought of as our window on the world, has become a dime-store mirror instead. Who needs images of the world's rich otherness, when you can watch these half-familiar avatars of yourself—these half-attractive half-persons—enacting ordinary life under weird conditions? Who needs talent, when the unashamed self-display of the talentless is constantly on offer?

5   I've been watching *Big Brother 2*, which has achieved the improbable feat of taking over the tabloid front pages in the final stages of a general election campaign. This, according to the conventional wisdom, is because the show is more interesting than the election. The "reality" may be even stranger. It may be that *Big Brother* is so popular because it's even more boring than the election. Because it is the most boring, and therefore most "normal," way of becoming famous, and, if you're lucky or smart, of getting rich as well.

"Famous" and "rich" are now the two most important concepts in western society, and ethical questions are simply obliterated by the potency of their appeal. In order to be famous and rich, it's OK—it's actually "good"—to be devious. It's "good" to be exhibitionistic. It's "good" to be bad. And what dulls the moral edge is boredom. It's impossible to maintain a sense of outrage about people being so trivially self-serving for so long.

Oh, the dullness! Here are people becoming famous for being asleep, for keeping a fire alight, for letting a fire go out, for videotaping their cliched thoughts, for flashing their breasts, for lounging around, for quarrelling, for bitching, for being unpopular, and (this is too interesting to happen often) for kissing! Here, in short, are people becoming famous for doing nothing much at all, but doing it where everyone can see them.

Add the contestants' exhibitionism to the viewers' voyeurism and you get a picture of a society sickly in thrall to what Saul Bellow called "event glamour." Such is the glamour of these banal but brilliantly spotlit events that anything resembling a real value—modesty, decency, intelligence, humour, selflessness; you can write your own list—is rendered redundant. In this inverted ethical universe, worse is better. The show presents "reality" as a prize fight, and suggests that in life, as on TV, anything goes, and the more deliciously contemptible it is, the more we'll like it. Winning isn't everything, as Charlie Brown once said, but losing isn't anything.

The problem with this kind of engineered realism is that, like all fads, it's likely to have a short shelf-life, unless it finds ways of renewing itself. The probability is that our voyeurism will become more demanding. It won't be enough to watch somebody being catty, or weeping when evicted from the house of hell, or "revealing everything" on subsequent talk shows, as if they had anything left to reveal.

10   What is gradually being reinvented is the gladiatorial combat. The TV set is the Colosseum and the contestants are both gladiators and lions; their job is to eat one another until only one remains alive. But how long, in our jaded culture, before "real" lions, actual dangers, are introduced to these various forms of fantasy island, to feed our hunger for more action, more pain, more vicarious thrills?

Here's a thought, prompted by the news that the redoubtable Gore Vidal has agreed to witness the execution by lethal injection of the Oklahoma bomber Timothy McVeigh. The witnesses at an execution watch the macabre proceedings through a glass window: a screen. This, too, is a kind of reality TV, and—to make a modest proposal—it may represent the future of such programmes. If we are willing to watch people stab one another in the back, might we not also be willing to actually watch them die?

In the world outside TV, our numbed senses already require increasing doses of titillation. One murder is barely enough; only the mass murderers make the front pages. You have to blow up a building full of people or machine-gun a whole royal family to get our attention. Soon, perhaps, you'll have to kill off a whole species of wildlife or unleash a virus that wipes out people by the thousand, or else you'll be small potatoes. You'll be on an inside page.

And as in reality, so on "reality TV." How long until the first TV death? How long until the second? By the end of Orwell's great novel 1984, Winston Smith has been brainwashed. "He loved Big Brother." As, now, do we. We are the Winstons now.

Responding to Reading

1. Salman Rushdie, a respected novelist with an international reputation, admits here that he knows little about reality TV and has only recently begun to watch *Big Brother 2*. Considering these admissions, do you think he has the credibility to criticize reality TV?
2. Rushdie's fear is that "our voyeurism will become more demanding" (9), leading to shows that will "feed our hunger for more action, more pain, more vicarious thrills" (10). Has this fear been realized in any way since this essay was published in 2001? Do you think Rushdie is correct to be alarmed, or do you think viewers will continue to be satisfied with the present level of thrills and action?
3. How is the reality TV Rushdie describes similar to Wendy Kaminer's description of TV talk shows (p. 278)? Are the programs Kaminer discusses also a form of "reality TV"? Explain.

Responding in Writing

Consulting a newspaper's TV listings, read the program descriptions of several different reality shows. List the features these programs seem to have in common. Then, write a paragraph in which you explain what it is about these shows that seems to appeal to viewers.

THE WORLD STILL WATCHES AMERICA

Neal Gabler

1950–

Neal Gabler was born in Chicago and attended the University of Michigan. A historian with advanced degrees in film and American culture, he has been a recipient of a Guggenheim Fellowship and a Freedom Forum Fellowship. His books include Life the Movie: How Entertainment Conquered Reality *(1998) and, with coauthors Frank Rich and Joyce Antler,* Television's Changing Image of American Jews *(2000). He is a regular contributor to periodicals, including* American Film, *the* New York Times Book Review, *and* Video Review. *The following selection appeared on the op-ed page of the* New York Times *in January 2003.*

Once again, we are told, America's cultural hegemony is cracking. The latest proof: American television programs, which had dominated prime-time viewing in Europe and Asia for decades, are now being consigned to the late-night fringes of the schedule.

One European TV executive was quoted as saying that you can no longer win a prime-time slot with an American show. In markets as diverse as Malaysia, France and Latin America, where "Dallas" and "Baywatch" were once blockbusters, locally produced soap operas and crime shows rule the ratings. Today, "C.S.I.," the top-rated show in this country, cannot attract even 3 percent of the viewers in South Korea.

Explanations for the decline range from general anti-American political sentiment to growing resentment of American cultural influence (which has led to restrictions on United States programming in some countries) to the rising cost of American shows. There is also the privatization of the old state-run networks, which has resulted in increased competition and greater demand for programs to fill expanded schedules, even as, paradoxically, the popularity of each individual show plummets.

Still, one shouldn't mourn the end of American cultural domination quite yet. There will always be the movies. And the truth is, American movies, not TV shows, are the truly potent examples of our cultural imperialism.

5   Films are far more costly than television programs and also face increased local competition, yet American movies don't seem to be suffering a similar diminution in popularity—they continue to rake in nearly 80 percent of the film industry's worldwide take. Even in France, where sensitivity to alleged American bullying and belief in native cultural superiority may be stronger than anywhere else in the world, Hollywood movies continue to account for 50 percent to 70 percent of box office receipts every year.

All of which leads one to suspect that the reason American television shows are losing popularity has less to do with resentments or economics than with fundamental differences between American television and American film. Movies are universal, TV is not.

In the United States, the film exhibition industry erupted in the early 1900's in working-class urban neighborhoods and movies were regarded, in the words of The Nation magazine in 1913, as a "democratic art" intended specifically for the masses.

By the 1920's, however, film became the medium of the middle, cutting a wide swath through every demographic group. The studios, which owned the theaters, had made a concerted effort to broaden their films' appeal—making them longer and better, using marketing to establish the first heartthrobs and sirens, and erecting lavish movie palaces that would elevate the movie-going experience. By decade's end, 90 million Americans were attending the movies each week, three attendees for each American household.

It was the ability of the movies to appeal to people of all ages, religions, ethnicities and regions that enabled Hollywood to export them. Already by 1925, 30 percent of the studios' profits came from overseas. (Today it is around 60 percent.) Part of this universality was aesthetic. Even after the silent era ended, the scale of American films, their speed and their action made them accessible to anyone.

Part of the attraction was ideological. American films, concentrat-   10
ing on stars framed in close-ups, promoted the centrality and the efficacy of individual action—a world that conformed to our vicarious will. Taken together, the artistry and the values made movie-going an otherworldly experience. Movies may be the medium of the middle in the composition of their audiences, but they are the medium of the exceptional in the way they grab those audiences.

Though television arrived in this country in the late 1940's amid fears in Hollywood that it would usurp film's audience, those concerns obviously proved ungrounded. Television couldn't have been more different a medium. Whereas the movies were made to mesmerize hundreds gathered in the dark, television was pitched to families huddled in their living rooms and dens. Whereas the movies emphasized the extraordinary, television relied on the familiar.

From its inception, television was a medium not of the intrepid or the glamorous individual but of ensembles, and it required an understanding of group dynamics that was not always easily translatable to other cultures. A German colleague of mine told me that "ER" is virtually unintelligible (and unwatched) in his country because Germans don't understand the easy camaraderie between different races and classes on the show.

To this aesthetic barrier was added a sociological one. Since it was sponsor-supported, television pitched itself to clusters of viewers—

potential buyers—rather than to the undifferentiated mass. It tried to attract what one might call a vertical audience rather than the large horizontal audience for which the movies aimed.

While Hollywood didn't tailor its product to blacks or Catholics or children, television always has. In its early days there was. "The Goldbergs," about a Jewish family living in a Bronx tenement, "Beulah," starring Ethel Waters as a black maid, and "Life Is Worth Living," a prime-time religious program featuring Bishop Fulton Sheen. (Although there is more of a niche market in movies these days, no studio depends on movies of, say, black interest or religious appeal to hold up the bottom line.)

15   Television now reaches almost every household in America, but it has never lost its narrowcast mindset. It is still demographically driven, with programs aimed at slices of the audience. The result is that television has a kind of clubbiness, using references, gestures and attitudes that don't always cross our country's demographic lines, much less international borders.

Indeed, the American shows that have traveled best around the globe are those that deal in the basics—sex ("Baywatch") and melodrama ("Dallas")—and even with these shows part of the appeal for foreign markets was that they reinforced the stereotype of American vulgarity.

The decline of American shows around the world, then, should be seen as a fulfillment of television's destiny, a destiny that had only been postponed until local markets gained the know-how, the money and the corporate structure to make their own programs for slices of their own audience. It also reflects a technological advance—the new panoply of cable and satellite channels that are breaking TV audiences down into niche groups—that perfectly mirrors what has been happening in America for the last three decades.

Our movies continue to be universal, exporting the primal aesthetic of excitement and individualism. Our TV shows continue to be domestic. And the rest of world is likely to continue to be divided between the American movies they love and the American television shows they don't really understand and, more and more, don't really care to watch.

Responding to Reading

1. Gabler sees TV and movies as very different media. What specific differences does he identify in this essay? Can you think of others?
2. Gabler states in no uncertain terms, "Movies are universal, TV is not" (6). What does he mean? Can you think of exceptions—that is, TV shows that are "universal" in their appeal and movies that are not?

3. Do you think Gabler believes that the "cultural imperialism" (4) he describes is a good thing? Do you? What do you see as the pluses and minuses of "American cultural domination" (4) in the media?

Responding in Writing

Compare a movie and a TV show of the same genre—for example, two contemporary romances, two family comedies, or two science fiction or spy thrillers—assessing their relative suitability for viewing outside the US. Do your observations support Gabler's conclusions?

THE MOVIE THAT CHANGED MY LIFE
David Bradley
1950–

David Bradley, whose father, grandfather, and great-grandfather were all preachers, was born in Bedford, Pennsylvania. Bradley studied English and creative writing at the University of Pennsylvania, where he received a BA degree (1972). He has taught at Temple University, the College of William and Mary, and the University of Oregon, where he currently directs the creative writing program. His books include South Street *(1975, reprinted 1986) and* The Chaneysville Incident *(1981). The following excerpt is taken from one of 23 essays by different writers collected in the book* The Movie That Changed My Life.

I might never have seen *The Birth of a Nation*[1] had I not been trained from puberty to abhor prejudice. But I had, and when I learned that the movie was being shown on campus as part of a film festival, it struck me that, despite my research, I'd formed an opinion based only on printed hearsay and some shadows on a wall.[2] So at the appointed hour I made my way to the designated hall.

I was happy to see that the audience, apart from being all white, was very different from the brotherhood of the Animal House. Not only were they sober; they were serious, notebook-toting, graduate-student and professor types. The film was preceded by an equally

---

[1]Based on a play called *The Clansmen, The Birth of a Nation* is a three-hour silent movie, a Civil War epic that covers the war, the assassination of Abraham Lincoln, and the rise of the Ku Klux Klan. When released in 1915, the movie sparked protests but sold more tickets than any other movie, setting a record that stood for decades. Directed by D. W. Griffith, the film conveys a condescending attitude toward black slaves and excitement surrounding the founding of the Ku Klux Klan. [Eds.]
[2]Earlier in this essay, Bradley described being terrified as scenes from the film were projected on the wall of a fraternity house. [Eds.]

serious lecture delivered by an ancient-looking scholar in chambray, corduroy, and chukka boots who gave an outline of Griffith's biography, ending with a description of the director's view of life: idyllic, sentimental, naive, romantic, based on traditional values—family, fidelity, chastity, the Golden Rule, Christian charity. But mostly he spoke of Griffith's cinematic innovations: the fade-in and the fade-out, the close-up, the montage, crosscutting, flashbacks, pre-shot rehearsals, masking, the use of a film stock called Peach Blossom, which gave the black-and-white an antiquated-looking tint. Griffith had not necessarily invented these techniques, the lecturer said, but he had brought them all together to their fullest advantage in *The Birth of a Nation*. Listening, I began to look forward to a brilliant artistic expression. That anticipation didn't last beyond the first caption: "The bringing of the African to America sowed the first seed of dis-Union."

It got worse, of course. Absent the realization that the "blacks" were whites in blackface, I could not have watched it. By the end I understood how the images of these pseudo-blacks—slavering, slobbering *things* which would make even a merciful God avert His sight—could cause havoc in the cities. Take a bunch of ignorant immigrants, show them a black-faced beast chasing a girl—not a woman, but a child—until she leaps to her death; then show them the man being shot in the back and the bastard being strung up and then dumped on the lawn of a mulatto named Lynch; get 'em fired up with *Die Walküre*[3] (an anticipation of Munich and Kristallnacht, *nicht wahr*)?[4]—then have them salute a flag. How could the audience not think that nigger-bashing, not baseball, was the national pastime? How could they not riot?

But what almost made me riot, what surely made my stomach turn, was the scene in which the intrepid hero bathes the cross in the lynched man's blood—"the sweetest blood ever shed," he says—turning it into a veritable calvary for the Klan cavalry. It made me want to vomit. I didn't; I couldn't; I merely wished to—more, I wished that I could expel the images from my memory like bile from the belly.

5   The lights came up. The audience applauded. The lecturer invited questions. Someone inquired about Griffith's symbolism. The lecturer responded with a sophomoric discussion of kittens, cooing doves,

---

[3]*Die Walküre* is an opera in three acts. Its libretto and music were written by Richard Wagner (1813–1883), whose music was appropriated by the Third Reich and often played during public events in Nazi Germany. [Eds.]

[4]*Kristallnacht*, "the Night of Broken Glass," was a government-sanctioned massacre of Jews in November 1938 in Germany and its territories. During two nights of violence, mobs freely attacked Jews in public, in their homes, and at their places of work and worship. Nearly 100 Jews were killed, more than 1,000 synagogues were burned, and almost 7,500 Jewish businesses were destroyed. Approximately 30,000 Jews were arrested and sent to concentration camps. [Eds.]

and bedposts rampant with references to Freud. That was it. I couldn't believe my ears. Or my eyes; the rest of the audience seemed quite happy with the film.

And so I rose—trembling, for reasons I did not then understand—and asked the lecturer quite politely if he was an idiot, or merely blind? How could he speak of symbols and make no mention of the cross, or note that when the lynching starts the cross is a spindly, anemic thing, but once it's bathed with a black man's blood it becomes an engorged shaft, licked by flame brandished by a horseman? How could he ignore the Freudian symbolism of that?

And didn't he know—didn't any of them know—that it wasn't just empty symbolism? Didn't they know that *The Birth of a Nation* had been the birth of a symbol, that the flaming cross, never seen before that night on Stone Mountain, was surely seen again? And didn't they know that *The Birth of a Nation* had been the rebirth of the Klan, a "High Class Order for Men of Intelligence and Character" with a taste for terrorism? Didn't they know how many black folk died at the Klan's fraternal hands, how many black women were raped by fraternal phalluses, how many families had fled in fear of a fraternal visitation? Didn't they understand what had been inspired by this misbegotten movie? Didn't they care?

The audience was silent, made uneasy by my outburst, unsure of what further form it might take. I'm sure they thought that I was angry. In fact, I was afraid to a degree beyond my simple togaed terror. Because until this night I'd felt safe in the Ivy League, no matter that it was so alien. Certainly I'd felt safer than I'd ever felt in Bedford, surrounded by poor white trash. I'd felt safe because I'd believed that at the university I would be surrounded by people who, though mostly white, were surely not poor, and probably not trash; people whose tradition of free inquiry elevated them above—if not bigotry, then prejudice; if not hatred, then violence. The Animal House, I'd thought, was the exception that proved the rule—it was called the Animal House because it was an unwelcome aberration from a cultured norm. I had been scared out of my toga while inside; I had felt safe as soon as I was outside. And I had felt safe tonight, entering a lecture hall to confront the very images that had inspired my prior terror, because I'd believed that this audience would not countenance racist drivel. But they *had* countenanced it. They'd *applauded* it. They'd pronounced it wonderful. They'd pronounced it art. And now I knew that I had not been safe, that I was not safe, that I would never be safe.

The lecturer was angry, too, although he seemed calm as he decried my objections as the very ones that had been used by those who'd tried to suppress Griffith's magnificent film. He recalled the restraint of Griffith's responses: a pamphlet on "freedom of the screen" and another great film, *Intolerance*, an examination of intellectual prejudice through the ages, symbolized in the end by the crucifixion of Christ. But, perhaps because I'd stayed standing, or because he saw some danger in my face, he added, "What you say happened, happened. But you have to get beyond history and deal with the aesthetics." I have hated men before and since, but I have never hated any man more.

10   On a cold day in February, twenty years later, I gave a reading for a national organization of writing teachers which had come to Philadelphia for its annual convention. I decided to read from my first novel, *South Street*, a sort of Dickensian Western set in inner-city Philadelphia, to give the visitors a glimpse of life they would not see on the standard Independence Hall–Liberty Bell–Art Museum tour.

I had thought the reading went all right, until the next morning, at the business meeting, when a nervous, thin-faced white woman "responded" to my reading, which, she said, had been so offensive in its brutal treatment of women that it had made her tearful and nauseated; she'd had to leave the room. The organization, she said, should not permit such things to be read.

When she was finished, a feminist friend of mine rose and said that while she could see the woman's point, she knew I would neither write nor read with hurtful intent, and . . . I interrupted; point of personal privilege.

I thanked my friend for her faith, I said, and hoped it was not misplaced. But I believed a writer, an artist, had the right, indeed the responsibility, to create or publish—or, in this case, perform—material that reflected his—or her—vision. If I could not exercise that right before an organization of writers, if I even had to explain it, I was misplaced. Then I went to the bar, ordered several shots of bourbon, and had a silent, solitary fit. I will not recount my rantings; suffice it to say that had that nervous liberal-Nazi bitch been present she would have again been moved to tears and nausea. But it came to me that there wasn't much difference between what that nervous liberal-Nazi bitch had said about *South Street* and what I had once said about *The Birth of a Nation*. Or, to put it a better way, somehow my work had made her feel the same way Griffith's work had made me feel.

The thought did not move me to retract the names I'd called her, but it forced me to apply them to myself. And—and this was hard—to Du Bois[5] Not that he'd ever been happy with his position; he'd called

---

[5]W. E. B. Du Bois (1868–1963), author, educator, and social reformer, was prominent in early movements for racial equality and helped create the National Association for the Advancement of Colored People (NAACP) in 1909. Du Bois is also known for his widely read book *The Souls of Black Folk* (1903). [Eds.]

it a "miserable dilemma."[6] But Du Bois, no fool, knew what evil lurked in the hearts and minds of Americans; that was why he'd hated and feared the film. Just as I had hated and feared it. Just as that poor nervous woman had hated and feared a depiction of violence done to women.

I had to view *The Birth of a Nation* because I'd agreed, for reasons I 15 had not yet understood, to write about it. I found I didn't know what to say. And I frankly couldn't face the thought of watching that drivel again. Then one morning came a letter from an old classmate, a fellow chip, who is now director of Alumni Relations. It was addressed "Dear Alumni Leader"—which I'm not, so maybe I got it by mistake—and said that the president of the university had formed a Committee to Diversify Locust Walk and was requesting "opinions and advice for consideration" so that the university could "communicate symbolically and more accurately to ourselves and to our visitors the wonderfully varied texture of this human community."

Oh hell, I thought, this is where I came in. If you're "diversified," who needs the symbols? And if you're not, aren't your symbols lies? It made me mad enough to do what I should have been doing: fire up the VCR and watch *The Birth of a Nation*.

You know, it wasn't all that good. It struck me, watching it, that a lot of the hoopla about the film is because it was innovative, not good; Griffith was the first to do a lot of things—sort of like Ed Brooke, the first black to get elected senator since Reconstruction. (Also, please note, the last.)[7] That long-ago lecturer should have listened to himself; get beyond history, deal with the aesthetics. The results would have been different. I mean, Naismith invented basketball, but that don't make him Michael Jordan.

To tell the truth, I thought the film was kind of funny. Especially the part where the white liberal congratulates the mulatto on wanting to marry a white woman, and then goes crazy when he finds out it's *his* daughter. And I think those puppies pissed on Ben Cameron's shoe.

But to tell more truth, finding out I could laugh at something that used to make my gorge rise if I only *thought* about it made me feel

---

[6]In August 1897, the *Atlantic Monthly* published "Strivings of the Negro People," in which Du Bois defined the problem of African American duality: "It is a peculiar sensation, this double-consciousness. . . . One ever feels his twoness—an American, a Negro; two souls, two thoughts, two unreconciled strivings; two warring ideals in one dark body, whose dogged strength alone keeps it from being torn asunder." The essay is available on the magazine's Web site, http://www.theatlantic.com/unbound/flashbks/black/dubstriv.htm. [Eds.]

[7]Carol Moseley Braun (1947–) has served as a United States Senator (1992–1998) and as the US Ambassador to New Zealand (1999–2001). The Illinois Democrat, the first African-American woman ever elected to the Senate by a major political party, was a Democratic candidate for president in 2004. [Eds.]

giddy as a geetchie on the first of August. But then came the scene, that cross engorged, and I had another thought: symbolism matters. Just not as much as people think. Enough to cause suffering; not enough to end it, forever and for all. And so, while it is wrong to make war on shadows, it is just as wrong to forget that sometimes shadows lead to acts.

20   So hear me now, my Klans and terrors: rest easy in your dens. Drink your bourbon and play "Dixie" on your comb kazoos, get weepy over the Stars and Bars, and, yes, sit back and watch *The Birth of a Nation*. And afterward, if you need some air, put on your bed-sheets and slouch up a mountain like rough beasts bound for Bethlehem. And if it makes you feel like men, go ahead, burn a cross. But as you gambol in its fiery light, know that that symbol, your symbol, is my symbol, too. And if you should come snaking down with mischief on your scaly mind, this Christian soldier will be waiting with hob-nailed heels.

Responding to Reading

1. What first motivates Bradley to see *The Birth of a Nation* despite what he has heard about it—and despite the strong negative response he had to scenes he glimpsed at a fraternity party? How does he react? How is his reaction different when he sees it a second time?
2. In paragraph 9, the lecturer tells Bradley that he needs to " 'get beyond history and deal with the aesthetics'." Do you believe it is possible to judge a film—or a piece of music or work of art—on the basis of aesthetics alone, regardless of its content or message? Explain.
3. Do you think *The Birth of a Nation* really changed Bradley in any way? Has he achieved any kind of closure or resolved his feelings about the film? For example, do you think he really accepts the fact that the white woman's reaction to his book is not much different from his own reaction 20 years earlier to the film? (Note that he is not motivated to take back the hostile names he called her.) Read the essay's last paragraph carefully before you respond.

Responding in Writing

What movie changed your life? Briefly summarize the film, and then explain the impact its characters and plot had on you.

WHY THE RECORD INDUSTRY
IS IN TROUBLE
Jann S. Wenner
1946–

At the age of twenty, after a few years of study at the University of California at Berkeley, Jann S. Wenner borrowed $7,500 and founded Rolling Stone *magazine. He currently serves as its publisher and as chairman of Wenner Media Incorporated, which publishes* US: The Entertainment Magazine *and* Men's Journal. *Wenner is the author of numerous articles and of the book* Lennon Remembers *(2000), a collection of interviews published on the twentieth anniversary of John Lennon's death. He is also vice-chairman of the Rock and Roll Hall of Fame Foundation. The following selection appeared in* Rolling Stone *in September 2002.*

Album sales are now down almost twenty percent from two years ago, and the record business is facing the biggest retail slide since the Great Depression. Yet rather than seek new ways to market, price and distribute music, the record labels have raised CD prices and continued their futile efforts to shut down Internet file-sharing sites, surely the most important innovation in music technology in the last twenty years. The industry insists on blaming music fans for its troubles.

Digital technology is not going away. We are growing accustomed to getting our music on demand, through our computers, one song at a time. The labels have played defense instead of embracing the Internet age and have spent millions of dollars trying to shut down trading sites—from Napster to Kazaa—rather than recognize the potential of the Web to market, promote and sell music. They've done the same thing with Internet radio, lobbying for prohibitive royalty rates that threaten to push thousands of independent stations—potentially great places to promote new and niche artists—out of business.

Several labels, including Sony and Universal, are offering limited songs online for ninety-nine cents each. But this is not enough: The labels must get together to put all of their music online—from the newest singles to the oldest catalog material—and allow fans to download what they want, for a fair price. "The kids have already stated. 'All of the music, all of the time,'" says Lyor Cohen, president of Island Def Jam Music Group. "Meanwhile, the record companies have responded with, 'Some of the music, some of the time.'"

A new distribution system could work like basic cable television, where users download as much as they want monthly, with premium offers and pay-per-download-style events. If 10 million people sign up for the new service, gross revenues could be enormous, with little of the current costs that record companies incur for manufacturing, marketing and retailing.

5   Still, the labels' unwillingness to move online, and their insistence on keeping prices too high, are just the obvious parts of the problem. The more complicated matter is the quality of the music itself. Labels have been unable to find ways to develop and broadly expose new bands and are too willing to put out albums with only two or three good songs. How many people spend eighteen dollars for a CD, then discover that the one song getting played on the radio or MTV is the single decent track? That has to happen only a few times before fans start looking for more cost-efficient ways to get music.

The labels say they can't compete with free—that CD-burning piracy and file swapping are the principal reasons for the industry's troubles. They claim that CD burning alone has cost $4.3 billion in lost revenues, and that file swapping costs them billions more. But there are no conclusive studies to prove that digital downloading cuts into album sales—in fact, some studies suggest that free downloading encourages fans to hear and buy more music. Further, there is ample evidence that the most active music fans today are both the biggest downloaders and the biggest music buyers. So why is the record industry going to war against its best customers?

While the costs of CD manufacturing has dropped—it costs record labels about forty cents to manufacture a CD, packaging included—retail prices have continued to rise. And consumers aren't willing to spend twenty dollars for a CD with two or three decent tracks. It's a question of simple marketplace common sense: Labels must give consumers product they want at a fair price. And artists play a role in this, too. Successful musicians have the power to demand and participate in price reductions for their releases, past and present.

The music business should take a cue from the hugely profitable DVD industry. In the past year, prices for DVDs have dropped, from about twenty dollars to seventeen dollars—and many DVDs come with excellent bonus materials that give additional value for the money.

Some of the year's biggest new artists, such as Ashanti and Norah Jones, have benefited from lower prices: $8.99 to $13.99. Avril Lavigne's debut, *Let Go*, sold for $5.99 in some outlets. All three of these artists are currently among the Top Twenty in the *Billboard* 200, and their success shows that people are still willing to pay for music. But they're not willing to be ripped off.

10   If the labels continue to blame the public for their own mistakes, rather than lowering prices and finding ways to effectively deliver music online, then music fans will grow even more alienated than they already are. And then, by comparison, the current sales slump will look like a boom.

Responding to Reading

1. In simple terms, why does Wenner believe the record industry is in trouble? What steps does he think the industry must take to survive?
2. According to Wenner, how has "the quality of the music itself" (5) hurt the record industry? Can you give additional examples to support his criticism?
3. In what sense does Wenner see "the record industry going to war against its best customers" (6)? To what degree does he believe artists are to blame?

Responding in Writing

What is the biggest problem you yourself have with the record industry? The high cost of CDs? The quality of the music? The content of the lyrics? Write a paragraph that identifies a problem and proposes some solutions.

Who Shot Mohammed al-Dura?

James Fallows

1949–

Journalist James M. Fallows, known for his insightful analysis of social and political issues, has written on a wide range of subjects, including computer software, immigration, economics, and national defense. At Harvard, where he earned his BA degree in 1970, he was president of the Crimson, *the student newspaper. He went on to study economics as a Rhodes Scholar at Oxford University in England and then served as President Jimmy Carter's chief speech writer. He has been an editor at* U.S. News and World Report *and the Washington editor of the* Atlantic Monthly *magazine, where he currently works as a national correspondent. His book* National Defense *won the American Book Award in 1981; he has also written* Breaking the News: How the Media Undermine American Democracy *(1996). In the following essay, Fallows examines the incendiary power of television news coverage.*

The name Mohammed al-Dura is barely known in the United States. Yet to a billion people in the Muslim world it is an infamous symbol of grievance against Israel and—because of this country's support for Israel—against the United States as well.

Al-Dura was the twelve-year-old Palestinian boy shot and killed during an exchange of fire between Israeli soldiers and Palestinian demonstrators on September 30, 2000. The final few seconds of his life, when he crouched in terror behind his father, Jamal, and then slumped to the ground after bullets ripped through his torso, were captured by a television camera and broadcast around the world. Through repetition they have become as familiar and significant to

Arab and Islamic viewers as photographs of bombed-out Hiroshima are to the people of Japan—or as footage of the crumbling World Trade Center is to Americans. Several Arab countries have issued postage stamps carrying a picture of the terrified boy. One of Baghdad's main streets was renamed The Martyr Mohammed Aldura Street. Morocco has an al-Dura Park. In one of the messages Osama bin Laden released after the September 11 attacks and the subsequent U.S. invasion of Afghanistan, he began a list of indictments against "American arrogance and Israeli violence" by saying, "In the epitome of his arrogance and the peak of his media campaign in which he boasts of 'enduring freedom,' Bush must not forget the image of Mohammed al-Dura and his fellow Muslims in Palestine and Iraq. If he has forgotten, then we will not forget, God willing."

But almost since the day of the episode evidence has been emerging in Israel, under controversial and intriguing circumstances, to indicate that the official version of the Mohammed al-Dura story is not true. It now appears that the boy cannot have died in the way reported by most of the world's media and fervently believed throughout the Islamic world. Whatever happened to him, he was not shot by the Israeli soldiers who were known to be involved in the day's fighting—or so I am convinced, after spending a week in Israel talking with those examining the case. The exculpatory evidence comes not from government or military officials in Israel, who have an obvious interest in claiming that their soldiers weren't responsible, but from other sources. In fact, the Israel Defense Forces, or IDF, seem to prefer to soft-pedal the findings rather than bring any more attention to this gruesome episode. The research has been done by a variety of academics, ex-soldiers, and Web-loggers who have become obsessed with the case, and the evidence can be cross-checked.

No "proof" that originates in Israel is likely to change minds in the Arab world. The longtime Palestinian spokesperson Hanan Ashrawi dismissed one early Israeli report on the topic as a "falsified version of reality [that] blames the victims." Late this spring Said Hamad, a spokesman at the PLO office in Washington, told me of the new Israeli studies, "It does not surprise me that these reports would come out from the same people who shot Mohammed al-Dura. He was shot of course by the Israeli army, and not by anybody else." Even if evidence that could revise the understanding of this particular death were widely accepted (so far it has been embraced by a few Jewish groups in Europe and North America), it would probably have no effect on the underlying hatred and ongoing violence in the region. Nor would evidence that clears Israeli soldiers necessarily support the overarching Likud policy of sending soldiers to occupy territories and protect settlements. The Israelis still looking into the al-Dura case

do not all endorse Likud occupation policies. In fact, some strongly oppose them.

The truth about Mohammed al-Dura is important in its own right, 5 because this episode is so raw and vivid in the Arab world and so hazy, if not invisible, in the West. Whatever the course of the occupation of Iraq, the United States has guaranteed an ample future supply of images of Arab suffering. The two explosions in Baghdad markets in the first weeks of the war, killing scores of civilians, offered an initial taste. Even as U.S. officials cautioned that it would take more time and study to determine whether U.S. or Iraqi ordnance had caused the blasts, the Arab media denounced the brutality that created these new martyrs. More of this lies ahead. The saga of Mohammed al-Dura illustrates the way the battles of wartime imagery may play themselves out.

The harshest version of the al-Dura case from the Arab side is that it proves the ancient "blood libel"—Jews want to kill gentile children—and shows that Americans count Arab life so cheap that they will let the Israelis keep on killing. The harshest version from the Israeli side is that the case proves the Palestinians' willingness to deliberately sacrifice even their own children in the name of the war against Zionism. In Tel Aviv I looked through hour after hour of videotape in an attempt to understand what can be known about what happened, and what it means.

The Day

The death of Mohammed al-Dura took place on the second day of what is now known as the second intifada, a wave of violent protests throughout the West Bank and Gaza. In the summer of 2000 Middle East peace negotiations had reached another impasse. On September 28 of that year, a Thursday, Ariel Sharon, then the leader of Israel's Likud Party but not yet Prime Minister, made a visit to the highly contested religious site in Jerusalem that Jews know as the Temple Mount and Muslims know as Haram al-Sharif, with its two mosques. For Palestinians this was the trigger—or, in the view of many Israelis, the pretext—for the expanded protests that began the next day.

On September 30 the protest sites included a crossroads in the occupied Gaza territory near the village of Netzarim, where sixty families of Israeli settlers live. The crossroads is a simple right-angle intersection of two roads in a lightly developed area. Three days earlier a roadside bomb had mortally wounded an IDF soldier there. At one corner of the intersection were an abandoned warehouse, two six-story office buildings known as the "twin towers," and a two-story building. (These structures and others surrounding the crossroads have since been torn down.) A group of IDF soldiers had made the two-story building their outpost, to guard the road leading to the Israeli settlement.

Diagonally across the intersection was a small, ramshackle building and a sidewalk bordered by a concrete wall. It was along this wall that Mohammed al-Dura and his father crouched before they were shot. (The father was injured but survived.) The other two corners of the crossroads were vacant land. One of them contained a circular dirt berm, known as the Pita because it was shaped like a pita loaf. A group of uniformed Palestinian policemen, armed with automatic rifles, were on the Pita for much of the day.

10   Early in the morning of Saturday, September 30, a crowd of Palestinians gathered at the Netzarim crossroads. TV crews, photographers, and reporters from many news agencies, including Reuters, AP, and the French television network France 2, were also at the ready. Because so many cameras were running for so many hours, there is abundant documentary evidence of most of the day's

events—with a few strange and crucial exceptions, most of them concerning Mohammed al-Dura.

"Rushes" (raw footage) of the day's filming collected from these and other news organizations around the world tell a detailed yet confusing story. The tapes overlap in some areas but leave mysterious gaps in others. No one camera, of course, followed the day's events from beginning to end; and with so many people engaged in a variety of activities simultaneously, no one account could capture everything. Gabriel Weimann, the chairman of the communications department at the University of Haifa, whose book *Communicating Unreality* concerns the media's distorting effects, explained to me on my visit that the footage in its entirety has a *"Rashomon* effect."[1] Many separate small dramas seem to be under way. Some of the shots show groups of young men walking around, joking, sitting and smoking and appearing to enjoy themselves. Others show isolated moments of intense action, as protesters yell and throw rocks, and shots ring out from various directions. Only when these vignettes are packaged together as a conventional TV news report do they seem to have a narrative coherence.

Off and on throughout the morning some of the several hundred Palestinian civilians at the crossroads mounted assaults on the IDF outpost. They threw rocks and Molotov cocktails. They ran around waving the Palestinian flag and trying to pull down an Israeli flag near the outpost. A few of the civilians had pistols or rifles, which they occasionally fired; the second intifada quickly escalated from throwing rocks to using other weapons. The Palestinian policemen, mainly in the Pita area, also fired at times. The IDF soldiers, according to Israeli spokesmen, were under orders not to fire in response to rocks or other thrown objects. They were to fire only if fired upon. Scenes filmed throughout the day show smoke puffing from the muzzles of M-16s pointed through the slits of the IDF outpost.

To watch the raw footage is to wonder, repeatedly, What is going on here? In some scenes groups of Palestinians duck for cover from gunfire while others nonchalantly talk or smoke just five feet away. At one dramatic moment a Palestinian man dives forward clutching his leg, as if shot in the thigh. An ambulance somehow arrives to collect him exactly two seconds later, before he has stopped rolling from the momentum of his fall. Another man is loaded into an ambulance— and, in footage from a different TV camera, appears to jump out of it again some minutes later.

At around 3:00 P.M. Mohammed al-Dura and his father make their first appearance on film. The time can be judged by later comments

---

[1] *Rashomon*, a 1950 film by Japanese director Akira Kurosawa, in which different people give varying accounts of a murder. [Eds.]

from the father and some journalists on the scene, and by the length of shadows in the footage. Despite the number of cameras that were running that day, Mohammed and Jamal al-Dura appear in the footage of only one cameraman—Talal Abu-Rahma, a Palestinian working for France 2.

15   Jamal al-Dura later said that he had taken his son to a used-car market and was on the way back when he passed through the crossroads and into the crossfire. When first seen on tape, father and son are both crouched on the sidewalk behind a large concrete cylinder, their backs against the wall. The cylinder, about three feet high, is referred to as "the barrel" in most discussions of the case, although it appears to be a section from a culvert or a sewer system. On top of the cylinder is a big paving stone, which adds another eight inches or so of protection. The al-Duras were on the corner diagonally opposite the Israeli outpost. By hiding behind the barrel they were doing exactly what they should have done to protect themselves from Israeli fire.

Many news accounts later claimed that the two were under fire for forty-five minutes, but the action captured on camera lasts a very brief time. Jamal looks around desperately. Mohammed slides down behind him, as if to make his body disappear behind his father's. Jamal clutches a pack of cigarettes in his left hand, while he alternately waves and cradles his son with his right. The sound of gunfire is heard, and four bullet holes appear in the wall just to the left of the pair. The father starts yelling. There is another burst. Mohammed goes limp and falls forward across his father's lap, his shirt stained with blood. Jamal, too, is hit, and his head starts bobbling. The camera cuts away. Although France 2 or its cameraman may have footage that it or he has chosen not to release, no other visual record of the shooting or its immediate aftermath is known to exist. Other Palestinian casualties of the day are shown being evacuated, but there is no known on-tape evidence of the boy's being picked up, tended to, loaded into an ambulance, or handled in any other way after he was shot.

The footage of the shooting is unforgettable, and it illustrates the way in which television transforms reality. I have seen it replayed at least a hundred times now, and on each repetition I can't help hoping that this time the boy will get himself down low enough, this time the shots will miss. Through the compression involved in editing the footage for a news report, the scene acquired a clear story line by the time European, American, and Middle Eastern audiences saw it on television: Palestinians throw rocks. Israeli soldiers, from the slits in their outpost, shoot back. A little boy is murdered.

What is known about the rest of the day is fragmentary and additionally confusing. A report from a nearby hospital says that a dead boy was admitted on September 30, with two gun wounds to the left side of his torso. But according to the photocopy I saw, the report also says that the boy was admitted at 1:00 P.M.; the tape shows that Mohammed was shot later in the afternoon. The doctor's report also notes, without further explanation, that the dead boy had a cut down his belly about eight inches long. A boy's body, wrapped in a Palestinian flag but with his face exposed, was later carried through the streets to a burial site (the exact timing is in dispute). The face looks very much like Mohammed's in the video footage. Thousands of mourners lined the route. A BBC TV report on the funeral began, "A Palestinian boy has been martyred." Many of the major U.S. news organizations reported that the funeral was held on the evening of September 30, a few hours after the shooting. Oddly, on film the procession appears to take place in full sunlight, with shadows indicative of midday.

The Aftermath

Almost immediately news media around the world began reporting the tragedy. Print outlets were generally careful to say that Mohammed al-Dura was killed in "the crossfire" or "an exchange of fire" between Israeli soldiers and Palestinians. *The New York Times*, for instance, reported that he was "shot in the stomach as he crouched behind his father on the sidelines of an intensifying battle between Israeli and Palestinian security forces." But the same account included Jamal al-Dura's comment that the fatal volley had come from Israeli soldiers. Jacki Lyden said on NPR's *Weekend All Things Considered* that the boy had been "caught in crossfire." She then interviewed the France 2 cameraman, Talal Abu-Rahma, who said that he thought the Israelis had done the shooting.

> ABU-RAHMA: I was very sad. I was crying. And I was remembering my children. I was afraid to lose my life. And I was sitting on my knees and hiding my head, carrying my camera, and I was afraid from the Israeli to see this camera, maybe they will think this is a weapon, you know, or I am trying to shoot on them. But I was in the most difficult situation in my life. A boy, I cannot save his life, and I want to protect myself.
> LYDEN: Was there any attempt by the troops who were firing to cease fire to listen to what the father had to say? Could they even see what they were shooting at?
> ABU-RAHMA: Okay. It's clear it was a father, it's clear it was a boy over there for ever who [presumably meaning "whoever"] was shooting on them from across the street, you know, in front of them. I'm sure from that area, I'm expert in that area, I've been in that area many times. I know every [unintelligible] in that area. Whoever was shooting, he got to see them, because that base is not far away from the boy and the father. It's about a hundred and fifty meters [about 500 feet].

20   On that night's broadcast of *ABC World News Tonight*, the correspondent Gillian Findlay said unambiguously that the boy had died "under Israeli fire." Although both NBC and CBS used the term "crossfire" in their reports, videos of Israeli troops firing and then the boy dying left little doubt about the causal relationship. Jamal al-Dura never wavered in his view that the Israelis had killed his son. "Are you sure they were Israeli bullets?" Diane Sawyer, of ABC News, asked him in an interview later that year. "I'm a hundred percent sure," he replied, through his translator. "They were Israelis." In another interview he told the Associated Press, "The bullets of the Zionists are the bullets that killed my son."

By Tuesday, October 3, all doubt seemed to have been removed. After a hurried internal investigation the IDF concluded that its troops were probably to blame. General Yom-Tov Samia, then the head of the IDF's Southern Command, which operated in Gaza, said, "It could very much be—this is an estimation—that a soldier in our position, who has a very narrow field of vision, saw somebody hiding behind a cement block in the direction from which he was being fired at, and he shot in that direction." General Giora Eiland, then the head of IDF operations, said on an Israeli radio broadcast that the boy was apparently killed by "Israeli army fire at the Palestinians who were attacking them violently with a great many petrol bombs, rocks, and very massive fire."

The further attempt to actually justify killing the boy was, in terms of public opinion, yet more damning for the IDF. Eiland said, "It is known that [Mohammed al-Dura] participated in stone throwing in the past." Samia asked what a twelve-year-old was doing in such a dangerous place to begin with. Ariel Sharon, who admitted that the footage of the shooting was "very hard to see," and that the death was "a real tragedy," also said, "The one that should be blamed is only the one . . . that really instigated all those activities, and that is Yasir Arafat."

Palestinians, and the Arab-Islamic world in general, predictably did not agree. Sweatshirts, posters, and wall murals were created showing the face of Mohammed al-Dura just before he died. "His face, stenciled three feet high, is a common sight on the walls of Gaza," Matthew McAllester, of *Newsday*, wrote last year. "His name is known to every Arab, his death cited as the ultimate example of Israeli military brutality." In modern warfare, Bob Simon said on CBS's *60 Minutes*, "one picture can be worth a thousand weapons," and the picture of the doomed boy amounted to "one of the most disastrous setbacks Israel has suffered in decades." Gabriel Weimann, of Haifa University, said that when he first heard of the case, "it made me sick to think this was done in my name." Amnon Lord, an Israeli columnist who has investigated the event, told me in an e-mail message that it was important "on the mythological level," because it was "a framework story, a paradigmatic event," illustrating Israeli brutality. Dan Schueftan, an Israeli strategist and military thinker, told me that the case was uniquely damaging. He said, "[It was] the ultimate symbol of what the Arabs want to think: the father is trying to protect his son, and the satanic Jews—there is no other word for it—are trying to kill him. These Jews are people who will come to kill our children, because they are not human."

Two years after Mohammed al-Dura's death his stepmother, Amal, became pregnant with another child, the family's eighth. The parents named him Mohammed. Amal was quoted late in her pregnancy as saying, "It will send a message to Israel: 'Yes, you've killed one, but God has compensated for him. You can't kill us all.'"

Second Thoughts

In the fall of last year Gabriel Weimann mentioned the Mohammed 25 al-Dura case in a special course that he teaches at the Israeli Military Academy, National Security and Mass Media. Like most adults in Israel, Weimann, a tall, athletic-looking man in his early fifties, still performs up to thirty days of military-reserve duty a year. His reserve rank is sergeant, whereas the students in his class are lieutenant colonels and above.

To underscore the importance of the media in international politics, Weimann shows some of his students a montage of famous images from past wars: for World War II the flag raising at Iwo Jima; for Vietnam the South Vietnamese officer shooting a prisoner in the head and the little girl running naked down a path with napalm on her back. For the current intifada, Weimann told his students, the lasting iconic image would be the frightened face of Mohammed al-Dura.

One day last fall, after he discussed the images, a student spoke up. "I was there," he said. "We didn't do it."

"Prove it," Weimann said. He assigned part of the class, as its major research project, a reconsideration of the evidence in the case. A surprisingly large amount was available. The students began by revisiting an investigation undertaken by the Israeli military soon after the event.

Shortly after the shooting General Samia was contacted by Nahum Shahaf, a physicist and engineer who had worked closely with the IDF on the design of pilotless drone aircraft. While watching the original news broadcasts of the shooting Shahaf had been alarmed, like most viewers inside and outside Israel. But he had also noticed an apparent anomaly. The father seemed to be concerned mainly about a threat originating on the far side of the barrel behind which he had taken shelter. Yet when he and his son were shot, the barrel itself seemed to be intact. What, exactly, did this mean?

30   Samia commissioned Shahaf and an engineer, Yosef Duriel, to work on a second IDF investigation of of the case. "The reason from my side is to check and clean up our values," Samia later told Bob Simon, of CBS. He said he wanted "to see that we are still acting as the IDF." Shahaf stressed to Samia that the IDF should do whatever it could to preserve all physical evidence. But because so much intifada activity continued in the Netzarim area, the IDF demolished the wall and all related structures. Shahaf took one trip to examine the crossroads, clad in body armor and escorted by Israeli soldiers. Then, at a location near Beersheba, Shahaf, Duriel, and others set up models of the barrel, the wall, and the IDF shooting position, in order to re-enact the crucial events.

Bullets had not been recovered from the boy's body at the hospital, and the family was hardly willing to agree to an exhumation to re-examine the wounds. Thus the most important piece of physical evidence was the concrete barrel. In the TV footage it clearly bears a mark from the Israeli Bureau of Standards, which enabled investigators to determine its exact dimensions and composition. When they placed the equivalent in front of a concrete wall and put mannequins representing father and son behind it, a conclusion emerged: soldiers in the Israeli outpost could not have fired the shots whose impact was shown on TV. The evidence was cumulative and reinforcing. It involved the angle, the barrel, the indentations, and the dust.

Mohammed al-Dura and his father looked as if they were sheltering themselves against fire from the IDF outpost. In this they were successful. The films show that the barrel was between them and the Israeli guns. The line of sight from the IDF position to the pair was blocked by concrete. Conceivably, some other Israeli soldier was present and fired from some other angle, although there is no evidence of this and no one has ever raised it as a possibility; and there were Palestinians in all the other places, who would presumably have noticed the presence of additional IDF troops. From the one location where Israeli soldiers are known to have been, the only way to hit the boy would have been to shoot through the concrete barrel.

This brings us to the nature of the barrel. Its walls were just under two inches thick. On the test range investigators fired M-16 bullets at a similar barrel. Each bullet made an indentation only two fifths to four fifths of an inch deep. Penetrating the barrel would have required multiple hits on both sides of the barrel's wall. The videos of the shooting show fewer than ten indentations on the side of the barrel facing the IDF, indicating that at some point in the day's exchanges of fire the Israelis did shoot at the barrel. But photographs taken after the shooting show no damage of any kind on the side of the barrel facing the al-Duras—that is, no bullets went through.

Further evidence involves the indentations in the concrete wall. The bullet marks that appear so ominously in the wall seconds before the fatal volley are round. Their shape is significant because of what it indicates about the angle of the gunfire. The investigators fired volleys into a concrete wall from a variety of angles. They found that in order to produce a round puncture mark, they had to fire more or less straight on. The more oblique the angle, the more elongated and skid-like the hole became.

The dust resulting from a bullet's impact followed similar rules. A head-on shot produced the smallest, roundest cloud of dust. The more oblique the angle, the larger and longer the cloud of dust. In the video of the shooting the clouds of dust near the al-Duras' heads are small and round. Shots from the IDF outpost would necessarily have been oblique. 35

In short, the physical evidence of the shooting was in all ways inconsistent with shots coming from the IDF outpost—and in all ways consistent with shots coming from someplace behind the France 2 cameraman, roughly in the location of the Pita. Making a positive case for who might have shot the boy was not the business of the investigators hired by the IDF. They simply wanted to determine whether the soldiers in the outpost were responsible. Because the investigation was overseen by the IDF and run wholly by Israelis, it stood no chance of being taken seriously in the Arab world. But its fundamental point—that the concrete barrel lay between the outpost and the boy, and no bullets had gone through the barrel—could be confirmed independently from news footage.

It was at this point that the speculation about Mohammed al-Dura's death left the realm of geometry and ballistics and entered the world of politics, paranoia, fantasy, and hatred. Almost as soon as the second IDF investigation was under way, Israeli commentators started questioning its legitimacy and Israeli government officials distanced themselves from its findings. "It is hard to describe in mild terms the stupidity of this bizarre investigation," the liberal newspaper *Ha'aretz* said in an editorial six weeks after the shooting. The newspaper claimed that Shahaf and Duriel were motivated not by a need for dispassionate inquiry but by the belief that Palestinians had staged the whole shooting. (Shahaf told me that he began his investigation out of curiosity but during the course of it became convinced that the multiple anomalies indicated a staged event.) "The fact that an organized body like the IDF, with its vast resources, undertook such an amateurish investigation—almost a pirate endeavor—on such a sensitive issue, is shocking and worrying," *Ha'aretz* said.

As the controversy grew, Samia abbreviated the investigation and subsequently avoided discussing the case. Most government officials,

I was told by many sources, regard drawing any further attention to Mohammed al-Dura as self-defeating. No new "proof" would erase images of the boy's death, and resurrecting the discussion would only ensure that the horrible footage was aired yet again. IDF press officials did not return any of my calls, including those requesting to interview soldiers who were at the outpost.

So by the time Gabriel Weimann's students at the Israeli Military Academy, including the one who had been on the scene, began looking into the evidence last fall, most Israelis had tried to put the case behind them. Those against the Likud policy of encouraging settlements in occupied territory think of the shooting as one more illustration of the policy's cost. Those who support the policy view Mohammed al-Dura's death as an unfortunate instance of "collateral damage," to be weighed against damage done to Israelis by Palestinian terrorists. Active interest in the case was confined mainly to a number of Israelis and European Jews who believe the event was manipulated to blacken Israel's image. Nahum Shahaf has become the leading figure in this group.

40   Shahaf is a type familiar to reporters: the person who has given himself entirely to a cause or a mystery and can talk about its ramifications as long as anyone will listen. He is a strongly built man of medium height, with graying hair combed back from his forehead. In photos he always appears stern, almost glowering, whereas in the time I spent with him he seemed to be constantly smiling, joking, having fun. Shahaf is in his middle fifties, but like many other scientists and engineers, he has the quality of seeming not quite grown up. He used to live in California, where, among other pursuits, he worked as a hang-gliding instructor. He moves and gesticulates with a teenager's lack of self-consciousness about his bearing. I liked him.

Before getting involved in the al-Dura case, Shahaf was known mainly as an inventor. He was only the tenth person to receive a medal from the Israeli Ministry of Science, for his work on computerized means of compressing digital video transmission. "But for two and a half years I am spending time only on the al-Dura case," he told me. "I left everything for it, because I believe that this is most important." When I arrived at his apartment, outside Tel Aviv, to meet him one morning, I heard a repeated sound from one room that I assumed was from a teenager's playing a violent video game. An hour later, when we walked into that room—which has been converted into a video-research laboratory, with multiple monitors, replay devices, and computers—I saw that it was one mob scene from September 30, being played on a continuous loop.

Shahaf's investigation for the IDF showed that the Israeli soldiers at the outpost did not shoot the boy. But he now believes that everything that happened at Netzarim on September 30 was a ruse. The boy on the film may or may not have been the son of the man who held him. The boy and the man may or may not actually have been shot. If shot, the boy may or may not actually have died. If he died, his killer may or may not have been a member of the Palestinian force, shooting at him directly. The entire goal of the exercise, Shahaf says, was to manufacture a child martyr, in correct anticipation of the damage this would do to Israel in the eyes of the world—especially the Islamic world. "I believe that one day there will be good things in common between us and the Palestinians," he told me. "But the case of Mohammed al-Dura brings the big flames between Israel and the Palestinians and Arabs. It brings a big wall of hate. They can say this is the proof, the ultimate proof, that Israeli soldiers are boy-murderers. And that hatred breaks any chance of having something good in the future."

The reasons to doubt that the al-Duras, the cameramen, and hundreds of onlookers were part of a coordinated fraud are obvious. Shahaf's evidence for this conclusion, based on his videos, is essentially an accumulation of oddities and unanswered questions about the chaotic events of the day. Why is there no footage of the boy after he was shot? Why does he appear to move in his father's lap, and to clasp a hand over his eyes after he is supposedly dead? Why is one Palestinian policeman wearing a Secret Service-style earpiece in one ear? Why is another Palestinian man shown waving his arms and yelling at others, as if "directing" a dramatic scene? Why does the funeral appear—based on the length of shadows—to have occurred before the apparent time of the shooting? Why is there no blood on the father's shirt just after they are shot? Why did a voice that seems to be that of the France 2 cameraman yell, in Arabic, "The boy is dead" before he had been hit? Why do ambulances appear instantly for seemingly everyone else and not for al-Dura?

A handful of Israeli and foreign commentators have taken up Shahaf's cause. A Web site called masada2000.org says of the IDF's initial apology, "They acknowledged guilt, for never in their collective minds would any one of them have imagined a scenario whereby Mohammed al-Dura might have been murdered by his *own* people . . . a cruel plot staged and executed by Palestinian sharp-shooters and a television cameraman!" Amnon Lord, writing for the magazine *Makor Rishon*, referred to a German documentary directed by Esther Schapira that was "based on Shahaf's own decisive conclusion" and that determined "that Muhammad Al-Dura was not killed by IDF gunfire at Netzarim junction." "Rather," Lord continued, "the Palestinians, in cooperation with foreign journalists and the UN, arranged a well-staged production of his death." In March of this year a French writer, Gérard Huber, published a book called *Contre expertise d'une mise en scène* (roughly, *Re-evaluation of a Re-enactment*). It, too, argues that the entire event was staged. In an e-mail message to me Huber said that before knowing of Shahaf's studies he had been aware that "the images of little Mohammed were part of the large war of images between Palestinians and Israelis." But until meeting Shahaf, he said, "I had not imagined that it involved a fiction"—a view he now shares. "The question of 'Who killed little Mohammed?'" he said, "has become a screen to disguise the real question, which is: 'Was little Mohammed actually killed?'"

45   The truth about this case will probably never be determined. Or, to put it more precisely, no version of truth that is considered believable by all sides will ever emerge. For most of the Arab world, the rights and wrongs of the case are beyond dispute: an innocent boy was murdered, and his blood is on Israel's hands. Mention of contrary evidence or hypotheses only confirms the bottomless dishonesty of the guilty parties—much as Holocaust-denial theories do in the the Western world. For the handful of people collecting evidence of a staged event, the truth is also clear, even if the proof is not in hand. I saw Nahum Shahaf lose his good humor only when I asked him what he thought explained the odd timing of the boy's funeral, or the contradictions in eyewitness reports, or the other loose ends in the case. "I don't 'think,' I know!" he said several times. "I am a physicist. I work from the evidence." Schapira had collaborated with him for the German documentary and then produced a film advancing the "minimum" version of his case, showing that the shots did not, could not have, come from the IDF outpost. She disappointed him by not embracing the maximum version—the all-encompassing hoax—and counseled him not to talk about a staged event unless he could produce a living boy or a cooperative eyewitness. Shahaf said that he still thought well of her, and that he was not discouraged. "I am only two and a half years into this work," he told me. "It took twelve years for the truth of the Dreyfus case to come out."

For anyone else who knows about Mohammed al-Dura but is not in either of the decided camps—the Arabs who are sure they know what happened, the revisionists who are equally sure—the case will remain in the uncomfortable realm of events that cannot be fully explained or understood. "Maybe it was an accidental shooting," Gabriel Weimann told me, after reading his students' report, which, like the German documentary, supported the "minimum" conclusion—the Israeli soldiers at the outpost could not have killed the boy. (He could not show the report to me, he said, on grounds of academic confidentiality.) "Maybe even it was staged—although I don't think my worst enemy is so inhuman as to shoot a boy for the sake of publicity. Beyond that, I do not know." Weimann's recent work involves the way that television distorts reality in attempting to reconstruct it, by putting together loosely related or even random events in what the viewer imagines is a coherent narrative flow. The contrast between the confusing, contradictory hours of raw footage from the Netzarim crossroads and the clear, gripping narrative of the evening news reports assembled from that footage is a perfect example, he says.

The significance of this case from the American perspective involves the increasingly chaotic ecology of truth around the world. In Arab and Islamic societies the widespread belief that Israeli soldiers shot this boy has political consequences. So does the belief among some Israelis and Zionists in Israel and abroad that Palestinians will go to any lengths to smear them. Obviously, these beliefs do not create the basic tensions in the Middle East. The Israeli policy of promoting settlements in occupied territory, and the Palestinian policy of terror, are deeper obstacles. There would never have been a showdown at the Netzarim crossroads, or any images of Mohammed al-Dura's shooting to be parsed in different ways, if there were no settlement nearby for IDF soldiers to protect. Gabriel Weimann is to the left of Dan Schueftan on Israel's political spectrum, but both believe that Israel should end its occupation. I would guess that Nahum Shahaf thinks the same thing, even though he told me that to preserve his "independence" as a researcher, he wanted to "isolate myself from any kind of political question."

The images intensify the self-righteous determination of each side. If anything, modern technology has aggravated the problem of mutually exclusive realities. With the Internet and TV, each culture now has a more elaborate apparatus for "proving," dramatizing, and disseminating its particular truth.

In its engagement with the Arab world the United States has assumed that what it believes are noble motives will be perceived as such around the world. We mean the best for the people under our control; stability, democracy, prosperity, are our goals; why else would we have risked so much to help an oppressed people achieve them? The case of Mohammed al-Dura suggests the need for much more modest assumptions about the way other cultures—in particular today's embattled Islam—will perceive our truths.

Responding to Reading

1. Do you think Fallows is presenting an unbiased report, or do you believe he has a particular agenda in reporting the events the way he does?
2. As Fallows notes, "To watch the raw footage is to wonder, repeatedly, What is going on here?" (13): a media expert he consults sees the footage as having a "'*Rashomon* effect'" (11), and Fallows repeatedly acknowledges

information gaps, inconsistencies, and confusion. Do you accept Fallows's conclusion that "The truth about this case will probably never be determined" (45)? What do you think actually happened?

3. If, as Fallows admits, the "proof" he assembles here is not at all "likely to change minds in the Arab world" (4), where the image of Mohammed al-Dura has been so inflammatory, what positive outcome can Fallows's article possibly have?

Responding in Writing

In paragraph 17, Fallows describes the footage of the shooting as "unforgettable," adding that "it illustrates the way television transforms reality." Later, he notes that "modern technology has aggravated the problem of mutually exclusive realities. With the Internet and TV, each culture now has a more elaborate apparatus for 'proving,' dramatizing, and disseminating its particular truth" (48). How, specifically, have you seen TV and the Internet "transform reality"?

FOCUS

Does Media Violence Hurt?

Scene from the video game *Carmageddon* depicting two people crushed by a truck.

Responding to the Image

1. Look carefully at the image above. What is actually taking place in the scene? What do you imagine happened before the scene? What do you think will happen next?
2. How would you expect a six-year-old child to respond to this image? How might a twelve-year-old respond? How do you respond?

GLOBAL MEDIA MAYHEM

George Gerbner

1919–

Born in Hungary, George Gerbner studied at the University of Budapest but left to escape the fascist regime in power there at that time. He immigrated to the United States in 1939, earned a BA degree from the University of California at Berkeley (1942), and became a naturalized citizen in 1943. After working as a journalist, Gerbner joined the US Army and earned the Bronze Star during World War II. He later earned an MS degree (1951) and a PhD (1955) from the University of Southern California and went on to devote more than forty years to studying the effects that television has on its view-ers. His books include The Future of Media: Digital Democracy or More Corporate Control? *(1999) and* Against the Mainstream: Selected Works of George Gerbner *(2002). The following essay appeared in the* Global Media Journal, *an electronic publication devoted to the study of communication, http://lass.calumet.purdue.edu/cca/gmj/.*

Humankind may have had more bloodthirsty eras, but none as filled with images of violence as the present. We are awash in a tide of violent representations such as the world has never seen. Images of ex-pertly choreographed brutality drench our homes. There is no escape from the mass-produced mayhem pervading the life space of ever larger areas of the world.

Violence is but the tip of the iceberg of a massive underlying con-nection to television's role as universal story-teller and an industry de-pendent on global markets.

The roles children grow into are no longer home-made, hand-crafted, community-inspired. They are products of a complex, inte-grated and globalized manufacturing and marketing system. Television violence, defined as overt physical action that hurts or kills (or threat-ens to do so), is an integral part of that system.

Representations of violence are not necessarily undesirable. There is blood in fairy tales, gore in mythology, murder in Shakespeare. Not all violence is alike. In some contexts, violence can be a legitimate and even necessary cultural expression. Individually crafted, historically in-spired, sparingly and selectively used expressions of symbolic violence can indicate the tragic costs of deadly compulsions. However, such tragic sense of violence has been swamped by "happy violence" pro-duced on the dramatic assembly-line. This "happy violence" is cool, swift, painless, and often spectacular, even thrilling, but usually sani-tized. It always leads to a happy ending; it must deliver the audience to the next commercial in a receptive mood.

5   The majority of network viewers have little choice of thematic con-text or cast of character types, and virtually no chance of avoiding vio-lence. Nor has the proliferation of channels led to greater diversity of actual viewing. If anything, the dominant dramatic patterns penetrate more deeply into viewer choices through more outlets managed by fewer owners airing programs produced by fewer creative sources.

The average viewer of prime time television drama (serious as well as comedic) sees in a typical week an average of 21 criminals arrayed against an army of 41 public and private law enforcers. There are 14 doctors, 6 nurses, 6 lawyers, and 2 judges to handle them. An average of 150 acts of violence and about 15 murders entertain them and their children every week, and that does not count cartoons and the news. Those who watch over 3 hours a day (more than half of all viewers) absorb much more.

Violence takes on an even more defining role for major characters. It involves more than half of all major characters (58 percent of men and 41 percent of women). Most likely to be involved either as perpetrators or victims, or both, are characters portrayed as mentally ill (84 percent), characters with mental or other disability (70 percent), young adult males (69 percent), and Latino/Hispanic Americans (64 percent). Children, lower class, and mentally ill or otherwise disabled characters, pay the highest price—13–16 victims for every 10 perpetrators.

Lethal victimization extends the pattern. About 5 percent of all characters and 10 percent of major characters are involved in killing (kill or get killed, or both). Being Latino/Hispanic, or lower class means bad trouble: they are the most likely to kill and be killed. Being poor, old, Hispanic or a woman of color means double-trouble, a disproportionate chance of being killed; they pay the highest relative price for taking another's life.

Among major characters, for every 10 "good" (positively valued) men who kill, about 4 are killed. But for every 10 "good" women who kill, 6 are killed, and for every 10 women of color who kill 17 are killed. Older women characters get involved in violence only to be killed.

We calculated a violence "pecking order" by ranking the risk ratios 10 of the different groups. Women, children, young people, lower class, disabled and Asian Americans are at the bottom of the heap. When it comes to killing, older and Latino/Hispanic characters also pay a higher-than-average price. In other words, hurting and killing by most majority groups extracts a tooth for a tooth. But minority groups tend tend to pay a higher price for their show of force. That imbalance of power is, in fact, what makes them minorities even when, as women, they are a numerical majority.

What are the consequences? The symbolic overkill takes its toll on all viewers. However, heavier viewers in every subgroup express a greater sense of apprehension than do light viewers in the same groups. They are more likely than comparable groups of light viewers to overestimate their chances of involvement in violence; to believe that their neighborhoods are unsafe; to state that fear of crime is a very serious personal problem and to assume that crime is rising, regardless of the facts of the case. Heavy viewers are also more likely to buy new locks, watchdogs, and guns "for protection." It makes no difference what they watch because only light viewers watch more selectively; heavy viewers watch more of everything that is on the air. Our studies show that they cannot escape watching violence.

Moreover, viewers who see members of their own group underrepresented but overvictimzed seem to develop a greater sense of apprehension, mistrust, and alienation, what we call the "mean world syndrome." Insecure, angry people may be prone to violence but are even more likely to be dependent on authority and susceptible to deceptively simple, strong, hard-line postures. They may accept and even welcome repressive measures such as more jails, capital punishment, harsher sentences—measures that have never reduced crime but never fail to get votes—if that promises to relieve their anxieties. That is the deeper dilemma of violence-laden television.

Formula-driven violence in entertainment and news is, therefore, not an expression of freedom, viewer preference, or even crime statistics. The frequency of violence in the media seldom, if ever, reflects the actual occurrence of crime in a community. It is, rather, the product of a complex manufacturing and marketing machine.

Mergers, consolidation, conglomeratization, and globalization speed the machine. Concentration brings denial of access to new entries and alternative perspectives. It places greater emphasis on dramatic ingredients most suitable for aggressive international promotion. Having fewer buyers for their products forces program producers into deficit financing. That means that most producers cannot break even on the license fees they receive for domestic airings. They are forced into syndication and foreign sales to make a profit. They need a dramatic ingredient that requires no translation, "speaks action" in any language and fits any culture. That ingredient is violence.

15 The rationalization for all that is that violence "sells." But what does it sell to whom, and at what price? There is no evidence that, other factors being equal, violence per se is giving most viewers, countries, and citizens "what they want." The most highly rated programs are usually not violent. In other words, violence may help sell programs cheaply to broadcasters in many countries despite the dislike of their audiences. But television audiences do not buy programs, and advertisers, who do, pay for reaching the available audience at the least cost.

We compared data from over 100 violent and the same number of non-violent prime-time programs stored in the Cultural Indicators database. The average Nielsen rating of the violent sample was 11.1; the same for the non-violent sample was 13.8. The share of viewing households in the violent and nonviolent samples was 18.9 and 22.5, respectively. The amount and consistency of violence in a series further increased the gap. Furthermore, the non-violent sample was more highly rated than the violent sample for each of the five seasons studied.

However, despite their low average popularity, what violent programs lose on general domestic audiences they more than make up by grabbing younger viewers the advertisers want to reach and by extending their reach to the global market hungry for a cheap product. Even though these imports are typically also less popular abroad than quality shows produced at home, their extremely low cost, compared to local production, makes them attractive to the broadcasters who buy them.

Most television viewers suffer the violence daily inflicted on them with diminishing tolerance. Organizations of creative workers in media, health-professionals, law enforcement agencies, and virtually all other media-oriented professional and citizen groups have come out against "gratuitous" television violence. A March 1985 Harris survey showed that 78 percent disapprove of violence they see on television. A Gallup poll of October 1990 found 79 percent in favor of "regulating" objectionable content in television. A *Times-Mirror* national poll in 1993 showed that Americans who said they were "personally bothered" by violence in entertainment shows jumped to 59 percent from 44 percent in 1983. Furthermore, 80 percent said entertainment violence was "harmful" to society, compared with 64 percent in 1983.

Local broadcasters, legally responsible for what goes on the air, also oppose the overkill and complain about loss of control. *Electronic Media* reported on August 2, 1993 the results of its own survey of 100 general managers across all regions and in all market sizes. Three out of four said there is too much needless violence on television; 57 percent would like to have "more input on program content decisions."

The Hollywood Caucus of Producers, Writers and Directors, speaking for the creative community, said in a statement issued in August 1993: "We stand today at a point in time when the country's dissatisfaction with the quality of television is at an all-time high, while our own feelings of helplessness and lack of power, in not only choosing material that seeks to enrich, but also in our ability to execute to the best of our ability, is at an all-time low." 20

Far from reflecting creative freedom, the marketing of formula violence restricts freedom and chills originality. The violence formula is, in fact, a de facto censorship extending the dynamics of domination, intimidation, and repression domestically and globally.

There is a liberating alternative. It exists in various forms in democratic countries. It is public participation in making decisions about cultural investment and cultural policy. Independent grass-roots citizen organization and action can provide the broad support needed for loosening the global marketing noose around the necks of producers, writers, directors, actors and journalists.

More freedom from violent and other inequitable and intimidating formulas, not more censorship, is the effective and acceptable way to increase diversity and reduce the dependence of program producers on the violence formula, and to reduce television violence to its legitimate role and proportion. The role of Congress, if any, is to turn its anti-trust and civil rights oversight on the centralized and globalized industrial structures and marketing strategies that impose violence on creative people and foist it on the children and adults of the world. It is high time to develop a vision of the right of children to be born into a reasonable free, fair, diverse and non-threatening cultural environment. It is time for citizen involvement in cultural decisions that shape our lives and the lives of our children.

Responding to Reading

1. In paragraph 3, Gerbner defines TV violence as "overt physical action that hurts or kills (or threatens to do so)." Do you think this definition is too broad? Too narrow? Can you give examples of TV violence that is not covered by Gerbner's definition—or actions that are covered by his definition but that you do not consider violent?
2. Whom or what does Gerbner blame for the "expertly choreographed brutality" (1) the media produces? According to Gerbner, whose responsibility is it to solve the problem?
3. Gerbner observes that TV violence is disproportionally associated with members of minority groups, who tend to be "underrepresented but overvictimized" (12). What attitudes and behavior result from this disparity? Why does Gerbner see it as such a serious problem? How are his concerns about the effects of media violence different from John Leo's (p. 327)?

Responding in Writing

In discussing the negative effects of media violence, Gerbner focuses mainly on television, but his comments could certainly be applied to other media as well. Reread paragraphs 5 through 12, and write a paragraph in which you use examples from movies you have seen to support Gerbner's argument.

HOLLOW CLAIMS ABOUT FANTASY VIOLENCE

Richard Rhodes

1937–

Journalist Richard Rhodes writes and edits essays, nonfiction books, and novels covering a wide range of topics, from nuclear bombs to mad cow disease. He was born in Kansas City and earned a Bachelor's degree in history from Yale University (1959). His book The Making of the Atomic Bomb *(1986) won a Pulitzer Prize in general nonfiction and a National Book Award. His recent books include* Deadly Feasts: Tracking the Secrets of a Terrifying New Plague *(1997);* Visions of Technology: A Century of Vital Debate about Machines, Systems, and the Human World *(1999);* Why They Kill: The Discoveries of a Maverick Criminologist *(1999); and* Masters of Death: The SS-Einsatgruppen and the Invention of the Holocaust

(2002). Rhodes has been a fellow of the Guggenheim, Ford, MacArthur, and Alfred P. Sloan foundations and of the National Endowment for the Arts. The following essay appeared on the op-ed page of the New York Times.

The moral entrepreneurs are at it again, pounding the entertainment industry for advertising its Grand Guignolesque confections to children. If exposure to this mock violence contributes to the development of violent behavior, then our political leadership is justified in its indignation at what the Federal Trade Commission has reported about the marketing of violent fare to children. Senators John McCain and Joseph Lieberman have been especially quick to fasten on the F.T.C. report as they make an issue of violent offerings to children.

But is there really a link between entertainment and violent behavior?

The American Medical Association, the American Psycological Association, the American Academy of Pediactrics and the National Institute of Mental Health all say yes. They base their claims on social science research that has been sharply criticized and disputed within the social science profession, especially outside the United States. In fact, no direct, causal link between exposure to mock violence in the media and subsequent violent behavior has ever been demonstrated, and the few claims of modest correlation have been contradicted by other findings, sometimes in the same studies.

History alone should call such a link into question. Private violence has been declining in the West since the media-barren late Middle Ages, when homicide rates are estimated to have been 10 times what they are in Western nations today. Historians attribute the decline to improving social controls over violence—police forces and commons access to courts of law—and to a shift away from brutal physical punishment in child-rearing (a practice that still appears as a common factor in the background of violent criminals today).

The American Medical Association has based its endorsement of   5 the media violence theory in major part on the studies of Brandon Centerwall, a psychiatrist in Seattle. Dr. Centerwall compared the murder rates for whites in three countries from 1945 to 1974 with numbers for television set ownership. Until 1975, television broadcasting was banned in South Africa, and "white homicide rates remained stable" there, Dr. Centerwall found, while corresponding rates in Canada and the United States doubled after television was introduced.

A spectacular finding, but it is meaningless. As Franklin E. Zimring and Gordon Hawkins of the University of California at Berkeley subsequently pointed out, homicide rates in France, Germany, Italy and Japan either failed to change with increasing television ownership in the same period or actually declined, and American homicide rates have more recently been sharply decling despite a proliferation of popular media outlets—not only movies and television, but also video games and the Internet.

Other social science that supposedly undergrids the theory, too, is marginal and problematic. Laboratory studies that expose children to selected incidents of televised mock violence and then assess changes in the children's behavior have sometimes found more "aggressive" behavior after the exposure—usually verbal, occasionally physical.

But sometimes the control group, shown incidents judged not to be violent, behaves more aggressively afterward then the test group; sometimes comedy produces the more aggressive behavior; and sometimes there's no change. The only obvious conclusion is that sitting and watching television stimulates subsequent physical activity. Any kid could tell you that.

As for those who claim that entertainment promotes violent behavior by desensitizing people to violence, the British scholar Martin Barker offers this critique: "Their claim is that the materials they judge to be harmful can only influence us by trying to make us be the same as them. So horrible things will make us horrible—not horrified. Terrifying things will make us terrifying—not terrified. To see something aggressive makes us feel aggressive—not aggressed against. This idea is so odd, it is hard to know where to begin in challenging it."

10   Even more influential on national policy has been a 22-year study by two University of Michigan psychologists, Leonard D. Eron and L. Rowell Huesmann, of boys exposed to so-called violent media. The Telecommunications Act of 1996, which mandated the television V-chip, allowing parents to screen out unwanted programming, invoked these findings, asserting, "Studies have shown that children exposed to violent video programming at a young age have a higher tendency for violent and aggressive behavior later in life than children not so exposed."

Well, not exactly. Following 875 children in upstate New York from third grade through high school, the psychologists found a correlation between a preference for violent television at age 8 and aggressiveness at age 18. The correlation—0.31—would mean television accounted for about 10 percent of the influence that led to this behavior. But the correlation only turned up in one of three measures of aggression: the assessment of students by their peers. It didn't show up in students' reports about themselves of in psychological testing. And for girls, there was no correlation at all.

Despite the lack of evidence, politicians can't resist blaming the media for violence. They can stake out the moral high ground confident that the First Amendment will protect them from having to actually write legislation that would be likely to alienate the entertainment industry. Some use the issue as a smokescreen to avoid having to confront gun control.

But violence isn't learned from mock violence. There is good evidence—casual evidence, not correlational—that it's learned in personal violent encounters, beginning with the brutalization of children by their parents or their peers.

The money spent on all the social science research I've described was diverted from the National Institute of Mental Health budget by reducing support for the construction of community mental health centers. To this day there is no standardized reporting system for emergency-room findings of physical child abuse. Violence is on the decline in America, but if we want to reduce it even further, protecting children from real violence in their real lives—not the pale shadow of mock violence—is the place to begin.

Responding to Reading

1. In paragraph 3, Rhodes states emphatically that "no direct, causal link between exposure to mock violence in the media and subsequent violent behavior has ever been demonstrated." Why, then, do so many people—such as George Gerbner (p. 319)—believe that such a link exists?
2. Rhodes is sharply critical of the social science research he summarizes, and he often includes irreverent or sarcastic comments, such as the following:
   - "A spectacular finding, but it is meaningless" (6).
   - "Any kid could tell you that" (8).
   - (Quoting British scholar Martin Barker) "'This idea is so odd, it is hard to know where to begin in challenging it'" (9).

   Do statements like these make you less inclined to accept Rhodes's position, or does his essay stand on its evidence?
3. Beyond setting the record straight on the question of the link between "mock violence" and actual violent acts, what other purpose or purposes does Rhodes hope to accomplish in this essay? For example, on whom does he place the blame for the central misconception he identifies?

Responding in Writing

Write a paragraph in which you describe a violent video game that you believe could actually incite violent behavior in its participants. Be sure to describe the setting and characters thoroughly and to explain how the action on screen might actually translate into real-life actions.

WHEN LIFE IMITATES VIDEO

John Leo

1935–

Columnist John Leo is a social commentator who often presents outspoken views on controversial topics in books and articles about current social issues and cultural trends, from political correctness to the immorality of popular song lyrics. Leo has a weekly syndicated column, "On Society," in U.S. News and World Report, where he has worked since 1988. He has also

been a staff writer for Time *magazine, the* New York Times, Common-
weal, *and the* Village Voice. *His books include* How the Russians Invented Baseball and Other Essays of Enlightenment *(1969),* Two Steps
ahead of the Thought Police *(1994), and* Incorrect Thoughts: Notes
on Our Wayward Culture *(2000). The following essay appeared in* US
News and World Report *in 1999, shortly after the deadly shootings at
Columbine High School in Littleton, Colorado.*

Was it real life or an acted-out video game?

Marching through a large building using various bombs and guns
to pick off victims is a conventional video-game scenario. In the Colorado massacre, Dylan Klebold and Eric Harris used pistolgrip shot-
guns, as in some video-arcade games. The pools of blood, screams of
agony, and pleas for mercy must have been familiar—they are featured
in some of the newer and more realistic kill-for-kicks games. "With
each kill," the *Los Angeles Times* reported, "the teens cackled and
shouted as though playing one of the morbid video games they loved."
And they ended their spree by shooting themselves in the head, the
final act in the game Postal, and, in fact, the only way to end it.

Did the sensibilities created by the modern, video kill games play a
role in the Littleton massacre? Apparently so. Note the cool and casual
cruelty, the outlandish arsenal of weapons, the cheering and laughing
while hunting down victims one by one. All of this seems to reflect the
style and feel of the video killing games they played so often.

No, there isn't any direct connection between most murderous
games and most murders. And yes, the primary responsibility for protecting children from dangerous games lies with their parents, many of
whom like to blame the entertainment industry for their own failings.

5   But there is a cultural problem here: We are now a society in which
the chief form of play for millions of youngsters is making large numbers of people die. Hurting and maiming others is the central fun activity in video games played so addictively by the young. A widely cited
survey of 900 fourth-through-eighth-grade students found that almost
half of the children said their favorite electronic games involve violence. Can it be that all this constant training in make-believe killing
has no social effects?

Dress Rehearsal

The conventional argument is that this is a harmless activity among
children who know the difference between fantasy and reality. But the
games are often played by unstable youngsters unsure about the difference. Many of these have been maltreated or rejected and left alone
most of the time (a precondition for playing the games obsessively).

Adolescent feelings of resentment, powerlessness and revenge pour into the killing games. In these children, the games can become a dress rehearsal for the real thing.

Psychologist David Grossman of Arkansas State University, a retired Army officer, thinks "point and shoot" video games have the same effect as military strategies used to break down a soldier's aversion to killing. During World War II, only 15 to 20 percent of all American soldiers fired their weapon in battle. Shooting games in which the target is a manshaped outline, the Army found, made recruits more willing to "make killing a reflex action."

Video games are much more powerful versions of the military's primitive discovery about overcoming the reluctance to shoot. Grossman says Michael Carneal, the schoolboy shooter in Paducah, Ky., showed the effects of video-game lessons in killing. Carneal coolly shot nine times, hitting eight people, five of them in the head or neck. Head shots pay a bonus in many video games. Now the Marine Corps is adapting a version of Doom, the hyperviolent game played by one of the Littleton killers, for its own training purposes.

More realistic touches in video games help blur the boundary between fantasy and reality—guns carefully modeled on real ones, accurate-looking wounds, screams, and other sound effects, even the recoil of a heavy rifle. Some newer games seem intent on erasing children's empathy and concern for others. Once the intended victims of video slaughter were mostly gangsters or aliens. Now some games invite players to blow away ordinary people who have done nothing wrong—pedestrians, marching bands, an elderly woman with a walker. In these games, the shooter is not a hero, just a violent sociopath. One ad for a Sony game says: "Get in touch with your gun-toting, testosterone-pumping, cold-blooded murdering side."

These killings are supposed to be taken as harmless over-the-top 10 jokes. But the bottom line is that the young are being invited to enjoy the killing of vulnerable people picked at random. This looks like the final lesson in a course to eliminate any lingering resistance to killing.

SWAT teams and cops now turn up as the intended victims of some video-game killings. This has the effect of exploiting resentments toward law enforcement and making real-life shooting of cops more likely. This sensibility turns up in the hit movie *Matrix*: world-saving hero Keanu Reeves, in a mandatory Goth-style, long black coat packed with countless heavy-duty guns, is forced to blow away huge numbers of uniformed law-enforcement people.

"We have to start worrying about what we are putting into the minds of our young," says Grossman. "Pilots train on flight simulators, drivers on driving simulators, and now we have our children on murder simulators." If we want to avoid more Littleton-style massacres, we will begin taking the social effects of the killing games more seriously.

Responding to Reading

1. In paragraph 1, Leo asks a question about the 1999 Littleton, Colorado, massacre: "Was it real life or an acted-out video game?" How would you answer this question?
2. Leo quotes psychologist David Grossman extensively. What is Grossman's position? Does Leo share this position? Would his essay be more convincing if he cited additional sources?
3. In paragraph 5, Leo identifies a "cultural problem": "We are now," he says, "a society in which the chief form of play for millions of youngsters is making large numbers of people die." In your opinion, *is* this kind of "play" a problem?

Responding in Writing

Write a letter to the editor from the point of view of a teenager who enjoys playing video games. In your letter, argue that video games that depict violence are just a "harmless activity among children who know the difference between fantasy and reality" (6). Briefly describe the violence in the games you play, but focus on the positive aspects of your life.

—— WIDENING THE FOCUS ——

The following readings can suggest additional perspectives for thinking and writing about the subject of media violence. You may also want to do further research about this subject on the Internet.

- Sharon Olds, "Rite of Passage" (p. 406)
- Christina Hoff Sommers, "The War against Boys" (p. 453)
- George Orwell, "Shooting an Elephant" (p. 673)
- Andrew Sullivan, "What's So Bad about Hate" (p. 745)

For Internet Research: Debates about media violence often draw on arguments relating to artistic expression, consumer choice, cultural norms, free speech, and public policy. Visit the Web site of the Media Awareness Network, a Canadian research group, at http://www .media-awareness.ca/english/issues/violence/index.cfm, and read the articles covering media violence. Also read journalist Richard Rhodes's essay "The Media Violence Myth," which is available on the Web site of the American Booksellers Foundation for Free Expression, http://www.abffe.com/myth1.htm. Then, write an essay in which you evaluate the arguments presented by both sides of this debate, and explain which arguments you find most effective and why.

—————————————— WRITING ——————————————

Media and Society

1. What do you think the impact of the various media discussed in this chapter will be in the years to come? What trends do you see emerging that you believe will change the way you think or the way you live? Write an essay in which you speculate about future trends and their impact.

2. Write an essay in which you consider the representation of women, the elderly, or people with disabilities—in movies, on television, or in magazine ads. Do you believe the group you have chosen to write about is adequately represented? Do you think its members are portrayed fairly and accurately, or do you think they are stereotyped? Support your conclusions with specific examples.

3. Keep a daily log of the programs you listen to on the radio and watch on television, the movies you see, the Web sites you visit, and the newspapers and magazines you read (in print and online). After one week, review your log, and consider how these different kinds of media informed, provoked, or entertained you. Then, write a report explaining why you made the choices you did and evaluating the impact of various media on you.

4. Do films and television shows present an accurate image of your gender, race, religion, or ethnic group? In what ways, if any, is the image you see unrealistic? In what ways, if any, is it demeaning? If possible, include recommendations for improving the media image of the group you discuss. What should be done to challenge—or change—simplistic or negative images? Whose responsibility should it be to effect change?

5. Should the government continue to support public television and radio? What, if anything, do public radio and television provide that commercial programming does not offer? (Before beginning this essay, compare newspaper listings of public and commercial programming, and try to spend a few hours screening public television and radio programs if you are not familiar with them.)

6. What kind of "family values" are promoted on television? Would you say that TV is largely "profamily" or "antifamily"? Using the essays in this chapter by Winn (p. 270), Rushdie (p. 289), and Kaminer (p. 278) for background, choose several films and television programs that support your position. Then, write an essay that takes a strong stand on this issue. (Be sure to define exactly what you mean by *family* and *family values*.)

7. To what extent, if any, should sexual content—for example, explicitly sexual images in magazine ads, on TV, or on the Internet—be censored? Write an essay in which you take a stand on this issue.

8. What danger, if any, do you see for young people in the seductive messages of the music they listen to? Do you believe that parents and educators are right to be concerned about the effect the messages in rock and rap music have on teenagers and young adults, or do you think they are overreacting? Support your position with quotations from popular music lyrics. If you like, you can also interview friends and relatives and use their responses to help you develop your argument.

9. Some argue that the Internet brings people together—for example, by providing constant dialogue in email exchanges and chat rooms and by creating a common cultural frame of reference. Others believe that the Internet actually divides and isolates people, enabling them to receive only information that appeals to their own narrow interests and allowing them to avoid face-to-face contact. Do you see the Internet as a unifying or a dividing force in our society?

10. Exactly how can media violence hurt? Whom do you think it hurts most? After reading the three essays in the Focus section of this chapter, write an essay that answers these questions. Be sure to provide specific examples from a variety of different media and to refer to the essays by George Gerbner ("Global Media Mayhem," p. 319), Richard Rhodes ("Hollow Claims about Fantasy Violence," p. 324), and John Leo ("When Life Imitates Video," p. 327).

5

THE WAY
WE LIVE NOW

PREPARING TO READ AND WRITE

The way we live now is very different from the way we lived just a generation or two ago. Early science fiction writers imagined time travel, but few envisioned the scope of the changes that would occur in where we live, what we wear and eat, how we spend our leisure time, and what electronic "toys" we rely on.

In Rick Moody's 1995 novel *The Ice Storm,* set in 1973, the narrator sets the scene in a way that reminds readers how different things were just twenty years earlier:

People in airport pay-phone booths, St. Louis, MO, 1966.

No answering machines. And no call waiting. No Caller I.D. No compact disc recorders or laser discs or holography or cable television or MTV. No multiplex cinemas or word processors or laser printers or modems. No virtual reality. No grand unified theory or Frequent Flyer mileage or fuel injection systems or turbo or premenstrual syndrome or rehabilitation centers or Adult Children of Alcoholics. No codependency. No punk rock, or postpunk, or hardcore, or grunge. No hip-hop. No Acquired Immune Deficiency Syndrome or Human Immunodeficiency Virus or mysterious AIDS-like illnesses. No computer viruses. No cloning or genetic engineering or biospheres or full-color photocopying or desktop copying and especially no facsimile transmission. . . .

And, of course, the world has continued to change in the years since 1995. Now, in the early years of the new millennium, life as we know it would hold surprises not only for a time traveler from 100 years ago or from the 1973 of Moody's novel, but for one from ten years ago as well: houses, televisions, SUVs, and portion sizes have gotten bigger; cell phones have gotten smaller; and the popularity of the Internet has exploded.

With these and other changes, both sudden and gradual, have come inevitable problems: As we applaud technology, we fear its misuse; as we discover new forms of entertainment, we find we must work harder to afford them (leaving us with less time to enjoy them);

Business people talking on cell phones, 2001.

as we celebrate our increasingly diverse society, we struggle to find common ground while retaining our unique cultures; and even as we learn more about health and nutrition, we have less time to exercise and monitor our diets.

The essays in this chapter look at some of these (and other) issues, commenting on how our lives have changed and suggesting changes still to come. The Focus section of this chapter, a photo essay entitled "What Do Our Clothes Tell Us about Ourselves?" looks at change from another perspective, tracing fashion trends through the past hundred years or so.

Each of the writers whose essays are collected in this chapter has a different way of looking at the world. Some look ahead; others look back. Some are optimistic; others are pessimistic. Perhaps your own view of present-day society is more similar to one of theirs; more likely, you see the world from a different angle, one that is unlike the one any of them describes.

As you read the selections in this chapter and prepare to write about them, you may consider the following questions:

- Does the writer present a primarily positive or negative picture of society?

- Is the writer looking forward or backward?

- On what issue or issues does the writer focus?

- Would you say the writer's primary objective is to understand an issue and its effect, to inform readers, or to change readers' minds?

- Does the writer have a personal stake in the issue? If so, does your awareness of this involvement weaken or strengthen the selection's impact on you?

- If the selection identifies a problem, does it focus on finding solutions, speculating about long-term effects, or warning about consequences?

- Does the writer focus on the need for change—for example, in basic attitudes, in habits, or in the law? Is the writer optimistic or pessimistic about the possibility of change?

- Are you emotionally connected to the issue under discussion, or are you relatively detached from it?

- What areas of common concern do the writers explore? How are their views alike? How are they different? In what ways are they like and unlike your own?

- How are the writers' hopes and dreams for the future alike? How are they different? In what ways are they like and unlike your own?

THE WORLD IS TOO MUCH WITH US
William Wordsworth
1770–1850

One of the best-known English poets, William Wordsworth graduated from Cambridge University in 1791, traveled abroad, and returned to live in the rural Lake District of England, where he stayed for the remainder of his life. Wordsworth's work was deeply influenced by his natural surroundings and by a close association with another English poet, Samuel Taylor Coleridge. Together they led the English Romantic Movement in literature, writing poetry in the language of ordinary people and focusing on ideas of freedom, individualism, and Nature. In the following 1807 sonnet, "The World Is Too Much with Us," Wordsworth contrasts the natural world with the world of materialism. Nearly 200 years ago—long before fast food, interstates, shopping malls, and suburban living—Wordsworth lamented human separation from the natural world.

The world is too much with us; late and soon,
Getting and spending, we lay waste our powers;
Little we see in Nature that is ours;
We have given our hearts away, a sordid boon!
This Sea that bares her bosom to the moon;   5
The winds that will be howling at all hours,
And are up-gathered now like sleeping flowers;
For this, for everything, we are out of tune;
It moves us not. Great God! I'd rather be
A Pagan suckled in a creed outworn;   10
So might I, standing on this pleasant lea,
Have glimpses that would make me less forlorn;
Have sight of Proteus[1] rising from the sea;
Or hear old Triton[2] blow his wreathèd horn.

Responding to Reading

1. What does the poem's speaker think is wrong with the world in which he lives? Do any of his complaints apply to the twenty-first-century world as well?
2. What do you think the speaker means by "Getting and spending" (2)?
3. With whom, or what, is the speaker "out of tune" (8)?

---

[1]A Greek sea god capable of assuming different forms. [Eds.]
[2]A son of Poseidon, the Greek god of the sea, described as a demigod of the sea with the lower part of his body like that of a fish. [Eds.]

Responding in Writing

What in our own world is "too much with us" (1)? Can you suggest a solution for this problem?

THE TRANSFORMATION OF EVERYDAY LIFE

Richard Florida

1957–

Born in Newark, New Jersey, Richard Florida earned a BA degree from Rutgers University (1979), studied at the Massachusetts Institute of Technology, and earned his PhD from Columbia University (1986). He is a professor of economic development at Carnegie Mellon University and has authored and coauthored several books and more than 100 articles in academic journals. The following selection is taken from his popular book, The Rise of the Creative Class: And How It's Transforming Work, Leisure, Community, and Everyday Life *(2002). Based on the author's research, the book illustrates how creativity can be an economic force, one that leads to changes in the workplace, in American culture, and in people's everyday lives. To learn more about this author, visit his Web site, http://www.creative class.org/.*

Something's happening here but you don't know what it is, do you, Mr. Jones?

—Bob Dylan

Here's a thought experiment. Take a typical man on the street from the year 1900 and drop him into the 1950s. Then take someone from the 1950s and move him Austin Powers-style into the present day. Who would experience the greater change?

At first glance the answer seems obvious. Thrust forward into the 1950s, a person from the turn of the twentieth century would be awestruck by a world filled with baffling technological wonders. In place of horse-drawn carriages, he would see streets and highways jammed with cars, trucks and buses. In the cities, immense skyscrapers would line the horizon, and mammoth bridges would span rivers and inlets where once only ferries could cross. Flying machines would soar overhead, carrying people across the continent or the oceans in a matter of hours rather than days. At home, our 1900-to-1950s time-traveler would grope his way through a strange new environment filled with appliances powered by electricity: radios and televisions emanating musical sounds and even human images, refrigerators to keep things cold, washing machines to clean his clothes automatically, and much more. A massive new super market would replace daily trips to the market with an array of technologically enhanced foods, such as instant coffee or frozen vegetables to put into the refrigerator. Life itself would be dramatically extended. Many once-fatal ailments could be prevented with an injection or cured with a pill. The newness of this time-traveler's physical surroundings—the speed and power of everyday machines—would be profoundly disorienting.

On the other hand, someone from the 1950s would have little trouble navigating the physical landscape of today. Although we like to think ours is the age of boundless technological wonders, our second time-traveler would find himself in a world not all that different from the one he left. He would still drive a car to work. If he took the train, it would likely be on the same line leaving from the same station. He could probably board an airplane at the same airport. He might still live in a suburban house, though a bigger one. Television would have more channels, but it would basically be the same, and he could still catch some of his favorite 1950s shows on reruns. He would know how, or quickly learn how, to operate most household appliances—even the personal computer, with its familiar QWERTY keyboard. In fact with just a few exceptions, such as the PC, the Internet, CD and DVD players, the cash machine and a wireless phone he could carry with him, he would be familiar with almost all current-day technology. Perhaps disappointed by the pace of progress, he might ask: "Why haven't we conquered outer space?" or "Where are all the robots?"

On the basis of big, obvious technological changes alone, surely the 1900-to-1950s traveler would experience the greater shift, while the other might easily conclude that we'd spent the second half of the twentieth century doing little more than tweaking the great waves of the first half.[1]

But the longer they stayed in their new homes, the more each time-traveler would become aware of subtler dimensions of change. Once the glare of technology had dimmed, each would begin to notice their respective society's changed norms and values, and the ways in which everyday people live and work. And here the tables would be turned. In terms of adjusting to the social structures and the rhythms and patterns of daily life, our second time-traveler would be much more disoriented.

Someone from the early 1900s would find the social world of the 1950s remarkably similar to his own. If he worked in a factory, he might find much the same divisions of labor, the same hierarchical systems of control. If he worked in an office, he would be immersed in the same bureaucracy, the same climb up the corporate ladder. He would come to work at 8 or 9 each morning and leave promptly at 5, his life neatly segmented into compartments of home and work. He would wear a suit and tie. Most of his business associates would be white and male. Their values and office politics would hardly have changed. He would seldom see women in the workplace, except as secretaries, and almost never interact professionally with someone of another race. He would marry young, have children quickly thereafter, stay married to the same person and probably work for the same company for the rest of his life. In his leisure time, he'd find that movies and TV had largely superseded live stage shows, but otherwise his recreational activities would be much the same as they were in 1900: taking in a baseball game or a boxing match, maybe playing a round of golf. He would join the clubs and civic groups befitting his socioeconomic class, observe the same social distinctions, and fully expect his children to do likewise. The tempo of his life would be structured by the values and norms of organizations. He would find himself living the life of the "company man" so aptly chronicled by writers from Sinclair Lewis and John Kenneth Galbraith to William Whyte and C. Wright Mills.[2]

Our second time-traveler, however, would be quite unnerved by the dizzying social and cultural changes that had accumulated between the 1950s and today. At work he would find a new dress code, a new schedule, and new rules. He would see office workers dressed like folks relaxing on the weekend, in jeans and open-necked shirts, and be shocked to learn they occupy positions of authority. People at the office would seemingly come and go as they pleased. The younger ones might sport bizarre piercings and tattoos. Women and even non-whites would be managers. Individuality and self-expression would be valued over conformity to organizational norms—and yet these people would seem strangely puritanical to this time-traveler. His ethnic jokes would fall embarrassingly flat. His smoking would get him banished to the parking lot, and his two-martini lunches would raise genuine concern. Attitudes and expressions he had never thought about would cause repeated offense. He would continually suffer the painful feeling of not knowing how to behave.

Out on the street, this time-traveler would see different ethnic groups in greater numbers than he ever could have imagined—Asian, Indian-, and Latin-Americans and others—all mingling in ways he found strange and perhaps inappropriate. There would be mixed-race couples, and same-sex couples carrying the upbeat-sounding moniker "gay." While some of these people would be acting in familiar ways—a woman shopping while pushing a stroller, an office worker having lunch at a counter—others, such as grown men clad in form-fitting gear whizzing by on high-tech bicycles, or women on strange new roller skates with their torsos covered only by "brassieres"—would appear to be engaged in alien activities.

People would seem to be always working and yet never working when they were supposed to. They would strike him as lazy and yet obsessed with exercise. They would seem career-conscious yet fickle—doesn't anybody stay with the company more than three years?—and caring yet anti-social: What happened to the ladies' clubs, Moose Lodges and bowling leagues? While the physical surroundings would be relatively familiar, the *feel* of the place would be bewilderingly different.

Thus, although the first time-traveler had to adjust to some drastic technological changes, it is the second who experiences the deeper, more pervasive transformation. It is the second who has been thrust into a time when lifestyles and worldviews are most assuredly changing—a time when the old order has broken down, when flux and uncertainty themselves seem to be part of the everyday norm.

The Force Behind the Shift

What caused this transformation? What happened between the 1950s and today that did not happen in the earlier period? Scholars and pundits have floated many theories, along with a range of opinions on whether the changes are good or bad. Some bemoan the passing of traditional social and cultural forms, while others point to a rosy future based largely on new technology. Yet on one point most of them agree. Most tend to see the transformation as something that's being done to us unwittingly. Some complain that certain factions of society have imposed their values on the rest of us; others say that our own inventions are turning around to reshape us. They're wrong.

Society is changing in large measure because we want it to. Moreover it is changing neither in random chaotic ways nor in some mysterious collective-unconscious way, but in ways that are perfectly sensible and rational. The logic behind the transformation has been unclear to this point because the transformation is still in progress. But lately a number of diverse and seemingly unconnected threads are starting to come together. The deeper pattern, the force behind the shift, can now be discerned.

That driving force is the rise of human creativity as the key factor in our economy and society. Both at work and in other spheres of our lives, we value creativity more highly than ever, and cultivate it more intensely. The creative impulse—the attribute that distinguishes us, as humans, from other species—is now being let loose on an unprecedented scale. The purpose of this book is to examine how and why this is so, and to trace its effects as they ripple through our world.

Consider first the realm of economics. Many say that we now live in an "information" economy or a "knowledge" economy. But what's more fundamentally true is that we now have an economy powered by human creativity. Creativity—"the ability to create meaningful new forms," as Webster's dictionary puts it—is now the *decisive* source of competitive advantage. In virtually every industry, from automobiles to fashion, food products, and information technology itself, the winners in the long run are those who can create and keep creating. This has always been true, from the days of the Agricultural Revolution to the Industrial Revolution. But in the past few decades we've come to recognize it clearly and act upon it systematically.

15   Creativity is multidimensional and comes in many mutually reinforcing forms. It is a mistake to think, as many do, that creativity can be reduced to the creation of new blockbuster inventions, new products and new firms. In today's economy creativity is pervasive and ongoing: We constantly revise and enhance every product, process and activity imaginable, and fit them together in new ways. Moreover, technological and economic creativity are nurtured by and interact with artistic and cultural creativity. This kind of interplay is evident in the rise of whole new industries from computer graphics to digital music and animation. Creativity also requires a social and economic environment that can nurture its many forms. Max Weber said long ago that the Protestant ethic provided the underlying spirit of thrift, hard work and efficiency that motivated the rise of early capitalism. In similar fashion, the shared commitment to the creative spirit in its many, varied manifestations underpins the new creative ethos that powers our age.

Thus creativity has come to be the most highly prized commodity in our economy—and yet it is not a "commodity." Creativity comes from people. And while people can be hired and fired, their creative capacity cannot be bought and sold, or turned on and off at will. This is why, for instance, we see the emergence of a new order in the workplace. Hiring for diversity, once a matter of legal compliance, has become a matter of economic survival because creativity comes in all colors, genders and personal preferences. Schedules, rules and dress codes have become more flexible to cater to how the creative process works. Creativity must be motivated and nurtured in a multitude of ways, by employers, by people themselves and by the communities where they locate. Small wonder that we find the creative ethos bleeding out from the sphere of work to infuse every corner of our lives.

At the same time, entirely new forms of economic infrastructure, such as systematic spending on research and development, the high-tech startup company and an extensive system of venture finance, have evolved to support creativity and mobilize creative people around promising ideas and products. Capitalism has also expanded its reach to capture the talents of heretofore excluded groups of eccentrics and nonconformists. In doing so, it has pulled off yet another astonishing mutation: taking people who would once have been viewed as bizarre mavericks operating at the bohemian fringe and setting them at the very heart of the process of innovation and economic growth. These changes in the economy and in the workplace have in turn helped to propagate and legitimize similar changes in society at large. The creative individual is no longer viewed as an iconoclast. He—or she—is the new mainstream.

In tracing economic shifts, I often say that our economy is moving from an older corporate-centered system defined by large companies to a more people-driven one. This view should not be confused with the unfounded and silly notion that big companies are dying off. Nor do I buy the fantasy of an economy organized around small enterprises and independent "free agents."[3] Companies, including very big ones, obviously still exist, are still influential and probably always will be. I simply mean to stress that as the fundamental source of creativity, people are the critical resource of the new age. This has far-reaching effects—for instance, on our economic and social geography and the nature of our communities.

It's often been said that in this age of high technology, "geography is dead" and place doesn't matter any more.[4] Nothing could be further from the truth: Witness how high-tech firms themselves concentrate in specific places like the San Francisco Bay Area or Austin or Seattle. Place has become the central organizing unit of our time, taking on many of the functions that used to be played by firms and other organizations. Corporations have historically played a key economic role in matching people to jobs, particularly given the long-term employment system of the post–World War II era. But today corporations are far less committed to their employees and people change jobs frequently, making the employment contract more contingent. In this environment, it is geographic place rather than the corporation that provides the organizational matrix for matching people and jobs. Access to talented and creative people is to modern business what access to coal and iron ore was to steelmaking. It determines where companies will choose to locate and grow, and this in turn changes the ways cities must compete. As Hewlett-Packard CEO Carly Fiorina once told this nation's governors: "Keep your tax incentives and highway interchanges; we will go where the highly skilled people are."[5]

Creative people, in turn, don't just cluster where the jobs are. 20 They cluster in places that are centers of creativity and also where they like to live. From classical Athens and Rome, to the Florence of the Medici and Elizabethan London, to Greenwich Village and the San Francisco Bay Area, creativity has always gravitated to specific locations. As the great urbanist Jane Jacobs pointed out long ago, successful places are multidimensional and diverse—they don't just cater to a single industry or a single demographic group; they are full of stimulation and creativity interplay.[6] In my consulting work, I often tell business and political leaders that places need a people climate—or a creativity climate—as well as a business climate. Cities like Seattle, Austin, Toronto and Dublin recognize the multidimensional nature of this transformation and are striving to become broadly creative communities, not just centers of technological innovation and high-tech industry. If places like Buffalo, Grand Rapids, Memphis and Louisville do not follow suit, they will be hard-pressed to survive.

Our fundamental social forms are shifting as well, driven by forces traceable to the creative ethos. In virtually every aspect of life, weak ties have replaced the stronger bonds that once gave structure to society. Rather than live in one town for decades, we now move about. Instead of communities defined by close associations and deep commitments to family, friends and organizations, we seek places where we can make friends and acquaintances easily and live quasi-anonymous lives. The decline in the strength of our ties to people and institutions is a product of the increasing number of ties we have. As a retired industrialist who was the head of a technology transfer center in Ottawa, Canada, told me: "My father grew up in a small town and worked for the same company. He knew the same fourteen people in his entire life. I meet more people than that in any given day."[7] Modern life is increasingly defined by contingent commitments. We progress from job to job with amazingly little concern or effort. Where people once found themselves bound together by social institutions and formed their identities in groups, a fundamental characteristic of life today is that we strive to create our own identities.[8] It is this creation and re-creation of the self, often in ways that reflect our creativity, that is a key feature of the creative ethos.

In this new world, it is no longer the organizations we work for, churches, neighborhoods or even family ties that define us. Instead, we do this ourselves, defining our identities along the varied dimensions of our creativity. Other aspects of our lives—what we consume, new forms of leisure and recreation, efforts at community-building—then organize themselves around this process of identity creation.

Notes

1. For a careful empirical comparison of technological change at the turn of the twentieth century versus modern times, see Robert Gordon, "Does the New Economy Measure Up to the Great Inventions of the Past?" Cambridge, Mass.: National Bureau of Economic Research, Working Paper No. 7833, August 2000. His answer is a resounding no. The great majority of the technological inventions in the National Academy of Engineering's "Greatest Engineering Accomplishments of the 20th Century" occurred prior to 1950. Only two of the top ten occurred after World War II (semiconductor electronics, no. 5, and computers, no. 8), while the Internet, the subject of so

much New Economy hype, ranks thirteenth. See www.greatachievements .org.

2. Among the most popular, indeed classic works in this vein, see Sinclair Lewis, *Main Street*. New York: Harcourt, Brace and Company, 1920; and *Babbitt*. New York: Harcourt, Brace and World, 1922; William H. Whyte, Jr., *The Organization Man*. New York: Simon and Schuster, 1956; David Riesman, *The Lonely Crowd: A Study of the Changing American Character*. New Haven: Yale University Press, 1950; C. Wright Mills, *White Collar: The American Middle Classes*. New York: Oxford University Press, 1951; John Kenneth Galbraith, *The New Industrial State*. New York: Houghton-Mifflin, 1967. Also see Anthony Sampson, *Company Man: The Rise and Fall of Corporate Life*. New York: Times Books, 1995.

3. There are many statements of the free agent view, but the most notable is Daniel Pink, *Free Agent Nation: How America's New Independent Workers Are Transforming the Way We Live*. New York: Warner Books, 2001.

4. Again there are many statements of this view, but for a contemporary one see Kevin Kelly, *New Rules for the New Economy: 10 Radical Strategies for a Connected World*. New York: Viking, 1998.

5. Fiorina preceded me in speaking to the Annual Meeting of the National Governors Association in Washington, D.C., in winter 2000, where she made these remarks.

6. Jacobs's work is the classic statement of these themes. See Jane Jacobs, *The Death and Life of Great American Cities*. New York: Random House, 1961; *The Economy of Cities*. New York: Random House, 1969; *Cities and the Wealth of Nations*. New York: Random House, 1984.

7. Personal interview by author, Ottawa, Canada, September 2001.

Responding to Reading

1. In answering the question he poses in paragraph 1, do you think Florida is correct to emphasize the importance of "society's changed norms and values, and the ways in which everyday people live and work" (5) rather than the technological changes that have occurred? Do you think he might be underestimating the importance of the impact of technology and overestimating the impact of "dizzying social and cultural changes" (7)?

2. According to Florida, the "driving force" behind the social and cultural transformation that occurred between 1950 and the present is "the rise of human creativity" (13). What does he mean?

3. How, according to Florida, have "our economic and social geography and the nature of our communities" (18) been transformed in recent years? What role have "creative" individuals played in this transformation?

Responding in Writing

Interview one or both of your parents (in person or by phone or email), and ask them to list five items they rely on now but had never heard of when they were children and five social or cultural changes they have observed over the past twenty years. Which do they see as more important, the technological changes or the social changes?

PUTTING UP THE GATES
Edward J. Blakely
1938–

Born in San Bernardino, California, Edward J. Blakely was a promising football and basketball player who left athletics to pursue a career in academia. He earned an associate's degree from San Bernardino Valley College (1958), a bachelor's degree from the University of California at Riverside (1960), master's degrees from the University of California at Berkeley (1964) and Pasadena College (1967), and a PhD in management and education from the University of California at Los Angeles (1971). He is now the dean of the School of Urban and Regional Planning at the University of Southern California. His books include Planning Local Economic Development *(1994) and* Separate Societies *(1993). For his work in the field of development and planning, Blakely has won several awards, including service awards from the Community Development Society of America and the NAACP.*

Mary Gail Snyder
1965–

Mary Gail Snyder earned a BA degree in political science from Mills College in Oakland, California (1987), and a PhD in housing and community development from the University of California at Berkeley (2002). She has authored and coauthored articles and book reviews as well as reports for municipalities. She teaches at the University of New Orleans.

Blakely and Snyder are coauthors of Fortress America: Gated Communities in the United States *(1997). The following essay, which is adapted from their book, was published in* Shelterforce, *an online journal published by the National Housing Institute. To read more about community development and gated communities, visit these Web sites:*

- National Housing Institute, *http://www.nhi.org/*
- Gated Communities Research Network, *http://www.gated-communities.de/*
- US Private Communities, *http://www.private-communities.org/*
- PrivateCommunities.com, *http://www.privatecommunities.com/*

Gated communities provoke impassioned reactions from supporters and critics alike. In our book, *Fortress America: Gated Communities in the United States,* to be published in October by the Brookings Institution Press, we question the ability of this increasingly pervasive design tool to meet its security goals and strengthen the sense of community in America.

Over eight million Americans have sought refuge from crime and other problems of urbanization by installing gates and fences to limit access to their communities—and their numbers are growing. Since the mid-1980s, gates have become ubiquitous in many areas of the country. New towns are routinely built with gated villages, and some entire incorporated cities feature guarded entrances. Along with the trend toward gating in new residential developments, existing neighborhoods are increasingly installing barricades and gates to seal themselves off.

Gated communities physically restrict access so that normally public spaces are privatized. They differ from apartment buildings with guards or doormen, which exclude public access to the private space of lobbies and hallways. Instead, gated communities exclude people from traditionally public areas like sidewalks and streets.

Gates—along with fences, private security forces, "residents only" restrictions on public parks, policies to control the homeless, land use policies, large-lot zoning, and other planning tools—are part of a trend throughout the country to restrict or limit access to residential, commercial, and public areas. These turf wars, representing a retreat from the public realm, are a troubling trend. Gated communities are a dramatic manifestation of the fortress mentality growing in America.

The context for the gated community trend is an America increas- 5
ingly separated by income, race, and economic opportunity, although people with a range of backgrounds live in gated communities. In *Fortress America: Gated Communities in the United States,* we classify gated communities into three major categories. First are the Lifestyle communities, where the gates provide security and separation for the leisure activities within. These include retirement communities and golf and country club leisure developments. Second are the Prestige communities, which lack the amenities of the Lifestyle communities, but where the gates still are valued as markers of distinction and status. The Lifestyle and Prestige communities are developer-built, and primarily suburban. They range from the enclaves of the rich and famous to the subdivisions of the working class.

The third category is the Security Zone, where trouble with crime or traffic and fear of outsiders are the most common motivations. In these cases residents, not developers, install gates and fences to their previously open neighborhoods. While the image of the neighborhood that retrofits itself with gates or barricades is of the embattled moderate-income city community, such closures occur in the inner city and in the suburbs, in neighborhoods of great wealth and in areas of great poverty. Gating is easily done in open private-street subdivisions. In neighborhoods with public streets, it is usually very controversial, as the streets must be taken over from the city before they can be gated off.

This third type of gated community also includes areas, such as Dayton's Five Oaks . . . , with street barricades that create mazes of blocked streets to reduce vehicular access and deter outsiders. Such street barricading occurs in very wealthy neighborhoods and very poor ones, in places where crime is very high and where it is low. This partial solution is used most often in cases of public streets where residents cannot privatize their streets, either because they cannot afford to or they are not legally allowed to. The street barricaded neighborhoods lack the private amenities and complete closure of the others, but are a form of gated community nonetheless. The reasons given for the gates are usually the same—to reduce traffic, deter crime, and make the neighborhood more livable.

Movements to gate public streets in Los Angeles, Houston, Miami, Chicago, and other large cities often lead to bitter battles within and between neighborhoods. Proponents support street closures as an effective crime deterrent that helps maintain neighborhoods, homeownership, and curb middle-class flight to the suburbs. Opponents point to division, the displacement of crime and traffic, and other negative impacts on neighboring areas. Some opponents charge that racism or classism is the real root of a barricade plan, as in the case of the upscale community of Miami Shores, which borders on a poor African-American section of Miami. And when a small, middle-class, ethnically diverse neighborhood in Maplewood, New Jersey, decided to install five barricades near its border with Newark, ostensibly to reduce the flow of traffic using the neighborhood as a short cut, charges by Newark's mayor and other opponents that the closures were elitist and destructive caused a national media stir.

Exclusion and Control

Social distance has long been a goal of American settlement patterns; the suburbs were built on separation and segregation. Today, with a new set of problems pressing on our metropolitan areas, Americans still turn to separation as a solution.

10   Suburbanization has not meant a lessening of segregation, but only a redistribution of the urban patterns of discrimination. Gated communities are a microcosm of the larger spatial pattern of segmentation and separation. In the suburbs, gates are the logical extension of the original suburban drive. In the city, gates and barricades are sometimes called "cul-de-sac-ization," a term that clearly reflects the design goal to create out of the existing urban grid a street pattern as close to the suburbs as possible.

Exclusion imposes social costs on those left outside. It reduces the number of public spaces that all can share, and thus the contacts that people from different socioeconomic groups might otherwise have with each other. The growing divisions between city and suburb and rich and poor are creating new patterns which reinforce the costs that isolation and exclusion impose on some at the same time that they benefit others. Even where the dividing lines are not clearly ones of wealth, this pattern of fragmentation affects us all.

Forts or Communities?

Some argue that gates and barricades are unfortunate but necessary. They feel that such measures are the only way for beleaguered neighborhoods to reclaim their streets and for better-off neighborhoods to protect themselves in the future. But are these expectations realistic? In the course of our field work, we interviewed local law enforcement and analyzed local studies of streets closures. We found no firm evidence of any general permanent reductions of crime in fully gated communities or in the barricaded streets of the Security Zone. In part, this is because most evidence is anecdotal, and it varies greatly. Some Security Zone communities report drops in crime after streets are closed. Some report only temporary drops, and some no change at all. And still other places have removed barricades as failures, such as in Sepulveda, California, where local gangs used the maze of blocked streets to evade police and control their turf.

In addition to this wide variation in the reported effects of street closures, there is the problem that many available reports simply give "before and after" crime rates. Because such information often does not include comparisons with the crime rate in the overall area, or with longer-term trends, it is hard to conclude what effect the barricades themselves really had.

Gates and fences are not impenetrable to serious criminals, and they do nothing to reduce crime arising from residents. They do not necessarily protect, and they often cause dissension and controversy.

Efforts of neighborhoods to take back their streets are inspira-   15
tional and sorely needed. That many are turning to barricades is understandable. But the issues that stimulate gates, walls, and private security stem in part from the inattention we have paid to building communities. Without community, we have no hope of solving our social problems, or ever really gaining control of our deteriorated neighborhoods. Physical design does have a place in building community and fighting crime; our choices in architecture, street layout, landscaping and design, and lighting all can help neighborhoods to protect themselves from threats. But these physical design choices are best used to facilitate and encourage social, community responses.

Ever since Jane Jacobs,[1] urban designers and planners have recognized that "eyes on the street" are basic defenses against crime. This is the social control of a tightly-knit community. Overall, such socially-based mechanisms are more effective than additional hardware like gates.

We must also remember that the reasons for gating are not always entirely, or even primarily, the laudable reasons of crime and traffic control. Hopes of rising property values, the lure of prestige, and even the desire to build barriers against a poorer neighborhood or one of different race are also common reasons behind gated communities.

What is the measure of nationhood when the divisions between neighborhoods require security patrols and fencing to keep out other citizens? When public services and even local government are privatized, when the community of responsibility stops at the gates, the function and the very idea of democracy is threatened. Gates and barricades that separate people from one another also reduce people's potential to understand one another and commit to any common or collective purpose. In short, gates reduce the opportunity for social contact, and without social contact, this nation becomes less likely to fulfill its social contract.

Responding to Reading

1. What three kinds of gated communities do Blakely and Snyder identify? What do the three have in common? How are they different? Do you see any one of the three as more desirable, or more justifiable, than the others? Explain.
2. How do Blakely and Snyder explain the recent trend in the US toward a "fortress mentality" (4)? Can you think of additional explanations?
3. Blakely and Snyder see the rise of gated communities as an alarming trend. What specific problems do they think such barricades create? Do you agree that gated communities pose more problems than solutions?

Responding in Writing

To what extent are your home, school, and workplace "gated communities"?

---

[1]Writer and activist Jane Jacobs (1916–) has been credited with changing the way many Americans view cities and their future. Her books, which examine the ways in which cities operate, include *Death and Life of Great American Cities* (1961), *The Economy of Cities* (1969), and *Cities and the Wealth of Nations* (1984). For decades, Jacobs has advocated a common-sense approach to urban development. [Eds.]

HOW NOT TO USE THE CELLULAR PHONE

Umberto Eco

1932–

Born in Alessandria, Italy, Umberto Eco is popularly known as the author of the international bestselling books The Name of the Rose *(1980) and* Foucault's Pendulum *(1988). Long before writing these novels, however, Eco had established himself as a scholar and literary critic. He earned a PhD from the University of Turin (1954) and, after several years working as an editor for cultural programs for RAI (Italian Radio-Television), he switched careers and began teaching and doing research. Eco worked at several universities in Italy and the US and became widely known for his academic study of language and signs. Over four decades, he has been a versatile writer, producing academic studies, popular essays, and whimsical children's books, in addition to three novels. The following essay appeared in the collection* How to Travel with a Salmon and Other Essays *(1994).*

It is easy to take cheap shots at the owners of cellular phones. But before doing so, you should determine to which of the five following categories they belong.

First come the handicapped. Even if their handicap is not visible, they are obliged to keep in constant contact with their doctor or the 24-hour medical service. All praise, then, to the technology that has placed this beneficent instrument at their service. Second come those who, for serious professional reasons, are required to be on call in case of emergency (fire chiefs, general practitioners, organ-transplant specialists always awaiting a fresh corpse, or President Bush,[1] because if he is ever unavailable, the world falls into the hands of Quayle). For them the portable phone is a harsh fact of life, endured, but hardly enjoyed. Third, adulterers. Finally, for the first time in their lives, they are able to receive messages from their secret lover without the risk that family members, secretaries, or malicious colleagues will intercept the call. It suffices that the number be known only to him and her (or to him and him, or to her and her; I can't think of any other possible combinations). All three categories listed above are entitled to our respect. Indeed, for the first two we are willing to be disturbed even while dining in a restaurant, or during a funeral; and adulterers are very discreet, as a rule.

Two other categories remain. These, in contrast, spell trouble (for us and for themselves as well). The first comprises those persons who are unable to go anywhere unless they have the possibility of

---

[1]George Herbert Walker Bush, father of President George W. Bush. Dan Quayle was his vice president. [Eds.]

chattering about frivolous matters with the friends and relations they
have just left. It is hard to make them understand why they shouldn't
do it. And finally, if they cannot resist the compulsion to interact, if
they cannot enjoy their moments of solitude and become interested in
what they themselves are doing at that moment, if they cannot avoid
displaying their vacuity and, indeed, make it their trademark, their
emblem, well, the problem must be left to the psychologist. They irk
us, but we must understand their terrible inner emptiness, be grateful
we are not as they are, and forgive them—without, however, gloating
over our own superior natures, and thus yielding to the sins of spiritual pride and lack of charity. Recognize them as your suffering
neighbor, and turn the other ear.

In the last category (which includes, on the bottom rung of the social ladder, the purchasers of fake portable phones) are those people
who wish to show in public that they are greatly in demand, especially for complex business discussions. Their conversations, which
we are obliged to overhear in airports, restaurants, or trains, always
involve monetary transactions, missing shipments of metal sections,
an unpaid bill for a crate of neckties, and other things that, the
speaker believes, are very Rockefellerian.

5   Now, helping to perpetuate the system of class distinctions is an
atrocious mechanism ensuring that, thanks to some atavistic proletarian defect, the nouveau riche, even when he earns enormous sums,
won't know how to use a fish knife or will hang a plush monkey in
the rear window of his Ferrari or put a San Gennaro on the dashboard
of his private jet, or (when speaking his native Italian) use English
words like "management." Therefore he will not be invited by the
Duchesse de Guermantes (and he will rack his brain trying to figure
out why not; after all, he has a yacht so long it could almost serve as a
bridge across the English Channel).

What these people don't realize is that Rockefeller doesn't need a
portable telephone; he has a spacious room full of secretaries so efficient that at the very worst, if his grandfather is dying, the chauffeur
comes and whispers something in his ear. The man with power is the
man who is not required to answer every call; on the contrary, he is
always—as the saying goes—in a meeting. Even at the lowest managerial level, the two symbols of success are a key to the executive wash-
room and a secretary who asks, "Would you care to leave a message?"

So anyone who flaunts a portable phone as a symbol of power is,
on the contrary, announcing to all and sundry his desperate, subaltern
position, in which he is obliged to snap to attention, even when making love, if the CEO happens to telephone; he has to pursue creditors
day and night to keep his head above water; and he is persecuted by
the bank, even at his daughter's First Holy Communion, because of
an overdraft. The fact that he uses, ostentatiously, his cellular phone is

proof that he doesn't know these things, and it is the confirmation of his social banishment, beyond appeal.

Responding to Reading

1. This essay, written in 1991, was originally published in Italy. Is the essay dated in any way? Do Eco's observations apply to cell phone use in the US today?

2. Is Eco entirely serious here, or is he having fun with readers? How can you tell?

3. What five categories of cell phone users does Eco discuss? Do his categories cover all the cell phone users you know? Can you think of any categories he does not include? In what category, if any, would you put yourself?

Responding in Writing

Write a love letter to your cell phone (or to another electronic device that you are attached to or dependent on).

BARBIE AT 35

Anna Quindlen

1953–

Anna Quindlen earned an AB degree from Barnard College (1974) and began her career in journalism with the New York Post *before she graduated. She moved to the* New York Times *in 1977, where her plainspoken style of writing made her columns—like the following selection—a popular feature for more than a decade. Her "Public and Private" column won a Pulitzer Prize in 1992, and a collection of those columns was published as* Thinking Out Loud *(1994). Quindlen is the author of two children's books, two collections of essays, and several bestselling novels, including* Object Lessons *(1991),* One True Thing *(1995),* Black and Blue *(1998), and* Blessings *(2002). She is now a contributing editor at* Newsweek *magazine, and her most recent column is available on the magazine's Web site, http://www.newsweek.com/.*

My theory is that to get rid of Barbie you'd have to drive a silver stake through her plastic heart. Or a silver lamé stake, the sort of thing that might accompany Barbie's Dream Tent.

This is not simply because the original Barbie, launched lo these 35 years ago, was more than a little vampiric in appearance, more Natasha of "Rocky and Bullwinkle" than the "ultimate girl next door" Mattel describes in her press kit.

It's not only that Barbie, like Dracula, can appear in guises that mask her essential nature: Surgeon, Astronaut, Unicef Ambassador. Or that she is untouched by time, still the same parody of the female form she's been since 1959. She's said by her manufacturers to be "eleven and one-half stylish inches" tall. If she were a real live woman she would not have enough body fat to menstruate regularly. Which may be why there's no PMS Barbie.

The silver stake is necessary because Barbie—the issue, not the doll—simply will not be put to rest.

5   "Mama, why can't I have Barbie?"

"Because I hate Barbie. She gives little girls the message that the only thing that's important is being tall and thin and having a big chest and lots of clothes. She's a terrible role model."

"Oh, Mama, don't be silly. She's just a toy."

It's an excellent comeback; if only it were accurate. But consider the recent study at the University of Arizona investigating the attitudes of white and black teen-age girls toward body image.

The attitudes of the white girls were a nightmare. Ninety percent expressed dissatisfaction with their own bodies and many said they saw dieting as a kind of all-purpose panacea. "I think the reason I would diet would be to gain self-confidence," said one. "I'd feel like it was a way of getting control," said another.

10   And they were curiously united in their description of the perfect girl. She's 5 feet 7 inches, weighs just over 100 pounds, has long legs and flowing hair. The researchers concluded, "The ideal girl was a living manifestation of the Barbie doll."

While the white girls described an impossible ideal, black teenagers talked about appearance in terms of style, attitude, pride and personality. White respondents talked "thin," black ones "shapely." Seventy percent of the black teen-agers said they were satisfied with their weight, and there was little emphasis on dieting. "We're all brought up and taught to be realistic about life," said one, "and we don't look at things the way you want them to be. You look at them the way they are."

There's a quiet irony in that. While black women correctly complain that they are not sufficiently represented in advertisements, commercials, movies, even dolls, perhaps the scarcity of those idealized and unrealistic models may help in some fashion to liberate black teen-agers from ridiculous standards of appearance. When the black teen-agers were asked about the ideal woman, many asked: Whose ideal? The perfect girl projected by the white world simply didn't apply to them or their community, which set beauty standards from within. "White girls," one black participant in the Arizona study wrote, "have to look like Barbie dolls."

There are lots of reasons teen-age girls have such a distorted fun-house mirror image of their own bodies, so distorted that one study found that 83 percent wanted to lose weight, although 62 percent were in the normal range. Fashion designers still showcase anorexia chic; last year the supermodel Kate Moss was reduced to insisting that, yes, she did eat.

But long before Kate and Ultra Slimfast came along, hanging over the lives of every little girl born in the second half of the twentieth century was the impossible curvy shadow (40-18-32 in life-size terms) of Barbie. That preposterous physique, we learn as kids, is what a woman looks like with her clothes off. "Two Barbie dolls are sold every second," says Barbie's résumé, which is more extensive than that of Hillary Rodham Clinton. "Barbie doll has had more than a bil-lion pairs of shoes . . . has had over 500 professional makeovers . . . has become the most popular toy ever created."

Has been single-handedly responsible for the popularity of the silicone implant?   15

Maybe, as my daughter suggests while she whines in her Barbie-free zone, that's too much weight to put on something that's just a toy. Maybe not. Happy birthday, Babs. Have a piece of cake. Have two.

Responding to Reading

1. In paragraph 3, Quindlen says, "Barbie, like Dracula, can appear in guises that mask her essential nature. . . ." What does she think Barbie's "essential nature" is?
2. In paragraphs 8–15, Quindlen (like Marge Piercy in the poem "Barbie Doll," p. 354) discusses the distorted images that teenage girls, particularly white girls, have of their bodies, and she places the blame at least partly on Barbie. Whom (or what) else does she blame? Whom do you blame?
3. Is Barbie, as Quindlen's daughter says, "just a toy" (7), or is she really something more? Do you think Quindlen is correct to be alarmed, or do you think she is taking Barbie's influence too seriously?

Responding in Writing

In the years since 1994, when this essay was written, what new developments in our popular culture have come to influence teenage girls' body images? Has the situation Quindlen describes improved at all?

THE BOREDOM EFFECT
Ellen Ruppel Shell
1952–

Ellen Ruppel Shell is a correspondent for the Atlantic Monthly *magazine and writes regularly for the* New York Times Magazine, *the* New York Times Book Review, Smithsonian, *and the* Washington Post. *She researches and writes about science and public policy, including public health, infectious diseases, and environmental issues. She has worked as a visiting scholar at the Harvard School of Public Health and has been a Knight Journalism Fellow at the Massachusetts Institute of Technology. Born in Auburn, New York, Shell earned a BA degree from the University of Rochester (1974). She is a co-director of the Science Journalism Program at Boston University, where she is an associate Professor of Journalism. Her most recent book,* The Hungry Gene: The Science of Fat and the Future of Thin *(2002), is a study of the worldwide obesity epidemic. The following essay first appeared in* Hope *magazine.*

As a child I loved a vacant lot we called "the woods." I went there alone, to read or to wander around. I went there with friends, to build tree forts. Sometimes, one of us would bring a magnifying glass to burn ants or to light little teepee fires. Sometimes, one of the boys would pee on the fire to put it out, and we'd laugh our heads off. Our parents knew none of this, of course, but that was the point. Back then, parents pretty much stayed out of children's business, which is to say they stayed out of our play.

Play went mostly unsupervised, and it was deliciously freeform. Our parents wouldn't have thought of making "play dates" for us, or cramming our schedules with lessons. After school and on weekends we hung out on the street until another kid showed up. If no one showed up, we bounced a ball off a stoop, or played solitary jacks, or lolled on the grass. If we had roller skates or a bike, we'd use them, If it rained, we roamed around the house, bored. But most of us avoided letting on that we were bored, for fear that our parents would find us something to do. I'm not talking about a trip to the amusement park or an afternoon of miniature golf. Something to do meant scrubbing the kitchen floor or mowing the lawn or washing the family car. So, unlike many kids today, we took charge of our boredom. According to child development experts, this was probably a good thing.

Last April, Ann O'Bar, president of the American Association on the Child's Right to Play told *The New York Times:* "There's nothing wrong with letting children be bored. Boredom leads to exploration, which leads to creativity." One day last spring I decided to put Ms. O'Bar's theory to the test. My younger daughter Joanna, who's eight, was very, very bored. Her best friend was out of town, none of her other friends was free, and, to heap insult on injury, it was sunny outside. So rather than entertain her, I insisted she find something to do out of doors. I watched from the window, feeling a little guilty as she stomped, sulking, to the play structure in our back yard. She sat on the swing, scowling down at her bare feet (out of defiance, she'd refused to put on shoes). After a few minutes, boredom got the best of her. She had to do something. She twisted and twisted in the swing, then let go, twirling like a dervish. She did this a few more times, throwing her head back to study the cloudless sky. Then she climbed out of the swing and up to the top of the monkey bars, and peered over at the neighbor's parking lot. (We live behind a condominium complex.) She watched a neighbor scrub down his Honda for a while, until she spotted a squirrel. She followed the squirrel up a tree with her eyes, then did a skin-the-cat maneuver down from the monkey bars, back to solid ground. She gathered a bunch of pine cones and sticks, and made a tiny fort for her stuffed armadillo, Jessica. She got the hose and flooded the fort with water. She learned that stuffed armadillos can't swim. She charged into the house for her doctor's bag, then hustled back outside just in time to bring Jessica back to life. I watched all this with one eye, my other trained on the Sunday paper. Gradually my guilt dissolved into pride. Clearly, Ms. O'Bar is onto something.

It seems to me that we've lost trust in our kids. We don't believe that they can navigate the world, so we try to navigate it for them. We muck around in the details of their lives. We load them up with lessons and organized sports overseen by adults. We monitor their every move, demanding to know how and where and with whom they spend their time. And we schedule them so tightly that they lose their natural-born knack for spontaneous play. Put these over-scheduled kids in a room with crayons and markers and scissors and paper and, rather than dig in, they'll ask you what the assignment is. Stick them on a field with a ball, and they'll ask you about the rules. Put them in a room filled with blocks and dolls and trucks and they'll demand a television set or a video game, anything that will organize and structure their time for them.

I'm not sure why this happened, or when, but I am almost certain 5 it has something to do with marketing. Making sure children are endlessly stimulated costs money—money that we are told we must spend if our kids are to be successful, productive adults. We are told that computer games will sharpen their minds, karate lessons will make them assertive, and that gymnastics classes will teach them "invaluable social skills." Many of us are ripe for this kind of argument. We are incredibly busy, juggling careers and community service and parenting like so many hot potatoes. We fear that if we miss a beat, look away for a second, the whole mess will come crashing down. We worry about our children wasting time, missing an opportunity that could, some day, help them get ahead, or even just get by. Most of us know intuitively that children need the opportunity to experiment, to fail. But we are afraid to allow them to do so for fear of their falling behind. In these achievement-oriented times, we parents want our kids to work as hard as we do.

Earlier this year, the Atlanta public schools eliminated recess in elementary schools. Other districts have turned to "socialized recess," where children are supervised in structured activities. Games that teach reading and math, frequently with the help of a computer, are encouraged, as is physical education instruction to "enhance motor skills." Many parents support this trend. We like the idea of our children spending all of the school day in structured learning situations. And we don't mind that new schools are being built without playgrounds. As one school administrator put it, you don't improve academic performance "by having kids hanging on the monkey bars."

I beg to differ. Half a century ago, Swiss child psychologist Jean Piaget identified play as critical to the emotional, moral, and intellectual development of children. According to Piaget, kids learn a whole lot while hanging upside down from their knees. They learn that gravity makes their blood rush to their heads. They learn that all that rushing of blood can make them dizzy. And they learn that if they hang too long another kid will push them off. Play and the restless questing energy that provokes it, is, in a sense, childhood's greatest gift. As Susan Isaacs, a pioneering researcher in child development wrote in 1929: "How large a value children's play has for all sides of their growth. And how fatal to go against this great stream of healthy and active impulse in our children! That 'restlessness' and inability to sit still; that 'mischievousness' and 'looking inside' and eternal 'Why?' That indifference to soiled hands and torn clothes for the sake of running and climbing and digging and exploring—these are not unfortunate and accidental ways of childhood which are to be shed as soon as we can get rid of them. They are the glory of the human child, his human heritage. They are at once the representatives in him of human adventurousness and hard-won wisdom, and the means by which he in his turn will lay hold of knowledge and skill, and add to them."

The best play is spontaneous and unpredictable. Adults cannot control it, they can only sit back and let it happen. While we may spend hours building an architecturally correct structure, as pictured on the box of an expensive construction set, our children would rather brainstorm and build their own shaky pile of blocks. It is the *process* of creation, not the product, that naturally interests children, and it is this process that encourages their development as independent thinkers. But it's terribly easy to dampen a child's creativity, espe-

cially by insisting that there is a right and wrong way of doing everything, that life is a sort of multiple-choice quiz with adults holding the
answer key. By forcing children to follow rules imposed by others,
even during what is supposed to be their leisure time, adults can effectively discourage them from believing that they have anything significant to offer. They can turn them from confident and curious
explorers, to cautious over-achievers intent on getting it right. Kids
like this grow into adults who are edgy and averse to risk, adults who
have difficulty thinking for themselves, difficulty creating. Adults like
this make awfully good corporate cogs, because they do what they
are told. But they don't make particularly good participants in a
democratic system because they fail to grasp that "getting it" in the
truest sense often has nothing to do with "getting it right."

And "getting it right" is often what "structured play" is all
about—organized sports being a prime example. Last fall, Joanna enrolled in a local soccer league. Not surprisingly, neither she nor many
of the other seven-year-olds on her team were terribly interested in
the rules of the game. What they wanted to do was kick the ball
around, schmooze with their friends, and pick three-leaf clovers on
the field. But the coaches and the parents would have none of this.
Girls whose attention wandered were called back to focus. Girls who
stooped to pick a clover were commanded to keep their eyes on the
ball. One father, a professor of mathematics who, from his appearance, has spent little time on playing fields himself, pulled his daughter onto his lap and barked in her ear "be A-G-G-R-E-S-S-I-V-E,
AGGRESSIVE!" Another dad threw up his hands in disgust when his
daughter kicked the ball into the opposing team's goal. Later I heard
her promise that she'd "do better" next time. If kept to a minimum,
this sort of adult meddling will probably do the girls little harm. But
we're fooling ourselves when we gush over all the good such sessions
can do for the pre-preteen set. Team spirit and competition are wonderful things, of course, but no thinking person would consider them
essential to the psychic or moral development of a second grader. By
projecting our own ambitions and needs onto our kids, by insisting,
for instance, that kicking a soccer ball into a goal is more important
than searching out clovers, we are making implicit judgments—judgments we may come to regret.

Which returns me to the concept of boredom. Maybe it's time we 10
reconsider the concept. Perhaps boredom is not, as we often regard
it, a symptom of neglect. Perhaps it's every child's natural-born
right. Rather than supervise and coach and guide our children toward some predetermined goal, perhaps we should encourage them
to follow their fancy to a goal we can't even imagine. Maybe it's time
we gave childhood back to children. Maybe it's time we let them
play.

Responding to Reading

1. How does Shell explain why children today are so much more closely supervised than she was as a child? How, specifically, do the lives of today's children differ from the life Shell led as a child?
2. What kinds of structured activities does Shell mention? What others can you think of? What does Shell see as the disadvantages of this kind of activity? What does she see as the advantages of boredom?
3. This essay, written in 1998, does not mention the barriers to boredom instituted in recent years—for example, TV/DVDs installed in back seats of minivans. Can you list other such innovations? Do you see these as positive or negative?

Responding in Writing

Do you think Shell's childhood world still exists anywhere today? Do you think overstructured, overscheduled children can still be "rescued" and taught to use their boredom creatively? If so, how? If not, why not?

SUPERSIZE ME[1]

Greg Critser

1954–

Journalist Greg Critser writes on nutrition, obesity, health, and medical issues, and his work appears regularly in USA Today, *where he is a member of the board of contributors. He is author of two books,* National Geographic California *(2000), and* Fat Land: How Americans Became the Fattest People in the World *(2003), from which the following selection is taken. Critser, a native of Steubenville, Ohio, lives in Pasadena, California.*

If the wobbly economy of the 1970s had left consumers fulminating over high food prices and the forces that caused them, the same economy had driven David Wallerstein, a peripatetic director of the McDonald's Corporation, to rage against a force even more primal: cultural mores against gluttony. He hated the fifth deadly sin because it kept people from buying more hamburgers.

Wallerstein had first waged war on the injunction against gluttony as a young executive in the theater business. At the staid Balaban Theaters chain in the early 1960s, Wallerstein had realized that the movie business was really a margin business; it wasn't the sale of low-markup movie tickets that generated profits but rather the sale of high-markup snacks like popcorn and Coke. To sell more of such items, he had, by the mid-1960s, tried about every trick in the conven-

---

[1]In 2004, McDonald's announced that it would phase out supersized portions by the end of the year, citing "menu simplification" as its reason. [Eds.]

tional retailer's book: two-for-one specials, combo deals, matinee specials, etc. But at the end of any given day, as he tallied up his receipts, Wallerstein inevitably came up with about the same amount of profit.

Thinking about it one night, he had a realization: People did not want to buy two boxes of popcorn *no matter what.* They didn't want to be seen eating two boxes of popcorn. It looked . . . piggish. So Wallerstein flipped the equation around: Perhaps he could get more people to spend just a little more on popcorn if he made the boxes bigger and increased the price only a little. The popcorn cost a pittance anyway, and he'd already paid for the salt and the seasoning and the counter help and the popping machine. So he put up signs advertising jumbo-size popcorn.

The results after the first week were astounding. Not only were individual sales of popcorn increasing; with them rose individual sales of that other high-profit item, Coca-Cola.

Later, at McDonald's in the mid-1970s, Wallerstein faced a similar 5 problem: With consumers watching their pennies, restaurant customers were coming to the Golden Arches less and less frequently. Worse, when they did, they were "cherry-picking," buying only, say, a small Coke and a burger, or, worse, just a burger, which yielded razor-thin profit margins. How could he get people back to buying more fries? His popcorn experience certainly suggested one solution—sell them a jumbo-size bag of the crispy treats.

Yet try as he may, Wallerstein could not convince Ray Kroc, McDonald's founder, to sign on to the idea. As recounted in interviews with his associates and in John F. Love's 1985 book, *McDonald's: Behind the Arches,* the exchange between the two men could be quite contentious on the issue. "If people want more fries," Kroc would say, "they can buy two bags."

"But Ray," Wallerstein would say, "they don't want to eat two bags—they don't want to look like a glutton."

To convince Kroc, Wallerstein decided to do his own survey of customer behavior, and began observing various Chicago-area McDonald's. Sitting in one store after another, sipping his drink and watching hundreds of Chicagoans chomp their way through their little bag of fries, Wallerstein could see: People *wanted* more fries.

"How do you know that?" Kroc asked the next morning when Wallerstein presented his findings.

"Because they're eating the entire bagful, Ray," Wallerstein said. 10 "They even scrape and pinch around at the bottom of the bag for more and eat the salt!"

Kroc gave in. Within months receipts were up, customer counts were up, and franchisees—the often truculent heart and soul of the McDonald's success—were happier than ever.

Many franchisees wanted to take the concept even further, offering large-size versions of other menu items. At this sudden burst of entrepreneurism, however, McDonald's mid-level managers hesitated. Many of them viewed large-sizing as a form of "discounting," with all the negative connotations such a word evoked. In a business where "wholesome" and "dependable" were the primary PR watchwords, large-sizing could become a major image problem. Who knew what the franchisees, with their primal desires and shortcutting ways, would do next? No, large-sizing was something to be controlled tightly from Chicago, if it were to be considered at all.

Yet as McDonald's headquarters would soon find out, large-sizing was a new kind of marketing magic—a magic that could not so easily be put back into those crinkly little-size bags.

Max Cooper, a Birmingham franchisee, was not unfamiliar with marketing and magic; for most of his adult life he had been paid to conjure sales from little more than hot air and smoke. Brash, blunt-spoken, and witty, Cooper had acquired his talents while working as an old-fashioned public relations agent—the kind, as he liked to say, who "got you into the newspaper columns instead of trying to keep you out." In the 1950s with his partner, Al Golin, he had formed what later became Golin Harris, one of the world's more influential public relations firms. In the mid-1960s, first as a consultant and later as an executive, he had helped create many of McDonald's most successful early campaigns. He had been the prime mover in the launch of Ronald McDonald.

15   By the 1970s Cooper, tired of "selling for someone else," bought a couple of McDonald's franchises in Birmingham, moved his split-off ad agency there, and set up shop as an independent businessman. As he began expanding, he noticed what many other McDonald's operators were noticing: declining customer counts. Sitting around a table and kibitzing with a few like-minded associates one day in 1975, "we started talking about how we could build sales—how we could do it and be profitable," Cooper recalled in a recent interview. "And we realized we could do one of three things. We could cut costs, but there's a limit to that. We could cut prices, but that too has its limits. Then we could raise sales profitably—sales, after all, could be limitless when you think about it. We realized we could do that by taking the high-profit drink and fry and then packaging it with the low-profit burger. We realized that if you could get them to buy three items for what they perceived as less, you could substantially drive up the number of walk-ins. Sales would follow."

But trying to sell that to corporate headquarters was next to impossible. "We were maligned! Oh were we maligned," he recalls. "A 99-cent anything was heresy to them. They would come and say 'You're just cutting prices! What are we gonna look like to everybody else?'"

"No no no," Cooper would shoot back. "You have to think of the analogy to a fine French restaurant. You always pay less for a *table d'hôte* meal than you pay for *à la carte*, don't you?"

"Yes, but—"

"Well, this is a *table d'hôte,* dammit! You're getting more people to the table spending as much as they would before—and coming more often!"

Finally headquarters relented, although by now it hardly mattered. Cooper had by then begun his own rogue campaign. He was selling what the industry would later call "value meals"—the origin of what we now call supersizing. Using local radio, he advertised a "Big Mac and Company," a "Fish, Fry, Drink and Pie," a "4th of July Value Combo."

Sales, Cooper says, "went through the roof. Just like I told them they would."

* * *

Selling more for less, of course, was hardly a revolutionary notion, yet in one sense it was, at least to the purveyors of restaurant food in post-Butzian[2] America. Where their prewar counterparts sold individual meals, the profitability of which depended on such things as commodity prices and finicky leisure-time spending, the fast-food vendors of the early 1980s sold a product that obtained its profitability from a consumer who increasingly viewed their product as a necessity. Profitability came by maintaining the total average tab.

The problem with maintaining spending levels was inflation. By the early Reagan years, inflation—mainly through rising labor costs—had driven up the average fast-food tab, causing a decline in the average head count. To bring up the customer count by cutting prices was thus viewed as a grand and—despite the anecdotal successes of people like Wallerstein and Cooper—largely risky strategy. But one thing was different: Thanks to Butz, the baseline costs of meat, bread, sugar, and cheese were rising much more slowly. There was some "give" in the equation if you could somehow combine that slight advantage with increased customer traffic. But how to get them in the door?

In 1983 the Pepsi Corporation was looking for such a solution when it hired John Martin to run its ailing Taco Bell fast-food operation. A Harley-riding, Hawaiian shirt–wearing former Burger King executive, Martin arrived with few attachments to fast-food tradition. "Labor, schmabor!" he liked to say whenever someone sat across from him explaining why, for the millionth time, you couldn't get average restaurant payroll costs down.

But Martin quickly found out that, as Max Cooper had divined a decade before, traditional cost-cutting had its limits. If you focused on it too much, you were essentially playing a zero-sum game, cutting up the same pie over and over again. You weren't creating anything new. And all the while there were those customers—just waiting to chomp away if you could give them just a nudge to do so.

[2]Earl L. Butz (1909–) served as US Secretary of Agriculture from 1971 to 1976. He was sentenced to five years in prison for tax evasion in 1981. [Eds.]

But did Americans really want to eat more tacos? "We had always viewed ourselves as a kind of 'one-off' brand," Martin recalled in a recent interview. Tacos—or, for that matter, pizza—would always be the second choice to buying a burger. "That caused us to view ourselves as in a small pond—that the competition was other Mexican outlets."

Then Martin met a young marketing genius named Elliot Bloom. A student of the so-called "smart research" trend in Europe, which emphasized the placing of relative "weights" on consumer responses so as to understand what really mattered to a customer, Bloom had completely different ideas about the market for Mexican food. Almost immediately he began running studies on Taco Bell customers. What he found startled: Fast-food consumers were much more sophisticated and open to innovation than previously thought. In fact, they were bored with burgers. Martin loved the idea of competing with McDonald's, and immediately launched a $200 million national ad campaign, the centerpiece of which was a commercial depicting a man threatening to jump off a ledge if he had to eat another hamburger. The results of the campaign were mixed. Sales of some new products, most notably the taco salad, blossomed, but overall customer counts remained vexingly low.

Meantime, Bloom was still playing with consumer surveys, which now revealed something even more surprising: While almost 90 percent of fast-food buyers had already tried Taco Bell, the repeat visit rate of the average consumer was flat. "Reach" wasn't the problem. Frequency was. And when you started studying the customers who *were* coming back—the "heavy users"—price and value—not taste and presentation—were the key. "That was shocking," Martin recalls. "Value was the number-one issue for these guys—and there were a lot of them—30 percent of our customers accounted for 70 percent of sales. For a lot of us, that was disturbing. Our whole culture was sort of 'out of the kitchen,' you know, the notion that taste, cleanliness, and presentation was the key. But that's not what this new kind of customer was about. His message was loud and clear: more for less. So the business question became—how do you create *more* of these guys?"

One way, of course, was to give them what they wanted. But that was discounting, Martin's financial people warned. "I argued with them. I said, 'Look, this isn't stupid discounting, this is a way to right-price the business after a decade of inflation.'"

30   Bloom suggested an unscientific test of the idea. Let's not make a lot of national noise about this, he said. Let's go someplace where we might get some clean data. There was, in fact, an ideal place to do so. It was Texas, which in the mid-1980s was suffering from one of the worst recessions the oil patch had seen for decades. "We went in and really cut prices and got a dramatic increase in business," Martin

says. "We did not make money but it showed us the potential for upping the number of visits per store."

After Martin widened the test, Bloom reported something even better. "Everyone had thought that if we cut 25 percent off the average price of, say, a taco, that the average check size would drop," Martin says. "I never believed that—that satiety was satiety—and, in fact, I was right. Within seven days of initiating the test, the average check was right back to where it was before—it was just four instead of three items." In other words, the mere presence of more for less induced people to eat more.

To get the profit margins back up, Martin turned to what he knew best: cost-cutting. He fired whole swaths of middle managers, then looked at the stores themselves. In them he found what he called a "just plain weird thing, when you thought about it: 30 percent of the typical Taco Bell store was dining area, 70 percent was kitchen. What was that about?" Martin reversed the ratio, ripping out old-fashioned kitchens and sending the bulk of the cooking to off-site preparation centers.

With his margins back up enough to quell upper management fears, Martin took the value meal concept nationwide in 1988. The response was rapid, dramatic, and, ultimately for Taco Bell, transformative. Between 1988 and 1996 sales grew from $1.6 billion to $3.4 billion.

And the value meal was spreading—to Burger King, to Wendy's, to Pizza Hut and Domino's and just about every player worth its salt except . . . David Wallerstein's McDonald's Corporation.

Not that McDonald's was hurting. Its aggressive advertising and 35 marketing had by the late 1980s turned it into a global force unparalleled in the history of the restaurant business. It could, in a sense, afford to call its own tune. (Or at least deal with PR disasters, as was the case in the late 1980s, when the firm was under attack by nutritionists and public health advocates for its use of saturated fats.) But by 1990, Martin's Taco Bell value meals were taking their toll on McDonald's sales. Worse, McDonald's lack of a value meal had become a hot topic on Wall Street, where its stock was slumping. Analysts were restless. On December 17, 1990, one of them, a sharp-eyed fast-food specialist at Shearson Lehman named Carolyn Levy, gave an uncharacteristically frank interview to a reporter at *Nation's Restaurant News*. "McDonald's must bite the bullet," she said. "Some people I know in Texas told me it's cheaper to take their kids for a burger and fries at Chili's than to take them to McDonald's." In McDonald's board meetings, Wallerstein and his supporters used the bad press to good effect. Two weeks later the front page of the same newspaper read: "MCDONALD'S KICKS OFF VALUE MENU BLITZ!"

Though it is difficult to gauge the exact impact of supersizing upon the appetite of the average consumer, there are clues about it in the now growing field of satiety—the science of understanding human satisfaction. A 2001 study by nutritional researchers at Penn State University, for example, sought to find out whether the presence of larger portions *in themselves* induced people to eat more. Men and women volunteers, all reporting the same level of hunger, were served lunch on four separate occasions. In each session, the size of the main entree was increased, from 500 to 625 to 750 and finally to 1000 grams. After four weeks, the pattern became clear: As portions increased, all participants ate increasingly larger amounts, despite their stable hunger levels. As the scholars wrote: "Subjects consumed approximately 30 percent more energy when served the largest as opposed to the smallest portion." They had documented exactly what John Martin had realized fifteen years earlier: that satiety is not satiety. Human hunger could be expanded by merely offering more and bigger options.

Certainly the best nutritional data suggest so as well. Between 1970 and 1994, the USDA reports, the amount of food available in the American food supply increased 15 percent—from 3300 to 3800 calories or by about 500 calories per person per day. During about the same period (1977–1995), average individual caloric intake increased by almost 200 calories, from 1876 calories a day to 2043 calories a day. One could argue which came first, the appetite or the bigger burger, but the calories—they were on the plate and in our mouths.

By the end of the century, supersizing—the ultimate expression of the value meal revolution—reigned. As of 1996 some 25 percent of the $97 billion spent on fast food came from items promoted on the basis of either larger size or extra portions. A serving of McDonald's french fries had ballooned from 200 calories (1960) to 320 calories (late 1970s) to 450 calories (mid-1990s) to 540 calories (late 1990s) to the present 610 calories. In fact, everything on the menu had exploded in size. What was once a 590-calorie McDonald's meal was now . . . 1550 calories. By 1999 heavy users—people who eat fast food more than twenty times a month and Martin's holy grail—accounted for $66 billion of the $110 billion spent on fast food. Twenty times a month is now McDonald's marketing goal for every fast-food eater. The average Joe or Jane thought nothing of buying Little Caesar's pizza "by the foot," of supersizing that lunchtime burger or supersupersizing an afternoon snack. Kids had come to see bigger everything—bigger sodas, bigger snacks, bigger candy, and even bigger doughnuts—as the norm; there was no such thing as a fixed, immutable size for anything, because anything could be made a lot bigger for just a tad more.

There was more to all of this than just eating more. Bigness: The concept seemed to fuel the marketing of just about everything, from cars (SUVs) to homes (mini-manses) to clothes (super-baggy) and then back again to food (as in the Del Taco Macho Meal, which weighed four pounds). The social scientists and the marketing gurus were going crazy trying to keep up with the trend. "Bigness is addictive because it is about power," commented Irma Zall, a teen marketing consultant, in a page-one story in *USA Today*. While few teenage boys can actually finish a 64-ounce Double Gulp, she added, "it's empowering to hold one in your hand."

The pioneers of supersize had achieved David Wallerstein's 40 dream. They had banished the shame of gluttony and opened the maw of the American eater wider than even they had ever imagined.

Responding to Reading

1. The subtitle of this essay (a chapter from a book called *Fat Land*) is "Who Got the Calories into Our Bellies." According to Critser, who got us to consume these calories? Why?
2. Assuming his readers will be familiar with the key terms he mentions, Critser does not define them. Define the terms *fast food, supersizing,* and *value meal,* and give several examples of each.
3. Critser does not consider the long-term effects of supersizing here. What might those effects be? How does satiety, "the science of understanding human satisfaction" (36), explain the probable long-term effects of supersizing?

Responding in Writing

Just as former smokers have successfully sued tobacco makers, several individuals have recently sued McDonald's for contributing to their obesity. Based on what you have read here about supersizing and satiety, do you think McDonald's owes these individuals compensation? Or do you believe that they themselves are responsible for their weight problems?

SWEET EROSIONS OF EMAIL
Geert Lovink
1959–

Media theorist, Internet critic, and activist Geert Lovink was born in Amsterdam in the Netherlands. He studied political science at the University of Amsterdam, where he earned an MA degree, and he received a PhD from the University of Melbourne in Australia (2003). Lovink worked as the editor of the media art magazine Mediamatic *(1989–1994), taught media theory at schools throughout Europe, and is currently a postdoctoral fellow at the University of Queensland in Brisbane, Australia. The following selection is taken from his collection of essays on Internet culture,* Dark Fiber

> *(2002). Lovink has also published* Uncanny Networks *(2002), a collection of interviews with artists, critics, and theorists who are intimately involved in building the content, interfaces, and architectures of new media. To read more works by Lovink, visit his online text archive, http://laudanum.net/geert/.*

> NORTH FALMOUTH, Mass.—(BUSINESS WIRE)—June 8, 2000—(NAS-DAQ: BTHS) Benthos, Inc. In an historic breakthrough in underwater communications made possible by the use of a Benthos ATM 885 Telesonar Acoustic Modem, the US Navy has completed its latest series of tests in which the submarine USS Dolphin, while cruising at a depth of 400 feet, was able to successfully send several email messages via the Internet to facilities located ashore.

It is a popular saying that email is the ultimate killer application of the Internet.[1] No matter how opinions may divide over the possible economic, social, or cultural impact of new technologies, there seems to be a next to global consensus about the blessings of electronic mail. Unlike the bandwidth consuming multi-media content on the web, email, as a medium, has well positioned itself beyond any criticism. It is being said that streaming media are for the happy few, with their T1, DSL, or cable modems, whereas email is regarded as the big equalizer. With broadband technology widening the "digital divide," low-tech email has the historical task to empower those with less access to technology. Lately I have started feeling increasing uncomfortable about this almighty, unquestioned assumption which is not addressing what is actually happening.

> In Greek mythology, Sisyphus, an evil king, was condemned to Hades to forever roll a big rock to the top of a mountain, and then the rock always rolled back down again. Similar version of Hell is suffered every day by people with forever full e-email boxes.
>
> —Nikolai Bezroukov[2]

Ever since its invention, there has been a well known list of complaints about email. Spam is certainly one of them. The use of email by telemarketers is still on the increase, despite the filter software which is constantly being upgraded and developed further. Like other biological and electronic viruses, spam is gaining intelligence and keeps breaking through the immune systems. Porn, ads for financial services and business proposal from Africa are well known genres. But that's still old school. What is new are good willed individuals and organizations, who, without any sense of right or wrong, subscribe to thousands of email addresses out of some database, without having consulted their niche market beforehand. These are the merits of direct marketing. In most cases it is not even possible to unsubscribe, and if one starts complaining, the conversation easily turns into a flame war. You are supposed to be happy to be informed. Friends and colleges are not sending anonymous spam, they are actually doing a great service for you. So why make trouble? You have been chosen as an ideal target audience for this or that service or opinion. There is little to do against the growing tide of electronic goodwill. The right not to be informed is a yet unknown phenomena, but one with a strong growth potential.

> NEW YORK—(BUSINESS WIRE)—June 8, 2000—Despite nationwide firings that resulted from improper email use at the workplace, fifty eight percent of the 1,004 employees recently surveyed by Vault.com are "not worried" about their employers monitoring their email accounts.

Unwanted mail is part of the growing anxiety over information overload, an ancient disease associated with email ever since its introduction in the 1970s. The amount of email per day, in some circles still proudly mentioned as a status symbol, was once associated with the ability to master the new medium, but has turned into a nuisance for most IT workers. Folders are being created in order not be confronted with the bulk of email. Online web archives are on the increase, used by those with enough connectivity. We can expect a growth in the use of customized personal filters.

With the democratization of the Internet and its default dissemination into all social spheres, the diversity of usage of email is growing too. It is tempting at this point to start complaining about a loss of values. The invasion of the common folks is lowering the quality of the conversations, so they say. I don't take that line. What is interesting to observe is how new users are responding to email communication in a diverse way. All I can do here is present some of my subjective observations:

- The more users online, the more unpredictable it is how fast people are responding to incoming email. Three weeks is not unusual. Most of the email is not dealt with within the same working day. If you work on a global level, time differences have to be taken into account as well. All in all, a response in the next day seems very unlikely. So, instead of the popular mythology that we are communicating at the speed of light on a 24-7 basis, the average speed of computer mediated communication is slowing down, getting remarkably close to the times when overland postal systems were fast and reliable (assuming that this is not a myth either). If you really want to reach someone it is better to grab the phone. This is a clear sign of the dirty reality invading the terrain of the virtual, messing up the perfection of technology. Instead of having to be afraid of the loss of identity, locality and global standards, we can look forward to a much more carnivalesque Internet full of unpredictable ruptures and reversals of meaning.

- More and more emails remain unanswered. This is a fascinating phenomenon. Apparently email has lost its aura, if it had any in the first place. It is tempting but dangerous to interpret the fact that someone is not responding as a bad sign. People are busy, or lazy, and the Internet is just a tiny aspect of their lives (which cannot be said of the IT professionals and those reporting about tendencies in the net). The immaterial, fluid character of the e-messages only adds to the growing indifference towards the virtual in times of its almighty economic and imaginative presence. It has never been easier to ignore, and delete, incoming messages.

- As a response to the erosion of speed and efficiency of email people will do anything to grab attention on the other side of the screen. One can use CAPITALS, write "Important" or "Urgent" in the subject line and attach a red flag onto the mail, indicating its "high priority" status. Alternatively you can also send someone a fax saying that you have just sent them an email, or you can leave a text message on someone's mobile phone. Results of these desperate attempts vary, though the tendency is clear: for the overworked, email has turned into a stress channel instead of a relief.

- Regional and local cultural aspects obviously have to be taken into account. National and private holidays are interrupting exchanges constantly. So does language. Limited knowledge and an uncertainty about the ability to write in English is one of the main reasons why international communication is hampered. In some cultures it seems to be less embarrassing not to answer than to end up with a badly written letter, which will most likely fuel global misunderstanding. The reason could be shyness or politeness, or is the act of non-communication an even more sophisticated one? Some cultures protect themselves from (post-colonial) co-option by active forms of disconnection. This act should not be read as technophobia or as a symptom of unfamiliarity with new media. Internet use will never be universal. Policies concerned with bridging the "digital divide" should aim at empowering regional and local use and development of technologies rather than importing global recipes.

- Breakdown of connectivity on a technical level is another fact most email users still have to get used to. Servers are going down all the time, everywhere, not just in the so-called developing world. Systems are attacked by viruses and hackers. Mailboxes easily get deleted, or simply disappear, especially of those using free web mail services such as hotmail.

With the next hundred million email users entering the Internet over the next year, one should not get angry or be disappointed about the expected disfunctionalities. The net is as good as its users which, in many places, in demographic terms is getting nearer to the average citizen. The rapid spreading of the technology is something people have dreamed of, and anticipated throughout the last decades. In no way will the Internet alter, lift, or cool down human nature so there is a lot we can still expect to happen, beyond good or evil, from jubilees, charities, parties and other types of celebrations to rape, murders, genocide, and other known or not yet known e-crimes.

The quality of the email communication ranges from deep friend- 5 ships, fierce debates, significant periods of silence, sudden flame wars and touching miscommunications, resulting in all too human activities such as love affairs, marriage, e-business, and everything between rumors, gossip, casual talk, propaganda, discourse, and noise. At best, the net will be a mirror of the societies, countries, and cultures which use it—not the sweet and innocent, sleepy global village but a vibrant crawling and crashing bunch of complexities, as chaotic and unfinished as the world we live in.

Notes

1. Originally written for *Billedkunst* magazine (Oslo) during Communication Front, Plovdiv, Bulgaria, June 2000 (www.cfront.org). Posted on nettime June 13, 2000.
2. See the Information/Workload Annotated Webliography, maintained by Nikolai Bezroukov (http://www.softpanorama.org/Social/overload .shtml).

Responding to Reading

1. Why does Lovink question the idea that email is "the big equalizer," with the ability to "empower those with less access to technology" (1)?
2. What specific effects does Lovink attribute to the expansion of the Internet in general and email in particular? Does your own experience confirm his observations?
3. Does Lovink see the "information overload" he describes as just a nuisance or as a serious problem? On balance, is he optimistic or pessimistic about the future of email communication?

Responding in Writing

Imagine you are in the direct mail business and have a product to sell. Write a brief advertising message to be sent to hundreds of thousands of email subscribers. Consider carefully what subject line will get people to open your message and what kind of wording and format will keep them from deleting the message once they have opened it. Remember, the goal of your message is to entice people to buy your product.

LEAD US INTO TEMPTATION
James B. Twitchell
1943–

Cultural critic James B. Twitchell has written on a wide range of topics, from vampires in literature to the effect of advertising on American culture. Born in Burlington, Vermont, Twitchell earned a BA degree at the University of Vermont (1962) and then received an MA degree (1966) and a PhD (1969) from the University of North Carolina at Chapel Hill. He is a professor of English at the University of Florida, where he has taught since 1972. His books include The Living Dead: The Vampire in Romantic Literature *(1980),* Dreadful Pleasures: An Anatomy of Modern Horror *(1985),* Carnival Culture: The Trashing of Taste in America *(1992),* Adcult USA: The Triumph of Advertising in America *(1995), and* Lead Us Into Temptation: The Triumph of American Materialism *(1999), from which the following selection was taken. His most recent work is* Living It Up: Why We Love Luxury *(2002).*

To speak of American "materialism" is . . . both an understatement and a misstatement. The material goods that historically have been the symbols which elsewhere separated men from one another have become, under American conditions, symbols which hold men together. From the moment of our rising in the morning, the breakfast food we eat, the coffee we drink, the automobile we drive to work— all these and nearly all the things we consume become thin, but not negligible, bonds with thousands of other Americans.

—Daniel J. Boorstin, *The Decline of Radicalism:*
Reflections on America Today

Of all "-isms" of the twentieth century none has been more misunderstood, more criticized, and more important than materialism. Who but fools, toadies, hacks, and occasional loopy Libertarians have ever risen to its defense? Yet the fact remains that while materialism may be the most shallow of the twentieth century's various -isms, it has been the one to ultimately triumph. The world of commodities seems so antithetical to the world of ideas that it seems almost heresy to point out the obvious: most of the world most of the time spends most of its energy producing and consuming more and more stuff.

The really interesting question may be not Why are we so materialistic? but Why are we so unwilling to acknowledge and explore what seems to be the central characteristic of modern life?

When the French wished to disparage the English in the nineteenth century, they called them a nation of shopkeepers. When the rest of the world now wishes to disparage Americans, they call us a nation of consumers. And they are right. Almost all mature American cities have a Market Street and almost all of us have been there. No longer. We are developing and rapidly exporting a new material culture, a "mallcondo" culture.

The bus lines today terminate not at Market Street but at the Mall, the heart of our new modern urbia. All around mallcondoville is a vast continuum of interconnected structures and modes of organizing work, shopping, and living, all based on principles of enclosure, control, and consumption.

Most of us have not entered the mallcondo cocoon . . . yet. But we are on our way. We have the industrial "park," the "gated" community, the corporate "campus," the "domed" stadium, all of which play on the same conception of Xanadu's pleasure dome. Get inside. In the modern world the Kubla Khan down at the bank or over at the insurance company is not building a mallcondo dome around the natural world, but around a commercial one. Few are willing or able to live outside except, of course, the poor. "If you lived here, you'd be home by now" is no idle billboard; it is the goal of middle-class life.

To the rest of the world we do indeed seem not just born to shop, but alive to shop. We spend more time tooling around the mallcondo—three to four times as many hours as our European counterparts—and we have more stuff to show for it. According to some estimates we have about four times as many things as Middle Europeans, and who knows how much more than the less developed parts of the world (Schor, *The Overworked American* 107). The quantity and disparity is increasing daily, even though, as we see in Russia and China, the "emerging nations" are playing a frantic game of catch up.

The Impact of the Baby Boom

This burst of mallcondo commercialism has happened recently—in my lifetime—and it is moving outward around the world at the speed of television. The average American consumes twice as many goods and services as in 1950; in fact, the poorest fifth of the current population buys more than the average fifth did in 1955. Little wonder that the average new home of today is twice as large as the average house constructed after World War II (Bennett). We have to put that stuff somewhere—quick!—before it turns to junk.

Manufacturing both things and their meanings is what mallcondo culture is all about, especially for the baby boomers. If Greece gave the world philosophy, Britain gave drama, Austria gave music, Germany gave politics, and Italy gave art, then America has recently contributed mass-produced and mass-consumed objects. "We bring good things to life" is no offhand claim but the contribution of the last century. Think about it: did anyone before the 1950s—except the rich—ever shop just for fun? Now the whole world wants to do it.

Sooner or later we are going to have to acknowledge the uncomfortable fact that this amoral commercial culture has proved potent because human beings love things. In fact, to a considerable degree, we live for things. Humans like to exchange things. In all cultures we buy things, steal things, and hoard things. From time to time, some of us collect vast amounts of things such as tulip bulbs, paint drippings on canvases, bits of minerals. Others collect such stuff as thimbles, shoes, even libraries of videocassettes. Often these objects have no observable use.

10   We live through things. We create ourselves through things. And we change ourselves by changing our things. We often depend on such material for meaning. In the West, we have even developed the elaborate algebra of commercial law to decide how things are exchanged, divested, and recaptured. Remember, we call these things goods as in "goods and services." Academics aside, we do not call them bads. This sounds simplistic, but it is crucial to understanding the powerful allure of materialism, consumption, mallcondo culture, and all that it carries with it.

Things are in the saddle, no doubt about it. We put them there. If some of us want to think that things are riding us, that's fine. The rest of us know better.

The Complexity of Consuming Commercialism

That consumption gives meaning to life seems to be rearranging the terms, getting things backwards. But think about it: do we work in order to have the leisure to buy things, or is the leisure to buy things how we make work necessary? We forever talk about how work gives meaning—labore est orare—but it may be consumption that we are referring to. Give a banana to a monkey and he eats it right away. Give him a bundle and he gets confused. He has no idea what to do with surplus. Should he hoard, should he gorge himself, should he share? This used to be a problem only for the rich; now the rest of us can share the perplexity.

I never want to imply that, in creating order in our lives, consumption is doing something to us that we are not covertly responsible for. We are not victims of consumption. Just as we make our media, our media make us. Again, commercialism is not making us behave against our "better judgment." Commercialism is our better judgment. Not only are we willing to consume, and not only does consuming make us happy, "getting and spending"[1] is what gives our lives order and purpose. We have a deluding tendency to consider advertising, packaging, fashion, branding, and the rest of the movement of goods in the way we consider many other cultural sequences, like politics and religion, as somehow "out there" beyond our control. Not so.

Our desire to individualize experience causes us to forget that there is a continual interaction between forces—between people and their leaders, between males and females, between readers and writers, between young and old, even between producers and consumers—in which there is a struggle not for dominance, but for expansion. In the language of William Blake, the endeavor is not to separate the Prolific and the Devourers, not to blame one for the condition of the other, but to realize that in the shifting of forces is the excitement and the danger of change. In this sense, commercialism is just another site in which the sometimes opposing forces of a culture are brought to bear on each other. The resulting friction is often quite hot.

I make this point now because commercial speech—how we talk   15
about manufactured things—has become one of the primary hotspots of modern culture. It has been blamed for the rise of eating disorders, the spreading of affluenza, the epidemic of depression, the despoiling of cultural icons, the corruption of politics, the carnivalization of holy times like Christmas, and the gnat-life attention span of our youth. All of this is true. Commercialism contributes. But it is by no means the whole truth. Commercialism is more a mirror than a lamp. That we demonize it, that we see ourselves as helpless and innocent victims of its overpowering force, that it has become scapegoat du jour, tells far more about our eagerness to be passive in the face of complexity than about our understanding of how it does its work.

Anthropologists tell us that consumption habits are gender specific. Men seem to want stuff in early adolescence and post-midlife. That's when the male collecting impulse seems to be felt. Boys gather playing marbles first, Elgin marbles later. Women seem to gain potency as consumers after childbirth, almost as if getting and spending is a nesting impulse. There are no women stamp collectors of note. They do save letters, however, far more often then men do.

Historians, however, tell us to be careful about such stereotyping. While it is clear that women are the primary consumers of commercial objects today, this has only been the case since the Industrial

---

[1]Twitchell is quoting a poem by William Wordsworth (see p. 337). [Eds.]

Revolution. Certainly in the pre-industrial world, men were the chief hunter-gatherers. If we can trust works of art to accurately portray how booty was split (and art historians like John Berger and Simon Schama think we can), then males were the prime consumers of fine clothes, heavily decorated furniture, gold and silver articles and, of course, paintings in which they could be shown displaying their stuff.

Once a surplus was created, as happened in the nineteenth century, women joined the fray in earnest. They were not duped. The hegemonic, phallocentric patriarchy did not brainwash them into thinking goods mattered. The Industrial Revolution produced more and more things not because production is what machines do, and not because nasty producers twisted their handlebar mustaches and whispered, "We can talk women into buying anything," but because both sexes are powerfully attracted to the world of things. Stuff is not nonsense. The material world magnetizes us and we focus much energy on our relationship with it.

Marx himself knew this better than anyone else. In the Communist Manifesto he writes:

> The bourgeoisie, by the rapid improvement of all instruments of production, by the immensely facilitated means of communication, draws all, even the most barbarian nations into civilization. The cheap prices of its commodities are the heavy artillery with which it batters down all Chinese walls . . . It compels all nations, on pain of extinction, to adopt the bourgeois mode of production; it compels them to introduce what it calls civilization into their midst, i.e., to become bourgeois themselves. In one word, it creates a world after its own image. (9)

Marx uses this insight to motivate the heroic struggle against capitalism. But as we have seen, especially in the last few decades, it proved feckless. The struggle should not be to deter capitalism and its mad consumptive ways, but to appreciate how it works so its furious energy may be understood and exploited.

My Argument in a Nutshell

20 I am going to put forward a seemingly naive thesis to understand the triumph of our commodity culture: (1) Humans are consumers by nature. We are tool users because we like to use what tool using can produce. In other words, tools are not the ends but the means. Further, materialism does not crowd out spiritualism; spiritualism is more likely a substitute when objects are scarce. When we have few things, we make the next world holy. When we have plenty, we enchant the objects around us. The hereafter becomes the here and now. You deserve a break today, not in the next life. (2) Consumers are rational.

They are often fully aware that they are more interested in consuming aura than objects, sizzle than steak, meaning than material, packaging than product. In fact, if you ask them—as academic critics are usually loath to do—they are quite candid in explaining that the Nike swoosh, the Polo pony, the Guess? label, the DKNY logo are what they are after. They are not duped by advertising, packaging, branding, fashion, or merchandising. They actively seek and enjoy what surrounds the object, especially when they are young. (3) We need to question the criticism that consumption almost always leads to "buyer's remorse." Admittedly the circular route from desire to purchase to disappointment to renewed desire is never-ending, but it may be followed because the other route from melancholy to angst is worse. In other words, in a world emptied of external values, consuming what looks to be overpriced kitsch may be preferable to consuming nothing. And (4) we need to rethink the separation between production and consumption, for they are more alike than separate, and occur not at different times and places but simultaneously.

Ironically the middle-aged critic, driving about in his well-designed Volvo (unattractive and built to stay that way), is unable to provide much insight into his own consumption practices, although he can certainly criticize the bourgeois afflictions of others. Ask him to explain the difference between "Hilfiger" inscribed on the oversize shirts worn outside pants slopped down to the thighs, and his rear window university decal (My child goes to Yale, sorry about yours), and you will be met with a blank stare. If you were to then suggest that what that decal and automotive nameplate represent is as overpriced as Calvin Klein's initials on a plain white T-shirt, he would pout that you can't compare apples and whatevers. If you were to say next that aspiration and affiliation is at the heart of both displays, he would say that you just don't get it, just don't get it at all.

But don't talk to critics if you want to understand the potency of American consumer culture. Ask any group of teenagers what democracy means to them and you will hear an extraordinary response. Democracy is the right to buy anything you want. Freedom's just another word for lots of things to buy. Appalling perhaps, but there is something to their answer. Being able to buy what you want when and where you want it was, after all, the right that made 1989 a watershed year in Eastern Europe.

Recall as well that freedom to shop was another way to describe the right to be served in a restaurant that provided a focus for the early civil rights movement. Go back farther. It was the right to consume freely that sparked the fires of separation of this country from England. The freedom to buy what you want (even if you can't pay for it) is what most foreigners immediately spot as what they like about our culture, even though in the next breath they will understandably criticize it.

Paradoxically, buying stuff is not just our current popular culture, it is how we understand the world. High culture has pretty much disappeared, desperately needing such infusions of life-preserving monies from taxpayer-supported endowments and tax-free foundations to keep it from gasping away. One might well wonder if there is anything more to American life than shopping. After all, we are all consumers now, consumers of everything—consumers of health services, consumers of things and ideas, consumers of political representation, even consumers of what high culture there is left.

25   The new model citizen wearing his Calvins and eating his Paul Newman popcorn while applying his Michael Jordan cologne, described by both Left and Right, is the citizen consumer, the one who makes rational choices based on assimilating all the available information. Thinking ends in action and that action is buying. W. H. Auden may have lampooned this creature as the drone of the modern state (The Unknown Citizen), but it seems it is not the state that makes the drone, but the drone that makes the state.

The Case of Seven-Year-Old Mollie

We learn early that shopping around is the way to organize experience. Enid Nemy reports in my favorite part of the *New York Times*, "Metropolitan Diary," this passing tidbit: "Seven-year-old Mollie Kurshan of Ridgewood, N.J., recently attended The Nutcracker with her grandmother at the New York State Theater at Lincoln Center. There was a Sugar Plum Fairy and beautiful costumes, Mollie told her mother, and, best of all 'They stopped in the middle so you could go shopping.' The Kurshans now have a cute little wooden nutcracker, bought at the gift shop during intermission" (A27).

By the time she gets to school, Mollie may see her education as something to purchase. Many of my students think of themselves as buyers of a degree. They can even tell you how much a credit hour costs. In addition, when we talk about how much a credit hour is worth, we mean in dollars and cents. A diploma is valued for how much it improves your starting wage.

Just look at the admission process, complete with competition for financial assistance. Schools live and die by what *US News & World Report* or *Money* magazine says about them. You make a deal with one school. You show the deal to other schools. They make counteroffers. It's just like car shopping.

Why go to a prestigious school? Not for good teaching—you are almost assured of being treated poorly in the full professor/teaching assistant configuration. No, you go because the school name improves the relative worth of the line on the vita, the certificate. The assumption is that you pay your money, you get your degree.

Mollie will also learn that what she experienced in Lincoln Center 30 is the norm for what was once called High Culture. Art today is almost always commodified. Juliet B. Schor, a Harvard economist who wrote *The Overworked American* and then *The Overspent American*, quotes a museum curator sheepishly explaining why his museum had to be combined with a shopping mall: "The fact is that shopping is the chief cultural activity in the United States" (1991:108). He is right, as the endless catalogs from the Metropolitan or the Museum of Modern Art attest. Not only are all major museum shows sponsored by corporate interests, but they all end in the same spot: the gift shop.

Mollie may discover that shopping for stuff is so powerful that it sets not just mallcondo culture but our biological clocks. The weekend developed so that shopping day—Saturday—would be set aside and formalized for consuming. Blue laws were passed because clearly Saturday was not enough, and the desire was spilling over to the Sabbath. The year is punctuated by shopping extravaganzas from Christmas to Valentine's Day to Mother's Day to Halloween. By the age of ten, we all know what Mollie Kurshan is learning: what to buy and when. We even know when prices fall: Washington's birthday, Labor Day, after Christmas.

Mollie even knows that objects themselves have seasons. Take candy, for instance. She knows exactly what kind of candy to expect as these days pass by: candy canes, sugar hearts, chocolate, candy corn. As she grows up she will even know what to buy during the day. Take fluids; we have coffee breaks, teatime, cocktail hour, and nightcap. The night belongs to Michelob. One of the biggest marketing problems Coca-Cola had was being thought of only as a hot weather drink. It created the image of Santa Claus, the one recognized by Mollie—a construction of adman Haddon Sundbloom—in order to show Santa drinking a summertime beverage in the dead of winter.

Shopping is so powerful that it even generates our urban architecture. Since the 1950s, towns and cities have grown in grids around not office buildings or schools but malls. Look at Atlanta or Los Angeles. The city of the future is spoked outward from a shopping hub. What of transportation? Every fifth time Mollie's mom gets in the car it is to go buy something. Why do people go to New York City? The third most important reason is to go shopping. Shopping—as Mollie will learn—is not just how we organize our life at various times. It is our life, especially when we are young.

Is this hyperbole? Is it possible for any of us to take a trip and not buy a souvenir? Getting there may be half the fun, but when you return home the experience may be forgotten without the aide memoire. The anxiety of returning empty-handed means we may lose the event. Kodak used this as a way to sell cameras. Show pictures of faraway places and people will travel to faraway places and take pictures of exactly what the ad showed. They were not duped or tricked by this process. We were there, we saw the picture, we "took" a picture just like it. We brought it home. Of course perception is reality, as the ad says. Is there any other kind?

The Carnivalization of Shopping

35 "Fill 'er up," we say as we motor through life from one defining purchase to another. On our journeying juggernauts we tape tributes onto our bumpers so all can see that we have been there, done that. Sometimes what we memorialize is not the trip but the purchase, not the thing but the image of it. On the bumpers of self we slap stickers: "Shop 'til you drop," "He who dies with the most toys wins," "People who say money can't buy happiness, don't know where to shop," "When the going gets tough, the tough go shopping," "But I can't be overdrawn! I still have some checks left!," "I'm spending my grandchildren's inheritance," "Nouveau riche is better than no riche at all," "A woman's place is in the mall." For those who want a thought larger than what fits on a car bumper, here is a greeting card. It says, "Work to Live, Live to Love, Love to Shop, so you see . . . if I buy enough things I'll never have to work at love again." Wink wink, we say, but under the irony is truth.

Let me reiterate what is central to my thesis and so overlooked in much academic cultural criticism. We were not suddenly transformed from customers to consumers by wily manufacturers eager to unload a surplus of crapular products. We are many things, but what we are not are victims of capitalism. With few exceptions (food, shelter, sex), our needs are cultural, not natural. We have created a surfeit of things because we enjoy the process of getting and spending. The consumption ethic may have started in the early 1900s and hit full tilt after the midcentury, but the desire is ancient. Whereas kings and princes once thought they could solve problems by possessing and amassing things, we now say, "Count us in." Whereas the Duchess of Windsor once said, "All my friends know that I'd rather shop than eat," we now say, "Hey, wait for me."

Generations ago, consumption played out its Saturnalian excesses alongside the church, literally, at the carnival. Mardi Gras and Lent were connected. Consumption, then denial. It was the world turned upside down, then fight side up. We used to go into the dark cathedral looking for life's meaning and then do a little shopping on the side. Now we just go straight to the mall. If you travel about the globe, you will find that millions are quietly queuing up waiting their turn to start shopping. Woe to that government or church that tries to turn them back.

By standards of stuff, the last half century of our national life has been wildly successful. We have achieved unprecedented prosperity and personal freedom. We are healthier, we work at less exhausting jobs, and we live longer than ever. Most of this has been made possible by consuming things, ironically spending more and more time at the carnival, less and less in church.

The Mixed Blessing

"Wanting," "desiring," "needing" are the gerunds that lubricated this strain of capitalism and made our culture so compelling for have-nots around the world. In the last generation we have almost completely reversed the poles of shame so that where we were once ashamed of consuming too much (religious shame), we are now often ashamed of consuming the wrong brands (shoppers' shame).

Was it worth it? Are we happier for it? Was it fair? Did some of us 40 suffer inordinately for the excesses of others? What are we going to do when all this stuff we have shopped for becomes junk? How close is the connection between the accumulation of goods and the fact that America also leads the industrialized world in rates of murder, violent crime, juvenile violent crime, imprisonment, divorce, abortion, single-parent households, obesity, teen suicide, cocaine consumption, per capita consumption of all drugs, pornography production, and pornography consumption?

These are important questions and we need to continually talk about them. I'm not going to. However, there is a mixed aspect of the material world that I will have to confront. The cornucopia of stuff— which I will address under the rubrics of advertising, fashion, branding, and marketing—is to a considerable number of people an experience that is not just boring but banal, almost obscene. The fact is that the carnival is a world of brazen excess, full of sound and excitement but signifying little in the way of philosophical depth. Most critics of mallcondo culture usually feel this antipathy toward commercialism in midlife, after they have chased the meaning of objects and have settled into a routine of low and simplified consumption. In advertising lingo, they no longer change brands because they have made their affiliations. For them the carnival is over and the church is beckoning.

Where the Generation Gap Begins

Yeats forecast this split between wanting and no longer interested via a sexual metaphor. In "Sailing to Byzantium" he wrote of the world of youthful urges from which the speaker is now alien:

That is no country for old men. The young
In one another's arms, birds in trees—
Those dying generations—at their song,
The salmon-falls, the mackerel-crowded seas,
Fish, flesh, or fowl, commend all summer long
Whatever is begotten, born, and dies.
Caught in that sensual music all neglect
Monuments of unaging intellect. (1–8)

To translate this "sensual music" into a consumerist apology: once you have passed through "prime-branding time" you are almost impossible to sell to. The mall carnival is not for you. You become in our culture, "a paltry thing, / A tattered coat upon a stick" . . . forgotten. Very little entertainment, let alone information, flows your way because no one is willing to pay the freight to send it. You better find your own Byzantium in far off High Aesthetica because you are not going to find it here in Lower Vulgaria. No one really makes movies for you (blockbusters are for the kids), programs television for you (check who watches primetime), publishes books and magazines for you (look at the bestseller lists or the flood of magazines like *Details, Rolling Stone, Wired*) because, although you have the money, your kids spend it. No wonder you become a critic of a culture that has made you a pariah.

There was no generation gap two generations ago. Fashions, like moral and ethical values, flowed down from above, from old to young, rich to poor. But the money in materialism is to be made from tapping those with excess disposable time and money—the young. Ironically, the only way to return to a culture that served the mature would be if everyone over forty made it a habit to change brands of everything every week or so just like the kids.

45   This generation gap and the hostility it has engendered is part of the reason we have recently been so passionate about condemning commercialism, and yet so unwilling to examine its workings. These are our kids. We have raised them. They have (gasp!) our values. Clearly we are perplexed about how they act, and just as clearly we have selectively forgotten how important consumption was for us. Their excitement in consumption has been little studied, perhaps because while it is so unfocused, so common, so usual, it is also so youthful. . . .

Responding to Reading

1. What is the "'mallcondo culture'" (3)? How does Twitchell account for the "potency of American consumer culture" (22)? How does he use the story of Mollie in paragraphs 26–32 to bolster his argument about the power of shopping?

2. In paragraph 13, Twitchell says, "Not only are we willing to consume, and not only does consuming make us happy, 'getting and spending' is what gives our lives order and purpose." Do you accept this statement as fact, or do you find it shocking, or even frightening?

3. How might Twitchell respond to "The Fashion Victim's Ten Commandments" (below)? (Note that in paragraph 13, he says, "We are not victims of consumption" and in paragraph 36, he reiterates, "We are many things, but what we are not are victims of capitalism.")

Responding in Writing

In addition to the anthropological and historical context Twitchell brings to his discussion, he also makes a number of references to poetry. For example, he quotes Wordsworth in paragraph 13, paraphrases Blake in paragraph 14, refers to W. H. Auden in paragraph 25, and quotes Yeats in paragraph 42. Why does he make these literary references? What is your reaction to them?

THE FASHION VICTIM'S TEN COMMANDMENTS

Michelle Lee

Michelle Lee is a frequent contributor to leading fashion publications and has held editorial positions at several national magazines, including Glamour, Us Weekly, CosmoGirl, *and* Mademoiselle. *In 1997 she won a William Randolph Hearst Award for feature writing. She lives and shops in New York City. Read more about this author and take her fashion victim quiz online at http://www.michelleklee.com.*

We Fashion Victims hold certain truths to be self-evident. Without so much as a raised eyebrow, we allow a set of ridiculous, yet compelling, rules to govern our wardrobes, our purchases, our desires, even our own sense of self-worth. It's these unquestioned tenets that have helped bring us to the sorry state we find ourselves in today.

Thou Shalt Pay More to Appear Poor

It takes a great deal of time and money to look as though you put no effort into dressing. Since a garment today rarely remains a popular item in our wardrobes beyond a few months, we require it to be worn out before we buy it. Fabrics are prewashed and grayed out to appear less new. Designers sew on decorative patches, slash gaping holes into the knees of jeans, and fray the hems. Dresses and shirts are prewrinkled. Jeans are stonewashed, sandblasted, acid-washed, and lightened; they're iron-creased and bleached to "whisker" at the upper-thigh as if they were passed down to you by your mother, who inherited them from her father, who had worn them in the wheat fields a century ago. Designers add "character" to clothes by messing them up, like Helmut Lang's famous $270 paint-spattered jeans. Jeans, blasted and stained dust-brown, by CK, Levi's, and Dolce & Gabbana, cost up to $200. In fact, Calvin Klein's "dirty" jeans sold for $20 more than a pair of his basic, unblemished ones. In 2001, Commes des Garçons produced a peasant dress, priced at a very unpeasantlike $495, described by discount shopping website Bluefly.com as "given a chic tattered look."

Fashion may be bent on newness, but we apparently can't stand it when something looks *too* new (who can bear the blinding whiteness of new sneakers?). The industry has taken to calling the shabby, imperfect look "distressed"—a word that carries a connotation of pain and suffering. This fashion agony doesn't come cheap, from Jean-Paul Gaultier's distressed leather pants for $1,560 and two-piece distressed leather jacket and bustier for $2,740 to Versace's distressed ball gowns and midpriced shoe maker Aldo's distressed leather pumps for $70.

On most new clothes, a flaw is reason to return a garment to the store; on others, it's a reason to love the garment with even more fervor. The Fashion Victim understands that ready-to-wear clothes are mostly mass produced, and that a handsewn article somehow possesses more soul and uniqueness. Minute blemishes in a fabric's color prove that a gown was hand-dipped by a dressmaker in Paris; slightly raised threads on a vest attest that it was handcrafted by the real wives of authentic sherpas in Nepal. Some clothes, like a sweater I bought years ago, come with tags explaining how the pills and flecks you may see in the fabric are not flaws at all but rather intentional imperfections, there to add to the garment's charm.

5   In our hunt for substance in style, we covet clothes that evoke the blue-collar world, like the Authentic Prison Blues shirts (actually made by inmates!) that Bruce Willis and Billy Bob Thornton wore in the 2001 movie *Bandits*. Why do we do it? Fashion is our way of visually signaling to others how we want to be seen, and even though we all want to be considered stylish, we don't want to look like we've put too much planning and money into doing so. Glamour and neatness have their place, but premeditated nonchalance is the Fashion Victim's Holy Grail. We shop at stores like Filthmart, the Manhattan vintage store co-owned by Drea de Matteo of *The Sopranos* and featuring Hell's Angels–meets–Jewel wares. Hip-hop fans spend exorbitant amounts of cash on urbanwear to prove they're still "street": a pair of denim and Ultrasuede pants from Phat Farm for $150, an Enyce "bulletproof" nylon vest for $97, puffy down jackets from the North Face for $199. Even a simple wifebeater tank top can sell for over $100 if it has the right label. We buy peasant blouses at faux-boho Anthropologie because we want to look like we churn butter on a farm in

Provence, or grungy $80 pants at Urban Outfitters to show our down-town cool. For his fall 2002 Marc by Marc Jacobs show, Jacobs sent models down the runway in mismatched grandma knits, oversized seventies scarves, rainbow-striped sweaters, jeans, and corduroys—the ultimate home-grown poor-girl look for the woman who has everything. In early 2000, John Galliano took the dressed-down look one step further: he stunned the fashion crowd in Paris with his Homeless Chic couture show for Christian Dior, featuring models draped in torn clothes held together by string and strewn with kitchen utensils and miniature liquor bottles.

In the world of the Fashion Victim, shopping at a thrift store is cool . . . unless you're actually on welfare and have to buy *all* your clothes there. Some hard-core fashionistas insist they only shop second hand. But it's usually not all from the buck-a-pound bin at the local thrift store. In recent years, designers like Imitation of Christ who re-work vintage and thrift have become hip. The Fashion Victim drools over these born-again garments, which still possess some of the old, dirty charm but at twenty times the price. Today, even the mere impli-cation that a garment is old can suffice. Gap and Abercrombie & Fitch have pilfered the word "vintage" for use on their fresh-from-the-factory shirts and jeans to suggest classic style. Are we really fooled by a crisp new T-shirt that spells Gap Vintage in faded letters?

Today, it's fun to think you're shopping downmarket. "Cheap chic" stores like H&M, Target, Japan's Uniqlo, and Spain's Mango have made fortunes in recent years selling cut-rate trends. But no true fashionista worth her salt would buy her entire wardrobe at one of these stores, so she engages in cheap chic in her own way, to the point at which "cheap" becomes a completely relative term. Moschino's lower-priced line, called Moschino Cheap & Chic, is far from cheap for most shoppers. A "Leopard" coat and scarf retails for $1,340, and a Petal Trim Sweater for $615. Frugality at its finest, indeed.

Thou Shalt Covet Useless Utility

To the Fashion Victim, there's nothing wrong with clothes that serve no purpose other than looking cool. But if a garment can create the il-lusion that it's functional as well, it's all the better. A part of us knows that fashion is frivolous, so we attempt to justify our participation in it by making our clothes seem useful. We're grasping at straws to ra-tionalize making some of our unnecessary purchases. Shirts come with hoods whose sole purpose is to hang behind one's neck. The polar fleece vest was pitched as functional in a climbing-the-Alps sort of way, but if you really wanted something to keep you warm, wouldn't you give it sleeves? Cargo pants, with their multitude of pockets, seemed infinitely useful . . . imagine all the odds and ends you could carry. Countless designers, including Calvin Klein, Gucci, and Versace, interpreted the military style for the runway, and mall retailers followed suit with their versions, like Abercrombie's Paratroops and American Eagle's Cargo Trek Pant. Ralph Lauren even produced an army-green cargo bikini with pockets at the hip (for toting beach grenades?). The fashion world's idealized image of the utilitarian future appears to involve lots of zippers, buckles, Velcro, pull closures, straps, and strings—no matter if they actually serve a purpose or not.

Judging by the creations we've seen of late, fashions of the future won't serve just one purpose—they'll serve purposes we never knew needed serving. In 2001, women's magazines touted a new pair of panty hose that dispense a tiny bit of lotion onto the legs with each wearing. The Fuji Spinning Company in Japan has developed a T-shirt and lace underwear that will give wearers their daily dose of vitamin C. Newly developed shirts can monitor vital signs like heart rate and breathing patterns by using optical fibers that send and receive electrical impulses. For years, techies have drooled over the advent of "smart clothes," ultramodern garments with fully operational computers implanted in them. The first samples, furnished with round-the-clock Internet access, have been revealed in fashion shows at tech conferences, with models wearing headset microphones and built-in keyboard sleeves. For all the innovation that's been shoveled into fashion, you'd think inventors would be able to come up with something truly useful—like snag-proof cashmere sweaters. Is that so much to ask?

Thou Shalt Own Minutely Differing Variations of the Same Thing

10 At least part of the Fashion Victim's closet looks like that of a cartoon character, with rows of essentially identical items hanging next to one another. There are multiple pairs of sneakers: a pair for running, a pair for walking, a pair for shopping, a pair for going out, a pair for jeans, a pair for shorts. Then there are the multiple pairs of black pants: wide-legged, skinny-legged, fitted, baggy, flat-front, zipper, button-fly, pleated, wool, stretch, rayon, linen. Former Filipino first lady Imelda Marcos, who once famously defended herself by stating, "I did not have three thousand pairs of shoes, I had one thousand and sixty," surely had some overlapping styles hanging in her gigantic closet.

Fashion Victims own duplicates of items that are just different enough to not be *exactly* the same. The average American owns seven pairs of blue jeans. Certainly, each pair could be cut and colored differently, but are those seven pairs really that different? Rosa, a twenty-six-year-old office manager in Chicago, owns more than fifteen pairs of navy-blue jeans that she's amassed over the last two years, picking up one or two pairs a month. "Some are regular-waisted, some are boot-cut, others are tapered, one has red stitching on the sides and on the pockets, some are button-fly, some are a bit darker," she explains. "Even though they all look the same, they each have their special style." All that variety means she doesn't wear each pair very often. "I have a few clothes that I have in my closet that I've only worn once or twice," she says. "But it's hard to part with them because I always feel like, 'Maybe I'll wear it *one* more time.' " Fashion Victims all share in this mind-set, and as a result, we could have two walk-in closets stuffed to the gills and still never feel like we have enough. So we continue to buy.

Fashion Victims convince themselves that they need variety in their wardrobes; often they aren't aware of how similar all their clothes really are. "Many of my clients are really surprised at the end of an organizing project to learn they own five pairs of black slacks," says Debbie Williams, a personal organizing coach in Houston, Texas, and publisher of *Organized Times*. "They wouldn't dream of wearing black slacks each and every day of the work week, so having five pairs is overkill to say the least—they really could get by with two or three pairs." When the time comes that our closets begin to burst at the seams and a clean-out is necessary, we moan about the effort it takes to dispose of all our unwanted items.

Nevertheless, it's the nature of the Fashion Victim to be a clothing pack rat, to act as an apparel archivist, to collect superfluous garments for the sake of collecting superfluous garments, to fool herself into thinking she needs a new jacket—even though she already owns its lookalike.

Thou Shalt Believe Submissively in the Fashion Label's Reach

Today when you buy a designer's clothes, you're also buying a lifestyle. Ralph Lauren (a.k.a. Ralph Lifschitz from the Bronx) knew this when he created Polo, a brand meant to evoke the image of the affluent, holiday-in-Hyannisport set. As a result, our favorite clothing brands can sell us practically anything else—hand cream, lipstick, perfume, nail polish, dishes, pillows, candles, duvets, music. You can not only wear Ralph Lauren, Calvin Klein, Banana Republic, Eddie Bauer, Donna Karan, Liz Claiborne, Nautica, and Versace, but you can dress your bedroom in them, too. Love how Club Monaco clothes look? Buy the retailer's line of cosmetics. Hooked on Victoria's Secret bras? Well, they must have good skin-care products if they make

good bras, right? Like Armani suits? Buy their line of gourmet chocolates. Just as automakers like Jaguar, Vespa, and Harley-Davidson
have their own branded clothing lines, retailers and designers have
left their mark on the automotive world with special-edition cars like
the Eddie Bauer Ford Explorer and Expedition, the Coach-edition
Lexus, the Subaru Outback LL Bean edition, the Joseph Abboud Special Edition Buick Regal, and the Louis Vuitton edition of Chrysler's
PT Cruiser.

15   A fashion label may be able to excel at auxiliary products, but
don't always assume they're made by who you think they are. For
decades, designers have known that their illustrious names alone can
sell nearly anything, so they engage in multimillion-dollar licensing
deals, offering their names for use by others to make and promote a
variety of products. In the 1970s, designers like Valentino and Pierre
Cardin began to license their names for everything from sheets to luggage to toilet-seat covers (by 1970, the House of Cardin had licensed
its name for use on more than six hundred products). Donna Karan
reported that its fastest growth segment was in its licensing division—including accessories, jeans, home, and bath—which grew to
over a billion dollars in sales in 2000. Kenneth Cole has admitted that
his company licenses out most of what it does, except for shoes and
women's handbags.

Some well-known brands actually make the products of *other*
well-known brands. Fossil designs, manufactures, markets, and dis-
tributes Burberry watches. Perry Ellis manufactures apparel, bags,
and accessories under the Nautica label. Liz Claiborne holds the exclusive license to design and produce DKNY jeans. Estée Lauder
holds exclusive licensing agreements to make fragrances for both
Tommy Hilfiger and Donna Karan. Procter and Gamble, home of
Noxzema, Oil of Olay, and Old Spice, also holds licenses for Hugo
Boss, Giorgio, Helmut Lang, and Hervé Leger fragrances. Luxottica
makes eyewear for Armani, Brooks Brothers, Anne Klein, Moschino,
Ungaro, and Ferragamo. Women's outerwear for Kenneth Cole and
Nine West is made by the same company—G-III Apparel, which also
holds the license for Tommy Hilfiger's leather outerwear for men.

Licensing may help designers expand their businesses, but it's
historically been frowned upon in the fashion world. Cardin's new-
found middle-brow appeal made him the world's richest couturier
but also got him booted out of the Chambre Syndicale, the exclusive
supervisory body for haute couture in Paris. By the late 1990s, licensing had fallen out of favor with many luxury designers, with many
like Gucci and Armani beginning to buy back their licensing agreements in an attempt to regain brand control. Then there was the
much-publicized lawsuit between Calvin Klein and licensee Warnaco
in 2000. In his countersuit, Klein alleged that Warnaco CEO Linda

Wachner damaged his brand's image by selling to discount stores and putting his name on designs he hadn't approved. Prior to the lawsuit, an unbelievable 90 percent of Klein's revenues came from licenses. The case shed much unwanted light on the practice of licensing. Consumers fretted, "Could our designer clothes actually be made by lesser manufacturers?" Quite the contrary, say designers—licensing actually improves the quality of products, because they pair with the pros. For instance, an expert in hosiery may do a better job at creating a line of silk stockings under the designer's name than the designer could do himself. Frankly, it works both ways. A good number of licensed products are well made while others are essentially generics with designer labels slapped on them. Luckily for them, either will do just fine for the Fashion Victim.

Thou Shalt Require Validation of Thine Own Stylishness

I've always wondered how people felt after they appeared in one of those "On the Street" photos in the *New York Times* Sunday Styles section, taken by fashion historian/scholar/journalist Bill Cunningham, a thirty-year veteran of the paper, a man whose job it is to catch the latest fashion trends on real people on the street. Clotheshorses are snapped as they're walking to Saks during their lunch break or browsing an outdoor vendor or exiting a bistro with co-workers. Some of the subjects are unknown; others, like Ivana Trump, *Vogue* editor Anna Wintour, and socialite/painter Anh Duong are career fashion plates. Some are clearly posing for the camera; others are caught unexpectedly, typically engaging in the Manhattanite's favorite outdoor pastime—nattering on the cell phone.

Cunningham, who camps out on the sidewalk day in and day out for up to a month just to photograph enough subjects for one story, says he never consciously goes out with a specific trend in mind. During Spring Fashion Week 2001, his discerning lens fell upon a former co-worker of mine outside one of the shows as she flaunted her cute metal-studded handbag. It was perhaps the least flattering angle at which I've ever seen her, but ego stroking nonetheless, in a "you have good enough taste in bags to be in the *New York Times*" kind of way. Many "On the Street" subjects are proud to be featured there. Cunningham has photographed Patrick McDonald, a public-relations director for a dressmaker, at least a dozen times. McDonald, who keeps a book of all his clips, told *New York* magazine in 2000, "I have friends who say, 'I look in the Style section as soon as I get home from the Hamptons to see if you're in it.' "

The art of dress is quite frequently built on the opinions of others. 20 We may like to think that how we dress is an extension of how we see ourselves, but more commonly, it's an expression of how we want *others* to see us. "We dress to communicate our social identities to others," says Kim Johnson, Ph.D., a professor at the University of Minnesota who teaches courses on the social psychology of clothing. "Dress informs others of how willing you are to participate in fashion and at what levels you're playing." In our appearance-centered society, one of the most common ways we butter up strangers and acquaintances is to compliment them on their clothes. We shower people with praise for their sense of style and expect to receive praise in return, like the sometimes sincere "You look great," which never fails to elicit the awkward yet gushing "You do *too*."

Fashion Victims dress deliberately, and whether the validation of their stylishness comes in the form of a photograph or a random compliment, that confirmation is all they need to keep going. A few years back I attended *Paper* magazine's "Beautiful People Party," held at the ultra-swanky restaurant of the moment, The Park, in Manhattan's meatpacking district. As guests entered, a photographer selected certain fashionable people to snap, letting others pass. To be waved through sans photo was like being dissed by the doorman at some snooty nightclub. I was swept up into the crowd and ended up standing next to a six-foot-five-inch gentleman dressed in full Dandy garb, complete with white jacket and chapeau. Sure enough, the photographer thought I was the dapper Dandy's date and encouraged us to smile for the camera. Was it because I, in my rather plain strapless dress, looked particularly smashing that night? Unfortunately, no. I had simply become fashionable by association. Did I feel like one of the Beautiful People that night? You bet.

Thou Shalt Dress Vicariously Through Thy Children and Pets

It's not enough for Fashion Victims to dress themselves in designer clothes; they often feel it necessary to share their impeccable taste with others. Someone once told me, "You give what you want to receive." People choose items for others that reflect their own taste, rather than the recipient's. We Fashion Victims live by this. We dress our kids (and others' children when we buy gifts) in mini-me lines like Moschino kids, GapKids, babyGap, Old Navy Kids, Diesel Kids, Ralph Lauren kids, Prada kids, and Guess? Kids. Small sizes don't mean small prices. A baby leather jacket costs $200 at Polo. A jean jacket from Diesel Kids costs $109—more than a grown-up size at many stores. Then there's the $125 tulle dress for girls by Christian Dior, the $175 sweater by Missoni Kids, the pink knit pant set by Baby Dior, $93 trousers by Young Versace, and $68 bootleg jeans by Diesel. Before Dolce & Gabbana's kiddy line, D&G Junior, ran into some trouble in 2000 when its licensee Nilva went belly up, it carried several categories of clothing like "Denim Rock Star," "Lord Rapper," and "Logomania." There were gold denim jackets, tiny shearling coats, and a red leather racing-team jacket for $599. With most kids' clothes, there's not even the possibility of an outfit becoming a long-lasting part of a wardrobe because they outgrow things so quickly, so laying out exorbitant amounts of cash is truly like throwing money into a bottomless pit.

Fashion Victims also know that true style must rub off on one's pets. We ooh and ahh over cutesy pet fashions, not just the doggy sweaters, bandannas, and plastic booties sold in most pet stores, but rather real designer duds that mirror our own dress. Illustrious labels like Hermès, Louis Vuitton, Prada, Salvatore Ferragamo, and Gucci have gotten in on the act, offering high-priced beds, bags, collars, and leashes. Gucci ignited the trend in 1997 when it released a collar and leash. Louis Vuitton and Prada followed in 1998, and Coach and Burberry in the following years. Gucci sells a brown doggy raincoat for $117. Louis Vuitton introduced LV-monogram leather dog carriers in the seventies; they are still available today for just under $1,000. And for those with financial constraints, there's always Old Navy's line of poochy fashions. In L.A., Hollywood's pet owners shop at chi-chi Fifi & Romeo, a luxurious boutique that sells a line of hand-knitted cashmere sweaters and wool coats for little dogs that come in sizes like "teacup" and "mini," priced from $100 to $300.

Models tote their grapefruit-sized Yorkies in their Fendi bags as they sit in the makeup chairs at fashion shows. And fashionable folk dine at sidewalk cafés with their debonair doggies fastened to a table leg with $300 leashes. If it's true what they say about dogs looking like their owners, the Fashion Victim must be quite the pampered human.

Thou Shalt Feign Athleticism

Today, our fascination with sports goes beyond wearing the jerseys 25 and caps of athletes and teams we like. Shoppers at American Eagle Outfitters can lounge around the house on a Sunday afternoon wearing one of the store's football shirts, a Vintage Rugby, Spin Cycle Trek T, or Motocross T. Few of us have ever taken a hit on the rugby field, but we can dress like those robust lads with rugby shirts from stores like J. Crew, Polo Ralph Lauren, H&M, and the Gap.

Abercrombie & Fitch carries such faux-sporty wares as the Morrill Athletic Knit with a number eight stitched over the heart, Field Events Vintage Track Pants, Mountaineering Windpant, Rock Climbing Crew, Sculling Hooded Fleece (basically just a hooded sweatshirt with a big green 9 sewn on), and the Goal Keeper Nylon Pant for women. Gap carries an entire Gap Athletic line. There's Prada Sport,

Polo Sport, and Tommy Sport. Designers even create sport perfumes and colognes that emit clean scents fitting for the fashion-conscious wannabe athlete, like Escada Sport, Benetton Sport, Boss Sport, and Liz Sport. We wear shoes with technical-sounding names like Reebok's Trailzilla III and Nike's Air Terra Humara Slip-on. Fila's Pininfarina shoe was designed in conjunction with the sports car manufacturer of the same name.

Most of our lives are wholly un-rugged, so we attempt to reinsert that missing ruggedness through our wardrobes. Labels like the North Face and Patagonia, which create functional garb for the mountaineering über-athlete, have become fashionable brands to traipse around town in. Timberland boots are as ideal for digging through CDs at the Virgin Megastore as they are for hiking through backwoods Montana. Columbia Sportswear recently produced a parka that detects when the wearer's skin temperature has dropped and releases stored body heat, which will no doubt become a must-have item for those climbing the Himalayas—or picking up an iced latte at Starbucks (*brrrr*).

Those of us who aren't triathletes or marathoners still enjoy examining the sole of a sneaker and seeing very scientific-looking springs, air pockets, gel, and pumps. Employees at the Nike Sport Research Laboratory hold Ph.D.'s or master's degrees in human biomechanics and bioengineering. In March 2002, Adidas introduced ClimaCool sneakers, designed to keep feet cool with a "360-degree ventilation system." Athletic shoe makers spend millions of dollars on research to develop supersneakers that add more bounce, absorb shock, improve traction, and cushion arches. And when the Fashion Victim buys these supersneakers, he is delighted over his purchase and can't wait to wear them when he meets his buddies for a drink, no doubt at the local sports bar.

Thou Shalt Be a Walking Billboard

The fashion industry is filled with bright ideas thought up by marketing opportunists, from the famous logo print of Louis Vuitton to the ubiquitous Polo emblem, the conspicuous A/X printed on Armani Exchange T-shirts, the unmistakable Nike swoosh, and the name of skatewear company Fuct emblazoned on a sweatshirt. In 2001, Kenneth Cole, Tommy Hilfiger, and Aldo shoes released lines of handbags that touted their designers' names in Steven Sprouse—like graffiti. When Ja Rule wears Burberry's signature plaid in his videos, he provides the company with a free subliminal ad that reaches millions of people, without even uttering the word *Burberry*.

30   Logophilia hit a high in the 1980s, then dipped in the less showy 1990s. But in 2000, it kicked into full gear again with brand names and

logo prints splashed across everything from the most downmarket to the most luxurious items. "Quite a bizarre trend if you analyze it too deeply," says Shelly Vella, fashion director of *Cosmopolitan* UK. "People normally associate wearing logoed merchandise with the need to advertise wealth and buying power: 'Look at my Versace sweatshirt, Gucci jeans, etc.' In decades past, sophisticated designer-ism was about quiet elegance and style—connoisseurs could recognize the cut of a good designer garment. Somehow, in the late nineties, Louis Vuitton logo-itis caught on and everything from Macs to bags, shoes, and tops bore a logo. I saw that whole trend as an attempt—very successful—by designers to reestablish the 'cult of the designer' and to market conspicuous consumption as cool."

In a way, wearing a logo is like wearing gang colors. Just as the Bloods and Crips brandish red and blue bandannas, the Fashion Victim wears the designer logo as a proud badge of membership. It's an act that's tribal at its core. "It's like schoolchildren all nagging for the coolest trainers [sneakers, for you non-Anglophiles]," says Vella. "If you're seen to be wearing the right thing, you're in."

A brand name can add immediate "worth" to two identical products. "Branding is unfortunately the cornerstone of many fashion labels today—not the design, the innovation, the cut, or any other skill honed by the designer. And what the brand stands for is everything," says Debi Hall, fashion-branding strategist for JY&A Consulting in London. "As the Japanese say, name is the first thing—without a name, a garment in today's highly capitalistic, value-added culture is worth very little. Take the vintage phenomenon: even if a secondhand YSL dress is without a label, because it once had a name, it is still worth something. If, however, it is simply a secondhand dress with a name nobody has heard of, then it will go for pennies."

Still, not every Fashion Victim is so taken with the visible logo. Some fashion-conscious folk have been known to consider a visible label such a dealbreaker that they'll take the time to remove it. A few years back, hipsters in London started a trend by tearing the *N* off their New Balance sneakers. And according to *New York* magazine, the late Carolyn Bessette Kennedy once had employees cut the labels out of skiwear she had bought. Emily Cinader Woods, cofounder and chairman of J. Crew, says that unlike her friend Michael Jeffries—CEO of Abercrombie & Fitch, a company notorious for slapping its name conspicuously on everything—she's always been adamant about no logos. "There are so many brands that you might love an item or the color but the logo keeps you from buying it," she says. On the other hand, when you're around people who are familiar with various brands—as is typical for the Fashion Victim—it's possible to be a walking billboard without ever displaying the brand name on your body. I once wore a sleeveless J. Crew top to the office, and two co-workers that day remarked in passing, "I like that—J. Crew?" The brand's familiar look and prevalence in their mail-order catalogs had made the clothes recognizable enough that they didn't need an obvious swoosh, polo player, or little green alligator sewn across the chest. I had been a moving J. Crew billboard all day without the presence of any visible logos.

Thou Shalt Care about Paris Hilton's Gaultier Micro-mini

Although some might argue that the socialite as we once knew her is dead, her successor's social calendar is still jam packed, and her list of contacts in the fashion industry is growing by the New York minute. Fashion glossies like *W* and *Vogue* regularly feature young butterflies like Alexandra Von Furstenberg, Rena Sindi, Aerin Lauder, Brooke de Ocampo, and the Hilton sisters mugging for photographers amid the hip DJs, models, movie stars, and artists who are typically their fellow revelers. The Fashion Victim devours the photos with delight, checking out the Dior gown that Karen Groos wore to an AIDS benefit or the Celine sheath that Pia Getty wore to a summer soiree, knowing little about who these people are except that they're in a magazine, they're rich, and they're incredibly well dressed.

35   Our fascination with the Junior Jet-setter is somewhat puzzling. She sometimes holds a glamorous job, like contributing editor at a magazine, or even perhaps heads up a relative's business empire, but it's an occupation that would not necessarily garner the same level of press attention for some other person in a similar position. For example, Aerin Lauder may be the executive director of creative marketing for family biz Estée Lauder, but you certainly wouldn't see someone with the same title at Lancôme or Elizabeth Arden in the pages of *Vogue* eight times a year. The Junior Jet-setter often has a famous last name, like Rockefeller or Von Furstenberg, but, again, a well-known surname on its own doesn't necessarily guarantee anyone an overwhelming number of glam photo ops (just look at Sean Lennon).

The socialite's role in the fashion game is to look stunning at events in couture gowns, and casually upper class when attending a summer soiree in the Hamptons. A gossipworthy socialite should be trailed by at least one rumor of out-of-control partying, like making out with someone other than her date or accidentally letting her Galliano gown slip down and flashing her fellow partygoers. Her job is to *be* the answer to the question: "Who actually wears those clothes?" These are the women who can afford the Fendi furs and Gucci pantsuits, but like celebrities, they are also the frequent recipients of loans and freebies from designers—residing below the A-List celebrity, but above B-List TV actresses and pop stars in the fashion hierarchy. In magazines, they seem somehow superhuman. Mostly whippet-thin (perfect for fitting into the sample size), the pretty and privileged attend trunk shows, where they're wined, dined, and shown exquisite new designs. Their job description also includes sitting front row at catwalk shows. Of course, these women are expected to do something in return: they are obliged to wear (and showcase) the designer's clothes. It would be social suicide for a Junior Jet-setter to show up in a Gucci dress at a Versace show. The smart socialite knows this: a few seasons back in Paris, Brooke de Ocampo was seen in Celine at the Celine show and then Dior at the Dior show—both on the same day.

The fashion system is built on want. Looking at socialites' clothes in *Vogue* is like drooling over the estates in *Architectural Digest* or flipping through the *DuPont Registry* to catch a glimpse of the Bentleys and Aston Martins you'll never be able to afford. We live vicariously through the socialite—who has deep enough pockets to buy designer threads of a caliber most of us will never even see in person. Perplexing as our interest may be, the Fashion Victim eats up every morsel, but not without a tinge of jealousy, of course. "I *love* looking at those rich bitches," says Rita, a forty-nine-year-old website editor in Stamford, Connecticut. "But what kills me is that a lot of them don't really have great taste—they just have great resources. If they had to put together a wardrobe like the rest of us mere mortals—from the Gap, Banana Republic, etc.—I doubt they'd be so fabulous. But you do get good fashion ideas from looking and it's nice to daydream."

Thou Shalt Want without Seeing

Curiously, selling clothes today does not always require actually *showing* the clothes. "Sex sells, sells, and keeps selling," says Marc Berger, fashion director of *GQ*. "A sexy woman in an ad will always grab the attention of a man. It's a great marketing ploy." The no-show advertising technique is frequently justified with "We're selling an image." Ads are another example of fashion's hypnotic power over us. All a company needs to do is get our attention—whether or not we love the clothes is insignificant. In recent years, Abercrombie & Fitch's controversial magalog, the *A&F Quarterly*, has raised eyebrows with its photos of tanned all-American dudes and dudettes, often with zero body fat and zero clothing—a buff naked guy holding a film reel in front of his privates, a couple wearing nothing but body paint, a group of disrobed guys flashing their smiles (and nearly everything else) by the pool. The image: cool, horny coeds. In 1999, a Sisley campaign shot by Terry Richardson simply showed the faces of two female models in a half-sexy, half-goofy liplock. Two years later, an ad for the retailer featured a self-portrait of the moustached Richardson wearing a snake around his neck and nothing else. The image: sexy, slightly dirty. Then there was an Ungaro print ad a few years back showing a werewolf licking a woman's bare body, which was widely condemned for being overly graphic. The image? Anyone's guess. Perhaps the most controversial campaign of late comes from French Connection. To announce the opening of its largest store ever, the retailer took out a full-page ad in a London paper that read. "The World's Biggest FCUK," flaunting the company's easily misread acronym (think of the poor dyslexics!).

Some industry experts think the sex pitch has gone too far. Others say it's all in the *way* it's done. Fashion straddles the line between art and commerce, and so do its ads. In 2001, a magazine and billboard ad campaign for Yves Saint Laurent featuring a nude Sophie Dahl laid out on her back as if in orgasmic rapture created a firestorm of controversy. Some people viewed it as art, like a nude painting or sculpture, while others considered it a shameless ploy for attention. *Vogue* Australia editor Kirstie Clements has nixed ads in the past for being too overtly sexual. "Sex sells *Cosmo,* but not so much *Vogue,*" says Clements. "I've rejected an ad for sex aids, but I have no problem with the Sophie Dahl YSL ads. I think they're very chic. Sexy for us has to be chic and sexy. A sexy-looking Gisele sells, yes. But a girl in bondage, no. Depends on your product."

40   Sex isn't the only trick in the book. Today, premeditated weirdness has just as much pull as a gratuitous glimpse of flesh. In 2000, menswear label Daniel Christian's fall ad campaign showed only the face of a wrinkly old woman with the message "buy a Daniel Christian shirt or pair of jeans and the bag comes free." Who *wouldn't* want to buy a pair of jeans after seeing that? "These ads also work because there's so much word of mouth and so many articles about them in the newspapers and other media," says Arthur Asa Berger, author of *Ads, Fads and Consumer Culture.* "If you can create an ad that gets talked about in television news shows and written about in newspapers, you're getting a lot of free publicity . . . for the brand." One of the revolutionaries in this seemingly illogical method of advertising was Benetton, whose ads in the eighties and nineties ranged from the harmless (two smiling children) to the provocative (a duck covered in crude oil) to the controversial (death row inmates). Oliviero Toscani, who photographed the confrontational ads and was dropped shortly after the death row campaign, always maintained that it wasn't *his* duty to sell the clothes—it was the company's. Oh, Oliviero, how we miss you.

Responding to Reading

1. Lee begins her essay by stating that fashion victims like herself "allow a set of ridiculous, yet compelling, rules to govern our wardrobes, our purchases, our desires, even our sense of self-worth" (1). In what sense are the rules she lists "compelling"? In what sense are they "ridiculous"? Who (or what) do you think is responsible for creating "fashion victims"?

2. Which of Lee's rules do you see as essentially harmless? Which, if any, do you find depressing, or even alarming? What is Lee's attitude toward the "ten commandments" she lists? Does she actually accept these commandments as articles of faith, or does she convey impatience or even contempt?

3. Look through the images in the Focus section of this chapter (p. 398). Which of Lee's "ten commandments" could each photo illustrate? Which of her rules do you yourself follow? Why do you do so?

Responding in Writing

Write a paragraph that uses the second sentence of Lee's essay as your topic sentence. Support this topic sentence with ten additional sentences, each of which paraphrases one of Lee's "ten commandments" and supplies an illustration. Add a final sentence that summarizes the paragraph's main idea. When you edit your paragraph, make sure you have included appropriate transitions between sentences.

FOCUS

What Do Our Clothes Tell Us about Ourselves?

The eight images that follow illustrate some of the key fashion trends from the late nineteenth century to the present. Look closely at the images, and read the captions that accompany them. Then, answer the questions below.

Responding to the Images

1. Which of the fashions pictured on the following pages would you characterize as restrictive or controlling? Which would you characterize as liberating? Why?

2. How different are the men's and women's clothes of the same period? Would you agree with Deborah Tannen (p. 430) that women's clothes have more "markers"?

3. What do the fashion accessories in these pictures tell you about the people who wear them? What does the absence of accessories tell you?

4. What information do the women's hairstyles give you about their lives?

5. Which photos convey a sense that the people are conforming to the dominant fashions of the time? Which suggest that they are using fashion to express their individuality? How can you tell?

6. What do you think body piercing and tattoos (present in just one of these photos) reveal about the people who display them? What messages do you think piercing and tattoos convey to your parents, teachers, and peers?

7. As the earlier photos suggest, hats were once part of nearly every outfit. Although hat wearing declined in the 1960s, it has reemerged today in a different form. What kinds of hats do you observe today? Who wears hats, and why?

8. Richard Florida (p. 338) suggests that the social changes that occurred between 1950 and today are more striking than those that took place between 1900 and 1950. Do these fashion photos support his observation?

9. According to Michelle Lee's criteria (p. 383), which, if any, of the individuals pictured would qualify as "fashion victims"?

10. Apart from those depicted in the last image, which people would attract the least attention on the street in your community? Which would attract the most attention? Why?

Family at home, 1890s.

Woman in typical "flapper" outfit, 1920s.

Men and women in business attire, 1950s.

Young woman listening to transistor radio, 1950s.

Hippie couple, late 1960s.

Man and woman disco dancing, 1970s.

Punk rockers, 1980s.

Contemporary men and women in casual clothing.

——————————— WIDENING THE FOCUS ———————————

The following readings can suggest additional perspectives for thinking and writing about what our clothing tells us about ourselves (and
what it tells others about us). You may also want to do further research
about this subject on the Internet.

- Michelle Lee, "The Fashion Victim's Ten Commandments" (p. 383)

- Deborah Tannen, "Marked Women" (p. 430)

- Marge Piercy, "Barbie Doll" (p. 405)

- Paul Fussell, "Deliverers" (p. 571)

For Internet Research: In their attempts to sell a wide range of products, advertisers often emphasize the importance of physical attractiveness. Researchers, however, fear that this emphasis pressures both
men and women to value physical appearance too highly. Visit the
Web site of the Adbusters Media Foundation, http://adbusters.org/
creativeresistance/spoofads/fashion/, and review some of its spoofs
of fashion advertisements. Choose one of the spoof advertisements,
and write an essay in which you analyze the purpose of that image.
What argument does the image present? Is the image persuasive? Why
or why not? How would you change the image to make it more persuasive? (You may want to review the "Reacting to Visual Texts" section on page 7 in the Introduction before you begin to write.)

WRITING

The Way We Live Now

1. Who are the heroes for the way we live now? Are they real or fictional? Are they famous? Are they living? Write an essay in which you establish some criteria to define heroism and explain why the figures you chose qualify as heroes.

2. Identify several visual "signs of the times," familiar images from advertising, movies, or Web sites, which you believe typify the way we live now, and write an essay explaining what these images tell you about your world.

3. Many contemporary writers have expressed concern about the gap beween the poor and the rest of society, a gap that is widening along with the expansion of computer technology. How do you think the dramatic technological changes the nation is experiencing will affect those who live in poverty? Do you see the "savage inequalities" between rich and poor (identified by Jonathan Kozol in his essay "The Human Cost of an Illiterate Society" on page 212) as inevitably widening? Explain what you believe needs to be done to resolve any problems you identify.

4. Several of the selections in this chapter suggest that some of modern-day society's problems are caused (or at least aggravated) by the media. Do you believe the media make social problems worse—or even create social problems? Support your conclusion with examples from essays in this chapter and Chapter 4 as well as from your own experence.

5. In an essay called "The Making of a Generation," writer Arthur Levine says, "Every . . . generation is defined by the social events of its age." Identify several pivotal social and political events—local or national—that have had an impact on you and others your age, and explain how these events define your generation.

6. What do you predict for our society's future? In light of these predictions, are you optimistic or pessimistic about what lies ahead? You may focus on any of the issues discussed in this chapter.

7. Although none of the essays in this chapter focus on the role of the family in the twenty-first century, the trends they discuss might certainly be seen to have an impact (positive or negative) on family life. Do you believe the ties that connect family members are weakening? If so, what contemporary social forces do you hold responsible? If not, how do you explain the family's continued strength in light of all that has changed in our society?

8. Keep a diary in which you record all the food you eat in a week (including brand names and approximate portion size). What do your food choices reveal about who you are and the way you live? Which of these choices do you suppose might surprise a time traveler from the 1950s? from the 1970s?

9. Richard Florida (p. 338), Edward J. Blakely and Mary Gail Snyder (p. 346), and Ellen Ruppel Shell (p. 356) discuss the concept of community in very different ways. Write an essay in which you use their observations to help you develop and support a thesis of your own about how our concept of community is changing.

10. Review the photos in the Focus section of this chapter as well as those in a variety of contemporary fashion magazines. Then, write an essay in which you answer the question, "What do our clothes tell us about ourselves?"

6

GENDER AND IDENTITY

PREPARING TO READ AND WRITE

Attitudes about gender have changed dramatically over the past thirty years, and they continue to change. For some, these changes have resulted in confusion and anger as well as liberation. One reason for this confusion is that people can no longer rely on fixed gender roles to tell them how to behave in public and how to function within their families. Still, many men and women—uncomfortable with the de-

Smash and Crash Hulk action figure.

mands of confining gender roles and unhappy with the expectations those roles create—yearn for even less rigidity, for an escape from stereotypes into a society where roles are not defined by gender.

Interestingly, many people still see men and women in terms of outdated or unrealistic stereotypes. Men are strong, tough, and brave, and women are weak, passive, and in need of protection. Men understand mathematics and science and have a natural aptitude for mechanical tasks. They also have the drive, the aggressiveness, the competitive edge, and the power to succeed. They are never sentimental and never cry. Women are better at small, repetitive tasks and shy away from taking bold, decisive actions. They enjoy, and are good at, domestic activities, and they have a natural aptitude for nurturing. They may like their jobs, but they will leave them to devote themselves to husband and children.

As you read the preceding list of stereotypes, you may react neutrally (or even favorably), or you may react with annoyance; how we react tells us something about our society and something about

Girl playing with Barbie dolls.

ourselves. But as a number of writers in this chapter point out, stereotypes are not just inaccurate; they also limit the way people think, the roles they chose to assume, and, ultimately, the positions they occupy in society.

As the Focus section of this chapter, "Who Has It Harder, Women or Men?," illustrates, both men and women have had problems living up to the images they believe they should conform to and filling the roles that have been set for them. For example, some believe that the emphasis in recent years on improving the self-image of young girls has been largely unsuccessful, and that "Generation X" is a generation of girls who hate themselves and their bodies. Others believe that it is boys who have suffered, for as parents and teachers have focused on girls, they have neglected the needs of boys. Some social critics point out that the disparity between boys and girls has gotten so pronounced that there is now a double standard: while it is acceptable to make fun of men in commercials, movies, and everyday conversation, it is sexist to make fun of women. Some blame the feminist movement for the problems faced by males and females; others blame society. The central questions seem to be "Who (if anyone) is suffering?" and "Who is at fault?" Beyond those questions, of course, lies the more important question: "What can be done to improve the lives of both women and of men?"

As you read and prepare to write about the essays in this chapter, you may consider the following questions:

- Is the writer male or female? Are you able to determine the writer's gender without reading his or her name or the headnote? Does the writer's gender really matter?

- Is the writer's focus on males, on females, or on both?

- When was the essay written? Does the date of publication affect its content?

- Does the essay seem fair? Balanced?

- Does the writer discuss gender as a sexual, political, economic, or social issue?

- What does the writer suggest are the specific advantages or disadvantages of being male? Of being female?

- Does the writer support the status quo, or does he or she suggest that change is necessary? That change is possible? That change is inevitable?

- Does the writer recommend specific changes? What are they?

- Is your interpretation of the issue the same as the writer's interpretation?

- Does the writer express the view that men and women are fundamentally different? If so, does he or she suggest that these differences can (or should) be overcome, or at least lessened?

- Does the writer see gender differences as the result of environment or of heredity?

- Does the essay challenge any of your ideas about male or female roles?

- In what ways is the essay like other essays in this chapter?

BARBIE DOLL

Marge Piercy
1936–

A native of Detroit, Piercy received a BA degree from the University of Michigan (1957) and a Master's degree from Northwestern University (1958). Her work includes the novels Small Changes *(1972);* He, She, and It *(1991);* The Longings of Women; *and* Three Women *(1999) and the poetry collections* Mars and Her Children *(1992) and* The Art of Blessing the Day *(1999), as well as the memoir* Sleeping with Cats *(2002). Piercy lives in Cape Cod, Massachusetts, and works at Leapfrog Press, which she founded with her husband in 1997. According to Piercy, who has been active in the women's movement since 1969, the movement "has been a great source (as well as energy sink!) and healer of the psyche for me." Piercy wants her poems to be useful; she hopes, as she explains in* Circles in the Water *(1988), "that readers will find poems that speak to and for them." "Barbie Doll," an ironic look at the influence of the controversial icon, is a poem from that collection. To learn more about Piercy, visit her Web site, http://www.margepiercy.com.*

This girlchild was born as usual
and presented dolls that did pee-pee
and miniature GE stoves and irons
and wee lipsticks the color of cherry candy.
Then in the magic of puberty, a classmate said: 5
You have a great big nose and fat legs.

She was healthy, tested intelligent,
possessed strong arms and back,
abundant sexual drive and manual dexterity.
She went to and fro apologizing.   10
Everyone saw a fat nose on thick legs.

She was advised to play coy,
exhorted to come on hearty,
exercise, diet, smile and wheedle.
15 Her good nature wore out
like a fan belt.
So she cut off her nose and her legs
and offered them up.

In the casket displayed on satin she lay
20 with the undertaker's cosmetics painted on,
a turned-up putty nose,
dressed in a pink and white nightie.
Doesn't she look pretty? everyone said.
Consummation at last.
25 To every woman a happy ending.

Responding to Reading

1. What is the significance of the poem's title? To whom or what does it refer? What toys was the "girlchild" (1) given after she was born? What effect does Piercy imply that these toys had on the child?
2. What happens to the "girlchild" when she reaches "the magic of puberty" (5)? Do you think this change is inevitable? Explain.
3. Piercy ends on a cynical note. Is this an effective conclusion? What does she gain (or lose) with this kind of ending?

Responding in Writing

What toy (or toys) did you have as a child that defined your "femaleness" or "maleness"? Do you think Piercy exaggerates the impact of such toys on children?

RITE OF PASSAGE

Sharon Olds

1942–

Born in San Francisco, Sharon Olds earned her Bachelor's degree at Stanford University (1964) and a PhD from Columbia University (1972). She has taught at many universities and currently teaches in the graduate creative writing program at New York University. Olds was thirty-seven years old when she published her first book of poems. Her collections include Waiting for My Life *(1981),* The Gold Cell *(1987),* The Wellspring

(1996), and Blood, Tin, Straw *(1999). Much of her poetry focuses on family relationships. Olds is active in community outreach programs, such as the writing workshop at Goldwater Hospital in New York City. In her poetry, Olds often dwells on family and relationships among parents and children, using plain language the reveals surprising emotional depths. According to one critic, "out of private revelations she makes poems of universal truth of sex, death, fear, and love."*

As the guests arrive at my son's party
they gather in the living room—
short men, men in first grade
with smooth jaws and chins.
Hands in pockets, they stand around   5
jostling, jockeying for place, small fights
breaking out and calming. One says to another
How old are you? Six. I'm seven. So?
They eye each other, seeing themselves
tiny in the other's pupils. They clear their   10
throats a lot, a room of small bankers,
they fold their arms and frown. *I could beat you
up,* a seven says to a six,
the dark cake, round and heavy as a
turret, behind them on the table. My son,   15
freckles like specks of nutmeg on his cheeks,
chest narrow as the balsa keel[1] of a
model boat, long hands
cool and thin as the day they guided him
out of me, speaks up as a host   20
for the sake of the group.
We could easily kill a two-year-old,
he says in his clear voice. The other
men agree, they clear their throats
like Generals, they relax and get down to   25
playing war, celebrating my son's life.

Responding to Reading

1. What is a "rite of passage"? Why do you think Olds gives her poem this title?
2. Why does Olds refer to the children at her son's birthday party as "men"?
3. What comment do you think Olds is making about what it means to be male in contemporary American society?

---

[1]The long, narrow bottom of a wooden ship. [Eds.]

Responding in Writing

Do you think that Olds's portrayal of boys is accurate, or do you think it is exaggerated? Why do you think that she characterizes boys as she does?

THE MEN WE CARRY IN OUR MINDS
Scott Russell Sanders
1945–

The author of novels, children's books, science fiction, and essays, Scott Russell Sanders teaches creative writing at Indiana University. He was born in Memphis, Tennessee, and earned a BA degree from Brown University (1967) and a PhD from Cambridge University in England (1971). His essay collections include The Paradise of Bombs *(1988),* Secrets of the Universe: Scenes from the Journey Home *(1991),* Staying Put in a Restless World *(1993),* Hunting for Hope: A Father's Journey *(1998), and* The Force of Spirit *(2000). An ardent environmentalist, Sanders has said, "If my writing does not help my neighbors to live more alertly, pleasurably, or wisely, then it is worth little." In "The Men We Carry in Our Minds," he recalls how he—a poor rural boy at an elite Ivy League college—first encountered upper-class women who railed at the "joys and privileges of men," privileges that did not apply to the working-class men he knew. To learn more about Sanders, visit his Web site, http://www.indiana.edu/~mfawrite/ sanders.html/.*

When I was a boy, the men I knew labored with their bodies. They were marginal farmers, just scraping by, or welders, steelworkers, carpenters; they swept floors, dug ditches, mined coal, or drove trucks, their forearms ropy with muscle; they trained horses, stoked furnaces, built tires, stood on assembly lines wrestling parts onto cars and refrigerators. They got up before light, worked all day long whatever the weather, and when they came home at night they looked as though somebody had been whipping them. In the evenings and on weekends they worked on their own places, tilling gardens that were lumpy with clay, fixing broken-down cars, hammering on houses that were always too drafty, too leaky, too small.

The bodies of the men I knew were twisted and maimed in ways visible and invisible. The nails of their hands were black and split, the hands tattooed with scars. Some had lost fingers. Heavy lifting had given many of them finicky backs and guts weak from hernias. Racing against conveyor belts had given them ulcers. Their ankles and knees ached from years of standing on concrete. Anyone who had worked for long around machines was hard of hearing. They squinted, and the skin of their faces was creased like the leather of old work gloves. There were times, studying them, when I dreaded growing up. Most of them coughed, from dust or cigarettes, and most of them drank cheap wine or whiskey, so their eyes looked bloodshot and bruised. The fathers of my friends always seemed older than the mothers. Men wore out sooner. Only women lived into old age.

As a boy I also knew another sort of men, who did not sweat and break down like mules. They were soldiers, and so far as I could tell they scarcely worked at all. During my early school years we lived on a military base, an arsenal in Ohio, and every day I saw GIs in the guardshacks, on the stoops of barracks, at the wheels of olive drab Chevrolets. The chief fact of their lives was boredom. Long after I left the Arsenal I came to recognize the sour smell the soldiers gave off as that of souls in limbo. They were all waiting—for wars, for transfers, for leaves, for promotions, for the end of their hitch—like so many braves waiting for the hunt to begin. Unlike the warriors of older tribes, however, they would have no say about when the battle would start or how it would be waged. Their waiting was broken only when they practiced for war. They fired guns at targets, drove tanks across the churned-up fields of the military reservation, set off bombs in the wrecks of old fighter planes. I knew this was all play. But I also felt certain that when the hour for killing arrived, they would kill. When the real shooting started, many of them would die. This was what soldiers were *for,* just as a hammer was for driving nails.

Warriors and toilers: those seemed, in my boyhood vision, to be the chief destinies for men. They weren't the only destinies, as I learned from having a few male teachers, from reading books, and from watching television. But the men on television—the politicians, the astronauts, the generals, the savvy lawyers, the philosophical doctors, the bosses who gave orders to both soldiers and laborers— seemed as removed and unreal to me as the figures in tapestries. I could no more imagine growing up to become one of these cool, potent creatures than I could imagine becoming a prince.

A nearer and more hopeful example was that of my father, who 5 had escaped from a red-dirt farm to a tire factory, and from the assembly line to the front office. Eventually he dressed in a white shirt and tie. He carried himself as if he had been born to work with his mind. But his body, remembering the earlier years of slogging work, began to give out on him in his fifties, and it quit on him entirely before he turned sixty-five. Even such a partial escape from man's fate as he had accomplished did not seem possible for most of the boys I knew. They joined the Army, stood in line for jobs in the smoky plants, helped build highways. They were bound to work as their fathers had worked, killing themselves or preparing to kill others.

A scholarship enabled me not only to attend college, a rare enough feat in my circle, but even to study in a university meant for the children of the rich. Here I met for the first time young men who had assumed from birth that they would lead lives of comfort and power. And for the first time I met women who told me that men were guilty of having kept all the joys and privileges of the earth for themselves. I was baffled. What privileges? What joys? I thought about the maimed, dismal lives of most of the men back home. What had they stolen from their wives and daughters? The right to go five days a week, twelve months a year, for thirty or forty years to a steel mill or a coal mine? The right to drop bombs and die in war? The right to feel every leak in the roof, every gap in the fence, every cough in the engine, as a wound they must mend? The right to feel, when the lay-off comes or the plant shuts down, not only afraid but ashamed?

I was slow to understand the deep grievances of women. This was because, as a boy, I had envied them. Before college, the only people I had ever known who were interested in art or music or literature, the only ones who read books, the only ones who ever seemed to enjoy a sense of ease and grace were the mothers and daughters. Like the menfolk, they fretted about money, they scrimped and made-do. But, when the pay stopped coming in, they were not the ones who had failed. Nor did they have to go to war, and that seemed to me a blessed fact. By comparison with the narrow, ironclad days of fathers, there was an expansiveness, I thought, in the days of mothers. They went to see neighbors, to shop in town, to run errands at school, at the library, at church. No doubt, had I looked harder at their lives, I would have envied them less. It was not my fate to become a woman, so it was easier for me to see the graces. Few of them held jobs outside the home, and those who did filled thankless roles as clerks and waitresses. I didn't see, then, what a prison a house could be, since houses seemed to me brighter, handsomer places than any factory. I did not realize—because such things were never spoken of—how often women suffered from men's bullying. I did learn about the wretchedness of abandoned wives, single mothers, widows; but I also learned about the wretchedness of lone men. Even then I could see how exhausting it was for a mother to cater all day to the needs of young children. But if I had been asked, as a boy, to choose between tending a baby and tending a machine, I think I would have chosen the baby. (Having now tended both, I know I would choose the baby.)

So I was baffled when the women at college accused me and my sex of having cornered the world's pleasures. I think something like my bafflement has been felt by other boys (and by girls as well) who grew up in dirt-poor farm country, in mining country, in black ghettos, in Hispanic barrios, in the shadows of factories, in Third World nations—any place where the fate of men is as grim and bleak as the fate of women. Toilers and warriors. I realize now how ancient these identities are, how deep the tug they exert on men, the undertow of a thousand generations. The miseries I saw, as a boy, in the lives of nearly all men I continue to see in the lives of many—the body-breaking toil, the tedium, the call to be tough, the humiliating power-lessness, the battle for a living and for territory.

When the women I met at college thought about the joys and privileges of men, they did not carry in their minds the sort of men I had known in my childhood. They thought of their fathers, who were bankers, physicians, architects, stockbrokers, the big wheels of the big cities. These fathers rode the train to work or drove cars that cost more than any of my childhood houses. They were attended from morning to night by female helpers, wives and nurses and secretaries. They were never laid off, never short of cash at month's end, never lined up for welfare. These fathers made decisions that mattered. They ran the world.

The daughters of such men wanted to share in this power, this 10 glory. So did I. They yearned for a say over their future, for jobs worthy of their abilities, for the right to live at peace, unmolested, whole. Yes, I thought, yes yes. The difference between me and these daughters was that they saw me, because of my sex, as destined from birth to become like their fathers, and therefore as an enemy to their desires. But I knew better. I wasn't an enemy, in fact or in feeling. I was an ally. If I had known, then, how to tell them so, would they have believed me? Would they now?

Responding to Reading

1. What do the men Sanders carries in his mind have in common? How have they helped to shape his attitude toward gender?
2. Do you agree with Sanders that women believe all men have greater access to power than they themselves do? Do you agree that women who believe this are mistaken?
3. In his conclusion, Sanders says that contrary to what they themselves believed, he was an "ally" of women who wanted to better themselves (10). What does he mean by this statement? Do you think the women about whom he is talking could be persuaded to see him as an ally?

Responding in Writing

How are your female friends' attitudes toward men and power different from (or similar to) those of the women Sanders describes in his essay?

WHY I WANT A WIFE

Judy Brady

1937–

Born in San Francisco, Judy Brady studied art at the University of Iowa and earned a BA degree before getting married, having a family, and starting her writing career. A breast cancer survivor, Brady co-founded the Toxic Links Coalition, an environmental advocacy group based in California. She has edited two books about cancer, including Women and Cancer *(1980) and a collection of essays and poems written by cancer victims,* One in Three: Women with Cancer Confront an Epidemic *(1991). Her popular essay "Why I Want a Wife" appeared in the first issue of* Ms. *magazine in 1972.*

I belong to that classification of people known as wives. I am A Wife. And, not altogether incidentally, I am a mother.

Not too long ago a male friend of mine appeared on the scene fresh from a recent divorce. He had one child, who is, of course, with his ex-wife. He is looking for another wife. As I thought about him while I was ironing one evening, it suddenly occurred to me that I, too, would like to have a wife. Why do I want a wife?

I would like to go back to school so that I can become economically independent, support myself, and, if need be, support those dependent upon me. I want a wife who will work and send me to school. And while I am going to school I want a wife to take care of my children. I want a wife to keep track of the children's doctor and dentist appointments. And to keep track of mine, too. I want a wife to make sure my children eat properly and are kept clean. I want a wife who will wash the children's clothes and keep them mended. I want a wife who is a good nurturant attendant to my children, who arranges for their schooling, makes sure that they have an adequate social life with their peers, takes them to the park, the zoo, etc. I want a wife who takes care of the children when they are sick, a wife who arranges to be around when the children need special care, because, of course, I cannot miss classes at school. My wife must arrange to lose time at work and not lose the job. It may mean a small cut in my wife's income from time to time, but I guess I can tolerate that. Needless to say, my wife will arrange and pay for the care of the children while my wife is working.

I want a wife who will take care of *my* physical needs. I want a wife who will keep my house clean. A wife who will pick up after me. I want a wife who will keep my clothes clean, ironed, mended, replaced when need be, and who will see to it that my personal things are kept in their proper place so that I can find what I need the minute I need it. I want a wife who cooks the meals, a wife who is a *good* cook. I want a wife who will plan the menus, do the necessary grocery shopping, prepare the meals, serve them pleasantly, and then do the cleaning up while I do my studying. I want a wife who will care for me when I am sick and sympathize with my pain and loss of time from school. I want a wife to go along when our family takes a vacation so that someone can continue to care for me and my children when I need a rest and change of scene.

I want a wife who will not bother me with rambling complaints 5 about a wife's duties. But I want a wife who will listen to me when I feel the need to explain a rather difficult point I have come across in my course of studies. And I want a wife who will type my papers for me when I have written them.

I want a wife who will take care of the details of my social life. When my wife and I are invited out by friends, I want a wife who will take care of the babysitting arrangements. When I meet people at school that I like and want to entertain, I want a wife who will have the house clean, will prepare a special meal, serve it to me and my friends, and not interrupt when I talk about the things that interest me and my friends. I want a wife who will have arranged that the children are fed and ready for bed before my guests arrive so that the children do not bother us. I want a wife who takes care of the needs of my guests so that they feel comfortable, who makes sure that they have an ashtray, that they are passed the hors d'oeuvres, that they are offered a second helping of the food, that their wine glasses are replenished when necessary, that their coffee is served to them as they like it. And I want a wife who knows that sometimes I need a night out by myself.

I want a wife who is sensitive to my sexual needs, a wife who makes love passionately and eagerly when I feel like it, a wife who makes sure that I am satisfied. And, of course, I want a wife who will not demand sexual attention when I am not in the mood for it. I want a wife who assumes the complete responsibility for birth control, because I do not want more children. I want a wife who will remain sexually faithful to me so that I do not have to clutter up my intellectual life with jealousies. And I want a wife who understands that *my* sexual needs may entail more than strict adherence to monogamy. I must, after all, be able to relate to people as fully as possible.

If, by chance, I find another person more suitable as a wife than the wife I already have, I want the liberty to replace my present wife with another one. Naturally, I will expect a fresh, new life; my wife will take the children and be solely responsible for them so that I am left free.

When I am through with school and have a job, I want my wife to quit working and remain at home so that my wife can more fully and completely take care of a wife's duties.

My God, who *wouldn't* want a wife?   10

Responding to Reading

1. Why does Brady begin her essay by saying that she is both a wife and a mother? How does her encounter with a male friend lead her to decide that she would like to have a wife?
2. This essay, written nearly thirty years ago, has been anthologized many times. To what do you attribute its continued popularity? In what ways, if any, is the essay dated? In what ways is it still relevant?
3. Brady wrote her essay to address a stereotype and a set of social conventions that she thought were harmful to women. Could you make the case that Brady's characterization of a "wife" is harmful both to women and to feminism?

Responding in Writing

What is your definition of a wife? How is it different from Brady's?

STAY-AT-HOME DADS

Glenn Sacks

1964–

Glenn Sacks is a columnist who writes about men's and fathers' issues and hosts the radio talk show "His Side" in Los Angeles. Sacks earned a Bachelor's degree in English from the University of Oregon (1986) and a Master's degree in Latin American Studies from UCLA (1999). His columns have appeared in the Chicago Tribune, *the* Los Angeles Times, Newsday, *the* Philadelphia Inquirer, Insight Magazine, *and other publications. Before embarking on a career as a columnist and radio personality, Sacks taught high school, elementary school, and adult education courses in Los Angeles and Miami. To read more of Sacks's columns, visit his Web site, http://www.glennsacks.com/.*

The subtext to the wave of concern over the recently announced epidemic of childlessness in successful career women is that women can't have it all after all—and it's men's fault. Why? Because men interfere with their wives' career aspirations by their refusal to become their children's primary caregivers, forcing women to sidetrack their careers if they want children.

Despite the criticism, men generally focus on their careers not out of selfishness but because most women still expect men to be their family's primary breadwinners. For women willing to shoulder this burden themselves, replacing the two-earner couple with a female breadwinner and a stay-at-home dad (SAHD) can be an attractive option. I became a SAHD with the birth of my daughter four years ago, and the arrangement has benefited my family immensely.

My wife and I sometimes remark that if we had met in the era before women had real career opportunities, we'd both be pretty unhappy. As a lone breadwinner I would feel deprived of time with my children. My wife, an ambitious woman who loves her career, would feel stifled as a stay-at-home mom. Since each of us would want to be doing what the other is doing, we would probably resent each other. Instead, the freedom to switch gender roles has allowed each of us to gravitate towards what we really want in life.

Men need not fear a loss of power when they become a SAHD. While SAHDs are sometimes stereotyped as being at the mercy of their stronger wives' commands, in reality, I have more power in the family now than I ever did when I was the family breadwinner. The most important issue in any marriage is deciding how to raise the children. While my wife is an equal partner in any major decision regarding the children, I supervise the children on a day to day basis and I make sure that things are done the way I want them done.

Women also benefit from SAHDs because, with reduced familial 5 responsibilities, they can compete on a level playing field with career-oriented men. For men, it is an opportunity to witness the countless magical, irreplaceable moments of a young child's life, and to enjoy some of the subtle pleasures our fathers never knew, like making dinner with a three year-old's "help," or putting the baby down for a midday nap in a hammock.

Still, there are adjustments that both men and women will need to make. Women will need to discard the popular yet misguided notion that men "have it all," and understand that being the breadwinner comes with disadvantages as well as advantages.

One disadvantage can be the loss of their primary status with their young children. Mom is #1 not because of biology or God's law but because mom is the one who does most of the child care. This can change when dad becomes the primary caregiver. When my young daughter has a nightmare and cries at 2 AM, my wife is relieved that she's not the one who has to get up and comfort her. The price that my wife has had to accept is that her child insists on being comforted not by her but by "yaddy."

Another disadvantage is that taking on the main breadwinner role reduces a woman's ability to cut back her work schedule or look for a more rewarding job if her career disappoints her. This is one of the reasons many women prefer life as a frazzled two-earner couple—keeping the man on career track as the main breadwinner helps to preserve women's options.

Men will also have to make adjustments. For one, they will have to endure the unconscious hypocrisy of a society which often wrings its hands over the lot of the housewife yet at the same time views SAHDs as freeloaders who have left their working wives holding the bag.

10   SAHDs also have to contend with the societal perception that being a househusband is unmanly. The idea is so pervasive that even I still tend to think "wimp" when I first hear about a SAHD.

Working women sometimes complain that men in the workplace don't take them as seriously as they take men. As a SAHD I have the same complaint. For example, last year I attended a school meeting with my wife, my son's elementary school teacher, and some school officials, most of whom knew that I drove my son to and from school, met with his teachers, and did his spelling words with him every day. Yet the woman who chaired the meeting introduced herself to my wife, began the meeting, and then, only as an afterthought, looked at me and said "and who might you be?"

In addition, while many stay-at-home parents face boredom and social isolation, it can be particularly acute for SAHDs, since there are few other men at home, and connections with stay-at-home moms can be difficult to cultivate.

None of these hurdles are insurmountable, and they pale in comparison to the benefits children derive from having a parent as a primary caregiver—particularly a parent grateful for the once-in-a-lifetime opportunity that he never knew he wanted, and never thought he would have.

Responding to Reading

1. According to Sacks, what is the "subtext to the wave of concern over the recently announced epidemic of childlessness in successful career women" (1)? Why does he think most men concentrate on their careers? What does he think is a good alternative to this situation?
2. What are the advantages of being a stay-at-home dad? What does Sacks see as the disadvantages? How practical do you think Sacks's solution is?
3. Could you make the argument that Sacks and his wife are simply switching traditional male/female roles? Are there any other models for work and childcare that Sacks and his wife could use? Do any of these seem preferable to the one they currently employ?

Responding in Writing

Would you want your husband to be (or would you want to be) a stay-at-home dad? Why or why not?

TITLE IX: GENDER EQUALITY
IN COLLEGE SPORTS

Robyn E. Blumner
1961–

Robyn E. Blumner, a syndicated columnist and reporter for the Saint
Petersburg Times, *specializes in writing from the perspective of a civil libertarian, analyzing current events and social trends based on how they affect the
individual rights guaranteed by the US Constitution. Blumner, who is a native
of Bayside, New York, challenges readers to think about the constitutionality of
entitlements, such as Title IX, which is discussed in the following essay. To read
more of Blumner's columns, visit the* Saint Petersburg Times *Web site,
http://www.sptimes.com/columns/blumner.shtml.*

Thanks to the way it's been enforced, Title IX, the 1972 law pro-
hibiting sex discrimination in education—including college athletics
programs—has turned college athletic directors into bean counters.
Rather than worry about the quality of their programs, they are busy
making sure they have enough players with the right chromosomes.

The University of Wisconsin at Madison is a prime example. After
a complaint was filed against the university in the 1980s, charging
that women athletes at the school were being shortchanged, bureaucrats from the Office for Civil Rights in the Department of Education
swooped in and aggressively nit-picked the UW program.

When the school in 2000 had successfully recruited enough female athletes onto sports teams, and pared down enough men's
sports so the ratio of male to female athletes was nearly even—there
were 425 women athletes and 429 men—federal regulators said the effort still fell short. Because the student body was 53 percent female,
said OCR in a letter, the school would have to add another 25 women
in order to be viewed as in compliance with the law.

Steve Malchow, assistant athletic director for communications at
the University of Wisconsin at Madison, said in order to keep the regulators happy, his department is deeply involved in "roster management." "We are constantly trying to manipulate numbers to reach
equity," Malchow said. The school does so by keeping women's
teams as full as possible and turning away men looking for walk-on
opportunities.

It is this kind of experience repeated in athletic programs at col-   5
leges and universities around the country that has led to a call for
change. In the hands of zealous government bureaucrats, Title IX has
been transformed from a needed tool to open opportunities for
women in college athletics to a rigidly applied formula that uses the

radical feminist pipe dream that men and women have an equal interest in athletic competition, as the basis for law.

It wasn't supposed to be this way. According to Department of Education guidelines, there are three ways to demonstrate compliance with Title IX: Show that the number of female athletes is substantially proportional to the number of female undergraduates; that athletic opportunities for women are being steadily increased over time; or that the school is meeting the athletic interests of female students.

But schools have learned through hard experience that meeting the proportionality test is the only "safe harbor" and, according to Jessica Gavora, a senior policy adviser at the U.S. Department of Justice and author of the book *Tilting the Playing Field: Schools, Sports, Sex and Title IX*, the courts have supported this view.

Gavora points to a 1996 case involving Brown University, which was sued after it attempted to demote two women's varsity teams, the gymnastics and volleyball teams, from university-funded to donor-funded. It didn't matter that the school also demoted the men's water polo and golf teams. According to Gavora, at the time Brown was sued, its women's athletics program was the second most generous in the country. Yet the university still lost because it had a 13 percent disparity between female athletes and female student enrollment. Gavora said the ruling broadcast that "proportionality is the only means of compliance with Title IX."

While girls' interest in sports has exploded, partly thanks to the impact of Title IX, girls are still not as interested as are boys. These lingering gender tendencies may be due to biology or culture, but either way they are real. To say women must be represented on sports teams relative to their presence in the student body is social engineering.

10   For many schools, reaching proportionality has meant dumping men's sports (though clearly some of the thinning has been done for budgetary reasons). The non-revenue generating sports, where there are no corresponding women's teams, have been hit hardest.

According to the National Wrestling Coaches Association, hundreds of wrestling teams have been cut as a direct and indirect application of Title IX. Out of desperation, the association has sued the Department of Education, alleging that the way the law is being enforced discriminates against males. The federal lawsuit includes the experiences of wrestling programs such as that at Marquette University, where the wrestling team was disbanded even though it was fully funded by private donations. The team's continued existence would have thrown the university's Title IX numbers out of whack.

The problem for men's shrinking opportunities is exacerbated because OCR counts only actual participants. If a women's basketball team offers 14 roster spots but only 11 women join, the school only gets credit for 11 players. So, for every women who is too uninterested in sports to show up, another motivated male athlete has to be shown the door.

Let's hope some sanity will come soon. A special commission constituted by Secretary of Education Roderick Paige has been studying this problem since June. Its recommendations are expected by the end of next month. Hopefully, one of them will be to banish proportionality as a test of Title IX compliance. Then universities would no longer have to worry about being penalized for having an extra man on the field.

Responding to Reading

1. What problem does Blumner see with the way Title IX is being enforced? Why does she think that this situation violates the intent of the law? What effect has this type of enforcement had on Title IX?
2. According to Department of Education guidelines, how are schools supposed to demonstrate compliance with Title IX? What is the "proportionality test"? Why is it the only "'safe harbor'" (7)? According to Blumner, what is the problem with the "proportionality test"?
3. How have schools attempted to reach proportionality? How have these actions affected men's teams? What does Blumner think the schools should do differently?

Responding in Writing

Do you think your college or university's sports programs offer equal opportunities to men and women?

SEXISM IN ENGLISH:
EMBODIMENT AND LANGUAGE
Alleen Pace Nilsen
1936–

A native of Phoenix, Arizona, Alleen Pace Nilsen is an educator and essayist who earned a BA degree from Brigham Young University (1958), an MEd degree from American University (1961), and a PhD from the University of Iowa (1973). Currently, she lives in Tempe, Arizona, and teaches English at Arizona State University. Her most recent book, coauthored with her husband, is the Encyclopedia of 20th-Century American Humor *(2000). When Nilsen lived in Afghanistan, she observed the subordinate position of women in that society. When she returned to the United States, she studied American English for its cultural biases toward men and women. Nilsen says of that project, "As I worked my way through the dictionary, I concentrated on the way particular usages, metaphors, slang terms, and*

*definitions reveal society's attitude toward males and females." The following
essay is an updated version of Nilsen's findings from her dictionary study.*

During the late 1960s, I lived with my husband and three young
children in Kabul, Afghanistan. This was before the Russian invasion,
the Afghan civil war, and the eventual taking over of the country by
the Taleban Islamic movement and its resolve to return the country to
a strict Islamic dynasty, in which females are not allowed to attend
school or work outside their homes.

But even when we were there and the country was considered
moderate rather than extremist, I was shocked to observe how different were the roles assigned to males and females. The Afghan version
of the *chaderi*[1] prescribed by Moslem women was particularly confining. Women in religious families were required to wear it whenever
they were outside their family home, with the result being that most
of them didn't venture outside.

The household help we hired were made up of men, because
women could not be employed by foreigners. Afghan folk stories and
jokes were blatantly sexist, as in this proverb: "If you see an old man,
sit down and take a lesson; if you see an old woman, throw a stone."

But it wasn't only the native culture that made me question women's roles, it was also the American community within Afghanistan.

5   Most of the American women were like myself—wives and mothers whose husbands were either career diplomats, employees of
USAID, or college professors who had been recruited to work on various contract teams. We were suddenly bereft of our traditional roles:
The local economy provided few jobs for women and certainly none
for foreigners; we were isolated from former friends and the social
goals we had grown up with. Some of us became alcoholics, others
got very good at bridge, while still others searched desperately for
ways to contribute either to our families or to the Afghans.

When we returned in the fall of 1969 to the University of Michigan
in Ann Arbor, I was surprised to find that many other women were
also questioning the expectations they had grown up with. Since I had
been an English major when I was in college, I decided that for my
part in the feminist movement I would study the English language
and see what it could tell me about sexism. I started reading a desk
dictionary and making note cards on every entry that seemed to tell
something different about male and female. I soon had a dog-eared
dictionary, along with a collection of note cards filling two shoe boxes.

The first thing I learned was that I couldn't study the language
without getting involved in social issues. Language and society are as
intertwined as a chicken and an egg. The language a culture uses is

---

[1]A *chaderi* is a heavily draped cloth covering the entire head and body. [Eds.]

telltale evidence of the values and beliefs of that culture. And because there is a lag in how fast a language changes—new words can easily be introduced, but it takes a long time for old words and usages to disappear—a careful look at English will reveal the attitudes that our ancestors held and that we as a culture are therefore predisposed to hold. My note cards revealed three main points. While friends have offered the opinion that I didn't need to read a dictionary to learn such obvious facts, the linguistic evidence lends credibility to the sociological observations.

Women Are Sexy: Men Are Successful

First, in American culture a woman is valued for the attractiveness and sexiness of her body, while a man is valued for his physical strength and accomplishments. A woman is sexy. A man is successful.

A persuasive piece of evidence supporting this view are the eponyms—words that have come from someone's name—found in English. I had a two-and-a-half-inch stack of cards taken from men's names but less than a half-inch stack from women's names, and most of those came from Greek mythology. In the words that came into American English since we separated from Britain, there are many eponyms based on the names of famous American men: Bartlett pear, boysenberry, Franklin stove, Ferris wheel, Gatling gun, mason jar, sideburns, sousaphone, Schick test, and Winchester rifle. The only common eponyms that I found taken from American women's names are Alice blue (after Alice Roosevelt Longworth), bloomers (after Amelia Jenks Bloomer), and Mae West jacket (after the buxom actress). Two out of the three feminine eponyms relate closely to a woman's physical anatomy, while the masculine eponyms (except for "sideburns" after General Burnsides) have nothing to do with the namesake's body, but, instead, honor the man for an accomplishment of some kind.

In Greek mythology women played a bigger role than they did in 10 the biblical stories of the Judeo-Christian cultures, and so the names of goddesses are accepted parts of the language in such place names as Pomona, from the goddess of fruit, and Athens, from Athena, and in such common words as *cereal* from Ceres, *psychology* from Psyche, and *arachnoid* from Arachne. However, there is the same tendency to think of women in relation to sexuality as shown through the eponyms *aphrodisiac* from Aphrodite, the Greek name for the goddess of love and beauty, and *venereal disease* from Venus, the Roman name for Aphrodite.

Another interesting word from Greek mythology is *Amazon*. According to Greek folk etymology, the *a-* means "without," as in *atypical* or *amoral*, while *-mazon* comes from *mazos*, meaning "breast," as still seen in *mastectomy*. In the Greek legend, Amazon women cut off their right breasts so they could better shoot their bows. Apparently, the storytellers had a feeling that for women to play the active, "masculine" role the Amazons adopted for themselves, they had to trade in part of their femininity.

This preoccupation with women's breasts is not limited to the Greeks; it's what inspired the definition and the name for "mammals" (from Indo-European *mammae* for "breasts"). As a volunteer for the University of Wisconsin's *Dictionary of American Regional English (DARE)*, I read a western trapper's diary from the 1830s. I was to make notes of any unusual usages or language patterns. My most interesting finding was that the trapper referred to a range of mountains as "The Teats," a metaphor based on the similarity between the shapes of the mountains and women's breasts. Because today we use the French wording "The Grand Tetons," the metaphor isn't as obvious, but I wrote to mapmakers and found the following listings: Nipple Top and Little Nipple Top near Mount Marcy in the Adirondacks; Nipple Mountain in Archuleta County, Colorado; Nipple Peak in Coke County, Texas; Nipple Butte in Pennington, South Dakota; Squaw Peak in Placer County, California (and many other locations); Maiden's Peak and Squaw Tit (they're the same mountain) in the Cascade Range in Oregon; Mary's Nipple near Salt Lake City, Utah; and Jane Russell Peaks near Stark, New Hampshire.

Except for the movie star Jane Russell, the women being referred to are anonymous—it's only a sexual part of their body that is mentioned. When topographical features are named after men, it's probably not going to be to draw attention to a sexual part of their bodies but instead to honor individuals for an accomplishment.

Going back to what I learned from my dictionary cards, I was surprised to realize how many pairs of words we have in which the feminine word has acquired sexual connotations while the masculine word retains a serious businesslike aura. For example, a callboy is the person who calls actors when it is time for them to go on stage, but a callgirl is a prostitute. Compare sir and madam. *Sir* is a term of respect, while *madam* has acquired the specialized meaning of a brothel manager. Something similar has happened to master and mistress. Would you rather have a painting "by an old master" or "by an old mistress"?

15   It's because the word *woman* had sexual connotations, as in "She's his woman," that people began avoiding its use, hence such terminology as ladies' room, lady of the house, and girl's school or school for young ladies. Those of us who in the 1970s began asking that speakers use the term *woman* rather than *girl* or *lady* were rejecting the idea that *woman* is primarily a sexual term.

I found two-hundred pairs of words with masculine and feminine forms; for example, *heir/heiress, hero/heroine, steward/stewardess, usher/usherette*. In nearly all such pairs, the masculine word is considered the base, with some kind of a feminine suffix being added. The masculine form is the one from which compounds are made; for example, from king/queen comes kingdom but not queendom, from sportsman/ sportslady comes sportsmanship but not sportsladyship. There is one—and only one—semantic area in which the masculine word is not the base or more powerful word. This is in the area dealing with sex, marriage, and motherhood. When someone refers to a virgin, a listener will probably think of a female unless the speaker specifies male or uses a masculine pronoun. The same is true for prostitute.

In relation to marriage, linguistic evidence shows that weddings are more important to women than to men. A woman cherishes the wedding and is considered a bride for a whole year, but a man is referred to as a groom only on the day of the wedding. The word *bride* appears in *bridal attendant, bridal gown, bridesmaid, bridal shower,* and even *bridegroom. Groom* comes from the Middle English *grom,* meaning "man," and in that sense is seldom used outside of the wedding. With most pairs of male/female words, people habitually put the masculine word first: *Mr. and Mrs., his and hers, boys and girls, men and women, kings and queens, brothers and sisters, guys and dolls, and host and hostess.* But it is the bride and groom who are talked about, not the groom and bride.

The importance of marriage to a woman is also shown by the fact that when a marriage ends in death, the woman gets the title of widow. A man gets the derived title of widower. This term is not used in other phrases or contexts, but widow is seen in widowhood, widow's peak, and widow's walk. A widow in a card game is an extra hand of cards, while in typesetting it is a leftover line of type.

Changing cultural ideas bring changes to language, and since I did my dictionary study three decades ago the word *singles* has largely replaced such gender-specific and value-laden terms as *bachelor, old maid, spinster, divorcee, widow,* and *widower.* In 1970 I wrote that when people hear a man called "a professional," they usually think of him as a doctor or a lawyer, but when people hear a woman referred to as "a professional," they are likely to think of her as a prostitute. That's not as true today because so many women have become doctors and lawyers, it's no longer incongruous to think of women in those professional roles.

Another change that has taken place is in wedding announce- 20 ments. They used to be sent out from the bride's parents and did not even give the name of the groom's parents. Today, most couples choose to list either all or none of the parents' names. Also it is now much more likely that both the bride and groom's picture will be in the newspaper, while twenty years ago only the bride's picture was published on the "Women's" or the "Society" page. In the weddings I have recently attended, the official has pronounced the couple "husband and wife" instead of the traditional "man and wife," and the bride has been asked if she promises to "love, honor, and cherish," instead of to "love, honor, and obey."

Women Are Passive; Men Are Active

However, other wording in the wedding ceremony relates to a second point that my cards showed, which is that women are expected to play a passive or weak role while men play an active or strong role. In the traditional ceremony, the official asks, "Who gives the bride away?" and the father answers, "I do." Some fathers answer, "Her mother and I do," but that doesn't solve the problem inherent in the question. The idea that a bride is something to be handed over from one man to another bothers people because it goes back to the days when a man's servants, his children, and his wife were all considered to be his property. They were known by his name because they belonged to him, and he was responsible for their actions and their debts.

The grammar used in talking or writing about weddings as well as other sexual relationships shows the expectation of men playing the active role. Men *wed* women while women *become* brides of men. A man *possesses* a woman; he *deflowers* her; he *performs*; he *scores*; he *takes away* her virginity. Although a woman can *seduce* a man, she cannot offer him her virginity. When talking about virginity, the only way to make the woman the actor in the sentence is to say that "she lost her virginity," but people lose things by accident rather than by purposeful actions, and so she's only the grammatical, not the real-life, actor.

The reason that women brought the term Ms. into the language to replace Miss and Mrs. relates to this point. Many married women resent being identified in the "Mrs. Husband" form. The dictionary cards showed what appeared to be an attitude on the part of the editors that it was almost indecent to let a respectable woman's name march unaccompanied across the pages of a dictionary. Women were listed with male names whether or not the male contributed to the woman's reason for being in the dictionary or whether or not in his own right he was as famous as the woman. For example:

> Charlotte Brontë = Mrs. Arthur B. Nicholls
> Amelia Earhart = Mrs. George Palmer Putnam
> Helen Hayes = Mrs. Charles MacArthur
> Jenny Lind = Mme. Otto Goldschmit
> Cornelia Otis Skinner = daughter of Otis
> Harriet Beecher Stowe = sister of Henry Ward Beecher
> Dame Edith Sitwell = sister of Osbert and Sacheverell[2]

Only a small number of rebels and crusaders got into the dictionary without the benefit of a masculine escort: temperance leaders Frances

---

[2]Charlotte Brontë (1816–1855), author of *Jane Eyre*; Amelia Earhart (1898–1937), first woman to fly over the Atlantic; Helen Hayes (1900–1993), actress; Jenny Lind (1820–1887), Swedish soprano; Cornelia Otis Skinner (1901–1979), actress and writer; Harriet Beecher Stowe (1811–1896), author of *Uncle Tom's Cabin*; Edith Sitwell (1877–1964), English poet and critic. [Eds.]

Elizabeth Caroline Willard and Carry Nation, women's rights leaders Carrie Chapman Catt and Elizabeth Cady Stanton, birth control educator Margaret Sanger, religious leader Mary Baker Eddy, and slaves Harriet Tubman and Phillis Wheatley.

Etiquette books used to teach that if a woman had Mrs. in front of her name, then the husband's name should follow because Mrs. is an abbreviated form of Mistress and a woman couldn't be a mistress of herself. As with many arguments about "correct" language usage, this isn't very logical because Miss is also an abbreviation of Mistress. Feminists hoped to simplify matters by introducing Ms. as an alternative to both Mrs. and Miss, but what happened is that Ms. largely replaced Miss to become a catch-all business title for women. Many married women still prefer the title Mrs., and some even resent being addressed with the term Ms. As one frustrated newspaper reporter complained, "Before I can write about a woman I have to know not only her marital status but also her political philosophy." The result of such complications may contribute to the demise of titles, which are already being ignored by many writers who find it more efficient to simply use names; for example, in a business letter: "Dear Joan Garcia," instead of "Dear Mrs. Joan Garcia," "Dear Ms. Garcia," or "Dear Mrs. Louis Garcia."

Titles given to royalty show how males can be disadvantaged by 25 the assumption that they always play the more powerful role. In British royalty, when a male holds a title, his wife is automatically given the feminine equivalent. But the reverse is not true. For example, a count is a high political officer with a countess being his wife. The same pattern holds true for a duke and a duchess and a king and a queen. But when a female holds the royal title, the man she marries does not automatically acquire the matching title. For example, Queen Elizabeth's husband has the title of prince rather than king, but when Prince Charles married Diana, she became Princess Diana. If they had stayed married and he had ascended to the throne, then she would have become Queen Diana. The reasoning appears to be that since masculine words are stronger, they are reserved for true heirs and withheld from males coming into the royal family by marriage. If Prince Phillip were called "King Phillip," British subjects might forget who had inherited the right to rule.

The names that people give their children show the hopes and dreams they have for them, and when we look at the differences between male and female names in a culture, we can see the cumulative expectations of that culture. In our culture girls often have names taken from small, aesthetically pleasing items; for example, Ruby, Jewel, and Pearl. Esther and Stella mean "star," and Ada means "ornament." One of the few women's names that refers to strength is Mildred, and it means "mild strength." Boys often have names with meanings of power and strength; for example, Neil means "champion"; Martin is from Mars, the God of war; Raymond means "wise protection"; Harold means "chief of the army"; Ira means "vigilant"; Rex means "king"; and Richard means "strong king."

We see similar differences in food metaphors. Food is a passive substance just sitting there waiting to be eaten. Many people have recognized this and so no longer feel comfortable describing women as "delectable morsels." However, when I was a teenager, it was considered a compliment to refer to a girl (we didn't call anyone a "woman" until she was middle-aged) as a cute tomato, a peach, a dish, a cookie, honey, sugar, or sweetie-pie. When being affectionate, women will occasionally call a man honey or sweetie, but in general, food metaphors are used much less often with men than with women. If a man is called "a fruit," his masculinity is being questioned. But it's perfectly acceptable to use a food metaphor if the food is heavier and more substantive than that used for women. For example, pin-up pictures of women have long been known as "cheesecake," but when Burt Reynolds posed for a nude centerfold the picture was immediately dubbed "beefcake," that is, a hunk of meat. That such sexual references to men have come into the language is another reflection of how society is beginning to lessen the differences between their attitudes toward men and women.

Something similar to the fruit metaphor happens with references to plants. We insult a man by calling him a "pansy," but it wasn't considered particularly insulting to talk about a girl being a wallflower, a clinging vine, or a shrinking violet, or to give girls such names as Ivy, Rose, Lily, Iris, Daisy, Camelia, Heather, and Flora. A positive plant metaphor can be used with a man only if the plant is big and strong; for example, Andrew Jackson's nickname of Old Hickory. Also, the phrases *blooming idiots* and *budding geniuses* can be used with either sex, but notice how they are based on the most active thing a plant can do, which is to bloom or bud.

Animal metaphors also illustrate the different expectations for males and females. Men are referred to as studs, bucks, and wolves, while women are referred to with such metaphors as kitten, bunny, beaver, bird, chick, and lamb. In the 1950s, we said that boys went "tom catting," but today it's just "catting around," and both boys and girls do it. When the term foxy, meaning that someone was sexy, first became popular it was used only for females, but now someone of either sex can be described as a fox. Some animal metaphors that are used predominantly with men have negative connotations based on the size and/or strength of the animals; for example, beast, bullheaded, jackass, rat, loanshark, and vulture. Negative metaphors used with women are based on smaller animals; for example, social butterfly, mousey, catty, and vixen. The feminine terms connote action, but not the same kind of large scale action as with the masculine terms.

Women Are Connected with Negative Connotations; Men with Positve Connotations

The final point that my note cards illustrated was how many positive 30 connotations are associated with the concept of masculinity, while there are either trivial or negative connotations connected with the corresponding feminine concept. An example from the animal metaphors makes a good illustration. The word *shrew* taken from the name of a small but especially vicious animal was defined in my dictionary as "an ill-tempered scolding woman," but the word *shrewd* taken from the same root was defined as "marked by clever, discerning awareness" and was illustrated with the phrase "a shrewd businessman."

Early in life, children are conditioned to the superiority of the masculine role. As child psychologists point out, little girls have much more freedom to experiment with sex roles than do little boys. If a little girl acts like a tomboy, most parents have mixed feelings, being at least partially proud. But if their little boy acts like a sissy (derived from *sister*), they call a psychologist. It's perfectly acceptable for a little girl to sleep in the crib that was purchased for her brother, to wear his hand-me-down jeans and shirts, and to ride the bicycle that he has outgrown. But few parents would put a boy baby in a white-and-gold crib decorated with frills and lace, and virtually no parents would have their little boy wear his sister's hand-me-down dresses, nor would they have their son ride a girl's pink bicycle with a flower-bedecked basket. The proper names given to girls and boys show this same attitude. Girls can have "boy" names—Cris, Craig, Jo, Kelly, Shawn, Teri, Toni, and Sam—but it doesn't work the other way around. A couple of generations ago, Beverly, Frances, Hazel, Marion, and Shirley were common boys' names. As parents gave these names to more and more girls, they fell into disuse for males, and some older men who have these names prefer to go by their initials or by such abbreviated forms as Haze or Shirl.

When a little girl is told to be a lady, she is being told to sit with her knees together and to be quiet and dainty. But when a little boy is told to be a man, he is being told to be noble, strong, and virtuous—to have all the qualities that the speaker looks on as desirable. The concept of manliness has such positive connotations that it used to be a compliment to call someone a he-man, to say that he was doubly a man. Today many people are more ambivalent about this term and respond to it much as they do to the word *macho*. But calling someone a manly man or a virile man is nearly always meant as a compliment. Virile comes from the Indo-European *vir*, meaning "man," which is also the basis of *virtuous*. Consider the positive connotations of both virile and virtuous with the negative connotations of *hysterical*. The Greeks took this latter word from their name for uterus (as still seen in *hysterectomy*). They thought that women were the only ones who experienced uncontrolled emotional outbursts, and so the condition must have something to do with a part of the body that only women have. But how word meanings change is regularly shown at athletic events where thousands of *virtuous* women sit quietly beside their *hysterical* husbands.

Differences in the connotations between positive male and negative female connotations can be seen in several pairs of words that differ denotatively only in the matter of sex. Bachelor as compared to spinster or old maid has such positive connotations that women try to adopt it by using the term *bachelor-girl* or *bachelorette*. Old maid is so negative that it's the basis for metaphors: pretentious and fussy old men are called "old maids," as are the leftover kernels of unpopped popcorn and the last card in a popular children's card game.

Patron and *matron* (Middle English for "father" and "mother") have such different levels of prestige that women try to borrow the more positive masculine connotations with the word *patroness*, literally "female father." Such a peculiar term came about because of the high prestige attached to patron in such phrases as a *patron of the arts* or a *patron saint*. Matron is more apt to be used in talking about a woman in charge of a jail or a public restroom.

35   When men are doing jobs that women often do, we apparently try to pay the men extra by giving them fancy titles. For example, a male cook is more likely to be called a "chef" while a male seamstress will get the title of "tailor." The armed forces have a special problem in that they recruit under such slogans as "The Marine Corps builds men!" and "Join the Army! Become a Man." Once the recruits are enlisted, they find themselves doing much of the work that has been traditionally thought of as "women's work." The solution to getting the work done and not insulting anyone's masculinity was to change the titles as shown below:

> waitress = orderly
> nurse = medic or corpsman
> secretary = clerk-typist
> assistant = adjutant
> dishwasher = KP (kitchen police) or kitchen helper

Compare *brave* and *squaw*. Early settlers in America truly admired Indian men and hence named them with a word that carried connotations of youth, vigor, and courage. But for Indian women they used an Algonquin slang term with negative sexual connotations that are almost opposite to those of brave. Wizard and witch contrast almost as much. The masculine *wizard* implies skill and wisdom combined with magic, while the feminine *witch* implies evil intentions combined with magic. When witch is used for men, as in witch-doctor, many mainstream speakers feel some carry-over of the negative connotations.

Part of the unattractiveness of both witch and squaw is that they have been used so often to refer to old women, something with which our culture is particularly uncomfortable, just as the Afghans were. Imagine my surprise when I ran across the phrases *grandfatherly advice* and *old wives' tales* and realized that the underlying implication is the same as the Afghan proverb about old men being worth listening to while old women talk only foolishness.

Other terms that show how negatively we view old women as compared to young women are *old nag* as compared to *filly, old crow* or *old bat* as compared to *bird,* and being *catty* as compared to being *kittenish.* There is no matching set of metaphors for men. The chicken metaphor tells the whole story of a woman's life. In her youth she is a chick. Then she marries and begins feathering her nest. Soon she begins feeling cooped up, so she goes to hen parties where she cackles with her friends. Then she has her brood, begins to henpeck her husband, and finally turns into an old biddy.

I embarked on my study of the dictionary not with the intention of prescribing language change but simply to see what the language would tell me about sexism. Nevertheless, I have been both surprised and pleased as I've watched the changes that have occurred over the past three decades. I'm one of those linguists who believes that new language customs will cause a new generation of speakers to grow up with different expectations. This is why I'm happy about people's efforts to use inclusive languages, to say "he or she" or "they" when speaking about individuals whose names they do not know. I'm glad that leading publishers have developed guidelines to help writers use language that is fair to both sexes. I'm glad that most newspapers and magazines list women by their own names instead of only by their husbands' names. And I'm so glad that educated and thoughtful people no longer begin their business letters with "Dear Sir" or "Gentlemen," but instead use a memo form or begin with such salutations as "Dear Colleagues," "Dear Reader," or "Dear Committee Members." I'm also glad that such words as *poetess, authoress, conductress,* and *aviatrix* now sound quaint and old-fashioned and that *chairman* is giving way to *chair* or *head, mailman* to *mail carrier, clergyman* to *clergy,* and *stewardess* to *flight attendant.* I was also pleased when the National Oceanic and Atmospheric Administration bowed to feminist complaints and in the late 1970s began to alternate men's and women's names for hurricanes. However, I wasn't so pleased to discover that the change did not immediately erase sexist thoughts from everyone's mind, as shown by a headline about Hurricane David in a 1979 New York tabloid, "David Rapes Virgin Islands." More recently a similar metaphor appeared in a headline in the *Arizona Republic* about Hurricane Charlie, "Charlie Quits Carolinas, Flirts with Virginia."

40   What these incidents show is that sexism is not something existing independently in American English or in the particular dictionary that I happened to read. Rather, it exists in people's minds. Language is like an X-ray in providing visible evidence of invisible thoughts. The best thing about people being interested in and discussing sexist language is that as they make conscious decisions about what pronouns they will use, what jokes they will tell or laugh at, how they will write their names, or how they will begin their letters, they are forced to think about the underlying issue of sexism. This is good because as a problem that begins in people's assumptions and expectations, it's a problem that will be solved only when a great many people have given it a great deal of thought.

Responding to Reading

1. What point is Nilsen making about American culture? Does your experience support her conclusions?
2. Does Nilsen use enough examples to support her claims? What others can you think of? In what way do her examples—and your own—illustrate the power of language to define the way people think?
3. Many of the connotations of the words Nilsen discusses are hundreds of years old and are also found in languages other than English. Given these widespread and long-standing linguistic patterns, do you think attempts by Nilsen and others to change this situation can succeed?

Responding in Writing

List some words and phrases that you routinely use that reinforce the stereotypes Nilsen discusses. What alternatives could you employ? What would be gained and lost if you used these alternatives?

MARKED WOMEN

Deborah Tannen

1945–

Deborah Tannen lives in Washington, DC, where she is a professor of linguistics at Georgetown University. A native of Brooklyn, New York, Tannen earned a BA degree from the State University of New York at Binghamton (1966) and an MA degree in English literature from Wayne State University (1970) and then began studying linguistics at the University of California, Berkeley, where she earned a PhD (1979). She has written books for both scholarly and popular audiences, with most of her work focusing on commu-

nication between men and women. Tannen is best known for her bestseller You Just Don't Understand: Women and Men in Conversation *(1990); her most recent book is* I Only Say This Because I Love You: How the Way We Talk Can Make or Break Family Relationships throughout Our Lives *(2001). The following essay, written in 1993, is something of a departure from Tannen's usual work. Here she focuses not on different communication styles but on the striking contrast she finds between the neutral way men in our culture present themselves to the world and the more message-laden way women present themselves. To read more about Tannen, visit her Web site, http://www.georgetown.edu/faculty/tannend/index.htm/.*

Some years ago I was at a small working conference of four women and eight men. Instead of concentrating on the discussion I found myself looking at the three other women at the table, thinking how each had a different style and how each style was coherent.

One woman had dark brown hair in a classic style, a cross between Cleopatra and Plain Jane. The severity of her straight hair was softened by wavy bangs and ends that turned under. Because she was beautiful, the effect was more Cleopatra than plain.

The second woman was older, full of dignity and composure. Her hair was cut in a fashionable style that left her with only one eye, thanks to a side part that let a curtain of hair fall across half her face. As she looked down to read her prepared paper, the hair robbed her of bifocal vision and created a barrier between her and the listeners.

The third woman's hair was wild, a frosted blond avalanche falling over and beyond her shoulders. When she spoke she frequently tossed her head, calling attention to her hair and away from her lecture.

Then there was makeup. The first woman wore facial cover that made her skin smooth and pale, a black line under each eye and mascara that darkened already dark lashes. The second wore only a light gloss on her lips and a hint of shadow on her eyes. The third had blue bands under her eyes, dark blue shadow, mascara, bright red lipstick and rouge; her fingernails flashed red. 5

I considered the clothes each woman had worn during the three days of the conference: In the first case, man-tailored suits in primary colors with solid-color blouses. In the second, casual but stylish black T-shirts, a floppy collarless jacket and baggy slacks or a skirt in neutral colors. The third wore a sexy jump suit; tight sleeveless jersey and tight yellow slacks; a dress with gaping armholes and an indulged tendency to fall off one shoulder.

Shoes? No. 1 wore string sandals with medium heels; No. 2, sensible, comfortable walking shoes; No. 3, pumps with spike heels. You can fill in the jewelry, scarves, shawls, sweaters—or lack of them.

As I amused myself finding coherence in these styles, I suddenly wondered why I was scrutinizing only the women. I scanned the eight men at the table. And then I knew why I wasn't studying them. The men's styles were unmarked.

The term "marked" is a staple of linguistic theory. It refers to the way language alters the base meaning of a word by adding a linguistic particle that has no meaning on its own. The unmarked form of a word carries the meaning that goes without saying—what you think of when you're not thinking anything special.

10   The unmarked tense of verbs in English is the present—for example, *visit*. To indicate past, you mark the verb by adding *ed* to yield *visited*. For future, you add a word: *will visit*. Nouns are presumed to be singular until marked for plural, typically by adding *s* or *es*, so *visit* becomes *visits* and *dish* becomes *dishes*.

The unmarked forms of most English words also convey "male." Being male is the unmarked case. Endings like *ess* and *ette* mark words as "female." Unfortunately, they also tend to mark them for frivolousness. Would you feel safe entrusting your life to a doctorette? Alfre Woodard, who was an Oscar nominee for best supporting actress, says she identifies herself as an actor because "actresses worry about eyelashes and cellulite, and women who are actors worry about the characters we are playing." Gender markers pick up extra meanings that reflect common associations with the female gender: not quite serious, often sexual.

Each of the women at the conference had to make decisions about hair, clothing, makeup and accessories, and each decision carried meaning. Every style available to us was marked. The men in our group had made decisions, too, but the range from which they chose was incomparably narrower. Men can choose styles that are marked, but they don't have to, and in this group none did. Unlike the women, they had the option of being unmarked.

Take the men's hair styles. There was no marine crew cut or oily longish hair falling into eyes, no asymmetrical, two-tiered construction to swirl over a bald top. One man was unabashedly bald; the others had hair of standard length, parted on one side, in natural shades of brown or gray or graying. Their hair obstructed no views, left little to toss or push back or run fingers through and, consequently, needed and attracted no attention. A few men had beards. In a business setting, beards might be marked. In this academic gathering, they weren't.

There could have been a cowboy shirt with string tie or a three-piece suit or a necklaced hippie in jeans. But there wasn't. All eight men wore brown or blue slacks and nondescript shirts of light colors. No man wore sandals or boots; their shoes were dark, closed, comfortable and flat. In short, unmarked.

15   Although no man wore makeup, you couldn't say the men didn't wear makeup in the sense that you could say a woman didn't wear makeup. For men, no makeup is unmarked.

I asked myself what style we women could have adopted that would have been unmarked, like the men's. The answer was none. There is no unmarked woman.

There is no woman's hair style that can be called standard, that says nothing about her. The range of women's hair styles is staggering, but a woman whose hair has no particular style is perceived as not caring about how she looks, which can disqualify her for many positions, and will subtly diminish her as a person in the eyes of some.

Women must choose between attractive shoes and comfortable shoes. When our group made an unexpected trek, the woman who wore flat, laced shoes arrived first. Last to arrive was the woman in spike heels, shoes in hand and a handful of men around her.

If a woman's clothing is tight or revealing (in other words, sexy), it sends a message—an intended one of wanting to be attractive, but also a possibly unintended one of availability. If her clothes are not sexy, that too sends a message, lent meaning by the knowledge that they could have been. There are thousands of cosmetic products from which women can choose and myriad ways of applying them. Yet no makeup at all is anything but unmarked. Some men see it as a hostile refusal to please them.

Women can't even fill out a form without telling stories about   20 themselves. Most forms give four titles to choose from. "Mr." carries no meaning other than that the respondent is male. But a woman who checks "Mrs." or "Miss" communicates not only whether she has been married but also whether she has conservative tastes in forms of address—and probably other conservative values as well. Checking "Ms." declines to let on about marriage (checking "Mr." declines nothing since nothing was asked), but it also marks her as either liberated or rebellious, depending on the observer's attitudes and assumptions.

I sometimes try to duck these variously marked choices by giving my title as "Dr."—and in so doing risk marking myself as either uppity (hence sarcastic responses like *"Excuse me!"*) or an overachiever (hence reactions of congratulatory surprise like "Good for you!").

All married women's surnames are marked. If a woman takes her husband's name, she announces to the world that she is married and has traditional values. To some it will indicate that she is less herself, more identified by her husband's identity. If she does not take her husband's name, this too is marked, seen as worthy of comment: she has done something; she has "kept her own name." A man is never said to have "kept his own name" because it never occurs to anyone that he might have given it up. For him using his own name is unmarked.

A married woman who wants to have her cake and eat it too may use her surname plus his, with or without a hyphen. But this too announces her marital status and often results in a tongue-tying string. In a list (Harvey O'Donovan, Jonathan Feldman, Stephanie Woodbury McGillicutty), the woman's multiple name stands out. It is marked.

I have never been inclined toward biological explanations of gender differences in language, but I was intrigued to see Ralph Fasold bring biological phenomena to bear on the question of linguistic marking in his book "The Sociolinguistics of Language." Fasold stresses that language and culture are particularly unfair in treating women as the marked case because biologically it is the male that is marked. While two X chromosomes make a female, two Y chromosomes make nothing. Like the linguistic markers *s*, *es* or *ess*, the Y chromosome doesn't "mean" anything unless it is attached to a root form—an X chromosome.

25   Developing this idea elsewhere, Fasold points out that girls are born with fully female bodies, while boys are born with modified female bodies. He invites men who doubt this to lift up their shirts and contemplate why they have nipples.

In his book, Fasold notes "a wide range of facts which demonstrates that female is the unmarked sex." For example, he observes that there are a few species that produce only females, like the whiptail lizard. Thanks to parthenogenesis, they have no trouble having as many daughters as they like. There are no species, however, that produce only males. This is no surprise, since any such species would become extinct in its first generation.

Fasold is also intrigued by species that produce individuals not involved in reproduction, like honeybees and leaf-cutter ants. Reproduction is handled by the queen and a relatively few males; the workers are sterile females. "Since they do not reproduce," Fasold says, "there is no reason for them to be one sex or the other, so they default, so to speak, to female."

Fasold ends his discussion of these matters by pointing out that if language reflected biology, grammar books would direct us to use "she" to include males and females and "he" only for specifically male referents. But they don't. They tell us that "he" means "he or she," and that "she" is used only if the referent is specifically female. This use of "he" as the sex-indefinite pronoun is an innovation introduced into English by grammarians in the 18th and 19th centuries, according to Peter Mühlhäusler and Rom Harré in "Pronouns and People." From at least about 1500, the correct sex-indefinite pronoun was "they," as it still is in casual spoken English. In other words, the female was declared by grammarians to be the marked case.

Writing this article may mark me not as a writer, not as a linguist, not as an analyst of human behavior, but as a feminist—which will have positive or negative, but in any case powerful, connotations for readers. Yet I doubt that anyone reading Ralph Fasold's book would put that label on him.

30   I discovered the markedness inherent in the very topic of gender after writing a book on differences in conversational style based on

geographical region, ethnicity, class, age and gender. When I was interviewed, the vast majority of journalists wanted to talk about the differences between women and men. While I thought I was simply describing what I observed—something I had learned to do as a researcher—merely mentioning women and men marked me as a feminist for some.

When I wrote a book devoted to gender differences, in ways of speaking, I sent the manuscript to five male colleagues, asking them to alert me to any interpretation, phrasing or wording that might seem unfairly negative toward men. Even so, when the book came out, I encountered responses like that of the television talk show host who, after interviewing me, turned to the audience and asked if they thought I was male-bashing.

Leaping upon a poor fellow who affably nodded in agreement, she made him stand and asked, "Did what she said accurately describe you?" "Oh, yes," he answered. "That's me exactly." "And what she said about women—does that sound like your wife?" "Oh yes," he responded. "That's her exactly." "Then why do you think she's male-bashing?" He answered, with disarming honesty, "Because she's a woman and she's saying things about men."

To say anything about women and men without marking oneself as either feminist or anti-feminist, male-basher or apologist for men seems as impossible for a woman as trying to get dressed in the morning without inviting interpretations of her character.

Sitting at the conference table musing on these matters, I felt sad to think that we women didn't have the freedom to be unmarked that the men sitting next to us had. Some days you just want to get dressed and go about your business. But if you're a woman, you can't, because there is no unmarked woman.

Responding to Reading

1. Tannen notes that men "can choose styles that are marked, but they don't have to" (12); however, she believes that women do not have the "option of being unmarked" (12). What does she mean? Can you give some examples of women's styles that you believe are unmarked? (Note that in paragraph 16, Tannen says there are no such styles.)

2. In paragraph 33, Tannen says, "To say anything about women and men without marking oneself as either feminist or anti-feminist, male-basher or apologist for men seems as impossible for a woman as trying to get dressed in the morning without inviting interpretations of her character." Do you agree?

3. In paragraphs 24–28, Tannen discusses Ralph Fasold's book *The Sociolinguistics of Language*. Why does she include this material? Could she have made her point just as effectively without it?

Responding in Writing

Look at the men and women around you. Does their appearance support Tannen's thesis?

THE TRUE CLASH OF CIVILIZATIONS
Ronald Inglehart
1934–

Born in Milwaukee, Wisconsin, Ronald Inglehart earned a BA degree from Northwestern University (1956) and an MA degree (1962) and PhD (1967) from the University of Chicago. He also studied as a Fulbright Scholar at Leiden University in The Netherlands (1963–1964). He has worked as a professor of political science at the University of Michigan since 1978, where he also directs the Center for Political Studies at the Institute for Social Research. Inglehart's ongoing research focuses on global cultural change and its consequences. He has coordinated a worldwide survey of mass values and attitudes, the World Values Survey, which has shown that cultural values and beliefs are integral to the presence or absence of democratic institutions and ideals. With Miguel Basanez and Alejandro Moreno, Inglehart authored the book Human Values and Beliefs: A Cross-Cultural Sourcebook *(1998). To learn more about the World Values Survey, visit http://wvs.isr .umich.edu/index.html.*

Pippa Norris
1953–

Born in London, England, Pippa Norris earned a BA degree from the University of Warwick and an MSc degree and PhD from the London School of Economics and Political Science. She does research on elections, political communications, and gender politics and teaches comparative politics at the John F. Kennedy School of Government at Harvard University. Her books include Democratic Phoenix: Political Activism Reinvented *(2002) and, with Inglehart,* Rising Tide: Gender Equality and Cultural Change *(2003).*

Inglehart and Norris coauthored the following essay, which appeared in the online publication Foreign Policy, *http://www.foreignpolicy.com, which is published by the Carnegie Endowment for International Peace.*

Democracy promotion in Islamic countries is now one of the Bush administration's most popular talking points. "We reject the conde-scending notion that freedom will not grow in the Middle East," Secretary of State Colin Powell declared last December as he unveiled the White House's new Middle East Partnership Initiative to encourage political and economic reform in Arab countries. Likewise, Condoleezza Rice, President George W. Bush's national security advisor, promised last September that the United States is committed to "the march of freedom in the Muslim world."

But does the Muslim world march to the beat of a different drummer? Despite Bush's optimistic pronouncement that there is "no clash of civilizations" when it comes to "the common rights and needs of men and women," others are not so sure. Samuel Huntington's controversial 1993 thesis—that the cultural division between "Western Christianity" and "Orthodox Christianity and Islam" is the new fault line for conflict—resonates more loudly than ever since September 11. Echoing Huntington, columnist Polly Toynbee argued in the British Guardian last November, "What binds together a globalized force of some extremists from many continents is a united hatred of Western values that seems to them to spring from Judeo-Christianity." Meanwhile, on the other side of the Atlantic, Democratic Rep. Christopher Shays of Connecticut, after sitting through hours of testimony on U.S.-Islamic relations on Capitol Hill last October, testily blurted, "Why doesn't democracy grab hold in the Middle East? What is there about the culture and the people and so on where democracy just doesn't seem to be something they strive for and work for?"

Huntington's response would be that the Muslim world lacks the core political values that gave birth to representative democracy in Western civilization: separation of religious and secular authority, rule of law and social pluralism, parliamentary institutions of representative government, and protection of individual rights and civil liberties as the buffer between citizens and the power of the state. This claim seems all too plausible given the failure of electoral democracy to take root throughout the Middle East and North Africa. According to the latest Freedom House rankings, almost two thirds of the 192 countries around the world are now electoral democracies. But among the 47 countries with a Muslim majority, only one fourth are electoral democracies—and none of the core Arabic-speaking societies falls into this category.

Yet this circumstantial evidence does little to prove Huntington correct, since it reveals nothing about the underlying beliefs of Muslim publics. Indeed, there has been scant empirical evidence whether Western and Muslim societies exhibit deeply divergent values—that is, until now. The cumulative results of the two most recent waves of the World Values Survey (WVS), conducted in 1995–96 and 2000–2002, provide an extensive body of relevant evidence. Based on questionnaires that explore values and beliefs in more than 70 countries, the WVS is an investigation of sociocultural and political change that encompasses over 80 percent of the world's population.

5   A comparison of the data yielded by these surveys in Muslim and non-Muslim societies around the globe confirms the first claim in Huntington's thesis: Culture does matter—indeed, it matters a lot. Historical religious traditions have left an enduring imprint on contemporary values. However, Huntington is mistaken in assuming that the core clash between the West and Islam is over political values. At this point in history, societies throughout the world (Muslim and Judeo-Christian alike) see democracy as the best form of government. Instead, the real fault line between the West and Islam, which Huntington's theory completely overlooks, concerns gender equality and sexual liberalization. In other words, the values separating the two cultures have much more to do with eros than demos. As younger generations in the West have gradually become more liberal on these issues, Muslim nations have remained the most traditional societies in the world.

This gap in values mirrors the widening economic divide between the West and the Muslim world. Commenting on the disenfranchisement of women throughout the Middle East, the United Nations Development Programme observed last summer that "no society can achieve the desired state of well-being and human development, or compete in a globalizing world, if half its people remain marginalized and disempowered." But this "sexual clash of civilizations" taps into far deeper issues than how Muslim countries treat women. A society's commitment to gender equality and sexual liberalization proves time and again to be the most reliable indicator of how strongly that society supports principles of tolerance and egalitarianism. Thus, the people of the Muslim world overwhelmingly want democracy, but democracy may not be sustainable in their societies.

Testing Huntington

Huntington argues that "ideas of individualism, liberalism, constitutionalism, human rights, equality, liberty, the rule of law, democracy, free markets, [and] the separation of church and state" often have little resonance outside the West. Moreover, he holds that Western efforts to promote these ideas provoke a violent backlash against "human rights imperialism." To test these propositions, we categorized the countries included in the WVS according to the nine major contemporary civilizations, based largely on the historical religious legacy of each society. The survey includes 22 countries representing Western Christianity (a West European culture that also encompasses North America, Australia, and New Zealand), 10 Central European nations (sharing a Western Christian heritage, but which also lived under Communist rule), 11 societies with a Muslim majority (Albania, Algeria, Azerbaijan, Bangladesh, Egypt, Indonesia, Iran, Jordan, Morocco, Pakistan, and Turkey), 12 traditionally Orthodox societies (such as Russia and Greece), 11 predominately Catholic Latin American countries, 4 East Asian societies shaped by Sino-Confucian values, 5 sub-Saharan Africa countries, plus Japan and India.

Despite Huntington's claim of a clash of civilizations between the West and the rest, the WVS reveals that, at this point in history, democracy has an overwhelmingly positive image throughout the world. In country after country, a clear majority of the population describes "having a democratic political system" as either "good" or "very good." These results represent a dramatic change from the 1930s and 1940s, when fascist regimes won overwhelming mass approval in many societies; and for many decades, Communist regimes had widespread support. But in the last decade, democracy became virtually the only political model with global appeal, no matter what the culture. With the exception of Pakistan, most of the Muslim countries surveyed think highly of democracy: In Albania, Egypt, Bangladesh, Azerbaijan, Indonesia, Morocco, and Turkey, 92 to 99 percent of the public endorsed democratic institutions—a higher proportion than in the United States (89 percent).

Yet, as heartening as these results may be, paying lip service to democracy does not necessarily prove that people genuinely support basic democratic norms—or that their leaders will allow them to have democratic institutions. Although constitutions of authoritarian states such as China profess to embrace democratic ideals such as freedom of religion, the rulers deny it in practice. In Iran's 2000 elections, reformist candidates captured nearly three quarters of the seats in parliament, but a theocratic elite still holds the reins of power. Certainly, it's a step in the right direction if most people in a country endorse the idea of democracy. But this sentiment needs to be complemented by deeper underlying attitudes such as interpersonal trust and tolerance of unpopular groups—and these values must ultimately be accepted by those who control the army and secret police.

The WVS reveals that, even after taking into account differences 10 in economic and political development, support for democratic institutions is just as strong among those living in Muslim societies as in Western (or other) societies. For instance, a solid majority of people living in Western and Muslim countries gives democracy high marks as the most efficient form of government, with 68 percent disagreeing with assertions that "democracies are indecisive" and "democracies aren't good at maintaining order." (All other cultural regions and countries, except East Asia and Japan, are far more critical.) And an equal number of respondents on both sides of the civilizational divide (61 percent) firmly reject authoritarian governance, expressing disapproval of "strong leaders" who do not "bother with parliament and elections." Muslim societies display greater support for religious authorities playing an active societal role than do Western societies. Yet this preference for religious authorities is less a cultural division between the West and Islam than it is a gap between the West and many other less secular societies around the globe, especially in sub-Saharan Africa and Latin America. For instance, citizens in some Muslim societies agree overwhelmingly with the statement that "politicians who do not believe in God are unfit for public office" (88 percent in Egypt, 83 percent in Iran, and 71 percent in Bangladesh), but this statement also garners strong support in the Philippines (71 percent), Uganda (60 percent), and Venezuela (52 percent). Even in the United States, about two fifths of the public believes that atheists are unfit for public office.

However, when it comes to attitudes toward gender equality and sexual liberalization, the cultural gap between Islam and the West widens into a chasm. On the matter of equal rights and opportunities for women—measured by such questions as whether men make better political leaders than women or whether university education is more important for boys than for girls—Western and Muslim countries score 82 percent and 55 percent, respectively. Muslim societies are also distinctively less permissive toward homosexuality, abortion, and divorce.

These issues are part of a broader syndrome of tolerance, trust, political activism, and emphasis on individual autonomy that constitutes "self-expression values." The extent to which a society emphasizes these self-expression values has a surprisingly strong bearing on the emergence and survival of democratic institutions. Among all the countries included in the WVS, support for gender equality—a key indicator of tolerance and personal freedom—is closely linked with a society's level of democracy.

In every stable democracy, a majority of the public disagrees with the statement that "men make better political leaders than women." None of the societies in which less than 30 percent of the public rejects this statement (such as Jordan, Nigeria, and Belarus) is a true democracy. In China, one of the world's least democratic countries, a majority of the public agrees that men make better political leaders than women, despite a party line that has long emphasized gender equality (Mao Zedong once declared, "women hold up half the sky"). In practice, Chinese women occupy few positions of real power and face widespread discrimination in the workplace. India is a borderline case. The country is a long-standing parliamentary democracy with an independent judiciary and civilian control of the armed forces, yet it is also marred by a weak rule of law, arbitrary arrests, and extrajudicial killings. The status of Indian women reflects this duality. Women's rights are guaranteed in the constitution, and Indira Gandhi led the nation for 15 years. Yet domestic violence and forced prostitution remain prevalent throughout the country, and, according to the WVS, almost 50 percent of the Indian populace believes only men should run the government.

The way a society views homosexuality constitutes another good litmus test of its commitment to equality. Tolerance of well-liked groups is never a problem. But if someone wants to gauge how tolerant a nation really is, find out which group is the most disliked, and then ask whether members of that group should be allowed to hold public meetings, teach in schools, and work in government. Today, relatively few people express overt hostility toward other classes, races, or religions, but rejection of homosexuals is widespread. In response to a WVS question about whether homosexuality is justifiable, about half of the world's population say "never." But, as is the case with gender equality, this attitude is directly proportional to a country's level of democracy. Among authoritarian and quasi-democratic states, rejection of homosexuality is deeply entrenched: 99 percent in both Egypt and Bangladesh, 94 percent in Iran, 92 percent in China, and 71 percent in India. By contrast, these figures are much lower among respondents in stable democracies: 32 percent in the United States, 26 percent in Canada, 25 percent in Britain, and 19 percent in Germany.

Muslim societies are neither uniquely nor monolithically low on 15 tolerance toward sexual orientation and gender equality. Many of the Soviet successor states rank as low as most Muslim societies. However, on the whole, Muslim countries not only lag behind the West but behind all other societies as well. Perhaps more significant, the figures reveal the gap between the West and Islam is even wider among younger age groups. This pattern suggests that the younger generations in Western societies have become progressively more egalitarian than their elders, but the younger generations in Muslim societies have remained almost as traditional as their parents and grandparents, producing an expanding cultural gap.

Clash of Conclusions

"The peoples of the Islamic nations want and deserve the same freedoms and opportunities as people in every nation," President Bush declared in a commencement speech at West Point last summer. He's right. Any claim of a "clash of civilizations" based on fundamentally different political goals held by Western and Muslim societies represents an oversimplification of the evidence. Support for the goal of democracy is surprisingly widespread among Muslim publics, even among those living in authoritarian societies. Yet Huntington is correct when he argues that cultural differences have taken on a new importance, forming the fault lines for future conflict. Although nearly the entire world pays lip service to democracy, there is still no global consensus on the self-expression values—such as social tolerance, gender equality, freedom of speech, and interpersonal trust—that are crucial to democracy. Today, these divergent values constitute the real clash between Muslim societies and the West.

But economic development generates changed attitudes in virtually any society. In particular, modernization compels systematic, predictable changes in gender roles: Industrialization brings women into the paid work force and dramatically reduces fertility rates. Women become literate and begin to participate in representative government but still have far less power than men. Then, the postindustrial phase brings a shift toward greater gender equality as women move into higher-status economic roles in management and gain political influence within elected and appointed bodies. Thus, relatively industrialized Muslim societies such as Turkey share the same views on gender equality and sexual liberalization as other new democracies.

Even in established democracies, changes in cultural attitudes—and eventually, attitudes toward democracy—seem to be closely linked with modernization. Women did not attain the right to vote in most historically Protestant societies until about 1920, and in much of Roman Catholic Europe until after World War II. In 1945, only 3 percent of the members of parliaments around the world were women. In 1965, the figure rose to 8 percent, in 1985 to 12 percent, and in 2002 to 15 percent.

The United States cannot expect to foster democracy in the Muslim world simply by getting countries to adopt the trappings of democratic governance, such as holding elections and having a parliament. Nor is it realistic to expect that nascent democracies in the Middle East will inspire a wave of reforms reminiscent of the velvet revolutions that swept Eastern Europe in the final days of the Cold War. A real commitment to democratic reform will be measured by the willingness to commit the resources necessary to foster human development in the Muslim world. Culture has a lasting impact on how societies evolve. But culture does not have to be destiny.

Responding to Reading

1. What would Samuel Huntington's answer be to the question of why democracy does not take hold in the Muslim world? What is Inglehart and Norris's response to Huntington?

2. According to Inglehart and Norris, how do people in Muslim countries feel about democracy? What do they see as the core clash between the West and Islam? What is the most reliable indicator of a society's commitment to the "principles of tolerance and egalitarianism" (6)?

3. What are the attitudes toward women in Muslim countries? According to Inglehart and Norris, what can the United States do to change these attitudes? What would be the result of this change of attitudes?

What historical precedents do Inglehart and Norris present to support this idea?

Responding in Writing

Do you think Inglehart and Norris are optimistic or pessimistic about the future of democracy in the Muslim world? Do you agree or disagree?

---------------------------------- FOCUS ----------------------------------

Who Has It Harder, Women or Men?

Man and woman playing basketball.

Responding to the Image

1. In a game such as the one depicted in the picture on page 444, what advantages does a woman have? What advantages does a man have? Judging from the picture, who do you think will win?
2. What quality do you think will determine the winner: strength, skill, or some other factor?

THE GIRLS OF GEN X

Barbara Dafoe Whitehead

1944–

A native of Rochester, Minnesota, Whitehead did her undergraduate work at the University of Wisconsin and earned a PhD from the University of Chicago (1976). A frequent lecturer on marriage and the family, she (along with behavioral scientist David Popenoe) directs the National Marriage Project, a research and public education organization that issues annual reports on the state of marriage in the United States. Whitehead gained notoriety in 1993 when her Harper's *magazine article "Dan Quayle Was Right" sparked national debate about the effects of single-parent households on children. In* The Divorce Culture *(1997), she continued her argument that two-parent families produce better-adjusted children than single-parent families do. Her latest book is* Why There Are No Good Men Left *(2003). The following essay was published online by the American Enterprise Institute in 1998. To learn more about this author, visit her Web site, http://www .barbaradafoewhitehead.com/.*

All is not well with the women of Generation X.

Consider the evidence: Close to 40 percent of college women are frequent binge drinkers, a behavior related to date rapes and venereal disease. Young women suffer higher levels of depression, suicidal thoughts and attempts than men from early adolescence on. Between 1980 and '92, the rate of completed suicides more than tripled among white girls and doubled among black girls. For white women between 15 and 24, suicide is the third leading cause of death. And there is evidence that young women are less happy today than 20 years ago. Using data from a survey of high school seniors, sociologist Norval D. Glenn has tracked the trends of reported happiness for young men and women. Since 1977, the "happiness index" has been trending downward for young women. Moreover, this decline is specific to girls. Young men's reported happiness has risen slightly over the same Time. Gen X women seem to experience the greatest discontent in two areas: Men, and their own bodies. Young women can find sex easily, but they have a hard time finding a caring and sexually faithful partner who will share their lives. Marline Pearson, who teaches at a large community college in Madison, Wisconsin, recently asked her women students to identify the greatest obstacle facing women today. The difficulty of "finding and keeping a loving partner" topped the list, outranking obstacles such as job discrimination, sexual harassment in the workplace, and domestic violence. In addition to being disappointed in their intimate relationships with men, women are discontented with their own bodies. Healthy young women of normal weight describe themselves as fat or "gross." At puberty or even earlier, girls begin restricting what they eat. Two-thirds of ninth-grade girls report attempts to lose weight in the previous month. Of course, dieting is not new, but Gen X women do more than watch calories. Some starve themselves. Others eat but are afraid to keep food in their body. Instead, they chew their food and spit it out, vomit it up, or purge it with laxatives. Even more widespread than eating disorders is disordered eating, the restrictive and obsessive monitoring of food consumption. According to some experts, most college women today suffer from disordered eating. Indeed, it is the rare college or university today that does not have at least one specialist in eating disturbances on its counseling staff. According to one survey, the number-one wish among young women, outranking the desire to end homelessness, poverty, or racism, is to get and stay thin.

These conditions afflict some of the most privileged young women of the generation. This comes as a shock to older, baby-boom women. After all, college-educated Gen X women—the first full beneficiaries of the achievements of the women's movement—have grown up with more freedom, opportunity and choice than their mothers or grandmothers. More to the point, they have been the beneficiaries of what might be called the girlhood project: the systematic and self-conscious effort to change the culture and prepare girls for lives as liberated, self-determined individuals with successful careers, sexual freedoms, and nearly limitless personal choice.

As a mother raising daughters in the 1970s and '80s, I remember the heady sense of possibility that accompanied the girlhood project. Sons were sons, but daughters were a social experiment. We gave them books like Marlo Thomas's *Free To Be You and Me* and read them stories in *Ms.* like "The Princess Who Could Stand on Her Own Two Feet." We dressed them in jeans and sneakers. We fought for their right to play Little League baseball. We pushed for more sex education in the schools. We urged them to please themselves rather than to please men.

5 Given our optimistic expectations, it is bitterly disappointing to reach the '90s only to discover that young women's happiness index is falling, not rising. What is happening to our bright and talented daughters?

Several feminist writers have grappled with this question. Therapist Mary Pipher was the first to describe the dark side of American girlhood in her best-selling book *Revivng Ophelia*. Pipher's case histories present a disturbing portrait of depressed and angry adolescent girls, self-mutilating, self-starving, self-loathing. Two more recent books offer a thoughtful analysis and criticism of the changing nature of American girlhood. In *Promiscuities,* her memoir of growing up fast and sexy in the '70s, Naomi Wolf describes the confused sexual awakening of privileged girls raised by self-absorbed parents too busy sampling the pleasures of the sexual revolution themselves to guide or protect their daughters. Historian Joan Jacobs Brumberg's *The Body Project: An Intimate History of Girlhood* meticulously documents the downward slide of girls' aspirations and ambitions over the past century, from improving one's character through good works to improving one's body through grueling workouts.

All three accounts point to one source of trouble: the passage between girlhood and womanhood. Growing up has never been easy for girls, of course, but it is more prolonged and perilous than ever before. Puberty can begin as early as eight; first sexual intercourse commonly occurs between 15 and 17; and women remain single and sexually active into their middle or late twenties. Forty-five percent of women who came of age in the 1950s and '60s were still virgins at age 19, and for many of those 19-year-old women, their first sexual intercourse occurred on their wedding night. But only 17 percent of women who came of age in the 1970s and '80s were virgins at 19. Since many Gen X women postpone marriage until their late twenties, few are likely to be virgins on their wedding night. As a consequence, girls are exposed to the problems associated with unmarried sex at an earlier age and for a longer period of time than a generation ago.

A rough consensus exists on some key factors that make coming of age more difficult for girls today: a cultural emphasis on thinness which makes the normal weight gains of puberty a source of anxiety and self-loathing; a media saturated with sexually explicit images and misogynistic messages; the sexual revolution and the availability of the Pill; which relieved men of any significant burden of responsibility for the negative consequences of unmarried sex; the high rate of family breakup and dysfunction; and the erosion of adult supervision. Puberty is now fraught with danger and anxiety.

Young girls are now at greater risk for early and traumatic sexualization, often by adult men. According to Brumberg, there have also been dramatic shifts in the social controls governing the sexuality of adolescent girls. Professional providers of contraceptive and abortion services have replaced mothers as the main source of authority on sexual matters. This shift has contributed to the demoralization of female sexuality and the decline in chastity.

At age 15, Naomi Wolf tells us, she followed the responsible, [10] "healthy," medically approved approach to getting rid of her virginity. With her boyfriend, she went to a clinic to be fitted for a diaphragm, a business "easier than getting a learner's permit to drive a car." Yet as she prepared for the procedure, she missed a sense of occasion. "It was weird to have these adults just hand you the keys to the kingdom, ask 'Any questions?,' wave and return to their paperwork. . . . The end of our virginity passed unmarked," she writes, "neither mourned or celebrated."

Both Brumberg and Wolf are critical of the medicalization of girls' sexuality, with its emphasis on sexual health and self-management. (In the words of one sex education book, the goal for girls is to stay "healthy, safe, and in charge.") This places an unsupportable burden on young girls to protect themselves from predatory males. It also neglects girls' emotional needs for affiliation and affection, as well as their desire to have their sexuality invested with some larger meaning.

These revisionist-feminist writers seek to remoralize girlhood, but not with the morals of yesteryear. Instead, they call upon older women to take responsibility for (and pride in) younger womens' sexuality, and they look to senior women and especially mothers to instruct girls more actively. This advice overlooks at least one crucial point. Older women are already involved in shaping the passage to womanhood and have been for more than 20 years. It is feminist women who write and edit books and magazines for teen girls. It is feminist women who have fought for abortion rights and the end to parental consent laws for girls. It is feminist women who have championed the right of girls to be as sexually free as boys. In short, these older women are the authors of the girlhood project. Are they now the right parties to repair the damage done?

The girlhood project was rooted in rebellion against traditional conceptions of girlhood. According to feminist critics, earlier generations of girls were raised primarily to be wives and mothers. From puberty on, parents taught daughters to be modest, nice, nurturing, accomplished in the domestic arts, and virginal. Since a young woman's virginity was a moral as well as a physical condition, family and church conspired to keep women pure.

Whether this is actually a fair summary of prevailing American sex roles prior to the 1960s is dubious. Even in the 1830s, Alexis de Tocqueville commented that Americans "have calculated that there was little chance of repressing in woman the most tyrannical passions of the human heart and that it was a safer policy to teach her to control them herself. Unable to prevent her chastity from being often in danger, they want her to know how to defend herself, and they count on the strength of her free determination more than on safeguards which have been shaken or overthrown. . . . Unable or unwilling to keep a girl in perpetual ignorance, they are in a hurry to give her precocious knowledge of everything."

15   In any case, the activists who undertook the girlhood project declared war on what they viewed as Victorian double standards for boys and girls, which they blamed for unhappy marriages and unfulfilled female desires. Feminists called instead for a new single sexual stan-

dard—based on traditional boyhood. In their play and pursuits, little girls were to be made more like boys. Among liberal elites, a traditionally feminine daughter became a mild social embarrassment, while a feisty tomboy daughter was a source of pride.

In everything from sports to sex, girls gained experiences that were once off-limits. Twenty-five years ago, only one in 27 high school girls participated in team sports. By 1994, one in three did. A copy-the-boys approach was also applied to sexuality. Increasingly, the timing of girls' sexual awakening resembled boys. Today, the most frequent age of first intercourse is 17 for girls, 16 for boys. In frequency of intercourse and number of sexual partners, the traditional gender gap is closing as well. Modesty has also disappeared. Girls can be as profane, sexually frank, and "horny" as the guys. "Girls talk in the casual, expletive-laced manner stereotypically attributed to men," one 18-year-old college male writes. "Sex is discussed in all its variations, and bizarre or deviant sexual practices are often explored. This sort of talk is considered 'flirting'."

Amidst its success at ending different standards for the sexes, the girlhood project has created new discontents. For one thing, it contributes to girls' unhappiness with their bodies. The tomboy ideal is demanding. It favors the few girls who are naturally wiry and athletic, and leaves the majority of girls displeased with their own shapes. The rapturous acclaim for tiny Olympic gymnasts and lithe skaters gives nonathletic girls still another reason to feel disappointed in their normal forms.

The more masculine body ideal shifts the locus of body shame from sexual organs to more visible body parts. Today's college women know how to find their clitoris in a mirror, but they can't bear to look at their "thunder thighs." Fashion magazines, which girls begin to read at age nine or ten and continue to consult well into their 20s, provoke body shame. Virtually all these magazines send one clear message: Your body is a mess. For example, the cover of the December 1997 *Jump,* a magazine for young teens, features stories entitled, "Body Bummers: How to go from feeling flawed to fab" and "Sizing up boobs." Such magazines tell girls to like themselves, whatever their size or shape, but they only feature flat-chested models who are six feet tall and 105 pounds. Indeed, a recurrent rumor among teenage girls is that these models are really boys.

Girls respond to body shame with rigid technocratic monitoring of their bodies. Again the strenuous pursuit of feminine virtue has not disappeared but shifted location. The virtue of staying sexually pure has been replaced by the virtue of staying physically fit. In my corner of western Massachusetts, swarms of college women descend on the local health club each fall. They work out in the weight room or on the treadmills, their pony tails bobbing, their arms pumping, their faces sweaty and serious. Some read fashion magazines as they work out.

20   It does not take a degree in cultural anthropology to figure out that more is going on here than mere exercise. In girl culture today, "working out" is the new self-purification ritual, deeply invested with positive moral meaning. Good girls work out. Bad girls let themselves go. In the same way, eating has become a means of self-purification, and food itself has been moralized. There are good foods that one takes into the body and bad foods that one avoids or throws up. This helps explain why so many college women see "bad" foods as far more dangerous than drugs or alcohol, and why young women who drink and take recreational drugs will simultaneously refuse to eat anything but "pure" pesticide free, fat-free organic food. Food is entirely divorced from pleasure and sociability while the other ingested substances are not.

If the girlhood project leads young women on a quest for a masculinized body, it also sets them on the path toward a more masculinized emotional life. There is now a single sex standard for men and women, but it favors Hugh Hefner, not Betty Friedan.

As much as young women's sexual lives resemble men's in the timing of first sex and the number of sex partners, their reasons for having sex remain very different. The nation's most comprehensive and up-to-date sex survey reports that 48 percent of women have intercourse for the first time out of "affection for their partner," compared to only 25 percent of men. The researchers add, "Young women often go along with intercourse the first time, finding little physical pleasure in it, and a substantial number report being forced to have intercourse. These facts reflect the dramatic costs for young women, and they seem to be increasing as young women have intercourse earlier in the life course."

Even when young women deliberately set out to lose their virginity, they often experience feelings of sadness, emptiness, and disappointment afterward. Women may want affection, tenderness, and commitment in their relationships, but what they actually get is "more naked, loss-filled sex," says Warren Schumacher, who teaches courses in marriage and the family at the University of Massachusetts. Thus, though the girlhood project prepares girls for sex, it says nothing to them about love.

With the decoupling of sex and love, intense passion and romance are vanishing. Loveless sex has become a routine pleasure of the single life, on a par with a good movie. Sexless love is also part of singlehood. According to psychologist Joanna Gutmann, a counselor at the University of Chicago, asexual couplings are increasingly common. Gen X men and women may share beds without ever having sex, or they may start out in a sexual relationship and then eventually shift to a comfy, asexual living-together relationship for the sake of companionship and convenience. Passionate, romantic love between young men and women is increasingly rare, says Gutmann.

By the time they reach their late twenties, many educated women 25 in urban areas complain that all the good men are "taken" (or not available because they are gay). Some single women find it easier to hook up with different people for different purposes. "It doesn't make sense to rely on one person to meet all your needs," one 28-year-old woman told me. "Our generation diversifies. We might have one person for sex, one to go out club-hopping, another to share thoughts and feelings." Comradeship has replaced courtship and marriage as the preferred path to intimacy. To use a political metaphor, the aspiration to union has been abandoned for the more modest goal of confederacy.

Two decades after the girlhood project began, it may be judged not only by its aspirations but also by its decidedly mixed results. In important respects, it has improved the lot of girls. Adolescent girls now receive more serious mentoring attention from important men in their lives, including fathers, teachers, and coaches. Their participation in sports prepares them for a work world still largely shaped by male codes of conduct rooted in competition, combat, and conquest. More importantly, they are no longer bound by the marriage-and-motherhood script. They are free to follow their own desires as they make choices about their work and private lives.

At the same time, the girlhood project has shortchanged young women. The passage from girlhood to womanhood now entails a remarkably strenuous effort to transcend biology. Most girls are not cut out to be tomboys forever. Too often now, normal female physical and psychological maturation is taken as a problem, a worrisome sign that girls are "falling behind boys."

Today, all that is naturally womanly—especially anything related to childbearing—is treated by elites as something to be managed, minimized, and somehow overcome. Nearly all women still want motherhood, but they have grown up with the idea that it is a trauma that must be "worked into" a career. The only trouble-free times in the female life course are now defined as the periods when women are least connected to their womanliness: in childhood and again in old age. A woman's life between ages 10 and 60 has been medicalized and problematized, with a host of products and technologies like birth control and abortion, hormone replacement therapy, and cosmetic surgery being offered to ward off or manage what is natural. Is it any wonder that Gen X women look at adult life with a measure of fear and trembling?

The attempt to remake American girlhood is deeply connected to feminist aspirations. So how are feminists responding to signs of trouble popping up among Generation Xers? Many are ringing alarm bells—and blaming society or men. Others are urging their fellow feminists to offer more personal guidance to the young. Liberal women, say Brumberg and others, must make a new commitment to girl advocacy.

30   More mentoring is a worthwhile goal, but the state of American girlhood won't improve unless older feminists acknowledge their own responsibility for creating some of the difficulties today's young women face. To begin, women may have to confront their own anxieties about body image. Many American girls now grow up with mothers who are dieting, working out, and always complaining about their bodies. Indeed, it is often mothers who feel shame over their daughters' weight gains in puberty and rush their 11-year-olds to a fat camp or a pediatrician for a medically supervised diet.

Older feminist women, not the patriarchy, also edit the fashion magazines girls so eagerly consult. Nowhere else on a newsstand will you find as much body worship and emphasis on dress and dieting, or as many models made up like drug-addled prostitutes, or as many articles romanticizing casual sex. The same magazines are obsessed with money, things, and the trappings of celebrity. They assume every girl is focused on her self and her sex life, rather than her family and community, and they ignore any topic of civic, religious, or intellectual seriousness.

In addition, the firsthand models that today's girls grow up with are too often no more responsible or inspiring than this magazine fare. Revisionist feminists themselves acknowledge that it is the nice progressive parents of Gen Xers who turned self-actualization, divorce, live-in lovers, the drug habit (stretching from pot to Prozac), latch-key childhood, New Age therapies, and feel-good morals into mass phenomena.

Older women who aspire to be advocates to today's girls ought to consult the desires of the girls themselves. They will find that, more than sex, girls are interested in love and the business of finding a male worthy of love. Contemporary liberal institutions give these girls hundreds of books and articles devoted to the mechanics of sex, and many warnings about the dangers of penises not wearing condoms, but almost no information about how to make a life with the boys attached to them.

Older women must recognize that their feminist critique of 1950s girlhood, which inspired the effort to remake female upbringing, may not fit the realities of girls' lives now. Maybe the problem then was the tyranny of the feminine mystique. But the solution today is not a more unnatural and therefore even more tyrannical masculine mystique.

Responding to Reading

1. In paragraph 6, Whitehead introduces three feminist writers—Mary Pipher, Naomi Wolf, and Joan Jacobs Brumberg—whose theories and findings she refers to later in her essay. How does she evaluate the ideas of these writers? Does she agree with their views?

2. What is the "girlhood project"? What problems does Whitehead believe this project has caused?
3. Why, according to Whitehead, do "Gen X women look at adult life with a measure of fear and trembling" (28)? Whom does she blame for the problems faced by Gen X women? Where does she believe the solution to these problems lies? Do you agree with her?

Responding in Writing

Based on your own observations and experiences, do you think that Whitehead accurately describes the problems young women experience in the transition between girlhood and womanhood?

THE WAR AGAINST BOYS
Christina Hoff Sommers
1950–

Christina Hoff Sommers received her BA degree from New York University (1971) and studied philosophy at Brandeis University, from which she received a PhD (1979). After teaching at several universities, Sommers became a fellow at the American Enterprise Institute, a conservative public policy organization in Washington, DC. A frequent television commentator, Sommers is also the author of essays in a wide variety of periodicals and has published several books, including Who Stole Feminism? How Women Have Betrayed Women *(1994) and* The War against Boys: How Misguided Feminism Is Harming Our Young Men *(2000). The following selection is the opening section of an essay that appeared in the* Atlantic Monthly. *To learn more about Sommers, visit the American Enterprise Institute Web page, http://www.aei.org/.*

It's a bad time to be a boy in America. The triumphant victory of the U.S. women's soccer team at the World Cup last summer has come to symbolize the spirit of American girls. The shooting at Columbine High last spring might be said to symbolize the spirit of American boys.

That boys are in disrepute is not accidental. For many years women's groups have complained that boys benefit from a school system that favors them and is biased against girls. "Schools shortchange girls," declares the *American Association of University Women.* Girls are "undergoing a kind of psychological foot-binding," two prominent educational psychologists say. A stream of books and pamphlets cite research showing not only that boys are classroom favorites but also that they are given to schoolyard violence and sexual harassment.

In the view that has prevailed in American education over the past decade, boys are resented, both as unfairly priviledged sex and as obstacles on the path to gender justice for girls. This perspective is promoted in schools of education, and many a teacher now feels that girls need and deserve special indemnifying condsideration. "It is really clear that boys are Number One in this society and in most of the world," says Patricia O'Reilly, a professor of education and the director of the Gender Equity Center, at the University of Cincinnati.

The idea that schools and society grind girls down has given rise to an array of laws and policies intended to curtail the advantage boys have and to redress the harm done to girls. That girls are treated as the second sex in school and consequently suffer, that boys are accorded privileges and consequently benefit—these are things everyone is presumed to know. But they are not true.

5   The research commonly cited to support claims of male privilege and male sinfulness is riddled with errors. Almost none of it has been published in peer-reviewed professional journals. Some of the data turn out to be mysteriously missing. A review of the facts shows boys, not girls, on the weak side of an education gender gap. The typical boy is a year and a half behind the typical girl in reading and writing; he is less committed to school and less likely to go to college. In 1997 college fulltime enrollments were 45 percent male and 55 percent female. The Department of Education predicts that the proportion of boys in college classes will continue to shrink.

Data from the U.S. Department of Education and from several recent university studies show that far from being shy and demoralized, today's girls outshine boys. They get better grades. They have higher educational aspirations. They follow more rigorous academic programs and participate in advanced-placement classes at higher rates. According to the National Center for Education Statistics, slightly more girls than boys enroll in high-level math and science courses. Girls, allegedly timorous and lacking in confidence, now outnumber boys in student government, in honor societies, on school newspapers, and in debating clubs. Only in sports are boys ahead, and women's groups are targeting the sports gap with a vengeance. Girls read more books. They outperform boys on tests for artistic and musical ability. More girls than boys study abroad. More join the Peace Corps. At the same time, more boys than girls are suspended from school. More are held back and more drop out. Boys are three times as likely to receive a diagnosis of attention-deficit hyperactivity disorder. More boys than girls are involved in crime, alcohol, and drugs. Girls attempt suicide more often than boys, but it is boys who more often succeed. In 1997, a typical year, 4,483 young people aged five to twenty-four committed suicide: 701 females and 3,782 males.

In the technical language of education experts, girls are academically more "engaged." Last year an article in *The CQ Researcher* about male and female academic achievement described a common parental observation: "Daughters want to please their teachers by spending extra time on projects, doing extra credit, making homework as neat as possible. Sons rush through homework assignments and run outside to play, unconcerned about how the teacher will regard the sloppy work."

School engagement is a critical measure of student success. The U.S. Department of Education gauges student commitment by the following criteria: "How much time do students devote to homework each night?" and "Do students come to class prepared and ready to learn? (Do they bring books and pencils? Have they completed their homework?)". According to surveys of fourth, eighth, and twelfth graders, girls consistently do more homework than boys. By the twelfth grade boys are four times as likely as girls not to do homework. Similarly, more boys than girls report that they "usually" or "often" come to school without supplies or without having done their homework.

The performance gap between boys and girls in high school leads directly to the growing gap between male and female admissions to college. The Department of Education reports that in 1996 there were 8.4 million women but only 6.7 million men enrolled in college. It predicts that women will hold on to and increase their lead well into the next decade, and that by 2007 the numbers will be 9.2 million women and 6.9 million men.

Deconstructing the Test-Score Gap

Feminists cannot deny that girls get better grades, are more engaged 10 academically, and are now the majority sex in higher education. They argue, however, that these advantages are hardly decisive. Boys, they point out, get higher scores than girls on almost every significant standardized test—especially the Scholastic Assessment Test and law school, medical school, and graduate school admissions tests.

In 1996 I wrote an article for *Education Week* about the many ways in which girl students were moving ahead of boys. Seizing on the test-score data that suggest boys are doing better than girls, David Sadker, a professor of education at American University and a co-author with his wife, Myra, of *Failing at Fairness: How America's Schools Cheat Girls* (1994), wrote, "If females are soaring in school, as Christina Hoff Sommers writes, then these tests are blind to their flight." On the 1998 SAT boys were thirty-five points (out of 800) ahead of girls in math and seven points ahead in English. These results seem to run counter to all other measurements of achievement in school. In almost all other areas boys lag behind girls. Why do they test better? Is Sadker right in suggesting that this is a manifestation of boys' privileged status?

The answer is no. A careful look at the pool of students who take the SAT and similar tests shows that the girls' lower scores have little or nothing to do with bias or unfairness. Indeed, the scores do not even signify lower achievement by girls. First of all, according to *College Bound Seniors,* an annual report on standardized-test takers published by the College Board, many more "at risk" girls than "at risk" boys take the SAT—girls from lower-income homes or with parents who never graduated from high school or never attended college. "These characteristics," the report says, "are associated with lower than average SAT scores." Instead of wrongly using SAT scores as evidence of bias against girls, scholars should be concerned about the boys who never show up for the tests they need if they are to move on to higher education.

Another factor skews test results so that they appear to favor boys. Nancy Cole, the president of the Educational Testing Service, calls it the "spread" phenomenon. Scores on almost any intelligence or achievement test are more spread out for boys than for girls—boys include more prodigies and more students of marginal ability. Or, as the political scientist James Q. Wilson once put it, "There are more male geniuses and more male idiots."

Boys also dominate dropout lists, failure lists, and learning-disability lists. Students in these groups rarely take college-admissions tests. On the other hand, exceptional boys who take school seriously show up in disproportionately high numbers for standardized tests. Gender-equity activists like Sadker ought to apply their logic consistently: if the shortage of girls at the high end of the ability distribution is evidence of unfairness to girls, then the excess of boys at the low end should be deemed evidence of unfairness to boys.

15   Suppose we were to turn our attention away from the highly motivated, self-selected two fifths of high school students who take the SAT and consider instead a truly representative sample of American schoolchildren. How would girls and boys then compare? Well, we have the answer. The National Assessment of Educational Progress started in 1969 and mandated by Congress, offers the best and most comprehensive measure of achievement among students at all levels of ability. Under the NAEP program 70,000 to 100,000 students, drawn from forty-four states, are tested in reading, writing, math, and science at ages nine, thirteen, and seventeen. In 1996, seventeen-year-old boys outperformed seventeen-year-old girls by five points in math and eight points in science, whereas the girls outperformed the boys by fourteen points in reading and seventeen points in writing. In the past few years girls have been catching up in math and science while boys have continued to lag far behind in reading and writing.

In the July, 1995, issue of *Science*, Larry V. Hedges and Amy Nowell, researchers at the University of Chicago, observed that girls' deficits in math were small but not insignificant. These deficits, they noted, could adversely affect the number of women who "excel in scientific and technical occupations." Of the deficits in boys' writing skills they wrote, "The large sex differences in writing . . . are alarming. . . . The data imply that males are, on average, at a rather profound disadvantage in the performance of this basic skill." They went on to warn,

> The generally larger numbers of males who perfom near the bottom of the distribution on reading comprehension and writing also have policy implications. It seems likely that individuals with such poor literacy skills will have difficulty finding employment in an increasingly information-driven economy. Thus, some intervention may be required to enable them to participate constructively.

Hedges and Nowell were describing a serious problem of national scope, but because the focus elsewhere has been on girls' deficits, few Americans know much about the problem or even suspect that it exists.

Indeed, so accepted has the myth of girls in crisis become that even teachers who work daily with male and female students tend to reflexively dismiss any challenge to the myth, or any evidence pointing to the very real crisis among boys. Three years ago Scarsdale High School, in New York, held a gender-equity workshop for faculty members. It was the standard girls-are-being-shortchanged fare, with one notable difference. A male student gave a presentation in which he pointed to evidence suggesting that girls at Scarsdale High were well ahead of boys. David Greene, a social-studies teacher, thought the student must be mistaken, but when he and some colleagues analyzed department grading patterns, they discovered that the student was right. They found little or no difference in the grades of boys and girls in advanced-placement social-studies classes. But in standard classes the girls were doing a lot better.

And Greene discovered one other thing: few wanted to hear about his startling findings. Like schools everywhere, Scarsdale High has been strongly influenced by the belief that girls are systematically deprived. That belief prevails among the school's gender-equity committee and has led the school to offer a special senior elective on gender equity. Greene has tried to broach the subject of male underperformance with his colleagues. Many of them concede that in the classes they teach, the girls seem to be doing better than the boys, but they do not see this as part of a larger pattern. After so many years of hearing about silenced, diminished girls, teachers do not take seriously the suggestion that boys are not doing as well as girls even if they see it with their own eyes in their own classrooms.

Responding to Reading

1. In paragraph 4, Sommers states her essay's thesis: "That girls are treated as the second sex in school and consequently suffer, that boys are accorded privileges and consequently benefit—these are things everyone is presumed to know. But they are not true." Do you agree that the supposed privileged position of boys is something "everyone is presumed to know"? Do you accept it as true?

2. Paragraph 6 of this essay presents a long list of areas in which "girls outshine boys." Compare this paragraph with the first three paragraphs of Barbara Dafoe Whitehead's pessimistic portrait of the women of Generation X (p. 445). Is it possible that both writers' observations are accurate? Explain.

3. Sommers believes that "the myth of girls in crisis" is so entrenched that "even teachers who work daily with male and female students tend to reflexively dismiss any challenge to the myth" (17). If what she says is true, would you expect this belief among teachers to benefit boys or girls in the long run? Why?

Responding in Writing

Based on your experience, who is more successful in school—girls or boys?

MAN BASHING: TRIVIAL PURSUIT OR A TRUTH WITH CONSEQUENCES?

Warren Farrell

1943–

Warren Farrell was born in New York City and earned a BA degree from Montclair State College (1965), an MA from the University of California, Los Angeles (1966), and a PhD from New York University (1974). He has taught at the School of Medicine at the University of California, San Diego, as well as at Georgetown University, Rutgers University, and American University. Farrell has been described as "the Gloria Steinem of Men's Liberation." His books include The Myth of Male Power *(1993);* Women Can't Hear What Men Don't Say *(1999), from which the following selection has been excerpted; and* Father and Child Reunion: How to Bring the Dads We Need to the Children We Love *(2001). To learn more about Farrell, visit his Web site, http://www.warrenfarrell.com.*

Man bashers focus on the problems *with* men and ignore the problems *of* men. They usually become man bashers by focusing on the problems of women and blaming those problems on men. The combination is misandry.

Misandry—or man hating—is the equivalent of misogyny. If you are unaware of misandry, welcome to the club. Our failure to see it is so complete that even the most careful observer of the human vocabulary, *Webster's Unabridged Dictionary*, is blind to it. One writer calls misandry "the hate that dares us to breathe its name."

Is misandry not acknowledged because it does not exist? A week after you read this chapter, misandry will become apparent in commercials, in films, in everyday conversations. But the bias that is hardest to see is the bias we share. Even allegedly gender-neutral words like "sexist" imply slights only against women.

Man bashing is *not* a problem per se. A person who cannot laugh at her- or himself has a serious problem. But when one group gets singled out far more often than others—whether it be "dumb Poles," "dumb blondes," or "corrupt lawyers"—then a red flag is sent up. And I find man bashing now runs about 9 to 1 over woman bashing. As *Time* magazine puts it, it's as if "masculinity were a bad smell in the room."

The lopsided objectification of a group as the devil always makes ₅ us callous to its deaths. Men's life expectancy was one year less than women's in 1920; today, it is seven years less, yet the federal government has only an Office of Research on Women's Health. It's part of what leads us to our blindness toward domestic violence against men and to caring more about saving whales than males.

On a personal level, man bashing hurts women because it undermines the one thing that has most motivated men to work for women and die for women throughout history: appreciation. **I've never seen a greeting card for thanking mentors, or for thanking volunteer firemen.**

The Double Standard and Its Consequences

Today, misandry is also in the double standard of our response: **Woman bashing is a lawsuit; man bashing is a Hallmark card.** Public woman bashing is illegal; public man bashing is institutionalized.

Is man bashing less damaging than woman bashing because boys spend a lifetime putting each other down? The two are different. When boys put each other down, there is an unwritten rule that *it goes both ways*. Not true when women put men down. If she implies he's inept, it's a joke; if he implies she's inept, it might be a joke, or it might be a "hostile work environment." If she considers it a joke at the time, but a year later fails to get promoted, yesterday's joke can become tomorrow's lawsuit. And an end to the "joker's" career.

A man whose career ends in shame is often a man whose marriage ends, which often leads to his children calling him visitor (as in "she has the children . . . he has visitation"). When the U.S. Coast Guard's top spokesperson, Captain Ernie Blanchard, told much less offensive jokes than the ones we'll see below, Coast Guard feminists complained.

Captain Blanchard apologized. The apologies weren't good enough. He was subjected to a *criminal* probe. He offered to resign to spare his family—on the condition the probe would stop. The Coast Guard refused. Beside himself, he took his grandfather's Smith & Wesson revolver, pointed it to his head, and shot a bullet through his brains.

10 Why would the Coast Guard refuse to stop a criminal probe for a joke? Once the machinery of a sexual harassment complaint is set into motion, few officers or corporate executives have the guts to stop the machinery for fear they'll become part of the complaint.

This double standard ultimately violates women. Mentors have proven crucial to female success, and women consistently seek male mentors—the higher up, the better. But the higher up the man, the farther he has to fall. Sexual harassment legislation has left potential mentors increasingly feeling there is a thin line between helping a woman advance her career and helping himself hurt his career. Mentoring requires intimacy that includes joking, criticism, and time alone. A joke that seems safe during the intimacy of mentoring can become a lawsuit when the woman being mentored begins to want to create an identity independent of the mentor. Then she often goes through a period of rebellion similar to any adolescent trying to create identity. The jokes and intimacies can come back to haunt him. Once a man sees this happen to someone in the company, or a friend, he thinks twice about being a mentor. Which is why the double standard hurts women.

Misandry's double standard is also in our language.

Doublespeak

When we make positive references, it is politically correct to include women: chairman becomes chairperson; spokesman becomes spokesperson; yet when the reference is negative, no one cries, "Don't say gunman, say gunperson."

When a wealthy older man marries a younger woman, we say, "He's robbing the cradle." We don't say "She's robbing the bank." When Warren Beatty was single, he was called a "womanizer," as if his women friends were victims; when Madonna was single, she was never called a "manizer." She was called either liberated or promiscuous. The difference? Neither liberated nor promiscuous suggests her men friends were victims. The old double standard of labeling women promiscuous while suggesting men were sowing their wild oats has reversed itself: Women with many partners are now liberated; their male counterparts, womanizers.

15 Even self-help writers voice only women's complaint that men leave the toilet seat up. No one suggests thanking the man for putting it up so he gets nothing on it. **And no one asks why a woman expects the toilet to always be as it is in women's rooms, and never as half the**

toilets are in men's rooms: urinals. Why, when a woman enters the picture, do her rules prevail? When she doesn't prevail, why is *he* criticized—why don't *they* compromise? When self-help writers help only her, are they really just helping themselves?

Unfortunately, the strongest opponents of misogyny are often the greatest misandrists. Feminists rightly ask us to reconsider references to women as "baby," "honey," "doll," and "spinster," but are often the first to call men dead-beats, jerks, perverts, macho, rapists, and womanizers. And should a man protest, he risks being labeled a wimp, whiner, chauvinist, or misogynist. . . .

Haven't Men Always Dished It Out? Why Can't They Take It?

When man bashing first appears on someone's radar screen, it is almost always dismissed as a function of the pendulum swinging too far—from woman bashing to man bashing. Not true. Comics like *Dagwood* have portrayed man-as-fool since the 1920s. Prior to the women's movement, shows like *The Three Stooges* made a joke of both verbal and physical man bashing. In *The Honeymooners,* the louder Ralph Kramden said "One of these days, *pow,* right in the kisser," or "To the moon, Alice," the farther *he* would fall. Every *Honeymooners* episode followed this formula—or Ralph's fall from man-as-boastful-jerk to the rediscovery of the greater superiority and wisdom of his wife. Only *he* was wrong; only *he* apologized.

On the other hand, shows like *I Love Lucy* mocked both sexes for the excesses of their sex role. And still others idealized both sexes' role (from the *Father Knows Best* image of masculinity to the "motherhood-and-apple-pie" image of *I Remember Mama*).

In the past, when *either* sex deviated from its role, it was a target of epithets. A woman was cheap, easy, promiscuous, a bitch; a man was a jerk, asshole, bastard, motherfucker, faggot. I am not aware of any time in the past in which men were not also the subject of ridicule. Feminists, though, have specialized in uncovering only the ridicule against women, making the pendulum appear to have been off balance, thus justifying man bashing as returning to balance.

Now the pendulum *is* off to one side. While epithets against women can end a man's career track, epithets against men can begin a career track for writers of cards, comedies, cartoons, and commercials.

Are Men *Called* Jerks Because Men *Are* Jerks?

A study of thousands of commercials found that if both sexes appeared in the commercial but only one was portrayed as a jerk, *it was the man who was the jerk 100 percent of the time.*

Would men be called jerks less often if they were jerks less often? Yes and no. Men are jerks more often in part because they take risks more often. A woman who doesn't receive a call from a man for a long time after a date often calls her woman friend and they both label him a "jerk." **No one asks why she's expecting** *him* **to make the call.** He doesn't call her a jerk if she doesn't call *him.*

Suppose he promised to call? That's part of their lopsided expectations—that he will make the promise to do something, not she. Those expected to take most of the risks, make most of the promises, do most of the performing, are most often called a jerk when they fail. When they do it perfectly, they're a hero. **A jerk is a potential hero who messes it up along the way.** Women who repeatedly fall in love with jerks have usually fallen in love with risk-takers rather than take the risks themselves.

Does man bashing make women believe men are getting worse even in areas in which they are improving? Yes. Remember how we saw in the chapter on housework that even though men were doing much more housework, women believed they were doing less? The only thing consistent with that belief was the male-bashing headlines about men and housework.

25   Obviously, something deeper is going on to generate this anger.

Why Are Women So Angry at Men?

The anger from women to men . . . can easily make us fell angry toward women. But understanding what creates that anger, and what can be done to change what creates it provides more compassion toward women, and is far more productive to loving each other. Both for ourselves and our children.

Are women angry because they're powerless, and anger is the way the powerless are heard? Yes and no. Never in history has any large single group of people had, on the surface, more options, wealth, education, personal power, privilege, and respect than women in middle- and upper-middle-class industrialized societies today. And never has such a large group been so angry. Why?

Until recently, there was no social permission for divorce. Marriage guaranteed for a lifetime meant economic security guaranteed for a lifetime. Any man who didn't provide that was ostracized, ridiculed, or ignored. Black men, Indian men, homeless men, and gay men have the toughest time among American males. *And they all have something in common: They do not provide an economic security blanket for women.*

Divorce altered the economic relationship between men and women, and, therefore, the psychological relationship between men and women. When divorce was not permitted, men's addiction to sex and the twenty-year-old woman worked for her—the addiction made him agree to support her for a lifetime; the taboo on divorce made him stick to his agreement. When the taboo on divorce weakened and she was forty, his addiction to the twenties worked against her. She felt disposable.

While this was true for all divorced women, the more beautiful the woman was when she was younger, the more she had been treated like a celebrity—what I call a "genetic celebrity." The more she had been a genetic celebrity, the more likely, she was to feel anger as age brought feelings of invisibility in the beauty contest of everyday life in which she used to be the winner.

Many divorced women with children feel they are not being treated as a woman, but as a package deal: a woman with children. A woman friend of mine deeply loved a man, but he was supporting his ex and their children and was already working more than he wanted. When he saw my woman friend's guilt about not spending more time with her children, he became afraid marriage would lead to her quitting work as his previous wife had. Thus he would never commit. My woman friend broke up with him and, after that, I noticed she would often make digs at men—digs that never quite disappeared.

Feminism had a powerful effect on helping women become stronger, more independent. But it had almost no impact on the type of man a woman would find suitable if she did marry. In workshops, **when I ask women, "On your wedding day, did you believe the man you married would consistently earn less than you?" almost no woman says "yes."** That is, almost every woman who *marries* still believes her future husband will earn equal to or more than she. If she feels he doesn't "have potential," she might have sex with him, might even live with him, but rarely marries him. Why?

This evolved as part of women's historic and biological obligation to find a good provider and protector, not just for themselves, but for their children. Her search for a successful man was her first step to becoming a responsible mother. But women's biology, like men's, created a barrier to our struggle not to treat each other as objects. Men treated women as sex objects; women treated men as success objects. Feminism confronted men's addiction to women as "sex objects," but no one confronted women's addiction to men as "success objects."

So worldwide, women are still set up with "The Princess Diana Fantasy." President Clinton made clear the problem with the male fantasy, but no one asked Monica to re-examine the problem with the female fantasy. Which is . . .?

When two-and-a-half-billion people, mostly women, are comparing their own lives to that of the future Princess Diana as they watch the TV broadcast of her marrying the prince, more than a few are likely to find their own lives disappointing. When 25 million American women read an average of twelve romance novels per month, often with *Bridges of Madison County*–type themes of married moms being swept away by roving Clint Eastwoods, again, more than a few are likely to find their own lives disappointing.

Even in the late '60s, the National Longitudinal Survey found that 70 percent of younger women believed they would not be working at age thirty-five, yet when they actually reached age thirty-five, more than 70 percent of them *were* working. *These women's dreams, of being swept away, had been swept away.* This created disappointment and anger.

Then, when women like Diana, who do marry the prince, are themselves disappointed, and that disappointment resonates with her own, and men are not offering their perspective, *marital* problems become interpreted as problems of women, *with* men.

Women's greater-than-ever wealth and power fails to predict happiness, then, because it fails to consider disappointed expectations, the hurt and pain of being rejected, and the hopelessness many women feel when they have less beauty power and more children than they did when they were twenty—thus making the princes who were interested in her when she had external beauty be less interested in her now that she has more internal beauty.

The degree to which we help our daughters resist the temptation to feel entitled to a prince is the degree to which they will feel less angry when the prince they marry is half prince and half frog . . . a bit like themselves. When I have seen, in my workshops, women without these expectations, or women who can see the world from men's perspectives without denying their own, I see the anger soften, and openings for love be created.

Responding to Reading

1. What is "man bashing"? According to Farrell, when does it become a problem? What harm does it do?
2. What does Farrell mean when he says that when it comes to bashing, there is a double standard? What form does this double standard take? In what way does man bashing hurt women?
3. Why does Farrell think that women are so angry with men? What does he think should be done to lessen this anger?

Responding in Writing

Make a list of examples of man bashing that you encounter every day—in movies, commercials, and conversation. Do you agree with Farrell that man bashing can have negative consequences?

———————— WIDENING THE FOCUS ————————

The following readings can suggest additional perspectives for thinking and writing about the roles of men and women. You may also want to do further research about this subject on the Internet.

- Michelle Lee, "The Fashion Victim's Ten Commandments" (p. 383)

- Judith Wallerstein, "The Unexpected Legacy of Divorce" (p. 85)

- Judith Ortiz Cofer, "The Myth of the Latin Woman: I Just Met a Girl Named Maria" (p. 491)

- Arlie Hochschild, "The Second Shift" (p. 554)

For Internet Research: Differences in the ways men and women are treated in school, business, sports, and society remain a contentious discussion topic. In preparation for writing an essay about the gender gap as it relates to an area of interest to you, open one of the popular Web search engines that compiles news stories—http://news.google .com or http://news.yahoo.com—and enter the search term *gender gap*. From the search results, select readings about your topic. Use information from these sources to support your essay. You can begin by reading one or all of the following readings, which were found through the Google news site:

- Conlin, Michelle. "The New Gender Gap." *Business Week Online.* May 26, 2003. http://www.businessweek.com:/print/magazine/ content/03_21/b3834001_mz001.htm?mz (Sept. 7, 2003).

- Suggs, Welch. "Colleges Make Slight Progress Toward Gender Equity in Sports." *The Chronicle of Higher Education.* July 25, 2003. http://chronicle.com/prm/weekly/v49/i46/46a03001.htm (Sept. 7, 2003).

- "Girls Get Extra School Help while Boys Get Ritalin." *USA Today.* Aug. 29, 2003. http://story.news.yahoo.com/news?tmpl=story&u=/ usatoday/20030829/cm_usatoday/11731917 (Sept. 7, 2003).

—————————— WRITING ——————————

Gender and Identity

1. In her well-known work *A Room of One's Own,* novelist and critic Virginia Woolf observes that "any woman born with a great gift in the sixteenth century would certainly have gone crazed, shot herself, or ended her days in some lonely cottage outside the village, half witch, half wizard, feared and mocked at." Write an essay in which you discuss in what respects this statement may still apply to gifted women of your own generation or of your parents' generation. You may want to read Marge Piercy's poem "Barbie Doll" (p. 405) and Barbara Dafoe Whitehead's essay "The Girls of Gen X" (p. 445) before you plan your paper.

2. List all the stereotypes of women—and of men—identified in the selections you read in this chapter. Then, write an essay in which you discuss those that have had the most negative effects on your life. Do you consider these stereotypes just annoying, or actually dangerous?

3. Several of the selections in this chapter—for example, "The Men We Carry in Our Minds" (p. 408), "Stay-at-Home Dads" (p. 414), and "Why I Want a Wife" (p. 412)—draw distinctions, implicitly or explicitly, between "men's work" and "women's work." Write an essay in which you consider the extent to which such distinctions exist today, and explain how they have affected your professional goals.

4. The title of a best-selling self-help book by John Gray, *Men Are from Mars, Women Are from Venus,* suggests that men and women are so completely different that they may as well be from different planets. Write an essay in which you support or contradict this title's claim. You may focus on men's and women's actions, tastes, values, preferences, or behavior.

5. Write a letter to Judy Brady in which you update (or challenge) her characterization of a wife in "Why I Want a Wife," p. 412.

6. Could all-male (or all-female) schools solve the problems encountered by boys and girls in school? Write an essay in which you present your views on this issue.

7. In her essay "Marked Women" (p. 430), Deborah Tannen discusses the distinction between the terms *marked* and *unmarked*. Study the men and women around you, or those you see in films or on television, and determine whether or not your observations support Tannen's point that unlike women, men have "the option of being unmarked." Write an essay in which you agree or disagree with Tannen's conclusion, citing her essay as well as your own observa-

tions. (Be sure to define the terms *marked* and *unmarked* in your introduction.)

8. Scott Russell Sanders and Sharon Olds express definite ideas about what it means to be male. Write an essay in which you present your view of what society expects from men. In addition to Sanders's "The Men We Carry in Our Minds" (p. 408) and Olds's "Rite of Passage" (p. 406), you may also consider Glenn Sacks's "Stay-at-Home Dads" (p. 414).

9. Do you think mixed male and female teams could be the answer to some of the problems created by government enforcement of Title IX? Write an essay in which you take a stand on this issue. Be sure to refer specifically to Robyn Blumner's "Title IX: Gender Equality in College Sports" (p. 417).

10. After reading the three essays in the Focus section of this chapter—Whitehead's "The Girls of Gen X" (p. 445), Sommers's "The War against Boys" (p. 453), and Farrell's "Man Bashing" (p. 458)—write an essay in which you answer the question "Who has it harder, women or men?" You may limit your discussion to family, sports, education, or any other area you choose.

7

THE AMERICAN DREAM

--- PREPARING TO READ AND WRITE ---

The American Dream—of political and religious freedom, equal access to education, equal opportunity in the workplace, and ultimately, success and wealth—is often elusive. Still, it continues to attract many who have heard its call. In the process of working toward the dream, individuals and groups struggle to overcome their status as newcomers or outsiders—to fit in, to belong, to be accepted. As they work toward their goals, however, some must make painful decisions, for full participation

Italian immigrant family on ferry from docks to Ellis Island, New York City, 1905.

in American society may mean giving up language, custom, and culture and becoming more like others. Thus, although the American Dream may ultimately mean winning something, it can often mean losing something—a vital part of oneself—as well.

Many of the essays in this chapter are written from the point of view of outsiders looking in. These writers want to be accepted, and they believe that the American Dream's reward is worth the struggle. Still, while some eagerly anticipate full acceptance, with all the rights and responsibilities that this entails, others are more cautious, afraid of the personal or cultural price they will have to pay for full acceptance into the American mainstream.

In "What Is the American Dream?" the Focus section that concludes this chapter, Thomas Jefferson, poet Emma Lazarus, President John F. Kennedy, and Martin Luther King, Jr., explore the political, historical, and emotional ties that bind Americans to their country and to one another. These readings showcase the idealism with which Americans approach their dream, reminding us that achieving this dream is worth the struggle.

As you read and prepare to write about the essays in this chapter, you may consider the following questions:

- What does the American Dream mean to the writer?

- Is the essay a personal narrative? An analysis of a problem facing a group? Both of these?

Italian-American couple celebrating fiftieth wedding anniversary with family.

- Has the writer been able to achieve the American Dream? If so, by what means? If not, why not?

- What are the greatest obstacles that stand between the writer (or the group he or she writes about) and the American Dream? Would you characterize these obstacles as primarily cultural, social, political, racial, economic, religious, or educational?

- Who has the easiest access to the American Dream? For whom is access most difficult? Why?

- Is the writer looking at the United States from the point of view of an insider or an outsider?

- Does the writer want to change his or her status? To change the status of others? What steps, if any, does he or she take to do so? What additional steps could he or she take?

- With what ethnic, racial, geographic, or economic group does the writer most identify? What is the writer's attitude toward this group? What is the writer's attitude toward what he or she identifies as mainstream American culture?

- Does the writer speak as an individual or as a representative of a particular group?

- Which writers' views of the American Dream are most similar? Most different? Most like your own?

WE MAY BE BROTHERS

Chief Seattle

1786?–1866

Son of a Suquamish chief and a Duwamish chief's daughter, Seattle was chief of the Suquamish, Duwamish, and other saltwater tribes occupying the area around Puget Sound in what is now the state of Washington. As white settlers arrived in the region in the early 1850s, Seattle used his diplomacy and speaking skills to help maintain peace between his followers and the settlers. (Unable to pronounce his name in the original Salish tongue, the whites changed its pronunciation to "Seattle" and eventually named their new settlement after him.) In 1854, during treaty negotiations with the US territorial governor, the chief delivered a moving speech in which he described the inevitable displacement of his people by the better-armed, more technologically advanced newcomers. This speech was not transcribed until some thirty years later, and then by a white onlooker who wrote in the flowery English popular at the time. As a result, it is impossible to say how closely what is reprinted here corresponds to Seattle's words. The message, however, is a timeless one that reflects Seattle's passionate beliefs.

Yonder sky that has wept tears of compassion upon my people for centuries untold, and which to us appears changeless and eternal, may change. Today is fair. Tomorrow it may be overcast with clouds. My words are like the stars that never change. Whatever Seattle says the great chief at Washington can rely upon with as much certainty as he can upon the return of the sun or the seasons. The White Chief says that Big Chief at Washington sends us greetings of friendship and goodwill. That is kind of him for we know he has little need of our friendship in return. His people are many. They are like the grass that covers vast prairies. My people are few. They resemble the scattering trees of a storm-swept plain. . . . I will not dwell on, nor mourn over, our untimely decay, nor reproach our paleface brothers with hastening it, as we too may have been somewhat to blame. . . .

Your God is not our God. Your God loves your people and hates mine. He folds his strong and protecting arms lovingly about the paleface and leads him by the hand as a father leads his infant son— but He has forsaken His red children—if they really are His. Our God, the Great Spirit, seems also to have forsaken us. Your God makes your people strong every day. Soon they will fill the land. Our people are ebbing away like a rapidly receding tide that will never return. The white man's God cannot love our people or He would protect them. They seem to be orphans who can look nowhere for help. How then can we be brothers? . . *!.* We are two distinct races with separate origins and separate destinies. There is little in common between us.

To us the ashes of our ancestors are sacred and their resting place is hallowed ground. You wander far from the graves of your ancestors and seemingly without regret. Your religion was written upon tables of stone by the iron finger of your God so that you could not forget. The Red Man could never comprehend nor remember it. Our religion is the traditions of our ancestors—the dreams of our old men, given them in solemn hours of night by the Great Spirit; and the visions of our sachems; and it is written in the hearts of our people.

Your dead cease to love you and the land of their nativity as soon as they pass the portals of the tomb and wander way beyond the stars. They are soon forgotten and never return. Our dead never forget the beautiful world that gave them being.

Day and night cannot dwell together. The Red Man has ever fled 5 the approach of the White Man, as the morning mist flees before the morning sun. However, your proposition seems fair and I think that my people will accept it and will retire to the reservation you offer them. Then we will dwell apart in peace. . . . It matters little where we pass the remnant of our days. They will not be many. A few more moons; a few more winters—and not one of the descendants of the mighty hosts that once moved over this broad land or lived in happy homes, protected by the Great Spirit, will remain to mourn over the graves of a people once more powerful and hopeful than yours. But why should I mourn at the untimely fate of my people? Tribe follows tribe, and nation follows nation, like the waves of the sea. It is the order of nature, and regret is useless. Your time of decay may be distant, but it will surely come, for even the White Man whose God walked and talked with him as friend with friend cannot be exempt from the common destiny. We may be brothers after all. We will see. . . .

Every part of this soil is sacred in the estimation of my people. Every hillside, every valley, every plain and grove, has been hallowed by some sad or happy event in days long vanished. The very dust upon which you now stand responds more lovingly to their footsteps than to yours, because it is rich with the blood of our ancestors and our bare feet are conscious of the sympathetic touch. Even the little children who lived here and rejoiced here for a brief season will love these somber solitudes and at eventide they greet shadowy returning spirits. And when the last Red Man shall have perished, and the memory of my tribe shall have become a myth among the White Men, these shores will swarm with the invisible dead of my tribe, and when your children's children think themselves alone in the field, the store, the shop, upon the highway, or in the silence of the pathless woods, they will not be alone. At night when the streets of your cities and villages are silent and you think them deserted, they will throng with the returning hosts that once filled and still love this beautiful land. The White Man will never be alone.

Let him be just and deal kindly with my people, for the dead are not powerless. Dead, did I say? There is no death, only a change of worlds.

Responding to Reading

1. The point is made in paragraph 2 that Native Americans and whites are "two distinct races with separate origins and separate destinies." What differences are then identified? Are there any similarities between the two groups?
2. Is the speech's tone primarily hopeful, resigned, conciliatory, angry, or bitter? What dreams, if any, does the speech suggest for Chief Seattle's people? Do you think these dreams have been realized?
3. Paragraph 5 offers the observation, "We may be brothers after all. We will see." What do you suppose Chief Seattle means? Do you agree?

Responding in Writing

Chief Seattle's comments were delivered in a speech. How do you picture the setting and audience for this speech?

WHY THE AMERICANS ARE SO RESTLESS IN THE MIDST OF THEIR PROSPERITY

Alexis de Tocqueville

1805–1859

Historian and political scientist Alexis de Tocqueville was born in Verneuil, France. After studying law, he entered politics and went on to serve in the Chamber of Deputies and as minister of foreign affairs. In 1831, the French government sent him on a mission to the United States to draft a report on the penal system. His stay led him to write De la Democratie en Amerique *(1835), the first comprehensive study of the political and social institutions of the United States as well as of the character of the American people. Translated as* Democracy in America, *the book was published here between 1835 and 1840 and remains a classic political science text.*

In certain remote corners of the Old World you may still sometimes stumble upon a small district that seems to have been forgotten amid the general tumult, and to have remained stationary while everything around it was in motion. The inhabitants, for the most part, are extremely ignorant and poor; they take no part in the business of the country and are frequently oppressed by the government, yet their countenances are generally placid and their spirits light.

In America I saw the freest and most enlightened men placed in the happiest circumstances that the world affords; it seemed to me as if a cloud habitually hung upon their brow, and I thought them serious and almost sad, even in their pleasures.

The chief reason for this contrast is that the former do not think of the ills they endure, while the latter are forever brooding over advantages they do not possess. It is strange to see with what feverish ardor the Americans pursue their own welfare, and to watch the vague dread that constantly torments them lest they should not have chosen the shortest path which may lead to it.

A native of the United States clings to this world's goods as if he were certain never to die; and he is so hasty in grasping at all within his reach that one would suppose he was constantly afraid of not living long enough to enjoy them. He clutches everything, he holds nothing fast, but soon loosens his grasp to pursue fresh gratifications.

In the United States a man builds a house in which to spend his 5 old age, and he sells it before the roof is on; he plants a garden and lets it just as the trees are coming into bearing; he brings a field into tillage and leaves other men to gather the crops; he embraces a profession and gives it up; he settles in a place, which he soon afterwards leaves to carry his changeable longings elsewhere. If his private affairs leave him any leisure, he instantly plunges into the vortex of politics; and if at the end of a year of unremitting labor he finds he has a few days' vacation, his eager curiosity whirls him over the vast extent of the United States, and he will travel fifteen hundred miles in a few days to shake off his happiness. Death at length overtakes him, but it is before he is weary of his bootless chase of that complete felicity which forever escapes him.

At first sight there is something surprising in this strange unrest of so many happy men, restless in the midst of abundance. The spectacle itself, however, is as old as the world; the novelty is to see a whole people furnish an exemplification of it.

Their taste for physical gratifications must be regarded as the original source of that secret disquietude which the actions of the Americans betray and of that inconstancy of which they daily afford fresh examples. He who has set his heart exclusively upon the pursuit of worldly welfare is always in a hurry, for he has but a limited time at his disposal to reach, to grasp, and to enjoy it. The recollection of the shortness of life is a constant spur to him. Besides the good things that he possesses, he every instant fancies a thousand others that death will prevent him from trying if he does not try them soon. This thought fills him with anxiety, fear, and regret and keeps his mind in ceaseless trepidation, which leads him perpetually to change his plans and his abode.

If in addition to the taste for physical well-being a social condition be added in which neither laws nor customs retain any person in his place, there is a great additional stimulant to this restlessness of temper. Men will then be seen continually to change their track for fear of missing the shortest cut to happiness.

It may readily be conceived that if men passionately bent upon physical gratifications desire eagerly, they are also easily discouraged; as their ultimate object is to enjoy, the means to reach that object must be prompt and easy or the trouble of acquiring the gratification would be greater than the gratification itself. Their prevailing frame of mind, then, is at once ardent and relaxed, violent and enervated. Death is often less dreaded by them than perseverance in continuous efforts to one end.

10 The equality of conditions leads by a still straighter road to several of the effects that I have here described. When all the privileges of birth and fortune are abolished, when all professions are accessible to all, and a man's own energies may place him at the top of any one of them, an easy and unbounded career seems open to his ambition and he will readily persuade himself that he is born to no common destinies. But this is an erroneous notion, which is corrected by daily experience. The same equality that allows every citizen to conceive these lofty hopes renders all the citizens less able to realize them; it

circumscribes their powers on every side, while it gives freer scope to their desires. Not only are they themselves powerless, but they are met at every step by immense obstacles, which they did not at first perceive. They have swept away the privileges of some of their fellow creatures which stood in their way, but they have opened the door to universal competition; the barrier has changed its shape rather than its position. When men are nearly alike and all follow the same track, it is very difficult for any one individual to walk quickly and cleave a way through the dense throng that surrounds and presses on him. This constant strife between the inclination springing from the equality of condition and the means it supplies to satisfy them harasses and wearies the mind.

It is possible to conceive of men arrived at a degree of freedom that should completely content them; they would then enjoy their independence without anxiety and without impatience. But men will never establish any equality with which they can be contented. Whatever efforts a people may make, they will never succeed in reducing all the conditions of society to a perfect level; and even if they unhappily attained that absolute and complete equality of position, the inequality of minds would still remain, which, coming directly from the hand of God, will forever escape the laws of man. However democratic, then, the social state and the political constitution of a people may be, it is certain that every member of the community will always find out several points about him which overlook his own position; and we may foresee that his looks will be doggedly fixed in that direction. When inequality of conditions is the common law of society, the most marked inequalities do not strike the eye; when everything is nearly on the same level, the slightest are marked enough to hurt it. Hence the desire of equality always becomes more insatiable in proportion as equality is more complete.

Among democratic nations, men easily attain a certain equality of condition, but they can never attain as much as they desire. It perpetually retires from before them, yet without hiding itself from their sight, and in retiring draws them on. At every moment they think they are about to grasp it; it escapes at every moment from their hold. They are near enough to see its charms, but too far off to enjoy them; and before they have fully tasted its delights, they die.

To these causes must be attributed that strange melancholy which often haunts the inhabitants of democratic countries in the midst of their abundance, and that disgust at life which sometimes seizes upon them in the midst of calm and easy circumstances. Complaints are made in France that the number of suicides increases; in America suicide is rare, but insanity is said to be more common there than anywhere else. These are all different symptoms of the same disease. The Americans do not put an end to their lives, however disquieted they may be, because their religion forbids it; and among them materialism may be said hardly to exist, notwithstanding the general passion for physical gratification. The will resists, but reason frequently gives way.

In democratic times enjoyments are more intense than in the ages of aristocracy, and the number of those who partake in them is vastly larger: but, on the other hand, it must be admitted that man's hopes and desires are oftener blasted, the soul is more stricken and perturbed, and care itself more keen.

Responding to Reading

1. De Tocqueville's essay was published in 1835. Does his characterization of Americans' "unrest" hold true today? If so, do you see this restlessness as a problem?
2. De Tocqueville speaks about Americans in very general, abstract terms. Can you supply concrete, specific examples to support (or contradict) his characterizations?
3. What does de Tocqueville see as the cause of Americans' restlessness? In what sense is "equality" to blame? Does he offer a cure for the national malady? Given the premise of equality upon which our society rests, do you think a cure is possible? Explain.

Responding in Writing

Write a brief letter to de Tocqueville supporting or challenging his characterization of Americans.

THE LIBRARY CARD

Richard Wright

1908–1960

Born on a former plantation near Natchez, Mississippi, Richard Wright spent much of his childhood in an orphanage or with various relatives. He attended schools in Jackson and in 1934 moved to Chicago, where he worked at a number of unskilled jobs before joining the Federal Writer's Project. When his politics became radical, he wrote poetry for leftist publications. In 1938, he published his first book, Uncle Tom's Children: Four Novellas; *two years later, his novel* Native Son *made him famous. After World War II, Wright lived as an expatriate in Paris, where he wrote his autobiography,* Black Boy *(1945), a book that celebrates African-American resilience and courage much as nineteenth-century slave narratives do. In this excerpt from* Black Boy, *Wright tells how he took advantage of an opportunity to feed his hunger for an intellectual life. To learn more about Wright, visit the Hurston Wright Foundation Web site, http://www.hurston-wright.org/ wright.html/.*

One morning I arrived early at work and went into the bank lobby where the Negro porter was mopping. I stood at a counter and picked up the Memphis *Commercial Appeal* and began my free reading of the press. I came finally to the editorial page and saw an article dealing with one H. L. Mencken.[1] I knew by hearsay that he was the editor of the *American Mercury*, but aside from that I knew nothing about him. The article was a furious denunciation of Mencken, concluding with one hot, short sentence: Mencken is a fool.

I wondered what on earth this Mencken had done to call down upon him the scorn of the South. The only people I had ever heard denounced in the South were Negroes, and this man was not a Negro. Then what ideas did Mencken hold that made a newspaper like the *Commercial Appeal* castigate him publicly? Undoubtedly he must be advocating ideas that the South did not like. Were there, then, people other than Negroes who criticized the South? I knew that during the Civil War the South had hated northern whites, but I had not encountered such hate during my life. Knowing no more of Mencken than I did at that moment, I felt a vague sympathy for him. Had not the South, which had assigned me the role of a non-man, cast at him its hardest words?

Now, how could I find out about this Mencken? There was a huge library near the riverfront, but I knew that Negroes were not allowed to patronize its shelves any more than they were the parks and playgrounds of the city. I had gone into the library several times to get books for the white men on the job. Which of them would now help me to get books? And how could I read them without causing concern to the white men with whom I worked? I had so far been successful in hiding my thoughts and feelings from them, but I knew that I would create hostility if I went about this business of reading in a clumsy way.

I weighed the personalities of the men on the job. There was Don, a Jew; but I distrusted him. His position was not much better than mine and I knew that he was uneasy and insecure; he had always treated me in an offhand, bantering way that barely concealed his contempt. I was afraid to ask him to help me to get books; his frantic desire to demonstrate a racial solidarity with the whites against Negroes might make him betray me.

Then how about the boss? No, he was a Baptist and I had the suspicion that he would not be quite able to comprehend why a black 5

---

[1] Henry Louis Mencken (1880–1956), journalist, critic, and essayist, who was known for his pointed, outspoken, and satirical comments about the blunders and imperfections of democracy and the cultural awkwardness of Americans. [Eds.]

boy would want to read Mencken. There were other white men on the job whose attitudes showed clearly that they were Kluxers or sympathizers, and they were out of the question.

There remained only one man whose attitude did not fit into an anti-Negro category, for I had heard the white men refer to him as a "Pope lover." He was an Irish Catholic and was hated by the white Southerners. I knew that he read books, because I had got him volumes from the library several times. Since he, too, was an object of hatred, I felt that he might refuse me but would hardly betray me. I hesitated, weighing and balancing the imponderable realities.

One morning I paused before the Catholic fellow's desk.

"I want to ask you a favor," I whispered to him.

"What is it?"

10   "I want to read. I can't get books from the library. I wonder if you'd let me use your card?"

He looked at me suspiciously.

"My card is full most of the time," he said.

"I see," I said and waited, posing my question silently.

"You're not trying to get me into trouble, are you, boy?" he asked, staring at me.

15   "Oh, no, sir."

"What book do you want?"

"A book by H. L. Mencken."

"Which one?"

"I don't know. Has he written more than one?"

20   "He has written several."

"I didn't know that."

"What makes you want to read Mencken?"

"Oh, I just saw his name in the newspaper," I said.

"It's good of you to want to read," he said. "But you ought to read the right things."

25   I said nothing. Would he want to supervise my reading?

"Let me think," he said. "I'll figure out something."

I turned from him and he called me back. He stared at me quizzically.

"Richard, don't mention this to the other white men," he said.

"I understand," I said. "I won't say a word."

30   A few days later he called me to him.

"I've got a card in my wife's name," he said. "Here's mine."

"Thank you, sir."

"Do you think you can manage it?"

"I'll manage fine," I said.

35   "If they suspect you, you'll get in trouble," he said.

"I'll write the same kind of notes to the library that you wrote when you sent me for books," I told him. "I'll sign your name."

He laughed.

"Go ahead. Let me see what you get," he said.

That afternoon I addressed myself to forging a note. Now, what were the names of books written by H. L. Mencken? I did not know any of them. I finally wrote what I thought would be a foolproof note: *Dear Madam: Will you please let this nigger boy*—I used the word "nigger" to make the librarian feel that I could not possibly be the author of the note—*have some books by H. L. Mencken?* I forged the white man's name.

I entered the library as I had always done when on errands for 40 whites, but I felt that I would somehow slip up and betray myself. I doffed my hat, stood a respectful distance from the desk, looked as unbookish as possible, and waited for the white patrons to be taken care of. When the desk was clear of people, I still waited. The white librarian looked at me.

"What do you want, boy?"

As though I did not possess the power of speech, I stepped forward and simply handed her the forged note, not parting my lips.

"What books by Mencken does he want?" she asked.

"I don't know, ma'am," I said, avoiding her eyes.

"Who gave you this card?"   45

"Mr. Falk," I said.

"Where is he?"

"He's at work, at the M—— Optical Company," I said. "I've been in here for him before."

"I remember," the woman said. "But he never wrote notes like this."

Oh, God, she's suspicious. Perhaps she would not let me have the 50 books? If she had turned her back at that moment, I would have ducked out the door and never gone back. Then I thought of a bold idea.

"You can call him up, ma'am," I said, my heart pounding.

"You're not using these books, are you?" she asked pointedly.

"Oh, no, ma'am. I can't read."

"I don't know what he wants by Mencken," she said under her breath.

I knew now that I had won; she was thinking of other things and 55 the race question had gone out of her mind. She went to the shelves. Once or twice she looked over her shoulder at me, as though she was still doubtful. Finally she came forward with two books in her hand.

"I'm sending him two books," she said. "But tell Mr. Falk to come in next time, or send me the names of the books he wants. I don't know what he wants to read."

I said nothing. She stamped the card and handed me the books. Not daring to glance at them, I went out of the library, fearing that the woman would call me back for further questioning. A block away from the library I opened one of the books and read a title: *A Book of Prefaces*. I was nearing my nineteenth birthday and I did not know how to pronounce the word "preface." I thumbed the pages and saw strange

words and strange names. I shook my head, disappointed. I looked at
the other book; it was called *Prejudices*. I knew what that word meant; I
had heard it all my life. And right off I was on guard against
Mencken's books. Why would a man want to call a book *Prejudices?*
The word was so stained with all my memories of racial hate that I
could not conceive of anybody using it for a title. Perhaps I had made a
mistake about Mencken? A man who had prejudices must be wrong.

When I showed the books to Mr. Falk, he looked at me and frowned.

"That librarian might telephone you," I warned him.

60   "That's all right," he said. "But when you're through reading
those books, I want you to tell me what you get out of them."

That night in my rented room, while letting the hot water run
over my can of pork and beans in the sink, I opened *A Book of Prefaces*
and began to read. I was jarred and shocked by the style, the clear,
clean, sweeping sentences. Why did he write like that? And how did
one write like that? I pictured the man as a raging demon, slashing
with his pen, consumed with hate, denouncing everything American,
extolling everything European or German, laughing at the weaknesses of people, mocking God, authority. What was this? I stood up,
trying to realize what reality lay behind the meaning of the words. . . .
Yes, this man was fighting, fighting with words. He was using words
as a weapon, using them as one would use a club. Could words be
weapons? Well, yes, for here they were. Then, maybe, perhaps, I
could use them as a weapon? No. It frightened me. I read on and
what amazed me was not what he said, but how on earth anybody
had the courage to say it.

Occasionally I glanced up to reassure myself that I was alone in
the room. Who were these men about whom Mencken was talking so
passionately? Who was Anatole France? Joseph Conrad? Sinclair
Lewis, Sherwood Anderson, Dostoevski, George Moore, Gustave
Flaubert, Maupassant, Tolstoy, Frank Harris, Mark Twain, Thomas
Hardy, Arnold Bennett, Stephen Crane, Zola, Norris, Gorky, Bergson,
Ibsen, Balzac, Bernard Shaw, Dumas, Poe, Thomas Mann, O. Henry,
Dreiser, H. G. Wells, Gogol, T. S. Eliot, Gide, Baudelaire, Edgar Lee
Masters, Stendhal, Turgenev, Huneker, Nietzsche, and scores of oth-
ers? Were these men real? Did they exist or had they existed? And
how did one pronounce their names?

I ran across many words whose meanings I did not know, and I
either looked them up in a dictionary or, before I had a chance to do
that, encountered the word in a context that made its meaning clear.
But what strange world was this? I concluded the book with the conviction that I had somehow overlooked something terribly important
in life. I had once tried to write, had once reveled in feeling, had let
my crude imagination roam, but the impulse to dream had been
slowly beaten out of me by experience. Now it surged up again and I
hungered for books, new ways of looking and seeing. It was not a

matter of believing or disbelieving what I read, but of feeling something new, of being affected by something that made the look of the
world different.

As dawn broke I ate my pork and beans, feeling dopey, sleepy. I
went to work, but the mood of the book would not die; it lingered,
coloring everything I saw, heard, did. I now felt that I knew what the
white men were feeling. Merely because I had read a book that had
spoken of how they lived and thought, I identified myself with that
book. I felt vaguely guilty. Would I, filled with bookish notions, act in
a manner that would make the whites dislike me?

I forged more notes and my trips to the library became frequent.   65
Reading grew into a passion. My first serious novel was Sinclair
Lewis's *Main Street*.[2] It made me see my boss, Mr. Gerald, and identify him as an American type. I would smile when I saw him lugging
his golf bags into the office. I had always felt a vast distance separating me from the boss, and now I felt closer to him, though still distant.
I felt now that I knew him, that I could feel the very limits of his narrow life. And this had happened because I had read a novel about a
mythical man called George F. Babbitt.[3]

The plots and stories in the novels did not interest me so much as
the point of view revealed. I gave myself over to each novel without
reserve, without trying to criticize it; it was enough for me to see and
feel something different. And for me, everything was something different. Reading was like a drug, a dope. The novels created moods in
which I lived for days. But I could not conquer my sense of guilt, my
feeling that the white men around me knew that I was changing, that
I had begun to regard them differently.

Whenever I brought a book to the job, I wrapped it in newspaper—a habit that was to persist for years in other cities and under
other circumstances. But some of the white men pried into my packages when I was absent and they questioned me.

"Boy, what are you reading those books for?"

"Oh, I don't know, sir."

"That's deep stuff you're reading, boy."   70

"I'm just killing time, sir."

"You'll addle your brains if you don't watch out."

I read Dreiser's *Jennie Gerhardt* and *Sister Carrie*[4] and they revived
in me a vivid sense of my mother's suffering; I was overwhelmed. I

---

[2]*Main Street*, published in 1920, examines the smugness, intolerance, and lack of imagination that
characterize small-town American life. [Eds.]

[3]The central character in Sinclair Lewis's *Babbit* (1922), who believed in the virtues of home, the Republican Party, and middle-class conventions. To Wright, Babbitt symbolizes the mindless complacency of white middle-class America. [Eds.]

[4]Both *Jennie Gerhardt* (1911) and *Sister Carrie* (1900), by Theodore Dreiser, tell the stories of working
women who struggle against poverty and social injustice. [Eds.]

grew silent, wondering about the life around me. It would have been impossible for me to have told anyone what I derived from these novels, for it was nothing less than a sense of life itself. All my life had shaped me for the realism, the naturalism of the modern novel, and I could not read enough of them.

Steeped in new moods and ideas, I bought a ream of paper and tried to write; but nothing would come, or what did come was flat beyond telling. I discovered that more than desire and feeling were necessary to write and I dropped the idea. Yet I still wondered how it was possible to know people sufficiently to write about them. Could I ever learn about life and people? To me, with my vast ignorance, my Jim Crow station in life, it seemed a task impossible of achievement. I now knew what being a Negro meant. I could endure the hunger. I had learned to live with hate. But to feel that there were feelings denied me, that the very breath of life itself was beyond my reach, that more than anything else hurt, wounded me. I had a new hunger.

75   In buoying me up, reading also cast me down, made me see what was possible, what I had missed. My tension returned, new, terrible, bitter, surging, almost too great to be contained. I no longer *felt* that the world about me was hostile, killing; I *knew* it. A million times I asked myself what I could do to save myself, and there were no answers. I seemed forever condemned, ringed by walls.

I did not discuss my reading with Mr. Falk, who had lent me his library card; it would have meant talking about myself and that would have been too painful. I smiled each day, fighting desperately to maintain my old behavior, to keep my disposition seemingly sunny. But some of the white men discerned that I had begun to brood.

"Wake up there, boy!" Mr. Olin said one day.

"Sir!" I answered for the lack of a better word.

"You act like you've stolen something," he said.

80   I laughed in the way I knew he expected me to laugh, but I resolved to be more conscious of myself, to watch my every act, to guard and hide the new knowledge that was dawning within me.

If I went north, would it be possible for me to build a new life then? But how could a man build a life upon vague, unformed yearnings? I wanted to write and I did not even know the English language. I bought English grammars and found them dull. I felt that I was getting a better sense of the language from novels than from grammars. I read hard, discarding a writer as soon as I felt that I had grasped his point of view. At night the printed page stood before my eyes in sleep.

Mrs. Moss, my landlady, asked me one Sunday morning: "Son, what is this you keep on reading?"

"Oh, nothing. Just novels."

"What you get out of 'em?"

85   "I'm just killing time," I said.

"I hope you know your own mind," she said in a tone which implied that she doubted if I had a mind.

I knew of no Negroes who read the books I liked and I wondered if any Negroes ever thought of them. I knew that there were Negro doctors, lawyers, newspapermen, but I never saw any of them. When I read a Negro newspaper I never caught the faintest echo of my preoccupation in its pages. I felt trapped and occasionally, for a few days, I would stop reading. But a vague hunger would come over me for books, books that opened up new avenues of feeling and seeing, and again I would forge another note to the white librarian. Again I would read and wonder as only the naïve and unlettered can read and wonder, feeling that I carried a secret, criminal burden about with me each day.

That winter my mother and brother came and we set up housekeeping, buying furniture on the installment plan, being cheated and yet knowing no way to avoid it. I began to eat warm food and to my surprise found that regular meals enabled me to read faster. I may have lived through many illnesses and survived them, never suspecting that I was ill. My brother obtained a job and we began to save toward the trip north, plotting our time, setting tentative dates for departure. I told none of the white men on the job that I was planning to go north; I knew that the moment they felt I was thinking of the North they would change toward me. It would have made them feel that I did not like the life I was living, and because my life was completely conditioned by what they said or did, it would have been tantamount to challenging them.

I could calculate my chances for life in the South as a Negro fairly clearly now.

I could fight the southern whites by organizing with other ₉₀ Negroes, as my grandfather had done. But I knew that I could never win that way; there were many whites and there were but few blacks. They were strong and we were weak. Outright black rebellion could never win. If I fought openly I would die and I did not want to die. News of lynchings were frequent.

I could submit and live the life of a genial slave, but that was impossible. All of my life had shaped me to live by my own feelings and thoughts. I could make up to Bess and marry her and inherit the house. But that, too, would be the life of a slave; if I did that, I would crush to death something within me, and I would hate myself as much as I knew the whites already hated those who had submitted. Neither could I ever willingly present myself to be kicked, as Shorty had done. I would rather have died than do that.

I could drain off my restlessness by fighting with Shorty and Harrison. I had seen many Negroes solve the problem of being black by transferring their hatred of themselves to others with a black skin and fighting them. I would have to be cold to do that, and I was not cold and I could never be.

I could, of course, forget what I had read, thrust the whites out of my mind, forget them; and find release from anxiety and longing in sex and alcohol. But the memory of how my father had conducted himself made that course repugnant. If I did not want others to violate my life, how could I voluntarily violate it myself?

I had no hope whatever of being a professional man. Not only had I been so conditioned that I did not desire it, but the fulfillment of such an ambition was beyond my capabilities. Well-to-do Negroes lived in a world that was almost as alien to me as the world inhabited by whites.

95   What, then, was there? I held my life in my mind, in my consciousness each day, feeling at times that I would stumble and drop it, spill it forever. My reading had created a vast sense of distance between me and the world in which I lived and tried to make a living, and that sense of distance was increasing each day. My days and nights were one long, quiet, continuously contained dream of terror, tension, and anxiety. I wondered how long I could bear it.

Responding to Reading

1. In what sense did access to books bring Wright closer to achieving the American Dream? What new obstacles did books introduce?
2. In paragraph 74, Wright mentions his "Jim Crow station in life." The term *Jim Crow*, derived from a character in a minstrel show, refers to laws enacted in Southern states that legalized racial segregation. What is Wright's "station in life"? In what ways does he adapt his behavior to accommodate this Jim Crow image? In what ways does he defy this stereotype?
3. After World War II, Wright left the United States to live in Paris. Given what you have read in this essay, does his decision surprise you? Do you think he made the right choice?

Responding in Writing

If Wright were alive today, what books and magazines would you recommend he read? Why?

BECOMING AMERICAN

Dinesh D'Souza

1961–

Dinesh D'Souza was born in Bombay, India, and immigrated to United States with his family in 1978. He studied at Dartmouth College, where he received an AB degree (1983). Working as a journalist, D'Souza began writing essays about social and political issues and moved on to serve as a domestic policy analyst at the White House during the Reagan administration.

He now works as a fellow at the Hoover Institution of Stanford University. D'Souza's books include the bestseller Illiberal Education *(1991),* The Virtue of Prosperity: Finding Values in an Age of Techno-Affluence *(2000), and the bestseller* What's So Great About America *(2002), from which the following essay is taken. His articles on culture and politics have appeared in* Vanity Fair, Forbes, Harper's, *the* Wall Street Journal, Atlantic Monthly, *the* Washington Post, *and the* New York Times. *To learn more about D'Souza, visit his Web site, http://www.dineshdsouza.com/.*

Critics of America, both at home and abroad, have an easy explanation for why the American idea is so captivating, and why immigrants want to come here. The reason, they say, is money. America represents "the bitch goddess of success." That is why poor people reach out for the American idea: they want to touch some of that lucre. As for immigrants, they allegedly flock to the United States for the sole purpose of getting rich. This view, which represents the appeal of America as the appeal of the almighty dollar, is disseminated on Arab streets and in multicultural textbooks taught in U.S. schools. It is a way of demeaning the United States by associating it with what is selfish, base, and crass: an unquenchable appetite for gain.

It is not hard to see why this view of America has gained a wide currency. When people in foreign countries turn on American TV shows, they are stupefied by the lavish displays of affluence: the sumptuous homes, the bejeweled women, the fountains and pools, and so on. Whether reruns of *Dallas* and *Dynasty* are true to the American experience is irrelevant here; the point is that this is how the United States appears to outsiders who have not had the chance to come here. And even for those who do, it is hard to deny that America represents the chance to live better, even to become fantastically wealthy. For instance, there are several people of Indian descent on the *Forbes* 400 list. And over the years I have heard many Indians now living in the United States say, "We want to live an Indian lifestyle, but at an American standard of living."

If this seems like a crass motive for immigration, it must be evaluated in the context of the harsh fate that poor people endure in much of the Third World. The lives of many of these people are defined by an ongoing struggle to exist. It is not that they don't work hard. On the contrary, they labor incessantly and endure hardships that are almost unimaginable to people in the West. In the villages of Asia and Africa, for example, a common sight is a farmer beating a pickax into the ground, women wobbling under heavy loads, children carrying stones. These people are performing very hard labor, but they are getting nowhere. The best they can hope for is to survive for another day. Their clothes are tattered, their teeth are rotted, and disease and death constantly loom over their horizon. For the poor of the Third World, life is characterized by squalor, indignity, and brevity.

I emphasize the plight of the poor, but I recognize, of course, that there are substantial middle classes even in the underdeveloped world. For these people basic survival may not be an issue, but still, they endure hardships that make everyday life a strain. One problem is that the basic infrastructure of the Third World is abysmal: the roads are not properly paved, the water is not safe to drink, pollution in the cities has reached hazardous levels, public transportation is overcrowded and unreliable, and there is a two-year waiting period to get a telephone. Government officials, who are very poorly paid, are inevitably corrupt, which means that you must pay bribes on a regular basis to get things done. Most important, there are limited prospects for the children's future.

5   In America, the immigrant immediately recognizes, things are different. The newcomer who sees America for the first time typically experiences emotions that alternate between wonder and delight. Here is a country where *everything works*: the roads are clean and paper smooth, the highway signs are clear and accurate, the public toilets function properly, when you pick up the telephone you get a dial tone, you can even buy things from the store and then take them back. For the Third World visitor, the American supermarket is a thing to behold: endless aisles of every imaginable product, fifty different types of cereal, multiple flavors of ice cream. The place is full of countless unappreciated inventions: quilted toilet paper, fabric softener, cordless telephones, disposable diapers, roll-on luggage, deodorant. Most countries even today do not have these benefits: deodorant, for example, is unavailable in much of the Third World and unused in much of Europe.

What the immigrant cannot help noticing is that America is a country where the poor live comparatively well. This fact was dramatized in the 1980s, when CBS television broadcast an anti-Reagan documentary, "People Like Us," which was intended to show the miseries of the poor during an American recession. The Soviet Union also broadcast the documentary, with a view to embarrassing the Reagan administration. But by the testimony of former Soviet leaders, it had the opposite effect. Ordinary people across the Soviet Union saw that the poorest Americans have television sets and microwave ovens and cars. They arrived at the same perception of America that I witnessed in a friend of mine from Bombay who has been unsuccessfully trying to move to the United States for nearly a decade. Finally I asked him, "Why are you so eager to come to America?" He replied, "Because I really want to live in a country where the poor people are fat."

The point is that the United States is a country where the ordinary guy has a good life. This is what distinguishes America from so many other countries. Everywhere in the world, the rich person lives well.

Indeed, a good case can be made that if you are rich, you live better in countries other than America. The reason is that you enjoy the pleasures of aristocracy. This is the pleasure of being treated as a superior person. Its gratification derives from subservience: in India, for example, the wealthy enjoy the satisfaction of seeing innumerable servants and toadies grovel before them and attend to their every need.

In the United States the social ethic is egalitarian, and this is unaffected by the inequalities of wealth in the country. Tocqueville noticed this egalitarianism a century and a half ago, but it is, if anything, more prevalent today. For all his riches, Bill Gates could not approach a homeless person and say, "Here's a $100 bill. I'll give it to you if you kiss my feet." Most likely the homeless guy would tell Gates to go to hell! The American view is that the rich guy may have more money, but he isn't in any fundamental sense better than you are. The American janitor or waiter sees himself as performing a service, but he doesn't see himself as inferior to those he serves. And neither do the customers see him that way: they are generally happy to show him respect and appreciation on a plane of equality. America is the only country in the world where we call the waiter "Sir," as if he were a knight.

The moral triumph of America is that it has extended the benefits of comfort and affluence, traditionally enjoyed by very few, to a large segment of society. Very few people in America have to wonder where their next meal is coming from. Even sick people who don't have proper insurance can receive medical care at hospital emergency rooms. The poorest American girls are not humiliated by having to wear torn clothes. Every child is given an education, and most have the chance to go on to college. The common man can expect to live long enough and have free time to play with his grandchildren.

Ordinary Americans enjoy not only security and dignity, but also 10 comforts that other societies reserve for the elite. We now live in a country where construction workers regularly pay $4 for a nonfat latte, where maids drive very nice cars, where plumbers take their families on vacation to Europe. As Irving Kristol once observed, there is virtually no restaurant in America to which a CEO can go to lunch with the absolute assurance that he will not find his secretary also dining there. Given the standard of living of the ordinary American, it is no wonder that socialist or revolutionary schemes have never found a wide constituency in the United States. As sociologist Werner Sombart observed, all socialist utopias in America have come to grief on roast beef and apple pie.*

---

*Werner Sombart, *Why Is There No Socialism in the United States?* (White Plains: International Arts and Sciences Press, 1976), 109–10.

Thus it is entirely understandable that people would associate the idea of America with a better life. For them, money is not an end in itself; money is the means to a longer, healthier, and fuller life. Money allows them to purchase a level of security, dignity, and comfort that they could not have hoped to enjoy in their native countries. Money also frees up time for family life, community involvement, and spiritual pursuits: thus it produces not just material, but also moral, gains. All of this is true, and yet in my view it offers an incomplete picture of why America is so appealing to so many. Let me illustrate with the example of my own life.

Not long ago, I asked myself: what would my life have been like if I had never come to the United States, if I had stayed in India? Materially, my life has improved, but not in a fundamental sense. I grew up in a middle-class family in Bombay. My father was a chemical engineer; my mother, an office secretary. I was raised without great luxury, but neither did I lack for anything. My standard of living in America is higher, but it is not a radical difference. My life has changed far more dramatically in other ways.

If I had remained in India, I would probably have lived my entire existence within a one-mile radius of where I was born. I would undoubtedly have married a woman of my identical religious, socioeconomic, and cultural background. I would almost certainly have become a medical doctor, an engineer, or a software programmer. I would have socialized within my ethnic community and had cordial relations, but few friends, outside that group. I would have a whole set of opinions that could be predicted in advance; indeed, they would not be very different from what my father believed, or his father before him. In sum, my destiny would to a large degree have been given to me.

This is not to say that I would have no choice; I would have choice, but within narrowly confined parameters. Let me illustrate with the example of my sister, who got married several years ago. My parents began the process by conducting a comprehensive survey of all the eligible families in our neighborhood. First they examined primary criteria, such as religion, socioeconomic position, and educational background. Then my parents investigated subtler issues: the social reputation of the family, reports of a lunatic uncle, the character of the son, and so on. Finally my parents were down to a dozen or so eligible families, and they were invited to our house for dinner with suspicious regularity. My sister was, in the words of Milton Friedman, "free to choose." My sister knew about, and accepted, the arrangement; she is now happily married with two children. I am not quarreling with the outcome, but clearly my sister's destiny was, to a considerable extent, choreographed by my parents.

By coming to America, I have seen my life break free of these tra- 15
ditional confines. I came to Arizona as an exchange student, but a
year later I was enrolled at Dartmouth College. There I fell in with a
group of students who were actively involved in politics; soon I had
switched my major from economics to English literature. My reading
included books like Plutarch's *Moralia*; Hamilton, Madison, and Jay's
Federalist Papers; and Evelyn Waugh's *Brideshead Revisited*. They trans-
ported me to places a long way from home and implanted in my
mind ideas that I had never previously considered. By the time I
graduated, I decided that I should become a writer, which is something you can do in this country. America permits many strange careers: this is a place where you can become, say, a comedian. I would
not like to go to my father and tell him that I was thinking of becoming a comedian. I do not think he would have found it funny.

Soon after graduation I became the managing editor of a policy
magazine and began to write freelance articles in the *Washington Post*.
Someone in the Reagan White House was apparently impressed by
my work, because I was called in for an interview and promptly hired
as a senior domestic policy analyst. I found it strange to be working at
the White House, because at the time I was not a United States citizen.
I am sure that such a thing would not happen in India or anywhere
else in the world. But Reagan and his people didn't seem to mind; for
them, ideology counted more than nationality. I also met my future
wife in the Reagan administration, where she was at the time a White
House intern. (She has since deleted it from her résumé.) My wife was
born in Louisiana and grew up in San Diego; her ancestry is English,
French, Scotch-Irish, German, and American Indian.

I notice that Americans marry in a rather peculiar way: by falling
in love. You may think that I am being ironic, or putting you on, so let
me hasten to inform you that in many parts of the world, romantic
love is considered a mild form of insanity. Consider a typical situation:
Anjali is in love with Arjun. She considers Arjun the best-looking man
in the world, the most intelligent, virtually without fault, a paragon of
humanity! But everybody else can see that Arjun is none of these
things. What, then, persuades Anjali that Arjun possesses qualities that
are nowhere in evidence? There is only one explanation: Anjali is
deeply deluded. It does not follow that her romantic impulses should
be ruthlessly crushed. But, in the view of many people and many traditions around the world, they should be steered and directed and
prevented from ruining Anjali's life. This is the job of parents and the
community, to help Anjali see beyond her delusions and to make decisions that are based on practical considerations and common sense.

If there is a single phrase that encapsulates life in the Third
World, it is that "birth is destiny." I remember an incident years ago
when my grandfather called in my brother, my sister, and me, and

asked us if we knew how lucky we were. We asked him why he felt this way: was it because we were intelligent, or had lots of friends, or were blessed with a loving family? Each time he shook his head and said, "No." Finally we pressed him: why did he consider us so lucky? Then he revealed the answer: "Because you are Brahmins!"

The Brahmin, who is the highest ranking in the Hindu caste system, is traditionally a member of the priestly class. As a matter of fact, my family had nothing to do with the priesthood. Nor are we Hindu: my ancestors converted to Christianity many generations ago. Even so, my grandfather's point was that before we converted, hundreds of years ago, our family used to be Brahmins. How he knew this remains a mystery. But he was serious in his insistence that nothing that the three of us achieved in life could possibly mean more than the fact that we were Brahmins.

20   This may seem like an extreme example, revealing my grandfather to be a very narrow fellow indeed, but the broader point is that traditional cultures attach a great deal of importance to data such as what tribe you come from, whether you are male or female, and whether you are the eldest son. Your destiny and your happiness hinge on these things. If you are a Bengali, you can count on other Bengalis to help you, and on others to discriminate against you; if you are female, then certain forms of society and several professions are closed to you; and if you are the eldest son, you inherit the family house and your siblings are expected to follow your direction. What this means is that once your tribe, caste, sex, and family position have been established at birth, your life takes a course that is largely determined for you.

In America, by contrast, you get to write the script of your own life. When your parents say to you, "What do you want to be when you grow up?" the question is open-ended; it is you who supply the answer. Your parents can advise you: "Have you considered law school?" "Why not become the first doctor in the family?" It is considered very improper, however, for them to try and force your decision. Indeed, American parents typically send their teenage children away to college, where they live on their own and learn independence. This is part of the process of forming your mind and choosing a field of interest for yourself and developing your identity. It is not uncommon in the United States for two brothers who come from the same gene pool and were raised in similar circumstances to do quite different things: the eldest becomes a gas station attendant, the younger moves up to be vice president at Oracle; the eldest marries his high-school sweetheart and raises four kids, the youngest refuses to settle down, or comes out of the closet as a homosexual; one is the Methodist that he was raised to be, the other becomes a Christian Scientist or a Buddhist. What to be, where to live, whom to love, whom to marry, what to believe, what religion to practice—these are all decisions that Americans make for themselves.

In most parts of the world your identity and your fate are to a large extent handed to you; in America, you determine them for yourself. In America your destiny is not prescribed; it is constructed. Your life is like a blank sheet of paper, and you are the artist. This notion of you being the architect of your own destiny is the incredibly powerful idea that is behind the worldwide appeal of America. Young people especially find irresistible the prospect of being in the driver's seat, of authoring the narrative of their own lives. So too the immigrant discovers that America permits him to break free of the constraints that have held him captive, so that the future becomes a landscape of his own choosing.

Responding to Reading

1. D'Souza seems to agree with those who claim that many immigrants come to the United States "for the sole purpose of getting rich" (1), but he does not criticize these immigrants who are motivated by dreams of wealth. How does he justify their motivation?
2. What is D'Souza's purpose in introducing the story of his own life? Does he achieve this purpose?
3. What specific differences does D'Souza observe between life in America and life in Third World nations? Between his own life in the United States and the life he would have led in India?

Responding in Writing

In paragraph 21, D'Souza says, "In America, . . . you get to write the script of your own life." Do you agree, or do you think D'Souza is too optimistic about what his adopted country has to offer?

THE MYTH OF THE LATIN WOMAN: I JUST MET A GIRL NAMED MARIA
Judith Ortiz Cofer
1952–

Born in Hormigueros, Puerto Rico, and raised in Paterson, New Jersey, Judith Ortiz Cofer earned a BA degree from Augusta College (1974) and an MA degree from Florida Atlantic University (1977); she also attended Oxford University. Cofer now teaches creative writing at the University of Georgia. An award-winning poet and novelist, Cofer wrote the novels The Line of the Sun *(1989) and* Silent Dancing *(1990) as well as a collection of biographical essays,* The Latin Deli: Prose and Poetry *(1993), from which the following essay is taken. In this essay, Cofer describes the stereotypes she has confronted as a Latina. For more information about Cofer, visit her Web site, http://parallel.park.uga.edu/~jcofer/.*

On a bus trip to London from Oxford University where I was earning some graduate credits one summer, a young man, obviously fresh from a pub, spotted me and as if struck by inspiration went down on his knees in the aisle. With both hands over his heart he broke into an Irish tenor's rendition of "Maria" from *West Side Story.*[1] My politely amused fellow passengers gave his lovely voice the round of gentle applause it deserved. Though I was not quite as amused, I managed my version of an English smile: no show of teeth, no extreme contortions of the facial muscles—I was at this time of my life practicing reserve and cool. Oh, that British control, how I coveted it. But "Maria" had followed me to London, reminding me of a prime fact of my life: you can leave the island, master the English language, and travel as far as you can, but if you are a Latina, especially one like me who so obviously belongs to Rita Moreno's[2] gene pool, the island travels with you.

This is sometimes a very good thing—it may win you that extra minute of someone's attention. But with some people, the same things can make *you* an island—not a tropical paradise but an Alcatraz, a place nobody wants to visit. As a Puerto Rican girl living in the United States[3] and wanting like most children to "belong," I resented the stereotype that my Hispanic appearance called forth from many people I met.

Growing up in a large urban center in New Jersey during the 1960s, I suffered from what I think of as "cultural schizophrenia." Our life was designed by my parents as a microcosm of their *casas*[4] on the island. We spoke in Spanish, ate Puerto Rican food bought at the *bodega,*[5] and practiced strict Catholicism at a church that allotted us a one-hour slot each week for mass, performed in Spanish by a Chinese priest trained as a missionary for Latin America.

As a girl I was kept under strict surveillance by my parents, since my virtue and modesty were, by their cultural equation, the same as their honor. As a teenager I was lectured constantly on how to behave

---

[1]A popular Broadway musical, loosely based on *Romeo and Juliet,* about two rival street gangs, one Anglo and one Puerto Rican, in New York City. [Eds.]

[2]Puerto Rico–born actress who won an Oscar for her role in the 1960 movie version of *West Side Story.* [Eds.]

[3]Although it is an island, Puerto Rico is part of the United States (it is a self-governing commonwealth). [Eds.]

[4]Homes. [Eds.]

[5]Small grocery store. [Eds.]

as a proper *senorita*. But it was a conflicting message I received, since the Puerto Rican mothers also encouraged their daughters to look and act like women and to dress in clothes our Anglo friends and their mothers found too "mature" and flashy. The difference was, and is, cultural; yet I often felt humiliated when I appeared at an American friend's party wearing a dress more suitable to a semi-formal than to a playroom birthday celebration. At Puerto Rican festivities, neither the music nor the colors we wore could be too loud.

I remember Career Day in our high school, when teachers told us 5 to come dressed as if for a job interview. It quickly became obvious that to the Puerto Rican girls "dressing up" meant wearing their mother's ornate jewelry and clothing, more appropriate (by mainstream standards) for the company Christmas party than as daily office attire. That morning I had agonized in front of my closet, trying to figure out what a "career girl" would wear. I knew how to dress for school (at the Catholic school I attended, we all wore uniforms), I knew how to dress for Sunday mass, and I knew what dresses to wear for parties at my relatives' homes. Though I do not recall the precise details of my Career Day outfit, it must have been a composite of these choices. But I remember a comment my friend (an Italian American) made in later years that coalesced my impressions of that day. She said that at the business school she was attending, the Puerto Rican girls always stood out for wearing "everything at once." She meant, of course, too much jewelry, too many accessories. On that day at school we were simply made the negative models by the nuns, who were themselves not credible fashion experts to any of us. But it was painfully obvious to me that to the others, in their tailored skirts and silk blouses, we must have seemed "hopeless" and "vulgar." Though I now know that most adolescents feel out of step much of the time, I also know that for the Puerto Rican girls of my generation that sense was intensified. The way our teachers and classmates looked at us that day in school was just a taste of the cultural clash that awaited us in the real world, where prospective employers and men on the street would often misinterpret our tight skirts and jingling bracelets as a "come-on."

Mixed cultural signals have perpetuated certain stereotypes—for example, that of the Hispanic woman as the "hot tamale" or sexual firebrand. It is a one-dimensional view that the media have found easy to promote. In their special vocabulary, advertisers have designated "sizzling" and "smoldering" as the adjectives of choice for describing not only the foods but also the women of Latin America. From conversations in my house I recall hearing about the harassment that Puerto Rican women endured in factories where the "bossmen" talked to them as if sexual innuendo was all they understood, and worse, often gave them the choice of submitting to their advances or being fired.

It is custom, however, not chromosomes, that leads us to choose scarlet over pale pink. As young girls, it was our mothers who influenced our decisions about clothes and colors—mothers who had grown up on a tropical island where the natural environment was a riot of primary colors, where showing your skin was one way to keep cool as well as to look sexy. Most important of all, on the island, women perhaps felt freer to dress and move more provocatively since, in most cases, they were protected by the traditions, mores, and laws of a Spanish/Catholic system of morality and machismo whose main rule was: *You may look at my sister, but if you touch her I will kill you.* The extended family and church structure could provide a young woman with a circle of safety in her small pueblo on the island; if a man "wronged" a girl, everyone would close in to save her family honor.

My mother has told me about dressing in her best party clothes on Saturday nights and going to the town's plaza to promenade with her girlfriends in front of the boys they liked. The males were thus given an opportunity to admire the women and to express their admiration in the form of *piropos:* erotically charged street poems they composed on the spot. (I have myself been subjected to a few *piropos* while visiting the island, and they can be outrageous, although custom dictates that they must never cross into obscenity.) This ritual, as I understand it, also entails a show of studied indifference on the woman's part; if she is "decent," she must not acknowledge the man's impassioned words. So I do understand how things can be lost in translation. When a Puerto Rican girl dressed in her idea of what is attractive meets a man from the mainstream culture who has been trained to react to certain types of clothing as a sexual signal, a clash is likely to take place. I remember the boy who took me to my first formal dance leaning over to plant a sloppy, over-eager kiss painfully on my mouth; when I didn't respond with sufficient passion, he remarked resentfully: "I thought you Latin girls were supposed to mature early," as if I were expected to *ripen* like a fruit or vegetable, not just grow into womanhood like other girls.

It is surprising to my professional friends that even today some people, including those who should know better, still put others "in their place." It happened to me most recently during a stay at a classy metropolitan hotel favored by young professional couples for weddings. Late one evening after the theater, as I walked toward my room with a colleague (a woman with whom I was coordinating an arts program), a middle-aged man in a tuxedo, with a young girl in satin and lace on his arm, stepped directly into our path. With his champagne glass extended toward me, he exclaimed "Evita!"[6]

---

[6]A Broadway musical, later made into a movie, about Eva Duarte de Perón, the former first lady of Argentina. [Eds.]

Our way blocked, my companion and I listened as the man half- 10
recited, half-bellowed "Don't Cry for Me, Argentina." When he finished, the young girl said: "How about a round of applause for my
daddy?" We complied, hoping this would bring the silly spectacle to
a close. I was becoming aware that our little group was attracting the
attention of the other guests. "Daddy" must have perceived this too,
and he once more barred the way as we tried to walk past him. He
began to shout-sing a ditty to the tune of "La Bamba"—except the
lyrics were about a girl named Maria whose exploits rhymed with her
name and gonorrhea. The girl kept saying "Oh, Daddy" and looking
at me with pleading eyes. She wanted me to laugh along with the others. My companion and I stood silently waiting for the man to end his
offensive song. When he finished, I looked not at him but at his
daughter. I advised her calmly never to ask her father what he had
done in the army. Then I walked between them and to my room. My
friend complimented me on my cool handling of the situation, but I
confessed that I had really wanted to push the jerk into the swimming
pool. This same man—probably a corporate executive, well-educated,
even worldly by most standards—would not have been likely to re-
gale an Anglo woman with a dirty song in public. He might have
checked his impulse by assuming that she could be somebody's wife
or mother, or at least *somebody* who might take offense. But, to him,
I was just an Evita or a Maria: merely a character in his cartoon-
populated universe.

Another facet of the myth of the Latin woman in the United States
is the menial, the domestic—Maria the housemaid or countergirl. It's
true that work as domestics, as waitresses, and in factories is all that's
available to women with little English and few skills. But the myth of
the Hispanic menial—the funny maid, mispronouncing words and
cooking up a spicy storm in a shiny California kitchen—has been perpetuated by the media in the same way that "Mammy" from *Gone
with the Wind* became America's idea of the black woman for generations. Since I do not wear my diplomas around my neck for all to see,
I have on occasion been sent to that "kitchen" where some think I obviously belong.

One incident has stayed with me, though I recognize it as a minor
offense. My first public poetry reading took place in Miami, at a
restaurant where a luncheon was being held before the event. I was
nervous and excited as I walked in with notebook in hand. An older
woman motioned me to her table, and thinking (foolish me) that she
wanted me to autograph a copy of my newly published slender volume of verse, I went over. She ordered a cup of coffee from me, assuming that I was the waitress. (Easy enough to mistake my poems
for menus, I suppose.) I know it wasn't an intentional act of cruelty.
Yet of all the good things that happened later, I remember that scene

most clearly, because it reminded me of what I had to overcome before anyone would take me seriously. In retrospect I understand that
my anger gave my reading fire. In fact, I have almost always taken
any doubt in my abilities as a challenge, the result most often being
the satisfaction of winning a convert, of seeing the cold, appraising
eyes warm to my words, the body language change, the smile that indicates I have opened some avenue for communication. So that day as
I read, I looked directly at that woman. Her lowered eyes told me she
was embarrassed at her faux pas, and when I willed her to look up at
me, she graciously allowed me to punish her with my full attention.
We shook hands at the end of the reading and I never saw her again.
She has probably forgotten the entire incident, but maybe not.

Yet I am one of the lucky ones. There are thousands of Latinas
without the privilege of an education or the entrees into society that I
have. For them life is a constant struggle against the misconceptions
perpetuated by the myth of the Latina. My goal is to try to replace the
old stereotypes with a much more interesting set of realities. Every time
I give a reading, I hope the stories I tell, the dreams and fears I examine
in my work, can achieve some universal truth that will get my audience
past the particulars of my skin color, my accent, or my clothes.

I once wrote a poem in which I called all Latinas "God's brown
daughters." This poem is really a prayer of sorts, offered upward, but
also, through the human-to-human channel of art, outward. It is a
prayer for communication and for respect. In it, Latin women pray
"in Spanish to an Anglo God/with a Jewish heritage," and they are
"fervently hoping/that if not omnipotent,/at least He be bilingual."

Responding to Reading

1. What exactly is the "myth of the Latin woman"? According to Cofer, what
   has perpetuated this stereotype? Do you see this "myth" as simply demeaning, or as potentially dangerous?
2. In paragraph 1, Cofer says, "you can leave [Puerto Rico], master the English language, and travel as far as you can, but if you are a Latina, . . . the island travels with you." What does she mean? Do you think this is also true
   of people from other ethnic groups (and other nations)?
3. Throughout this essay, Cofer speaks of the "'cultural schizophrenia'" (3)
   she felt, describing the "conflicting message" (4), the "cultural clash" (5),
   and the "mixed cultural signals" (6) she received from the two worlds she
   inhabited. Do you see this kind of "schizophrenia" as inevitable? Do you
   see it as an obstacle to the American Dream? Explain.

Responding in Writing

What stereotypes are associated with your own ethnic group? Do you see these
stereotypes as benign or harmful?

JUST WALK ON BY

Brent Staples

1951–

Born in Chester, Pennsylvania, Brent Staples earned a BA degree from Widener University (1973) and a PhD in psychology from the University of Chicago (1977). Staples then turned to journalism, writing for the Chicago Sun-Times and the New York Times. He worked as an editor of the New York Times Book Review and in 1990 joined the editorial board of the Times, where his columns appear regularly. His memoir Parallel Time (1994), which was sparked by his brother's murder in a dispute over a co-caine deal, describes Staples's own internal struggles as he straddled the black and white worlds. Originally published in Ms. in 1986, the following essay conveys Staples's reactions to white people's images of black men. To read more of Staples's work, search the Web site of the New York Times, www.nytimes.com.

My first victim was a woman—white, well dressed, probably in her early twenties. I came upon her late one evening on a deserted street in Hyde Park, a relatively affluent neighborhood in an other-wise mean, impoverished section of Chicago. As I swung onto the av-enue behind her, there seemed to be a discreet, uninflammatory distance between us. Not so. She cast back a worried glance. To her, the youngish black man—a broad six feet two inches with a beard and billowing hair, both hands shoved into the pockets of a bulky military jacket—seemed menacingly close. After a few more quick glimpses, she picked up her pace and was soon running in earnest. Within sec-onds she disappeared into a cross street.

That was more than a decade ago. I was 22 years old, a graduate student newly arrived at the University of Chicago. It was in the echo of that terrified woman's footfalls that I first began to know the un-wieldy inheritance I'd come into—the ability to alter public space in ugly ways. It was clear that she thought herself the quarry of a mug-ger, a rapist, or worse. Suffering a bout of insomnia, however, I was stalking sleep, not defenseless wayfarers. As a softy who is scarcely able to take a knife to a raw chicken—let alone hold it to a person's throat—I was surprised, embarrassed, and dismayed all at once. Her flight made me feel like an accomplice in tyranny. It also made it clear that I was indistinguishable from the muggers who occasionally seeped into the area from the surrounding ghetto. That first en-counter, and those that followed, signified that a vast, unnerving gulf lay between nighttime pedestrians—particularly women—and me. And I soon gathered that being perceived as dangerous is a hazard in itself. I only needed to turn a corner into a dicey situation, or crowd some frightened, armed person in a foyer somewhere, or make an errant move after being pulled over by a policeman. Where fear and weapons meet—and they often do in urban America—there is always the possibility of death.

In that first year, my first away from my hometown, I was to become thoroughly familiar with the language of fear. At dark, shadowy intersections in Chicago, I could cross in front of a car stopped at a traffic light and elicit the *thunk, thunk, thunk, thunk* of the driver—black, white, male, or female—hammering down the door locks. On less traveled streets after dark, I grew accustomed to but never comfortable with people who crossed to the other side of the street rather than pass me. Then there were the standard unpleasantries with police, doormen, bouncers, cab drivers, and others whose business it is to screen out troublesome individuals *before* there is any nastiness.

I moved to New York nearly two years ago and I have remained an avid night walker. In central Manhattan, the near-constant crowd cover minimizes tense one-on-one street encounters. Elsewhere—visiting friends in SoHo, where sidewalks are narrow and tightly spaced buildings shut out the sky—things can get very taut indeed.

5   Black men have a firm place in New York mugging literature. Norman Podhoretz in his famed (or infamous) 1963 essay, "My Negro Problem—And Ours," recalls growing up in terror of black males; they "were tougher than we were, more ruthless," he writes—and as an adult on the Upper West Side of Manhattan, he continues, he cannot constrain his nervousness when he meets black men on certain streets. Similarly, a decade later, the essayist and novelist Edward Hoagland extols a New York where once "Negro bitterness bore down mainly on other Negroes." Where some see mere panhandlers, Hoagland sees "a mugger who is clearly screwing up his nerve to do more than just *ask* for money." But Hoagland has "the New Yorker's quickhunch posture for broken-field maneuvering," and the bad guy swerves away.

I often witness that "hunch posture," from women after dark on the warrenlike streets of Brooklyn where I live. They seem to set their faces on neutral and, with their purse straps strung across their chests bandolier style, they forge ahead as though bracing themselves against being tackled. I understand, of course, that the danger they perceive is not a hallucination. Women are particularly vulnerable to street violence, and young black males are drastically overrepresented among the perpetrators of that violence. Yet these truths are no solace against the kind of alienation that comes of being ever the suspect, against being set apart, a fearsome entity with whom pedestrians avoid making eye contact.

It is not altogether clear to me how I reached the ripe old age of 22 without being conscious of the lethality nighttime pedestrians attributed to me. Perhaps it was because in Chester, Pennsylvania, the small, angry industrial town where I came of age in the 1960s, I was scarcely noticeable against a backdrop of gang warfare, street knifings, and murders. I grew up one of the good boys, had perhaps a half-dozen fist fights. In retrospect, my shyness of combat has clear sources.

Many things go into the making of a young thug. One of those things is the consummation of the male romance with the power to intimidate. An infant discovers that random flailings send the baby bottle flying out of the crib and crashing to the floor. Delighted, the joyful babe repeats those motions again and again, seeking to duplicate the feat. Just so, I recall the points at which some of my boyhood friends were finally seduced by the perception of themselves as tough guys. When a mark cowered and surrendered his money without resistance, myth and reality merged—and paid off. It is, after all, only manly to embrace the power to frighten and intimidate. We, as men, are not supposed to give an inch of our lane on the highway; we are to seize the fighter's edge in work and in play and even in love; we are to be valiant in the face of hostile forces.

Unfortunately, poor and powerless young men seem to take all this nonsense literally. As a boy, I saw countless tough guys locked away; I have since buried several, too. They were babies, really—a teenage cousin, a brother of 22, a childhood friend in his mid-twenties—all gone down in episodes of bravado played out in the streets. I came to doubt the virtues of intimidation early on. I chose, perhaps even unconsciously, to remain a shadow—timid, but a survivor.

The fearsomeness mistakenly attributed to me in public places   10 often has a perilous flavor. The most frightening of these confusions occurred in the late 1970s and early 1980s when I worked as a journalist in Chicago. One day, rushing into the office of a magazine I was writing for with a deadline story in hand, I was mistaken for a burglar. The office manager called security and, with an ad hoc posse, pursued me through the labyrinthine halls, nearly to my editor's door. I had no way of proving who I was. I could only move briskly toward the company of someone who knew me.

Another time I was on assignment for a local paper and killing time before an interview. I entered a jewelry store on the city's affluent Near North Side. The proprietor excused herself and returned with an enormous red Doberman pinscher straining at the end of a leash. She stood, the dog extended toward me, silent to my questions, her eyes bulging nearly out of her head. I took a cursory look around, nodded, and bade her good night. Relatively speaking, however, I never fared as badly as another black male journalist. He went to nearby Waukegan, Illinois, a couple of summers ago to work on a story about a murderer who was born there. Mistaking the reporter for the killer, police hauled him from his car at gunpoint and but for his press credentials would probably have tried to book him. Such episodes are not uncommon. Black men trade tales like this all the time.

In "My Negro Problem—And Ours," Podhoretz writes that the hatred he feels for blacks makes itself known to him through a variety of avenues—one being his discomfort with that "special brand of paranoid touchiness" to which he says blacks are prone. No doubt he is speaking here of black men. In time, I learned to smother the rage I felt at so often being taken for a criminal. Not to do so would surely have led to madness—via that special "paranoid touchiness" that so annoyed Podhoretz at the time he wrote the essay.

I began to take precautions to make myself less threatening. I move about with care, particularly late in the evening. I give a wide berth to nervous people on subway platforms during the wee hours, particularly when I have exchanged business clothes for jeans. If I happen to be entering a building behind some people who appear skittish, I may walk by, letting them clear the lobby before I return, so as not to seem to be following them. I have been calm and extremely congenial on those rare occasions when I've been pulled over by the police.

And on late-evening constitutionals along streets less traveled by, I employ what has proved to be an excellent tension-reducing measure: I whistle melodies from Beethoven and Vivaldi and the more popular classical composers. Even steely New Yorkers hunching toward nighttime destinations seem to relax, and occasionally they even join in the tune. Virtually everybody seems to sense that a mugger wouldn't be warbling bright, sunny selections from Vivaldi's *Four Seasons*. It is my equivalent of the cowbell that hikers wear when they know they are in bear country.

Responding to Reading

1. Staples speaks quite matter-of-factly of the fear he inspires. Does your experience support his assumption that black men have the "ability to alter public space" (2)? Why or why not? Do you believe white men also have this ability? Explain.

2. In paragraph 13, Staples suggests some strategies that he believes make him "less threatening." What else, if anything, do you think he could do? Do you believe he *should* adopt such strategies? Explain your position.

3. Although Staples says he arouses fear in others, he also admits that he himself feels fearful. Why? Do you think he has reason to be fearful? What does this sense of fear say about his access to the American Dream?

Responding in Writing

Imagine you are the woman Staples describes in paragraph 1. Write a letter to Staples in which you explain why you reacted as you did.

ON DUMPSTER DIVING
Lars Eighner
1948–

When Lars Eighner was eighteen years old, his mother threw him out of her house after she learned he was gay. Then a student at the University of Texas at Austin (1966–1969), Eighner began a series of part-time and dead-end jobs that ended in 1988, when he was fired from his position at an Austin mental hospital and soon after evicted from his apartment. At that point, he headed for Los Angeles and spent three years homeless on the streets, shuttling between California and Texas with Lizbeth, his Labrador retriever. During his travels, he kept a journal and later published these entries, along with letters he wrote to a friend, as Travels with Lizbeth: Three Years on the Road and on the Streets *(1993), portions of which had been published previously in several different magazines and journals. The essay that follows, a chapter from Eighner's book, was originally published in the* Threepenny Review *in 1991. His most recent book is the novel* Pawn to Queen Four *(1995). To find out more about Eighner, visit his Web site, http://www.io.com/~eighner/.*

This chapter was composed while the author was homeless. The present tense has been preserved.

Long before I began Dumpster diving I was impressed with Dumpsters, enough so that I wrote the Merriam-Webster research service to discover what I could about the word *Dumpster*. I learned from them that it is a proprietary word belonging to the Dempsey Dumpster company. Since then I have dutifully capitalized the word, although it was lowercased in almost all the citations Merriam-Webster photocopied for me. Dempsey's word is too apt. I have never heard these things called anything but Dumpsters. I do not know anyone who knows the generic name for these objects. From time to time I have heard a wino or hobo give some corrupted credit to the original and call them Dipsy Dumpsters.

I began Dumpster diving about a year before I became homeless.

I prefer the word *scavenging* and use the word *scrounging* when I mean to be obscure. I have heard people, evidently meaning to be polite, use the word *foraging*, but I prefer to reserve that word for gathering nuts and berries and such which I do also according to the season and the opportunity. *Dumpster diving* seems to me to be a little too cute and, in my case, inaccurate because I lack the athletic ability to lower myself into the Dumpsters as the true divers do, much to their increased profit.

I like the frankness of the word *scavenging*, which I can hardly think of without picturing a big black snail on an aquarium wall. I live from the refuse of others. I am a scavenger. I think it a sound and honorable niche, although if I could I would naturally prefer to live the comfortable consumer life, perhaps—and only perhaps—as a slightly less wasteful consumer, owing to what I have learned as a scavenger.

5   While Lizbeth and I were still living in the shack on Avenue B as my savings ran out, I put almost all my sporadic income into rent. The necessities of daily life I began to extract from Dumpsters. Yes, we ate from them. Except for jeans, all my clothes came from Dumpsters. Boom boxes, candles, bedding, toilet paper, a virgin male love doll, medicine, books, a typewriter, dishes, furnishings, and change, sometimes amounting to many dollars—I acquired many things from the Dumpsters.

I have learned much as a scavenger. I mean to put some of what I have learned down here, beginning with the practical art of Dumpster diving and proceeding to the abstract.

What is safe to eat?

After all, the finding of objects is becoming something of an urban art. Even respectable employed people will sometimes find something tempting sticking out of a Dumpster or standing beside one. Quite a number of people, not all of them of the bohemian type, are willing to brag that they found this or that piece in the trash. But eating from Dumpsters is what separates the dilettanti from the professionals. Eating safely from the Dumpsters involves three principles: using the senses and common sense to evaluate the conditions of the found materials, knowing the Dumpsters of a given area and checking them regularly, and seeking always to answer the question "Why was this discarded?"

Perhaps everyone who has a kitchen and a regular supply of groceries has, at one time or another, made a sandwich and eaten half of it before discovering mold on the bread or got a mouthful of milk before realizing the milk had turned. Nothing of the sort is likely to happen to a Dumpster diver because he is constantly reminded that most food is discarded for a reason. Yet a lot of perfectly good food can be found in Dumpsters.

10   Canned goods, for example, turn up fairly often in the Dumpsters I frequent. All except the most phobic people would be willing to eat from a can, even if it came from a Dumpster. Canned goods are among the safest of foods to be found in Dumpsters but are not utterly foolproof.

Although very rare with modern canning methods, botulism is a possibility. Most other forms of food poisoning seldom do lasting harm to a healthy person, but botulism is most certainly fatal and often the first symptom is death. Except for carbonated beverages, all canned goods should contain a slight vacuum and suck air when first punctured. Bulging, rusty, and dented cans and cans that spew when punctured should be avoided, especially when the contents are not very acidic or syrupy.

Heat can break down the botulin, but this requires much more cooking than most people do to canned goods. To the extent that botulism occurs at all, of course, it can occur in cans on pantry shelves as well as in cans from Dumpsters. Need I say that home-canned goods are simply too risky to be recommended.

From time to time one of my companions, aware of the source of my provisions, will ask, "Do you think these crackers are really safe to eat?" For some reason it is most often the crackers they ask about.

This question has always made me angry. Of course I would not offer my companion anything I had doubts about. But more than that, I wonder why he cannot evaluate the condition of the crackers for himself. I have no special knowledge and I have been wrong before. Since he knows where the food comes from, it seems to me he ought to assume some of the responsibility for deciding what he will put in his mouth. For myself I have few qualms about dry foods such as crackers, cookies, cereal, chips, and pasta if they are free of visible contaminants and still dry and crisp. Most often such things are found in the original packaging, which is not so much a positive sign as it is the absence of a negative one.

Raw fruits and vegetables with intact skins seem perfectly safe to me, excluding of course the obviously rotten. Many are discarded for minor imperfections that can be pared away. Leafy vegetables, grapes, cauliflower, broccoli, and similar things may be contaminated by liquids and may be impractical to wash. 15

Candy, especially hard candy, is usually safe if it has not drawn ants. Chocolate is often discarded only because it has become discolored as the cocoa butter de-emulsified. Candying, after all, is one method of food preservation because pathogens do not like very sugary substances.

All of these foods might be found in any Dumpster and can be evaluated with some confidence largely on the basis of appearance. Beyond these are foods that cannot be correctly evaluated without additional information.

I began scavenging by pulling pizzas out of the Dumpster behind a pizza delivery shop. In general, prepared food requires caution, but in this case I knew when the shop closed and went to the Dumpster as soon as the last of the help left.

Such shops often get prank orders; both the orders and the products made to fill them are called *bogus*. Because help seldom stays long at these places, pizzas are often made with the wrong topping, refused on delivery for being cold, or baked incorrectly. The products to be discarded are boxed up because inventory is kept by counting boxes: A boxed pizza can be written off; an unboxed pizza does not exist.

20   I never placed a bogus order to increase the supply of pizzas and I believe no one else was scavenging in this Dumpster. But the people in the shop became suspicious and began to retain their garbage in the shop overnight. While it lasted I had a steady supply of fresh, sometimes warm pizza. Because I knew the Dumpster I knew the source of the pizza, and because I visited the Dumpster regularly I knew what was fresh and what was yesterday's.

The area I frequent is inhabited by many affluent college students. I am not here by chance; the Dumpsters in this area are very rich. Students throw out many good things, including food. In particular they tend to throw everything out when they move at the end of a semester, before and after breaks, and around midterm, when many of them despair of college. So I find it advantageous to keep an eye on the academic calendar.

Students throw food away around breaks because they do not know whether it has spoiled or will spoil before they return. A typical discard is a half jar of peanut butter. In fact, nonorganic peanut butter does not require refrigeration and is unlikely to spoil in any reasonable time. The student does not know that, and since it is Daddy's money, the student decides not to take a chance. Opened containers require caution and some attention to the question "Why was this discarded?" But in the case of discards from student apartments, the answer may be that the item was thrown out through carelessness, ignorance, or wastefulness. This can sometimes be deduced when the item is found with many others, including some that are obviously perfectly good.

Some students, and others, approach defrosting a freezer by chucking out the whole lot. Not only do the circumstances of such a find tell the story, but also the mass of frozen goods stays cold for a long time and items may be found still frozen or freshly thawed.

Yogurt, cheese, and sour cream are items that are often thrown out while they are still good. Occasionally I find a cheese with a spot of mold, which of course I just pare off, and because it is obvious why such a cheese was discarded, I treat it with less suspicion than an apparently perfect cheese found in similar circumstances. Yogurt is often discarded, still sealed, only because the expiration date on the carton had passed. This is one of my favorite finds because yogurt will keep for several days, even in warm weather.

25   Students throw out canned goods and staples at the end of semesters and when they give up college at midterm. Drugs, pornography, spirits, and the like are often discarded when parents are expected— Dad's day, for example. And spirits also turn up after big party weekends, presumably discarded by the newly reformed. Wine and spirits, of course, keep perfectly well even once opened, but the same cannot be said of beer.

My test for carbonated soft drinks is whether they still fizz vigorously. Many juices or other beverages are too acidic or too syrupy to cause much concern, provided they are not visibly contaminated. I have discovered nasty molds in vegetable juices, even when the product was found under its original seal; I recommend that such products be decanted slowly into a clear glass. Liquids always require some care. One hot day I found a large jug of Pat O'Brien's Hurricane mix. The jug had been opened, but it was still ice cold. I drank three large glasses before it became apparent to me that someone had added the rum to the mix, and not a little rum. I never tasted the rum, and by the time I began to feel the effects I had already ingested a very large quantity of the beverage. Some divers would have considered this a boon, but being suddenly intoxicated in a public place in the early afternoon is not my idea of a good time.

I have heard of people maliciously contaminating discarded food and even handouts, but mostly I have heard of this from people with vivid imaginations who have had no experience with Dumpsters them selves. Just before the pizza shop stopped discarding its garbage at night, jalapeños began showing up on most of the discarded pizzas. If indeed this was meant to discourage me it was a wasted effort because I am native Texan.

For myself, I avoid game, poultry, pork, and egg-based foods, whether I find them raw or cooked. I seldom have the means to cook what I find, but when I do I avail myself of plentiful supplies of beef, which is often in very good condition. I suppose fish becomes disagreeable before it becomes dangerous. Lizbeth is happy to have any such thing that is past its prime and, in fact, does not recognize fish as food until it is quite strong.

Home leftovers, as opposed to surpluses from restaurants, are very often bad. Evidently, especially among students, there is a common type of personality that carefully wraps up even the smallest leftover and shoves it into the back of the refrigerator for six months or so before discarding it. Characteristic of this type are the reused jars and margarine tubs to which the remains are committed. I avoid ethnic foods I am unfamiliar with. If I do not know what it is supposed to look like when it is good, I cannot be certain I will be able to tell if it is bad.

No matter how careful I am I still get dysentery at least once a 30 month, oftener in warm weather. I do not want to paint too romantic a picture. Dumpster diving has serious drawbacks as a way of life.

I learned to scavenge gradually, on my own. Since then I have initiated several companions into the trade. I have learned that there is a predictable series of stages a person goes through in learning to scavenge.

At first the new scavenger is filled with disgust and self-loathing. He is ashamed of being seen and may lurk around, trying to duck behind things, or he may try to dive at night. (In fact, most people instinctively look away from a scavenger. By skulking around, the novice calls attention to himself and arouses suspicion. Diving at night is ineffective and needlessly messy.)

Every grain of rice seems to be a maggot. Everything seems to stink. He can wipe the egg yolk off the found can, but he cannot erase from his mind the stigma of eating garbage.

That stage passes with experience. The scavenger finds a pair of running shoes that fit and look and smell brand-new. He finds a pocket calculator in perfect working order. He finds pristine ice cream, still frozen, more than he can eat or keep. He begins to understand: People throw away perfectly good stuff, a lot of perfectly good stuff.

35   At this stage, Dumpster shyness begins to dissipate. The diver, after all, has the last laugh. He is finding all manner of good things that are his for the taking. Those who disparage his profession are the fools, not he.

He may begin to hang on to some perfectly good things for which he has neither a use nor a market. Then he begins to take note of the things that are not perfectly good but are nearly so. He mates a Walkman with broken earphones and one that is missing a battery cover. He picks up things that he can repair.

At this stage he may become lost and never recover. Dumpsters are full of things of some potential value to someone and also of things that never have much intrinsic value but are interesting. All the Dumpster divers I have known come to the point of trying to acquire everything they touch. Why not take it, they reason, since it is all free? This is, of course, hopeless. Most divers come to realize that they must restrict themselves to items of relatively immediate utility. But in some cases the diver simply cannot control himself. I have met several of these pack-rat types. Their ideas of the values of various pieces of junk verge on the psychotic. Every bit of glass may be a diamond, they think, and all that glistens, gold.

I tend to gain weight when I am scavenging. Partly this is because I always find far more pizza and doughnuts than water-packed tuna, nonfat yogurt, and fresh vegetables. Also I have not developed much faith in the reliability of Dumpsters as a food source, although it has been proven to me many times. I tend to eat as if I have no idea where my next meal is coming from. But mostly I just hate to see food go to waste and so I eat much more than I should. Something like this drives the obsession to collect junk.

As for collecting objects, I usually restrict myself to collecting one kind of small object at a time, such as pocket calculators, sunglasses, or campaign buttons. To live on the street I must anticipate my needs to a certain extent: I must pick up and save warm bedding I find in August because it will not be found in Dumpsters in November. As I have no access to health care, I often hoard essential drugs, such as antibiotics and antihistamines. (This course can be recommended only to those with some grounding in pharmacology. Antibiotics, for example, even when indicated are worse than useless if taken in insufficient amounts.) But even if I had a home with extensive storage space, I could not save everything that might be valuable in some contingency.

I have proprietary feelings about my Dumpsters. As I have men- 40 tioned, it is no accident that I scavenge from ones where good finds are common. But my limited experience with Dumpsters in other areas suggests to me that even in poorer areas, Dumpsters, if attended with sufficient diligence, can be made to yield a livelihood. The rich students discard perfectly good kiwifruit; poorer people discard perfectly good apples. Slacks and Polo shirts are found in the one place; jeans and T-shirts in the other. The population of competitors rather than the affluence of the dumpers most affects the feasibility of survival by scavenging. The large number of competitors is what puts me off the idea of trying to scavenge in places like Los Angeles.

Curiously, I do not mind my direct competition, other scavengers, so much as I hate the can scroungers.

People scrounge cans because they have to have a little cash. I have tried scrounging cans with an able-bodied companion. Afoot a can scrounger simply cannot make more than a few dollars a day. One can extract the necessities of life from the Dumpsters directly with far less effort than would be required to accumulate the equivalent value in cans. (These observations may not hold in places with container redemption laws.)

Can scroungers, then, are people who must have small amounts of cash. These are drug addicts and winos, mostly the latter because the amounts of cash are so small. Spirits and drugs do, like all other commodities, turn up in Dumpsters and the scavenger will from time to time have a half bottle of a rather good wine with his dinner. But the wino cannot survive on these occasional finds; he must have his daily dose to stave off the DTs. All the cans he can carry will buy about three bottles of Wild Irish Rose.

I do not begrudge them the cans, but can scroungers tend to tear up the Dumpsters, mixing the contents and littering the area. They become so specialized that they can see only cans. They earn my contempt by passing up change, canned goods, and readily hockable items.

There are precious few courtesies among scavengers. But it is com- 45 mon practice to set aside surplus items: pairs of shoes, clothing, canned goods, and such. A true scavenger hates to see good stuff go to waste, and what he cannot use he leaves in good condition in plain sight.

Can scroungers lay waste to everything in their path and will stir one of a pair of good shoes to the bottom of a Dumpster, to be lost or ruined in the muck. Can scroungers will even go through individual garbage cans, something I have never seen a scavenger do.

Individual garbage cans are set out on the public easement only on garbage days. On other days going through them requires trespassing close to a dwelling. Going through individual garbage cans without scattering litter is almost impossible. Litter is likely to reduce the public's tolerance of scavenging. Individual cans are simply not as productive as Dumpsters; people in houses and duplexes do not move so often and for some reason do not tend to discard as much useful material. Moreover, the time required to go through one garbage can that serves one household is not much less than the time required to go through a Dumpster that contains the refuse of twenty apartments.

But my strongest reservation about going through individual garbage cans is that this seems to me a very personal kind of invasion to which I would object if I were a householder. Although many things in Dumpsters are obviously meant never to come to light, a Dumpster is somehow less personal.

I avoid trying to draw conclusions about the people who dump in the Dumpsters I frequent. I think it would be unethical to do so, although I know many people will find the idea of scavenger ethics too funny for words.

50   Dumpsters contain bank statements, correspondence, and other documents, just as anyone might expect. But there are also less obvious sources of information. Pill bottles, for example. The labels bear the name of the patient, the name of the doctor, and the name of the drug. AIDS drugs and antipsychotic medicines, to name but two groups, are specific and are seldom prescribed for any other disorders. The plastic compacts for birth-control pills usually have complete label information.

Despite all of this sensitive information, I have had only one apartment resident object to my going through the Dumpster. In that case it turned out the resident was a university athlete who was taking bets and who was afraid I would turn up his wager slips.

Occasionally a find tells a story. I once found a small paper bag containing some unused condoms, several partial tubes of flavored sexual lubricants, a partially used compact of birth-control pills, and the torn pieces of a picture of a young man. Clearly she was through with him and planning to give up sex altogether.

Dumpster things are often sad—abandoned teddy bears, shredded wedding books, despaired-of sales kits. I find many pets lying in state in Dumpsters. Although I hope to get off the streets so that Lizbeth can have a long and comfortable old age, I know this hope is not very realistic. So I suppose when her time comes she too will go into a Dumpster. I will have no better place for her. And after all, it is fitting, since for most of her life her livelihood has come from the Dumpster. When she finds something I think is safe that has been spilled from a Dumpster, I let her have it. She already knows the route around the best ones. I like to think that if she survives me she will have a chance of evading the dog catcher and of finding her sustenance on the route.

Silly vanities also come to rest in the Dumpsters. I am a rather accomplished needleworker. I get a lot of material from the Dumpsters. Evidently sorority girls, hoping to impress someone, perhaps themselves, with their mastery of a womanly art, buy a lot of embroider-by-number kits, work a few stitches horribly, and eventually discard the whole mess. I pull out their stitches, turn the canvas over, and work an original design. Do not think I refrain from chuckling as I make gifts from these kits.

I find diaries and journals. I have often thought of compiling a 55 book of literary found objects. And perhaps I will one day. But what I find is hopelessly commonplace and bad without being, even unconsciously, camp. College students also discard their papers. I am horrified to discover the kind of paper that now merits an A in an undergraduate course. I am grateful, however, for the number of good books and magazines the students throw out.

In the area I know best I have never discovered vermin in the Dumpsters, but there are two kinds of kitty surprise. One is alley cats whom I meet as they leap, claws first, out of Dumpsters. This is especially thrilling when I have Lizbeth in tow. The other kind of kitty surprise is a plastic garbage bag filled with some ponderous, amorphous mass. This always proves to be used cat litter.

City bees harvest doughnut glaze and this makes the Dumpster at the doughnut shop more interesting. My faith in the instinctive wisdom of animals is always shaken whenever I see Lizbeth attempt to catch a bee in her mouth, which she does whenever bees are present. Evidently some birds find Dumpsters profitable, for birdie surprise is almost as common as kitty surprise of the first kind. In hunting season all kinds of small game turn up in Dumpsters, some of it, sadly, not entirely dead. Curiously, summer and winter, maggots are uncommon.

The worst of the living and near-living hazards of the Dumpsters are the fire ants. The food they claim is not much of a loss, but they are vicious and aggressive. It is very easy to brush against some surface of the Dumpster and pick up half a dozen or more fire ants, usually in some sensitive area such as the underarm. One advantage of bringing Lizbeth along as I make Dumpster rounds is that, for obvious reasons, she is very alert to ground-based fire ants. When Lizbeth recognizes a fire-ant infestation around our feet, she does the Dance of the Zillion Fire Ants. I have learned not to ignore this warning from

Lizbeth, whether I perceive the tiny ants or not, but to remove ourselves at Lizbeth's first pas de bourrée.[1] All the more so because the
ants are the worst in the summer months when I wear flip-flops if I
have them. (Perhaps someone will misunderstand this. Lizbeth does
the Dance of the Zillion Fire Ants when she recognizes more fire ants
than she cares to eat, not when she is being bitten. Since I have
learned to react promptly, she does not get bitten at all. It is the isolated patrol of fire ants that falls in Lizbeth's range that deserves pity.
She finds them quite tasty.)

By far the best way to go through a Dumpster is to lower yourself
into it. Most of the good stuff tends to settle at the bottom because it is
usually weightier than the rubbish. My more athletic companions
have often demonstrated to me that they can extract much good material from a Dumpster I have already been over.

60 To those psychologically or physically unprepared to enter a
Dumpster, I recommend a stout stick, preferably with some barb or
hook at one end. The hook can be used to grab plastic garbage bags.
When I find canned goods or other objects loose at the bottom of a
Dumpster, I lower a bag into it, roll the desired object into the bag,
and then hoist the bag out—a procedure more easily described than
executed. Much Dumpster diving is a matter of experience for which
nothing will do except practice.

Dumpster diving is outdoor work, often surprisingly pleasant. It
is not entirely predictable; things of interest turn up every day and
some days there are finds of great value. I am always very pleased
when I can turn up exactly the thing I most wanted to find. Yet in
spite of the element of chance, scavenging more than most other pursuits tends to yield returns in some proportion to the effort and intelligence brought to bear. It is very sweet to turn up a few dollars in
change from a Dumpster that has just been gone over by a wino.

The land is now covered with cities. The cities are full of Dumpsters. If a member of the canine race is ever able to know what it is
doing, then Lizbeth knows that when we go around to the Dumpsters, we are hunting. I think of scavenging as a modern form of self-
reliance. In any event, after having survived nearly ten years of
government service, where everything is geared to the lowest common denominator, I find it refreshing to have work that rewards initiative and effort. Certainly I would be happy to have a sinecure
again, but I am no longer heartbroken that I left one.

I find from the experience of scavenging two rather deep lessons.
The first is to take what you can use and let the rest go by. I have

---

[1]A short walking or running step in ballet. [Eds.]

come to think that there is no value in the abstract. A thing I cannot use or make useful, perhaps by trading, has no value however rare or fine it may be. I mean useful in a broad sense—some art I would find useful and some otherwise.

I was shocked to realize that some things are not worth acquiring, but now I think it is so. Some material things are white elephants that eat up the possessor's substance. The second lesson is the transience of material being. This has not quite converted me to a dualist,[2] but it has made some headway in that direction. I do not suppose that ideas are immortal, but certainly mental things are longer lived than other material things.

Once I was the sort of person who invests objects with sentimental value. Now I no longer have those objects, but I have the sentiments yet. 65

Many times in our travels I have lost everything but the clothes I was wearing and Lizbeth. The things I find in Dumpsters, the love letters and rag dolls of so many lives, remind me of this lesson. Now I hardly pick up a thing without envisioning the time I will cast it aside. This I think is a healthy state of mind. Almost everything I have now has already been cast out at least once, proving that what I own is valueless to someone.

Anyway, I find my desire to grab for the gaudy bauble has been largely sated. I think this is an attitude I share with the very wealthy—we both know there is plenty more where what we have came from. Between us are the rat-race millions who nightly scavenge the cable channels looking for they know not what.

I am sorry for them.

Responding to Reading

1. In paragraph 6, Eighner explains, "I have learned much as a scavenger. I mean to put some of what I have learned down here, beginning with the practical art of Dumpster diving and proceeding to the abstract." Do you think Eighner's purpose goes beyond educating his readers? What other purpose do you think he might have?
2. What surprised you most about Eighner's essay? Did any information embarrass you? Repulse you? Make you feel guilty? Arouse your sympathy? Arouse your pity? Explain your response. Do you think Eighner intended you to feel the way you do?
3. How do you suppose Eighner would define the American Dream? What do you think he might have to say about its limits?

---

[2]One who believes that material things also exist as spiritual ideals or abstractions. [Eds.]

Responding in Writing

Assuming that Eighner wished to continue living on the streets, what could he do to make his life easier? Write a flyer, to be distributed to homeless men, advising them of resources available to them in your community (for example, public rest rooms).

TWO KINDS

Amy Tan

1952–

Amy Tan was born in Oakland, California, to parents who had emigrated from China only a few years earlier. She earned a bachelor's degree in English and a master's degree in Linguistics from San Jose State University (1973, 1974) and did postgraduate work at the University of California at Berkeley (1974–1976). She began her career as a business and technical writer but turned to fiction, driven by her need to tell stories. Her first novel, The Joy Luck Club *(1987), about Chinese-born mothers and their American-born daughters, became a best-seller and won the National Book Award. She has also written* The Kitchen God's Wife *(1991),* The Hundred Secret Senses *(1995),* The Bonesetter's Daughter *(2001), and* The Opposite of Fate: A Book of Musings *(2003) as well as the illustrated children's books* The Moon Lady *(1992) and* The Chinese Siamese Cat *(1994). The following short story, a chapter of* The Joy Luck Club, *offers several perspectives on the American Dream—the mother's, the narrator's as a young girl, and the narrator's as an adult.*

My mother believed you could be anything you wanted to be in America. You could open a restaurant. You could work for the government and get good retirement. You could buy a house with almost no money down. You could become rich. You could become instantly famous.

"Of course you can be prodigy, too," my mother told me when I was nine. "You can be best anything. What does Auntie Lindo know? Her daughter, she is only best tricky."

America was where all my mother's hopes lay. She had come here in 1949 after losing everything in China: her mother and father, her family home, her first husband, and two daughters, twin baby girls. But she never looked back with regret. There were so many ways for things to get better.

We didn't immediately pick the right kind of prodigy. At first my mother thought I could be a Chinese Shirley Temple. We'd watch Shirley's old movies on TV as though they were training films. My mother would poke my arm and say, *"Ni kan"*—You watch. And I would see Shirley tapping her feet, or singing a sailor song, or pursing her lips into a very round O while saying, "Oh my goodness."

"Ni kan," said my mother as Shirley's eyes flooded with tears. 5 "You already know how. Don't need talent for crying!"

Soon after my mother got this idea about Shirley Temple, she took me to a beauty training school in the Mission district and put me in the hands of a student who could barely hold the scissors without shaking. Instead of getting big fat curls, I emerged with an uneven mass of crinkly black fuzz. My mother dragged me off to the bathroom and tried to wet down my hair.

"You look like Negro Chinese," she lamented, as if I had done this on purpose.

The instructor of the beauty training school had to lop off these soggy clumps to make my hair even again. "Peter Pan is very popular these days," the instructor assured my mother. I now had hair the length of a boy's, with straight-across bangs that hung at a slant two inches above my eyebrows. I liked the haircut and it made me actually look forward to my future fame.

In fact, in the beginning, I was just as excited as my mother, maybe even more so. I pictured this prodigy part of me as many different images, trying each one on for size. I was a dainty ballerina girl standing by the curtains, waiting to hear the right music that would send me floating on my tiptoes. I was like the Christ child lifted out of the straw manger, crying with holy indignity. I was Cinderella stepping from her pumpkin carriage with sparkly cartoon music filling the air.

In all of my imaginings, I was filled with a sense that I would 10 soon become *perfect*. My mother and father would adore me. I would be beyond reproach. I would never feel the need to sulk for anything.

But sometimes the prodigy in me became impatient. "If you don't hurry up and get me out of here, I'm disappearing for good," it warned. "And then you'll always be nothing."

Every night after dinner, my mother and I would sit at the Formica kitchen table. She would present new tests, taking her examples from stories of amazing children she had read in *Ripley's Believe It or Not*, or *Good Housekeeping, Reader's Digest*, and a dozen other magazines she kept in a pile in our bathroom. My mother got these magazines from people whose houses she cleaned. And since she cleaned many houses each week, we had a great assortment. She would look through them all, searching for stories about remarkable children.

The first night she brought out a story about a three-year-old boy who knew the capitals of all the states and even most of the European countries. A teacher was quoted as saying the little boy could also pronounce the names of the foreign cities correctly.

"What's the capital of Finland?" my mother asked me, looking at the magazine story.

15   All I knew was the capital of California, because Sacramento was the name of the street we lived on in Chinatown. "Nairobi!" I guessed, saying the most foreign word I could think of. She checked to see if that was possibly one way to pronounce "Helsinki" before showing me the answer.

The tests got harder—multiplying numbers in my head, finding the queen of hearts in a deck of cards, trying to stand on my head without using my hands, predicting the daily temperatures in Los Angeles, New York, and London.

One night I had to look at a page from the Bible for three minutes and then report everything I could remember. "Now Jehoshaphat had riches and honor in abundance and . . . that's all I remember, Ma," I said.

And after seeing my mother's disappointed face once again, something inside of me began to die. I hated the tests, the raised hopes and failed expectations. Before going to bed that night, I looked in the mirror above the bathroom sink and when I saw only my face staring back—and that it would always be this ordinary face—I began to cry. Such a sad, ugly girl! I made high-pitched noises like a crazed animal, trying to scratch out the face in the mirror.

And then I saw what seemed to be the prodigy side of me—because I had never seen that face before. I looked at my reflection, blinking so I could see more clearly. The girl staring back at me was angry, powerful. This girl and I were the same. I had new thoughts, willful thoughts, or rather thoughts filled with lots of won'ts. I won't let her change me, I promised myself. I won't be what I'm not.

20   So now on nights when my mother presented her tests, I performed listlessly, my head propped on one arm. I pretended to be bored. And I was. I got so bored I started counting the bellows of the foghorns out on the bay while my mother drilled me in other areas. The sound was comforting and reminded me of the cow jumping over the moon. And the next day, I played a game with myself, seeing if my mother would give up on me before eight bellows. After a while I usually counted only one, maybe two bellows at most. At last she was beginning to give up hope.

Two or three months had gone by without any mention of my being a prodigy again. And then one day my mother was watching *The Ed Sullivan Show* on TV. The TV was old and the sound kept shorting out. Every time my mother got halfway up from the sofa to adjust the set, the sound would go back on and Ed would be talking. As soon as she sat down, Ed would go silent again. She got up, the TV broke into loud piano music. She sat down. Silence. Up and down, back and forth, quiet and loud. It was like a stiff embraceless dance between her and the TV set. Finally she stood by the set with her hand on the sound dial.

She seemed entranced by the music, a little frenzied piano piece with this mesmerizing quality, sort of quick passages and then teasing lilting ones before it returned to the quick playful parts.

"*Ni kan*," my mother said, calling me over with hurried hand gestures, "Look here."

I could see why my mother was fascinated by the music. It was being pounded out by a little Chinese girl, about nine years old, with a Peter Pan haircut. The girl had the sauciness of a Shirley Temple. She was proudly modest like a proper Chinese child. And she also did this fancy sweep of a curtsy, so that the fluffy skirt of her white dress cascaded slowly to the floor like the petals of a large carnation.

In spite of these warning signs, I wasn't worried. Our family had 25 no piano and we couldn't afford to buy one, let alone reams of sheet music and piano lessons. So I could be generous in my comments when my mother bad-mouthed the little girl on TV.

"Play note right, but doesn't sound good! No singing sound," complained my mother.

"What are you picking on her for?" I said carelessly. "She's pretty good. Maybe she's not the best, but she's trying hard." I knew almost immediately I would be sorry I said that.

"Just like you," she said. "Not the best. Because you not trying." She gave a little huff as she let go of the sound dial and sat down on the sofa.

The little Chinese girl sat down also to play an encore of "Anitra's Dance" by Grieg. I remember the song, because later on I had to learn how to play it.

Three days after watching *The Ed Sullivan Show*, my mother told 30 me what my schedule would be for piano lessons and piano practice. She had talked to Mr. Chong, who lived on the first floor of our apartment building. Mr. Chong was a retired piano teacher and my mother had traded housecleaning services for weekly lessons and a piano for me to practice on every day, two hours a day, from four until six.

When my mother told me this, I felt as though I had been sent to hell. I whined and then kicked my foot a little when I couldn't stand it anymore.

"Why don't you like me the way I am? I'm *not* a genius! I can't play the piano. And even if I could, I wouldn't go on TV if you paid me a million dollars!" I cried.

My mother slapped me. "Who ask you be genius?" she shouted. "Only ask you be your best. For you sake. You think I want you be genius? Hnnh! What for! Who ask you!"

"So ungrateful," I heard her mutter in Chinese. "If she had as much talent as she has temper, she would be famous now."

35   Mr. Chong, whom I secretly nicknamed Old Chong, was very strange, always tapping his fingers to the silent music of an invisible orchestra. He looked ancient in my eyes. He had lost most of the hair on top of his head and he wore thick glasses and had eyes that always looked tired and sleepy. But he must have been younger than I thought, since he lived with his mother and was not yet married.

    I met Old Lady Chong once and that was enough. She had this peculiar smell like a baby that had done something in its pants. And her fingers felt like a dead person's, like an old peach I once found in the back of the refrigerator; the skin just slid off the meat when I picked it up.

    I soon found out why Old Chong had retired from teaching piano. He was deaf. "Like Beethoven!" he shouted to me. "We're both listening only in our head!" And he would start to conduct his frantic silent sonatas.

    Our lessons went like this. He would open the book and point to different things, explaining their purpose: "Key! Treble! Bass! No sharps or flats! So this is C major! Listen now and play after me!"

    And then he would play the C scale a few times, a simple chord, and then, as if inspired by an old, unreachable itch, he gradually added more notes and running trills and a pounding bass until the music was really something quite grand.

40   I would play after him, the simple scale, the simple chord, and then I just played some nonsense that sounded like a cat running up and down on top of garbage cans. Old Chong smiled and applauded and then said, "Very good! But now you must learn to keep time!"

    So that's how I discovered that Old Chong's eyes were too slow to keep up with the wrong notes I was playing. He went through the motions in half-time. To help me keep rhythm, he stood behind me, pushing down on my right shoulder for every beat. He balanced pennies on top of my wrists so I would keep them still as I slowly played scales and arpeggios. He had me curve my hand around an apple and keep that shape when playing chords. He marched stiffly to show me how to make each finger dance up and down, staccato like an obedient little soldier.

    He taught me all these things, and that was how I also learned I could be lazy and get away with mistakes, lots of mistakes. If I hit the wrong notes because I hadn't practiced enough, I never corrected myself. I just kept playing in rhythm. And Old Chong kept conducting his own private reverie.

    So maybe I never really gave myself a fair chance. I did pick up the basics pretty quickly, and I might have become a good pianist at that young age. But I was so determined not to try, not to be anybody different that I learned to play only the most ear-splitting preludes, the most discordant hymns.

Over the next year, I practiced like this, dutifully in my own way. And then one day I heard my mother and her friend Lindo Jong both talking in a loud bragging tone of voice so others could hear. It was after church, and I was leaning against the brick wall wearing a dress with stiff white petticoats. Auntie Lindo's daughter, Waverly, who was about my age, was standing farther down the wall about five feet away. We had grown up together and shared all the closeness of two sisters squabbling over crayons and dolls. In other words, for the most part, we hated each other. I thought she was snotty. Waverly Jong had gained a certain amount of fame as "Chinatown's Littlest Chinese Chess Champion."

"She bring home too many trophy," lamented Auntie Lindo that 45 Sunday. "All day she play chess. All day I have no time do nothing but dust off her winnings." She threw a scolding look at Waverly, who pretended not to see her.

"You lucky you don't have this problem," said Auntie Lindo with a sigh to my mother.

And my mother squared her shoulders and bragged: "Our problem worser than yours. If we ask Jing-mei wash dish, she hear nothing but music. It's like you can't stop this natural talent."

And right then, I was determined to put a stop to her foolish pride.

A few weeks later, Old Chong and my mother conspired to have me play in a talent show which would be held in the church hall. By then, my parents had saved up enough to buy me a secondhand piano, a black Wurlitzer spinet with a scarred bench. It was the showpiece of our living room.

For the talent show, I was to play a piece called "Pleading Child" 50 from Schumann's *Scenes from Childhood*. It was a simple, moody piece that sounded more difficult than it was. I was supposed to memorize the whole thing, playing the repeat parts twice to make the piece sound longer. But I dawdled over it, playing a few bars and then cheating, looking up to see what notes followed. I never really listened to what I was playing. I daydreamed about being somewhere else, about being someone else.

The part I liked to practice best was the fancy curtsy: right foot out, touch the rose on the carpet with a pointed foot, sweep to the side, left leg bends, look up and smile.

My parents invited all the couples from the Joy Luck Club[1] to witness my debut. Auntie Lindo and Uncle Tin were there. Waverly and her two older brothers had also come. The first two rows were filled with children both younger and older than I was. The littlest ones got

---

[1]A name denoting the mother's circle of friends, all of whom were Chinese immigrants to the United States. [Eds.]

to go first. They recited simple nursery rhymes, squawked out tunes on miniature violins, twirled Hula Hoops, pranced in pink ballet tutus, and when they bowed or curtsied, the audience would sigh in unison, "Awww," and then clap enthusiastically.

When my turn came, I was very confident. I remember my childish excitement. It was as if I knew, without a doubt, that the prodigy side of me really did exist. I had no fear whatsoever, no nervousness. I remember thinking to myself, This is it! This is it! I looked out over the audience, at my mother's blank face, my father's yawn, Auntie Lindo's stiff-lipped smile, Waverly's sulky expression. I had on a white dress layered with sheets of lace, and a pink bow in my Peter Pan haircut. As I sat down I envisioned people jumping to their feet and Ed Sullivan rushing up to introduce me to everyone on TV.

And I started to play. It was so beautiful. I was so caught up in how lovely I looked that at first I didn't worry how I would sound. So it was a surprise to me when I hit the first wrong note and I realized something didn't sound quite right. And then I hit another and another followed that. A chill started at the top of my head and began to trickle down. Yet I couldn't stop playing, as though my hands were bewitched. I kept thinking my fingers would adjust themselves back, like a train switching to the right track. I played this strange jumble through two repeats, the sour notes staying with me all the way to the end.

55   When I stood up, I discovered my legs were shaking. Maybe I had just been nervous and the audience, like Old Chong, had seen me go through the right motions and had not heard anything wrong at all. I swept my right foot out, went down on my knee, looked up and smiled. The room was quiet, except for Old Chong, who was beaming and shouting, "Bravo! Bravo! Well done!" But then I saw my mother's face, her stricken face. The audience clapped weakly, and as I walked back to my chair, with my whole face quivering as I tried not to cry, I heard a little boy whisper loudly to his mother, "That was awful," and the mother whispered back, "Well, she certainly tried."

And now I realized how many people were in the audience, the whole world it seemed. I was aware of eyes burning into my back. I felt the shame of my mother and father as they sat stiffly throughout the rest of the show.

We could have escaped during intermission. Pride and some strange sense of honor must have anchored my parents to their chairs. And so we watched it all: the eighteen-year-old boy with a fake mustache who did a magic show and juggled flaming hoops while riding a unicycle. The breasted girl with white makeup who sang from *Madama Butterfly* and got honorable mention. And the eleven-year-old boy who won first prize playing a tricky violin song that sounded like a busy bee.

After the show, the Hsus, the Jongs, and the St. Clairs from the Joy Luck Club came up to my mother and father.

"Lots of talented kids," Auntie Lindo said vaguely, smiling broadly.

"That was somethin' else," said my father, and I wondered if he was referring to me in a humorous way, or whether he even remembered what I had done.

Waverly looked at me and shrugged her shoulders. "You aren't a genius like me," she said matter-of-factly. And if I hadn't felt so bad, I would have pulled her braids and punched her stomach.

But my mother's expression was what devastated me: a quiet, blank look that said she had lost everything. I felt the same way, and it seemed as if everybody were now coming up, like gawkers at the scene of an accident, to see what parts were actually missing. When we got on the bus to go home, my father was humming the busy-bee tune and my mother was silent. I kept thinking she wanted to wait until we got home before shouting at me. But when my father unlocked the door to our apartment, my mother walked in and then went to the back, into the bedroom. No accusations. No blame. And in a way, I felt disappointed. I had been waiting for her to start shouting, so I could shout back and cry and blame her for all my misery.

I assumed my talent-show fiasco meant I never had to play the piano again. But two days later, after school, my mother came out of the kitchen and saw me watching TV.

"Four clock," she reminded me as if it were any other day. I was stunned, as though she were asking me to go through the talent-show torture again. I wedged myself more tightly in front of the TV.

"Turn off TV," she called from the kitchen five minutes later.

I didn't budge. And then I decided. I didn't have to do what my mother said anymore. I wasn't her slave. This wasn't China. I had listened to her before and look what happened. She was the stupid one.

She came out from the kitchen and stood in the arched entryway of the living room. "Four clock," she said once again, louder.

"I'm not going to play anymore," I said nonchalantly. "Why should I? I'm not a genius."

She walked over and stood in front of the TV. I saw her chest was heaving up and down in an angry way.

"No!" I said, and I now felt stronger, as if my true self had finally emerged. So this was what had been inside me all along.

"No! I won't!" I screamed.

She yanked me by the arm, pulled me off the floor, snapped off the TV. She was frighteningly strong, half pulling, half carrying me toward the piano as I kicked the throw rugs under my feet. She lifted me up and onto the hard bench. I was sobbing by now, looking at her bitterly. Her chest was heaving even more and her mouth was open, smiling crazily as if she were pleased I was crying.

"You want me to be someone that I'm not!" I sobbed. "I'll never be the kind of daughter you want me to be!"

"Only two kinds of daughters," she shouted in Chinese. "Those who are obedient and those who follow their own mind! Only one kind of daughter can live in this house. Obedient daughter!"

75 "Then I wish I wasn't your daughter. I wish you weren't my mother," I shouted. As I said these things I got scared. It felt like worms and toads and slimy things crawling out of my chest, but it also felt good, as if this awful side of me had surfaced, at last.

"Too late change this," said my mother shrilly.

And I could sense her anger rising to its breaking point. I wanted to see it spill over. And that's when I remembered the babies she had lost in China, the ones we never talked about. "Then I wish I'd never been born!" I shouted. "I wish I were dead! Like them."

It was as if I had said the magic words. Alakazam!—and her face went blank, her mouth closed, her arms went slack, and she backed out of the room, stunned, as if she were blowing away like a small brown leaf, thin, brittle, lifeless.

It was not the only disappointment my mother felt in me. In the years that followed, I failed her so many times, each time asserting my own will, my right to fall short of expectations. I didn't get straight As. I didn't become class president. I didn't get into Stanford. I dropped out of college.

80 For unlike my mother, I did not believe I could be anything I wanted to be. I could only be me.

And for all those years, we never talked about the disaster at the recital or my terrible accusations afterward at the piano bench. All that remained unchecked, like a betrayal that was now unspeakable. So I never found a way to ask her why she had hoped for something so large that failure was inevitable.

And even worse, I never asked her what frightened me the most: Why had she given up hope?

For after our struggle at the piano, she never mentioned my playing again. The lessons stopped. The lid to the piano was closed, shutting out the dust, my misery, and her dreams.

So she surprised me. A few years ago, she offered to give me the piano, for my thirtieth birthday. I had not played in all those years. I saw the offer as a sign of forgiveness, a tremendous burden removed.

85 "Are you sure?" I asked shyly. "I mean, won't you and Dad miss it?"

"No, this your piano," she said firmly. "Always your piano. You only one can play."

"Well, I probably can't play anymore," I said. "It's been years."

"You pick up fast," said my mother, as if she knew this was certain. "You have natural talent. You could been genius if you want to."

"No I couldn't."

"You just not trying," said my mother. And she was neither angry 90
nor sad. She said it as if to announce a fact that could never be disproved. "Take it," she said.

But I didn't at first. It was enough that she had offered it to me. And after that, every time I saw it in my parents' living room, standing in front of the bay windows, it made me feel proud, as if it were a shiny trophy I had won back.

Last week I sent a tuner over to my parents' apartment and had the piano reconditioned, for purely sentimental reasons. My mother had died a few months before and I had been getting things in order for my father, a little bit at a time. I put the jewelry in special silk pouches. The sweaters she had knitted in yellow, pink, bright orange—all the colors I hated—I put those in moth-proof boxes. I found some old Chinese silk dresses, the kind with little slits up the sides. I rubbed the old silk against my skin, then wrapped them in tissue and decided to take them home with me.

After I had the piano tuned, I opened the lid and touched the keys. It sounded even richer than I remembered. Really, it was a very good piano. Inside the bench were the same exercise notes with handwritten scales, the same secondhand music books with their covers held together with yellow tape.

I opened up the Schumann book to the dark little piece I had played at the recital. It was on the left-hand side of the page, "Pleading Child." It looked more difficult than I remembered. I played a few bars, surprised at how easily the notes came back to me.

And for the first time, or so it seemed, I noticed the piece on the 95
right-hand side. It was called "Perfectly Contented." I tried to play this one as well. It had a lighter melody but the same flowing rhythm and turned out to be quite easy. "Pleading Child" was shorter but slower; "Perfectly Contented" was longer, but faster. And after I played them both a few times, I realized they were two halves of the same song.

Responding to Reading

1. Why does the narrator's mother believe that her daughter can become a prodigy? Does the daughter agree that this is possible?
2. What are the "two kinds" to which the story's title refers? Are these two categories completely irreconcilable, or do you see any common ground between them?

3. In what respects are the story's plot and characters unique to the Chinese-American experience? In what respects does the story reveal truths about other immigrant families as well?

Responding in Writing

The narrator's mother sees the child actress Shirley Temple as typically American. What prominent individuals—entertainers, politicians, sports figures, and so on—do you see as typically American? Why?

—————————————— FOCUS ——————————————

What Is the American Dream?

Immigrant families on board ship approaching Statue of Liberty, c. 1900.

Responding to the Image

1. What does this photograph suggest to you about the power of the American Dream? How might the immigrants pictured here define the American Dream?
2. What do you think the Statue of Liberty symbolizes to the people in the picture? Do you think the statue means something different to today's Americans? (Note that most immigrants no longer come to the US by ship.)

THE DECLARATION OF INDEPENDENCE

Thomas Jefferson

1743–1826

Thomas Jefferson—lawyer, statesman, diplomat, architect, scientist, politician, writer, education theorist, and musician—graduated from William and Mary College in 1762 and went on to lead an impressive political life. Jefferson served as a member of the Continental Congress, governor of Virginia, Secretary of State to George Washington, and Vice-President to John Adams and also served two terms as the US President (1801–1809), during which he oversaw the Louisiana Purchase. After retiring from public office, Jefferson founded the University of Virginia in 1819. He was an avid collector of books and owned nearly ten thousand, which later became the foundation of the Library of Congress. A firm believer in reason and the natural rights of individuals, Jefferson drafted The Declaration of Independence, which was later amended by the Continental Congress. To learn more about Jefferson, visit the Biographical Directory of the US Congress, http://bioguide .congress.gov.

In Congress, July 4, 1776: The Unanimous Declaration of the Thirteen United States of America

When in the Course of human events it becomes necessary for one people to dissolve the political bands which have connected them with another, and to assume among the powers of the earth, the separate and equal station to which the Laws of Nature and of Nature's God entitle them, a decent respect to the opinions of mankind requires that they should declare the causes which impel them to the separation.

We hold these truths to be self-evident, that all men are created equal, that they are endowed by their Creator with certain unalienable Rights, that among these are Life, Liberty and the pursuit of Happiness. That to secure these rights, Governments are instituted among Men, deriving their just powers from the consent of the governed. That whenever any Form of Government becomes destructive of these ends, it is the Right of the People to alter or to abolish it, and to institute new Government, laying its foundation on such principles and organizing its powers in such form, as to them shall seem most likely to effect their Safety and Happiness. Prudence, indeed, will dictate that Governments long established should not be changed for light and transient causes; and accordingly all experience hath shewn, that mankind are more disposed to suffer, while evils are sufferable, than to right themselves by abolishing the forms to which they are accustomed. But when a long train of abuses and usurpations, pursuing invariably the same Object, evinces a design to reduce them under absolute Despotism, it is their right, it is their duty, to throw off such Government, and to provide new Guards for their future security. Such has been the patient sufferance of these Colonies; and such is now the necessity which constrains them to alter their former Systems of Governors. The history of the present King of Great Britain is a history of repeated injuries and usurpations, all having in direct object the establishment of an absolute Tyranny over these States. To prove this, let Facts be submitted to a candid world.

He has refused his Assent to Laws, the most wholesome and necessary for the public good.

He has forbidden his Governors to pass laws of immediate and pressing importance, unless suspended in their operation till his Assent should be obtained; and when so suspended, he has utterly neglected to attend to them.

He has refused to pass other Laws for the accommodation of large 5 districts of people, unless those people would relinquish the right of Representation in the Legislature, a right inestimable to them and formidable to tyrants only.

He has called together legislative bodies at places unusual, uncomfortable, and distant from the depository of their Public Records, for the sole purpose of fatiguing them into compliance with his measures.

He has dissolved Representative Houses repeatedly, for opposing with manly firmness his invasions on the rights of the people.

He has refused for a long time, after such dissolutions, to cause others to be elected; whereby the Legislative Powers, incapable of Annihilation, have returned to the People at large for their exercise; the State remaining in the mean time exposed to all the dangers of invasion from without, and convulsions within.

He has endeavored to prevent the population of these States; for that purpose obstructing the Laws for Naturalization of Foreigners; refusing to pass others to encourage their migration hither, and raising the conditions of new Appropriations of Lands.

He has obstructed the Administration of Justice, by refusing his As- 10 sent to Laws for establishing Judiciary Powers.

He has made Judges dependent on his Will alone, for the tenure of their offices, and the amount and payment of their salaries.

He has erected a multitude of New Offices, and sent hither swarms of Officers to harass our people, and eat out their substance.

He has kept among us, in times of peace, Standing Armies without the Consent of our legislatures.

He has affected to render the Military independent of and superior to the Civil Power.

He has combined with others to subject us to a jurisdiction foreign 15 to our constitution, and unacknowledged by our laws; giving his

Assent to their Acts of pretended Legislation: For quartering large bodies of armed troops among us: For protecting them, by a mock Trial, from punishment for any Murders which they should commit on the Inhabitants of these States: For cutting off our Trade with all parts of the world: For imposing Taxes on us without our Consent: For depriving us in many cases, of the benefits of Trial by Jury; For transporting us beyond Seas to be tried for pretended offenses: For abolishing the free System of English Laws in a neighboring Province, establishing therein an Arbitrary government, and enlarging its Boundaries so as to render it at once an example and fit instrument for introducing the same absolute rule into these Colonies: For taking away our Charters, abolishing our most valuable Laws and altering fundamentally the Forms of our Governments: For suspending our own Legislatures, and declaring themselves invested with power to legislate for us in all cases whatsoever.

He has abdicated Government here, by declaring us out of his Protection and waging War against us.

He has plundered our seas, ravaged our Coasts, burnt our towns, and destroyed the lives of our people.

He is at this time transporting large Armies of foreign Mercenaries to complete the works of death, desolation and tyranny, already begun with circumstances of Cruelty & Perfidy scarcely paralleled in the most barbarous ages, and totally unworthy the Head of a civilized nation.

He has constrained our fellow Citizens taken Captive on the high Seas to bear Arms against their Country, to become the executioners of their friends and Brethren, or to fall themselves by their Hands.

20   He has excited domestic insurrections amongst us, and has endeavored to bring on the inhabitants of our frontiers, the merciless Indian Savages, whose known rule of warfare, is an undistinguished destruction of all ages, sexes, and conditions.

In every stage of these Oppressions We have Petitioned for Redress in the most humble terms: Our repeated Petitions have been answered only by repeated injury. A Prince, whose character is thus marked by every act which may define a Tyrant, is unfit to be the ruler of a free people.

Nor have We been wanting in attention to our British brethren. We have warned them from time to time of attempts by their legislature to extend an unwarrantable jurisdiction over us. We have reminded them of the circumstances of our emigration and settlement here. We have appealed to their native justice and magnanimity, and we have conjured them by the ties of our common kindred to disavow these usurpations, which would inevitably interrupt our connections and correspondence. They too have been deaf to the voice of justice and of consanguinity. We must, therefore, acquiesce in the necessity, which denounces our Separation, and hold them, as we hold the rest of mankind, Enemies in War, in Peace Friends.

We, THEREFORE, the Representatives of the UNITED STATES OF AMERICA, in General Congress, Assembled, appealing to the Supreme Judge of the world for the rectitude of our intentions, do, in the Name, and by Authority of the good People of these Colonies, solemnly publish and declare, That these United Colonies are, and of Right ought to be FREE AND INDEPENDENT STATES; that they are Absolved from all Allegiance to the British Crown, and that all political connection between them and the State of Great Britain, is and ought to be totally dissolved; and that as Free and Independent States, they have full Power to levy War, conclude Peace, contract Alliances, establish Commerce, and to do all other Acts and Things which Independent States may of right do. And for the support of this Declaration, with a firm reliance on the protection of Divine Providence, we mutually pledge to each other our Lives, our Fortunes, and our sacred Honor.

Responding to Reading

1. The Declaration of Independence was written in the eighteenth century, a time when logic and reason were thought to be the supreme achievements of human beings. Do you think this document appeals just to reason, or does it also appeal to the emotions? Explain.
2. Paragraphs 3 through 20 consist of a litany of grievances, expressed in forceful parallel language. How is this use of parallelism similar to (or different from) the language used by Kennedy (p. 528) and King (p. 532)?
3. Do you think it is fair, as some have done, to accuse the framers of the Declaration of Independence of being racist? Of being sexist?

Responding in Writing

Rewrite five or six sentences from paragraphs 3–20 of The Declaration of Independence in modern English, substituting contemporary examples for the injustices Jefferson enumerates.

THE NEW COLOSSUS

Emma Lazarus

1849–1887

Born to a wealthy family in New York City and educated by private tutors, Emma Lazarus became one of the foremost poets of her day. Today, she is remembered solely for her poem "The New Colossus," a sonnet written in 1883 as part of an effort to raise funds for the Statue of Liberty. The poem was later inscribed on the statue's base, and it remains a vivid reminder of the immigrant's American dream. Lazarus's collected works include Admetus and Other Poems (1871) *and* Songs of a Semite (1882); *she also wrote essays, translations, and a verse play. As a Jew, Lazarus decried the persecution of Jews in Russia and elsewhere. In two tours of Europe during the 1880s, she was received as an international celebrity, but she returned to New York, after having been diagnosed with cancer, and died at thirty-eight. For more information about Liberty and Ellis islands, visit http://www.nps.gov/stli/ and http://www.ellisisland.org/.*

Not like the brazen giant of Greek fame,
With conquering limbs astride from land to land;
Here at our sea-washed, sunset gates shall stand
A mighty woman with a torch, whose flame
5   Is the imprisoned lightning, and her name
Mother of Exiles. From her beacon-hand
Glows world-wide welcome; her mild eyes command
The air-bridged harbor that twin cities frame.
"Keep, ancient lands, your storied pomp!" cries she
10   With silent lips. "Give me your tired, your poor,
Your huddled masses yearning to breathe free,
The wretched refuse of your teeming shore.
Send these, the homeless, tempest-tost to me,
I lift my lamp beside the golden door!"

Responding to Reading

1. The Colossus of Rhodes, an enormous statue of the Greek god Apollo, was considered one of the seven wonders of the ancient world. It stood at the mouth of the harbor at Rhodes. Why do you think this poem is called "The New Colossus"?
2. Who is the poem's speaker? Who is being addressed?
3. What is the "golden door" to which the last line refers?

Responding in Writing

Look at the photograph on page 523. What elements of the Statue of Liberty has Lazarus captured in this poem? What characteristics, if any, has she failed to capture?

INAUGURAL ADDRESS

John F. Kennedy

1917–1963

Born in Brookline, Massachusetts, John Fitzgerald Kennedy received a Bachelor's degree from Harvard University and served in the Navy as a PT boat commander in the South Pacific. A highly charismatic politician, he was elected to the United States House of Representatives in 1947 and to the Senate in 1953. In 1960, defeating Republican candidate (and later President) Richard Nixon, Kennedy became the youngest man and first Catholic to be elected President. During his tenure, the government adopted policies promoting racial equality, aid to the poor and education, and increased availability of medical care; it also established the Peace Corps. However, Kennedy was also responsible for involving the country further in the doomed Vietnam conflict. He was assassinated in November of 1963, a year before the end of his first term. To learn more about Kennedy, visit the Biographical Directory of the US Congress, http://bioguide.congress.gov.

Vice President Johnson, Mr. Speaker, Mr. Chief Justice, President Eisenhower, Vice President Nixon, President Truman, Reverend Clergy, fellow citizens:

We observe today not a victory of party but a celebration of freedom—symbolizing an end as well as a beginning—signifying renewal as well as change. For I have sworn before you and Almighty God the same solemn oath our forebears prescribed nearly a century and three-quarters ago.

The world is very different now. For man holds in his mortal hands the power to abolish all forms of human poverty and all forms of human life. And yet the same revolutionary beliefs for which our forebears fought are still at issue around the globe—the belief that the rights of man come not from the generosity of the state but from the hand of God.

We dare not forget today that we are the heirs of that first revolution. Let the word go forth from this time and place, to friend and foe alike, that the torch has been passed to a new generation of Americans—born in this century, tempered by war, disciplined by a hard and bitter peace, proud of our ancient heritage—and unwilling to witness or permit the slow undoing of those human rights to which this nation has always been committed, and to which we are committed today at home and around the world.

Let every nation know, whether it wishes us well or ill, that we ₅ shall pay any price, bear any burden, meet any hardship, support any friend, oppose any foe to assure the survival and the success of liberty.

This much we pledge—and more.

To those old allies whose cultural and spiritual origins we share, we pledge the loyalty of faithful friends. United there is little we cannot do in a host of cooperative ventures. Divided there is little we can do—for we dare not meet a powerful challenge at odds and split asunder.

To those new states whom we welcome to the ranks of the free, we pledge our word that one form of colonial control shall not have passed away merely to be replaced by a far more iron tyranny. We shall not always expect to find them supporting our view. But we shall always hope to find them strongly supporting their own freedom—and to remember that, in the past, those who foolishly sought power by riding the back of the tiger ended up inside. To those people in the huts and villages of half the globe struggling to break the bonds of mass misery, we pledge our best efforts to help them help themselves, for whatever period is required—not because the communists may be doing it, not because we seek their votes, but because it is right. If a free society cannot help the many who are poor, it cannot save the few who are rich.

To our sister republics south of our border, we offer a special pledge—to convert our good words into good deeds—in a new alliance for progress—to assist free men and free governments in casting off the chains of poverty. But this peaceful revolution of hope cannot become the prey of hostile powers. Let all our neighbors know that we shall join with them to oppose aggression or subversion anywhere in the Americas. And let every other power know that this Hemisphere intends to remain the master of its own house.

10   To that world assembly of sovereign states, the United Nations, our last best hope in an age where the instruments of war have far outpaced the instruments of peace, we renew our pledge of support—to prevent it from becoming merely a forum for invective—to strengthen its shield of the new and the weak—and to enlarge the area in which its writ may run.

Finally, to those nations who would make themselves our adversary, we offer not a pledge but a request: that both sides begin anew the quest for peace, before the dark powers of destruction unleashed by science engulf all humanity in planned or accidental self-destruction.

We dare not tempt them with weakness. For only when our arms are sufficient beyond doubt can we be certain beyond doubt that they will never be employed.

But neither can two great and powerful groups of nations take comfort from our present course—both sides overburdened by the cost of modern weapons, both rightly alarmed by the steady spread of the deadly atom, yet both racing to alter that uncertain balance of terror that stays the hand of mankind's final war.

So let us begin anew—remembering on both sides that civility is not a sign of weakness, and sincerity is always subject to proof. Let us never negotiate out of fear. But let us never fear to negotiate.

15   Let both sides explore what problems unite us instead of belaboring those problems which divide us.

Let both sides, for the first time, formulate serious and precise proposals for the inspection and control of arms and bring the absolute power to destroy other nations under the absolute control of all nations.

Let both sides seek to invoke the wonders of science instead of its terrors. Together let us explore the stars, conquer the deserts, eradicate disease, tap the ocean depths and encourage the arts and commerce.

Let both sides unite to heed in all corners of the earth the command of Isaiah—to "undo the heavy burdens . . . (and) let the oppressed go free."

And if a beachhead of cooperation may push back the jungle of suspicion, let both sides join in creating a new endeavor, not a new balance of power, but a new world of law, where the strong are just and the weak secure and the peace preserved.

All this will not be finished in the first one hundred days. Nor 20 will it be finished in the first one thousand days, nor in the life of this Administration, nor even perhaps in our lifetime on this planet. But let us begin.

In your hands, my fellow citizens, more than mine, will rest the final success or failure of our course. Since this country was founded, each generation of Americans has been summoned to give testimony to its national loyalty. The graves of young Americans who answered the call to service surround the globe.

Now the trumpet summons us—again not as a call to bear arms, though arms we need—not as a call to battle, though embattled we are—but a call to bear the burden of a long twilight struggle, year in and year out, "rejoicing in hope, patient in tribulation"—a struggle against the common enemies of man: tyranny, poverty, disease and war itself. Can we forge against these enemies a grand and global alliance, North and South, East and West, that can assure a more fruitful life for all mankind? Will you join in that historic effort?

In the long history of the world, only a few generations have been granted the role of defending freedom in its hour of maximum danger. I do not shrink from this responsibility—I welcome it. I do not believe that any of us would exchange places with any other people or any other generation. The energy, the faith, the devotion which we bring to this endeavor will light our country and all who serve it— and the glow from that fire can truly light the world. And so, my fellow Americans: ask not what your country can do for you—ask what you can do for your country. My fellow citizens of the world: ask not what America will do for you, but what together we can do for the freedom of man.

Finally, whether you are citizens of America or citizens of the world, ask of us here the same high standards of strength and sacrifice which we ask of you. With a good conscience our only sure reward, with history the final judge of our deeds, let us go forth to lead the land we love, asking His blessing and His help, but knowing that here on earth God's work must truly be our own.

Responding to Reading

1. At the beginning of his speech, Kennedy alludes to the "revolutionary beliefs" of Jefferson (p. 524) and asserts, "We are the heirs of that first revolution" (4). What does he mean? Do you think his speech offers adequate support for this statement?

2. What, according to Kennedy, must we still achieve in order to fulfill Jefferson's dreams? Can you think of other problems that must still be solved before we can consider the American Dream a reality?

3. Near the end of his speech, Kennedy says, "And so, my fellow Americans: ask not what your country can do for you—ask what you can do for your country" (23). What does this famous, often-quoted passage actually mean in practical terms? Do you think this exhortation is realistic? Do you think it is fair? Explain.

Responding in Writing

Exactly what do you expect America to do for you, and what do you expect to do for your country?

I HAVE A DREAM

Martin Luther King, Jr.

1929–1968

One of the greatest civil rights leaders and orators of this century, Baptist minister Martin Luther King, Jr. was the winner of the 1964 Nobel Peace Prize. Born in Atlanta, Georgia, son and grandson of Baptist preachers, King earned a BA degree from Morehouse College (1948), a BD degree from Crozer Theological Seminary in Pennsylvania (1951), and a PhD from Boston University (1955). Influenced by Thoreau and Gandhi, King altered the spirit of African-American protest in the United States by advocating nonviolent civil disobedience to achieve racial equality. King was arrested more than twenty times and assaulted at least four times for his activities, but he was also awarded five honorary degrees and was named Man of the Year by Time *magazine in 1963. King's books include* Letter from Birmingham Jail *(1963) and* Where Do We Go from Here: Chaos or Community? *(1967). King was assassinated on April 4, 1968, in Memphis, Tennessee. He delivered the following speech from the steps of the Lincoln Memorial on August 28, 1963, during the March on Washington in support of civil rights. To learn more about Martin Luther King, Jr., visit the Web site of the King Center, founded by his widow in 1968, http://thekingcenter.com/.*

I am happy to join with you today in what will go down in history as the greatest demonstration for freedom in the history of our nation.

Fivescore years ago, a great American, in whose symbolic shadow we stand today, signed the Emancipation Proclamation. This momentous decree came as a great beacon light of hope to millions of Negro slaves who had been seared in the flames of withering injustice. It came as a joyous daybreak to end the long night of their captivity.

But one hundred years later, the Negro still is not free; one hundred years later, the life of the Negro is still sadly crippled by the manacles of segregation and the chains of discrimination; one hundred years later, the Negro lives on a lonely island of poverty in the midst of a vast ocean of material prosperity; one hundred years later, the Negro is still languishing in the corners of American society and finds himself in exile in his own land.

So we've come here today to dramatize a shameful condition. In a sense we've come to our nation's capital to cash a check. When the architects of our republic wrote the magnificent words of the Constitution and the Declaration of Independence, they were signing a promissory note to which every American was to fall heir. This note was the promise that all men, yes, black men as well as white men, would be guaranteed the unalienable rights of life, liberty, and the pursuit of happiness.

It is obvious today that America has defaulted on this promissory note in so far as her citizens of color are concerned. Instead of honoring this sacred obligation, America has given the Negro people a bad check; a check which has come back marked "insufficient funds." We refuse to believe that there are insufficient funds in the great vaults of opportunity of this nation. And so we've come to cash this check, a check that will give us upon demand the riches of freedom and the security of justice. 5

We have also come to this hallowed spot to remind America of the fierce urgency of now. This is no time to engage in the luxury of cooling off or to take the tranquilizing drug of gradualism. Now is the time to make real the promises of democracy; now is the time to rise from the dark and desolate valley of segregation to the sunlit path of racial justice; now is the time to lift our nation from the quicksands of racial injustice to the solid rock of brotherhood; now is the time to make justice a reality for all God's children. It would be fatal for the nation to overlook the urgency of the moment. This sweltering summer of the Negro's legitimate discontent will not pass until there is an invigorating autumn of freedom and equality.

Nineteen sixty-three is not an end, but a beginning. And those who hope that the Negro needed to blow off steam and will now be content, will have a rude awakening if the nation returns to business as usual.

There will be neither rest nor tranquility in America until the Negro is granted his citizenship rights. The whirlwinds of revolt will continue to shake the foundations of our nation until the bright day of justice emerges.

But there is something that I must say to my people who stand on the warm threshold which leads into the palace of justice. In the process of gaining our rightful place we must not be guilty of wrongful deeds.

10   Let us not seek to satisfy our thirst for freedom by drinking from the cup of bitterness and hatred. We must forever conduct our struggle on the high plane of dignity and discipline. We must not allow our creative protest to degenerate into physical violence. Again and again we must rise to the majestic heights of meeting physical force with soul force.

The marvelous new militancy which has engulfed the Negro community must not lead us to a distrust of all white people, for many of our white brothers, as evidenced by their presence here today, have come to realize that their destiny is tied up with our destiny and they have come to realize that their freedom is inextricably bound to our freedom. This offense we share mounted to storm the battlements of injustice must be carried forth by a biracial army. We cannot walk alone.

And as we walk, we must make the pledge that we shall always march ahead. We cannot turn back. There are those who are asking the devotees of civil rights, "When will you be satisfied?" We can never be satisfied as long as the Negro is the victim of the unspeakable horrors of police brutality.

We can never be satisfied as long as our bodies, heavy with fatigue of travel, cannot gain lodging in the motels of the highways and the hotels of the cities. We cannot be satisfied as long as the Negro's basic mobility is from a smaller ghetto to a larger one.

We can never be satisfied as long as our children are stripped of their selfhood and robbed of their dignity by signs stating "for whites only." We cannot be satisfied as long as a Negro in Mississippi cannot vote and a Negro in New York believes he has nothing for which to vote. No, we are not satisfied, and we will not be satisfied until justice rolls down like waters and righteousness like a mighty stream.

15   I am not unmindful that some of you have come here out of excessive trials and tribulation. Some of you have come fresh from narrow jail cells. Some of you have come from areas where your quest for freedom left you battered by the storms of persecution and staggered by the winds of police brutality. You have been the veterans of creative suffering. Continue to work with the faith that unearned suffering is redemptive.

Go back to Mississippi; go back to Alabama; go back to South Carolina; go back to Georgia; go back to Louisiana; go back to the slums and ghettos of the northern cities, knowing that somehow this situation can, and will be changed. Let us not wallow in the valley of despair.

So I say to you, my friends, that even though we must face the difficulties of today and tomorrow, I still have a dream. It is a dream deeply rooted in the American dream that one day this nation will rise up and live out the true meaning of its creed—we hold these truths to be self-evident, that all men are created equal.

I have a dream that one day on the red hills of Georgia, sons of former slaves and sons of former slave-owners will be able to sit down together at the table of brotherhood.

I have a dream that one day, even the state of Mississippi, a state sweltering with the heat of injustice, sweltering with the heat of oppression, will be transformed into an oasis of freedom and justice.

I have a dream my four little children will one day live in a nation 20
where they will not be judged by the color of their skin but by the content of their character. I have a dream today!

I have a dream that one day, down in Alabama, with its vicious racists, with its governor having his lips dripping with the words of interposition and nullification, that one day, right there in Alabama, little black boys and black girls will be able to join hands with little white boys and white girls as sisters and brothers. I have a dream today!

I have a dream that one day every valley shall be exalted, every hill and mountain shall be made low, the rough places shall be made plain, and the crooked places shall be made straight and the glory of the Lord will be revealed and all flesh shall see it together.

This is our hope. This is the faith that I go back to the South with.

With this faith we will be able to hew out of the mountain of despair a stone of hope. With this faith we will be able to transform the jangling discords of our nation into a beautiful symphony of brotherhood.

With this faith we will be able to work together, to pray together, 25
to struggle together, to go to jail together, to stand up for freedom together, knowing that we will be free one day. This will be the day when all of God's children will be able to sing with new meaning—"my country 'tis of thee; sweet land of liberty; of thee I sing; land where my fathers died, land of the pilgrim's pride; from every mountain side, let freedom ring"—and if America is to be a great nation, this must become true.

So let freedom ring from the prodigious hilltops of New Hampshire.

Let freedom ring from the mighty mountains of New York.

Let freedom ring from the heightening Alleghenies of Pennsylvania.

Let freedom ring from the snow-capped Rockies of Colorado.

Let freedom ring from the curvaceous slopes of California. 30

But not only that.

Let freedom ring from Stone Mountain of Georgia.

Let freedom ring from Lookout Mountain of Tennessee.

Let freedom ring from every hill and molehill of Mississippi, from every mountainside, let freedom ring.

And when we allow freedom to ring, when we let it ring from 35
every village and hamlet, from every state and city, we will be able to speed up that day when all of God's children—black men and white

men, Jews and Gentiles, Catholics and Protestants—will be able to join hands and to sing in the words of the old Negro spiritual, "Free at last, free at last; thank God Almighty, we are free at last."

Responding to Reading

1. What exactly is King's dream? Do you believe it has come true in any sense?
2. Speaking as a representative of his fellow African-American citizens, King tells his audience that African Americans find themselves "in exile in [their] own land" (3). Do you believe this is still true of African Americans? Of members of other minority groups? Which groups? Why?
3. Jefferson (p. 524) wrote in the eighteenth century; King, in the twentieth. Jefferson wrote as an insider, a man of privilege; King, as an outsider. What do their dreams have in common? How did each man intend to achieve his dream?

Responding in Writing

What dreams do you have for yourself and for your family? What dreams do you have for your country?

WIDENING THE FOCUS

The following readings can suggest additional perspectives for thinking and writing about the American Dream. You may also want to do further research on this subject on the Internet.

- Sherman Alexie, "The Unauthorized Autobiography of Me" (p. 53)
- Jonathan Kozol, "The Human Cost of an Illiterate Society" (p. 212)
- Martin Luther King, Jr., "Letter from Birmingham Jail" (p. 699)

For Internet Research: The American Dream was first defined more than two centuries ago, and it has changed along with our society. How would you define today's American Dream? For example, does it include access for all to education, employment, healthcare, and home ownership? Analyze Web sites that offer their visions of the American Dream, such as the following:

- *The Center for a New American Dream*, http://www.newdream.org/
- *A World Connected*, http://www.aworldconnected.org/
- *The American Dream Group*, http://achieve-the-dream.net/index.htm
- *America's Promise*, http://www.americaspromise.org/

Or, use a search engine to find discussion of the American Dream in online political magazines listed on the Yahoo! Directory, http://dir.yahoo.com/Government/U_S_Government/Politics/News_and_Media/Magazines/.

Then, write an essay in which you define what you think the American Dream should be for the twenty-first century.

[handwritten annotations: No your / No what you think / it for what America should be]

WRITING

The American Dream

1. Write an essay in which you support the idea that the strength of the United States comes from its ability to assimilate many different groups. In your essay, discuss specific contributions your own ethnic group and others have made to American society.

2. Some of the writers in this chapter respond to their feelings of being excluded from American society with anger and protest; others respond with resignation and acceptance. Considering several different writers and situations, write an essay in which you contrast these two kinds of responses. Under what circumstances, if any, does each kind of response make sense?

3. Several of the readings in this chapter—for example, "The Library Card" (p. 476) and "Two Kinds" (p. 512)—deal with the uniquely American concept of reinventing oneself, taking on a new identity. Some Americans reinvent themselves through education; others do so simply by changing their appearance. Write an essay in which you outline the options available to newcomers to the United States who wish to effect this kind of transformation.

4. What do you see as the greatest obstacle to full access to the American Dream? (You might, for example, consider the limitations posed by gender, race, religion, language, social class, ethnicity, physical disability, lack of education, or poverty.) Support your thesis with references to several selections in this chapter—and, if you like, to your own experiences.

5. Interview a first-generation American, a second-generation American, and a third-generation American. How are their views of the American Dream different? How are they like and unlike the dreams of various writers represented in this chapter? How do you account for those similarities and differences?

6. The mother in Amy Tan's "Two Kinds" (p. 512) believes "you could be anything you wanted to be in America" (1); in "Becoming American" (p. 484), Dinesh D'Souza says, "In America your destiny is not prescribed; it is constructed. Your life is like a blank sheet of paper, and you are the artist" (22). Do you agree? That is, do you think the United States is a land of opportunity? Support your position on this issue with references to readings in this chapter and elsewhere in this book.

7. Using the readings in this chapter as source material, write a manifesto that sets forth the rights and responsibilities of all Americans. (Begin by reading Kennedy's inaugural address, p. 528.)

8. Some Americans believe that before the American Dream can become a reality, the nation has an obligation to compensate members of minority groups for past injustices—in particular, to compensate African Americans for the evils of slavery. Do you believe that blacks are owed such compensation, or do you see the payment of reparations as inherently unfair, impractical, or unnecessary? For additional background, read Jonathan Kozol's "The Human Cost of an Illiterate Society" (p. 212) and Maya Angelou's "Graduation" (p. 123) as well as the essays in this chapter by Richard Wright ("The Library Card," p. 476) and Brent Staples ("Just Walk On By," p. 497).

9. Most of the writers whose works appear in this chapter are Americans, people who view the American Dream as something of their own. De Tocqueville, however, was clearly an outsider, looking at American institutions and aspirations from an objective point of view ("Why the Americans Are So Restless in the Midst of Their Prosperity," p. 473). What special insights did his outsider status give him? Which of the writers in this chapter might benefit from de Tocqueville's insights?

10. Read the selections by Jefferson (The Declaration of Independence, p. 524), Lazarus ("The New Colossus," p. 527), Kennedy (Inaugural Address, p. 528), and King ("I Have a Dream," p. 532) in the Focus section of this chapter. Then, try to answer the question "What is the American Dream?"

8

WHY WE WORK

PREPARING TO READ AND WRITE

Although work has always been a part of the human experience, the nature of work has evolved considerably—especially over the last two hundred years. During the Middle Ages and the Renaissance, work was often done by family units. Whether it involved planting and harvesting crops, tending livestock, or engaging in the manufacture of goods, parents, grandparents, and children (and possibly an apprentice or two) worked together, at home. With the advent of the Industrial

Auto workers making car radiators on assembly line, circa 1915.

Revolution, however, the nature of work changed. Manufacturing became centralized in factories, and tasks that were formerly divided among various members of a family were now carried out more efficiently by machines. People worked long hours—in many cases twelve to fifteen hours a day, six and sometimes seven days a week—and could be fired without cause. By the middle of the nineteenth century, most of the great manufacturing cities of Europe were overcrowded and polluted, teeming with unskilled factory workers. It is no wonder that labor unions became increasingly popular as they organized workers to fight for job security, shorter workdays, and minimum safety standards.

Thanks to the labor struggles of the past, many workers today have health insurance, sick leave, paid vacations, life insurance, and other benefits. In some respects, American workers are the most secure and highly compensated in history, but there is a dark side to their situation: workers in the United States work longer and harder than those in any other Western country—often working long hours without overtime and routinely forgoing vacation and personal leave days. Add to this the tendency of American companies to move manufacturing jobs overseas and to see workers as entities whose jobs can be phased out as the need arises, and it is no surprise that employees are often stressed, insecure, and unhappy. The result is that many of today's workers question the role that work plays in their lives and wonder if it is in their best interests to invest so much time and effort in their jobs.

Automotive manufacturing line with robotic arms, 1999.

The Focus section of this chapter addresses the question, "What is a living wage?" The essays in this section examine the condition of the many unskilled, minimum-wage workers that most of us encounter every day—in fast-food restaurants, in retail stores, and in many public facilities. This workforce is composed largely of teenagers, the elderly, minorities, and immigrants (both legal and illegal) who speak little English. Although these people work long hours, they exist on the fringes of the labor market and receive little compensation (and often, no overtime pay or benefits). These essays ask important questions: Is the minimum wage fair compensation for the work that minimum wage workers perform? Do we, as a society, have the obligation to guarantee workers a "living wage," a salary that reflects how much a family actually needs to live? Finally, is it prudent economic policy for the government to define a "living wage" and to require private businesses to adjust their pay scales accordingly?

As you read and prepare to write about the essays in this chapter, you may consider the following questions:

- What do you know about the writer? In what way does the writer's economic and social position affect his or her definition of work?

- Is the writer male or female? Does the writer's gender affect his or her attitude toward work?

- When was the essay written? Does the date of publication affect its content?

- Does the essay seem fair? Balanced? Does the writer seem to have any preconceived ideas about work and its importance?

- Is the writer generally sympathetic or unsympathetic toward workers?

- Does the writer have a realistic or unrealistic view of work?

- On what specific problems does the writer focus?

- What specific solutions does the writer suggest? Are these solutions sensible? Practical?

- Is your interpretation of the problem the same as or different from the interpretation presented in the essay?

- Are there any aspects of the problem that the writer ignores?

- Does the essay challenge any of your ideas about work?

- In what ways is the essay like other essays in this chapter?

WHY WE WORK
Andrew Curry
1976–

Andrew Curry, a reporter for U.S. News and World Report, *received a BS degree in international relations from Georgetown University (1998) and an MA degree in Russian and East European Studies from Stanford University (2000). Curry writes and reports for* U.S. News's *weekly magazine and its annual "America's Best Colleges" supplement. "Why We Work" was the cover story of the February 24, 2003 issue. To read more about Curry, visit his Web site, http://www.andrewcurry.com.*

In 1930, W. K. Kellogg made what he thought was a sensible decision, grounded in the best economic, social, and management theories of the time. Workers at his cereal plant in Battle Creek, Mich., were told to go home two hours early. Every day. For good.

The Depression-era move was hailed in Factory and Industrial Management magazine as the "biggest piece of industrial news since [Henry] Ford announced his five-dollar-a-day policy." President Herbert Hoover summoned the eccentric cereal magnate to the White House and said the plan was "very worthwhile." The belief: Industry and machines would lead to a workers' paradise where all would have less work, more free time, and yet still produce enough to meet their needs.

So what happened? Today, work dominates Americans' lives as never before, as workers pile on hours at a rate not seen since the Industrial Revolution. Technology has offered increasing productivity and a higher standard of living while bank tellers and typists are replaced by machines. The mismatch between available work and those available to do it continues, as jobs go begging while people beg for jobs. Though Kellogg's six-hour day lasted until 1985, Battle Creek's grand industrial experiment has been nearly forgotten. Instead of working less, our hours have stayed steady or risen—and today many more women work so that families can afford the trappings of suburbia. In effect, workers chose the path of consumption over leisure.

But as today's job market shows so starkly, that road is full of potholes. With unemployment at a nine-year high and many workers worried about losing their jobs—or forced to accept cutbacks in pay and benefits—work is hardly the paradise economists once envisioned.

Instead, the job market is as precarious today as it was in the 5 early 1980s, when business began a wave of restructurings and layoffs to maintain its competitiveness. Many workers are left feeling unsecure, unfulfilled, and underappreciated. It's no wonder surveys of today's workers show a steady decline in job satisfaction. "People are very emotional about work, and they're very negative about it," says David Rhodes, a principal at human resource consultants Towers Perrin. "The biggest issue is clearly workload. People are feeling crushed."

The backlash comes after years of people boasting about how hard they work and tying their identities to how indispensable they are. Ringing cellphones, whirring faxes, and ever present E-mail have blurred the lines between work and home. The job penetrates every aspect of life. Americans don't exercise, they work out. We manage our time and work on our relationships. "In reaching the affluent society, we're working longer and harder than anyone could have imagined," says Rutgers University historian John Gillis. "The work ethic and identifying ourselves with work and through work is not only alive and well but more present now than at any time in history."

Stressed Out

It's all beginning to take a toll. Fully one third of American workers—who work longer hours than their counterparts in any industrialized country—felt overwhelmed by the amount of work they had to do, according to a 2001 Families and Work Institute survey. "Both men and women wish they were working about 11 hours [a week] less," says Ellen Galinsky, the institute's president. "A lot of people believe if they do work less they'll be seen as less committed, and in a shaky economy no one wants that."

The modern environment would seem alien to pre-industrial laborers. For centuries, the household—from farms to "cottage" craftsmen—was the unit of production. The whole family was part of the enterprise, be it farming, blacksmithing, or baking. "In pre-industrial society, work and family were practically the same thing," says Gillis.

The Industrial Revolution changed all that. Mills and massive iron smelters required ample labor and constant attendance. "The factory took men, women and children out of the workshops and homes and put them under one roof and timed their movements to machines," writes Sebastian de Grazia in *Of Time, Work and Leisure*. For the first time, work and family were split. Instead of selling what they produced, workers sold their time. With more people leaving farms to move to cities and factories, labor became a commodity, placed on the market like any other.

10   Innovation gave rise to an industrial process based on machinery and mass production. This new age called for a new worker. "The only safeguard of order and discipline in the modern world is a standardized worker with interchangeable parts," mused one turn-of-the-century writer.

Business couldn't have that, so instead it came up with the science of management. The theories of Frederick Taylor, a Philadelphia factory foreman with deep Puritan roots, led to work being broken down into component parts, with each step timed to coldly quantify jobs that skilled craftsmen had worked a lifetime to learn. Workers resented Taylor and his stopwatch, complaining that his focus on process stripped their jobs of creativity and pride, making them irritable. Long before anyone knew what "stress" was, Taylor brought it to the workplace—and without sympathy. "I have you for your strength and mechanical ability, and we have other men paid for thinking," he told workers.

Long Hours

The division of work into components that could be measured and easily taught reached its apex in Ford's River Rouge plant in Dearborn, Mich., where the assembly line came of age. "It was this combination of a simplification of tasks . . . with moving assembly that created a manufacturing revolution while at the same time laying waste human potential on a massive scale," author Richard Donkin writes in *Blood, Sweat and Tears.*

To maximize the production lines, businesses needed long hours from their workers. But it was no easy sell. "Convincing people to work 9 to 5 took a tremendous amount of propaganda and discipline," says the University of Richmond's Joanne Ciulla, author of *The Working Life: The Promise and Betrayal of Modern Work.* Entrepreneurs, religious leaders, and writers like Horatio Alger created whole bodies of literature to glorify the work ethic.

Labor leaders fought back with their own propaganda. For more than a century, a key struggle for the labor movement was reducing the amount of time workers had to spend on the job. "They were pursuing shorter hours and increased leisure. In effect, they were buying their time," says University of Iowa Prof. Benjamin Hunnicutt, author of *Work Without End: Abandoning Shorter Hours for the Right to Work.*

The first labor unions were organized in response to the threat of 15 technology, as skilled workers sought to protect their jobs from mechanization. Later, semi- and unskilled workers began to organize as well, agitating successfully for reduced hours, higher wages, and better work conditions. Unions enjoyed great influence in the early 20th century, and at their height in the 1950s, 35 percent of U.S. workers belonged to one.

Union persistence and the mechanization of factories gradually made shorter hours more realistic. Between 1830 and 1930, work hours were cut nearly in half, with economist John Maynard Keynes famously predicting in 1930 that by 2030 a 15-hour workweek would be standard. The Great Depression pressed the issue, with job sharing proposed as a serious solution to widespread unemployment. Despite business and religious opposition over worries of an idle populace, the Senate passed a bill that would have mandated a 30-hour week in 1933; it was narrowly defeated in the House.

Franklin Delano Roosevelt struck back with a new gospel that lives to this very day: consumption. "The aim . . . is to restore our rich domestic market by raising its vast consuming capacity," he said. "Our first purpose is to create employment as fast as we can." And so began the modern work world. "Instead of accepting work's continuing decline and imminent fall from its dominant social position, businessmen, economists, advertisers, and politicians preached that there would never be 'enough,' " Hunnicutt writes in *Kellogg's Six-Hour Day*. "The entrepreneur and industry could invent new things for advertising to sell and for people to want and work for indefinitely."

The New Deal dumped government money into job creation, in turn encouraging consumption. World War II fueled the fire, and American workers soon found themselves in a "golden age"—40-hour workweeks, plenty of jobs, and plenty to buy. Leisure was the road not taken, a path quickly forgotten in the postwar boom of the 1950s and 1960s.

Discontent

Decades of abundance, however, did not bring satisfaction. "A significant number of Americans are dissatisfied with the quality of their working lives," said the 1973 report "Work in America" from the Department of Health, Education and Welfare. "Dull, repetitive, seemingly meaningless tasks, offering little challenge or autonomy, are causing discontent among workers at all occupational levels." Underlying the dissatisfaction was a very gradual change in what the "Protestant work ethic" meant. Always a source of pride, the idea that hard work was a calling from God dated to the Reformation and the teachings of Martin Luther. While work had once been a means to serve God, two centuries of choices and industrialization had turned work into an end in itself, stripped of the spiritual meaning that sustained the Puritans who came ready to tame the wilderness.

20   By the end of the '70s, companies were reaching out to spiritually drained workers by offering more engagement while withdrawing the promise of a job for life, as the American economy faced a stiff challenge from cheaper workers abroad. "Corporations introduced feel-good programs to stimulate jaded employees with one hand while taking away the elements of a 'just' workplace with the other," says Andrew Ross, author of *No Collar: The Humane Workplace and Its Hidden Costs*. Employees were given more control over their work and schedules, and "human relations" consultants and motivational speakers did a booming business. By the 1990s, technology made

working from home possible for a growing number of people. Seen as a boon at first, telecommuting and the rapidly proliferating "electronic leash" of cellphones made work inescapable, as employees found themselves on call 24/7. Today, almost half of American workers use computers, cellphones, E-mail, and faxes for work during what is supposed to be nonwork time, according to the Families and Work Institute. Home is no longer a refuge but a cozier extension of the office.

The shift coincided with a shortage of highly skilled and educated workers, some of whom were induced with such benefits as stock options in exchange for their putting the company first all the time. But some see a different explanation for the rise in the amount of time devoted to work. "Hours have crept up partly as a consequence of the declining power of the trade-union movement," says Cornell University labor historian Clete Daniel. "Many employers find it more economical to require mandatory overtime than hire new workers and pay their benefits." Indeed, the trend has coincided with the steady decline in the percentage of workers represented by unions, as the labor movement failed to keep pace with the increasing rise of white-collar jobs in the economy. Today fewer than 15 percent of American workers belong to unions.

Nirvana?

The Internet economy of the '90s gave rise to an entirely new corporate climate. The "knowledge worker" was wooed with games, gourmet chefs, and unprecedented freedom over his schedule and environment. Employees at Intuit didn't have to leave their desks for massages; Sun Microsystems offered in-house laundry, and Netscape workers were offered an on-site dentist. At first glance, this new corporate world seemed like nirvana. But "for every attractive feature, workers found there was a cost," says Ross. "It was both a worker's paradise and a con game."

When the stock market bubble burst and the economy fell into its recent recession, workers were forced to re-evaluate their priorities. "There used to be fat bonuses and back rubs, free bagels and foosball tables—it didn't really feel like work," says Allison Hemming, who organizes "pink-slip parties" for laid-off workers around the country and has written *Work It! How to Get Ahead, Save Your Ass, and Land a Job in Any Economy.* "I think people are a lot wiser about their choices now. They want a better quality of life; they're asking for more flextime to spend with their families."

In a study of Silicon Valley culture over the past decade, San Jose State University anthropologist Jan English-Lueck found that skills learned on the job were often brought home. Researchers talked to families with mission statements, mothers used conflict-resolution buzzwords with their squabbling kids, and engineers used flowcharts to organize Thanksgiving dinner. Said one participant: "I don't live life; I manage it."

25   In some ways, we have come full circle. "Now we're seeing the return of work to the home in terms of telecommuting," says Gillis. "We may be seeing the return of households where work is the central element again."

But there's still the question of fulfillment. In a recent study, human resources consultants Towers Perrin tried to measure workers' emotions about their jobs. More than half of the emotion was negative, with the biggest single factor being workload but also a sense that work doesn't satisfy their deeper needs. "We expect more and more out of our jobs," says Hunnicutt. "We expect to find wonderful people and experiences all around us. What we find is Dilbert."

Responding to Reading

1. Why does work "[dominate] Americans' lives as never before" (3)? According to Curry, what toll does this situation take on American workers?
2. How did the Industrial Revolution change the nature of work? What effect did Fredrick Taylor have on work? According to Curry, why were the first labor unions formed? Why was the New Deal "the golden age" for workers (18)?
3. Why does Curry think that workers today are unfulfilled? What evidence does he offer to support this contention? What view of work do you think he has? Do you agree or disagree with his assessment?

Responding in Writing

Why do the people you know work? Do their motives support or challenge Curry's conclusion?

PROFESSIONS FOR WOMEN

Virginia Woolf

1882–1941

Virginia Woolf was born into a literary family in London, England. Largely self-educated, she began writing criticism for the Times Literary Supplement *when she was in her early twenties and published her first novel,* The Voyage Out, *in 1915. In later novels, including* Mrs. Dalloway *(1925),* To the Lighthouse *(1927), and* The Waves *(1931), she experimented with stream of consciousness and other stylistic and narrative innovations. She published two collections of her essays under the title* The Common Reader *(1925, 1932) and two feminist tracts,* A Room of One's Own *(1929) and* Three Guineas *(1938). Troubled by mental illness from an early age, Woolf committed suicide by drowning herself in 1941. Her husband, Leonard, edited several posthumously published collections of her work, including* The Death of the Moth and Other Essays *(1942). The following essay was originally composed as a speech delivered in 1931 to a British women's organization, the Women's League of Service.*

When your secretary invited me to come here, she told me that your Society is concerned with the employment of women and she suggested that I might tell you something about my own professional experiences. It is true I am a woman; it is true I am employed, but what professional experiences have I had? It is difficult to say. My profession is literature; and in that profession there are fewer experiences for women than in any other, with the exception of the stage—fewer, I mean, that are peculiar to women. For the road was cut many years ago—by Fanny Burney, by Aphra Behn, by Harriet Martineau, by Jane Austen, by George Eliot—many famous women, and many more unknown and forgotten, have been before me, making the path smooth, and regulating my steps. Thus, when I came to write, there were very few material obstacles in my way. Writing was a reputable and harmless occupation. The family peace was not broken by the scratching of a pen. No demand was made upon the family purse. For ten and sixpence one can buy paper enough to write all the plays of Shakespeare—if one has a mind that way. Pianos and models, Paris, Vienna and Berlin, masters and mistresses, are not needed by a writer. The cheapness of writing paper is, of course, the reason why women have succeeded as writers before they have succeeded in the other professions.

But to tell you my story—it is a simple one. You have only got to figure to yourselves a girl in a bedroom with a pen in her hand. She had only to move that pen from left to right—from ten o'clock to one. Then it occurred to her to do what is simple and cheap enough after all—to slip a few of those pages into an envelope, fix a penny stamp in the corner, and drop the envelope in the red box at the corner. It was thus that I became a journalist; and my effort was rewarded on the first day of the following month—a very glorious day it was for me—by a letter from an editor containing a check for one pound ten shillings and sixpence. But to show you how little I deserve to be called a professional woman, how little I know of the struggles and difficulties of such lives, I have to admit that instead of spending that sum upon bread and butter, rent, shoes and stockings, or butcher's bills, I went out and bought a cat—a beautiful cat, a Persian cat, which very soon involved me in bitter disputes with my neighbors.

What could be easier than to write articles and to buy Persian cats with the profits? But wait a moment. Articles have to be about something. Mine, I seem to remember, was about a novel by a famous man. And while I was writing this review, I discovered that if I were going to review books I should need to do battle with a certain phantom. And the phantom was a woman, and when I came to know her better I called her after the heroine of a famous poem, The Angel in the House. It was she who used to come between me and my paper when I was writing reviews. It was she who bothered me and wasted my time and so tormented me that at last I killed her. You who come of a younger and happier generation may not have heard of her—you may not know what I mean by the Angel in the House. I will describe her as shortly as I can. She was intensely sympathetic. She was immensely charming. She was utterly unselfish. She excelled in the difficult arts of family life. She sacrificed herself daily. If there was chicken, she took the leg; if there was a draught she sat in it—in short she was so constituted that she never had a mind or a wish of her own but preferred to sympathize always with the minds and wishes of others. Above all—I need not say it—she was pure. Her purity was supposed to be her chief beauty—her blushes, her great grace. In those days—the last of Queen Victoria—every house had its Angel. And when I came to write I encountered her with the very first words. The shadow of her wings fell on my page; I heard the rustling of her skirts in the room. Directly, that is to say, I took my pen in hand to review that novel by a famous man, she slipped behind me and whispered: "My dear, you are a young woman. You are writing about a book that has been written by a man. Be sympathetic; be tender; flatter; deceive; use all the arts and wiles of our sex. Never let anybody guess that you have a mind of your own. Above all, be pure." And she made as if to guide my pen. I now record the one act for which I take some credit to myself, though the credit rightly belongs to some excellent ancestors of mine who left me a certain sum of money—shall we say five hundred pounds a year?—so that it was not necessary for me to depend solely on charm for my living. I turned upon her and caught her by the throat. I did my best to kill her. My excuse, if I were to be had up in a court of law, would be that I acted in self-defense. Had I not killed her she would have killed me. She would have plucked the heart out of my writing. For, as I found, directly I put pen to paper, you cannot review even a novel without having a mind of your own, without expressing what you think to be the truth about human relations, morality, sex. And all these questions, according to the Angel in the House, cannot be dealt with freely and openly by women; they must charm, they must conciliate, they must—to put it bluntly—tell lies if they are to succeed. Thus, whenever I felt the shadow of her wing or the radiance of her halo upon my page, I took up the inkpot and flung it at her. She died hard. Her fictitious nature was of great assistance to her. It is far harder to kill a phantom than a reality. She was always creeping back when I thought I had dispatched her. Though I flatter myself that I killed her in the end, the struggle was severe; it took much time that had better have been spent upon learning Greek grammar; or in roaming the world in search of adventures. But it was a real experience; it was an experience that was bound to befall all women writers at that time. Killing the Angel in the House was part of the occupation of a woman writer.

But to continue my story. The Angel was dead; what then remained? You may say that what remained was a simple and common object—a young woman in a bedroom with an inkpot. In other words, now that she had rid herself of falsehood, that young woman had only to be herself. Ah, but what is "herself"? I mean, what is a woman? I assure you, I do not know. I do not believe that you know. I do not believe that anybody can know until she has expressed herself in all the arts and professions open to human skill. That indeed is one of the reasons why I have come here—out of respect for you, who are in process of showing us by your experiments what a woman is, who are in process of providing us, by your failures and successes, with that extremely important piece of information.

But to continue the story of my professional experiences. I made 5 one pound ten and six by my first review; and I bought a Persian cat with the proceeds. Then I grew ambitious. A Persian cat is all very well, I said; but a Persian cat is not enough. I must have a motor car. And it was thus that I became a novelist—for it is a very strange thing that people will give you a motor car if you will tell them a story. It is a still stranger thing that there is nothing so delightful in the world as telling stories. It is far pleasanter than writing reviews of famous novels. And yet, if I am to obey your secretary and tell you my professional experiences as a novelist, I must tell you about a very strange experience that befell me as a novelist. And to understand it you must try first to imagine a novelist's state of mind. I hope I am not giving away professional secrets if I say that a novelist's chief desire is to be as unconscious as possible. He has to induce in himself a state of perpetual lethargy. He wants life to proceed with the utmost quiet and regularity. He wants to see the same faces, to read the same books, to do the same things day after day, month after month, while he is writing, so that nothing may break the illusion in which he is living—so that nothing may disturb or disquiet the mysterious nosings about, feelings round, darts, dashes and sudden discoveries of that very shy and illusive spirit, the imagination. I suspect that this state is the same both for men and women. Be that as it may, I want you to imagine me writing a novel in a state of trance. I want you to figure to yourselves a girl sitting with a pen in her hand, which for minutes, and indeed for hours, she never dips into the inkpot. The image that comes to my mind when I think of this girl is the image of a fisherman lying sunk in dreams on the verge of a deep lake with a rod held out over the water. She was letting her imagination sweep unchecked round every rock and cranny of the world that lies submerged in the depths of our unconscious being. Now came the experience, the experience that I believe to be far commoner with women writers than with men. The line raced through the girl's fingers. Her imagination had rushed away. It had sought the pools, the depths, the dark places where the largest fish slumber. And then there was a smash. There was an explosion. There was foam and confusion. The imagination had dashed itself against something hard. The girl was roused from her dream. She was indeed in a state of the most acute and difficult distress. To speak without figure she had thought of something, something about the body, about the passions which it was unfitting for her as a woman to say. Men, her reason told her, would be shocked. The consciousness of what men will say of a woman who speaks the truth about her passions had roused her from her artist's state of unconsciousness. She could write no more. The trance was over. Her imagination could work no longer. This I believe to be a very common experience with women writers—they are impeded by the extreme conventionality of the other sex. For though men sensibly allow themselves great freedom in these respects, I doubt that they realize or can control the extreme severity with which they condemn such freedom in women.

These then were two very genuine experiences of my own. These were two of the adventures of my professional life. The first—killing the Angel in the House—I think I solved. She died. But the second, telling the truth about my own experiences as a body, I do not think I solved. I doubt that any woman has solved it yet. The obstacles against her are still immensely powerful—and yet they are very difficult to define. Outwardly, what is simpler than to write books? Outwardly, what obstacles are there for a woman rather than for a man? Inwardly, I think the case is very different; she has still many ghosts to fight, many prejudices to overcome. Indeed it will be a long time still, I think, before a woman can sit down to write a book without finding a phantom to be slain, a rock to be dashed against. And if this is so in literature, the freest of all professions for women, how is it in the new professions which you are now for the first time entering?

Those are the questions that I should like, had I time, to ask you. And indeed, if I have laid stress upon these professional experiences of mine, it is because I believe that they are, though in different forms, yours also. Even when the path is nominally open—when there is nothing to prevent a woman from being a doctor, a lawyer, a civil servant—there are many phantoms and obstacles, as I believe, looming in her way. To discuss and define them is I think of great value and importance; for thus only can the labor be shared, the difficulties be solved. But besides this, it is necessary also to discuss the ends and the aims for which we are fighting, for which we are doing battle with these formidable obstacles. Those aims cannot be taken for granted; they must be perpetually questioned and examined. The whole position, as I see it—here in this hall surrounded by women practising for the first time in history I know not how many different professions— is one of extraordinary interest and importance. You have won rooms of your own in the house hitherto exclusively owned by men. You are able, though not without great labor and effort, to pay the rent. You are earning your five hundred pounds a year. But this freedom is only a beginning; the room is your own, but it is still bare. It has to be furnished; it has to be decorated; it has to be shared. How are you going to furnish it, how are you going to decorate it? With whom are you going to share it, and upon what terms? These, I think, are questions of the utmost importance and interest. For the first time in history you are able to ask them; for the first time you are able to decide for yourselves what the answers should be. Willingly would I stay and discuss those questions and answers—but not tonight. My time is up; and I must cease.

Responding to Reading

1. According to Woolf, why have women found success in writing? How does Woolf's explanation shed light on the fact that there were few female doctors, lawyers, or corporate executives in 1931—the year she delivered her address?

2. What does Woolf mean in paragraph 3 when she says that if she were going to review books, she would have to do battle with a phantom? Why does she call this phantom "The Angel in the House"? What does Woolf mean when she says, "Killing the Angel in the House was part of the occupation of a woman writer" (3)?

3. In paragraph 7, Woolf says that women writers now have a room in a house that was once "exclusively owned by men." What must women do to make the room their own? What does Woolf mean when she says, "It has to be furnished; it has to be decorated; it has to be shared" (7)?

Responding in Writing

In what ways would Woolf's speech be different if she were delivering it today to a graduating class at your college or university?

THE SECOND SHIFT

Arlie Hochschild

1940–

Arlie Hochschild was born in Boston and received a Bachelor's degree from Swarthmore College (1962) and a PhD from the University of California, Berkeley (1969), where she currently teaches in the sociology department. She is co-director of the Center for Working Families and has done extensive research into the role of work in personal and family life. Hochschild has published The Second Shift: Working Parents and the Revolution at Home *(1989), from which the following essay, republished in the* Utne Reader *in 1990, was taken; and* The Time Bind: When Work Becomes Home and Home Becomes Work *(1997). To learn more about Hochschild, visit her Web site, http://sociology.berkeley.edu/faculty/hochschild/.*

Every American household bears the footprints of economic and cultural trends that originate far outside its walls. A rise in inflation eroding the earning power of the male wage, an expanding service sector opening for women, and the inroads made by women into many professions—all these changes do not simply go on around the American family. They occur *within* a marriage or living-together arrangement and transform it. Problems between couples, problems that seem "unique" or "marital," are often the individual ripples of powerful economic and cultural shock waves. Quarrels between husbands and wives in households across the nation result mainly from a friction between faster-changing women and slower-changing men.

The exodus of women from the home to the workplace has not been accompanied by a new view of marriage and work that would make this transition smooth. Most workplaces have remained inflexible in the face of the changing needs of workers with families, and most men have yet to really adapt to the changes in women. I call the strain caused by the disparity between the change in women and the absence of change elsewhere the "stalled revolution."

If women begin to do less at home because they have less time, if men do little more, and if the work of raising children and tending a home requires roughly the same effort, then the questions of who does what at home and of what "needs doing" become a source of deep tension in a marriage.

Over the past 30 years in the United States, more and more women have begun to work outside the home, and more have divorced. While some commentators conclude that women's work *causes* divorce, my research into changes in the American family suggests something else. Since all the wives in the families I studied (over an eight-year period) worked outside the home, the fact that they worked did not account for why some marriages were happy and others were not. What *did* contribute to happiness was the husband's willingness to do the work at home. Whether they were traditional or more egalitarian in their relationship, couples were happier when the men did a sizable share of housework and child care.

In one study of 600 couples filing for divorce, researcher George 5 Levinger found that the second most common reason women cited for wanting to divorce—after "mental cruelty"—was their husbands' "neglect of home or children." Women mentioned this reason more often than financial problems, physical abuse, drinking, or infidelity.

A happy marriage is supported by a couple's being economically secure, by their enjoying a supportive community, and by their having compatible needs and values. But these days it may also depend on a shared appreciation of the work it takes to nurture others. As the role of the homemaker is being abandoned by many women, the homemaker's work has been continually devalued and passed on to low-paid house-keepers, baby-sitters, or day-care workers. Long devalued by men, the contribution of cooking, cleaning, and care-giving is now being devalued as mere drudgery by many women, too.

In the era of the stalled revolution, one way to make housework and child care more valued is for men to share in that work. Many working mothers are already doing all they can at home. Now it's time for men to make the move.

If more mothers of young children are working at full-time jobs outside the home, and if most couples can't afford household help, who's doing the work at home? Adding together the time it takes to do a paid job and to do housework and child care and using estimates from major studies on time use done in the 1960s and 1970s, I found that women worked roughly 15 more hours each week than men. Over a year, they worked an extra month of 24-hour days. Over a dozen years, it was an extra year of 24-hour days. Most women without children spend much more time that men on housework. Women with children devote more time to both housework and child care. Just as there is a wage gap between men and women in the workplace, there is a "leisure gap" between them at home. Most women work one shift at the office or factory and a "second shift" at home.

In my research, I interviewed and observed 52 couples over an eight-year period as they cooked dinner, shopped, bathed their children, and in general struggled to find enough time to make their complex lives work. The women I interviewed seemed to be far more deeply torn between the demands of work and family than were their husbands. They talked more about the abiding conflict between work and family. They felt the second shift was *their* issue, and most of their husbands agreed. When I telephoned one husband to arrange an interview with him, explaining that I wanted to ask him how he managed work and family life, he replied genially, "Oh, this will *really* interest my *wife.*"

10   Men who shared the load at home seemed just as pressed for time as their wives, and as torn between the demands of career and small children. But of the men I surveyed, the majority did not share the load at home. Some refused outright. Others refused more passively, often offering a loving shoulder to lean on, or an understanding ear, as their working wife faced the conflict they both saw as hers. At first it seemed to me that the problem of the second shift *was* hers. But I came to realize that those husbands who helped very little at home were often just as deeply affected as their wives—through the resentment their wives felt toward them and through their own need to steel themselves against that resentment.

A clear example of this phenomenon is Evan Holt, a warehouse furniture salesman who did very little housework and played with his four-year-old son, Joey, only at his convenience. His wife, Nancy, did the second shift, but she resented it keenly and half-consciously expressed her frustration and rage by losing interest in sex and becoming overly absorbed in Joey.

Even when husbands happily shared the work, their wives *felt* more responsible for home and children. More women than men kept track of doctor's appointments and arranged for kids playmates to come over. More mothers than fathers worried about a child's Halloween costume or a birthday present for a school friend. They were more likely to think about their children while at work and to check in by phone with the baby-sitter.

Partly because of this, more women felt torn between two kinds of urgency, between the need to soothe a child's fear of being left at daycare and the need to show the boss she's "serious" at work. Twenty percent of the men in my study shared housework equally. Seventy percent did a substantial amount (less than half of it, but more than a third), and 10 percent did less than a third. But even when couples more equitably share the work at home, women do two thirds of the daily jobs at home, such as cooking and cleaning up—jobs that fix them into a rigid routine. Most women cook dinner, for instance, while men change the oil in the family car. But, as one mother pointed out, dinner needs to be prepared every evening around six o'clock, whereas the car oil needs to be changed every six months, with no particular deadline. Women do more child care than men, and men repair more household appliances. A child needs to be tended to daily, whereas the repair of household appliances can often wait, said the men, "until I have time." Men thus have more control over when they make their contributions than women do. They may be very busy with family chores, but, like the executive who tells his secretary to "hold my calls," the man has more control over his time.

Another reason why women may feel under more strain than men is that women more often do two things at once—for example, write checks and return phone calls, vacuum and keep an eye on a three-year-old, fold laundry and think out the shopping list. Men more often will either cook dinner *or* watch the kids. Women more often do both at the same time.

Beyond doing more at home, women also devote proportionately, more of their time at home to housework than men and proportionately less of it to child care. Of all the time men spend working at home, a growing amount of it goes to child care. Since most parents prefer to tend to their children than to clean house, men do more of what they'd rather do. More men than women take their children on "fun" outings to the park, the zoo, the movies. Women spend more time on maintenance, such as feeding and bathing children—enjoyable activities, to be sure, but often less leisurely or "special" than going to the zoo. Men also do fewer of the most undesirable household chores, such as scrubbing the toilet.

As a result, women tend to talk more intensely about being overtired, sick, and emotionally, drained. Many women interviewed were fixated on the topic of sleep. They talked about how much they could "get by on" six and a half, seven, seven and a half, less, more. They talked about who they knew who needed more or less. Some apologized for how much sleep they needed—"I'm afraid I need eight hours of sleep"—as if eight was "too much." They talked about how to avoid fully waking up when a child called them at night, and how to get back to sleep. These women talked about sleep the way a hungry person talks about food.

If, all in all, the two-job family is suffering from a speedup of work and family life, working mothers are its primary victims. It is ironic, then, that often it falls to women to be the time-and-motion experts of family life. As I observed families inside their homes, I noticed it was often the mother who rushed children, saying, "Hurry up! It's time to go." "Finish your cereal now," "You can do that later," or "Let's go!" When a bath needed to be crammed into a slot between 7:45 and 8:00, it was often the mother who called out "Let's see who can take their bath the quickest." Often a younger child would rush out, scurrying to be first in bed, while the older and wiser one stalled, resistant, sometimes resentful: "Mother is always rushing us." Sadly, women are more often the lightning rods for family tensions aroused by this speedup of work and family life. They are the villains in a process in which they are also the primary victims. More than the longer hours and the lack of sleep, this is the saddest cost to women of their extra month of work each year.

Raising children in a nuclear family is still the overwhelming preference of most people. Yet in the face of new problems for this family mode we have not created an adequate support system so that the nuclear family can do its job well in the era of the two-career couple. Corporations have done little to accommodate the needs of working parents, and the government has done little to prod them.

We really need, as sociologist Frank Furstenberg has suggested, a Marshall Plan for the family. After World War II we saw that it was in our best interests to aid the war-torn nations of Europe. Now—it seems obvious in an era of growing concern over drugs, crime, and family instability—is in our best interests to aid the overworked two-job families right here at home. We should look to other nations for a model of what could be done. In Sweden, for example, upon the birth of a child every working couple is entitled to 12 months of paid parental leave—nine months at 90 percent of the worker's salary, plus an additional three months at about three hundred dollars a month. The mother and father are free to divide this year off between them as they wish. Working parents of a child under eight have the opportunity to work no more than six hours a day, at six hours' pay. Parental insurance offers parents money for work time lost while visiting a child's school or caring for a sick child. That's a true pro-family policy.

20   A pro-family policy in the United States could give tax breaks to companies that encourage job sharing, part-time work, flex time, and family leave for new parents. By implementing comparable worth policies we could increase pay scales for "women's" jobs. Another key element of a pro-family policy would be instituting, fewer-hour, more flexible options—called "family phases"—for all regular jobs filled by parents of young children.

Day-care centers could be made more warm and creative through generous public and private funding. If the best form of day-care comes from the attention of elderly neighbors, students, or grandparents, these people could be paid to care for children through social programs.

In these ways, the American government would create a safer environment for the two-job family. If the government encouraged corporations to consider the long-ranged interests of workers and their families, they would save on long-range costs caused by absenteeism, turnover, juvenile delinquency, mental illness, and welfare support for single mothers.

These are real pro-family reforms. If they seem utopian today, we should remember that in the past the eight-hour day, the abolition of child labor, and the vote for women seemed utopian, too. Among top rated employees listed in *The 100 Best Companies to Work for in America* are many offering country-club memberships, first-class air travel, and million-dollar fitness centers. But only a handful offer job shar-ing, flex time, or part-time work. Not one provides on-site day-care, and only three offer child-care deductions: Control Data, Polaroid, and Honeywell. In his book *Megatrends*, John Naisbitt reports that 83 percent of corporate executives believed that more men feel the need to share the responsibilities of parenting; yet only 9 percent of corpo-rations offer paternity leave.

Public strategies are linked to private ones. Economic and cul-tural trends bear on family relations in ways it would be useful for all of us to understand. The happiest two-job marriages I saw during my research were ones in which men and women shared the housework and parenting. What couples called good communication often meant that they were good at saying thanks to one another for small aspects of taking care of the family. Making it to the school play, helping a child read, cooking dinner in good spirit, remembering the grocery list, taking responsibility for cleaning up the bedrooms—these were the silver and gold of the marital exchange. Until now, couples com-mitted to an equal sharing of house-work and child care have been rare. But, if we as a culture come to see the urgent need of meeting the new problems posed by the second shift, and if society and govern-ment begin to shape new policies that allow working parents more flexibility then we will be making some progress toward happier times at home and work. And as the young learn by example, many more women and men will be able to enjoy the pleasure that arises when family life is family life, and not a second shift.

Responding to Reading

1. Hochschild coined the terms "second shift" and "stalled revolution." De-fine each of these terms. Are they appropriate for what they denote? Would other terms—for example, *late shift* or *swing shift* and *postponed revolution* or *failed revolution*—be more appropriate? Explain.
2. According to Hochschild, women *think* that they are "under more strain than men" (14) even when their husbands do their share of housework and child care. How does Hochschild account for this impression?
3. Beginning with paragraph 18, Hochschild recommends changes that she believes will ease the strain on working families—because, as she says in paragraph 24, "public strategies are linked to private ones." Given what Hochschild has said about the basic differences in men's and women's ap-proaches to family roles, do you believe that government and corporations can solve the problem she identifies? Explain your reasoning.

Responding in Writing

Would you say that your parents are committed to equal sharing of housework and childcare? What changes, if any, would you suggest?

BEHIND THE COUNTER

Eric Schlosser

1960–

Eric Schlosser was born in Manhattan and grew up there and in Los Angeles. He studied American history at Princeton University and British imperial history at Oxford University. Schlosser became a full-time journalist after writing a two-part article for Rolling Stone *magazine, which was later expanded into the book* Fast Food Nation *(2001). Schlosser is a correspondent for the* Atlantic Monthly *and has written about the families of homicide victims and the "prison-industrial complex." His magazine investigations into migrant labor, pornography, and marijuana gave him the background for his most recent book,* Reefer Madness: Sex, Drugs, and Cheap Labor in the American Black Market *(2003).*

Every Saturday Elisa Zamot gets up at 5:15 in the morning. It's a struggle, and her head feels groggy as she steps into the shower. Her little sisters, Cookie and Sabrina, are fast asleep in their beds. By 5:30, Elisa's showered, done her hair, and put on her McDonald's uniform. She's sixteen, bright-eyed and olive-skinned, pretty and petite, ready for another day of work. Elisa's mother usually drives her the half-mile or so to the restaurant, but sometimes Elisa walks, leaving home before the sun rises. Her family's modest townhouse sits beside a busy highway on the south side of Colorado Springs, in a largely poor and working-class neighborhood. Throughout the day, sounds of traffic fill the house, the steady whoosh of passing cars. But when Elisa heads for work, the streets are quiet, the sky's still dark, and the lights are out in the small houses and rental apartments along the road.

When Elisa arrives at McDonald's, the manager unlocks the door and lets her in. Sometimes the husband-and-wife cleaning crew are just finishing up. More often, it's just Elisa and the manager in the restaurant, surrounded by an empty parking lot. For the next hour or so, the two of them get everything ready. They turn on the ovens and grills. They go downstairs into the basement and get food and supplies for the morning shift. They get the paper cups, wrappers, cardboard containers, and packets of condiments. They step into the big freezer and get the frozen bacon, the frozen pancakes, and the frozen cinnamon rolls. They get the frozen hash browns, the frozen biscuits, the frozen McMuffins. They get the cartons of scrambled egg mix and orange juice mix. They bring the food upstairs and start preparing it before any customers appear, thawing some things in the microwave and cooking other things on the grill. They put the cooked food in special cabinets to keep it warm.

The restaurant opens for business at seven o'clock, and for the next hour or so, Elisa and the manager hold down the fort, handling all the orders. As the place starts to get busy, other employees arrive. Elisa works behind the counter. She takes orders and hands food to customers from breakfast through lunch. When she finally walks home, after seven hours of standing at a cash register, her feet hurt. She's wiped out. She comes through the front door, flops onto the living room couch, and turns on the TV. And the next morning she gets up at 5:15 again and starts the same routine.

Up and down Academy Boulevard, along South Nevada, Circle Drive, and Woodman Road, teenagers like Elisa run the fast food restaurants of Colorado Springs. Fast food kitchens often seem like a scene from *Bugsy Malone*, a film in which all the actors are children pretending to be adults. No other industry in the United States has a workforce so dominated by adolescents. About two-thirds of the nation's fast food workers are under the age of twenty. Teenagers open the fast food outlets in the morning, close them at night, and keep them going at all hours in between. Even the managers and assistant managers are sometimes in their late teens. Unlike Olympic gymnastics—an activity in which teenagers consistently perform at a higher level than adults—there's nothing about the work in a fast food kitchen that requires young employees. Instead of relying upon a small, stable, well-paid, and well-trained workforce, the fast food industry seeks out part-time, unskilled workers who are willing to accept low pay. Teenagers have been the perfect candidates for these jobs, not only because they are less expensive to hire than adults, but also because their youthful inexperience makes them easier to control.

The labor practices of the fast food industry have their origins in 5 the assembly line systems adopted by American manufacturers in the early twentieth century. Business historian Alfred D. Chandler has argued that a high rate of "throughput" was the most important aspect of these mass production systems. A factory's throughput is the speed and volume of its flow—a much more crucial measurement, according to Chandler, than the number of workers it employs or the value of its machinery. With innovative technology and the proper organization, a small number of workers can produce an enormous amount of goods cheaply. Throughput is all about increasing the speed of assembly, about doing things faster in order to make more.

Although the McDonald brothers had never encountered the term "throughput" or studied "scientific management," they instinctively grasped the underlying principles and applied them in the Speedee Service System. The restaurant operating scheme they developed has been widely adopted and refined over the past half century. The ethos of the assembly line remains at its core. The fast food industry's obsession with throughput has altered the way millions of Americans work, turned commercial kitchens into small factories, and changed familiar foods into commodities that are manufactured.

At Burger King restaurants, frozen hamburger patties are placed on a conveyer belt and emerge from a broiler ninety seconds later fully cooked. The ovens at Pizza Hut and at Domino's also use conveyer belts to ensure standardized cooking times. The ovens at McDonald's look like commercial laundry presses, with big steel hoods that swing down and grill hamburgers on both sides at once. The burgers, chicken, french fries, and buns are all frozen when they arrive at a McDonald's. The shakes and sodas begin as syrup. At Taco Bell restaurants the food is "assembled," not prepared. The guacamole isn't made by workers in the kitchen; it's made at a factory in Michoacán, Mexico, then frozen and shipped north. The chain's taco meat arrives frozen and precooked in vacuum-sealed plastic bags. The beans are dehydrated and look like brownish corn flakes. The cooking process is fairly simple. "Everything's add water," a Taco Bell employee told me. "Just add hot water."

Although Richard and Mac McDonald introduced the division of labor to the restaurant business, it was a McDonald's executive named Fred Turner who created a production system of unusual thoroughness and attention to detail. In 1958, Turner put together an operations and training manual for the company that was seventy-five pages long, specifying how almost everything should be done. Hamburgers were always to be placed on the grill in six neat rows; french fries had to be exactly 0.28 inches thick. The McDonald's operations manual today has ten times the number of pages and weighs about four pounds. Known within the company as "the Bible," it contains precise instructions on how various appliances should be used, how each item on the menu should look, and how employees should greet customers. Operators who disobey these rules can lose their franchises. Cooking instructions are not only printed in the manual, they are often designed into the machines. A McDonald's kitchen is full of buzzers and flashing lights that tell employees what to do.

At the front counter, computerized cash registers issue their own commands. Once an order has been placed, buttons light up and suggest other menu items that can be added. Workers at the counter are told to increase the size of an order by recommending special promotions, pushing dessert, pointing out the financial logic behind the purchase of a larger drink. While doing so, they are instructed to be upbeat and friendly. "Smile with a greeting and make a positive first impression," a Burger King training manual suggests. "Show them you are GLAD TO SEE THEM. Include eye contact with the cheerful greeting."

10   The strict regimentation at fast food restaurants creates standardized products. It increases the throughput. And it gives fast food com-

panies an enormous amount of power over their employees. "When management determines exactly how every task is to be done . . . and can impose its own rules about pace, output, quality, and technique," the sociologist Robin Leidner has noted, "[it] makes workers increasingly interchangeable." The management no longer depends upon the talents or skills of its workers—those things are built into the operating system and machines. Jobs that have been "de-skilled" can be filled cheaply. The need to retain any individual worker is greatly reduced by the ease with which he or she can be replaced.

Teenagers have long provided the fast food industry with the bulk of its workforce. The industry's rapid growth coincided with the baby-boom expansion of that age group. Teenagers were in many ways the ideal candidates for these low-paying jobs. Since most teenagers still lived at home, they could afford to work for wages too low to support an adult, and until recently, their limited skills attracted few other employers. A job at a fast food restaurant became an American rite of passage, a first job soon left behind for better things. The flexible terms of employment in the fast food industry also attracted housewives who needed extra income. As the number of baby-boom teenagers declined, the fast food chains began to hire other marginalized workers: recent immigrants, the elderly, and the handicapped.

English is now the second language of at least one-sixth of the nation's restaurant workers, and about one-third of that group speaks no English at all. The proportion of fast food workers who cannot speak English is even higher. Many know only the names of the items on the menu; they speak "McDonald's English."

The fast food industry now employs some of the most disadvantaged members of American society. It often teaches basic job skills—such as getting to work on time—to people who can barely read, whose lives have been chaotic or shut off from the mainstream. Many individual franchisees are genuinely concerned about the well-being of their workers. But the stance of the fast food industry on issues involving employee training, the minimum wage, labor unions, and overtime pay strongly suggests that its motives in hiring the young, the poor, and the handicapped are hardly altruistic.

At a 1999 conference on foodservice equipment, top American executives from Burger King, McDonald's, and Tricon Global Restaurants, Inc. (the owner of Taco Bell, Pizza Hut, and KFC) appeared together on a panel to discuss labor shortages, employee training, computerization, and the latest kitchen technology. The three corporations now employ about 3.7 million people worldwide, operate about 60,000 restaurants, and open a new fast food restaurant every two hours. Putting aside their intense rivalry for customers, the executives had realized at a gathering the previous evening that when it came to labor issues, they were in complete agreement. "We've come to the conclusion that we're in support of each other," Dave Brewer, the vice president of engineering at KFC, explained. "We are aligned as a team to support this industry." One of the most important goals they held in common was the redesign of kitchen equipment so that less money needed to be spent training workers. "Make the equipment intuitive, make it so that the job is easier to do right than to do wrong," advised Jerry Sus, the leading equipment systems engineer at McDonald's. "The easier it is for him [the worker] to use, the easier it is for us not to have to train him." John Reckert—director of strategic operations and of research and development at Burger King—felt optimistic about the benefits that new technology would bring the industry. "We can develop equipment that only works one way," Reckert said. "There are many different ways today that employees can abuse our product, mess up the flow . . . If the equipment only allows one process, there's very little to train." Instead of giving written instructions to crew members, another panelist suggested, rely as much as possible on photographs of menu items, and "if there are instructions, make them very simple, write them at a fifth-grade level, and write them in Spanish and English." All of the executives agreed that "zero training" was the fast food industry's ideal, though it might not ever be attained.

15   While quietly spending enormous sums on research and technology to eliminate employee training, the fast food chains have accepted hundreds of millions of dollars in government subsidies for "training" their workers. Through federal programs such as the Targeted Jobs Tax Credit and its successor, the Work Opportunity Tax Credit, the chains have for years claimed tax credits of up to $2,400 for each new low-income worker they hired. In 1996 an investigation by the U.S. Department of Labor concluded that 92 percent of these workers would have been hired by the companies anyway—and that their new jobs were part-time, provided little training, and came with no benefits. These federal subsidy programs were created to reward American companies that gave job training to the poor.

Attempts to end these federal subsidies have been strenuously opposed by the National Council of Chain Restaurants and its allies in Congress. The Work Opportunity Tax Credit program was renewed in 1996. It offered as much as $385 million in subsidies the following year. Fast food restaurants had to employ a worker for only four hundred hours to receive the federal money—and then could get more money as soon as that worker quit and was replaced. American taxpayers have in effect subsidized the industry's high turnover rate, providing company tax breaks for workers who are employed for just a few months and receive no training. The industry front group formed to defend these government subsidies is called the "Committee for Employment Opportunities." Its chief lobbyist, Bill Signer, told the *Houston Chronicle* there was nothing wrong with the use of federal subsidies to create low-paying, low-skilled, short-term jobs for the poor. Trying to justify the minimal amount of training given to these workers, Signer said, "They've got to crawl before they can walk."

The employees whom the fast food industry expects to crawl are by far the biggest group of low-wage workers in the United States today. The nation has about 1 million migrant farm workers and about 3.5 million fast food workers. Although picking strawberries is orders of magnitude more difficult than cooking hamburgers, both jobs are now filled by people who are generally young, unskilled, and willing to work long hours for low pay. Moreover, the turnover rates for both jobs are among the highest in the American economy. The annual turnover rate in the fast food industry is now about 300 to 400 percent. The typical fast food worker quits or is fired every three to four months.

The fast food industry pays the minimum wage to a higher proportion of its workers than any other American industry. Consequently, a low minimum wage has long been a crucial part of the fast food industry's business plan. Between 1968 and 1990, the years when the fast food chains expanded at their fastest rate, the real value of the U.S. minimum wage fell by almost 40 percent. In the late 1990s, the real value of the U.S. minimum wage still remained about 27 percent lower than it was in the late 1960s. Nevertheless, the National Restaurant Association (NRA) has vehemently opposed any rise in the minimum wage at the federal, state, or local level. About sixty large food-service companies—including Jack in the Box, Wendy's, Chevy's, and Red Lobster—have backed congressional legislation that would essentially eliminate the federal minimum wage by allowing states to disregard it. Pete Meersman, the president of the Colorado Restaurant Association, advocates creating a federal guest worker program to import low-wage foodservice workers from overseas.

While the real value of the wages paid to restaurant workers has declined for the past three decades, the earnings of restaurant company executives have risen considerably. According to a 1997 survey in *Nation's Restaurant News*, the average corporate executive bonus was $131,000, an increase of 20 percent over the previous year. Increasing the federal minimum wage by a dollar would add about two cents to the cost of a fast food hamburger.

In 1938, at the height of the Great Depression, Congress passed 20 legislation to prevent employers from exploiting the nation's most vulnerable workers. The Fair Labor Standards Act established the first federal minimum wage. It also imposed limitations on child labor. And it mandated that employees who work more than forty hours a week be paid overtime wages for each additional hour. The overtime wage was set at a minimum of one and a half times the regular wage.

Today few employees in the fast food industry qualify for overtime—and even fewer are paid it. Roughly 90 percent of the nation's fast food workers are paid an hourly wage, provided no benefits, and scheduled to work only as needed. Crew members are employed "at will." If the restaurant's busy, they're kept longer than usual. If business is slow, they're sent home early. Managers try to make sure that each worker is employed less than forty hours a week, thereby avoiding any overtime payments. A typical McDonald's or Burger King restaurant has about fifty crew members. They work an average of thirty hours a week. By hiring a large number of crew members for each restaurant, sending them home as soon as possible, and employing them for fewer than forty hours a week whenever possible, the chains keep their labor costs to a bare minimum.

A handful of fast food workers are paid regular salaries. A fast food restaurant that employs fifty crew members has four or five managers and assistant managers. They earn about $23,000 a year and usually receive medical benefits, as well as some form of bonus or profit sharing. They have an opportunity to rise up the corporate ladder. But they also work long hours without overtime—fifty, sixty, seventy hours a week. The turnover rate among assistant managers is extremely high. The job offers little opportunity for independent decision-making. Computer programs, training manuals, and the machines in the kitchen determine how just about everything must be done.

Fast food managers do have the power to hire, fire, and schedule workers. Much of their time is spent motivating their crew members. In the absence of good wages and secure employment, the chains try to inculcate "team spirit" in their young crews. Workers who fail to work hard, who arrive late, or who are reluctant to stay extra hours are made to feel that they're making life harder for everyone else, letting their friends and coworkers down. For years the McDonald's Corporation has provided its managers with training in "transactional analysis," a set of psychological techniques popularized in the book *I'm OK—You're OK* (1969). One of these techniques is called "stroking"—a form of positive reinforcement, deliberate praise, and recognition that many teenagers don't get at home. Stroking can make a worker feel that his or her contribution is sincerely valued. And it's much less expensive than raising wages or paying overtime.

The fast food chains often reward managers who keep their labor costs low, a practice that often leads to abuses. In 1997 a jury in Washington State found that Taco Bell had systematically coerced its crew members into working off the clock in order to avoid paying them overtime. The bonuses of Taco Bell restaurant managers were tied to their success at cutting labor costs. The managers had devised a number of creative ways to do so. Workers were forced to wait until things got busy at a restaurant before officially starting their shifts. They were forced to work without pay after their shifts ended. They were forced to clean restaurants on their own time. And they were sometimes compensated with food, not wages. Many of the workers involved were minors and recent immigrants. Before the penalty phase of the Washington lawsuit, the two sides reached a settlement; Taco Bell agreed to pay millions of dollars in back wages, but admitted no wrongdoing. As many as 16,000 current and former employees were owed money by the company. One employee, a high school dropout named Regina Jones, regularly worked seventy to eighty hours a week but was paid for only forty. In 2001, Taco Bell settled a class-action lawsuit in California, agreeing to pay $9 million in back wages for overtime and an Oregon jury found that Taco Bell managers had falsified the time cards of thousands of workers in order to get productivity bonuses.

Responding to Reading

1. Why does Schlosser begin his essay with a description of Eliza Zamot's daily routine? What does Schlosser mean when he says, "Fast food kitchens often seem like a scene from *Bugsy Malone*, a film in which all the actors are children pretending to be adults" (4)?
2. In what way do the labor practices of the Speedee Service system resemble those of an assembly line? What are the advantages of this system? What are the disadvantages?
3. Why are teenagers the ideal candidates for the fast-food workforce? What other types of worker does this industry employ? Overall, would you say that Schlosser presents a positive picture of the fast-food industry?

Responding in Writing

Have you (or has anyone you have known) worked in a fast-food restaurant? Do your experiences (or the experiences of someone you know) support Schlosser's conclusions?

SELLING IN MINNESOTA
Barbara Ehrenreich
1941–

Born in Butte, Montana, Barbara Ehrenreich labels herself an unabashed "feminist, populist, socialist, and secular humanist." She earned a BA degree from Reed College (1963) in Portland, Oregon, and a PhD from Rockefeller University (1968) in New York City. Ehrenreich has written about social, political, and economic issues for Mother Jones *magazine,* Time

magazine, and the Guardian. *Her books of social criticism include* Fear of
Falling: The Inner Life of the Middle Class *(1989);* The Worst Years of
Our Lives: Irreverent Notes on a Decade of Greed *(1990);* Nickel and
Dimed: On (Not) Getting by in America *(2001), from which the follow-
ing essay is taken; and* Global Woman: Nannies, Maids, and Sex Work-
ers in the New Economy *(2003).*

For sheer grandeur, scale, and intimidation value, I doubt if any
corporate orientation exceeds that of Wal-Mart. I have been told that
the process will take eight hours, which will include two fifteen-
minute breaks and one half-hour break for a meal, and will be paid
for like a regular shift. When I arrive, dressed neatly in khakis and
clean T-shirt, as befits a potential Wal-Mart "associate," I find there
are ten new hires besides myself, mostly young and Caucasian, and a
team of three, headed by Roberta, to do the "orientating." We sit
around a long table in the same windowless room where I was interviewed, each with a thick folder of paperwork in front of us, and hear
Roberta tell once again about raising six children, being a "people
person," discovering that the three principles of Wal-Mart philosophy
were the same as her own, and so on. We begin with a video, about
fifteen minutes long, on the history and philosophy of Wal-Mart, or,
as an anthropological observer might call it, the Cult of Sam. First
young Sam Walton, in uniform, comes back from the war. He starts a
store, a sort of five-and-dime; he marries and fathers four attractive
children; he receives a Medal of Freedom from President Bush, after
which he promptly dies, making way for the eulogies. But the company goes on, yes indeed. Here the arc of the story soars upward un-
stoppably, pausing only to mark some fresh milestone of corporate
expansion. 1992: Wal-Mart becomes the largest retailer in the world.
1997: Sales top $100 billion. 1998: The number of Wal-Mart associates
hits 825,000, making Wal-Mart the largest private employer in the nation. Each landmark date is accompanied by a clip showing throngs
of shoppers, swarms of associates, or scenes of handsome new stores
and their adjoining parking lots. Over and over we hear in voiceover
or see in graphic display the "three principles," which are madden-
ingly, even defiantly, nonparallel: "respect for the individual, exceed-
ing customers' expectations, strive for excellence."

"Respect for the individual" is where we, the associates, come in,
because vast as Wal-Mart is, and tiny as we may be as individuals,
everything depends on us. Sam always said, and is shown saying,
that "the best ideas come from the associates"—for example, the idea
of having a "people greeter," an elderly employee (excuse me, associate) who welcomes each customer as he or she enters the store. Three
times during the orientation, which began at three and stretches to
nearly eleven, we are reminded that this brainstorm originated in a
mere associate, and who knows what revolutions in retailing each one

of us may propose? Because our ideas are welcome, more than welcome, and we are to think of our managers not as bosses but as "servant leaders," serving us as well as the customers. Of course, all is not total harmony, in every instance, between associates and their servant-leaders. A video on "associate honesty" shows a cashier being caught on videotape as he pockets some bills from the cash register. Drums beat ominously as he is led away in handcuffs and sentenced to four years.

The theme of covert tensions, overcome by right thinking and positive attitude, continues in the twelve-minute video entitled *You've Picked a Great Place to Work*. Here various associates testify to the "essential feeling of family for which Wal-Mart is so well-known," leading up to the conclusion that we don't need a union. Once, long ago, unions had a place in American society, but they "no longer have much to offer workers," which is why people are leaving them "by the droves." Wal-Mart is booming; unions are declining: judge for yourself. But we are warned that "unions have been targeting Wal-Mart for years." Why? For the dues money of course. Think of what you would lose with a union: first, your dues money, which could be $20 a month "and sometimes much more." Second, you would lose "your voice" because the union would insist on doing your talking for you. Finally, you might lose even your wages and benefits because they would all be "at risk on the bargaining table." You have to wonder—and I imagine some of my teenage fellow orientees may be doing so—why such fiends as these union organizers, such outright extortionists, are allowed to roam free in the land.

There is more, much more than I could ever absorb, even if it were spread out over a semester-long course. On the reasonable assumption that none of us is planning to go home and curl up with the "Wal-Mart Associate Handbook," our trainers start reading it out loud to us, pausing every few paragraphs to ask, "Any questions?" There never are. Barry, the seventeen-year-old to my left, mutters that his "butt hurts." Sonya, the tiny African American woman across from me, seems frozen in terror. I have given up on looking perky and am fighting to keep my eyes open. No nose or other facial jewelry, we learn; earrings must be small and discreet, not dangling; no blue jeans except on Friday, and then you have to pay $1 for the privilege of wearing them. No "grazing," that is, eating from food packages that somehow become open; no "time theft." This last sends me drifting off in a sci-fi direction: *And as the time thieves headed back to the year 3420, loaded with weekends and days off looted from the twenty-first century* . . . Finally, a question. The old guy who is being hired as a people greeter wants to know, "What is time theft?" Answer: Doing anything other than working during company time, anything at all. Theft of *our* time is not, however, an issue. There are stretches amounting to many minutes when all three of our trainers wander off, leaving us to sit there in silence or take the opportunity to squirm. Or our junior trainers go through a section of the handbook, and then Roberta, returning from some other business, goes over the same section again. My eyelids droop and I consider walking out. I have seen time move more swiftly during seven-hour airline delays. In fact, I am getting nostalgic about seven-hour airline delays. At least you can read a book or get up and walk around, take a leak.

5   On breaks, I drink coffee purchased at the Radio Grill, as the in-house fast-food place is called, the real stuff with caffeine, more because I'm concerned about being alert for the late-night drive home than out of any need to absorb all the Wal-Mart trivia coming my way. Now, here's a drug the drug warriors ought to take a little more interest in. Since I don't normally drink it at all—iced tea can usually be counted on for enough of a kick—the coffee has an effect like reagent-grade Dexedrine: my pulse races, my brain overheats, and the result in this instance is a kind of delirium. I find myself overly challenged by the little kindergarten-level tasks we are now given to do, such as affixing my personal bar code to my ID card, then sticking on the punch-out letters to spell my name. The letters keep curling up and sticking to my fingers, so I stop at "Barb," or more precisely, "B*ARB*," drifting off to think of all the people I know who have gentrified their names in recent years—Patsy to Patricia, Dick to Richard, and so forth—while I am going in the other direction. Now we start taking turns going to the computers to begin our CBL, or Computer-Based Learning, and I become transfixed by the HIV-inspired module entitled "Bloodborne Pathogens," on what to do in the event that pools of human blood should show up on the sales floor. All right, you put warning cones around the puddles, don protective gloves, etc., but I can't stop trying to envision the circumstances in which these pools might arise: an associate uprising? a guest riot? I have gone through six modules, three more than we are supposed to do tonight—the rest are to be done in our spare moments over the next few weeks—when one of the trainers gently pries me away from the computer. We are allowed now to leave.

Responding to Reading

1.   Ehrenreich begins her essay with the statement, "For sheer grandeur, scale, and intimidation value, I doubt if any corporate orientation exceeds that of Wal-Mart" (1). Do you think Ehrenreich wants her readers to take this statement seriously? In what way do these remarks set the tone for the rest of the essay?

2.   Why does Ehrenreich describe the orientation process in such detail? What does she hope to accomplish with this strategy?

3. How would you describe Ehrenreich's attitude toward the orientation process? Toward Wal-Mart? Toward her co-workers? What words and phrases in the essay convey these attitudes?

Responding in Writing

Assume you are one of the trainers at Wal-Mart's orientation section. Write a one- or two-paragraph memo that explains the orientation process and its goals.

DELIVERERS

Paul Fussell

1924–

Born in Pasadena, California, Paul Fussell served in the US Army in World War II, receiving the Bronze Star and two purple hearts, and returned to the United States to earn a BA at Pomona College (1947) and an MA (1949) and PhD (1952) from Harvard University. Fussell has taught English literature at the University of Pennsylvania since 1983. He has authored and edited more than twenty books, including The Great War and Modern Memory *(1975), which won both the National Book Award and the National Book Critics Circle Award;* Doing Battle: The Making of a Skeptic *(1996); and* Uniforms: Why We Are What We Wear *(2002), from which the following selection is taken.*

Next to sailors and marines, perhaps the most enthusiastic devotees of their uniforms are postal workers. The Postal Service's reputation for probity helps assure respect for its uniformed personnel on the street and in stations. As one female letter carrier attested, "Uniform implies that you can be trusted, and so you are treated better." There would seem to be wide agreement that the check proffered by a uniformed postal worker will probably not bounce. The black stripe of the letter carrier's trousers, shorts, and culottes is like that of the military, and it betokens in many ways a similar status. It is strict discipline that helps postal workers, like United States Marines, to keep their honor clean.

For example, a letter carrier finished with his or her daily round may not, in uniform, pause at a bar on the way home. In a T-shirt, OK, but not in the uniform, which the service takes seriously. It provides each employee with an annual uniform allowance amounting to nearly $300, and it is precise in its insistence that only official garb may be worn. This includes shoes and socks. And because so many employees must be outdoors in all kinds of weather, there are official rubber overshoes and official rubber boots as well as twenty different styles of all-weather black shoes and three types of raincoats. Everything worn above the waist bears the postal logo, a stylized eagle's head in blue and white. There are official caps for all purposes and climates: sun helmets (reproductions of solar topees), also useful in the rain, and for hot temperatures there's a mesh model—that's when you wear your Bermuda shorts. There are visor caps for the old-fashioned, but the favorite cap now is the baseball cap, available in two models, one for hot weather, with a mesh back, and one for winter, with a solid back. For really frigid conditions there's a fur cap with ear flaps and a knitted watch cap with a knitted face mask. The service provides weatherproof parkas and windbreakers and heavy sweaters, and it is up-to-date on the facts of life, offering women official postal maternity blouses. Neckties for all are dark blue with tiny red and white dots. All kinds of official gloves can be had: "Sure-Grip," knit, leather with insulated lining, deerskin, and capeskin, and an official black belt too.

Workers indoors have their own uniform items. For men, a cardigan or a sweater vest; for women, dark blue jumper and skirt. For both, official shirts, white with blue pinstripes and long or short sleeves. And for "internal" workers, choice of necktie, either blue or red, with diagonal stripes in postal colors, that is, red or blue. It is clearly a service not at all shy about its patriotism. On each jacket, vest, and windbreaker, there's an inch-wide horizontal stripe in, of course, red, white, and blue. The postal police are vouchsafed their own special uniform, dark blue trousers with light blue stripes, jackets and shirts with shoulder straps and a place for the police badge. And even the vehicle maintenance people have their own outfits, no stripes on the trousers but warm jackets in several styles.

Everything has been so well thought out that even the socks are special. You can wear either postal white or blue, but the white socks (short, usually, but tall also for wear with short pants) have at the top two handsome dark-blue stripes. All these things may be had by mail from numerous approved manufacturers, but post offices in large cities hold occasional uniform fairs, when the manufacturers are invited to lay out their wares and sell on the spot. The whole variety of uniforms reveals remarkable imagination and even taste, and it's not surprising that those who wear them are happy—and trustworthy.

5   The theory of uniforms is full of inexplicables, paradoxes, and contradictions. For example, how to reconcile the loathing felt by soldiers for brown uniforms, while dirt- (and even worse-) brown attire seems to delight the employees of the United Parcel Service? And odder still, the UPS uniform doesn't please just UPS males but also hordes of their female customers, throwing them into something like ecstasy.

A United Parcel spokesman explained the color: what is wanted, he said, is a sedate uniform that doesn't show dirt—similar to khaki in the British army, but darker. The company won't allow its deliverers to take their trousers home overnight; they must be washed daily by the company, partly to keep them up to the standard of looking good, but partly to prevent their turning up in the fashion marketplace, where what the journalist Robert Frank calls *delivery chic* becomes more popular daily. Time was when military uniforms, dirty and disused, became all but obligatory among the trendy young. Now it's uniform wear from United Parcel, Federal Express, and—if you can get away with it—the Postal Service itself.

Frank, in the July 1995 issue of *Cosmopolitan*, offered the following potpourri of UPS erotics, disclosing the degree to which "UPS men, the humble couriers in tight brown polyester uniforms driving clunky package trucks, have become sex objects of the service world." It has gone so far that the company has had to turn down "adult" calendar makers who want to depict their drivers as lewd come-ons—although the company doesn't mind if people find its deliverymen cute. (About 93 percent of its deliverers are men.) Sometimes everything matches the dark brown of the uniform, causing one woman to say, "I think I've got a crush on him. He's got brown eyes." Some find even the company's phone number provocative: it's I-800-PICK-UPS. A teenager recalled how she and a friend would wait at her mother's store every morning at 11:00 for the UPS man—said to be a tan, blond, muscular hunk. "We scheduled our whole morning around it. He looked cool in the uniform and he always rolled his sleeves up so his muscles would show."

And female UPS deliverers have been equally exciting. Patti Anderson, a New Jersey UPS employee, has often been propositioned by dock workers, which, she says, never particularly bothers her. The impression seems to have gone around that there is no such thing as an ugly UPS man or woman. How much of this is evanescent folklore no one will ever know, but it's almost as if a vacuum is being filled and that the UPS deliverer occupies the role once enjoyed by the suburban iceman, who used to deliver great blocks of ice to housewives while the husband was safely out of the way at work.

If you lined up a number of letter carriers, they would resemble the troops of a well-disciplined army. If you lined up a number of Federal Express deliverers, they might remind you of a chorus line in a Broadway musical. Their current get-ups owe as little as possible to the military model, which they used to honor with navy blue trousers and shirts with shoulder strap epaulets.

Their new uniforms were created in 1991 by Stan Herman, the well-known New York fashion designer. They are nothing if not colorful, with emphasis on green, purple, and black in various mixtures. 10

They resemble leisure wear, especially what might be seen at a golf course. Few surprises there, for Herman also designs the uniforms for McDonald's. But he can do the quasi-military look when appropriate, as he has done for Amtrak and both TWA and American Airlines, and he can make single-color outfits attractive as he's done for FedEx's main competitor, United Parcel.

In the Elizabethen period, buffoons wore "motley"—a style of dress featuring tights with legs of different colors. "Motley" would describe the FedEx outfits, likely to present a purple sleeve on a dark blue or black shirt, or one green sleeve on a black or purple shirt. The technique seems to be a way of departing from the symmetry that used to govern livery or the wear of subordinates, like bellboys and doormen. Little of this sort of thing goes on below the FedEx waist; the trousers remain largely black.

The splashes of purple or green make the FedEx employees recognizable, according to Melinda Webber, an authority on uniforms at New York's Fashion Institute of Technology. She pointed out the special difficulty facing contemporary uniform designers for commercial enterprises. The uniforms must keep the wearers happy, proud, and comfortable, with some attention to aesthetics; they must project an unforgettable corporate image to please management; and they must be unique to prevent confusion among customers. What with Newman's rampant purples, greens, and blacks, there's little chance of anyone confusing a FedEx with a United Parcel.

With commercial uniforms developing in the most unlikely places, it's to be expected that more and more elaborate will become the behind-the-scenes trade administration, now the business of the National Association of Uniform Manufacturers and Distributors. It has popularized among its members the high-class euphemism "career apparel." The career apparel trade is doing very well, thank you, because, as the journalist Carina Chocano noted, "Recent decades have seen an explosion in the number of people who wear uniforms to work. An estimated ten percent of the American workforce is required to wear them every day." A tribute to the success of advertising in dominating American life, making mass consumption the only kind that succeeds.

Responding to Reading

1. How are postal workers' uniforms different from and similar to those of UPS personnel? According to Fussell, how do people feel about UPS uniforms? How do you think these uniforms help to convey the company's image?

2. What does Fussell mean when he says that the uniforms of Federal Express employees "owe as little as possible to the military model" (9)? Why do you think this is so? What message are these uniforms supposed to convey?

3. Why do you think corporations like UPS and FedEx want their employees to wear uniforms? Overall, do you think these uniforms are a clever marketing strategy or a waste of corporate money? Explain.

Responding in Writing

Assume you are starting a private delivery service. Describe the uniforms you would require your employees to wear. What impression would you want these uniforms to convey?

DELUSIONS OF GRANDEUR

Henry Louis Gates, Jr.
1950–

Henry Louis Gates, Jr. was born in Keyser, West Virginia, and earned a BA degree in history from Yale University (1973) and an MA degree (1974) and PhD (1979) in English Literature from Clare College at the University of Cambridge, where he was the first African American to do so. At age thirty, he received a Macarthur Foundation Genius Grant (1980). He has taught at Yale, Cornell, Duke, and Harvard. One of Gates's best-known works is Loose Canons: Notes on the Culture Wars, *in which he discusses gender, literature, and multiculturalism in American arts and letters. He is general editor of* The Norton Anthology of African-American Literature, *second edition (2003); a staff writer for the* New Yorker; *and the author of essays, reviews, and profiles in many other publications.*

Standing at the bar of an all-black VFW post in my hometown of Piedmont, W.Va., I offered five dollars to anyone who could tell me how many African-American professional athletes were at work today. There are 35 million African-Americans, I said.

"Ten million!" yelled one intrepid soul, too far into his cups.

"No way . . . more like 500,000," said another.

"You mean *all* professional sports," someone interjected, "including golf and tennis, but not counting the brothers from Puerto Rico?" Everyone laughed.

"Fifty thousand, minimum," was another guess.   5

Here are the facts:

There are 1,200 black professional athletes in the U.S.

There are 12 times more black lawyers than black athletes.

There are 2½ times more black dentists than black athletes.

There are 15 times more black doctors than black athletes.

Nobody in my local VFW believed these statistics; in fact, few people would believe them if they weren't reading them in the pages of *Sports Illustrated*. In spite of these statistics, too many African-American youngsters still believe that they have a much better chance of becoming another Magic Johnson or Michael Jordan than they do of matching the achievements of Baltimore Mayor Kurt Schmoke or neurosurgeon Dr. Benjamin Carson, both of whom, like Johnson and Jordan, are black.

In reality, an African-American youngster has about as much chance of becoming a professional athlete as he or she does of winning the lottery. The tragedy for our people, however, is that few of us accept that truth.

Let me confess that I love sports. Like most black people of my generation—I'm 40—I was raised to revere the great black athletic heroes, and I never tired of listening to the stories of triumph and defeat that, for blacks, amount to a collective epic much like those of the ancient Greeks: Joe Louis's demolition of Max Schmeling; Satchel Paige's dazzling repertoire of pitches; Jesse Owens's in-your-face performance in Hitler's 1936 Olympics; Willie Mays's over-the-shoulder basket catch; Jackie Robinson's quiet strength when assaulted by racist taunts; and a thousand other grand tales.

10   Nevertheless, the blind pursuit of attainment in sports is having a devastating effect on our people. Imbued with a belief that our principal avenue to fame and profit is through sport, and seduced by a win-at-any-cost system that corrupts even elementary school students, far too many black kids treat basketball courts and football fields as if they were classrooms in an alternative school system. "O.K., I flunked English," a young athlete will say. "But I got an A plus in slam-dunking."

The failure of our public schools to educate athletes is part and parcel of the schools' failure to educate almost everyone. A recent survey of the Philadelphia school system, for example, stated that "more than half of all students in the third, fifth and eighth grades cannot perform minimum math and language tasks." One in four middle school students in that city fails to pass to the next grade each year. It is a sad truth that such statistics are repeated in cities throughout the nation. Young athletes—particularly young black athletes—are especially ill-served. Many of them are functionally illiterate, yet they are passed along from year to year for the greater glory of good old Hometown High. We should not be surprised to learn, then, that only 26.6% of black athletes at the collegiate level earn their degrees. For every successful educated black professional athlete, there are thousands of dead and wounded. Yet young blacks continue to aspire to careers as athletes, and it's no wonder why; when the University of North Carolina recently commissioned a sculptor to create archetypes of its student body, guess which ethnic group was selected to represent athletes?

Those relatively few black athletes who do make it in the professional ranks must be prevailed upon to play a significant role in the education of all of our young people, athlete and nonathlete alike. While some have done so, many others have shirked their social obligations: to earmark small percentages of their incomes for the United Negro College Fund; to appear on television for educational purposes rather than merely to sell sneakers; to let children know the message that becoming a lawyer, a teacher or a doctor does more good for our people than winning the Super Bowl; and to form productive liaisons with educators to help forge solutions to the many ills that beset the black community. These are merely a few modest proposals.

A similar burden falls upon successful blacks in all walks of life. Each of us must strive to make our young people understand the realities. Tell them to cheer Bo Jackson but to emulate novelist Toni Morrison or businessman Reginald Lewis or historian John Hope Franklin or Spelman College president Johnetta Cole—the list is long.

Of course, society as a whole bears responsibility as well. Until colleges stop using young blacks as cannon fodder in the big-business wars of so-called nonprofessional sports, until training a young black's mind becomes as important as training his or her body, we will continue to perpetuate a system akin to that of the Roman gladiators, sacrificing a class of people for the entertainment of the mob.

Responding to Reading

1. Why does Gates begin his essay with an anecdote? What does this story reveal about African-American assumptions about sports? According to Gates, what harm do these assumptions do?
2. What does Gates mean when he says, "The failure of our public schools to educate athletes is part and parcel of the schools' failure to educate almost everyone" (11)? Do you agree? In addition to the public schools, who or what else could be responsible for the situation Gates describes?
3. Why does Gates say that colleges are using young blacks as "cannon fodder" (14)? According to Gates, how are young black athletes like Roman gladiators? Do you think that this comparison is accurate? Fair?

Responding in Writing

What were your reactions to the statistics presented in paragraph 6? Write the text of a children's picture book designed to convey this information accurately to preschoolers.

WHAT NURSES STAND FOR

Suzanne Gordon

1945–

Suzanne Gordon was born in New York City and received her BA from Cornell University and her MA from Johns Hopkins. A freelance writer and editor, she writes frequently about social issues and health care. She is coeditor of Caregiving: Readings in Knowledge, Practice, Ethics, and Politics *(1996); author of* Life Support: Three Nurses on the Front Lines *(1997); and coauthor of* From Silence to Voice: What Nurses Know and Must Communicate to the Public *(2000). In the following excerpt from* Life Support, *which appeared in the* Atlantic Monthly, *Gordon explains that nurses play a far greater role in medical caregiving than most people realize.*

At four o'clock on a Friday afternoon the hematology-oncology clinic at Boston's Beth Israel Hospital is quiet. Paddy Connelly and Frances Kiel, two of the eleven nurses who work in the unit, sit at the nurses' station—an island consisting of two long desks equipped with phones, which ring constantly, and computers. They are encircled by thirteen blue-leather reclining chairs, in which patients may spend only a brief time, for a short chemotherapy infusion, or an entire afternoon, to receive more complicated chemotherapy or blood products. At one of the chairs Nancy Rumplik is starting to administer chemotherapy to a man in his mid-fifties who has colon cancer.

Rumplik is forty-two and has been a nurse on the unit for seven years. She stands next to the wan-looking man and begins to hang the intravenous [IV] drugs that will treat his cancer. As the solution drips through the tubing and into his vein, she sits by his side, watching to make sure that he has no adverse reaction.

Today she is acting as triage nurse—the person responsible for patients who walk in without an appointment, for patients who call with a problem but can't reach their primary nurse, for the smooth functioning of the unit, and, of course, for responding to any emergencies. Rumplik's eyes thus constantly sweep the room to check on the other patients. She focuses for a moment on a heavy-set African-American woman in her mid-forties, dressed in a pair of navy slacks and a brightly colored shirt, who is sitting in the opposite corner. Her sister, who is younger and heavier, is by her side. The patient seems fine, so Rumplik returns her attention to the man next to her. Several minutes later she looks up again, checks the woman, and stiffens. There is now a look of anxiety on the woman's face. Rumplik, leaning forward in her chair, stares at her.

"What's she getting?" she mouths to Kiel.

Looking at the patient's chart, Frances Kiel names a drug that has 5 been known to cause severe allergic reactions. In that brief moment, as the two nurses confer, the woman suddenly clasps her chest. Her look of anxiety turns to terror. Her mouth opens and shuts in silent panic. Rumplik leaps up from her chair, as do Kiel and Connelly, and sprints across the room.

"I can't breathe," the woman sputters when Rumplik is at her side. Her eyes bulging, she grasps Rumplik's hand tightly; her eyes roll back as her head slips to the side. Realizing that the patient is having an anaphylactic reaction (her airway is swelling and closing), Rumplik immediately turns a small spigot on the IV tubing to shut off the drip. At the same instant Kiel calls a physician and the emergency-response team. By this time the woman is struggling for breath.

Kiel slips an oxygen mask over the woman's head and wraps a blood-pressure cuff around her arm. Connelly administers an antihistamine to stop the allergic reaction, and cortisone to decrease the inflammation blocking her airway. The physician, an oncology fellow, arrives within minutes. He assesses the situation and then notices the woman's sister standing paralyzed, watching the scene. "Get out of here!" he commands sharply. The woman moves away as if she had been slapped.

Just as the emergency team arrives, the woman's breathing returns to normal and the look of terror fades from her face. Taking Rumplik's hand again, she looks up and says, "I couldn't breathe. I just couldn't breathe." Rumplik gently explains that she has had an allergic reaction to a drug and reassures her that it has stopped.

After a few minutes, when the physician is certain that the patient is stable, he and the emergency-response team walk out of the treatment area, but the nurses continue to comfort the shaken woman. Rumplik then crosses the room to talk with her male patient, who is ashen-faced at this reminder of the potentially lethal effects of the medication that he and others are receiving. Responding to his unspoken fears, Rumplik says quietly, "It's frightening to see something like that. But it's under control."

He nods silently, closes his eyes, and leans his head back against 10 the chair. Rumplik goes over to the desk where Connelly and Kiel are breathing a joint sigh of relief. One of the nurses comments on the physician's treatment of the patient's sister. "Did you hear him? He just told her to get out."

Wincing with distress, Rumplik looks around for the sister. She goes into the waiting room, where the woman is sitting in a corner, looking bereft and frightened. Rumplik sits down next to her, explains what happened, and suggests that the patient could probably benefit from some overnight company. Then she adds, "I'm sorry the doctor talked to you like that. You know, it's a very anxious time for all of us."

At this gesture of respect and recognition the woman, who has every strike—race, class, and sex—against her when dealing with elite white professionals in this downtown hospital, smiles solemnly. "I understand. Thank you."

Nancy Rumplik returns to her patient.

"I Am Ready to Die"

It is 6:00 P.M. Today Jeannie Chaisson, a clinical nurse specialist, arrived at her general medical unit at seven in the morning and cared for patients until three-thirty in the afternoon. At home now, she makes herself a pot of coffee and sits down in the living room, cradling her cup. Just as she is shedding the strain of the day, the phone rings.

15 It's the husband of one of Chaisson's patients—a sixty-three-year-old woman suffering from terminal multiple myeloma, a cancer of the bone marrow. When Chaisson left the hospital, she knew the family was in crisis. Having endured the cancer for several years, the woman is exhausted from the pain, from the effects of the disease and failed treatments, and from the pain medication on which she has become increasingly dependent. Chaisson knows she is ready to let death take her. But her husband and daughter are not.

Now the crisis that was brewing has exploded. Chaisson's caller is breathless, frantic with anxiety, as he relays his wife's pleas. She wants to die. She is prepared to die. She says the pain is too much. "You've got to do something," he implores Chaisson. "Keep her going—stop her from doing this."

Chaisson knows that it is indeed time for her to do something—but, sadly, not what the anguished husband wishes. "Be calm," she tells him. "Please hold on. We'll all talk together. I'm coming right in." Leaving a note for her family, she gets into her car and drives back to the hospital.

When Chaisson walks into the patient's room, she is not surprised by what she finds. Seated next to the bed is the visibly distraught husband. Behind him the patient's twenty-five-year-old daughter paces in front of a picture window with a view across Boston. The patient is lying in a state somewhere between consciousness and coma, shrunken by pain and devoured by the cancer's progress. Chaisson has seen scenes like this many times before in her fifteen-year career as a nurse.

As she looks at the woman, she can understand why her husband and her daughter are so resistant. They remember her as she first appeared to Chaisson, three years ago—a bright, feisty sixty-year-old woman, her nails tapered and polished, her hair sleekly sculpted into a perfect silver pouf. Chaisson remembers the day, during the first of many admissions to the unit, when she asked the woman if she wanted her hair washed.

The woman replied in astonishment, "I do not wash my hair. I 20 have it done. Once a week."

Now her hair is unkempt, glued to her face with sweat. Her nails are no longer polished. Their main work these days is to dig into her flesh when the pain becomes too acute. The disease has slowly bored into her bones. Simply to stand is painful and could even be an invitation to a fracture. Her pelvis is disintegrating. The nurses have inserted an indwelling catheter, because having a bedpan slipped underneath her causes agony, but she has developed a urinary-tract infection. Because removing the catheter will make the infection easier to treat, doctors suggest this course of action. Yet if the catheter is removed, the pain will be intolerable each time she has to urinate.

When the residents and interns argued that failure to treat the infection could mean the patient would die, Chaisson responded, "She's dying anyway. It's her disease that is killing her, not a urinary tract infection." They relented.

Now the family must confront this reality.

Chaisson goes to the woman's bed and gently wakes her. Smiling at her nurse, the woman tries to muster the energy to explain to her husband and her daughter that the pain is too great and she can no longer attain that delicate balance, so crucial to dying patients, between fighting off pain and remaining alert for at least some of the day. Only when she is practically comatose from drugs can she find relief.

"I am ready to die," she whispers weakly. 25

Her husband and daughter contradict her—there is still hope.

Jeannie Chaisson stands silent during this exchange and then intervenes, asking them to try to take in what their loved one is telling them. Then she repeats the basic facts about the disease and its course. "At this point there is no treatment for the disease," she explains, "but there is treatment for the pain, to make the patient comfortable and ease her suffering." Chaisson spends another hour sitting with them, answering their questions and allowing them to feel supported. Finally the family is able to heed the patient's wishes—leave the catheter in and do not resuscitate her if she suffers a cardiac arrest. Give her enough morphine to stop the pain. Let her go.

The woman visibly relaxes, lies back, and closes her eyes. Chaisson approaches the husband and the daughter, with whom she has worked for so long, and hugs them both. Then she goes out to talk to the medical team.

Before leaving for home, Chaisson again visits her patient. The husband and the daughter have gone for a cup of coffee. The woman is quiet. Chaisson sits down at the side of her bed and takes her hand. The woman opens her eyes. Too exhausted to say a word, she merely squeezes the nurse's hand in gratitude. For the past three years Chaisson has helped her to fight her disease and live as long as possible. Now she is here to help her die.

The Endangered RN

30 When we hear the word "hospital," technology and scientific invention spring to mind: mechanical ventilators, dialysis machines, intravenous pumps, biomedical research, surgery, medication. These, many believe, are the life supports in our health-care system. This technology keeps people alive, and helps to cure and heal them.

In fact there are other, equally important life supports in our health care system: the 2.2 million nurses who make up the largest profession in health care, the profession with the highest percentage of women, and the second largest profession after teaching. These women and men weave a tapestry of care, knowledge, and trust that is critical to patients' survival.

Nancy Rumplik and Jeannie Chaisson have between them more than a quarter century's experience caring for the sick. They work in an acute-care hospital, one of Harvard Medical School's teaching hospitals. Beth Israel not only is known for the quality of its patient care but also is world-renowned for the quality of its nursing staff and its institutional commitment to nursing.

The for-profit, market-driven health care that is sweeping the nation is threatening this valuable group of professionals. To gain an advantage in the competitive new health-care marketplace, hospitals all over the country are trying to cut their costs. One popular strategy is to lay off nurses and replace them with lower-paid, less-skilled workers.

American hospitals already use 20 percent fewer nurses than their counterparts in other industrialized countries. Nursing does provide attractive middle-income salaries. In 1992 staff nurses earned, on average, $33,000 a year. Clinical nurse specialists, who have advanced education and specialize in a particular field, earned an average of $41,000, and nurse practitioners, who generally have a master's degree and provide primary-care services, earned just under $44,000. Yet RN salaries and benefits altogether represent only about 16 percent of total hospital costs.

35 Nevertheless, nurses are a major target of hospital "restructuring" plans, which in some cases have called for a reduction of 20 to 50 percent in registered nursing staff.

The process of job elimination, deskilling, and downgrading seriously erodes opportunities for stable middle-class employment in nursing as in other industries. However, as the late David Gordon documented in his book *Fat and Mean: The Corporate Squeeze of Working Americans and the Myth of Managerial "Downsizing,"* reduced "head counts" among production or service workers don't necessarily mean that higher-level jobs (and the pay and perquisites associated with them) are being chopped as well. In fact, Gordon argued, many headline grabbing exercises in corporate cost-cutting leave executive compensation untouched, along with other forms of managerial "bloat."

Even in this era of managed-care limits on physicians' compensation, nurses' pay is relatively quite modest. And the managers of care themselves—particularly hospital administrators and health-maintenance-organization executives—are doing so well that even doctors look underpaid by comparison.

According to the business magazine *Modern Healthcare's* 1996 physician-compensation report, the average salary in family practice is $128,096, in internal medicine $135,755, in oncology $164,621, in anesthesiology $193,242, and in general surgery $199,342. Some specialists earn more than a million dollars a year.

A survey conducted in 1995 by *Hospitals & Health Networks*, the magazine of the American Hospital Association, found that the average total cash compensation for hospital CEOs was $188,500. In large hospitals the figure went up to $280,900, and in for-profit chains far higher. In 1995, at age forty-three, Richard Scott, the CEO of Columbia/Healthcare Corporation, received a salary of $2,093,844. He controlled shares in Columbia/HCA worth $359.5 million.

In 1994 compensation for the CEOs of the seven largest for-profit 40 HMOs averaged $7 million. Even those in the not-for-profit sector of insurance earn startling sums: in 1995 John Burry Jr., the chairman and CEO of Ohio Blue Cross and Blue Shield, was paid $1.6 million.

According to a report in *Modern Healthcare*, a proposed merger with the for-profit Columbia/HCA would have paid him $3 million "for a decade-long no-compete contract . . . [and] up to $7 million for two consulting agreements."

At the other end of the new health-care salary spread are "unlicensed assistive personnel" (UAPs), who are now being used instead of nurses. They usually have little background in health care and only rudimentary training. Yet UAPs may insert catheters, read EKGs, suction tracheotomy tubes, change sterile dressings, and perform other traditional nursing functions. To keep patients from becoming unduly alarmed about—or even aware of—this development, some hospitals now prohibit nurses from wearing any badges that identify them as RNs. Thus everyone at the bedside is some kind of generic "patient-care technician"—regardless of how much or how little training and experience she or he has.

In some health-care facilities other nonprofessional staff—janitors, housekeepers, security guards, and aides—are also being "cross-trained" and transformed into "multi-skilled" workers who can be assigned to nursing duties. One such employee was so concerned about the impact of this on patient care that he recently wrote a letter to Timothy McCall, M.D., a critic of multi-skilling, after reading a magazine article the latter had written on the subject.

> I am an employee of a 95-bed, long-term care facility. My position is that of a security guard. Ninety-five percent of my job consists of maintenance, housekeeping, admitting persons into clinical lab to pick-up & leave specimens. Now a class, 45 minutes, is being given so employees can feed, give bedpans & move patients. My expertise is in law enforcement & security, 25 years. I am not trained or licensed in patient care, maintenance, lab work, etc. . . . This scares me. Having untrained, unlicensed people performing jobs, in my opinion, is dangerous.

Training of RN replacements is indeed almost never regulated by state licensing boards. There are no minimum requirements governing the amount of training that aides or cross-trained workers must have before they can be redeployed to do various types of nursing work. Training periods can range from a few hours to six weeks. One 1994 study cited in a 1996 report by the Institute of Medicine on nursing staffing found that

> 99 percent of the hospitals in California reported less than 120 hours of on-the-job training for newly hired ancillary nursing personnel. Only 20 percent of the hospitals required a high school diploma. The majority of hospitals (59 percent) provided less than 20 hours of classroom instruction and 88 percent provided 40 hours or less of instruction time.

45   Because the rapidly accelerating UAP trend is so new, its impact on patient care has not yet been fully documented. However, in a series of major studies over the past twenty years researchers have directly linked higher numbers and greater qualifications of registered nurses on hospital units to lower mortality rates and decreased lengths of hospital stay. Reducing the number of expert nurses in the hospital, the community, and homes endangers patients' lives and wastes scarce resources. Choosing to save money by reducing nursing care aggravates the impersonality of a medical system that tends to turn human beings into their diseases and the doctors who care for them into sophisticated clinical machines. When they're sick, patients do not ask only what pills they should take or what operations they should have. They are preoccupied with questions such as Why me? Why now? Nurses are there through this day-by-day, minute-by-minute attack on the soul. They know that for the patient not only a

sick or infirm body but also a life, a family, a community, a society, needs to heal.

Media Stereotypes

Although nurses help us to live and die, in the public depiction of health care patients seem to emerge from hospitals without ever having benefited from their assistance. Whether patients are treated in an emergency room in a few short hours or on a critical-care unit for months on end, we seem to assume that physicians are responsible for all the successes—and failures—in our medical system. In fact, we seem to believe that they are responsible not only for all of the curing but also for much of the caring.

Nurses remain shadowy figures moving mysteriously in the background. In television series they often appear as comic figures. On TV's short-lived *Nightingales*, on the sitcom *Nurses*, and on the medical drama *Chicago Hope* nurses are far too busy pining after doctors or racing off to aerobics classes to care for patients.

ER gives nurses more prominence than many other hospital shows, but doctors on *ER* are constantly barking out commands to perform the simplest duties—get a blood pressure, call the OR—to experienced emergency-room nurses. In reality the nurses would have thought of all this before the doctor arrived. In an emergency room as busy and sophisticated as the one on *ER*, the first clinician a patient sees is a triage nurse, who assesses the patient and dictates what he needs, who will see him, and when. Experienced nurses will direct less-experienced residents (and have sometimes done so on *ER*), suggesting a medication, a test, consultation with a specialist, or transfer to the operating room. The great irony of *ER* is that Carol Hathaway, the nurse in charge, is generally relegated to comforting a child or following a physician's orders rather than, as would occur in real life, helping to direct the staff in saving lives.

Not only do doctors dominate on television but they are the focus of most hard-news health-care coverage. Reporters rarely cover innovations in nursing, use nurses as sources, or report on nursing research. The health-care experts whom reporters or politicians consult are invariably physicians, representatives of physician organizations, or policy specialists who tend to look at health care through the prism of economics. "Who Counts in New Coverage of Health Care?," a 1990 study by the Women, Press & Politics Project, in Cambridge, Massachusetts, of healthcare coverage in *The New York Times*, the *Los Angeles Times*, and *The Washington Post*, found that out of 908 quotations that appeared in three months' worth of health-care stories, nurses were the sources for ten.

50   The revolution in health care has become big news. Occasionally reporters will turn their attention to layoffs in nursing, but the story is rarely framed as an important public-health issue. Rather, it is generally depicted as a labor-management conflict. Nursing unions are battling with management. Nurses say this; hospital administrators claim that. Whom can you believe?

Worse still, this important issue may be couched in the stereotypes of nursing or of women's work in general. A typical example appeared on *NBC Nightly News* in September of 1994. The show ran a story that involved a discussion of the serious problems, including deaths, resulting from replacing nurses with unlicensed aides. The anchor introduced it as "a new and controversial way of administering TLC."[1] Imagine how the issue would be characterized if 20 to 50 percent of staff physicians were eliminated in thousands of American hospitals. Would it not be front-page news, a major public-health catastrophe? Patients all over the country would be terrified to enter hospitals. Yet we learn about the equivalent in nursing with only a minimum of concern. If laying off thousands of nurses results only in the loss of a little TLC, what difference does it make if an aide replaces a nurse?

Nursing is not simply a matter of TLC. It's a matter of life and death. In hospitals, which employ 66 percent of America's nurses, nurses monitor a patient's condition before, during, and after high-tech medical procedures. They adjust medication, manage pain and the side effects of treatment, and instantly intervene if a life-threatening change occurs in a patient's condition.

In our high-tech medical system nurses care for the body and the soul. No matter how sensitive, caring, and attentive physicians are, nurses are often closer to the patient's needs and wishes. That's not because they are inherently more caring but because they spend far more time with patients and are likely to know them better. This time and knowledge allows them to save lives. Nurses also help people to adjust to the lives they must live after they have recovered. And when death can no longer be delayed, nurses help patients confront their own mortality with at least some measure of grace and dignity.

The Stigma of Sickness

There is another reason that nurses' work so often goes unrecognized. Even some of the patients who have benefited the most from nurses' critical care are unable to credit its importance publicly. Because

---

[1]That is, "tender, loving care." [Eds.]

nurses observe and cushion what the physician and writer Oliver Sacks has called human beings' falling "radically into sickness," they are a reminder of the pain, fear, vulnerability, and loss of control that adults find difficult to tolerate and thus to discuss. A man who has had a successful heart bypass will boast of his surgeon's accomplishments to friends at a dinner party. A woman who has survived a bone-marrow transplant will extol her oncologist's triumph in the war against cancer to her friends and relatives. But what nurses did for those two patients will rarely be mentioned. It was a nurse who bathed the cardiac patient and comforted him while he struggled with the terror of possible death. It was a nurse who held the plastic dish under the cancer patient's lips as she was wracked with nausea, and who wiped a bottom raw from diarrhea. As Claire Fagin and Donna Diers have explained in an eloquent essay titled "Nursing as Metaphor," nurses stand for intimacy. They are our secret sharers. Even though they are lifelines during illness, when control is restored the residue of our anxiety and mortality clings to them like dust, and we flee the memory.

At one moment a nurse like Nancy Rumplik or Jeannie Chaisson 55 may be involved in a sophisticated clinical procedure that demands expert judgment and advanced training in the latest technology. The next moment she may do what many people consider trivial or menial work, such as emptying a bedpan, giving a sponge bath, administering medication, or feeding or walking a patient.

The fact that nurses' work incorporates many so-called menial tasks that don't demand total attention is not a reason to replace nurses with less-skilled workers. This hands-on care allows nurses to explore patients' physical condition *and* to register their anxiety and fear. It allows them to save lives *and* to ascertain when it's appropriate to help patients die. It is only in watching nurses weave the tapestry of care that we grasp its integrity and its meaning for a society that too easily forgets the value of things that are beyond price.

Responding to Reading

1. Gordon begins her essay with two long narratives. What does each of these stories illustrate? How do they help Gordon make her point about nurses? How is this section of the essay different from the rest of the essay?
2. What new positions have for-profit health-care corporations created to save money? According to Gordon, how are the actions of these corporations compromising health care in the United States?
3. Why does Gordon think the work of nurses so often goes unnoticed? Why do the media contribute to this situation? Why do people's attitudes toward "nurses' work" add to the problem?

Responding in Writing

What attitude do you have toward nurses? Do you think your attitude "adds to the problem"?

OWNING IT ALL
William Kittredge
1932–

William Kittredge was born in Portland, Oregon, and raised on a ranch in the Warner Valley in Southeastern Oregon. He earned a BS in general agriculture from Oregon State University (1953) and worked as a rancher until 1967, when he enrolled at the Writer's Workshop at the University of Iowa and earned an MFA degree (1969). Kittredge writes short stories and essays, and his books include The Van Gogh Field and Other Stories *(1979);* We Are Not in This Together *(1982);* Owning It All: Essays *(1987), from which the following piece is excerpted;* Hole in the Sky: A Memoir *(1992); and* Who Owns the West? *(1996). Kittredge has also edited several books, including* The Portable Western Reader *(1997). He has taught creative writing at the University of Montana, Missoula, for more than twenty-five years, and his writing has appeared in* Harper's *and* Outside *magazines.*

Agriculture is often envisioned as an art, and it can be. Of course there is always survival, and bank notes, and all that. But your basic bottom line on the farm is again and again some notion of how life should be lived. The majority of agricultural people, if you press them hard enough, even though most of them despise sentimental abstractions, will admit they are trying to create a good place, and to live as part of that goodness, in the kind of connection which with fine reason we called rootedness. It's just that there is good art and bad art.

These are thoughts which come back when I visit eastern Oregon. I park and stand looking down into the lava-rock and juniper-tree canyon where Deep Creek cuts its way out of the Warner Mountains, and the great turkey buzzard soars high in the yellow-orange light above the evening. The fishing water is low, as it always is in late August, unfurling itself around dark and broken boulders. The trout, I know, are hanging where the currents swirl across themselves, waiting for the one entirely precise and lucky cast, the Renegade fly bobbing toward them.

Even now I can see it, each turn of water along miles of that creek. Walk some stretch enough times with a fly rod and its configurations will imprint themselves on your being with Newtonian exactitude. Which is beyond doubt one of the attractions of such fishing—the hours of learning, and then the intimacy with a living system that carries you beyond the sadness of mere gaming for sport.

What I liked to do, back in the old days, was pack in some spuds and an onion and corn flour and spices mixed up in a plastic bag, a small cast-iron frying pan in my wicker creel and, in the late twilight on a gravel bar by the water, cook up a couple of rainbows over a fire of snapping dead willow and sage, eating alone while the birds flitted through the last hatch, wiping my greasy fingers on my pants while the heavy trout began rolling at the lower ends of the pools.

The canyon would be shadowed under the moon when I walked 5 out to show up home empty-handed, to sit with my wife over a drink of whiskey at the kitchen table. Those nights I would go to bed and sleep without dreams, a grown-up man secure in the house and the western valley where he had been a child, enclosed in a topography of spirit he assumed he knew more closely than his own features in the shaving mirror.

So, I ask myself, if it was such a pretty life, why didn't I stay? The peat soil in Warner Valley was deep and rich, we ran good cattle, and my most sacred memories are centered there. What could run me off?

Well, for openers, it got harder and harder to get out of bed in the mornings and face the days, for reasons I didn't understand. More and more I sought the comfort of fishing that knowable creek. Or in winter the blindness of television.

My father grew up on a homestead place on the sagebrush flats outside Silver Lake, Oregon. He tells of hiding under the bed with his sisters when strangers came to the gate. He grew up, as we all did in that country and era, believing that the one sure defense against the world was property. I was born in 1932, and recall a life before the end of World War II in which it was possible for a child to imagine that his family owned the world.

Warner Valley was largely swampland when my grandfather bought the MC Ranch with no downpayment in 1936, right at the heart of the Great Depression. The outside work was done mostly by men and horses and mules, and our ranch valley was filled with life. In 1937 my father bought his first track-layer, a secondhand RD6 Caterpillar he used to build a 17-mile diversion canal to carry the spring floodwater around the east side of the valley, and we were on our way to draining all swamps. The next year he bought an RD7 and a John Deere 36 combine which cut an 18-foot swath, and we were deeper into the dream of power over nature and men, which I had begun to inhabit while playing those long-ago games of war.

The peat ground left by the decaying remnants of ancient tule 10 beds was diked into huge undulating grainfields—Houston Swamp with 750 irrigated acres, Dodson Lake with 800—a final total of almost 8,000 acres under cultivation, and for reasons of what seemed like common sense and efficiency, the work became industrialized. Our artistry worked toward a model whose central image was the machine.

The natural patterns of drainage were squared into drag-line ditches, the tules and the aftermath of the oat and barley crops were burned—along with a little more of the combustible peat soil every year. We flood-irrigated when the water came in spring, drained in late March, and planted in a 24-hour-a-day frenzy which began around April 25 and ended—with luck—by the 10th of May, just as leaves on the Lombardy poplar were breaking from their buds. We summered our cattle on more than a million acres of Taylor Grazing Land across the high lava-rock and sagebrush desert out east of the valley, miles of territory where we owned most of what water there was, and it was ours. We owned it all, or so we felt. The government was as distant as news on the radio.

The most intricate part of my job was called "balancing water," a night-and-day process of opening and closing pipes and redwood headgates and running the 18-inch drainage pumps. That system was the finest plaything I ever had. And despite the mud and endless hours, the work remained play for a long time, the making of a thing both functional and elegant. We were doing God's labor and creating a good place on earth, living the pastoral yeoman dream—that's how our mythology defined it, although nobody would ever had thought to talk about work in that way.

And then it all went dead, over years, but swiftly.

You can imagine our surprise and despair, our sense of having been profoundly cheated. It took us a long while to realize some unnamable thing was wrong, and then we blamed it on ourselves, our inability to manage enough. But the fault wasn't ours, beyond the fact that we had all been educated to believe in a grand bad factory-land notion as our prime model of excellence.

15   We felt enormously betrayed. For so many years, through endless efforts, we had proceeded in good faith, and it turned out we had wrecked all we had not left untouched. The beloved migratory rafts of waterbirds, the green-headed mallards and the redheads and canvasbacks, the cinnamon teal and the great Canadian honkers, were mostly gone along with their swampland habitat. The hunting, in so many ways, was no longer what it had been.

We wanted to build a reservoir, and litigation started. Our laws were being used against us, by people who wanted a share of what we thought of as our water. We could not endure the boredom of our mechanical work, and couldn't hire anyone who cared enough to do it right. We baited the coyotes with 1080, and rodents destroyed our alfalfa; we sprayed weeds and insects with 2-4-D Ethyl and Malathion, and Parathion for clover mite, and we shortened our own lives. In quite an actual way we had come to victory in the artistry of our playground warfare against all that was naturally alive in our native home. We had reinvented our valley according to the most persuasive ideal given us by our culture, and we ended with a landscape organized like a machine for growing crops and fattening cattle, a machine that creaked a little louder each year, a dreamland gone wrong.

One of my strongest memories comes from a morning when I was maybe 10 years old, out on the lawn before our country home in spring, beneath a bluebird sky. I was watching the waterbirds coming off the valley swamps and grainfields where they had been feeding overnight. They were going north to nesting grounds on the Canadian tundra, and that piece of morning, inhabited by the sounds of their wings and their calling in the clean air, was wonder-filled and magical. I was enclosed in a living place.

No doubt that memory has persisted because it was a sight of possibility which I will always cherish—an image of the great good place rubbed smooth over the years like a river stone, which I touch again as I consider why life in Warner Valley went so seriously haywire. But never again in my lifetime will it be possible for a child to stand out on a bright spring morning in Warner Valley and watch the waterbirds come through in enormous, rafting, vee-shaped flocks of thousands—and I grieve.

My father is a very old man. A while back we were driving up the Bitterroot Valley of Montana, and he was gazing away to the mountains. "They'll never see it the way we did," he said, and I wonder what he saw.

We shaped our piece of the West according to the model provided 20 by our mythology, and instead of a great good place such order had given us enormous power over nature, and a blank perfection of fields.

Responding to Reading

1. What was work like on the MC Ranch when Kittredge's grandfather bought it in 1936? What does Kittredge mean when he says, "the work remained play for a long time, the making of a thing both functional and elegant" (12)? Why does Kittredge call this attitude toward work a "mythology" (12)?

2. What does Kittredge imply when he says, "we owned it all, or so we felt" (11)? What was the "factory-land notion" that he and his family had all "been educated to believe" (14)? Why did everyone feel betrayed?

3. Kittredge says that his family eventually came to operate the ranch "like a machine for growing crops and fattening cattle" (16). What was wrong with this method of running the ranch? According to Kittredge, how *should* his family have run the ranch? Is this proposal realistic?

Responding in Writing

Search the Internet for a description of farm work during the early part of the twentieth century. How is this description similar to or different from Kittredge's description of the work he did?

GIRL

Jamaica Kincaid

1949–

Born Elaine Potter Richardson in Saint Johns, Antigua-Barbuda, Jamaica Kincaid moved to the United States and worked as a nanny and a receptionist before attending the New School for Social Research in New York and Franconia College in New Hampshire. She has written for the New Yorker since 1976 and has taught at Bennington College and Harvard University. Kincaid writes novels, essays, and short stories and has published At the Bottom of the River *(1983),* Annie John *(1985),* Lucy *(1991),* The Autobiography of My Mother *(1996), and* Talk Stories *(2000). In the following short story, published in 1978, a young girl is being taught a lesson in life.*

Wash the white clothes on Monday and put them on the stone heap; wash the color clothes on Tuesday and put them on the clothesline to dry; don't walk barehead in the hot sun; cook pumpkin fritters in very hot sweet oil; soak your little cloths right after you take them off; when buying cotton to make yourself a nice blouse, be sure that it doesn't have gum on it, because that way it won't hold up well after a wash; soak salt fish overnight before you cook it; is it true that you sing benna in Sunday school?; always eat your food in such a way that it won't turn someone else's stomach; on Sundays try to walk like a lady and not like the slut you are so bent on becoming; don't sing benna in Sunday school; you mustn't speak to wharf-rat boys, not even to give directions; don't eat fruits on the street—flies will follow you; *but I don't sing benna on Sundays at all and never in Sunday school;* this is how to sew on a button; this is how to make a buttonhole for the button you have just sewed on; this is how to hem a dress when you see the hem coming down and so to prevent yourself from looking like the slut I know you are so bent on becoming; this is how you iron your father's khaki shirt so that it doesn't have a crease; this is how you iron your father's khaki pants so that they don't have a crease; this is how you grow okra—far from the house, because okra tree harbors red ants; when you are growing dasheen, make sure it gets plenty of water or else it makes your throat itch when you are eating it; this is how you sweep a corner; this is how you sweep a whole house; this is how you sweep a yard; this is how you smile to someone you don't like too much; this is how you smile to someone you don't like at all; this is how you smile to someone you like completely; this is how you set a table for tea; this is how you set a table for dinner; this is how you set a table for dinner with an important guest; this is how you set a table for lunch; this is how you set a table for breakfast; this is how to behave in the presence of men who don't know you very well, and this way they won't recognize immediately the slut I have warned you against becoming; be sure to wash every day, even if it is with your own spit; don't squat down to play marbles—you are not a boy, you know; don't pick people's flowers— you might catch something; don't throw stones at blackbirds, because it might not be a blackbird at all; this is how to make a bread pudding; this is how to make doukona; this is how to make pepper pot; this is how to make a good medicine for a cold; this is how to make a good medicine to throw away a child before it even becomes a child; this is how to catch a fish; this is how to throw back a fish you don't like, and that way something bad won't fall on you; this is how to bully a man; this is how a man bullies you; this is how to love a man, and if this doesn't work there are other ways, and if they don't work don't feel too bad about giving up; this is how to spit up in the air if you feel like it, and this is how to move quick so that it doesn't fall on you; this is how to make ends meet; always squeeze bread to make sure it's fresh; *but what if the baker won't let me feel the bread?*; you mean to say that after all you are really going to be the kind of women who the baker won't let near the bread?

Responding to Reading

1. How would you describe the kind of work the narrator of the story is being taught to do? Who is instructing her? Why must she learn the tasks she is being taught?

2. How old do you think the narrator is? Does she like the work she is being taught to do? What choices in life does she seem to have? What kind of future do you envision for her?

3. To whom is the narrator speaking? What clues in the story indicate what the listener is thinking?

Responding in Writing

Rewrite a portion of the story, filling in the responses of the silent listener to the narrator.

—————————— FOCUS ——————————

What Is a Living Wage?

A typical McDonald's restaurant.

Responding to the Image

1. What is your response to the golden arches? The signs? The adjacent playground? The flag? How do they reinforce the McDonald's company image?

2. Recently, some people have criticized McDonald's for its aggressive marketing to children. Do any details in the picture indicate that McDonald's is trying to appeal specifically to children?

THE POLITICS OF INEQUALITY
Manning Marable
1950–

Writer and activist Manning Marable was born in Dayton, Ohio, and earned an AB degree at Earlham College (1971), an MA degree at the University of Wisconsin, Madison (1972), and a PhD at the University of Maryland (1976). He is a professor of history and political science at Columbia University, where he directs the Institute for Research in African-American Studies. Marable has written hundreds of articles for academic journals, and his recent books include Black Liberation in Conservative America *(1997),* Black Leadership *(1998), and* What Black America Thinks: Race, Ideology, and Political Power *(2002). The following essay appeared in* Z Magazine Online, *http://zmag.org/, in December 1999.*

The fundamental issue that will define U.S. politics in the first decade of the twenty-first century is the spiraling growth of inequality in American life.

One might respond that "inequality" is not new in U.S. society, and has always existed. What is "new" is the degree of income stratification and class polarization we are now experiencing, which is really unlike anything since the Robber Barons of the nineteenth century's Gilded Era.

Most Americans know that household income levels are sharply stratified by race. For example, in 1998, the median household income for African Americans was $25,351, only 60 percent of the median white household income of $42,439. According to a recent report by United For a Fair Economy, "Shifting Fortunes," the average white household in 1995 had $18,000 in financial wealth (net worth minus equity in owner-occupied housing). By contrast, the average African American household possessed a grand total of two hundred dollars. The typical Hispanic household's financial wealth was zero.

But these statistics don't reveal the growing class stratification that in many ways cuts across racial boundaries. Alan Wolfe, the director of the Center for Religion and American Public Life, recently observed in the New York Times that "the 1990s will be remembered as a time of Reaganism without Reagan." During the decade, "the incomes of the best-off Americans have risen twice as fast as those of middle-class Americans." Back in 1980, the average top corporate executive's salary was 42 times higher than the median income of a factory worker. By 1998, the top executives were taking home 419 times more than factory workers.

Although Wolfe is not a political progressive, he makes some excellent points about the growing class hostility of most Americans about 5 the wealthy. "The fact that Americans hope to become rich does not mean that they admire the rich," Wolfe states. Corporate executives' salaries, stock options and company perks deeply trouble people "because such rewards have become disconnected from the efforts that go into earning them." The upper one percent of all U.S. households has a greater combined net wealth than the bottom ninety-five percent of all households.

Most working Americans resent all this, because through their practical experiences, they know that they are working harder and for longer hours, but their wages are smaller than a decade ago. Last August, the Economic Policy Institute reported that in 1997, the median inflation-adjusted earnings of the average worker were 3.1 percent lower than in 1989. Six out of ten U.S. workers earn either the same or less than they did ten years ago. The Economic Policy Institute also notes that the typical married couple family in the U.S. worked a total of 247 more hours in 1996 than in 1989. That is six additional weeks of work for less income.

The other dimension of income and class stratification is what is happening within the working class itself. There is increasingly a two-tiered stratification, a growing division between working class households whose incomes have held steady or slightly improved vs. the "working poor," people just above the poverty level but below the income level that would be a "living wage." Since the draconian Welfare Act of 1996, growing numbers of children are being trapped into poverty or near-poverty. In 1996, more than one in five children were poor, up from 16.4 percent in 1979. The Economic Policy Institute also notes that 39.9 percent of all African-American children and 40.3 percent of all Latino children live in poverty today.

The economic crisis for the poor and working poor can be measured in cities and states across the country. In New York State, for example, according to a recent study by the Fiscal Policy Institute, the number of New Yorkers in poverty increased by one-third since 1989 to 3 million. Twenty-five percent of the state's children, and 40 percent of the children in New York City, live in poverty. For New York State's working poor, "the median hourly wage fell 6.3 percent in the 1990s despite a 7.9 percent increase in productivity per worker." The median wages for New York State's black and Latino workers "fell at least one and a half times as much" as for white workers. In New York City, "the number of working poor families has jumped by 84 percent in the 1990s, more than three times greater than the U.S. increase." Conversely, the Wall Street bull market has affected only a small number of households. The top seven percent of New York's households, states that Fiscal Policy Institute, "receives 85 percent of all capital gains."

The challenges for black politics and the left is that most liberals and Democrats don't want to talk about class. After all, it was Clinton who signed the 1996 Welfare Act. Both political parties, in varying degrees, pursue policies that directly contribute to class stratification and the vast concentrations of wealth among the upper two or three percent of all U.S. households. One concrete step we may take to reverse these devastating trends should be to demand an increase and index in the minimum wage back to its 1968 level, which today would be $7.65 in inflation-adjusted dollars. We should also support the various campaigns for a living wage, which is defined as the amount of money necessary to support a family of four above the poverty level. In the past five years, living wage initiatives have been approved in 32 cities and counties nationwide, with over 70 other campaigns being waged currently. Some cities have now begun to establish a two-tiered living wage. In Detroit, for instance, jobs with benefits must be offered at a minimum of $8.25 per hour; for jobs without benefits, the living wage mandated is $10.29 per hour. In San Jose, city contractors are required to pay workers at least $9.50 per hour, double the minimum wage.

What does all this mean to the future of black politics? As powerful 10 as race and racism are in determining the life chances to African Americans, the politics of inequality will play a more significant and central role, both inside the black community, and in its relations with other groups. In short, class matters, and the battle for economic fairness will in many respects be the most fundamental factor in the future of African-American politics.

Responding to Reading

1. According to Marable, what is "the fundamental issue that will define U.S. politics in the first decade of the twenty-first century" (1)? Do you agree?
2. What does Marable mean when he says that household income levels "don't reveal the growing class stratification that in many ways cuts across racial boundaries" (4)? How has growing class stratification affected the working class? What evidence does Marable provide to support his assertion that an economic crisis exists "for the poor and working poor" (8)?
3. Who or what does Marable blame for the class stratification he discusses? What does he think should be done about this situation? Do you think Marable strengthens or weakens his case by concluding his essay with a discussion of African-American politics? Explain.

Responding in Writing

Write a short editorial, which could appear in your school newspaper, that agrees or disagrees with Marable's contention that workers who do not receive benefits should be paid $10.29 an hour. Use the situation of workers on your campus to support your position.

HARVARD, DO THE RIGHT THING

Tom Jehn

1967–

Born in Milwaukee, Wisconsin, Tom Jehn received a BA degree from the University of Chicago (1989) and an MA degree (1992) and PhD (2003) in English from the University of Virginia. Jehn was a founder and organizer of a living wage campaign when he was a student at the University of Virginia and a faculty organizer for the living wage campaign at Harvard University. He has taught in Harvard's Expository Writing Program since 1997, serving as an administrator of the program since 2000, and since 2001 has coordinated its Harvard Writing Project, a program dedicated to improving writing pedagogy throughout the University. He has also written about contemporary and historical political protests. The following opinion piece appeared in the Christian Science Monitor *in May 2001.*

Cambridge, Mass.

Harvard University's administrators know the value of a dollar, especially the $19 billion in its endowment. The leaders of the world's second-richest nonprofit also say they know the value of a moral education. But the students sitting-in at Massachusetts Hall to demand a living wage for the university's 1,000-plus lowest-paid employees know something Harvard's leaders have apparently forgotten: Justice for those who clean, guard, and cook for the campus every day is priceless.

Justice could come relatively cheaply. A living wage of $10.25 an hour for its lowest tier of workers—who, making as little as $6.50 an hour, must work two or three jobs just to meet basic daily needs like rent and food—would cost Harvard $10 million a year. That's equivalent to less than one-half of 1 percent of the annual interest on its endowment.

Any concern that raising the floor on wages would destabilize the local labor market and cool investment is unfounded. Since 1999, Harvard's hometown, Cambridge, has abided by a living wage ordinance guaranteeing $10 an hour for all employees working for the city and for firms with major city contracts. The sky hasn't fallen there, or in other municipalities across the country with living-wage policies.

What then prevents Harvard's leaders from doing what's right? Perhaps indifference to the idealism they have publicly championed before.

5   In 1998, Harvard conferred an honorary degree on *Nobel Peace Laureate Nelson Mandela*. Harvard President Neil Rudenstine hailed the man who had struggled against apartheid in South Africa for inspiring "the betters angels of our nature."

That day, the robed ranks of Harvard's best joined with 25,000 spectators to celebrate a moral vision. Mr. Rudenstine honored Mr. Mandela's devotion to a just cause and his reconciliation with those who had hurt him. Mandela graciously accepted his degree and said nothing of Harvard's long resistance to divesting from South African companies.

Instead, he appealed to our better angels, exhorting us to match deed to word. While Mandela addressed the obligations of rich nations to poor ones, his message spoke to Americans' aspirations for democracy: "We constantly need to remind ourselves that the freedoms which democracy brings will remain empty shells if they are not accompanied by real and tangible improvements in the material lives of . . . millions of ordinary citizens."

Where the daily degradations of poverty persist, Mandela stressed, "talk of democracy and freedom that does not recognize these material aspects, can ring hollow and erode confidence in exactly those values we seek to promote."

Harvard's leaders can afford to pay their workers a living wage. They cannot, however, afford the rhetoric of equality if they cannot grant employees the dignity they deserve. As one campus guard said, "It's not what you do to the most powerful person. It is how you treat the least powerful people that determines whether you have honor."

Responding to Reading

1. According to Jehn, what have Harvard's administrators forgotten? Why does Jehn begin his essay by saying what Harvard should do? Would his essay have been more effective if he had waited until his conclusion to present his suggestions?

2. Throughout his essay, Jehn compares the struggle of workers at Harvard to the struggle of Nelslon Mandela in South Africa. Do you think this comparison is justified? What are the implications of this association?

3. According to Jehn, what prevents the leaders of Harvard from "doing what's right" (4)? What does Jehn mean when he says that Harvard's leaders cannot "afford the rhetoric of equality if they cannot grant employees the dignity they deserve" (9)? Do you agree?

Responding in Writing

Suppose the situation Jehn describes was occurring at your school. How would you respond to Jehn's suggestions if adopting them meant a 10 percent increase in your tuition?

THE EMPLOYMENT EFFECTS
OF LIVING WAGE LAWS

Bruce Bartlett

1951–

Born in Ann Arbor, Michigan, Bruce Bartlett earned a BA degree from Rutgers University (1973) and an MA degree from Georgetown University (1976). He worked as a legislative assistant and economist for several members of the US Congress and as the Deputy Assistant Secretary for Economic Policy at the US Treasury Department. Bartlett is a senior fellow at the National Center for Policy Analysis in Washington, DC. His column on economic policy is published twice a week in the Washington Times *and is syndicated nationally. His articles have appeared in the* Wall Street Journal, *the* New York Times, *the* Los Angeles Times, *the* Washington Post, Fortune *magazine, and other publications. To read more about Bartlett, visit the National Center for Policy Analysis Web site, http:// www.ncpa.org/.*

For some years, liberal groups like ACORN (Association of Community Organizations for Reform Now) have been pushing hard to get so-called living wage laws enacted in cities and counties throughout the country. They have been extremely successful, with more than 60 jurisdictions having enacted living wage ordinances since the first in Baltimore in 1994.

Typically, living wage laws require city contractors to pay their employees a wage significantly higher than the minimum wage as a condition for doing business with the city. Living wage rates are often tied to the poverty-level income for a family of four. In 2000 this figure was $17,761 per year. The equivalent figure for a single person was just $8,959.

Thus one effect of a living wage law is to pay single people and two-earner couples considerably more than a living wage, as defined by the poverty level. The former would get $8,802 more than he really needs, while a two-earner couple where both work in jobs covered by a living wage law would make twice as much.

Of course, it would be illegal to pay people working the same job differently depending on whether they are married, single, have children or a working spouse. But at the same time, it is silly to treat every worker as if he or she is the sole wage earner in a four-person family, as living wage advocates do. In principle, people should be paid according to the value of their output, irrespective of race, age, sex, family status or other extraneous factor.

5   Living wage advocates are not interested in hearing about productivity, supply and demand, or anything else to do with economics.

Their campaign is based on nothing but emotion. They simply assert that people who work for companies doing business with local governments ought to be paid more those doing the same work in companies not doing business with government. No explanation is given for why this should be the case. Somehow or other, it is just the fair thing to do, we are told.

The truth is that living wage campaigns are mainly fronts for municipal employee unions. Their goal is to raise labor costs for potential competitors. If government contractors have to pay their workers more because of living wage laws, then they are less likely to replace traditional government workers. This makes it easier for government employee unions to demand higher wages for their members, because the option of saving money by contracting out has been undercut.

A new study from the Public Policy Institute of California by economist David Neumark documents this fact. He finds that existing government employees are the primary beneficiaries of living wage laws, even though such laws do not apply to them, only to government contractors. This is the main reason why he finds that living wage laws do in fact raise wages in places where they are enacted.

However, Neumark also finds, as economic theory would predict, that forcing up wages causes demand for labor to fall. The higher wages for some workers are offset by higher unemployment for others. The former would see a 3.5 percent increase in their income under a typical living wage law, while there would be a 7 percent increase in unemployment among low-wage workers.

Economic theory tells us that it is improper to make interpersonal comparisons of value. There is simply no way for an economist to say that one person's higher wages offset someone else's unemployment. Contrary to this standard practice, Mr. Neumark asserts that the higher incomes of those benefiting from living wage laws does in fact compensate for the lost income of those unemployed by the law. He bases this conclusion on data showing that poverty rates fell slightly where living wage laws were enacted. This has made Neumark a hero to the living wage crowd.

Neumark also seems to have forgotten that someone is paying the 10 bill for the higher wages. That person is the taxpayer, who must pay higher taxes for the same government services. He may pay again when businesses relocate from places where living wage laws are enacted, thus reducing the tax base. The actual cost of the living wage law may not be very much, but why would a business want to locate in a place where a bunch of left-wing nuts seem to be running the show? What will be next, businessmen have to wonder when deciding where to locate?

Economists have an expression, "There ain't no such thing as a free lunch." Government can't give anyone anything it hasn't first taken from someone else. Understanding this simple point is all that is necessary to see the basic lunacy of living wage laws.

Responding to Reading

1. What is a "living wage"? How does it differ from a minimum wage? According to Bartlett, why is it silly to treat each worker as if he or she is the head of a family? Why does Bartlett think that the living wage campaign is "based on nothing but emotion" (5)?
2. According to Bartlett, how do living wage laws hurt low-wage workers? How do they affect taxpayers and businesspeople?
3. Bartlett ends his essay with the cliché, "'There ain't no such thing as a free lunch'" (11). Is this an effective strategy, or should he have thought of a more original way to express his ideas? How do you think Tom Jehn (p. 598) would respond to Bartlett's points?

Responding in Writing

Consult the "help wanted" section of your local newspaper, and list three jobs that pay the minimum wage. Do you think the minimum wage is adequate compensation for the duties these jobs require?

——————— WIDENING THE FOCUS ———————

The following readings can suggest additional perspectives for thinking and writing about how to address the plight of minimum-wage workers in the United States. You may also want to do further research about this subject on the Internet.

- Jonathan Kozol, "The Human Cost of an Illiterate Society" (p. 212)

- Scott Russell Sanders, "The Men We Carry in Our Minds" (p. 408)

- Lars Eighner, "On Dumpster Diving" (p. 501)

For Internet Research: What is your view of the living wage campaign? Is it a misguided effort to force employers to introduce a welfare program into the workplace? Or, is the living wage campaign a sensible way to address the economic conditions of the working poor? Write an essay in which you take a stand on this issue, summarizing the arguments on both sides of the debate.

Search online for the term *living wage* using Yahoo!, Google, or other search engines. To get started, you may want to consult the following documents:

- "The Living Wage Issue Guide," published by the Economic Policy Institute, http://www.epinet.org/content.cfm/issueguides _livingwage_livingwage

- "Living Wage FAQs," published by the Employment Policies Institute, http://www.epionline.org/lw_faq.cfm

- "Choosing the High Road: Businesses That Pay a Living Wage and Prosper," published by Responsible Wealth, http://www .responsiblewealth.org/living_wage/Choosing.html

————————————————— **WRITING** —————————————————

Why We Work

1. In "Professions for Women," (p. 548) Virginia Woolf speaks of the difficulties women writers face—the "many ghosts to fight, many prejudices to overcome" (6). Apply Woolf's ideas about the struggle of women artists to a contemporary woman writer or artist with whose career you are familiar.

2. In "What Nurses Stand For" (p. 578), Suzanne Gordon say that the public's lack of concern about the layoffs of nurses "may be couched in the stereotypes of nursing or of women's work in general" (51). Interview several of your friends and family members about their attitudes toward nurses. Find out whether they see them as highly trained professionals or as people who perform menial tasks. Then, write an essay in which you discuss your findings.

3. Write an essay in which you describe the worst job you ever had.

4. List the uniforms you see on the workers you encounter in your daily life. After reading Paul Fussell's "Deliverers" (p. 571), write an essay in which you discuss how these uniforms help to establish the images the companies wish to project. How successful do you think these uniforms are in projecting this message? How do the uniforms affect your impressions of the companies and of the workers themselves? If you like, you can also refer to Eric Schlosser's "Behind the Counter" (p. 560) and Barbara Ehrenreich's "Selling in Minnesota" (p. 567).

5. In "The Second Shift" (p. 554), Arlie Hochschild says that both society and the government should institute new policies that would allow workers to have more time at home. Write an essay in which you summarize Hochschild's ideas and explain in detail why people need more time with their families. Make sure that you refer specifically to Hochschild's essay.

6. In "Professions for Women" (p. 548), Virginia Woolf sees work as a way to achieve her full potential as a human being. In "Why We Work," (p. 543), however, Andrew Curry makes the point that most workers feel negatively about their jobs. Which of these two views of work do you hold? Write an essay in which you give the reasons for your belief. Illustrate your points with your own experiences as well as references to the essays by Woolf and Curry.

7. Imagine that you have been asked by your former high school to address this year's graduating class about how to get part-time and summer jobs to offset the high cost of college. Remember, your speech is supposed to be inspirational, but it is also supposed to contain specific advice.

8. Do you agree with Henry Louis Gates's contention that colleges place too much emphasis on sports—especially when it concerns the African-American athlete (see "Delusions of Grandeur," p. 575)? If you agree with Gates, present specific suggestions for rectifying the situation. If you do not agree with Gates, show where in the essay he is in error.

9. Suppose that you were attending the Wal-Mart orientation with Barbara Ehrenreich (see "Selling in Minnesota," p. 567). Write a letter to the manager of the store in which you point out the shortcomings of the program as well as your suggestions for improving it. Support your points with specific references to Ehrenreich's essay.

10. After reading the three essays in the Focus section of this chapter—Manning Marable's "The Politics of Inequality" (p. 595), Tom Jehn's "Harvard, Do the Right Thing" (p. 598), and Bruce Bartlett's "The Employment Effects of Living Wage Laws" (p. 600)—write an essay in which you answer the question "What Is a Living Wage?"

9

MEDICINE AND
HUMAN VALUES

PREPARING TO READ AND WRITE

Because medical science has made such great advances, it is easy to forget that until the 1930s, doctors could do little more than diagnose most diseases. With the discovery of sulfa drugs and penicillin, the situation changed dramatically, and physicians were actually able to cure diseases that had devastated human populations for centuries. Since the mid-1970s, medical science has made tremendous advances toward understanding basic biological processes and prolonging human life. Recently, however, new diseases and new forms of old diseases have

Engraving showing patients dying of the Plague in the streets of a seventeenth-century European city.

threatened to wipe out these gains. For example, AIDS, a disease almost unheard of thirty years ago, afflicts millions of people worldwide, and tuberculosis in new drug-resistant forms is making a deadly comeback in American cities. More recently, SARS (Severe Acute Respiratory Syndrome), first reported in Asia in 2003, spread over the next few months to more than two dozen countries. These developments suggest that scientists may have to face the uncomfortable fact that in the near future, epidemics might be as common as they were a hundred years ago.

Like our gains against disease, our advances in medical technology have proved to be a mixed blessing. Although doctors are armed with an array of high-tech equipment, they must face problems this technology has created. For example, how far should doctors go to preserve human life? At what point, if any, does a life become not worth saving? Ironically, as we are spending hundreds of millions of dollars on medical technology, we have not yet found a way to provide health care for the over 40 million people who cannot afford health insurance. These and other complex problems—such as soaring medical costs—that beset our health-care delivery systems will undoubtedly continue to challenge us well into the twenty-first century.

The Focus section of this chapter addresses the question "What is happening to medical care?" The essays in this section examine the quality of health care in the United States. For example, what is the

Chinese newlyweds wearing face masks for protection from SARS, 2003.

effect of managed care on both patients and physicians? Have the large number of malpractice suits and the high cost of malpractice insurance changed the way medicine is being practiced? Should limits be placed on the amount of money juries can award to plaintiffs? Finally, given the financial realities of the marketplace, can Americans continue to receive the high level of care they now take for granted?

As you read and prepare to write about the essays in this chapter, you may consider the following questions:

- Is the writer a physician? A scientist? A layperson? Does the writer's background make you more or less receptive to his or her ideas?

- On what issue does the writer focus?

- What position does the writer take on the issue? Do you agree or disagree with this position?

- Is the writer's emphasis on the theory or on the practice of medicine?

- What preconceptions do you have about the issue? Does the essay reinforce or contradict your preconceptions?

- What background in science or medicine does the writer assume readers have?

- Is the writer optimistic or pessimistic about the future of medicine? About the future in general?

- Is the writer's purpose to educate? To make readers think about a provocative idea? To persuade them? To warn them?

- In what ways is the essay similar to or different from others in this chapter?

THE BITTERSWEET SCIENCE

Austin Bunn

1973–

Journalist Austin Bunn writes articles and reviews on a wide variety of topics, including border patrols, books, and video games. A native of Princeton, New Jersey, Bunn graduated from Yale University. His work has appeared in the Village Voice, Salon, *the* Advocate, *and the* New York Times Magazine, *where the following essay, which traces the history of diabetes*

*and the discovery of insulin, appeared in March 2003. To read more of
Bunn's articles, visit his Web site: http://austinbunn.com/.*

Eleven-year-old Elizabeth Hughes was, in retrospect, the ideal patient: bright, obedient, uncomplaining and wholly unprepared to die.
Born in 1907 in the New York State governor's mansion, Elizabeth
was the daughter of Charles Evans Hughes, who later became a justice on the Supreme Court, ran against Woodrow Wilson in 1916 and
served as secretary of state under Harding.

Elizabeth had a perfectly normal, aristocratic youth until she
seemed to become allergic to childhood. She would come home from
friends' birthday parties with an insatiable thirst, drinking almost two
quarts of water at a sitting. By winter, she had become thin, constantly hungry and exhausted. Her body turned into a sieve: no matter how much water she drank, she was always thirsty.

In early 1919, Elizabeth's parents took her to a mansion in Morris-
town, N.J., recently christened the Physiatric Institute and run by Dr.
Frederick Allen. A severe, debt-ridden clinician with a pockmarked
résumé, Allen had written the authoritative account on treating her
condition. He prolonged hundreds of lives and was the girl's best
chance. Allen examined Elizabeth and diagnosed diabetes—her body
was not properly processing her food into fuel—and told her parents
what they would never tell their daughter: that her life expectancy
was one year, three at the outside. Even that was a magnificent extension of previous fatality rates. "The diagnosis was like knowing a
death sentence had been passed," wrote one historian. Then Dr. Allen
did what many doctors at the time would have done for Elizabeth, except that this doctor was exceptionally good, if not the finest in the
world, at it. He began to starve her.

The history of medicine "is like the night sky," says the historian
Roy Porter in his book "The Greatest Benefit to Mankind: A Medical
History of Humanity." "We see a few stars and group them into
mythic constellations. What is chiefly visible is the darkness."

Diabetes doesn't come from simply eating too much sugar; nor is 5
it cured, as was once thought, by a little horseback riding. It is not the
result of a failing kidney, overactive liver or phlegmy disposition,
though these were the authoritative answers for centuries. Diabetes
happens when the blood becomes saturated with glucose, the body's
main energy source, which is normally absorbed by the cells—which
is to say that the pathology of diabetes is subtle and invisible, so much
so that a third of the people who have it don't even know it. Until the
prohibition against autopsies was gradually lifted (by 1482, the pope
had informally sanctioned it), what we knew of human anatomy came
through the tiny window of war wounds and calamitous gashes—and
even then it took centuries for doctors to decide just what the long,
lumpy organ called the pancreas actually did or, in the case of

diabetes, didn't do. We like to think surgically about the history of medicine, that it moved purposefully from insight to insight, angling closer to cure. But that is only the luxury of contemporary life. Looked at over time, medicine doesn't advance as much as grope forward, with remedies—like bloodletting, quicksilver ointments and simple, unendurable hunger—that blurred the line between treatment and torture.

Diabetes was first diagnosed by the Greek physician Aretaeus of Cappadocia, who deemed it a "wonderful affection . . . being a melting down of the flesh and limbs into urine." For the afflicted, "life is disgusting and painful; thirst unquenchable . . . and one cannot stop them from drinking or making water." Since the classical period forbade dissection, Porter notes, "hidden workings had to be deduced largely from what went in and what came out." An early diagnostic test was to swill urine, and to the name diabetes, meaning "siphon," was eventually added "mellitus," meaning "sweetened with honey." Healers could often diagnose diabetes without the taste test. Black ants were attracted to the urine of those wasting away, drawn by the sugar content. Generations later, doctors would make a similar deduction by spotting dried white sugar spots on the shoes or pants of diabetic men with bad aim.

For the Greeks, to separate disease symptoms from individual pain while isolating them from magical causes was itself an enormous intellectual leap. "We should be really impressed with Aretaeus," says Dr. Chris Feudtner, author of the coming "Bittersweet: Diabetes, Insulin and the Transformation of Illness." "He was able to spot the pattern of diabetes in a dense thicket of illness and suffering."

But for centuries, this increasing precision in disease recognition was not followed by any effective treatment—more details didn't make physicians any less helpless. At the time, they were unknowingly confusing two kinds of diabetes: Type 1, known until recently as "juvenile diabetes," which is more extreme but less common than Type 2, or "adult onset," which seems to be related to obesity and overeating. With Type 1 (what Elizabeth Hughes had), the pancreas stops secreting insulin, a hormone that instructs the body to use the sugar in the blood for energy. With Type 2, the pancreas produces insulin (at least initially), but the tissues of the body stop responding appropriately. By 1776, doctors were still just boiling the urine of diabetics to conclusively determine that they were passing sugar, only to watch their patients fall into hyperglycemic comas and die.

If dangerous levels of glucose were pumping out of diabetics, one idea was obvious: stop it from going in. That demanded a more sophisticated understanding of food itself. In the long tradition of grotesque scientific experimentation, an insight came through a lucky break: a gaping stomach wound. In 1822, William Beaumont, a surgeon in the U.S. Army, went to the Canadian border to treat a 19-year-old trapper hit by a shotgun. The boy recovered, but he was left with a hole in his abdomen. According to Porter, Beaumont "took advantage of his patient's unique window" and dropped food in on a string. The seasoned beef took the longest to digest. Stale bread broke down the quickest. The digestion process clearly worked differently depending on what was eaten. Then during the 1871 siege of Paris by the Germans, a French doctor named Apollinaire Bouchardat noticed that, though hundreds were starving to death, his diabetic patients strangely improved. This became the basis for a new standard of treatment. Mangez le moins possible, he advised them. Eat as little as possible.

In the spring of 1919, when Elizabeth Hughes came under Dr. 10 Allen's care, she weighed 75 pounds and was nearly 5 feet tall. For one week, he fasted her. Then he put her on an extremely low-calorie diet to eradicate sugar from her urine. If the normal caloric intake for a girl her age is between 2,200 and 2,400 calories daily, Elizabeth took in 400 to 600 calories a day for several weeks, including one day of fasting each week. Her weight, not surprisingly, plummeted. As Michael Bliss notes in his book "The Discovery of Insulin," the Hughes family brought in a nurse to help weigh and supervise every gram of food that she ate. Desserts and bread were verboten. "She lived on lean meat, eggs, lettuce, milk, a few fruits, tasteless bran rusks and tasteless vegetables (boiled three times to make them almost totally carbohydrate-free)," Bliss writes. Instead of a birthday cake, she had to settle for "a hat box covered in pink and white paper with candles on it. On picnics in the summertime she had her own little frying pan to cook her omelet in while the others had chops, fresh fish, corn on the cob and watermelon."

You could say that Elizabeth Hughes was on a twisted precursor of the Zone diet: her menu relied on proteins and fats, with the abolishment of carbohydrates like bread and pasta. In fact, Allen's maniacal scrutiny of his patients' nutrition—fasting them, weighing each meal, counting calories—was one of the first "diets" in the modern sense. At the time Elizabeth entered the clinic, being well fed was a sign of good health. But the new science of nutrition fostered the idea of weight reduction as a standard of health and not illness.

Allen's "starvation diet" was a particular cruelty. Patients came to him complaining of hunger and rapid weight loss, and Allen demanded further restrictions, further weight loss. "Yes, the method was severe; yes, many patients could not or would not follow it," writes Bliss. "But what was the alternative?" Over the years, doctors recommended opium, even heaps of sugar (which only accelerated death, but since nothing else worked, why not enjoy the moment?). But nobody had a better way than Allen to extend lives. If the fasting wasn't working and symptoms got worse, Allen insisted on more rigorous undernourishment. In his campaigns to master their disease, Allen took his patients right to the edge of death, but he justified this by pointing out that patients faced a stark choice: die of diabetes or risk "inanition," which Allen explained as "starvation due to inability to acquire tolerance for any living diet." The Physiatric Institute became a famine ward.

Some of Allen's patients survived levels of inanition not thought possible, Bliss writes. One 12-year-old patient, blind from diabetes when he was admitted, still occasionally showed sugar in his urine. The clinic became convinced that the kid—so weak he could barely get out of bed—was somehow stealing food. "It turned out that his supposed helplessness was the very thing that gave him opportunities which other persons lacked," Allen later wrote in his book, "Total Dietary Regulation in the Treatment of Diabetes." "Among unusual things eaten were toothpaste and birdseed, the latter being obtained from the cage of a canary which he had asked for." The staff, thinking he was pilfering food, cut his diet back and further back. The boy weighed less than 40 pounds when he died from starvation.

No one explained to Elizabeth Hughes why the friends she made at Allen's clinic stopped writing her letters. Death was kept hidden, though it must have been obvious from the halls of the clinic, where rows of gaunt children stared from their beds. "It would have been unendurable if only there had not been so many others," one Allen nurse wrote. Dutifully, Elizabeth—strong enough just to read and sew—hardly ever showed sugar. Her attendant punished her severely the one time she caught her stealing turkey skin from the kitchen after Thanksgiving. Still, she was wasting away. By April 1921, 13 years old and two years into her treatment, Elizabeth was down to 52 pounds and averaged 405 calories a day. In letters to her parents, she talked about getting married and what she would do on her 21st birthday. Reading the letters "must have been heartbreaking," writes Bliss. "Elizabeth was a semi-invalid."

15   In the history of illness, there are countless medicines, over time and across cultures, with varying degrees of suffering and success. There is only one kind of cure—the one that invariably, irrefutably works. Insulin is not a cure. It is a treatment, but it changed everything. In the summer of 1922, two young clinicians in Toronto named Frederick Banting and Charles Best surgically removed the pancreases from dozens of dogs, causing the dogs to "get" diabetes. They found that by injecting the dogs with a filtered solution of macerated pancreas (either the dogs' own or from calf fetuses), the glucose level in the dogs' blood dropped to normal. The researchers had discovered insulin.

But in August 1922, Dr. Frederick Allen had patients who could not wait, like Elizabeth. Allen left for Toronto to secure insulin. While he was gone, word leaked through his clinic about the breakthrough. Patients "who had not been out of bed for weeks began to trail weakly about, clinging to walls and furniture," wrote one nurse. "Big stomachs, skin-and-bone necks, skull-like faces . . . they looked like an old Flemish painter's depiction of a resurrection after famine. It was a resurrection, a crawling stirring, as of some vague springtime."

On the night Allen returned to the clinic, he found his patients— "silent as the bloated ghosts they looked like"—waiting in the hallway for him, wrote the nurse. "When he appeared through the open doorway, he caught the full beseeching of a hundred pair of eyes. It stopped him dead. Even now I am sure it was minutes before he spoke to them. . . . 'I think,' he said. 'I think we have something for you.'"

He did, but not nearly enough. Though the results were striking—with the insulin, sugar vanished from the urine of "some of the most hopelessly severe cases of diabetes I have ever seen," wrote Allen—he did not have enough extract to treat all his patients, including Elizabeth. So her parents got her to Toronto. When Banting saw Elizabeth, she was three days away from her 15th birthday. She weighed 45 pounds. He wrote: "Patient extremely emaciated . . . hair brittle and thin . . . muscles extremely wasted. . . . She was scarcely able to walk."

He started her insulin treatment immediately. The first injections cleared the sugar from her urine, and by the end of the first week, she was up to 1,220 calories a day, still without sugar. By the next, she was at 2,200 calories. Banting advised her to eat bread and potatoes, but she was incredulous. It had been three and a half years since she had them. That fall, she was one of several hundred North American diabetics pulled back from the edge. By November, she went home to her parents in Washington, and by January, she weighed 105 pounds. The same year, the 31-year-old Banting won the Nobel Prize. Meanwhile, Dr. Allen, proprietor of an expensive clinic whose patients no longer needed him, went broke. Insulin was a miracle drug, resurrecting diabetics from comas and putting flesh on skeletons and, since it needed to be administered at least twice daily, it was a miracle that would be performed over and over. The era of chronic medical care had begun.

That may be the most poignant part of the history of Allen's 20 clinic. The end of the famine of Elizabeth Hughes is really the start of another hunger: for the drugs that will keep us well for the rest of our lives. Elizabeth went to Barnard, reared three children, drank and smoked but kept her diabetes a secret almost her entire life. She died of a heart attack in 1981, more than 43,000 injections of insulin later. But if the discovery of insulin took away the terror of diabetes, it replaced the miraculous with the routine. Healing lost one major ingredient: awe. "To think that I'll be leading a normal, healthy existence is beyond all comprehension," Elizabeth wrote to her mother, days after her first injection, in 1922. "It is simply too wonderful for words."

Responding to Reading

1. What does Bunn mean when he says, "Looked at over time, medicine doesn't advance as much as grope forward, with remedies . . . that blurred the line between treatment and torture" (5)? Why did it take so long for physicians to diagnose diabetes? How did the final "breakthrough" in diagnosis take place?
2. What treatment did Dr. Allen prescribe for Elizabeth Hughes? Why was this treatment considered unorthodox? Why did it work? Why, according to Bunn, was this treatment "a particular cruelty" (12)?
3. What effect did the discovery of insulin in 1922 have on the patents in Dr. Allen's clinic? What happened to Dr. Allen after the discovery of insulin? What does Bunn mean when he says that with the discovery of insulin, "the era of chronic medical care had begun" (18)?

Responding in Writing

Think of a friend or relative who has a medical condition that has existed over a long period of time—for example, asthma or heart disease. How has this person's treatment changed over the years? In what ways have these different treatments affected this person's quality of life?

THE TURBID EBB AND FLOW OF MISERY

Margaret Sanger

1883–1966

Born in Corning, New York, Margaret Sanger worked for many years as a public health nurse in New York City. The appalling conditions she witnessed among the city's poor led her to become an early advocate for birth control. Although Sanger publicly argued that having fewer children would improve the health and economic condition of poor families, her reasons for advocating birth control were complex. On the one hand, she saw birth control as a way of liberating women from the fear of pregnancy. On the other hand, she regarded family planning as a method of limiting the proliferation of those elements in society whom she saw as "unfit." Whatever her motives, it is clear that without Sanger's dedication and tireless work, the birth control movement would not have been as successful as it was. She opened the first birth control clinic in the United States in Brooklyn, New York, in 1916 and was arrested and sentenced to thirty days in jail. Eventually, she became president of the National Committee on Federal Legislation for Birth Control and was instrumental in the adoption of laws that legalized medically super-

vised birth control throughout the United States. The following essay is from Sanger's 1938 autobiography.

Every night and every morn
Some to misery are born.
Every morn and every night
Some are born to sweet delight.
Some are born to sweet delight,
Some are born to endless night.

—William Blake

During these years [about 1912] in New York trained nurses were in great demand. Few people wanted to enter hospitals; they were afraid they might be "practiced" upon, and consented to go only in desperate emergencies. Sentiment was especially vehement in the matter of having babies. A woman's own bedroom, no matter how inconveniently arranged, was the usual place for her lying-in. I was not sufficiently free from domestic duties to be a general nurse, but I could ordinarily manage obstetrical cases because I was notified far enough ahead to plan my schedule. And after serving my two weeks I could get home again.

Sometimes I was summoned to small apartments occupied by young clerks, insurance salesmen, or lawyers, just starting out, most of them under thirty and whose wives were having their first or second baby. They were always eager to know the best and latest method in infant care and feeding. In particular, Jewish patients, whose lives centered around the family, welcomed advice and followed it implicitly.

But more and more my calls began to come from the Lower East Side, as though I were being magnetically drawn there by some force outside my control. I hated the wretchedness and hopelessness of the poor, and never experienced that satisfaction in working among them that so many noble women have found. My concern for my patients was now quite different from my earlier hospital attitude. I could see that much was wrong with them which did not appear in the physiological or medical diagnosis. A woman in childbirth was not merely a woman in childbirth. My expanded outlook included a view of her background, her potentialities as a human being, the kind of children she was bearing, and what was going to happen to them.

The wives of small shopkeepers were my most frequent cases, but I had carpenters, truck drivers, dishwashers, and pushcart vendors. I admired intensely the consideration most of these people had for their own. Money to pay doctor and nurse had been carefully saved months in advance—parents-in-law, grandfathers, grandmothers, all contributing.

5   As soon as the neighbors learned that a nurse was in the building they came in a friendly way to visit, often carrying fruit, jellies, or gefüllter fish made after a cherished recipe. It was infinitely pathetic to me that they, so poor themselves, should bring me food. Later they drifted in again with the excuse of getting the plate, and sat down for a nice talk; there was no hurry. Always back of the little gift was the question, "I am pregnant (or my daughter, or my sister is). Tell me something to keep from having another baby. We cannot afford another yet."

I tried to explain the only two methods I had ever heard of among the middle classes, both of which were invariably brushed aside as unacceptable. They were of no certain avail to the wife because they placed the burden of responsibility solely upon the husband—a burden which he seldom assumed. What she was seeking was self-protection she could herself use, and there was none.

Below this stratum of society was one in truly desperate circumstances. The men were sullen and unskilled, picking up odd jobs now and then, but more often unemployed, lounging in and out of the house at all hours of the day and night. The women seemed to slink on their way to market and were without neighborliness.

These submerged, untouched classes were beyond the scope of organized charity or religion. No labor union, no church, not even the Salvation Army reached them. They were apprehensive of everyone and rejected help of any kind, ordering all intruders to keep out; both birth and death they considered their own business. Social agents, who were just beginning to appear, were profoundly mistrusted because they pried into homes and lives, asking questions about wages, how many were in the family, had any of them ever been in jail. Often two or three had been there or were now under suspicion of prostitution, shoplifting, purse snatching, petty thievery, and, in consequence, passed furtively by the big blue uniforms on the corner.

The utmost depression came over me as I approached this surreptitious region. Below Fourteenth Street I seemed to be breathing a different air, to be in another world and country where the people had habits and customs alien to anything I had ever heard about.

10   There were then approximately ten thousand apartments in New York into which no sun ray penetrated directly; such windows as they had opened only on a narrow court from which rose fetid odors. It was seldom cleaned, though garbage and refuse often went down into it. All these dwellings were pervaded by the foul breath of poverty, that moldy, indefinable, indescribable smell which cannot be fumigated out, sickening to me but apparently unnoticed by those who lived there. When I set to work with antiseptics, their pungent sting, at least temporarily, obscured the stench.

I remember one confinement case to which I was called by the doctor of an insurance company. I climbed up the five flights and entered the airless rooms, but the baby had come with too great speed. A boy of ten had been the only assistant. Five flights was a long way; he had wrapped the placenta in a piece of newspaper and dropped it out the window into the court.

Many families took in "boarders," as they were termed, whose small contributions paid the rent. These derelicts, wanderers, alternately working and drinking, were crowded in with the children; a single room sometimes held as many as six sleepers. Little girls were accustomed to dressing and undressing in front of the men, and were often violated, occasionally by their own fathers or brothers, before they reached the age of puberty.

Pregnancy was a chronic condition among the women of this class. Suggestions as to what to do for a girl who was "in trouble" or a married woman who was "caught" passed from mouth to mouth— herb teas, turpentine, steaming, rolling downstairs, inserting slippery elm, knitting needles, shoe-hooks. When they had word of a new remedy they hurried to the drugstore, and if the clerk were inclined to be friendly he might say, "Oh, that won't help you, but here's something that may." The younger druggists usually refused to give advice because, if it were to be known, they would come under the law; midwives were even more fearful. The doomed women implored me to reveal the "secret" rich people had, offering to pay me extra to tell them; many really believed I was holding back information for money. They asked everybody and tried anything, but nothing did them any good. On Saturday nights I have seen groups of from fifty to one hundred with their shawls over their heads waiting outside the office of a five-dollar abortionist.

Each time I returned to this district, which was becoming a recurrent nightmare, I used to hear that Mrs. Cohen "had been carried to a hospital, but had never come back," or that Mrs. Kelly "had sent the children to a neighbor and had put her head into the gas oven." Day after day such tales were poured into my ears—a baby born dead, great relief—the death of an older child, sorrow but again relief of a sort—the story told a thousand times of death from abortion and children going into institutions. I shuddered with horror as I listened to the details and studied the reasons back of them—destitution linked with excessive childbearing. The waste of life seemed utterly senseless. One by one worried, sad, pensive, and aging faces marshaled themselves before me in my dreams, sometimes appealingly, sometimes accusingly.

These were not merely "unfortunate conditions among the poor" 15 such as we read about. I knew the women personally. They were living, breathing, human beings, with hopes, fears, and aspirations like my own, yet their weary, misshapen bodies, "always ailing, never failing," were destined to be thrown on the scrap heap before they were thirty-five. I could not escape from the facts of their wretchedness; neither was I able to see any way out. My own cozy and comfortable family existence was becoming a reproach to me.

Then one stifling mid-July day of 1912 I was summoned to a Grand Street tenement. My patient was a small, slight Russian Jewess, about twenty-eight years old, of the special cast of feature to which suffering lends a madonna-like expression. The cramped three-room apartment was in a sorry state of turmoil. Jake Sachs, a truck driver scarcely older than his wife, had come home to find the three children crying and her unconscious from the effects of a self-induced abortion. He had called the nearest doctor, who in turn had sent for me. Jake's earnings were trifling, and most of them had gone to keep the none-too-strong children clean and properly fed. But his wife's ingenuity had helped them to save a little, and this he was glad to spend on a nurse rather than have her go to a hospital.

The doctor and I settled ourselves to the task of fighting the septicemia. Never had I worked so fast, never so concentratedly. The sultry days and nights were melted into a torpid inferno. It did not seem possible there could be such heat, and every bit of food, ice, and drugs had to be carried up three flights of stairs.

Jake was more kind and thoughtful than many of the husbands I had encountered. He loved his children, and had always helped his wife wash and dress them. He had brought water up and carried garbage down before he left in the morning, and did as much as he could for me while he anxiously watched her progress.

After a fortnight Mrs. Sachs' recovery was in sight. Neighbors, ordinarily fatalistic as to the results of abortion, were genuinely pleased that she had survived. She smiled wanly at all who came to see her and thanked them gently, but she could not respond to their hearty congratulations. She appeared to be more despondent and anxious than she should have been, and spent too much time in meditation.

20　　At the end of three weeks, as I was preparing to leave the fragile patient to take up her difficult life once more, she finally voiced her fears, "Another baby will finish me, I suppose?"

"It's too early to talk about that," I temporized.

But when the doctor came to make his last call, I drew him aside. "Mrs. Sachs is terribly worried about having another baby."

"She well may be," replied the doctor, and then he stood before her and said, "Any more such capers, young woman, and there'll be no need to send for me."

"I know, doctor," she replied timidly, "but," and she hesitated as though it took all her courage to say it, "what can I do to prevent it?"

25　　The doctor was a kindly man, and he had worked hard to save her, but such incidents had become so familiar to him that he had long since lost whatever delicacy he might once have had. He laughed good-naturedly. "You want to have your cake and eat it too, do you? Well, it can't be done."

Then picking up his hat and bag to depart he said, "Tell Jake to sleep on the roof."

I glanced quickly at Mrs. Sachs. Even through my sudden tears I could see stamped on her face an expression of absolute despair. We simply looked at each other, saying no word until the door had closed behind the doctor. Then she lifted her thin, blue-veined hands and clasped them beseechingly. "He can't understand. He's only a man. But you do, don't you? Please tell me the secret, and I'll never breathe it to a soul. *Please!*"

What was I to do? I could not speak the conventionally comforting phrases which would be of no comfort. Instead, I made her as physically easy as I could and promised to come back in a few days to talk with her again. A little later, when she slept, I tiptoed away.

Night after night the wistful image of Mrs. Sachs appeared before me. I made all sorts of excuses to myself for not going back. I was busy on other cases; I really did not know what to say to her or how to convince her of my own ignorance; I was helpless to avert such monstrous atrocities. Time rolled by and I did nothing.

The telephone rang one evening three months later, and Jake   30
Sachs' agitated voice begged me to come at once; his wife was sick again and from the same cause. For a wild moment I thought of sending someone else, but actually, of course, I hurried into my uniform, caught up my bag, and started out. All the way I longed for a subway wreck, an explosion, anything to keep me from having to enter that home again. But nothing happened, even to delay me. I turned into the dingy doorway and climbed the familiar stairs once more. The children were there, young little things.

Mrs. Sachs was in a coma and died within ten minutes. I folded her still hands across her breast, remembering how they had pleaded with me, begging so humbly for the knowledge which was her right. I drew a sheet over her pallid face. Jake was sobbing, running his hands through his hair and pulling it out like an insane person. Over and over again he wailed, "My God! My God! My God!"

I left him pacing desperately back and forth, and for hours I myself walked and walked and walked through the hushed streets. When I finally arrived home and let myself quietly in, all the household was sleeping. I looked out my window and down upon the dimly lighted city. Its pains and griefs crowded in upon me, a moving picture rolled before my eyes with photographic clearness: women writhing in travail to bring forth little babies; the babies themselves naked and hungry, wrapped in newspapers to keep them from the cold; six-year-old children with pinched, pale, wrinkled faces, old in concentrated wretchedness, pushed into gray and fetid cellars, crouching on stone floors, their small scrawny scuttling through rags, making lamp shades, artificial flowers; white coffins, black coffins, coffins, coffins interminably passing in never-ending succession. The scenes piled one upon another on another. I could bear it no longer.

As I stood there the darkness faded. The sun came up and threw its reflection over the house tops. It was the dawn of a new day in my life also. The doubt and questioning, the experimenting and trying, were now to be put behind me. I knew I could not go back merely to keeping people alive.

I went to bed, knowing that no matter what it might cost, I was finished with palliatives and superficial cures; I was resolved to seek out the root of evil, to do something to change the destiny of mothers whose miseries were vast as the sky.

Responding to Reading

1. What social classes does Sanger discuss? According to Sanger, what are the characteristics of each social class? Which is most needy? Why?
2. Why does Sanger tell the story of Mrs. Sachs? How did her situation change the direction of Sanger's life?
3. What attitudes does Sanger have toward her patients? Does she see them as her equals, or does she think she is better than they are? How can you tell?

Responding in Writing

Reread the headnote that precedes this essay. Do you think Sanger's motives for advocating birth control diminish her achievements in any way? Why or why not?

THE METAPHOR OF BLIGHT

Abraham Verghese

1955–

Born in Addis Ababa, Ethiopia, Abraham Verghese is a dean at the Center for Medical Humanities and Ethics in the School of Medicine at the University of Texas Health Science Center at San Antonio. He earned an MD at Madras University in Madras, India (1979), and an MFA degree from the Writer's Workshop at the University of Iowa (1991). His books include My Own Country: A Doctor's Story of a Town and Its People in the Age of AIDS *(1994) and* The Tennis Partner: A Story of Friendship and Loss *(1998), about coming to terms with the death of his best friend. In the following essay, which appeared in the* Wall Street Journal *in May 2003, Verghese discusses the breakout of severe acute respiratory syndrome (SARS).*

China's shame, Hong Kong's misfortune, America's good luck—
this is how we in America seem to view the disease severe acute respiratory syndrome (SARS), an illness caused by a virus whose
genetic vocabulary neither encodes for such adjectives, nor recognizes sovereign boundaries. Indeed, the tendency to ascribe
metaphors to disease (as Susan Sontag pointed out some years ago)
is a uniquely human enterprise, absurd on the one hand, and inevitable on the other.

Such metaphors take root and hold sway; they dictate our emotional responses to a disease. Thus, the cancer metaphor is historically
(and quite unfairly) one of failure, or personal weakness—cancer happens to the Hubert Humphreys of the world, to the perennial
runners-up. The metaphor of tuberculosis, by contrast, is that of unbridled passion affecting sensitive souls such as Keats.

SARS quickly became invested with its own metaphors, and, just
as when AIDS first came on the scene, the dominant metaphor of
SARS was that of a medieval plague. And plague, whether medieval
or postmodern, needs its scapegoats and its sacrificial lambs.

The SARS virus sprang up in a part of China known for its exotic
cuisine. The markets and kitchens of Canton (now Guangdong) could
in other times have been the subject for a colorful and even mouthwa-
tering story on one of the cable food channels. But in light of SARS,
that story has been recast as an epic and cautionary tale, the emphasis
no longer gustatory, but apocalyptic: Guangdong as an anti-Eden
where the flesh and blood of serpents, ducks, pigs, chicken and other
animals run together on the butchers board and on the floors of open
air markets. From this primordial ooze, so the new mythology goes, a
super villain—SARS—is born. Thus the first metaphor of SARS was
not simply that of plague, but a Chinese plague.

Then, as SARS spread out of China, to Hong Kong and then to 5
Vietnam and Singapore, the metaphor changed and SARS became an
Oriental plague and the metaphor began to affect business in the far-
flung Chinatowns of New York, San Francisco, Seattle and other
cities. Then the remarkable propensity of this disease to affect health-
care workers added a new wrinkle: In Singapore and Hong Kong,
doctors and hospitals became tainted by the metaphor. This was a
medical plague, and if you had a neighbor who was a physician or a
nurse, it was cause for alarm.

As an infectious disease specialist, I shuddered when I first read
the early reports of SARS. In the back of my mind was another
metaphor, namely the horrific 1918 Spanish influenza. That pandemic
had a relatively low mortality of about 5%, and yet it spread so
widely that it caused 25 million deaths worldwide. SARS seems to
have a higher mortality, anywhere from 5% to 50% depending on the

host and the setting, but fortunately the kind of rapid spread that characterizes influenza seems not to be occurring with SARS—thank heavens for that.

Meanwhile the metaphors—exaggerated, capricious, unfair and unjustified as they may be—are difficult to bottle back up once they have been invoked. When WHO issued travel advisories for the affected countries, the SARS metaphor now came to mean economic blight. Singapore, China and Hong Kong saw trade and tourism shrivel away (and it was not as if these economies were doing that well before SARS). At a time when international bodies such as the UN are divided and ineffective, the WHO has never seemed more virile and potent. Indeed, it was a WHO physician, Carlo Urbani, MD, who first identified the new outbreak and tragically became a martyr to the illness, one of many doctors to succumb to the disease.

The warning against travel to the Far East was accepted as prudent by most in the West, a tough pill that those countries would have to swallow. But when Toronto was added to the WHO list, there were howls of protest from that city as they objected to the metaphor of blight. A delegation from Toronto flew to Geneva to make the case that they had controlled the infection, and a surprisingly pliant WHO agreed to take them off the list. It turned out that new cases were popping up in Toronto even as their officials were flying to Geneva. Canadian officials claimed they did not know about the new cases when they made their pitch in Geneva. Embarrassed WHO officials seemed ready to reimpose the recommendation against travel, sensing that a double standard had been revealed. But in any case, the damage to Toronto was done and would take time to be reversed, no matter what the WHO or the city fathers now said.

America thus far has been most fortunate and has largely been spared the disease. More important from an economic point of view, it has been spared the metaphor. The CDC and regional public-health entities have done a great job of tracking potentially infected persons and isolating them, and also of raising awareness in the health-care settings most likely to see patients. Julie Gerberding, MD, of the CDC has been a much more reassuring figure than Tommy Thompson. But let's not kid ourselves: We have also been incredibly lucky to be spared the virus and the metaphor.

Reasons for Concern

10 America still has much to be concerned about. There are aspects of SARS we don't understand. For example, SARS, more than any disease I can recall, amplifies itself dramatically in some health-care set-

tings. At the Prince of Wales Hospital in Hong Kong, 138 health-care workers came down with SARS contracted from one patient. Similarly in Toronto, almost all the patients were traced to one hospitalized patient. Indeed, it is almost as if the virus uses a patient as its Trojan horse to get entry into the hospital, as if the hospital were its primary target.

And hospitals are not the only institutions we must worry about; one hotel, the Metropole in Hong Kong, had a single infected guest—a doctor, who later died—who somehow spread it to other guests who in turn carried the disease to several other countries. And then there is the story of the incredible spread of SARS within an apartment building at the Amoy Gardens in Hong Kong, where ultimately 286 people came down with the disease. All it will take to cause an outbreak in an American city is one patient, a superspreader, whose illness is not immediately recognized, and then we will find out what it is like to be tainted by the metaphor.

SARS has exposed the inequities and imbalances between the health systems of various countries—disorganized and secretive in China, well organized and accessible in the U.S. It has suggested how phenomenally important the element of luck is in a country's experience. And the metaphors SARS invokes reflect our biases and our prejudices; the disease reveals the cultural stereotypes hiding just below the surface. The virus, like so many before it, is democratic: It reminds us that we share one planet, and that even if we do not share the planet's wealth, we share its misfortunes.

Responding to Reading

1. What does Verghese mean when he says that human beings tend "to ascribe metaphors to disease" (1)? What metaphor is associated with SARS?
2. What are the effects of disease metaphors once they are invoked? What happened to the SARS metaphor once the World Health Organization got involved?
3. According to Verghese, why do Americans still have much to worry about concerning SARS? How has SARS "exposed the inequities and imbalances between the health systems of various countries" (12)? How does SARS reflect "our biases and our prejudices" (12)?

Responding in Writing

Do you think Verghese is optimistic or pessimistic about our ability to control future outbreaks of diseases like SARS? Do you share his views?

My World Now

Anna Mae Halgrim Seaver

1919–1994

In 1994, Anna Mae Halgrim Seaver died at the nursing home where she had lived for some time. When cleaning out her room, her son discovered some notes and was so moved by them that he arranged them into the following essay, which appeared as a "My Turn" column in Newsweek.

This is my world now; it's all I have left. You see, I'm old. And, I'm not as healthy as I used to be. I'm not necessarily happy with it but I accept it. Occasionally, a member of my family will stop in to see me. He or she will bring me some flowers or a little present, maybe a set of slippers—I've got 8 pair. We'll visit for awhile and then they will return to the outside world and I'll be alone again.

Oh, there are other people here in the nursing home. Residents, we're called. The majority are about my age. I'm 84. Many are in wheelchairs. The lucky ones are passing through—a broken hip, a diseased heart, something has brought them here for rehabilitation. When they're well they'll be going home.

Most of us are aware of our plight—some are not. Varying stages of Alzheimer's have robbed several of their mental capacities. We listen to endlessly repeated stories and questions. We meet them anew daily, hourly or more often. We smile and nod gracefully each time we hear a retelling. They seldom listen to my stories, so I've stopped trying.

The help here is basically pretty good, although there's a large turnover. Just when I get comfortable with someone he or she moves on to another job. I understand that. This is not the best job to have.

5　I don't much like some of the physical things that happen to us. I don't care much for a diaper. I seem to have lost the control acquired so diligently as a child. The difference is that I'm aware and embarrassed but I can't do anything about it. I've had 3 children and I know it isn't pleasant to clean another's diaper. My husband used to wear a gas mask when he changed the kids. I wish I had one now.

Why do you think the staff insists on talking baby talk when speaking to me? I understand English. I have a degree in music and am a certified teacher. Now I hear a lot of words that end in "y." Is this how my kids felt? My hearing aid works fine. There is little need for anyone to position their face directly in front of mine and raise their voice with those "y" words. Sometimes it takes longer for a meaning to sink in; sometimes my mind wanders when I am bored. But there's no need to shout.

I tried once or twice to make my feelings known. I even shouted once. That gained me a reputation of being "crotchety." Imagine me, crotchety. My children never heard me raise my voice. I surprised myself. After I've asked for help more than a dozen times and received nothing more than a dozen condescending smiles and a "Yes, deary, I'm working on it," something begins to break. That time I wanted to be taken to a bathroom.

I'd love to go out for a meal, to travel again. I'd love to go to my own church, sing with my own choir. I'd love to visit my friends. Most of them are gone now or else they are in different "homes" of their children's choosing. I'd love to play a good game of bridge but no one here seems to concentrate very well.

My children put me here for my own good. They said they would be able to visit me frequently. But they have their own lives to lead. That sounds normal. I don't want to be a burden. They know that. But I would like to see them more. One of them is here in town. He visits as much as he can.

Something else I've learned to accept is loss of privacy. Quite often 10 I'll close my door when my roommate—imagine having a roommate at my age—is in the TV room. I do appreciate some time to myself and believe that I have earned at least that courtesy. As I sit thinking or writing, one of the aides invariably opens the door unannounced and walks in as if I'm not there. Sometimes she even opens my drawers and begins rummaging around. Am I invisible? Have I lost my right to respect and dignity? What would happen if the roles were reversed? I am still a human being. I would like to be treated as one.

The meals are not what I would choose for myself. We get variety but we don't get a choice. I am one of the fortunate ones who can still handle utensils. I remember eating off such cheap utensils in the Great Depression. I worked hard so I would not have to ever use them again. But here I am.

Did you ever sit in a wheelchair over an extended period of time? It's not comfortable. The seat squeezes you into the middle and applies constant pressure on your hips. The armrests are too narrow and my arms slip off. I am luckier than some. Others are strapped into their chairs and abandoned in front of the TV. Captive prisoners of daytime television; soap operas, talk shows and commercials.

One of the residents died today. He was a loner who, at one time, started a business and developed a multimillion-dollar company. His children moved him here when he could no longer control his bowels. He didn't talk to most of us. He often snapped at the aides as though they were his employees. But he just gave up; willed his own demise. The staff has made up his room and another man has moved in.

A typical day. Awakened by the woman in the next bed wheezing—a former chain smoker with asthma. Call an aide to wash me and place me in my wheelchair to wait for breakfast. Only 67 minutes until breakfast. I'll wait. Breakfast in the dining area. Most of the residents are in wheelchairs. Others use canes or walkers. Some sit and wonder what they are waiting for. First meal of the day. Only 3 hours and 26 minutes until lunch. Maybe I'll sit around and wait for it. What is today? One day blends into the next until day and date mean nothing.

15   Let's watch a little TV. Oprah and Phil and Geraldo and who cares if some transvestite is having trouble picking a color-coordinated wardrobe from his husband's girlfriend's mother's collection. Lunch. Can't wait. Dried something with puréed peas and coconut pudding. No wonder I'm losing weight.

Back to my semiprivate room for a little semiprivacy or a nap. I do need my beauty rest, company may come today. What is today, again? The afternoon drags into early evening. This used to be my favorite time of the day. Things would wind down. I would kick off my shoes. Put my feet up on the coffee table. Pop open a bottle of Chablis and enjoy the fruits of my day's labor with my husband. He's gone. So is my health. *This* is my world.

Responding to Reading

1. Seaver's son compiled this essay from notes left in his mother's room after her death. Perhaps for this reason, it seems to jump from one subject to another. Are there any advantages to this choppy structure? Would a smoother, more unified structure have been more effective?
2. What picture of life in a nursing home does Seaver present? How does she characterize the people who live there?
3. In paragraph 9, Seaver says "My children put me here for my own good. . . . But they have their own lives to lead. . . . I don't want to be a burden." Do you think Seaver means what she says? What do you think her son hoped to accomplish by publishing her notes?

Responding in Writing

Write a paragraph or two in which you describe your typical day. As Seaver does, begin your discussion with the phrase, "This is my world now."

Do Not Go Gentle into That Good Night

Dylan Thomas
1914–1953

Born in Swansea, Wales, Dylan Thomas was one of the most popular poets of his day. His first collection, Eighteen Poems *(1934), was both hailed and condemned for its earthy vigor, but it immediately established his reputa-*

tion. *Other collections include* Twenty-Five Poems *(1936);* Deaths and Entrances *(1946);* In Country Sleep and Other Poems *(1952); and volumes of whimsical prose, including* Portrait of the Artist as a Young Dog *(1940). Thomas also wrote the play* Under Milkwood *(1954). Famous for his dramatic public readings of his work (as well as for his drinking), Thomas made several highly successful tours of the United States. He died in New York City in 1953 at the age of thirty-nine of complications arising from alcoholism.*

Do not go gentle into that good night,
Old age should burn and rave at close of day;
Rage, rage against the dying of the light.

Though wise men at their end know dark is right,
Because their words had forked no lightning they   5
Do not go gentle into that good night.

Good men, the last wave by, crying how bright
Their frail deeds might have danced in a green bay,
Rage, rage against the dying of the light.

Wild men who caught and sang the sun in flight,   10
And learn, too late, they grieved it on its way,
Do not go gentle into that good night.

Grave men, near death, who see with blinding sight
Blind eyes could blaze like meteors and be gay,
Rage, rage against the dying of the light.   15

And you, my father, there on the sad height,
Curse, bless, me now with your fierce tears, I pray,
Do not go gentle into that good night.
Rage, rage against the dying of the light.

Responding to Reading

1. What is the speaker's attitude toward death? How does he want people to act as they face death? How realistic are his wishes?
2. What different kinds of men are discussed in this poem? How does each of these types of men face death? What type of man is the speaker's father?
3. What is your opinion of the speaker? Do you think he is concerned primarily about his father or about himself?

Responding in Writing

Read a few obituaries in a newspaper. Then, in a paragraph or two, write your own obituary. Assume you lived to the age of 85 and accomplished many of your personal and professional goals.

ON THE FEAR OF DEATH

Elisabeth Kübler-Ross

1926–

Psychiatrist and physician Elisabeth Kübler-Ross was born in Zurich, Switzerland, received her MD at the University of Zurich (1957), and has had a distinguished career working with dying patients and their families. Her preoccupation with death was inspired by the concentration camps of World War II and her relief work in postwar Europe. She established a pioneering interdisciplinary seminar in the care of the terminally ill when she taught at the University of Chicago, and, for many years, she headed a center for terminal patients in rural Virginia. Her first book on the subject was On Death and Dying *(1969). Other works include* Death: The Final State *(1974),* On Childhood and Death *(1985),* AIDS: The Ultimate Challenge *(1987),* On Life After Death *(1991), and* The Wheel of Life: A Memoir of Living and Dying *(1997). In the following excerpt from* On Death and Dying, *Kübler-Ross argues that we should confront death directly in order to reduce our fear of it.*

> Let me not pray to be sheltered from dangers but to be fearless in facing them.
> Let me not beg for the stilling of my pain but for the heart to conquer it.
> Let me not look for allies in life's battlefield but to my own strength.
> Let me not crave in anxious fear to be saved but hope for the patience to win my freedom.
> Grant me that I may not be a coward, feeling your mercy in my success alone; but let me find the grasp of your hand in my failure.
>
> —Rabindranath Tagore, *Fruit-Gathering*

Epidemics have taken a great toll of lives in past generations. Death in infancy and early childhood was frequent and there were few families who didn't lose a member of the family at an early age. Medicine has changed greatly in the last decades. Widespread vaccinations have practically eradicated many illnesses, at least in western Europe and the United States. The use of chemotherapy, especially the antibiotics, has contributed to an ever decreasing number of fatalities in infectious diseases. Better child care and education have effected a low morbidity and mortality among children. The many diseases that have taken an impressive toll among the young and middle-aged have been conquered. The number of old people is on the rise, and with this fact come the number of people with malignancies and chronic diseases associated more with old age.

Pediatricians have less work with acute and life-threatening situations as they have an ever increasing number of patients with psychosomatic disturbances and adjustment and behavior problems. Physicians have more people in their waiting rooms with emotional problems than they have ever had before, but they also have more elderly patients who not only try to live with their decreased physical abilities and limitations but who also face loneliness and isolation with all its pains and anguish. The majority of these people are not seen by a psychiatrist. Their needs have to be elicited and gratified by other professional people, for instance, chaplains and social workers. It is for them that I am trying to outline the changes that have taken place in the last few decades, changes that are ultimately responsible for the increased fear of death, the rising number of emotional problems, and the greater need for understanding of and coping with the problems of death and dying.

When we look back in time and study old cultures and people, we are impressed that death has always been distasteful to man and will probably always be. From a psychiatrist's point of view this is very understandable and can perhaps best be explained by our basic knowledge that, in our unconscious, death is never possible in regard to ourselves. It is inconceivable for our unconscious to imagine an actual ending of our own life here on earth, and if this life of ours had to end, the ending is always attributed to a malicious intervention from the outside by someone else. In simple terms, in our unconscious mind we can only be killed; it is inconceivable to die of a natural cause or of old age. Therefore death in itself is associated with a bad act, a frightening happening, something that in itself calls for retribution and punishment.

One is wise to remember these fundamental facts as they are essential in understanding some of the most important, otherwise unintelligible communications of our patients.

The second fact that we have to comprehend is that in our unconscious mind we cannot distinguish between a wish and a deed. We are all aware of some of our illogical dreams in which two completely opposite statements can exist side by side—very acceptable in our dreams but unthinkable and illogical in our wakening state. Just as our unconscious mind cannot differentiate between the wish to kill somebody in anger and the act of having done so, the young child is unable to make this distinction. The child who angrily wishes his mother to drop dead for not having gratified his needs will be traumatized greatly by the actual death of his mother—even if this event is not linked closely in time with his destructive wishes. He will always take part or the whole blame for the loss of his mother. He will always say to himself—rarely to others—"I did it, I am responsible, I was bad, therefore Mommy left me." It is well to remember that the child will react in the same manner if he loses a parent by divorce, separation, or desertion. Death is often seen by a child as an impermanent thing and has therefore little distinction from a divorce in which he may have an opportunity to see a parent again.

Many a parent will remember remarks of their children such as, "I will bury my doggy now and next spring when the flowers come up again, he will get up." Maybe it was the same wish that motivated the ancient Egyptians to supply their dead with food and goods to keep them happy and the old American Indians to bury their relatives with their belongings.

When we grow older and begin to realize that our omnipotence is really not so omnipotent, that our strongest wishes are not powerful enough to make the impossible possible, the fear that we have contributed to the death of a loved one diminishes—and with it the guilt. The fear remains diminished, however, only so long as it is not challenged too strongly. Its vestiges can be seen daily in hospital corridors and in people associated with the bereaved.

A husband and wife may have been fighting for years, but when the partner dies, the survivor will pull his hair, whine and cry louder and beat his chest in regret, fear and anguish, and will hence fear his own death more than before, still believing in the law of talion—an eye for an eye, a tooth for a tooth—"I am responsible for her death, I will have to die a pitiful death in retribution."

Maybe this knowledge will help us understand many of the old customs and rituals which have lasted over the centuries and whose purpose is to diminish the anger of the gods or the people as the case may be, thus decreasing the anticipated punishment. I am thinking of the ashes, the torn clothes, the veil, the *Klage Weiber*[1] of the old days— they are all means to ask you to take pity on them, the mourners, and are expressions of sorrow, grief, and shame. If someone grieves, beats his chest, tears his hair, or refuses to eat, it is an attempt at self-punishment to avoid or reduce the anticipated punishment for the blame that he takes on the death of a loved one.

10   This grief, shame, and guilt are not very far removed from feelings of anger and rage. The process of grief always includes some qualities of anger. Since none of us likes to admit anger at a deceased person, these emotions are often disguised or repressed and prolong the period of grief or show up in other ways. It is well to remember that it is not up to us to judge such feelings as bad or shameful but to understand their true meaning and origin as something very human. In order to illustrate this I will again use the example of the child— and the child in us. The five-year-old who loses his mother is both blaming himself for her disappearance and being angry at her for having deserted him and for no longer gratifying his needs. The dead

---

[1]Wailing wives. [Eds.]

person then turns into something the child loves and wants very much but also hates with equal intensity for this severe deprivation.

The ancient Hebrews regarded the body of a dead person as something unclean and not to be touched. The early American Indians talked about the evil spirits and shot arrows in the air to drive the spirits away. Many other cultures have rituals to take care of the "bad" dead person, and they all originate in this feeling of anger which still exists in all of us, though we dislike admitting it. The tradition of the tombstone may originate in this wish to keep the bad spirits deep down in the ground, and the pebbles that many mourners put on the grave are left-over symbols of the same wish. Though we call the firing of guns at military funerals a last salute, it is the same symbolic ritual as the Indian used when he shot his spears and arrows into the skies.

I give these examples to emphasize that man has not basically changed. Death is still a fearful, frightening happening, and the fear of death is a universal fear even if we think we have mastered it on many levels.

What has changed is our way of coping and dealing with death and dying and our dying patients.

Having been raised in a country in Europe where science is not so advanced, where modern techniques have just started to find their way into medicine, and where people still live as they did in this country half a century ago, I may have had an opportunity to study a part of the evolution of mankind in a shorter period.

I remember as a child the death of a farmer. He fell from a tree 15 and was not expected to live. He asked simply to die at home, a wish that was granted without questioning. He called his daughters into the bedroom and spoke with each one of them alone for a few moments. He arranged his affairs quietly, though he was in great pain, and distributed his belongings and his land, none of which was to be split until his wife should follow him in death. He also asked each of his children to share in the work, duties, and tasks that he had carried on until the time of the accident. He asked his friends to visit him once more, to bid good-bye to them. Although I was a small child at the time, he did not exclude me or my siblings. We were allowed to share in the preparations of the family just as we were permitted to grieve with them until he died. When he did die, he was left at home, in his own beloved home which he had built, and among his friends and neighbors who went to take a last look at him where he lay in the midst of flowers in the place he had lived in and loved so much. In that country today there is still no make-believe slumber room, no embalming, no false makeup to pretend sleep. Only the signs of very disfiguring illnesses are covered up with bandages and only infectious cases are removed from the home prior to the burial.

Why do I describe such "old-fashioned" customs? I think they are an indication of our acceptance of a fatal outcome, and they help the dying patient as well as his family to accept the loss of a loved one. If a patient is allowed to terminate his life in the familiar and beloved environment, it requires less adjustment for him. His own family knows him well enough to replace a sedative with a glass of his favorite wine; or the smell of a home-cooked soup may give him the appetite to sip a few spoons of fluid which, I think, is still more enjoyable than an infusion. I will not minimize the need for sedatives and infusions and realize full well from my own experience as a country doctor that they are sometimes life-saving and often unavoidable. But I also know that patience and familiar people and foods could replace many a bottle of intravenous fluids given for the simple reason that it fulfills the physiological need without involving too many people and/or individual nursing care.

The fact that children are allowed to stay at home where a fatality has stricken and are included in the talk, discussions, and fears gives them the feeling that they are not alone in the grief and gives them the comfort of shared responsibility and shared mourning. It prepares them gradually and helps them view death as part of life, an experience which may help them grow and mature.

This is in great contrast to a society in which death is viewed as taboo, discussion of it is regarded as morbid, and children are excluded with the presumption and pretext that it would be "too much" for them. They are then sent off to relatives, often accompanied with some unconvincing lies of "Mother has gone on a long trip" or other unbelievable stories. The child senses that something is wrong, and his distrust in adults will only multiply if other relatives add new variations of the story, avoid his questions or suspicions, shower him with gifts as a meager substitute for a loss he is not permitted to deal with. Sooner or later the child will become aware of the changed family situation and, depending on the age and personality of the child, will have an unresolved grief and regard this incident as a frightening, mysterious, in any case very traumatic experience with untrustworthy grownups, which he has no way to cope with.

It is equally unwise to tell a little child who lost her brother that God loved little boys so much that he took little Johnny to heaven. When this little girl grew up to be a woman she never solved her anger at God, which resulted in a psychotic depression when she lost her own little son three decades later.

20   We would think that our great emancipation, our knowledge of science and of man, has given us better ways and means to prepare ourselves and our families for this inevitable happening. Instead the days are gone when a man was allowed to die in peace and dignity in his own home.

The more we are making advancements in science, the more we seem to fear and deny the reality of death. How is this possible?

We use euphemisms, we make the dead look as if they were asleep, we ship the children off to protect them from the anxiety and turmoil around the house if the patient is fortunate enough to die at home, we don't allow children to visit their dying parents in the hospitals, we have long and controversial discussions about whether patients should be told the truth—a question that rarely arises when the dying person is tended by the family physician who has known him from delivery to death and who knows the weaknesses and strengths of each member of the family.

I think there are many reasons for this flight away from facing death calmly. One of the most important facts is that dying nowadays is more gruesome in many ways, namely, more lonely, mechanical, and dehumanized; at times it is even difficult to determine technically when the time of death has occurred.

Dying becomes lonely and impersonal because the patient is often taken out of his familiar environment and rushed to an emergency room. Whoever has been very sick and has required rest and comfort especially may recall his experience of being put on a stretcher and enduring the noise of the ambulance siren and hectic rush until the hospital gates open. Only those who have lived through this may appreciate the discomfort and cold necessity of such transportation which is only the beginning of a long order—hard to endure when you are well, difficult to express in words when noise, light, pumps, and voices are all too much to put up with. It may well be that we might consider more the patient under the sheets and blankets and perhaps stop our well-meant efficiency and rush in order to hold the patient's hand, to smile, or to listen to a question. I include the trip to the hospital as the first episode in dying, as it is for many. I am putting it exaggeratedly in contrast to the sick man who is left at home—not to say that lives should not be saved if they can be saved by a hospitalization but to keep the focus on the patient's experience, his needs and his reactions.

When a patient is severely ill, he is often treated like a person 25 with no right to an opinion. It is often someone else who makes the decision if and when and where a patient should be hospitalized. It would take so little to remember that the sick person too has feelings, has wishes and opinions, and has—most important of all—the right to be heard.

Well, our presumed patient has now reached the emergency room. He will be surrounded by busy nurses, orderlies, interns, residents, a lab technician perhaps who will take some blood, an electrocardiogram technician who takes the cardiogram. He may be moved to X ray and he will overhear opinions of his condition and discussions and questions to members of the family. He slowly but surely is beginning to be treated like a thing. He is no longer a person. Decisions are made often without his opinion. If he tries to rebel he will be sedated and after hours of waiting and wondering whether he has the strength, he will be wheeled into the operating room or intensive treatment unit and become an object of great concern and great financial investment.

He may cry for rest, peace, and dignity, but he will get infusions, transfusions, a heart machine, or tracheotomy[2] if necessary. He may want one single person to stop for one single minute so that he can ask one single question—but he will get a dozen people around the clock, all busily preoccupied with his heart rate, pulse, electrocardiogram or pulmonary functions, his secretions or excretions but not with him as a human being. He may wish to fight it all but it is going to be a useless fight since all this is done in the fight for his life, and if they can save his life they can consider the person afterwards. Those who consider the person first may lose precious time to save his life! At least this seems to be the rationale or justification behind all this— or is it? Is the reason for this increasingly mechanical, depersonalized approach our own defensiveness? Is this approach our own way to cope with and repress the anxieties that a terminally or critically ill patient evokes in us? Is our concentration on equipment, on blood pressure, our desperate attempt to deny the impending death which is so frightening and discomforting to us that we displace all our knowledge onto machines, since they are less close to us than the suffering face of another human being which would remind us once more of our lack of omnipotence, our own limits and failures, and last but not least perhaps our own mortality?

Maybe the question has to be raised: Are we becoming less human or more human? . . . It is clear that whatever the answer may be, the patient is suffering more—not physically, perhaps, but emotionally. And his needs have not changed over the centuries, only our ability to gratify them.

Responding to Reading

1. Despite advances in medical science over the centuries, Kübler-Ross says, death remains "a fearful, frightening happening, and the fear of death is a universal fear even if we think we have mastered it on many levels" (12). Do you think she is correct?
2. To what extent do you agree with Kübler-Ross that we should confront the reality of death directly—for example, by being honest with children, keeping terminally ill patients at home, and allowing dying patients to deter-

---

[2]An incision in the trachea in the neck to allow the insertion of a breathing tube. [Eds.]

mine their own treatment? What arguments are there against each of her suggestions?

3. Instead of quoting medical authorities, Kübler-Ross supports her points with anecdotes. Do you find this support convincing? Would hard scientific data be more convincing? Explain.

Responding in Writing

What experiences have you had with death and dying? Did you confront the person's death directly, as Kübler-Ross recommends? Why or why not? Do you think you made the right choice?

THE HEALTH OF NATIONS
Phillip Longman
1956–

Phillip Longman, a William Schwartz fellow at the New America Foundation, has written numerous articles and books on demographics, economics, and public policy—including, most recently, The Empty Cradle: How Falling Birthrates Threaten World Prosperity *(Perseus 2004). His work has appeared in the* Atlantic Monthly, Foreign Affairs, Fortune, *the* New York Times Magazine, *the* New Republic, *the* Wall Street Journal, *and the* Washington Post. *He is a former senior writer and deputy assistant managing editor at* US News & World Report *and the recipient of numerous awards for business and financial writing. Born in Stuttgart, Germany, Longman graduated from Oberlin College and was a Knight-Baghot fellow at Columbia University. In the following essay, first printed in 2003 in the* Washington Monthly, *Longman takes a critical look at the American health-care system. To read more of Longman's work, visit the Web site of the New America Foundation, http://www.newamerica.net/, and look under the heading "Current Fellows."*

To get an idea of how wildly ineffective our health-care system is, consider this: The United States spends roughly $4,500 per person on health care each year. Costa Rica spends just $273. That small Central American country also has half as many doctors per capita as the United States. Yet the life expectancy of the average Costa Rican is virtually the same as the average American's: 76.1 years.

How can that be? According to public health researchers, the biggest reasons are behavior and environment. Costa Ricans consume about half as many cigarettes per person as we do. Not surprisingly, they are four times less likely to die of lung cancer. The car ownership rate in Costa Rica is a fraction of what it is in the United States. That not only means that fewer Costa Ricans die in auto accidents, but that they do a lot more walking, and hence they get more exercise. Thanks to a much lower McDonald's-to-citizen ratio, the average Costa Rican thrives on a traditional diet of rice, beans, fruits, vegetables, and a moderate amount of fried food—and therefore enjoys one of the world's lowest rates of heart disease and other stress-related illnesses.

The simple comparison between the health of Costa Ricans and Americans suggests a whole new way to think about how to fix America's increasingly dysfunctional health-care system—a system that these days seems to combine spiraling costs, declining coverage, and growing dissatisfaction with the quality of care. But instead of offering new ideas, both political parties in Washington are stuck in a hopeless rut, each trying to hawk plans that essentially expand the current system.

The battle over a Medicare prescription-drug benefit is a classic example. In March, President Bush unveiled a plan to provide partial drug discounts to all seniors, but full discounts only to those who leave traditional "fee-for-service" Medicare and join an HMO. Democrats derided the plan as a stealth attempt to "privatize" Medicare and argued instead for a much more generous plan that would give full discounts to all seniors, including those who remain in traditional Medicare.

5   Neither party seems to get it. Simply adding an expensive new benefit to a Medicare system whose costs are running out of control, as Democrats want to do, is fiscally irresponsible. Republicans, however, are deluded if they think funneling the elderly into HMOs will do much to cut health-care costs for long—HMO costs in the private sector are soaring. Moreover, when the Clinton administration experimented with a program to lure seniors into HMOs (Medicare+Choice), the result was chaos: Many HMOs went broke, others raised premiums, cut benefits, shifted costs, or simply dropped hundreds of thousands of seniors.

Both parties should pause and reflect. For all the additional money we're throwing into medicine, Americans aren't getting much healthier. Maybe it's time to try a different approach. The biggest opportunities for improving the health of Americans—and restraining health-care costs—lie in keeping people healthy, rather than treating them once they become sick. So instead of simply adding more benefits to a health-care system that is already financially unsustainable, or using new benefits to herd people into HMOs, why not offer a more sensible deal: Bribe people into taking better care of themselves. For instance, why not offer seniors who exercise bigger drug discounts than those who don't?

This may sound radical, and it is. But the more Americans learn about the costs and failings of contemporary medicine and the extraordinary benefits they can reap from simple behavioral changes like exercising, the more such plans will begin to make sense.

Clean Living

To understand the value of this approach, it is important to clarify a common misperception about health care. During the 20th century, the health and life expectancy of the average American improved dramatically. A child born today can expect to live a full 30 years longer than one born in 1900. Improvements in medicine, however, played a surprisingly small role in this achievement. Public health experts agree that it contributed no more than five of those 30 years.

This may seem counterintuitive given the attention society pays to medical breakthroughs. But the changes in living and working conditions over the last century are the real reason. American cities at the turn of the last century stank of coal dust, manure, and rotting garbage. Most people still used latrines and outhouses. As recently as 1913, industrial accidents killed 23,000 Americans annually. Milk and meat were often spoiled; the water supply untreated. Trichinellosis, a dangerous parasite found in meat, infected 16 percent of the population, while food-borne bacteria such as salmonella, clostridium, and staphylococcus killed millions, especially children, 10 percent of whom died before their first birthday.

During the first half of the 20th century, living and working conditions improved vastly for most Americans. Workplace fatalities dropped 90 percent. This, combined with public health measures such as mosquito control, quarantines, and food inspections, led to dramatic declines in premature death. In 1900, 194 of every 100,000 U.S. residents died from tuberculosis. By 1940, before the advent of any effective medical treatment, reductions in over-crowded tenements combined with quarantine efforts had reduced the death rate by three-fourths. ¹⁰

As the century progressed, medical care grew enormously more sophisticated and effective, particularly in managing pain and preventing sudden death from traumatic injury, infection, and heart attack. But the overall gains to public health remained modest. The greatest gains came from strategic vaccination campaigns, which have virtually eliminated once-common diseases, including diphtheria, tetanus, poliomyelitis, smallpox, measles, mumps, rubella, and meningitis. But even these triumphs involved treating people before they became sick. Modern medicine's ability to actually cure people is quite depressing. The consensus estimate, accepted by the Centers for Disease Control (CDC), is that medicine has contributed just two of the seven years in added life expectancy achieved since 1950.

The reason is that, strictly speaking, medicine doesn't "save" lives, but extends them. If you're like my son, who spent the first 60 days of his life in a neonatal intensive care unit, medical intervention could extend your lifespan 90 years or more—but that number diminishes if you're 50, much more so if you're 90.

This gets at an important truth about the role medicine plays in public health—it is concentrated primarily on the elderly, who consume about 38 percent of all health-care dollars, yet account for just 12.4 percent of the population. By definition, the elderly have fewer years of life to extend than the young. This simple fact goes a long way toward explaining medicine's modest role in improving life expectancy: It cannot stop aging.

Sure, many best-sellers and newsweeklies tout the "longevity revolution" prompted by advances in cutting-edge medicine. But overall longevity is due more to dramatic reductions in infant mortality, which allow more people to grow old, than to modestly extended lives among the elderly. Since 1950, life expectancy at 65 has increased by just 3.45 years; among women over 65, it has actually declined slightly since 1992.

Domino's Theory

15 Another reason for the medical system's limited role in extending life is that, frankly, it kills so many people. Each year nearly two million patients in U.S. hospitals get an infection, about 90,000 of whom die as a result. According to the CDC, the largest preventable cause is doctors and nurses with dirty hands. Then there is the institute of Medicine's well-publicized finding that "more people die in a given year as a result of medical errors than from motor vehicle accidents (43,458), breast cancer (42,297), or AIDS (16,516)." Such errors cause 2 to 4 percent of all deaths and derive not just from doctors' indecipherable handwriting or mix-ups in the lab, but also from a lack of the same kinds of systematic quality control procedures that are commonplace in workplaces from automakers to Domino's Pizza chains. Had the institute considered deaths caused by medical errors outside of hospitals—in doctors' offices, pharmacies, or outpatient clinics— the fatality rate would be even higher.

Overmedication and adverse reactions to prescription drugs also cause unnecessary deaths. In 1994, these accounted for 106,000 deaths, according to the *Journal of the American Medical Association*. More people are killed by adverse reactions to prescription drugs than by pulmonary disease or accidents. In fact, prescription drug deaths are surpassed only by heart disease, cancer, and stroke. The elderly, whose bodies often can't tolerate the dosages and combinations of pills doctors prescribe them, are particularly susceptible.

Moreover, many of the treatments the medical system provides are unnecessary, further limiting their effect. Consider the wide regional disparity in the intensity of care given to patients. In Miami, the average Medicare patient is treated by 25 specialists during the last six months of life; in Minneapolis, such patients see only four specialists. Yet the result is exactly the same: death within six months. Where specialists are abundant, they find elders to treat—and Medicare pays, spending, for example, $50,000 more per patient in Miami than Minneapolis, as my colleague Shannon Brownlee recently wrote in *The Atlantic*. But according to John Wennberg of Dartmouth Medical School, elder persons living in regions where the use of specialists is high have no greater life expectancy than their counterparts in regions where it is low. Wennberg and his colleagues estimate that nearly 20 percent of Medicare expenditures provide no benefit in terms of survival, nor does evidence show improvement in quality of life.

Then there is the growing problem of "pseudo-disease," defined by medical researchers Elliot S. Fischer and H. Gilbert Welch as "disease that would never become apparent to patients during their lifetime were it not for diagnostic tests." Most Americans have a binary view of illness: Either you have a disease or you don't. But the truth is often more subtle. Autopsy studies have shown that a third of adults have cancer cells in their thyroid; up to 40 percent of women in their 40s have ductal carcinoma in situ in their breasts; and half of men in their 60s have adenocarcinoma of the prostate. Yet each of the subjects died of other diseases. In other words, they died with their cancer, not from it, suggesting that many who have small cancers will never develop symptoms because they will die of something else before their cancers become noticeable.

Yet if your doctor discovers that you have cancer, there are two likely results: First, you will experience extraordinary and prolonged stress from the diagnosis, along with the attendant risks to health. Second, you and your doctor will try to fight the disease through radiation, chemotherapy, or surgery. Though it is difficult for a doctor and patient to know, even in terms of probability, whether such treatment is necessary, it is clear that for the broader population, the spread of diagnostic testing is causing an epidemic of "pseudo disease"—and vast commitments of medical resources that result in little, if any, gain in public health.

But what if we could get doctors and nurses to wash their hands, 20 fix the errors in the medical system, and adapt sensible, evidence-based medicine to prevent over-treatment, overmedication, and adverse drug reaction? This would dramatically improve our healthcare system and prevent millions of deaths. But the overall effect on the health and life expectancy of Americans, and on the future demand for health care, would remain startlingly small. That's because the health-care system kicks in after most people are already ill. As the poet Joseph Malines aptly put it, it's like an ambulance waiting at the bottom of a cliff. By the time most people receive treatment, their bodies are already compromised by stress, indulgent habits, environmental dangers, and injury. As Maline wrote in his poem, "A Fence or an Ambulance": "If the cliff we will fence, we might almost dispense/With the ambulance down in the valley."

Joint Survival

In a recent issue of *Health Affairs,* three researchers from the Robert Wood Johnson Foundation examined scores of studies dating back to the 1970s on what factors cause people to die prematurely. They reported that genetic predispositions account for 30 percent of premature deaths; social circumstances, 15 percent; environmental exposures, 5 percent; behavioral patterns, 40 percent; and shortfalls in medical care, 10 percent. As they note, these proportions are easily misinterpreted. Ultimately, nearly everyone's health is determined by a combination of factors. For example, while only about 2 percent of human diseases are caused by inherited genetic mutations alone, nearly everyone carries various genetic dispositions that, when combined with a hazardous environment or unhealthy lifestyle, can contribute to ill health. But this only underscores the relatively small role medicine plays in preventing premature death.

Consider the startling difference in mortality between Utah and Nevada. These two contiguous states are similar in demographics, climate, access to health care, and average income. Yet Nevada's infant mortality rate is 40 percent higher than Utah's, and Nevada adults face an increased likelihood of premature death. As health-care economists Victor Fuchs and Nathan Rosenberg have pointed out, it's hard not to attribute much of that difference to the fact that 70 percent of Utah's population follows the strictures of the Mormon Church, which requires abstinence from tobacco, alcohol, premarital sex, and divorce. Nevada, with its freewheeling, laissez-faire culture, has the highest incidence of smoking-related death in the country; Utah the lowest. Utah has the nation's highest birthrate, but the lowest incidence of unwed teenage mothers. Culture and behavior seem to trump access to health care in improving human life span.

Similarly, when comparing life expectancy in the United States to other countries, it becomes clear that the vast sums we spend on health care buy very little health. The roughly $4,500 per person the United States spends annually on health care far outpaces any other country. Yet three-fourths of developed countries outrank America in life expectancy and infant mortality. Indeed, for all our high-tech medicine, Jamaican seniors outlive American seniors. According to the World Health Organization, life expectancy at age 65 is roughly equal, and at 85 it's longer in Jamaica. An argument for medical marijuana? No, it's an argument for walking. Dr. Denise Eldemire of the University of West Indies notes that 60 percent of Jamaica's elderly live in rural areas, where "walking is the only reliable means of transport." According to her studies, 78 percent of Jamaican elders walk daily. By contrast, just 60 percent of the entire U.S. adult population exercises at all.

Further evidence of medicine's limited effect is the slow pace of progress against cancer. The percentage of the U.S. population dying of cancer, while modestly improved in recent years, remains higher than in 1973, while the incidence of many specific forms of cancers, including non-Hodgkin's lymphoma, melanoma, and female breast and lung cancer have gotten worse. Headlines often celebrate how many more Americans are surviving cancer, but the underlying data offer little to cheer about. The five-year survival rate for men diagnosed with prostate cancer has improved—but mainly because doctors are able to detect it earlier, including cases that may never have proven lethal or been so only at advanced ages. The five-year survival rate for lung cancer is unchanged since the early 1970s. Breast cancer survival rates have improved by a matter of months, but like prostate cancer, much of this is due to earlier diagnosis, not to the success of treatment. Though there has been real progress in detecting and treating cancer, much of the claimed advance in survivability is really just an increase in the incidence of pseudo-disease. Cancer still kills 1,500 Americans a day.

Mortality from diabetes, liver, and kidney disease, meanwhile, has hardly changed since the 1960s—while infectious diseases continue to grow more numerous and deadly. Thirty years ago, the surgeon general declared it time to "close the book" on infectious disease. Since then, at least 20 that were once thought conquered, from tuberculosis to salmonella, have reemerged, while 29 new ones have been identified, including HIV/AIDS, Lyme disease, and hepatitis C. Meanwhile, antibiotic-resistant strains of all sorts of microbes are cropping up, largely because doctors keep dispensing antibiotics to treat what are actually viral infections.

In the face of such trends, even a Cadillac health-insurance plan plays little, if any, measurable role in improving health and life expectancy. A RAND Corporation study compared two groups of families over 15 years, one with full medical coverage, the other with a large deductible. The families with full coverage consumed 40 percent more health-care dollars than the other groups, but researchers couldn't detect any measurable differences in health.

Death of a Salesman

These results may seem odd until one considers that the eight leading causes of death in the United States—heart disease, cancer, stroke, pulmonary diseases, accidents, pneumonia/influenza, diabetes, and suicide—are closely tied to living conditions and behavior. According to the Institute of Medicine, social and behavioral factors such as smoking, diet, alcohol use, and sedentary lifestyles contribute to approximately half of all deaths in this country. Scientists estimate that up to 75 percent of all cancer deaths result from behavior such as smoking, diet, and lack of exercise. Though modern medicine can help stave off death from such behavior, rarely can it mitigate these factors altogether. Chemotherapy, for example, may put a smoker's lung cancer into remission. But he'll continue to face the risk of dying from heart disease or other chronic conditions brought on by his behavior and environment—including the damage his body suffers from chemotherapy itself.

In contrast, large-scale changes in social arrangements or the environment do have profound effects on health. There is powerful statistical evidence, for instance, that hierarchy and inequality are among the major contributing causes of premature death. The first hint of this came in a famous 1967 study of British civil service workers, which found that, within a given office mortality rates would increase, step by step, as one moved down the organization chart. Those at the bottom suffered three times the death rate of those at the top. Since everyone had equal access to health care under Britain's universal, socialized system, the study suggested that one's socioeconomic status is a key determinant of health.

Since then, a cascade of studies has confirmed the relationship between equality and health. The healthiest states, such as Utah, Iowa, and New Hampshire, are also those with the least disparity of income, while states such as Louisiana, Mississippi, and New York lead the nation in both poor population health and income inequality. Similarly, wealthy nations with low income inequality, such as Sweden and Japan, have higher life expectancy than wealthy countries in which income is less evenly shared, such as the United States and Britain.

30   This phenomenon isn't associated simply with extreme concentrations of poverty or wealth. Across nations and races, under both single-payer systems that provide universal care and market-driven

systems, life expectancy gradually increases according to socio-economic status. There is a raging debate over why this is so. Some researchers suggest that a widening gap between the rich and every-one else leads to deepening stress, frustration, and ultimately self-destructive behavior among people struggling unsuccessfully toward the top. (Imagine the unhappy American salesman who relieves his stress with booze, cigarettes, and occasionally compulsive unpro-tected sex with strangers.) Others speculate that political support for government services critical to health, such as clean water and police protection, erodes when too many of a society's resources are con-trolled by a narrow elite.

Others turn the question on its head, suggesting that the rich get ahead because they are, on average, healthier than everyone else to begin with and smart enough to know how to stay that way. Or it may be that education plays a key role, too. Those who do well in school may learn a greater awareness of how to lead a healthy life, and they may also have greater discipline and ability to defer gratifi-cation. In any event, those with a bright financial future certainly have more to lose, in a monetary sense at least, by indulging in un-healthy behavior.

But there is one point of agreement among all serious students of public health, which is that environment and social conditions play an overwhelming role in determining the prevalence of diseases and premature death. Indeed, a study published in the *Journal of the American Medical Association* estimates that 40 percent of all deaths are caused by behavior patterns that could be prevented. And yet, ap-proximately 95 percent of the $1 trillion dollars the nation spends on health goes for direct medical care services to individuals. Only 5 per-cent goes for measures designed to promote more healthy behavior among the population as a whole.

Deadly Suburbs

Persuading Americans to take better care of themselves is no easy task. As prohibition and the drug war demonstrate, simply criminal-izing unhealthy behavior goes only so far. Moreover, most of the un-healthy behavior we're talking about—say, eating Big Macs—shouldn't be criminalized in the first place. Imposing "sin" taxes, while somewhat effective, can only do so much without creating black markets. And most Americans are appropriately resentful of government efforts to penalize them for lifestyle choices. That's why, instead of punishing citizens for unhealthy behavior, the government should concentrate on reducing the major environmental causes of premature death—not just pollution, but poverty and hazardous living conditions—while also paying you to clean up your act. Here are three ideas on how to do it:

Drugs for Jumping Jacks: The benefits to older people of even moderate exercise are overwhelming. As a report sponsored by the AARP and other health and aging groups concludes: "Scientific evidence increasingly indicates that physical activity can extend years of active independent life, reduce disability, and improve the quality of life for older persons." And yet approximately 34 percent of those ages 50 and older are sedentary, and fewer than half of older adults report that their physician has suggested exercise.

35   Meanwhile, with Medicare's insolvency looming in 2030, both political parties are competing to offer a plan that would subsidize prescription drugs for seniors. These plans attempt to meet a real problem: Higher prescription drug costs are eating away at the economic well being of many moderate-income seniors.

There's little evidence, however, that such an entitlement would increase longevity. According to the Department of Health and Human Services, only 2 percent of the nation's elderly report being unable to obtain a needed prescription drug even once in the course of the year. Moreover, an estimated 17 percent of all hospital admissions among persons over 70 result from harmful combinations of prescriptions drugs. Overmedication in hospitals and nursing homes is a leading form of elder abuse.

Death by Sprawl: On a statistical basis, what's most likely to get you killed in the next year: (A) living in Israel during the Intifada; (B) living in crime-ridden, inner-city Baltimore, Chicago, Dallas, Houston, Milwaukee, Minneapolis-St. Paul, Philadelphia, or Pittsburgh; or (C) living in the bucolic outer suburbs of those cities? The answer is overwhelmingly C. A recent study by University of Virginia professor William H. Lucy found that Americans' migration into sprawling outer suburbs is actually a huge cause of premature death. In the suburbs, you're less likely to be killed by a stranger—unless you count strangers driving cars. Residents of inner-city Houston, for example, face about a 1.5 in 10,000 chance of being killed in the coming year by either a murderous stranger or in an automobile accident. But in the Houston suburb of Montgomery County, residents are 50 percent more likely to die from one of those two causes because the incidence of automobile accidents is so much higher.

Sprawling, auto-dependent suburbs are unhealthy in other ways, too. In such an environment, almost no one walks—and for good reason. In 1999, 4,906 pedestrians died, 873 of them children under 14. Not surprisingly, metro areas marked by sprawling development and a high degree of auto dependency—Orlando, Tampa, West Palm Beach, and Memphis, among others—are the most dangerous regions to walk in.

But rarely walking or riding a bike can also be deadly. Largely because of sprawl, the number of trips people take on foot has dropped by 42 percent in the last 20 years. This is particularly true among children. In 1977, children ages 5 to 15 walked or biked 15.8 percent of the time. By 1995, the rate dropped to only 9.9 percent. Seventy percent of all trips children take today are in the back seats of cars. So sprawl not only substantially increases the odds of dying in an auto crash, it also discourages routine exercise.

This is no small matter. Walking 10 blocks or more per day reduces the chance of heart disease in women by a third. The risks associated with a sedentary lifestyle rival those of hypertension, high cholesterol, diabetes, and even smoking. According to the surgeon general, the economic costs of obesity total $117 billion a year, about 9.4 percent of health-care spending. Americans who never exercise cost the health-care system $76.6 billion a year. Sprawl does not fully account for our increasingly sedentary lives, but it is a major factor, and therefore a leading cause of premature death.

Sprawl also leads to high levels of social isolation, which has its own public-health implications. Lonely individuals who are cut off from regular contact with friends and neighbors face highly elevated risks for heart diseases and other disorders. What's cause and effect is not entirely clear, but Robert Putnam, a professor of public policy at Harvard University, has found that an isolated individual's chances of dying over the next year fall by half if he joins a group, two-thirds if he joins two.

The good news is that reducing subsidies for sprawl is among the biggest policy levers available to improve public health. This includes reforming gas taxes that are currently nowhere near high enough to recoup the environmental costs of driving, let alone to compensate for the losses to the economy caused by autorelated deaths and injuries. And it includes ending overinvestment in new roads and highways, and directing more toward mass transit, bike trails, and sidewalks. Thanks to the surgeon general's warnings and vastly increased tobacco taxes, millions of Americans have overcome their addiction to nicotine. It's equally important for the federal government to warn Americans about the health hazards of auto-dependent sprawl and provide financial incentives to encourage a healthier environment and lifestyle.

Instead of paying a fare, for example, transit users should receive a dollar's credit on their swipe cards for up to three rides a day, financed by drivers who will enjoy less traffic, cleaner air, and a smaller burden on the health care system. The government could also offer greater home mortgage deductions to homeowners who move to cities and developments served by mass transit. These measures might at first seem politically unfeasible, but presented to an aging population as a way to improve public health and fix a failing health-care system, they may gain real political traction.

The Americans Without Disabilities Act: The Americans With Disability Act mandates everything from how parking lots and public bathrooms are arranged to how employers organize workplaces. Yet it does nothing to prevent disability. Why not adapt parallel legislation that would prevent Americans from becoming disabled in the first place?

45   For instance, the National Cancer Institute recommends at least five servings of fruits and vegetables a day—but prices for fruits and vegetables have increased more than any other food category in recent years. Expand the Food Stamp program so that everyone is entitled to generous, free weekly allowances of fruits and vegetables. Or how about creating an Interstate Bicycle Highway System using abandoned railroad right-of-way? Instead of charging tolls, pay cyclists according to the number of miles they've pedaled. Or how about mandating that companies that employ 25 or more workers provide on-site exercise rooms or tax-free benefits to cover gym membership? Or offer a $200-a-month benefit increase to obese welfare recipients who shed at least 20 pounds, using the subsequent decrease in Medicaid expenditures to meet the cost? The ideas are practically limitless.

How might American life change for the better if we took this approach? Consider the problem of the uninsured. Currently, the cost of health care is outpacing economic growth, so maintaining the number of insured people would seem enough of a challenge. But the question of what health care costs depends overwhelmingly on how much is needed—and that is determined largely by how Americans conduct their lives. How fat are we? How sedentary? How much pollution do we create? How much do we suffer from loneliness, depression, and social isolation? How much do we smoke, drink, or abuse drugs? How productively do we age? What the Costa Rican example shows us is that with the right behavioral changes in lifestyle and social environment, we too could lower health-care costs—maybe not to $273 per person, but low enough to afford universal health-care access. And Americans wouldn't even need to forego superfluous treatments; Costa Rica boasts world-class plastic surgeons and cosmetic dentists and still offers free universal health.

That would, however, require more time walking. And some of us would have to be bribed to take better care of ourselves. And there would be big expenses for building better transit systems, and more compact, socially cohesive, less-polluted communities. But which system seems like the better bargain?

Greek Hygiene

There are clear signs that Americans are becoming fed up with the current health-care system and open to bold new approaches. Marcus Welby would be shocked, for example, to know what Americans think of doctors these days. In the late 1960s, when millions of viewers tuned in to watch the avuncular M.D. offer sage advice to his patients about the root causes of their illnesses, more than 70 percent of Americans had confidence in medical leaders; today, only 40 percent trust doctors. A mere 29 percent of the public agrees with the statement: "The health-care system would work better if doctors had full control of the system."

And it seems the more people know about health care, the less faith they have in doctors and their remedies. While half the public now says it lacks trust in "scientific solutions" for health care, nearly 80 percent of health-care policy professionals share this doubt. According to a study that appeared recently in the medical journal. *Milbank Quarterly,* the largest single factor driving down trust in doctors—among the general public, but especially among health-care-policy experts—is mounting concern about the ineffectiveness of modern medicine.

In Greek mythology, the god of medicine, Asclepios, had two 50 daughters. Hygeia was the daughter responsible for prevention, while, Panacea was responsible for cure. Today, to the detriment of our nation's health, we're fixated on the idea that medicine will produce a panacea. It's time to listen to her more powerful sister.

Responding to Reading

1. Why, according to Longman, is it time to try a different approach when it comes to health care? What approach does he advocate? Why does he think his approach would be more effective and cheaper than the one currently in place?
2. Why does Longman think that the medical system plays such a limited role in extending life? What does he think doctors and nurses could do to improve the health-care system?
3. In paragraph 32, Longman says, "environment and social conditions play an overwhelming role in determining the prevalence of diseases and premature death." How does this statement suggest a way to allocate the funds that our nation spends on health care?

Responding in Writing

In paragraphs 33 through 47, Longman suggests several ways of persuading Americans to take care of themselves. Which of these suggestions strike you as reasonable? Which seem unrealistic?

Focus

What Is Happening to Medical Care?

Saturday Evening Post cover by Norman Rockwell, March 9, 1929.

Responding to the Image

1. The picture on page 649 appeared on the cover of *The Saturday Evening Post* in 1929. How does the artist portray physicians? What assumptions has the artist made about his audience? Do you think the doctor in the picture is a family practitioner or a specialist? What makes you think so?
2. What do the age and gender of the doctor imply? How do you account for the expression on the doctor's face? For the expression on the child's face? How might this picture be different if it were painted today?

The Overtreated American

Shannon Brownlee

1956–

Born in Honolulu, Hawaii, Shannon Brownlee earned a bachelor's degree in biology and master's degree in marine science from the University of California, Santa Cruz. She has worked as a journalist, writing articles and essays on genetics, cancer research, and health-care policy that have appeared in publications such as Time *magazine, the* New York Times, *the* Washington Post, *the* New Republic, *and the* Wilson Quarterly. *Previously a staff writer at* Discover *magazine and a senior writer at* U.S. News & World Report, *Brownlee is now a senior fellow at the New America Foundation. More of her work is available online at the foundation's Web site, http://www.newamerica.net/, under the heading "Current Fellows."*

Americans enjoy the most sophisticated medical care that money can buy—and one of the most vexing health-care-delivery systems. We spend about $1.2 trillion each year, two to four times per capita what other developed nations spend, yet we can't find a way to provide health insurance for 41 million citizens. After a brief respite in the 1990s when HMOs held down expenses by squeezing profits from doctors and hospitals, medical costs are once again soaring by 10 to 12 percent a year. Yet reforms proposed by Congress and the White House are only nibbling around the edges of the problem.

Such political timidity is understandable, given the experience of would-be reformers of the past. Any attempt to expand coverage for the uninsured while holding down costs inevitably raises fear in the minds of voters that the only way to accomplish these seemingly opposing goals is by restricting access to expensive, life-saving medical treatment. Sure, we feel bad about the 18,000 or so of our fellow citizens who die prematurely each year because they lack health insurance, and about the seniors who are forced to choose between buying food and buying medicine. But Americans want nothing to do with a system like England's, which, for example, is reluctant to provide dialysis to the elderly, and most of us who are now covered by either Medicare or private insurance have little stomach for health-care reform that contains even a whiff of rationing.

Behind this fear lies an implicit assumption that more health care means better health. But what if that assumption is wrong? In fact, what if more medicine can sometimes be bad not just for our pocketbooks but also for our health?

An increasing body of evidence points to precisely that conclusion. "There is a certain level of care that helps you live as long and as well as possible," says John Wennberg, the director of the Center for Evaluative Clinical Sciences at Dartmouth Medical School. "Then there's excess care, which not only doesn't help you live longer but may shorten your life or make it worse. Many Americans are getting excess care." According to the center, 20 to 30 percent of health-care spending goes for procedures, office visits, drugs, hospitalization, and treatments that do absolutely nothing to improve the quality or increase the length of our lives. At the same time, the type of treatment that offers clear benefits is not reaching many Americans, even those who are insured.

That's a sobering thought, but it opens the possibility of a new 5 way to look at the conundrum of health-care reform. Lawmakers, insurers, and the health-care industry might be able to save money if they were to concentrate on improving the quality of medicine rather than on controlling costs. Better health care will of course mean more medicine for some Americans, particularly the uninsured; but for many of us it will mean less medicine.

Support for this idea can be found in *The Dartmouth Atlas of Health Care*, a compendium of statistics and patterns of medical spending in 306 regions of the country. The atlas is generated by a group of nearly two dozen doctors, epidemiologists, and health-care economists, using data from Medicare, large private insurers, and a variety of other sources. Wennberg is the group's leader and the patron saint of the idea that more medicine does not necessarily mean better health—a view that has not exactly endeared him to the medical establishment over the years. These days, however, his ideas are bolstered by the Institute of Medicine and other independent researchers, and by new results coming from his Dartmouth research team, which is showing precisely how the nation misspends its health-care dollars.

Take the regions surrounding Miami and Minneapolis, which represent the high and low ends, respectively, of Medicare spending. A sixty-five-year-old in Miami will typically account for $50,000 more in Medicare expenses over the rest of his life than a sixty-five-year-old in Minneapolis. During the last six months of life, a period that usually accounts for more than 20 percent of a patient's total Medicare expenditures, a Miamian spends, on average, twice as many days in the hospital as his counterpart in Minneapolis, and is twice as likely to see the inside of an intensive-care unit.

This type of regional variation would make perfect sense if regions where citizens were sickest were the ones that used the most medical services. After all, it's only fair that we should spend more and do more in places where people need more medical attention. But, as Wennberg and his colleagues Elliott Fisher and Jonathan Skinner point out in a recent paper, "Geography and the Debate Over Medicare Reform," which appeared online in the journal *Health Affairs*, rates of underlying illness do not account for the differences in spending among regions. If they did, the region around Provo, Utah, one of the healthiest in the country, would get 14 percent fewer Medicare dollars than the national average, because its citizens are less likely to smoke, drink, or suffer from strokes, heart attacks, and other ailments. Instead it receives seven percent more than the national average. In contrast, elderly people in the region around Richmond, Virginia, tend to be sicker than the average American, and should be receiving 11 percent more—rather than 21 percent less—than the national average. Nor are regional differences explained by variations in the cost of care. Provo doctors are not, for example, charging significantly more for office visits or lumpectomies than doctors in Richmond, and their patients aren't getting costlier artificial hips.

Rather, much of the variation among regions—about 41 percent of it, by the most recent estimate—is driven by hospital resources and numbers of doctors. In other words, it is the supply of medical services rather than the demand for them that determines the amount of care delivered. Where neonatal intensive-care units are more abundant, more babies spend more days in the NICU. Where there are more MRI machines, people get more diagnostic tests; where there are more specialty practices, people see more specialists. It's probably safe to assume that many people are gravely ill during the last six months of their lives no matter where they live; but Medicare beneficiaries see, on average, twenty-five specialists in a year in Miami versus two in Mason City, Iowa, largely because Miami is home to a lot more specialists.

10   It would be one thing if all this lavish medical attention were helping people in high-cost regions like Miami to live longer or better. But that doesn't appear to be the case. Recent studies are beginning to show that excess spending in high-cost regions does not buy citizens better health. Medicare patients visit doctors more frequently in high-cost regions, to be sure, but they are no more likely than citizens in low-cost regions to receive preventive care such as flu shots or careful monitoring of their diabetes, and they don't live any longer. In fact, their lives may be slightly shorter. The most likely explanation for the increased mortality seen in high-cost regions is that elderly people who live there spend more time in hospitals than do citizens in low-cost regions, Wennberg says, "and we

know that hospitals are risky places." Patients who are hospitalized run the risk of suffering from medical errors or drug interactions, receiving the wrong drug, getting an infection, or being subjected to diagnostic testing that leads to unnecessary treatment.

An obvious way we might cut excess medical care is to change the way we pay hospitals and doctors. "Medicine is the only industry where high quality is reimbursed no better than low quality," says David Cutler, a health economist at Harvard. "The reason we do all the wasteful stuff is that we pay for what's done, not what's accomplished." Although that's clearly the case, figuring out the right incentives for health-care providers is by no means easy. Let's say that Medicare decided to use low-cost regions as a benchmark and told providers in the rest of the country that their compensation would be capped at some level not far above the benchmark. Some doctors in high-cost regions would undoubtedly be encouraged to practice more conservatively, but many others would maintain their incomes by either dropping Medicare patients altogether or giving them even more hysterectomies and CT scans they don't need (thus compensating for lower fees by simply performing a greater number of procedures).

Even if policymakers come up with the right financial incentives, restructuring compensation will constitute only one small component of the reform that's needed to turn medicine into an efficient, effective industry. Think of it this way: at 13 to 14 percent of GDP, health care is the nation's largest single industry, and probably its most complex. Transforming this sprawling behemoth is going to involve a lot more upheaval than, say, the shift that took place in the auto industry when companies adopted the assembly line, or the shake-up that Hollywood and the music industry now face with the advent of Web entertainment.

Step No. 1 toward improving the quality of health care is reducing what the Dartmouth group calls "supply-sensitive" care—the excess procedures, hospital admissions, and doctor visits that are driven by the supply of doctors and hospital resources rather than by need. Organizations such as the American Medical Association and Kaiser Permanente will need to set standards for more-conservative practices, and for measuring patient outcomes. Benchmarks are also needed to ensure that doctors deliver more "evidence-based" medicine: procedures and practices whose benefits are proven. Three recent studies, conducted by the Institute of Medicine, the Rand Corporation, and the President's Advisory Commission on Consumer Protection and Quality in the Health Care Industry, report widespread underuse of evidence-based treatment, such as balloon angioplasty to open blocked arteries in heart-attack victims, even among citizens with gold-plated health insurance.

Probably the hardest part of reforming health care will be persuading policymakers and politicians that improving the quality of care can also save money. The Medical Quality Improvement Act, introduced last July by Vermont Senator James Jeffords, is a step in the right direction. It would call on several medical centers around the country to model high-quality medicine that also reins in costs.

15 But evidence already exists that improving quality can hold down costs. Franklin Health, a company based in Upper Saddle River, New Jersey, manages so-called "complex cases" for private insurers. Complex cases are the sickest of the sick, patients with multiple or terminal illnesses, who are also the most costly to treat. They typically make up only one or two percent of the average patient population while accounting for 30 percent of costs. Franklin employs a battalion of nurses, who make home visits and spend hours on the phone, sometimes every day, to help patients control pain and other symptoms and stay out of the hospital. For this low-tech but intensive service the company charges insurers an average of $6,000 to $8,000 per patient—but it saves them $14,000 to $18,000 per patient in medical bills.

How much money is at stake? If spending in high-cost regions could somehow be brought in line with spending in low-cost regions, Medicare alone could save on the order of 29 percent, or $59 billion a year—enough to keep the Medicare system afloat for an additional ten years, or to fund a generous prescription-drug benefit for seniors. And there's no reason to believe that doctors and hospitals behave any differently toward their non-Medicare patients. That means the system as a whole is wasting about $400 billion a year—more than enough to cover the needs of the 41 million uninsured citizens.

The last attempt at reforming the U.S. health-care system failed in large measure because of fears of rationing. Reform was viewed as an effort to cut costs, not to improve health, and voters believed, rightly or wrongly, that they would end up being denied the benefits of modern medicine. Future efforts at reform are going to have to persuade Americans and their doctors that sometimes less care is better.

Responding to Reading

1. What assumption about health care does Brownlee say Americans have? Does she think this assumption is correct? What is the difference between excess care and the kind of care that offers clear benefits? How does this distinction provide "a new way to look at the conundrum of health-care reform" (5)?

2. According to John Wennberg and his Dartmouth research team, what determines the amount of medical care that is delivered to a region? Does increased medical attention necessarily enable people to live longer or better? Explain.

3. According to Brownlee, what should be done to improve the current health-care situation? What would be the hardest part of instituting the reforms she says are necessary? Does Brownlee seem optimistic or pes-

simistic about convincing physicians and patients "that sometimes less care is better" (19)?

Responding in Writing

Do you believe that Americans are overtreated? As a patient, how would you react to the reforms that Brownlee proposes in paragraph 17?

Doctor Takes Her Own Advice
Kara M. Nakisbendi
1969–

Born and raised in Philadelphia, Kara M. Nakisbendi received her BS and MD degrees from Temple University and completed her internship and residency in obstetrics and gynecology at Thomas Jefferson University Hospital. Nakisbendi is board certified in obstetrics and gynecology and is a Fellow of the American College of Obstetricians and Gynecologists. For four years, she practiced obstetrics and gynecology in a fast-paced private practice, but, realizing that she could not provide the level of care she wanted to and still make a living, Nakisbendi established her own "fee-for-service" gynecology practice in which she helps women make the transition from adolescence to menopause. In the following essay, she expresses the frustrations that caused her to abandon obstetrics, a field that she loved.

Delivering babies has been one of the most incredible experiences of my life. Yet last year I became one of many doctors in Pennsylvania who gave up obstetrics.

I have prided myself on being called a midwife from time to time because of how I support women in labor. I believe I provided a perfect balance between the benefits of a midwife and those of an obstetrician.

The goal was a peaceful, controlled delivery, with each patient and her support person being an active part of that process. I would spend time with my patient while she was in active labor. I tried to make sure I didn't just come in at the end when she was ready to deliver.

However, after only four years, I have found it near impossible to sustain that level of care. And if I can't practice the way I believe is necessary for good patient care, I won't practice.

Because of low reimbursements and high malpractice premiums, 5 doctors must increase volume to meet overhead. With this increase in volume, they struggle to give the level of care patients need and deserve. Add in the physical and emotional stress we endure on a regular basis. We don't let pilots fly the number of hours we work.

We don't let truck drivers travel the number of hours we stay awake. Yet, we expect doctors to sacrifice family and health to meet the bottom line. Doesn't it make sense that physicians lead healthy, balanced lives so they are awake and alert, functioning at their best and reducing medical errors?

One of my last days shows the emotional and physical stresses obstetricians face every day.

One morning about 8, I already had two patients in labor. A nurse asked me to come into one patient's room. My resident was doing an ultrasound that showed no fetal heart activity. The baby had died sometime before admission. This woman had gone through an entire pregnancy ready to see her newborn daughter, and I had to tell her she was no longer alive.

My dear patient got down on her knees and said we had to pray. I joined her. There was nothing else I could do. She then got up and said look again with the ultrasound. So we did. No miracle had happened. All expectations of this newborn life were gone. Not one eye in that room was dry. There was no holding back.

10   We discussed her options, but because of her history, she had to go through a cesarean section. While the patient took some time and received her epidural, my office hours had begun. I had to go see all the patients who had been waiting while I provided emotional support to the woman in labor. I had to swallow my grief. There was no time for it. I held back tears for my pregnant patients and pretended that there was nothing they needed to worry about.

I was called to the operating room when the woman was ready. Gone was the usual hustle and bustle around a woman about to have a baby. The silence was so painful. I did the cesarean section feeling as if I had received anesthesia. I placed my hand into her uterus and delivered this beautiful girl who was perfect in every way. She looked like she was ready to take her first breath. But no breath came. There was no heartbeat. Her spirit had passed.

I placed the baby on the warmer. She was given her first bath. The operation was over, and we handed my patient her baby girl. We stared in awe of her. She was so perfect. I didn't want to leave my patient and her husband. I wanted to help them grieve. I wanted to grieve. I couldn't. I had to say I was sorry and move on.

I continued to see patients throughout the day, feeling drained from the morning. One patient every 15 minutes. Even when office hours were finally over, I was still not done. I was on call. I delivered another patient who had a healthy baby boy with a vigorous cry.

By 10 p.m. I was still in the hospital. While one patient was laboring, I went to visit another who had been admitted with a bad reaction to her chemotherapy. She had recently been diagnosed with metastatic cancer. All I could do was to hug her and sit with her. There was no medicine I could give her to make her better.

15   Shortly after that, my laboring patient needed assistance with natural childbirth. It was her third, and she wanted to try to do it without

anesthesia. Natural childbirths have always been my favorite experiences. She progressed quickly but not without pain. I helped her and her husband use different positions to help ease the pain. After many hours, she reached down to her crying baby girl and held her in her arms.

Inside, I was still mourning the baby girl who had not made it earlier that day.

I crawled into bed at 2 in the morning. Another day ended. Lying there, I wanted to cry, but the exhaustion and the overwhelming numbness prevented me from letting down. I awoke at 7, wondering what the work day would bring.

This has been my life for four years. No more. There was nothing left of me. I had no time to mourn the losses. I had to go from death to life to death to life every 24 hours. Yes, this is medicine. Yes, this is life, but no one can function at this level of stress for an entire career.

Some doctors try, but at what cost? Their health? Their family? Patient care? How can we teach patients to live healthy, well-balanced lives when we can't do this ourselves?

There are amazing doctors in the Philadelphia area. One by one, 20 they are leaving. I am joining them. I am not leaving the area, but I left the field I loved. I do not feel obligated to fix a broken system.

Instead, I now practice gynecology on the old-fashioned, fee-for-service model. Patients pay me, and they can get reimbursed from their insurance companies. But I'm not chasing down insurers for money, which reduces my overhead and lets me run an office more efficiently. I'm practicing the way I want, without the volume or time constraints. I am taking the advice I give to my patients: I am finding the balance in my life.

Responding to Reading

1. What was Nakisbendi's goal with each patient? According to her, why has she found it nearly "impossible to sustain that level of care" (4)? Why does she compare physicians to pilots and truck drivers? Do you think that this comparison is effective?

2. Much of Nakisbendi's essay consists of a long section in which she describes her typical day. Why does she include this narrative? Could she have conveyed the same idea more effectively with another strategy?

3. At the end of her essay, Nakisbendi says that her practice, which no longer includes obstetrics, is now limited to gynecology. What are the advantages of this change? Why do you think Nakisbendi wrote this essay? Do you think she accomplished her purpose?

Responding in Writing

Think about the last visit you made to the doctor's. Did the physician provide good patient care? Did he or she show any signs of the stress that Nakisbendi describes?

MALPRACTICE: BY LAWYERS

Mona Charen

1957–

*Born in New York City, Mona Charen is a syndicated columnist who began
her career as an editorial assistant at* National Review *magazine. In 1984, she
joined the White House staff, serving as Nancy Reagan's speechwriter. Charen
earned a BA degree from Columbia University (1979) and a law degree from
Washington University School of Law (1984). In 2003, Charen published the
book* Useful Idiots: How Liberals Got It Wrong in the Cold War and Still
Blame America *(2003). To read more of her opinion columns, visit the Web
site http://www.townhall.com/columnists/monacharen/archive.shtml.*

They did it in West Virginia, and now they're going to do it in New
Jersey. Doctors are staging strikes. They will of course continue to care for
emergencies, but office visits and non-emergency surgeries will have to
wait. No one is quite sure for how long. It may be a day or two, or possibly
a week. But doctors have been driven to this attention-getting extreme
by an out-of-control malpractice system. To quote the old movie "Network," they're "mad as hell and they're not going to take it anymore."

The doctors are outraged because the malpractice lottery has made
the practice of medicine a combat zone. It is making a few lawyers
very rich but driving up costs, causing good doctors to abandon medicine, and souring the relationships between physicians and patients.

The situation is particularly acute for obstetricians, whose malpractice insurance premiums have jumped by as much as 150 percent in
four years. About one in 11 obstetricians has scaled back his or her
practice to gynecology only to avoid these enormous costs.

In places like Las Vegas, it's getting difficult for pregnant women to
find doctors willing to deliver babies, as malpractice premiums have
jumped from $37,000 to $150,000 annually. Obstetricians are paying a
heavy price because most malpractice suits in America are not about
bad medicine, they are about bad outcomes. In obstetrics, more than in
other fields, a certain number of disabled children and bereft parents is
unavoidable. But trial lawyers seize upon every tragedy as an opportunity to enrich themselves.

5   While the total number of medical malpractice suits has held
steady over the past decade, the size of recoveries has not. The average
jury award rose to $3.39 million in 1999—a 79 percent rise since 1993.

The trial lawyers argue that malpractice suits improve medicine by
going after the few bad apples in the medical profession and holding
them accountable. But as the Harvard Medical School study of 30,000
New York City cases demonstrated, more than 80 percent of the lawsuits filed were without merit—i.e., no malpractice was found.

As Peter Huber, a tort reform advocate has pointed out, about 20 percent of the suits did not even involve an adverse event—yet these tended to be settled for an average cost of $29,000. (Fifty-seven percent of medical malpractice premiums pay for lawyers' fees.) The presence or absence of actual malpractice had nothing to do with the likely outcome of the case. Insurance companies settle with plaintiffs all the time in order to avoid the expense of litigation.

One factor that did correlate well with likely outcomes was the socio-economic status of the plaintiff. Wealthier plaintiffs were more likely to file malpractice claims and more likely to recover damages. Another good predictor of outcome was the severity of disability (whether caused by negligence or not). The more disabled a plaintiff was, the more likely a sympathetic jury would award large damages.

Not only are doctors passing along their higher costs to patients in the form of higher fees, they are also increasing overall medical spending by practicing defensive medicine—ordering tests by the bucketful and referring patients to specialists to cover themselves in the event of a lawsuit.

What is particularly galling to many doctors is the fact that merely   10
being named in a malpractice suit is enough to raise your premiums— even if the suit turns out to be dismissed as without merit and even if the doctor in question had nothing to do with the alleged malpractice. If an orthopedist saw a patient for a sprained wrist, and that patient later sued his partner for a poor surgical outcome on his knee, the first doctor is named in the suit anyway.

What the striking doctors are asking for is a rule of reason. California has capped recoveries for pain and suffering at a quarter million dollars and has limited attorneys' contingency fees. There is no limit to recoveries for lost wages, lost future earnings or medical expenses, including rehabilitation for plaintiffs. If such a system were adopted nationwide, critics of the current system argue, it could save the country more than $50 billion a year.

That's reason enough for reform. But an equally pressing reason is that curbing the lottery would be a victory for sobriety. Misfortune is a part of life, and Americans once faced it with fortitude, not lawsuits.

Responding to Reading

1. According to Charen, doctors are striking because of "an out-of-control malpractice system" (1). What effect has this situation had on the medical profession? How has it caused a shortage of obstetricians?

2. What does Charen mean when she says, "most malpractice suits in America are not about bad medicine, they are about bad outcomes" (4)? How does Charen respond to the trial lawyers' argument that malpractice suits actually improve the practice of medicine by eliminating "the few bad

apples" (6)? How does Charen support her charge that "trial lawyers seize upon every tragedy as an opportunity to enrich themselves" (4)?

3. What suggestions does Charen have for dealing with the problem she identifies? Does she provide enough facts to support her conclusion? Could she be accused of overstating her case? Can you think of reasons other than overzealous trial lawyers for the rise in malpractice insurance rates?

Responding in Writing

Assume that you are a trial lawyer. Write a short letter to Charen in which you address one or two of her charges.

————————————— WIDENING THE FOCUS —————————————

The following readings can suggest additional perspectives for thinking and writing about the state of medical care in the United States. You may also want to do further research about this subject on the Internet.

- Marie Winn, "Television: The Plug-In Drug" (p. 270)

- Greg Critser, "Supersize Me" (p. 360)

- Garrett Hardin, "Lifeboat Ethics" (p. 715)

- Claire McCarthy, "Dog Lab" (p. 724)

For Internet Research: According to many experts, the health-care
system in the United States is in trouble. Most people in the United
States get health care coverage from their employers. As health insurance premiums continue to rise, however, companies pass more and more costs on to their employees. In addition, because of constantly rising malpractice insurance premiums, many physicians can no longer afford to carry out certain procedures—for example, obstetrics or high-risk surgery. To make matters even worse, millions of Americans lack basic health insurance coverage.

Physicians for a National Health Program (PNHP), a not-for-profit organization of health-care professionals, has proposed sweeping changes to the health-care system. The group's report, *A National Health Program for the United States: A Physicians' Proposal*, argues for a comprehensive system that would

1. fully cover everyone under a single public insurance program,

2. pay hospitals and nursing homes a total annual amount for all operating expenses, and

3. establish regulated systems for paying for physicians' and ambulatory services.

This program would control billing and personnel costs by distributing funds from a single payment pool.

Read   the   group's   proposal   at   <http://www.pnhp.org/
publications/a_national_health_program_for_the_united_states.php>.
Then, write a paper in which you evaluate this proposal. Is it an effective proposal? Who is its intended audience? Does it address the needs of that audience? Why or why not? What arguments and evidence are presented? How would you change the proposal to make it more effective?

─────────────────── WRITING ───────────────────

Medicine and Human Values

1. In his essay "The Metaphor of Blight" (p. 620), Abraham Verghese says that human beings "ascribe metaphors to disease" (1). For example, cancer is historically associated with failure, and tuberculosis is associated with "unbridled passion" (2). Choose a disease—like AIDS, SARS, or Alzheimer's—and consider what metaphors are associated with it. Then, write an essay in which you discuss how these metaphors may discourage people from getting help.

2. In his essay "The Bittersweet Science" (p. 608), Austin Bunn describes how physicians treated diabetes before insulin was discovered. Choose a disease for which we currently have a treatment—cancer, polio, smallpox, or leprosy, for example—and use the Internet to help you determine how physicians dealt with this disease before there was a cure or preventive measure, such as a vaccine. Then, write an essay in which you compare how people with the disease were regarded before there was a treatment and how they are regarded now. In your essay, refer specifically to Bunn's essay.

3. Do you agree with Elisabeth Kübler-Ross when she says that many people choose not to face the reality of death because they are afraid of it? Interview several of your friends and family members about their attitudes toward death. Then, write a short report in which you sum up your findings. In your report, refer specifically to Kübler-Ross's essay, "On the Fear of Death" (p. 628) as well as to Dylan Thomas's poem "Do Not Go Gentle into That Good Night" (p. 626).

4. Search the Internet (or your school library), and find some information about Margaret Sanger. Then, assume you are Sanger's supervisor. Write a report in which you assess Sanger's actions as a visiting nurse, and explain why you support or oppose her decision to discuss birth control with her patients. (Keep in mind that to do so in 1912 was against the law.)

5. Write a letter to Mona Charen (p. 658) in which you either agree or disagree with her charge that trial lawyers are destroying the American medical system. In your letter, specifically address each of her points, and suggest reforms (other than the one Charen suggests) that you think could fix "the out-of-control malpractice system" (1).

6. Currently, there is a debate about how much medical care the government should provide. What obligation do you think that the

government has to provide health care? For example, should the government pay for all prescriptions for children and for the elderly? For routine office visits? For long-term care? What limitations, if any, do you think there should be? In addition, how should the government pay for the care that you think is necessary? Read Phillip Longman's "The Health of Nations" (p. 635) and Shannon Brownlee's "The Overtreated American" (p. 650), and then write an editorial for your local newspaper in which you present your recommendations.

7. Identify a medical advance that has changed either your own life or the life of someone you know. Write an essay in which you discuss how this development has affected you or the person you know—and, possibly, society as a whole.

8. Assume you are the new director of Anna Mae Halgrim Seaver's nursing home. Write a memo in which you outline changes that would make life in the nursing home better for its residents. In your memo, respond specifically to the points Seaver mentions in her essay, "My World Now" (p. 624).

9. Do you think that a person has a right to die? Under what circumstances? In what way? Write an essay in which you discuss these issues. Include information from Dylan Thomas's "Do Not Go Gentle into That Good Night" (p. 626), Anna Mae Halgrim Seaver's "My World Now" (p. 624), and Elisabeth Kübler-Ross's "On the Fear of Death" (p. 628).

10. What do you think is happening to medical care in the United States? Do you believe that Americans are paying more than they ever have for medical care and getting less in return? Do you think that physicians give patients the attention they deserve? Write an essay in which you discuss these issues. Include information from the three essays in the Focus section of this chapter: Sharon Brownlee's "The Overtreated American" (p. 650), Mona Charen's "Malpractice: By Lawyers" (p. 658), and Kara M. Nakisbendi's "Doctor Takes Her Own Advice" (p. 655).

10

MAKING CHOICES

—————— PREPARING TO READ AND WRITE ——————

As Robert Frost suggests in his poem "The Road Not Taken" (p. 667), making choices is fundamental to our lives. The ability—and, in fact, the need—to make complex decisions is part of what makes us human. On a practical level, we choose friends, mates, careers, and places to live. On a more abstract level, we struggle to make the moral and ethical choices that people have struggled with for many years.

Many times, complex questions have no easy answers; occasionally, they have no answers at all. For example, should we abide by a law even if we believe it to be morally wrong? Should we stand up to

Peace Corps volunteer teaching a health class in Guatemala.

authority even if our stand puts us at risk? Should we help less fortunate individuals if such help threatens our own social or economic status? Should we strive to do well or to do good? Should we act to save an endangered species if that action may put people out of work? Should we tell the truth even if the truth may hurt us—or hurt someone else? Which road should we take, the easy one or the hard one?

Most of the time, the choice we (and the writers whose works appear in this chapter) face is the same: to act or not to act. To make a decision, we must understand both the long- and short-term consequences of acting in a particular way or of choosing not to act. We must struggle with the possibility of compromise—and with the possibility of making a morally or ethically objectionable decision. And, perhaps most important, we must learn to take responsibility for our decisions.

The writers whose essays are included in the Focus section of this chapter, "Can We Be Both Free and Safe?" consider the difficult question of how to achieve a balance between liberty and security. In the

Young businessman at work.

wake of the terrible events of September 11, 2001, many strongly be-lieve that it is necessary to sacrifice some of our rights and institute measures (such as racial and ethnic profiling, increased electronic sur-veillance, and limitations on immigration) that may protect us. Others feel just as strongly that to sacrifice any of our precious rights (for ex-ample, the right to privacy), even in the name of personal safety or na-tional security, is to sacrifice what it means to be an American. Now more than ever, this is a question that we must struggle to answer.

As you read and prepare to write about the selections in this chap-ter, you may consider the following questions:

- On what specific choice or choices does the essay focus? Is the de-cision to be made moral? Ethical? Political?

- Does the writer introduce a dilemma, a choice between two equally problematic alternatives?

- Does the choice the writer presents apply only to one specific situ-ation or case, or does it also have a wider application?

- Is the writer emotionally involved with the issue he or she is dis-cussing? Does this involvement (or lack of involvement) affect the writer's credibility?

- What social, political, or religious ideas influence the writer? How can you tell? Are these ideas similar to or different from your own views?

- Does the choice being considered cause the writer to examine his or her own values? The values of others? The values of the society at large? Does the selection lead you to examine your own values?

- Does the writer offer a solution? If so, do you find it reasonable?

- Does the choice the writer advocates require sacrifice? If so, does the sacrifice seem worth it?

- Which writers' views seem most alike? Which seem most different?

THE ROAD NOT TAKEN

Robert Frost

1874–1963

Robert Frost, four-time Pulitzer Prize–winning poet of rural New England, lived most of his life in New Hampshire and taught at Amherst College, Harvard University, and Dartmouth College. His subjects at first seem

familiar and comfortable, as does his language, but the symbols and allu-
sions and underlying meanings in many of his poems are quite complex.
Some of Frost's most famous poems are "Birches," "Mending Wall," and
"Stopping by Woods on a Snowy Evening." Frost read a poem, "The Gift
Outright," which he composed for the occasion, at the inauguration of Presi-
dent John F. Kennedy. In the poem that follows, "The Road Not Taken," the
speaker hesitates before making a choice. To read more about Frost, visit
the Web sites of the Academy of American Poets, http://www.poets.org, and
the Friends of Robert Frost, http://www.frostfriends.org.

Two roads diverged in a yellow wood,
And sorry I could not travel both
And be one traveller, long I stood
And looked down one as far as I could
To where it bent in the undergrowth;   5

Then took the other, as just as fair,
And having perhaps the better claim,
Because it was grassy and wanted wear;
Though as for that the passing there
Had worn them really about the same,   10

And both that morning equally lay
In leaves no step had trodden black.
Oh, I kept the first for another day!
Yet knowing how way leads on to way,
I doubted if I should ever come back.   15

I shall be telling this with a sigh
Somewhere ages and ages hence:
Two roads diverged in a wood, and I—
I took the one less travelled by,
And that has made all the difference.   20

Responding to Reading

1. What is the difference between the two paths Frost's speaker considers?
    Why does he make the choice he does?
2. Is "The Road Not Taken" simply about two paths in the wood, or does it
    suggest more? What makes you think so? To what larger choices might the
    speaker be alluding?
3. What does the speaker mean by "that has made all the difference" (20)?

Responding in Writing

In your own words, write a short summary of this poem. Use first person and
past tense (as Frost does).

ETHICS

Linda Pastan

1932–

As a senior at Radcliffe College in 1954, poet Linda Pastan won the Mademoiselle *poetry award (the runner-up that year was Sylvia Plath). Pastan earned an MLS degree from Simmons College (1955) and an MA degree from Brandeis University (1957). Her first book of poetry,* A Perfect Circle of Sun, *was published in 1971. The winner of numerous prizes for her poetry, Pastan often focuses on the complexity of domestic life, using intense imagery to bring a sense of mystery to everyday matters. She has been a lecturer at Breadloaf Writers Conference in Vermont and an instructor at American University, and she has written fourteen collections of poetry, including* Waiting for My Life *(1981),* PM/AM: New and Selected Poems *(1983),* Carnival Evening: New and Selected Poems 1968–1998, *(1998), and* The Last Uncle: Poems *(2002). "Ethics" is from* Waiting for My Life. *To read more about Pastan, visit the Academy of American Poets Web site, http://www.poets.org/.*

In ethics class so many years ago
our teacher asked this question every fall:
if there were a fire in a museum
which would you save, a Rembrandt painting
5   or an old woman who hadn't many
years left anyhow? Restless on hard chairs
caring little for pictures or old age
we'd opt one year for life, the next for art
and always half-heartedly. Sometimes
10   the woman borrowed my grandmother's face
leaving her usual kitchen to wander
some drafty, half imagined museum.
One year, feeling clever, I replied
why not let the woman decide herself?
15   Linda, the teacher would report, eschews
the burdens of responsibility.
This fall in a real museum I stand
before a real Rembrandt, old woman,
or nearly so, myself. The colors
20   within this frame are darker than autumn,
darker even than winter—the browns of earth,
though earth's most radiant elements burn
through the canvas. I know now that woman
and painting and season are almost one
25   and all beyond saving by children.

Responding to Reading

1. What choice actually confronts Pastan's speaker? What answer do you think the teacher expects the students to give?
2. Do you agree with the teacher that refusing to choose means avoiding responsibility? Does Frost's speaker (p. 667) have the option not to choose?
3. When the speaker says that "woman / and painting and season are almost one" (23–24), what does she mean? Does she imply that the teacher's question really has no answer? That the children who would "opt one year for life, the next for art" (8) are right?

Responding in Writing

Confronted with the choice facing the speaker, would you save the Rembrandt painting or the elderly woman? Why? Would you find this a difficult choice to make?

THE DEER AT PROVIDENCIA
Annie Dillard
1945–

Naturalist and essayist Annie Dillard wrote of the Roanoke Valley of Virginia in her first book, Pilgrim at Tinker Creek, *for which she won the Pulitzer Prize in 1975. The Pittsburgh native received her BA and MA degrees from Hollins College (1967, 1968) and has worked as an editor at* Harper's *magazine and as a writing professor at Western Washington University and Wesleyan University. Dillard calls herself a "stalker" of nature and its mysteries, and she delights in both the wonders and the terrors it inspires. Her books include* Teaching a Stone to Talk *(1982),* An American Childhood *(1987),* The Writing Life *(1989),* The Living *(1992),* Mornings Like This: Found Poems *(1995), and* For the Time Being *(1999). Her articles have been published in* Harper's *and the* Atlantic Monthly, *among other magazines. In "The Deer at Providencia," first published in 1982, Dillard explores the paradoxical nature of suffering for animals and humans.*

There were four of us North Americans in the jungle, in the Ecuadoran jungle on the banks of the Napo River in the Amazon watershed. The other three North Americans were metropolitan men. We stayed in tents in one riverside village, and visited others. At the village called Providencia we saw a sight which moved us, and which shocked the men.

The first thing we saw when we climbed the riverbank to the village of Providencia was the deer. It was roped to a tree on the grass clearing near the thatch shelter where we would eat lunch.

The deer was small, about the size of a whitetail fawn, but apparently full-grown. It had a rope around its neck and three feet caught in the rope. Someone said that the dogs had caught it that morning and the villagers were going to cook and eat it that night.

This clearing lay at the edge of the little thatched-hut village. We could see the villagers going about their business, scattering feed corn for hens about their houses, and wandering down paths to the river to bathe. The village headman was our host; he stood beside us as we watched the deer struggle. Several village boys were interested in the deer; they formed part of the circle we made around it in the clearing. So also did four businessmen from Quito[1] who were attempting to guide us around the jungle. Few of the very different people standing in this circle had a common language. We watched the deer, and no one said much.

5   The deer lay on its side at the rope's very end, so the rope lacked slack to let it rest its head in the dust. It was "pretty," delicate of bone like all deer, and thin-skinned for the tropics. Its skin looked virtually hairless, in fact, and almost translucent, like a membrane. Its neck was no thicker than my wrist; it was rubbed open on the rope, and gashed. Trying to paw itself free of the rope, the deer had scratched its own neck with its hooves. The raw underside of its neck showed red stripes and some bruises bleeding inside the muscles. Now three of its feet were hooked in the rope under its jaw. It could not stand, of course, on one leg, so it could not move to slacken the rope and ease the pull on its throat and enable it to rest its head.

Repeatedly the deer paused, motionless, its eyes veiled, with only its rib cage in motion, and its breaths the only sound. Then, after I would think, "It has given up; now it will die," it would heave. The rope twanged; the tree leaves clattered; the deer's free foot beat the ground. We stepped back and held our breaths. It thrashed, kicking, but only one leg moved; the other three legs tightened inside the rope's loop. Its hip jerked; its spine shook. Its eyes rolled; its tongue, thick with spittle, pushed in and out. Then it would rest again. We watched this for fifteen minutes.

Once three young native boys charged in, released its trapped legs, and jumped back to the circle of people. But instantly the deer scratched up its neck with its hooves and snared its forelegs in the rope again. It was easy to imagine a third and then a fourth leg soon stuck, like Brer Rabbit and the Tar Baby.[2]

We watched the deer from the circle, and then we drifted on to lunch. Our palm-roofed shelter stood on a grassy promontory from which we could see the deer tied to the tree, pigs and hens walking

---

[1]Capital of Ecuador. [Eds.]

[2]Characters created by southern writer Joel Chandler Harris. In one of Harris's stories, Brer Rabbit become stuck to a figure made of tar. [Eds.]

under village houses, and black-and-white cattle standing in the river. There was even a breeze.

Lunch, which was the second and better lunch we had that day, was hot and fried. There was a big fish called *doncella*, a kind of catfish, dipped whole in corn flour and beaten egg, then deep fried. With our fingers we pulled soft fragments of it from its sides to our plates, and ate; it was delicate fish-flesh, fresh and mild. Someone found the roe, and I ate of that too—it was fat and stronger, like egg yolk, naturally enough, and warm.

There was also a stew of meat in shreds with rice and pale brown 10 gravy. I had asked what kind of deer it was tied to the tree; Pepe had answered in Spanish, *"Gama."* Now they told us this was *gama* too, stewed. I suspect the word means merely game or venison. At any rate, I heard that the village dogs had cornered another deer just yesterday, and it was this deer which we were now eating in full sight of the whole article. It was good. I was surprised at its tenderness. But it is a fact that high levels of lactic acid, which builds up in muscle tissues during exertion, tenderizes.

After the fish and meat we ate bananas fried in chunks and served on a tray; they were sweet and full of flavor. I felt terrific. My shirt was wet and cool from swimming; I had had a night's sleep, two decent walks, three meals, and a swim—everything tasted good. From time to time each one of us, separately, would look beyond our shaded roof to the sunny spot where the deer was still convulsing in the dust. Our meal completed, we walked around the deer and back to the boats.

That night I learned that while we were watching the deer, the others were watching me.

We four North Americans grew close in the jungle in a way that was not the usual artificial intimacy of travelers. We liked each other. We stayed up all that night talking, murmuring, as though we rocked on hammocks slung above time. The others were from big cities: New York, Washington, Boston. They all said that I had no expression on my face when I was watching the deer—or at any rate, not the expression they expected.

They had looked to see how I, the only woman, and the youngest, was taking the sight of the deer's struggles. I looked detached, apparently, or hard, or calm, or focused, still. I don't know. I was thinking. I remember feeling very old and energetic. I could say like Thoreau that I have traveled widely in Roanoke, Virginia.[3] I have thought a great deal about carnivorousness; I eat meat. These things are not issues; they are mysteries.

---

[3]In *Walden,* Henry David Thoreau (see p. 680) says, "I have traveled a good deal in Concord." [Eds.]

15   Gentlemen of the city, what surprises you? That there is suffering here, or that I know it?

We lay in the tent and talked, "If it had been my wife," one man said with special vigor, amazed, "she wouldn't have cared what was going on; she would have dropped *everything* right at that moment and gone in the village from here to there to there, she would not have *stopped* until that animal was out of its suffering one way or another. She couldn't *bear* to see a creature in agony like that."

I nodded.

Now I am home. When I wake I comb my hair before the mirror above my dresser. Every morning for the past two years I have seen in that mirror, beside my sleep-softened face, the blackened face of a burnt man. It is a wire-service photograph clipped from a newspaper and taped to my mirror. The caption reads: "Alan McDonald in Miami hospital bed." All you can see in the photograph is a smudged triangle of face from his eyelids to his lower lip; the rest is bandages. You cannot see the expression in his eyes; the bandages shade them.

The story, headed MAN BURNED FOR SECOND TIME, begins:

> "Why does God hate me?" Alan McDonald asked from his hospital bed.
> "When the gunpowder went off, I couldn't believe it," he said. "I just couldn't believe it. I said, 'No, God couldn't do this to me again.'"

20   He was in a burn ward in Miami, in serious condition. I do not even know if he lived. I wrote him a letter at the time, cringing.

He had been burned before, thirteen years previously, by flaming gasoline. For years he had been having his body restored and his face remade in dozens of operations. He had been a boy, and then a burnt boy. He had already been stunned by what could happen, by how life could veer.

Once I read that people who survive bad burns tend to go crazy; they have a very high suicide rate. Medicine cannot ease their pain; drugs just leak away, soaking the sheets, because there is no skin to hold them in. The people just lie there and weep. Later they kill themselves. They had not known, before they were burned, that the world included such suffering, that life could permit them personally such pain.

This time a bowl of gunpowder had exploded on McDonald.

> "I didn't realize what had happened at first," he recounted. "And then I heard that sound from 13 years ago. I was burning. I rolled to put the fire out and I thought, 'Oh God, not again.'
> "If my friend hadn't been there, I would have jumped into a canal with a rock around my neck."

His wife concludes the piece, "Man, it just isn't fair."

I read the whole clipping again every morning. This is the Big 25
Time here, every minute of it. Will someone please explain to Alan
McDonald in his dignity, to the deer at Providencia in his dignity,
what is going on? And mail me the carbon.

When we walked by the deer at Providencia for the last time, I
said to Pepe, with a pitying glance at the deer, "*Pobrecito*"—"poor little thing." But I was trying out Spanish. I knew at the time it was a
ridiculous thing to say.

Responding to Reading

1. Could Dillard have done anything to free the deer? Why do you think she
   chose to do nothing? Does she regret her decision not to act? Do you think
   she *should* regret it?
2. In paragraph 14, Dillard says, "I have thought a great deal about carnivorousness; I eat meat. These things are not issues; they are mysteries." What
   does she mean? Do you find this statement a satisfactory explanation of
   her ability to enjoy deer meat while she watches the trapped deer "convulsing in the dust" (11)? Why or why not?
3. What connection does Dillard see between Alan McDonald and the deer at
   Providencia? Do you see this as a reasonable association, or do you believe
   Dillard has exploited (or even invented) a connection?

Responding in Writing

Reread paragraphs 5 and 6, in which Dillard describes the deer's suffering.
Rewrite this passage from the deer's point of view, paraphrasing Dillard's language and deleting information that the deer could not know or observe.

SHOOTING AN ELEPHANT

George Orwell

1903–1950

*This detailed account of a cruel incident with an elephant in Burma is
George Orwell's most powerful criticism of imperialism and the impossible
position of British police officers—himself among them—in the colonies. Orwell says about the incident, "It was perfectly clear to me what I ought to
do," but then he thinks of "the watchful yellow faces from behind" and realizes that his choice is not so simple. (Also see Orwell's essay in Chapter 3,
p. 226.)*

In Moulmein, in lower Burma, I was hated by large numbers of
people—the only time in my life that I have been important enough

for this to happen to me. I was sub-divisional police officer of the town, and in an aimless, petty kind of way anti-European feeling was very bitter. No one had the guts to raise a riot, but if a European woman went through the bazaars alone somebody would probably spit betel juice over her dress. As a police officer I was an obvious target and was baited whenever it seemed safe to do so. When a nimble Burman tripped me up on the football field and the referee (another Burman) looked the other way, the crowd yelled with hideous laughter. This happened more than once. In the end the sneering yellow faces of young men that met me everywhere, the insults hooted after me when I was at a safe distance, got badly on my nerves. The young Buddhist priests were the worst of all. There were several thousands of them in the town and none of them seemed to have anything to do except stand on street corners and jeer at Europeans.

All this was perplexing and upsetting. For at that time I had already made up my mind that imperialism was an evil thing and the sooner I chucked up my job and got out of it the better. Theoretically—and secretly, of course—I was all for the Burmese and all against their oppressors, the British. As for the job I was doing, I hated it more bitterly than I can perhaps make clear. In a job like that you see the dirty work of Empire at close quarters. The wretched prisoners huddling in the stinking cages of the lock-ups, the grey, cowed faces of the long-term convicts, the scarred buttocks of the men who had been flogged with bamboos—all these oppressed me with an intolerable sense of guilt. But I could get nothing into perspective. I was young and ill-educated and I had had to think out my problems in the utter silence that is imposed on every Englishman in the East. I did not even know that the British Empire is dying, still less did I know that it is a great deal better than the younger empires that are going to supplant it.[1] All I knew was that I was stuck between my hatred of the empire I served and my rage against the evil-spirited little beasts who tried to make my job impossible. With one part of my mind I thought of the British Raj[2] as an unbreakable tyranny, as something clamped down, in *saecula saeculorum*,[3] upon the will of prostrate peoples; with another part I thought that the greatest joy in the world would be to drive a bayonet into a Buddhist priest's guts. Feelings like these are the normal by-products of imperialism; ask any Anglo-Indian official, if you can catch him off duty.

One day something happened which in a roundabout way was enlightening. It was a tiny incident in itself, but it gave me a better glimpse than I had had before of the real nature of imperialism—the

---

[1]This essay was written in 1936, three years before the start of World War II; Stalin and Hitler were in power. [Eds.]

[2]Sovereignty. [Eds.]

[3]From time immemorial. [Eds.]

real motives for which despotic governments act. Early one morning the sub-inspector at a police station the other end of the town rang me up on the phone and said that an elephant was ravaging the bazaar. Would I please come and do something about it? I did not know what I could do, but I wanted to see what was happening and I got on to a pony and started out. I took my rifle, an old .44 Winchester and much too small to kill an elephant, but I thought the noise might be useful *in terrorem.* Various Burmans stopped me on the way and told me about the elephant's doings. It was not, of course, a wild elephant, but a tame one which had gone "must." It had been chained up, as tame elephants always are when their attack of "must"[4] is due, but on the previous night it had broken its chain and escaped. Its mahout,[5] the only person who could manage it when it was in that state, had set out in pursuit, but had taken the wrong direction and was now twelve hours' journey away, and in the morning the elephant had suddenly reappeared in the town. The Burmese population had no weapons and were quite helpless against it. It had already destroyed somebody's bamboo hut, killed a cow, and raided some fruit-stalls and devoured the stock; also it had met the municipal rubbish van and, when the driver jumped out and took to his heels, had turned the van over and inflicted violences upon it.

The Burmese sub-inspector and some Indian constables were waiting for me in the quarter where the elephant had been seen. It was a very poor quarter, a labyrinth of squalid bamboo huts, thatched with palm-leaf, winding all over a steep hillside. I remember that it was a cloudy, stuffy morning at the beginning of the rains. We began questioning the people as to where the elephant had gone and, as usual, failed to get any definite information. That is invariably the case in the East; a story always sounds clear enough at a distance, but the nearer you get to the scene of events the vaguer it becomes. Some of the people said that the elephant had gone in one direction, some said that he had gone in another, some professed not even to have heard of any elephant. I had almost made up my mind that the whole story was a pack of lies, when we heard yells a little distance away. There was a loud, scandalized cry of "Go away, child! Go away this instant!" and an old woman with a switch in her hand came round the corner of a hut, violently shooing away a crowd of naked children. Some more women followed, clicking their tongues and exclaiming; evidently there was something that the children ought not to have seen. I rounded the hut and saw a man's dead body sprawling in the mud. He was an Indian, a black Dravidian coolie,[6] almost

---

[4]Frenzy. [Eds.]
[5]Keeper. [Eds.]
[6]An unskilled laborer. [Eds.]

naked, and he could not have been dead many minutes. The people said that the elephant had come suddenly upon him round the corner of the hut, caught him with its trunk, put its foot on his back, and ground him into the earth. This was the rainy season and the ground was soft, and his face had scored a trench a foot deep and a couple of yards long. He was lying on his belly with arms crucified and head sharply twisted to one side. His face was coated with mud, the eyes wide open, the teeth bared and grinning with an expression of unendurable agony. (Never tell me, by the way, that the dead look peaceful. Most of the corpses I have seen looked devilish.) The friction of the great beast's foot had stripped the skin from his back as neatly as one skins a rabbit. As soon as I saw the dead man I sent an orderly to a friend's house nearby to borrow an elephant rifle. I had already sent back the pony, not wanting it to go mad with fright and throw me if it smelt the elephant.

5   The orderly came back in a few minutes with a rifle and five cartridges, and meanwhile some Burmans had arrived and told us that the elephant was in the paddy fields below, only a few hundred yards away. As I started forward practically the whole population of the quarter flocked out of the houses and followed me. They had seen the rifle and were all shouting excitedly that I was going to shoot the elephant. They had not shown much interest in the elephant when he was merely ravaging their homes, but it was different now that he was going to be shot. It was a bit of fun to them, as it would be to an English crowd; besides they wanted the meat. It made me vaguely uneasy. I had no intention of shooting the elephant—I had merely sent for the rifle to defend myself if necessary—and it is always unnerving to have a crowd following you. I marched down the hill, looking and feeling a fool, with the rifle over my shoulder and an ever-growing army of people jostling at my heels. At the bottom, when you got away from the huts, there was a metalled road and beyond that a miry waste of paddy fields a thousand yards across, not yet ploughed but soggy from the first rains and dotted with coarse grass. The elephant was standing eight yards from the road, his left side towards us. He took not the slightest notice of the crowd's approach. He was tearing up bunches of grass, beating them against his knees to clean them and stuffing them into his mouth.

I had halted on the road. As soon as I saw the elephant I knew with perfect certainty that I ought not to shoot him. It is a serious matter to shoot a working elephant—it is comparable to destroying a huge and costly piece of machinery—and obviously one ought not to do it if it can possibly be avoided. And at that distance, peacefully eating, the elephant looked no more dangerous than a cow. I thought then and I think now that his attack of "must" was already passing off; in which case he would merely wander harmlessly about until the mahout came back and caught him. Moreover, I did not in the least want to shoot him. I decided that I would watch him for a little while to make sure that he did not turn savage again, and then go home.

But at that moment I glanced round at the crowd that had followed me. It was an immense crowd, two thousand at the least and growing every minute. It blocked the road for a long distance on either side. I looked at the sea of yellow faces above the garish clothes—faces all happy and excited over this bit of fun, all certain that the elephant was going to be shot. They were watching me as they would watch a conjurer about to perform a trick. They did not like me, but with the magical rifle in my hands I was momentarily worth watching. And suddenly I realized that I should have to shoot the elephant after all. The people expected it of me and I had got to do it; I could feel their two thousand wills pressing me forward, irresistibly. And it was at this moment, as I stood there with the rifle in my hands, that I first grasped the hollowness, the futility of the white man's dominion in the East. Here was I, the white man with his gun, standing in front of the unarmed native crowd—seemingly the leading actor of the piece; but in reality I was only an absurd puppet pushed to and fro by the will of those yellow faces behind. I perceived in this moment that when the white man turns tyrant it is his own freedom that he destroys. He becomes a sort of hollow, posing dummy, the conventionalized figure of a sahib.[7] For it is the condition of his rule that he shall spend his life in trying to impress the "natives," and so in every crisis he has got to do what the "natives" expect of him. He wears a mask, and his face grows to fit it. I had got to shoot the elephant. I had committed myself to doing it when I sent for the rifle. A sahib has got to act like a sahib; he has got to appear resolute, to know his own mind and do definite things. To come all that way, rifle in hand, with two thousand people marching at my heels, and then to trail feebly away, having done nothing—no, that was impossible. The crowd would laugh at me. And my whole life, every white man's life in the East, was one long struggle not to be laughed at.

But I did not want to shoot the elephant. I watched him beating his bunch of grass against his knees, with that preoccupied grandmotherly air that elephants have. It seemed to me that it would be murder to shoot him. At that age I was not squeamish about killing animals, but I had never shot an elephant and never wanted to. (Somehow it always seems worse to kill a *large* animal.) Besides, there was the beast's owner to be considered. Alive, the elephant was worth at least a hundred pounds; dead, he would only be worth the value of his tusks, five pounds, possibly. But I had got to act quickly. I turned to some experienced looking Burmans who had been there when we

---

[7]Term used by natives of colonial India when referring to a European of rank. [Eds.]

arrived, and asked them how the elephant had been behaving. They all said the same thing: he took no notice of you if you left him alone, but he might charge if you went too close to him.

It was perfectly clear to me what I ought to do. I ought to walk up to within, say, twenty-five yards of the elephant and test his behavior. If he charged, I could shoot; if he took no notice of me, it would be safe to leave him until the mahout came back. But also I knew that I was going to do no such thing. I was a poor shot with a rifle and the ground was soft mud into which one would sink at every step. If the elephant charged and I missed him, I should have about as much chance as a toad under a steam-roller. But even then I was not thinking particularly of my own skin, only of the watchful yellow faces behind. For at that moment, with the crowd watching me, I was not afraid in the ordinary sense, as I would have been if I had been alone. A white man mustn't be frightened in front of "natives"; and so, in general, he isn't frightened. The sole thought in my mind was that if anything went wrong those two thousand Burmans would see me pursued, caught, trampled on, and reduced to a grinning corpse like that Indian up the hill. And if that happened it was quite probable that some of them would laugh. That would never do. There was only one alternative. I shoved the cartridges into the magazine and lay down on the road to get a better aim.

10   The crowd grew very still, and a deep, low, happy sigh, as of people who see the theatre curtain go up at last, breathed from innumerable throats. They were going to have their bit of fun after all. The rifle was a beautiful German thing with cross-hair sights. I did not then know that in shooting an elephant one would shoot to cut an imaginary bar running from ear-hole to ear-hole. I ought, therefore, as the elephant was sideways on, to have aimed straight at his ear-hole; actually I aimed several inches in front of this, thinking the brain would be further forward.

When I pulled the trigger I did not hear the bang or feel the kick—one never does when a shot goes home—but I heard the devilish roar of glee that went up from the crowd. In that instant, in too short a time, one would have thought, even for the bullet to get there, a mysterious, terrible change had come over the elephant. He neither stirred nor fell, but every line of his body had altered. He looked suddenly stricken, shrunken, immensely old, as though the frightful impact of the bullet had paralysed him without knocking him down. At last, after what seemed a long time—it might have been five seconds, I dare say—he sagged flabbily to his knees. His mouth slobbered. An enormous senility seemed to have settled upon him. One could have imagined him thousands of years old. I fired again into the same spot. At the second shot he did not collapse but climbed with desperate slowness to his feet and stood weakly upright, with legs sagging and head dropping. I fired a third time. That was the shot that did for him. You could see the agony of it jolt his whole body and knock the last remnant of strength from his legs. But in falling he seemed for a moment to rise, for as his hind legs collapsed beneath him he seemed to tower upward like a huge rock toppling, his trunk reaching skywards like a tree. He trumpeted, for the first and only time. And then down he came, his belly towards me, with a crash that seemed to shake the ground even where I lay.

I got up. The Burmans were already racing past me across the mud. It was obvious that the elephant would never rise again, but he was not dead. He was breathing very rhythmically with long rattling gasps, his great mound of a side painfully rising and falling. His mouth was wide open—I could see far down into caverns of pale pink throat. I waited a long time for him to die, but his breathing did not weaken. Finally I fired my two remaining shots into the spot where I thought his heart must be. The thick blood welled out of him like red velvet, but still he did not die. His body did not even jerk when the shots hit him, the tortured breathing continued without a pause. He was dying, very slowly and in great agony, but in some world remote from me where not even a bullet could damage him further. I felt that I had got to put an end to that dreadful noise. It seemed dreadful to see the great beast lying there, powerless to move and yet powerless to die, and not even to be able to finish him. I sent back for my small rifle and poured shot after shot into his heart and down his throat. They seemed to make no impression. The tortured gasps continued as steadily as the ticking of a clock.

In the end I could not stand it any longer and went away. I heard later that it took him half an hour to die. Burmans were bringing dahs[8] and baskets even before I left, and I was told they had stripped his body almost to the bones by the afternoon.

Afterwards, of course, there were endless discussions about the shooting of the elephant. The owner was furious, but he was only an Indian and could do nothing. Besides, legally I had done the right thing, for a mad elephant has to be killed, like a mad dog, if its owner fails to control it. Among the Europeans opinion was divided. The older men said I was right, the younger men said it was a damn shame to shoot an elephant for killing a coolie, because an elephant was worth more than any damn Coringhee coolie. And afterwards I was very glad that the coolie had been killed; it put me legally in the right and it gave me a sufficient pretext for shooting the elephant. I often wondered whether any of the others grasped that I had done it solely to avoid looking a fool.

---

[8]Large knives. [Eds.]

Responding to Reading

1. The central focus of this essay is Orwell's struggle to decide how to control the elephant. Do you think he really has a choice? Explain.
2. Orwell says that his encounter with the elephant, although "a tiny incident in itself," gave him an understanding of "the real nature of imperialism— the real motives for which despotic governments act" (3). In light of this statement, do you think his purpose in this essay is to explore something about himself or something about the nature of British colonialism—or both?
3. In paragraphs 5–6, Orwell introduces the elephant as peaceful and inno- cent; in paragraphs 11–12, he describes the animal's misery. What do these paragraphs contribute to the essay?

Responding in Writing

Compare paragraphs 11–12 with paragraphs 5–6 of Annie Dillard's essay (p. 669). How are the descriptions alike? How are they different?

Civil Disobedience

Henry David Thoreau

1817–1862

American essayist, journalist, and intellectual Henry David Thoreau was a social rebel who loved nature and solitude. A follower of transcendentalism, a philosophic and literary movement that flourished in New England, he contributed to the Dial, *a publication that gave voice to the movement's ro- mantic, idealistic, and individualistic beliefs. For three years, Thoreau lived in a cabin near Walden Pond in Concord, Massachusetts, and he recorded his experiences there in his most famous book,* Walden *(1854). He left* Walden, *however, because, according to him, he had "several more lives to live and could not spare any more for that one." A canoe excursion in 1839 resulted in the chronicle* A Week on the Concord and Merrimack Rivers, *and other experiences produced books about Maine and Cape Cod. The fol- lowing impassioned and eloquent defense of civil disobedience, published in 1849, has influenced such leaders as Gandhi and Martin Luther King, Jr. To read more about Thoreau, visit, http://www.transcendentalists.com/lthorea .html.*

I heartily accept the motto,—"That government is best which governs least;" and I should like to see it acted up to more rapidly and systematically. Carried out, it finally amounts to this, which also I believe,—"That government is best which governs not at all"; and when men are prepared for it, that will be the kind of government which they will have. Government is at best but an expedient; but most governments are usually, and all governments are sometimes, inexpedient. The objections which have been brought against a standing army, and they are many and weighty, and deserve to prevail, may also at last be brought against a standing government. The standing army is only an arm of the standing government. The government itself, which is only the mode which the people have chosen to execute their will, is equally liable to be abused and perverted before the people can act through it. Witness the present Mexican war,[1] the work of comparatively a few individuals using the standing government as their tool; for, in the outset, the people would not have consented to this measure.

This American Government,—what is it but a tradition, though a recent one, endeavoring to transmit itself unimpaired to posterity, but each instant losing some of its integrity? It has not the vitality and force of a single living man; for a single man can bend it to his will. It is a sort of wooden gun to the people themselves. But it is not the less necessary for this; for the people must have some complicated machinery or other, and hear its din, to satisfy that idea of government which they have. Governments show thus how successfully men can be imposed on, even impose on themselves, for their own advantage. It is excellent, we must all allow. Yet this government never of itself furthered any enterprise, but by the alacrity with which it got out of its way. *It* does not keep the country free. *It* does not settle the West. *It* does not educate. The character inherent in the American people has done all that has been accomplished; and it would have done somewhat more, if the government had not sometimes got in its way. For government is an expedient by which men would fain succeed in letting one another alone; and, as has been said, when it is most expedient, the governed are most let alone by it. Trade and commerce, if they were not made of India-rubber, would never manage to bounce over the obstacles which legislators are continually putting in their way; and, if one were to judge these men wholly by the effects of their actions and not partly by their intentions, they would deserve to be classed and punished with those mischievous persons who put obstructions on the railroads.

But, to speak practically and as a citizen, unlike those who call themselves no-government men, I ask for, not at once no government, but *at once* a better government. Let every man make known what kind of government would command his respect, and that will be one step toward obtaining it.

---

[1] In December 1845, the US annexation of Texas, led to a war between the United States and Mexico (1846–1848). Thoreau opposed this war, thinking it served the interests of slaveholders, who believed that the land won from Mexico would be slave territory. In protest, he refused to pay the Massachusetts poll tax and was arrested for his act of civil disobedience. [Eds.]

After all, the practical reason why, when the power is once in the hands of the people, a majority are permitted, and for a long period continue, to rule is not because they are most likely to be in the right, nor because this seems fairest to the minority, but because they are physically the strongest. But a government in which the majority rule in all cases cannot be based on justice, even as far as men understand it. Can there not be a government in which majorities do not virtually decide right and wrong, but conscience?—in which majorities decide only those questions to which the rule of expediency is applicable? Must the citizen ever for a moment, or in the least degree, resign his conscience to the legislator? Why has every man a conscience, then? I think that we should be men first, and subjects afterward. It is not desirable to cultivate a respect for the law, so much as for the right. The only obligation which I have a right to assume is to do at any time what I think right. It is truly enough said, that a corporation has no conscience; but a corporation of conscientious men is a corporation *with* a conscience. Law never made men a whit more just; and, by means of their respect for it, even the well-disposed are daily made the agents of injustice. A common and natural result of any undue respect for law is, that you may see a file of soldiers, colonel, captain, corporal, privates, powder-monkeys, and all, marching in admirable order over hill and dale to the wars, against their wills, ay, against their common sense and consciences, which makes it very steep marching indeed, and produces a palpitation of the heart. They have no doubt that it is a damnable business in which they are concerned; they are all peaceably inclined. Now, what are they? Men at all? or small movable forts and magazines, at the service of some unscrupulous man in power? Visit the Navy-Yard, and behold a marine, such a man as an American government can make, or such as it can make a man with its black arts,—a mere shadow and reminiscence of humanity, a man laid out alive and standing, and already, as one may say, buried under arms with funeral accompaniments, though it may be,—

> "Not a drum was heard, not a funeral note,
> As his corse to the rampart we hurried;
> Not a soldier discharged his farewell shot
> O'er the grave where our hero we buried."[2]

5   The mass of men serve the state thus, not as men mainly, but as machines, with their bodies. They are the standing army, and the militia, jailers, constables, posse comitatus, etc. In most cases there is no free exercise whatever of the judgment or of the moral sense; but they

---

[2]From "The Burial of Sir John Moore at Corunna," by Irish poet Charles Wolfe (1791–1823). [Eds.]

put themselves on a level with wood and earth and stones; and wooden men can perhaps be manufactured that will serve the purpose as well. Such command no more respect than men of straw or a lump of dirt. They have the same sort of worth only as horses and dogs. Yet such as these even are commonly esteemed good citizens. Others—as most legislators, politicians, lawyers, ministers, and office-holders—serve the state chiefly with their heads; and, as they rarely make any moral distinctions, they are as likely to serve the Devil, without intending it, as God. A very few, as heroes, patriots, martyrs, reformers in the great sense, and men, serve the state with their consciences also, and so necessarily resist it for the most part; and they are commonly treated as enemies by it. A wise man will only be useful as a man, and will not submit to be "clay," and "stop a hole to keep the wind away,"[3] but leave that office to his dust at least:—

"I am too high-born to be propertied,
To be a secondary at control,
Or useful serving-man and instrument
To any sovereign state throughout the world."[4]

He who gives himself entirely to his fellow-men appears to them useless and selfish; but he who gives himself partially to them is pronounced a benefactor and philanthropist.

How does it become a man to behave toward this American government to-day? I answer, that he cannot without disgrace be associated with it. I cannot for an instant recognize that political organization as *my* government which is the *slave's* government also.

All men recognize the right of revolution; that is, the right to refuse allegiance to, and to resist, the government, when its tyranny or its inefficiency are great and unendurable. But almost all say that such is not the case now. But such was the case, they think, in the Revolution of '75. If one were to tell me that this was a bad government because it taxed certain foreign commodities brought to its ports, it is most probable that I should not make an ado about it, for I can do without them. All machines have their friction; and possibly this does enough good to counterbalance the evil. At any rate, it is a great evil to make a stir about it. But when the friction comes to have its machine, and oppression and robbery are organized, I say, let us not have such a machine any longer. In other words, when a sixth of the population of a nation which has undertaken to be the refuge of liberty are slaves, and a whole country is unjustly overrun and conquered by a foreign army, and subjected to military law, I think that it

---

[3]From *Hamlet* (act V, scene i) by William Shakespeare. [Eds.]
[4]From *King John* (act V, scene ii) by William Shakespeare. [Eds.]

is not too soon for honest men to rebel and revolutionize. What makes this duty the more urgent is the fact that the country so overrun is not our own, but ours is the invading army.

Paley,[5] a common authority with many on moral questions, in his chapter on the "Duty of Submission to Civil Government," resolves all civil obligation into expediency; and he proceeds to say, "that so long as the interest of the whole society requires it, that is, so long as the established government cannot be resisted or changed without public inconveniency, it is the will of God that the established government be obeyed, and no longer. . . . This principle being admitted, the justice of every particular case of resistance is reduced to a computation of the quantity of the danger and grievance on the one side, and of the probability and expense of redressing it on the other." Of this, he says, every man shall judge for himself. But Paley appears never to have contemplated those cases to which the rule of expediency does not apply, in which a people, as well as an individual, must do justice, cost what it may. If I have unjustly wrested a plank from a drowning man, I must restore it to him though I drown myself. This, according to Paley, would be inconvenient. But he that would save his life, in such a case, shall lose it. This people must cease to hold slaves, and to make war on Mexico, though it cost them their existence as a people.

10   In their practice, nations agree with Paley; but does any one think that Massachusetts does exactly what is right at the present crisis?

"A drab of state, a cloth-o'-silver slut,
To have her train borne up, and her soul trail in the dirt."[6]

Practically speaking, the opponents to a reform in Massachusetts are not a hundred thousand politicians at the South, but a hundred thousand merchants and farmers here, who are more interested in commerce and agriculture than they are in humanity, and are not prepared to do justice to the slave and to Mexico, *cost what it may*. I quarrel not with far-off foes, but with those who, near at home, coöperate with, and do the bidding of, those far away, and without whom the latter would be harmless. We are accustomed to say, that the mass of men are unprepared; but improvement is slow, because the few are not materially wiser or better than the many. It is not so important that many should be as good as you, as that there be some absolute goodness somewhere; for that will leaven the whole lump. There are thousands who are *in opinion* opposed to slavery and to the war, who yet in effect do nothing to put an end to them; who, esteeming themselves children of Washington and Franklin, sit down with their

---

[5]William Paley (1743–1805), English clergyman and philosopher. [Eds.]
[6]From act IV, scene iv, of Cyril Tourneur's *The Revenger's Tragedy* (1607). [Eds.]

hands in their pockets, and say that they know not what to do, and do nothing; who even postpone the question of freedom to the question of free-trade, and quietly read the prices-current along with the latest advices from Mexico, after dinner, and, it may be, fall asleep over them both. What is the price-current of an honest man and patriot to-day? They hesitate, and they regret, and sometimes they petition; but they do nothing in earnest and with effect. They will wait, well disposed, for others to remedy the evil, that they may no longer have it to regret. At most, they give only a cheap vote, and a feeble countenance and Godspeed, to the right, as it goes by them. There are nine hundred and ninety-nine patrons of virtue to one virtuous man. But it is easier to deal with the real possessor of a thing than with the temporary guardian of it.

All voting is a sort of gaming, like checkers or backgammon, with a slight moral tinge to it, a playing with right and wrong, with moral questions; and betting naturally accompanies it. The character of the voters is not staked. I cast my vote, perchance, as I think right; but I am not vitally concerned that that right should prevail. I am willing to leave it to the majority. Its obligation, therefore, never exceeds that of expediency. Even voting *for the right* is *doing* nothing for it. It is only expressing to men feebly your desire that it should prevail. A wise man will not leave the right to the mercy of chance, nor wish it to prevail through the power of the majority. There is but little virtue in the action of masses of men. When the majority shall at length vote for the abolition of slavery, it will be because they are indifferent to slavery, or because there is but little slavery left to be abolished by their vote. *They* will then be the only slaves. Only *his* vote can hasten the abolition of slavery who asserts his own freedom by his vote.

I hear of a convention to be held at Baltimore, or elsewhere, for the selection of a candidate for the Presidency, made up chiefly of editors, and men who are politicians by profession; but I think, what is it to any independent, intelligent, and respectable man what decision they may come to? Shall we not have the advantage of his wisdom and honesty, nevertheless? Can we not count upon some independent votes? Are there not many individuals in the country who do not attend conventions? But no: I find that the respectable man, so called, has immediately drifted from his position, and despairs of his country, when his country has more reason to despair of him. He forthwith adopts one of the candidates thus selected as the only *available* one, thus proving that he is himself *available* for any purposes of the demagogue. His vote is of no more worth than that of any unprincipled foreigner or hireling native, who may have been bought. O for a man who is a *man*, and, as my neighbor says, has a bone in his back which you cannot pass your hand through! Our statistics are at fault: the population has been returned too large. How many *men* are there to a square thousand miles in this country? Hardly one. Does not America offer any inducement for men to settle here? The American has dwindled into an Odd Fellow,—one who may be known by the development of his organ of gregariousness, and a manifest lack of intellect and cheerful self-reliance; whose first and chief concern, on coming into the world, is to see that Almshouses[7] are in good repair; and, before yet he has lawfully donned the virile garb, to collect a fund for the support of the widows and orphans that may be; who, in short, ventures to live only by the aid of the Mutual Insurance company, which has promised to bury him decently.

It is not a man's duty, as a matter of course, to devote himself to the eradication of any, even the most enormous wrong; he may still properly have other concerns to engage him; but it is his duty, at least, to wash his hands of it, and, if he gives it no thought longer, not to give it practically his support. If I devote myself to other pursuits and contemplations, I must first see, at least, that I do not pursue them sitting upon another man's shoulders. I must get off him first, that he may pursue his contemplations too. See what gross inconsistency is tolerated. I have heard some of my townsmen say, "I should like to have them order me out to help put down an insurrection of the slaves, or to march to Mexico—see if I would go;" and yet these very men have each, directly by their allegiance, and so indirectly, at least, by their money, furnished a substitute. The soldier is applauded who refuses to serve in an unjust war by those who do not refuse to sustain the unjust government which makes the war; is applauded by those whose own act and authority he disregards and sets at naught; as if the state were penitent to that degree that it hired one to scourge it while it sinned, but not to that degree that it left off sinning for a moment. Thus, under the name of Order and Civil Government, we are all made at last to pay homage to and support our own meanness. After the first blush of sin comes its indifference; and from immoral it becomes, as it were, *un*moral, and not quite unnecessary to that life which we have made.

15   The broadest and most prevalent error requires the most disinterested virtue to sustain it. The slight reproach to which the virtue of patriotism is commonly liable, the noble are most likely to incur. Those who, while they disapprove of the character and measures of a government, yield to it their allegiance and support are undoubtedly its most conscientious supporters, and so frequently the most serious obstacles to reform. Some are petitioning the state to dissolve the Union, to disregard the requisitions of the President. Why do they not dissolve it themselves,—the union between themselves and the state,—and refuse to pay their quota into its treasury? Do not they

---

[7]Poorhouses; county homes that provided for the needy. [Eds.]

stand in the same relation to the state that the state does to the Union? And have not the same reasons prevented the state from resisting the Union which have prevented them from resisting the state?

How can a man be satisfied to entertain an opinion merely, and enjoy *it?* Is there any enjoyment in it, if his opinion is that he is aggrieved? If you are cheated out of a single dollar by your neighbor, you do not rest satisfied with knowing that you are cheated, or with saying that you are cheated, or even with petitioning him to pay you your due; but you take effectual steps at once to obtain the full amount, and see that you are never cheated again. Action from principle, the perception and the performance of right, changes things and relations; it is essentially revolutionary, and does not consist wholly with anything which was. It not only divides states and churches, it divides families; ay, it divides the *individual,* separating the diabolical in him from the divine.

Unjust laws exist: shall we be content to obey them, or shall we endeavor to amend them, and obey them until we have succeeded, or shall we transgress them at once? Men generally, under such a government as this, think that they ought to wait until they have persuaded the majority to alter them. They think that, if they should resist, the remedy would be worse than the evil. But it is the fault of the government itself that the remedy is worse than the evil. *It* makes it worse. Why is it not more apt to anticipate and provide for reform? Why does it not cherish its wise minority? Why does it cry and resist before it is hurt? Why does it not encourage its citizens to be on the alert to point out its faults, and *do* better than it would have them? Why does it always crucify Christ, and excommunicate Copernicus and Luther, and pronounce Washington and Franklin rebels?

One would think, that a deliberate and practical denial of its authority was the only offense never contemplated by government; else, why has it not assigned its definite, its suitable and proportionate penalty? If a man who has no property refuses but once to earn nine shillings for the state, he is put in prison for a period unlimited by any law that I know, and determined only by the discretion of those who placed him there; but if he should steal ninety times nine shillings from the state, he is soon permitted to go at large again.

If the injustice is part of the necessary friction of the machine of government, let it go, let it go: perchance it will wear smooth,—certainly the machine will wear out. If the injustice has a spring, or a pulley, or a rope, or a crank, exclusively for itself, then perhaps you may consider whether the remedy will not be worse than the evil; but if it is of such a nature that it requires you to be the agent of injustice to another, then, I say, break the law. Let your life be a counter friction to stop the machine. What I have to do is to see, at any rate, that I do not lend myself to the wrong which I condemn.

20   As for adopting the ways which the state has provided for remedying the evil, I know not of such ways. They take too much time, and a man's life will be gone. I have other affairs to attend to. I came into this world, not chiefly to make this a good place to live in, but to live in it, be it good or bad. A man has not everything to do, but something; and because he cannot do *everything*, it is not necessary that he should do *something* wrong. It is not my business to be petitioning the Governor or the Legislature any more than it is theirs to petition me; and if they should not hear my petition, what should I do then? But in this case the state has provided no way: its very Constitution is the evil. This may seem to be harsh and stubborn and unconciliatory; but it is to treat with the utmost kindness and consideration the only spirit that can appreciate or deserve it. So is all change for the better, like birth and death, which convulse the body.

I do not hesitate to say, that those who call themselves Abolitionists should at once effectually withdraw their support, both in person and property, from the government of Massachusetts, and not wait till they constitute a majority of one, before they suffer the right to prevail through them. I think that it is enough if they have God on their side, without waiting for that other one. Moreover, any man more right than his neighbors constitutes a majority of one already.

I meet this American government, or its representative, the state government, directly, and face to face, once a year—no more—in the person of its tax-gatherer; this is the only mode in which a man situated as I am necessarily meets it; and it then says distinctly, Recognize me; and the simplest, the most effectual, and, in the present posture of affairs, the indispensablest mode of treating with it on this head, of expressing your little satisfaction with and love for it, is to deny it then. My civil neighbor, the tax-gatherer, is the very man I have to deal with,—for it is, after all, with men and not with parchment that I quarrel,—and he has voluntarily chosen to be an agent of the government. How shall he ever know well what he is and does as an officer of the government, or as a man, until he is obliged to consider whether he shall treat me, his neighbor, for whom he has respect, as a neighbor and well-disposed man, or as a maniac and disturber of the peace, and see if he can get over this obstruction to his neighborliness without a ruder and more impetuous thought or speech corresponding with his action. I know this well, that if one thousand; if one hundred, if ten men whom I could name,—if ten *honest* men only,—say if *one* HONEST man, in this State of Massachusetts, *ceasing to hold slaves,* were actually to withdraw from this copartnership, and be locked up in the county jail therefor, it would be the abolition of slavery in America. For it matters not how small the beginning may seem to be: what is once well done is done forever. But we love better to talk about it: that we say is our mission. Reform keeps many scores of newspapers in its service, but not one man. If my esteemed neighbor, the State's ambassador, who will devote his days to the settlement of the question of human rights in the Council Chamber, instead of being threatened with the prisons of Carolina, were to sit down the prisoner of Massachusetts, that State which is so anxious to foist the sin of slavery upon her sister,—though at present she can discover only an act of inhospitality to be the ground of a quarrel with her,— the Legislature would not wholly waive the subject the following winter.

Under a government which imprisons any unjustly, the true place for a just man is also a prison. The proper place to-day, the only place which Massachusetts has provided for her freer and less desponding spirits, is in her prisons, to be put out and locked out of the State by her own act, as they have already put themselves out by their principles. It is there that the fugitive slave, and the Mexican prisoner on parole, and the Indian come to plead the wrongs of his race should find them; on that separate, but more free and honorable ground, where the State places those who are not *with* her, but *against* her,— the only house in a slave State in which a free man can abide with honor. If any think that their influence would be lost there, and their voices no longer afflict the ear of the State, that they would not be as an enemy within its walls, they do not know by how much truth is stronger than error, nor how much more eloquently and effectively he can combat injustice who has experienced a little in his own person. Cast your whole vote, not a strip of paper merely, but your whole influence. A minority is powerless while it conforms to the majority; it is not even a minority then; but it is irresistible when it clogs by its whole weight. If the alternative is to keep all just men in prison, or give up war and slavery, the State will not hesitate which to choose. If a thousand men were not to pay their tax-bills this year, that would not be a violent and bloody measure, as it would be to pay them, and enable the State to commit violence and shed innocent blood. This is, in fact, the definition of a peaceable revolution, if any such is possible. If the tax-gatherer, or any other public officer, asks me, as one has done, "But what shall I do?" my answer is, "If you really wish to do anything, resign your office." When the subject has refused allegiance, and the officer has resigned his office, then the revolution is accomplished. But even suppose blood should flow. Is there not a sort of blood shed when the conscience is wounded? Through this wound a man's real manhood and immortality flow out, and he bleeds to an everlasting death. I see this blood flowing now.

I have contemplated the imprisonment of the offender, rather than the seizure of his goods,—though both will serve the same purpose,—because they who assert the purest right, and consequently are most dangerous to a corrupt State, commonly have not spent much time in accumulating property. To such the State renders comparatively small service, and a slight tax is wont to appear exorbitant, particularly if they are obliged to earn it by special labor with their hands. If there were one who lived wholly without the use of money, the State itself would hesitate to demand it of him. But the rich man—not to make any invidious comparison—is always sold to the institution which makes him rich. Absolutely speaking, the more money, the less virtue; for money comes between a man and his objects, and obtains them for him; and it was certainly no great virtue to obtain it. It puts to rest many questions which he would otherwise be taxed to answer; while the only new question which it puts is the hard but superfluous one, how to spend it. Thus his moral ground is taken from under his feet. The opportunities of living are diminished in proportion as what are called the "means" are increased. The best thing a man can do for his culture when he is rich is to endeavor to carry out those schemes which he entertained when he was poor. Christ answered the Herodians according to their condition. "Show me the tribute-money," said he;—and one took a penny out of his pocket;—if you use money which has the image of Caesar on it, which he has made current and valuable, that is, *if you are men of the State,* and gladly enjoy the advantages of Caesar's government, then pay him back some of his own when he demands it. "Render therefore to Caesar that which is Caesar's, and to God those things which are God's,"—leaving them no wiser than before as to which was which; for they did not wish to know.

25   When I converse with the freest of my neighbors, I perceive that, whatever they may say about the magnitude and seriousness of the question, and their regard for the public tranquility, the long and the short of the matter is, that they cannot spare the protection of the existing government, and they dread the consequences to their property and families of disobedience to it. For my own part, I should not like to think that I ever rely on the protection of the State. But, if I deny the authority of the State when it presents its tax-bill, it will soon take and waste all my property, and so harass me and my children without end. This is hard. This makes it impossible for a man to live honestly, and at the same time comfortably, in outward respects. It will not be worth the while to accumulate property; that would be sure to go again. You must hire or squat somewhere, and raise but a small crop, and eat that soon. You must live within yourself, and depend upon yourself always tucked up and ready for a start, and not have many affairs. A man may grow rich in Turkey even, if he will be in all respects a good subject of the Turkish government. Confucius said: "If a state is governed by the principles of reason, poverty and misery are subjects of shame; if a state is not governed by the principles of reason, riches and honors are the subjects of shame." No: until I want the

protection of Massachusetts to be extended to me in some distant Southern port, where my liberty is endangered, or until I am bent solely on building up an estate at home by peaceful enterprise, I can afford to refuse allegiance to Massachusetts, and her right to my property and life. It costs me less in every sense to incur the penalty of disobedience to the State than it would to obey. I should feel as if I were worth less in that case.

Some years ago, the State met me in behalf of the Church, and commended me to pay a certain sum toward the support of a clergyman whose preaching my father attended, but never I myself. "Pay," it said, "or be locked up in the jail." I declined to pay. But, unfortunately, another man saw fit to pay it. I did not see why the schoolmaster should be taxed to support the priest, and not the priest the schoolmaster; for I was not the State's schoolmaster, but I supported myself by voluntary subscription. I did not see why the lyceum should not present its tax-bill, and have the State to back its demand, as well as the Church. However, at the request of the selectmen, I condescended to make some such statement as this in writing:—"Know all men by these presents, that I, Henry Thoreau, do not wish to be regarded as a member of any incorporated society which I have not joined." This I gave to the town clerk; and he has it. The State, having thus learned that I did not wish to be regarded as a member of that church, has never made a like demand on me since; though it said that it must adhere to its original presumption that time. If I had known how to name them, I should have then signed off in detail from all the societies which I never signed on to; but I did not know where to find a complete list.

I have paid no poll-tax for six years. I was put into a jail once on this account, for one night; and, as I stood considering the walls of solid stone, two or three feet thick, the door of wood and iron, a foot thick, and the iron grating which strained the light, I could not help being struck with the foolishness of that institution which treated me as if I were mere flesh and blood and bones, to be locked up. I wondered that it should have concluded at length that this was the best use it could put me to, and had never thought to avail itself of my services in some way. I say that, if there was a wall of stone between me and my townsmen, there was a still more difficult one to climb or break through before they could get to be as free as I was. I did not for a moment feel confined, and the walls seemed a great waste of stone and mortar. I felt as if I alone of all my townsmen had paid my tax. They plainly did not know how to treat me, but behaved like persons who are underbred. In every threat and in every compliment there was a blunder; for they thought that my chief desire was to stand the other side of that stone wall. I could not but smile to see how industriously they locked the door on my meditations, which followed them out again without let or hindrance, and *they* were really all that was dangerous. As they could not reach me, they had resolved to punish my body; just as boys, if they cannot come at some person against whom they have a spite, will abuse his dog. I saw that the State was half-witted, that it was timid as a lone woman with her silver spoons, and that it did not know its friends from its foes, and I lost all my remaining respect for it, and pitied it.

Thus the State never intentionally confronts a man's sense, intellectual or moral, but only his body, his senses. It is not armed with superior wit or honesty; but with superior physical strength. I was not born to be forced. I will breathe after my own fashion. Let us see who is the strongest. What force has a multitude? They only can force me who obey a higher law than I. They force me to become like themselves. I do not hear of *men* being *forced* to live this way or that by masses of men. What sort of life were that to live? When I meet a government which says to me, "Your money or your life," why should I be in haste to give it my money? It may be in a great strait, and not know what to do: I cannot help that. It must help itself; do as I do. It is not worth the while to snivel about it. I am not responsible for the successful working of the machinery of society. I am not the son of the engineer. I perceive that, when an acorn and a chestnut fall side by side, the one does not remain inert to make way for the other, but both obey their own laws, and spring and grow and flourish as best they can, till one, perchance, over-shadows and destroys the other. If a plant cannot live according to its nature, it dies; and so a man.

The night in prison was novel and interesting enough. The prisoners in their shirt-sleeves were enjoying a chat and the evening air in the doorway, when I entered. But the jailer said, "Come, boys, it is time to lock up;" and so they dispersed, and I heard the sound of their steps returning into the hollow apartments. My room-mate was introduced to me by the jailer as "a first-rate fellow and a clever man." When the door was locked, he showed me where to hang my hat, and how he managed matters there. The rooms were whitewashed once a month; and this one, at least, was the whitest, most simply furnished, and probably the neatest apartment in the town. He naturally wanted to know where I came from, and what brought me there; and, when I had told him, I asked him in my turn how he came there, presuming him to be an honest man, of course; and, as the world goes, I believe he was. "Why," said he, "they accuse me of burning a barn; but I never did it." As near as I could discover, he had probably gone to bed in a barn when drunk, and smoked his pipe there; and so a barn was burnt. He had the reputation of being a clever man, had been there some three months waiting for his trial to come on, and would have to wait as much longer; but he was quite domesticated and contented, since he got his board for nothing, and thought that he was well treated.

He occupied one window, and I the other; and I saw that if one stayed there long, his principal business would be to look out the window. I had soon read all tracts that were left there, and examined where former prisoners had broken out, and where a grate had been sawed off, and heard the history of the various occupants of that room; for I found that even here there was a history and a gossip which never circulated beyond the walls of the jail. Probably this is the only house in the town where verses are composed, which are afterward printed in a circular form, but not published. I was shown quite a long list of verses which were composed by some young men who had been detected in an attempt to escape, who avenged themselves by signing them.

I pumped my fellow-prisoner as dry as I could, for fear I should never see him again; but at length he showed me which was my bed, and left me to blow out the lamp.

It was like traveling into a far country, such as I had never expected to behold, to lie there for one night. It seemed to me that I never had heard the town-clock strike before, nor the evening sounds of the village; for we slept with the windows open, which were inside the grating. It was to see my native village in the light of the Middle Ages, and our Concord was turned into a Rhine stream, and visions of knights and castles passed before me. They were the voices of old burghers that I heard in the streets. I was an involuntary spectator and auditor of whatever was done and said in the kitchen of the adjacent village-inn,—a wholly new and rare experience to me. It was a closer view of my native town. I was fairly inside of it. I never had seen its institutions before. This is one of its peculiar institutions; for it is a shire town.[8] I began to comprehend what its inhabitants were about.

In the morning, our breakfasts were put through the hole in the door, in small oblong-square tin pans, made to fit, and holding a pint of chocolate, with brown bread, and an iron spoon. When they called for the vessels again, I was green enough to return what bread I had left; but my comrade seized it, and said that I should lay that up for lunch or dinner. Soon after he was let out to work at haying in a neighboring field, whither he went every day, and would not be back till noon; so he bade me good-day, saying that he doubted if he should see me again.

When I came out of prison,—for some one interfered, and paid that tax,—I did not perceive that great changes had taken place on the common, such as he observed who went in a youth and emerged a tottering and gray-headed man; and yet a change had to my eyes come over the scene,—the town, and State, and country,—greater than any that mere time could effect. I saw yet more distinctly the

---

[8]County seat. [Eds.]

State in which I lived. I saw to what extent the people among whom I lived could be trusted as good neighbors and friends; that their friendship was for summer weather only; that they did not greatly propose to do right; that they were a distinct race from me by their prejudices and superstitions, as the Chinamen and Malays are; that in their sacrifices to humanity they ran no risks, not even to their property; that after all they were not so noble but they treated the thief as he had treated them, and hoped, by a certain outward observance and a few prayers, and by walking in a particular straight though useless path from time to time, to save their souls. This may be to judge my neighbors harshly; for I believe that many of them are not aware that they have such an institution as the jail in their village.

35   It was formerly the custom in our village; when a poor debtor came out of jail, for his acquaintances to salute him, looking through their fingers, which were crossed to represent the grating of a jail window, "How do ye do?" My neighbors did not thus salute me, but first looked at me, and then at one another, as if I had returned from a long journey. I was put into jail as I was going to the shoemaker's to get a shoe which was mended. When I was let out the next morning, I proceeded to finish my errand, and, having put on my mended shoe, joined a huckleberry party, who were impatient to put themselves under my conduct; and in half an hour,—for the horse was soon tackled,—was in the midst of a huckleberry field, on one of our highest hills, two miles off, and then the State was nowhere to be seen.

This is the whole history of "My Prisons."

I have never declined paying the highway tax, because I am as desirous of being a good neighbor as I am of being a bad subject; and as for supporting schools, I am doing my part to educate my fellow-countrymen now. It is for no particular item in the tax-bill that I refuse to pay it. I simply wish to refuse allegiance to the State, to withdraw and stand aloof from it effectually. I do not care to trace the course of my dollar, if I could, till it buys a man or a musket to shoot one with,—the dollar is innocent,—but I am concerned to trace the effects of my allegiance. In fact, I quietly declare war with the State, after my fashion, though I will still make what use and get what advantage of her I can, as is usual in such cases.

If others pay the tax which is demanded of me, from a sympathy with the State, they do but what they have already done in their own case, or rather they abet injustice to a greater extent than the State requires. If they pay the tax from a mistaken interest in the individual taxed, to save his property, or prevent his going to jail, it is because they have not considered wisely how far they let their private feelings interfere with the public good.

This, then, is my position at present. But one cannot be too much on his guard in such a case, lest his action be biased by obstinacy or an undue regard for the opinions of men. Let him see that he does only what belongs to himself and to the hour.

I think sometimes, Why, this people mean well, they are only ig- 40 norant; they would do better if they knew how: why give your neighbors this pain to treat you as they are not inclined to? But I think again, This is no reason why I should do as they do, or permit others to suffer much greater pain of a different kind. Again, I sometimes say to myself, When many millions of men, without heat, without ill will, without personal feeling of any kind, demand of you a few shillings only, without the possibility, such is their constitution, of retracting or altering their present demand, and without the possibility, on your side, of appeal to any other millions, why expose yourself to this overwhelming brute force? You do not resist cold and hunger, the winds and the waves, thus obstinately; you quietly submit to a thousand similar necessities. You do not put your head into the fire. But just in proportion as I regard this as not wholly a brute force, but partly a human force, and consider that I have relations to those millions as to so many millions of men, and not of mere brute or inanimate things, I see that appeal is possible, first and instantaneously, from them to the Maker of them, and, secondly, from them to themselves. But if I put my head deliberately into the fire, there is no appeal to fire or to the Maker of fire, and I have only myself to blame. If I could convince myself that I have any right to be satisfied with men as they are, and to treat them accordingly, and not accordingly, in some respects, to my requisitions and expectations of what they and I ought to be, then, like a good Mussulman[9] and fatalist, I should endeavor to be satisfied with things as they are, and say it is the will of God. And, above all, there is this difference between resisting this and a purely brute or natural force that I can resist this with some effect; but I cannot expect, like Orpheus,[10] to change the nature of the rocks and trees and beasts.

I do not wish to quarrel with any man or nation. I do not wish to split hairs, to make the fine distinctions, or set myself up as better than my neighbors. I seek rather, I may say, even an excuse for conforming to the laws of the land. I am but too ready to conform to them. Indeed, I have reason to suspect myself on this head; and each year, as the tax-gatherer comes round, I find myself disposed to review the acts and position of the general and State governments, and the spirit of the people, to discover a pretext for conformity.

---

[9]Muslim. [Eds.]

[10]Legendary Greek poet and musician who played the lyre so beautifully that wild beasts were transfixed by his music and rocks and trees moved. [Eds.]

"We must affect our country as our parents,
And if at any time we alienate
Our love or industry from doing it honor,
We must respect effects and teach the soul
Matter of conscience and religion,
And not desire of rule or benefit."[11]

I believe that the State will soon be able to take all my work of this sort out of my hands, and then I shall be no better a patriot than my fellow-countrymen. Seen from a lower point of view, the Constitution, with all its faults, is very good; the law and the courts are very respectable; even this State and this American government are, in many respects, very admirable, and rare things, to be thankful for, such as a great many have described them; but seen from a point of view a little higher, they are what I have described them; seen from a higher still, and the highest, who shall say what they are, or that they are worth looking at or thinking of at all?

However, the government does not concern me much, and I shall bestow the fewest possible thoughts on it. It is not many moments that I live under a government, even in this world. If a man is thought-free, fancy-free, imagination-free, that which *is not* never for a long time appearing *to be* to him, unwise rulers or reformers cannot fatally interrupt him.

I know that most men think differently from myself; but those whose lives are by profession devoted to the study of these or kindred subjects content me as little as any. Statesmen and legislators, standing so completely within the institution, never distinctly and nakedly behold it. They speak of moving society, but have no resting-place without it. They may be men of a certain experience and discrimination, and have no doubt invented ingenious and even useful systems, for which we sincerely thank them; but all their wit and usefulness lie within certain not very wide limits. They are wont to forget that the world is not governed by policy and expediency. Webster[12] never goes behind government, and so cannot speak with authority about it. His words are wisdom to those legislators who contemplate no essential reform in the existing government; but for thinkers, and those who legislate for all time, he never once glances at the subject. I know of those whose serene and wise speculations on this theme would soon reveal the limits of his mind's range and hospitality. Yet, compared with the cheap professions of most reformers, and the still cheaper wisdom and eloquence of politicians in general, his are almost the only sensible and valuable words, and we thank Heaven for

---

[11]From *The Battle of Alcazar* (1594), a play by George Peele (1558?–1597?). [Eds.]

[12]Daniel Webster (1782–1852), legendary American orator, lawyer, and statesman. [Eds.]

him. Comparatively, he is always strong, original, and, above all, practical. Still, his quality is not wisdom, but prudence. The lawyer's truth is not Truth, but consistency or a consistent expediency. Truth is always in harmony with herself, and is not concerned chiefly to reveal the justice that may consist with wrong-doing. He well deserves to be called, as he has been called, the Defender of the Constitution. There are really no blows to be given to him but defensive ones. He is not a leader, but a follower. His leaders are the men of '87.[13] "I have never made an effort," he says, "and never propose to make an effort; I have never countenanced an effort, and never mean to countenance an effort, to disturb the arrangement as originally made, by which the various States came into the Union." Still thinking of the sanction which the Constitution gives to slavery, he says, "Because it was a part of the original compact,—let it stand." Notwithstanding his special acuteness and ability, he is unable to take a fact out of its merely political relations, and behold it as it lies absolutely to be disposed of by the intellect,—what, for instance, it behooves a man to do here in America to-day with regard to slavery,—but ventures, or is driven, to make some such desperate answer as the following, while professing to speak absolutely, and as a private man,—from which what new and singular code of social duties might be inferred? "The manner," says he, "in which the governments of those States where slavery exists are to regulate it is for their own consideration, under their responsibility to their constituents, to the general laws of propriety, humanity, and justice, and to God. Associations formed elsewhere, springing from a feeling of humanity, or any other cause, have nothing whatever to do with it. They have never received any encouragement from me, and they never will."

They who know of no purer sources of truth, who have traced up   45
its stream no higher, stand, and wisely stand, by the Bible and the Constitution, and drink at it there with reverence and humility; but they who behold where it comes trickling into this lake or that pool, gird up their loins once more, and continue their pilgrimage toward its fountain-head.

No man with a genius for legislation has appeared in America. They are rare in the history of the world. There are orators, politicians, and eloquent men, by the thousand; but the speaker has not yet opened his mouth to speak who is capable of settling the much-vexed questions of the day. We love eloquence for its own sake, and not for any truth which it may utter, or any heroism it may inspire. Our legislators have not yet learned the comparative value of free-trade and of freedom, of union, and of rectitude, to a nation. They have no genius or talent for comparatively humble questions of taxation and finance,

---

[13]The 1787 framers of the Constitution. [Eds.]

commerce and manufacturers and agriculture. If we were left solely to the wordy wit of legislators in Congress for our guidance, uncorrected by the seasonable experience and the effectual complaints of the people, America would not long retain her rank among the nations. For eighteen hundred years, though perchance I have no right to say it, the New Testament has been written; yet where is the legislator who has wisdom and practical talent enough to avail himself of the light which it sheds on the science of legislation?

The authority of government, even such as I am willing to submit to,—for I will cheerfully obey those who know and can do better than I, and in many things even those who neither know nor can do so well,—is still an impure one: to be strictly just, it must have the sanction and consent of the governed. It can have no pure right over my person and property but what I concede to it. The progress from an absolute to a limited monarchy, from a limited monarchy to a democracy, is a progress toward a true respect for the individual. Even the Chinese philosopher was wise enough to regard the individual as the basis of the empire. Is a democracy, such as we know it, the last improvement possible in government? Is it not possible to take a further step towards recognizing and organizing the rights of man? There will never be a really free and enlightened State until the State comes to recognize the individual as a higher and independent power, from which all its own power and authority are derived, and treats him accordingly. I please myself with imagining a State at last which can afford to be just to all men, and to treat the individual with respect as a neighbor; which even would not think it inconsistent with its own repose if a few were to live aloof from it, not meddling with it, nor embraced by it, who fulfilled all the duties of neighbors and fellow-men. A State which bore this kind of fruit, and suffered it to drop off as fast as it ripened, would prepare the way for a still more perfect and glorious State, which also I have imagined, but not yet anywhere seen.

Responding to Reading

1. What moral or political choice does each of the following statements by Thoreau imply?
   - " 'That government is best which governs least' " (1).
   - "All men recognize the right of revolution" (8).
   - "All voting is a sort of gaming, like checkers or backgammon" (12).
   - "Under a government which imprisons any unjustly, the true place for a just man is also a prison" (23).
   - "I did not see why the schoolmaster should be taxed to support the priest, and not the priest the schoolmaster" (26).

2. Do you believe civil disobedience is ever necessary? If so, under what circumstances?
3. Do you see any advantages in obeying a law, however unjust, rather than disobeying it? Explain.

Responding in Writing

Thoreau, like Martin Luther King, Jr. (below), was jailed for his beliefs (Thoreau for refusing to pay his taxes, King for refusing to cease his civil rights demonstrations). What other forms of peaceful protest can you think of? Select several causes you believe in, and suggest an appropriate form of civil disobedience for each.

LETTER FROM BIRMINGHAM JAIL

Martin Luther King, Jr.

1929–1968

One of the greatest civil rights leaders and orators of this century, Martin Luther King, Jr., was a Baptist minister and winner of the 1964 Nobel Peace Prize. He was born in Atlanta, Georgia, and earned degrees from four institutions. Influenced by Thoreau and Gandhi, King altered the spirit of African-American protest in the United States by advocating nonviolent civil disobedience to achieve racial equality. His books include Letter from Birmingham Jail *(1963) and* Where Do We Go From Here: Chaos or Community? *(1967). King was assassinated on April 4, 1968. The following letter, written in 1963, is his eloquent and impassioned response to a public statement by eight fellow clergymen in Birmingham, Alabama, who appealed to the citizenry of the city to "observe the principles of law and order and common sense" rather than join in the principled protests that King was leading. (Also see King's essay in Chapter 7, p. 532.)*

MY DEAR FELLOW CLERGYMEN:[1]

While confined here in the Birmingham city jail, I came across your recent statement calling my present activities "unwise and untimely." Seldom do I pause to answer criticism of my work and ideas.

---

[1]This response to a published statement by eight fellow clergymen from Alabama (Bishop C. C. J. Carpenter, Bishop Joseph A. Durick, Rabbi Milton L. Grafman, Bishop Paul Hardin, Bishop Holan B. Harmon, the Reverend George M. Murray, the Reverend Edward V. Ramage and the Reverend Earl Stallings) was composed under somewhat constricting circumstances. Begun on the margins of the newspaper in which the statement appeared while I was in jail, the letter was continued on scraps of writing paper supplied by a friendly Negro trusty, and concluded on a pad my attorneys were eventually permitted to leave me. Although the text remains in substance unaltered, I have indulged in the author's prerogative of polishing it for publication.

If I sought to answer all the criticisms that cross my desk, my secretaries would have little time for anything other than such correspondence in the course of the day, and I would have no time for constructive work. But since I feel that you are men of genuine good will and that your criticisms are sincerely set forth, I want to try to answer your statement in what I hope will be patient and reasonable terms.

I think I should indicate that I am here in Birmingham, since you have been influenced by the view which argues against "outsiders coming in." I have the honor of serving as president of the Southern Christian Leadership Conference, an organization operating in every southern state, with headquarters in Atlanta, Georgia. We have some eighty-five affiliated organizations across the South, and one of them is the Alabama Christian Movement for Human Rights. Frequently we share staff, educational, and financial resources with our affiliates. Several months ago the affiliate here in Birmingham asked us to be on call to engage in a non-violent direct-action program if such were deemed necessary. We readily consented, and when the hour came we lived up to our promise. So I, along with several members of my staff, am here because I was invited here. I am here because I have organizational ties here.

But more basically, I am in Birmingham because injustice is here. Just as the prophets of the eighth century B.C. left their villages and carried their "thus saith the Lord" far beyond the boundaries of their home towns, and just as the Apostle Paul left his village of Tarsus and carried the gospel of Jesus Christ to the far corners of the Greco-Roman world, so am I compelled to carry the gospel of freedom beyond my own home town. Like Paul, I must constantly respond to the Macedonian call for aid.

Moreover, I am cognizant of the interrelatedness of all communities and states. I cannot sit idly by in Atlanta and not be concerned about what happens in Birmingham. Injustice anywhere is a threat to justice everywhere. We are caught in an inescapable network of mutuality, tied in a single garment of destiny. Whatever affects one directly, affects all indirectly. Never again can we afford to live with the narrow, provincial "outside agitator" idea. Anyone who lives inside the United States can never be considered an outsider anywhere within its bounds.

5   You deplore the demonstrations taking place in Birmingham. But your statement, I am sorry to say, fails to express a similar concern for the conditions that brought about the demonstrations. I am sure that none of you would want to rest content with the superficial kind of social analysis that deals merely with effects and does not grapple with underlying causes. It is unfortunate that demonstrations are taking place in Birmingham, but it is even more unfortunate that the

city's white power structure left the Negro community with no alternative.

In any nonviolent campaign there are four basic steps: collection of the facts to determine whether injustices exist; negotiation; self-purification; and direct action. We have gone through all these steps in Birmingham. There can be no gainsaying the fact that racial injustice engulfs this community. Birmingham is probably the most thoroughly segregated city in the United States. Its ugly record of brutality is widely known. Negroes have experienced grossly unjust treatment in the courts. There have been more unsolved bombings of Negro homes and churches in Birmingham than in any other city in the nation. These are the hard, brutal facts of the case. On the basis of these conditions, Negro leaders sought to negotiate with the city fathers. But the latter consistently refused to engage in good-faith negotiation.

Then, last September, came the opportunity to talk with leaders of Birmingham's economic community. In the course of the negotiations, certain promises were made by the merchants—for example, to remove the stores' humiliating racial signs. On the basis of these promises, the Reverend Fred Shuttlesworth and the leaders of the Alabama Christian Movement for Human Rights agreed to a moratorium on all demonstrations. As the weeks and months went by, we realized that we were the victims of a broken promise. A few signs, briefly removed, returned; the others remained.

As in so many past experiences, our hopes had been blasted, and the shadow of deep disappointment settled upon us. We had no alternative except to prepare for direct action, whereby we would present our very bodies as a means of laying our case before the conscience of the local and the national community. Mindful of the difficulties involved, we decided to undertake a process of self-purification. We began a series of workshops on nonviolence, and we repeatedly asked ourselves: "Are you able to accept blows without retaliating?" "Are you able to endure the ordeal of jail?" We decided to schedule our direct-action program for the Easter season, realizing that except for Christmas, this is the main shopping period of the year. Knowing that a strong economic-withdrawal program would be the by-product of direct action, we felt that this would be the best time to bring pressure to bear on the merchants for the needed change.

Then it occurred to us that Birmingham's mayoral election was coming up in March, and we speedily decided to postpone action until after election day. When we discovered that the Commissioner of Public Safety, Eugene "Bull" Connor,[2] had piled up enough votes to be in the run-off, we decided again to postpone action until the day

---

[2]An ardent segregationist, Connor ordered police officers to use police dogs and fire hoses to break up civil rights demonstrations. (Conner lost his bid for mayor.) [Eds.]

after the run-off so that the demonstrations could not be used to cloud the issues. Like many others, we wanted to see Mr. Connor defeated, and to this end we endured postponement after postponement. Having aided in this community need, we felt that our direct-action program could be delayed no longer.

10   You may well ask, "Why direct action? Why sit-ins, marches, and so forth? Isn't negotiation a better path?" You are quite right in calling for negotiation. Indeed, this is the very purpose of direct action. Nonviolent direct action seeks to create such a crisis and foster such a tension that a community which has constantly refused to negotiate is forced to confront the issue. It seeks so to dramatize the issue that it can no longer be ignored. My citing the creation of tension as part of the work of the nonviolent-resister may sound rather shocking. But I must confess that I am not afraid of the word "tension." I have earnestly opposed violent tension, but there is a type of constructive, nonviolent tension which is necessary for growth. Just as Socrates felt that it was necessary to create a tension in the mind so that individuals could rise from the bondage of myths and half-truths to the unfettered realm of creative analysis and objective appraisal, so must we see the need for nonviolent gadflies to create the kind of tension in society that will help men rise from the dark depths of prejudice and racism to the majestic heights of understanding and brotherhood.

The purpose of our direct-action program is to create a situation so crisis-packed that it will inevitably open the door to negotiation. I therefore concur with you in your call for negotiation. Too long has our beloved Southland been bogged down in a tragic effort to live in monologue rather than dialogue.

One of the basic points in your statement is that the action that I and my associates have taken in Birmingham is untimely. Some have asked: "Why didn't you give the new city administration time to act?" The only answer that I can give to this query is that the new Birmingham administration must be prodded about as much as the outgoing one, before it will act. We are sadly mistaken if we feel that the election of Albert Boutwell as mayor will bring the millennium to Birmingham. While Mr. Boutwell is a much more gentle person than Mr. Connor, they are both segregationists, dedicated to maintenance of the status quo. I have hoped that Mr. Boutwell will be reasonable enough to see the futility of massive resistance to desegregation. But he will not see this without pressure from devotees of civil rights. My friends, I must say to you that we have not made a single gain in civil rights without determined legal and nonviolent pressure. Lamentably, it is an historical fact that privileged groups seldom give up their privileges voluntarily. Individuals may see the moral light and volun-

tarily give up their unjust posture; but, as Reinhold Niebuhr[3] has reminded us, groups tend to be more immoral than individuals.

We know through painful experience that freedom is never voluntarily given by the oppressor; it must be demanded by the oppressed. Frankly, I have yet to engage in a direct-action campaign that
was "well timed" in the view of those who have not suffered unduly
from the disease of segregation. For years now I have heard the word
"Wait!" It rings in the ear of every Negro with piercing familiarity.
This "Wait!" has almost always meant "Never." We must come to see,
with one of our distinguished jurists, that "justice too long delayed is
justice denied."[4]

We have waited for more than 340 years for our constitutional
and God-given rights. The nations of Asia and Africa are moving with
jetlike speed toward gaining political independence, but we still creep
at horse-and-buggy pace toward gaining a cup of coffee at a lunch
counter. Perhaps it is easy for those who have never felt the stinging
darts of segregation to say, "Wait." But when you have seen vicious
mobs lynch your mothers and fathers at will and drown your sisters
and brothers at whim; when you have seen hate-filled policemen
curse, kick, and even kill your black brothers and sisters; when you
see the vast majority of your twenty million Negro brothers smother-
ing in an airtight cage of poverty in the midst of an affluent society;
when you suddenly find your tongue twisted and your speech stammering as you seek to explain to your six-year-old daughter why she
can't go to the public amusement park that has just been advertised
on television, and see tears welling up in her eyes when she is told
that Funtown is closed to colored children, and see ominous clouds of
inferiority beginning to form in her little mental sky, and see her beginning to distort her personality by developing an unconscious bitterness toward white people; when you have to concoct an answer for
a five-year-old son who is asking, "Daddy, why do white people treat
colored people so mean?"; when you take a cross-country drive and
find it necessary to sleep night after night in the uncomfortable corners of your automobile because no motel will accept you; when you
are humiliated day in and day out by nagging signs reading "white"
and "colored"; when your first name becomes "nigger," your middle
name becomes "boy" (however old you are) and your last name becomes "John," and your wife and mother are never given the respected title "Mrs."; when you are harried by day and haunted by
night by the fact that you are a Negro, living constantly at tiptoe

---

[3]American religious and social thinker (1892–1971). [Eds.]
[4]Attributed to British statesman William Ewart Gladstone (1809–1898), a stalwart of the Liberal
Party who also said, "You cannot fight the future. Time is on our side." [Eds.]

stance, never quite knowing what to expect next, and are plagued with inner fears and outer resentments; when you are forever fighting a degenerating sense of "nobodiness"—then you will understand why we find it difficult to wait. There comes a time when the cup of endurance runs over, and men are no longer willing to be plunged into the abyss of despair. I hope, sirs, you can understand our legitimate and unavoidable impatience.

15   You express a great deal of anxiety over our willingness to break laws. This is certainly a legitimate concern. Since we so diligently urge people to obey the Supreme Court's decision of 1954 outlawing segregation in the public schools, at first glance it may seem rather paradoxical for us consciously to break laws. One may well ask: "How can you advocate breaking some laws and obeying others?" The answer lies in the fact that there are two types of laws: just and unjust. I would be the first to advocate obeying just laws. One has not only a legal but a moral responsibility to obey just laws. Conversely, one has a moral responsibility to disobey unjust laws. I would agree with St. Augustine[5] that "an unjust law is no law at all."

Now, what is the difference between the two? How does one determine whether a law is just or unjust? A just law is a man-made code that squares with the moral law or the law of God. An unjust law is a code this is out of harmony with the moral law. To put it in the terms of St. Thomas Aquinas:[6] An unjust law is a human law that is not rooted in eternal law and natural law. Any law that uplifts human personality is just. Any law that degrades human personality is unjust. All segregation statutes are unjust because segregation distorts the soul and damages the personality. It gives the segregator a false sense of superiority and the segregated a false sense of inferiority. Segregation, to use the terminology of the Jewish philosopher Martin Buber,[7] substitutes an "I-it" relationship for an "I-thou" relationship and ends up relegating persons to the status of things. Hence segregation is not only politically, economically, and sociologically unsound, it is morally wrong and sinful. Paul Tillich[8] has said that sin is separation. Is not segregation an existential expression of man's tragic separation, his awful estrangement, his terrible sinfulness? Thus it is that I can urge men to obey the 1954 decision of the Supreme Court, for it is morally right; and I can urge them to disobey segregation ordinances, for they are morally wrong.

Let us consider a more concrete example of just and unjust laws. An unjust law is a code that a numerical or power majority group compels a minority group to obey but does not make binding on it-

---

[5]Italian-born missionary and theologian (?–c.604) [Eds.]
[6]Italian philosopher and theologian (1225–1274). [Eds.]
[7]Austrian existentialist philosopher and Judaic scholar (1878–1965). [Eds.]
[8]American philosopher and theologian (1886–1965). [Eds.]

self. This is *difference* made legal. By the same token, a just law is a code that a majority compels a minority to follow and that it is willing to follow itself. This is *sameness* made legal.

Let me give another explanation. A law is unjust if it is inflicted on a minority that, as a result of being denied the right to vote, had no part in enacting or devising the law. Who can say that the legislature of Alabama which set up that state's segregation laws was democratically elected? Throughout Alabama all sorts of devious methods are used to prevent Negroes from becoming registered voters, and there are some counties in which, even though Negroes constitute a majority of the population, not a single Negro is registered. Can any law enacted under such circumstances be considered democratically structured?

Sometimes a law is just on its face and unjust in its application. For instance, I have been arrested on a charge of parading without a permit. Now, there is nothing wrong in having an ordinance which requires a permit for a parade. But such an ordinance becomes unjust when it is used to maintain segregation and to deny citizens the First-Amendment privilege of peaceful assembly and protest.

I hope you are able to see the distinction I am trying to point out. 20 In no sense do I advocate evading or defying the law, as would the rabid segregationist. That would lead to anarchy. One who breaks an unjust law must do so openly, lovingly, and with a willingness to accept the penalty. I submit that an individual who breaks a law that conscience tells him is unjust, and who willingly accepts the penalty of imprisonment in order to arouse the conscience of the community over its injustice, is in reality expressing the highest respect for law.

Of course, there is nothing new about this kind of civil disobedience. It was evidenced sublimely in the refusal of Shadrach, Meshach, and Abednego to obey the laws of Nebuchadnezzar, on the ground that a higher moral law was at stake.[9] It was practiced superbly by the early Christians, who were willing to face hungry lions and the excruciating pain of chopping blocks rather than submit to certain unjust laws of the Roman Empire. To a degree, academic freedom is a reality today because Socrates practiced civil disobedience.[10] In our own nation, the Boston Tea Party represented a massive act of civil disobedience.

---

[9]In the book of Daniel, Nebuchadnezzar commanded the people to worship a golden statue or be thrown into a furnace of blazing fire. When Shadrach, Meshach, and Abednego refused to worship any god but their own, they were bound and thrown into a blazing furnace, but the fire had no effect on them. Their escape led Nebuchadnezzar to make a decree forbidding blasphemy against their god. [Eds.]

[10]The ancient Greek philosopher Socrates was tried by the Athenians for corrupting their youth through his use of questions to teach. When he refused to change his methods of teaching, he was condemned to death. [Eds.]

We should never forget that everything Adolf Hitler did in Germany was "legal" and everything the Hungarian freedom fighters[11] did in Hungary was "illegal." It was "illegal" to aid and comfort a Jew in Hitler's Germany. Even so, I am sure that, had I lived in Germany at the time, I would have aided and comforted my Jewish brothers. If today I lived in a Communist country where certain principles dear to the Christian faith are suppressed, I would openly advocate disobeying that country's anti-religious laws.

I must make two honest confessions to you, my Christian and Jewish brothers. First, I must confess that over the past few years I have been gravely disappointed with the white moderate. I have almost reached the regrettable conclusion that the Negro's great stumbling block in his stride toward freedom is not the White Citizen's Counciler or the Ku Klux Klanner, but the white moderate, who is more devoted to "order" than to justice; who prefers a negative peace which is the absence of tension to a positive peace which is the presence of justice; who constantly says, "I agree with you in the goal you seek, but I cannot agree with your methods of direct action"; who paternalistically believes he can set the timetable for another man's freedom; who lives by a mythical concept of time and who constantly advises the Negro to wait for a "more convenient season." Shallow understanding from people of good will is more frustrating than absolute misunderstanding from people of ill will. Lukewarm acceptance is much more bewildering than outright rejection.

I had hoped that the white moderate would understand that law and order exist for the purpose of establishing justice and that when they fail in this purpose they become the dangerously structured dams that block the flow of social progress. I had hoped that the white moderate would understand that the present tension in the South is a necessary phase of the transition from an obnoxious negative peace, in which the Negro passively accepted his unjust plight, to a substantive and positive peace, in which all men will respect the dignity and worth of human personality. Actually, we who engage in nonviolent direct action are not the creators of tension. We merely bring to the surface the hidden tension that is already alive. We bring it out in the open, where it can be seen and dealt with. Like a boil that can never be cured so long as it is covered up but must be opened with all its ugliness to the natural medicines of air and light, injustice must be exposed, with all the tension its exposure creates, to the light of human conscience and the air of national opinion, before it can be cured.

---

[11]The Hungarian anti-Communist uprising of 1956 was quickly crushed by the army of the USSR. [Eds.]

In your statement you assert that our actions, even though peace- 25
ful, must be condemned because they precipitate violence. But is this
a logical assertion? Isn't this like condemning a robbed man because
his possession of money precipitated the evil act of robbery? Isn't this
like condemning Socrates because his unswerving commitment to
truth and his philosophical inquiries precipitated the act by the misguided populace in which they made him drink hemlock? Isn't this
like condemning Jesus because his unique God-consciousness and
never-ceasing devotion to God's will precipitated the evil act of crucifixion? We must come to see that, as the federal courts have consistently affirmed, it is wrong to urge an individual to cease his efforts to
gain his basic constitutional rights because the quest may precipitate
violence. Society must protect the robbed and punish the robber.

I had also hoped that the white moderate would reject the myth
concerning time in relation to the struggle for freedom. I have just
received a letter from a white brother in Texas. He writes: "All Christians know that the colored people will receive equal rights eventually, but it is possible that you are in too great a religious hurry. It has
taken Christianity almost two thousand years to accomplish what it
has. The teachings of Christ take time to come to earth." Such an attitude stems from a tragic misconception of time, from the strangely irrational notion that there is something in the very flow of time that
will inevitably cure all ills. Actually, time itself is neutral; it can be
used either destructively or constructively. More and more I feel that
the people of ill will have used time much more effectively than have
the people of good will. We will have to repent in this generation not
merely for the hateful words and actions of the bad people, but for the
appalling silence of the good people. Human progress never rolls in
on wheels of inevitability; it comes through the tireless efforts of men
willing to be co-workers with God, and without this hard work, time
itself becomes an ally of the forces of social stagnation. We must use
time creatively, in the knowledge that the time is always ripe to do
right. Now is the time to make real the promise of democracy and
transform our pending national elegy into a creative psalm of brotherhood. Now is the time to lift our national policy from the quicksand
of racial injustice to the solid rock of human dignity.

You speak of our activity in Birmingham as extreme. At first I was
rather disappointed that fellow clergymen would see my nonviolent
efforts as those of an extremist. I began thinking about the fact that I
stand in the middle of two opposing forces in the Negro community.
One is a force of complacency, made up in part of Negroes who, as a
result of long years of oppression, are so drained of self-respect and a
sense of "somebodiness" that they have adjusted to segregation; and
in part of a few middle-class Negroes who, because of a degree of academic and economic security and because in some ways they profit

by segregation, have become insensitive to the problems of the masses. The other force is one of bitterness and hatred, and it comes perilously close to advocating violence. It is expressed in the various black nationalist groups that are springing up across the nation, the largest and best-known being Elijah Muhammad's Muslim movement. Nourished by the Negro's frustration over the continued existence of racial discrimination, this movement is made up of people who have lost faith in America, who have absolutely repudiated Christianity, and who have concluded that the white man is an incorrigible "devil."

I have tried to stand between these two forces, saying that we need emulate neither the "do-nothingism" of the complacent nor the hatred and despair of the black nationalist. For there is the more excellent way of love and nonviolent protest. I am grateful to God that, through the influence of the Negro church, the way of nonviolence became an integral part of our struggle.

If this philosophy had not emerged, by now many streets of the South would, I am convinced, be flowing with blood. And I am further convinced that if our white brothers dismiss as "rabblerousers" and "outside agitators" those of us who employ nonviolent direct action, and if they refuse to support our nonviolent efforts, millions of Negroes will, out of frustration and despair, seek solace and security in black-nationalist ideologies—a development that would inevitably lead to a frightening racial nightmare.

30   Oppressed people cannot remain oppressed forever. The yearning for freedom eventually manifests itself, and that is what has happened to the American Negro. Something within has reminded him of his birthright of freedom, and something without has reminded him that it can be gained. Consciously or unconsciously, he has been caught up by the *Zeitgeist*,[12] and with his black brothers of Africa and his brown and yellow brothers of Asia, South America, and the Caribbean, the United States Negro is moving with a sense of great urgency toward the promised land of racial justice. If one recognizes this vital urge that has engulfed the Negro community, one should readily understand why public demonstrations are taking place. The Negro has many pent-up resentments and latent frustrations, and he must release them. So let him march; let him make prayer pilgrimages to the city hall; let him go on freedom rides—and try to understand why he must do so. If his repressed emotions are not released in nonviolent ways, they will seek expression through violence; this is not a threat but a fact of history. So I have not said to my people, "Get rid of your discontent." Rather, I have tried to say that this normal and healthy discontent can be channeled into the creative outlet of nonviolent direct action. And now this approach is being termed extremist.

---

[12]The spirit of the times. [Eds.]

But though I was initially disappointed at being categorized as an extremist, as I continued to think about the matter I gradually gained a measure of satisfaction from the label. Was not Jesus an extremist for love: "Love your enemies, bless them that curse you, do good to them that hate you, and pray for them which despitefully use you, and persecute you." Was not Amos an extremist for justice: "Let justice roll down like waters and righteousness like an ever-flowing stream." Was not Paul an extremist for the Christian gospel: "I bear in my body the marks of the Lord Jesus." Was not Martin Luther an extremist: "Here I stand; I cannot do otherwise, so help me God." And John Bunyan: "I will stay in jail to the end of my days before I make a butchery of my conscience." And Abraham Lincoln: "This nation cannot survive half slave and half free." And Thomas Jefferson: "We hold these truths to be self-evident, that all men are created equal. . . ." So the question is not whether we will be extremists, but what kind of extremists we will be. Will we be extremists for hate or for love? Will we be extremists for the preservation of injustice or for the extension of justice? In that dramatic scene on Calvary's hill three men were crucified. We must never forget that all three were crucified for the same thing—the crime of extremism. Two were extremists for immorality, and thus fell below their environment. The other, Jesus Christ, was an extremist for love, truth, and goodness, and thereby rose above his environment. Perhaps the South, the nation, and the world are in dire need of creative extremists.

I had hoped that the white moderate would see this need. Perhaps I was too optimistic; perhaps I expected too much. I suppose I should have realized that few members of the oppressor race can understand the deep groans and passionate yearnings of the oppressed race, and still fewer have the vision to see that injustice must be rooted out by strong, persistent, and determined action. I am thankful, however, that some of our white brothers in the South have grasped the meaning of this social revolution and committed themselves to it. They are still all too few in quantity, but they are big in quality. Some—such as Ralph McGill, Lillian Smith, Harry Golden, James McBridge Dabbs, Ann Braden, and Sarah Patton Boyle—have written about our struggle in eloquent and prophetic terms. Others have marched with us down nameless streets of the South. They have languished in filthy, roach-infested jails, suffering the abuse and brutality of policemen who view them as "dirty nigger-lovers." Unlike so many of their moderate brothers and sisters, they have recognized the urgency of the moment and sensed the need for powerful "action" antidotes to combat the disease of segregation.

Let me take note of my other major disappointment. I have been so greatly disappointed with the white church and its leadership. Of course, there are some notable exceptions. I am not unmindful of the fact that each of you has taken some significant stands on this issue. I commend you, Reverend Stallings, for your Christian stand on this past Sunday, in welcoming Negroes to your worship service on a non-segregated basis. I commend the Catholic leaders of this state for integrating Spring Hill College several years ago.

But despite these notable exceptions, I must honestly reiterate that I have been disappointed with the church. I do not say this as one of those negative critics who can always find something wrong with the church. I say this as a minister of the gospel, who loves the church; who was nurtured in its bosom; who has been sustained by its spiritual blessings and who will remain true to it as long as the cord of life shall lengthen.

35 When I was suddenly catapulted into the leadership of the bus protest in Montgomery, Alabama, a few years ago, I felt we would be supported by the white church. I felt that the white ministers, priests, and rabbis of the South would be among our strongest allies. Instead, some have been outright opponents, refusing to understand the freedom movement and misrepresenting its leaders; all too many others have been more cautious than courageous and have remained silent behind the anesthetizing security of stained glass windows.

In spite of my shattered dreams, I came to Birmingham with the hope that the white religious leadership of this community would see the justice of our cause and, with deep moral concern, would serve as the channel through which our just grievances could reach the power structure. I had hoped that each of you would understand. But again I have been disappointed.

I have heard numerous southern religious leaders admonish their worshipers to comply with a desegregation decision because it is the law, but I have longed to hear white ministers declare: "Follow this decree because integration is morally right and because the Negro is your brother." In the midst of blatant injustices inflicted upon the Negro, I have watched white churchmen stand on the sideline and mouth pious irrelevancies and sanctimonious trivialities. In the midst of a mighty struggle to rid our nation of racial and economic injustice, I have heard many ministers say: "Those are social issues, with which the gospel has no real concern." And I have watched many churches commit themselves to a completely otherworldly religion which makes a strange, un-Biblical distinction between body and soul, between the sacred and the secular.

I have traveled the length and breadth of Alabama, Mississippi, and all the other southern states. On sweltering summer days and crisp autumn mornings I have looked at the South's beautiful churches with their lofty spires pointing heavenward. I have beheld the impressive outlines of her massive religious-education buildings. Over and over I have found myself asking: "What kind of people worship here? Who is their God? Where were their voices when the lips of Governor Barnett[13] dripped with words of interposition and nullification? Where were they when Governor Wallace[14] gave a clarion call for defiance and hatred? Where were their voices of support when bruised and weary Negro men and women decided to rise from the dark dungeons of complacency to the bright hills of creative protest?"

Yes, these questions are still in my mind. In deep disappointment I have wept over the laxity of the church. But be assured that my tears have been tears of love. There can be no deep disappointment where there is not deep love. Yes, I love the church. How could I do otherwise? I am in the rather unique position of being the son, the grandson, and the great-grandson of preachers. Yes, I see the church as the body of Christ. But, oh! How we have blemished and scarred that body through social neglect and through fear of being nonconformists.

There was a time when the church was very powerful—in the time when the early Christians rejoiced at being deemed worthy to suffer for what they believed. In those days the church was not merely a thermometer that recorded the ideas and principles of popular opinion; it was a thermostat that transformed the mores of society. Whenever the early Christians entered a town, the people in power became disturbed and immediately sought to convict the Christians for being "disturbers of the peace" and "outside agitators." But the Christians pressed on, in the conviction that they were "a colony of heaven," called to obey God rather than man. Small in number, they were big in commitment. They were too God-intoxicated to be "astronomically intimidated." By their effort and example they brought an end to such ancient evils as infanticide and gladiatorial contests.

Things are different now. So often the contemporary church is a weak, ineffectual voice with an uncertain sound. So often it is an archdefender to the status quo. Far from being disturbed by the presence of the church, the power structure of the average community is consoled by the church's silent—and often even vocal—sanction of things as they are.

But the judgment of God is upon the church as never before. If today's church does not recapture the sacrificial spirit of the early church, it will lose its authenticity, forfeit the loyalty of millions, and be dismissed as an irrelevant social club with no meaning for the twentieth century. Every day I meet young people whose disappointment with the church has turned into outright disgust.

---

[13]Ross Barnett, segregationist governor of Mississippi, who strongly resisted the integration of the University of Mississippi in 1962. [Eds.]

[14]George Wallace, segregationist governor of Alabama, best known for standing in the doorway of a University of Alabama building to block the entrance of two black students who were trying to register. [Eds.]

Perhaps I have once again been too optimistic. Is organized religion too inextricably bound to the status quo to save our nation and the world? Perhaps I must turn my faith to the inner spiritual church, the church within the church, as the true *ekklesia*[15] and the hope of the world. But again I am thankful to God that some noble souls from the ranks of organized religion have broken loose from the paralyzing chains of conformity and joined us as active partners in the struggle for freedom. They have left their secure congregations and walked the streets of Albany, Georgia, with us. They have gone down the highways of the South on tortuous rides for freedom. Yes, they have gone to jail with us. Some have been dismissed from their churches, have lost the support of their bishops and fellow ministers. But they have acted in the faith that right defeated is stronger than evil triumphant. Their witness has been the spiritual salt that has preserved the true meaning of the gospel in these troubled times. They have carved a tunnel of hope through the dark mountain of disappointment.

I hope the church as a whole will meet the challenge of this decisive hour. But even if the church does not come to the aid of justice, I have no despair about the future. I have no fear about the outcome of our struggle in Birmingham, even if our motives are at present misunderstood. We will reach the goal of freedom in Birmingham and all over the nation, because the goal of America is freedom. Abused and scorned though we may be, our destiny is tied up with America's destiny. Before the pilgrims landed at Plymouth, we were here. Before the pen of Jefferson etched the majestic words of the Declaration of Independence across the pages of history, we were here. For more than two centuries our forebears labored in this country without wages; they made cotton king; they built the homes of their masters while suffering gross injustice and shameful humiliation—and yet out of a bottomless vitality they continued to thrive and develop. If the inexpressible cruelties of slavery could not stop us, the opposition we now face will surely fail. We will win our freedom because the sacred heritage of our nation and the eternal will of God are embodied in our echoing demands.

45   Before closing I feel impelled to mention one other point in your statement that has troubled me profoundly. You warmly commended the Birmingham police force for keeping "order" and "preventing violence." I doubt that you would have so warmly commended the police force if you had seen its dogs sinking their teeth into unarmed, nonviolent Negroes. I doubt that you would so quickly commend the policemen if you were to observe their ugly and inhumane treatment of Negroes here in the city jail; if you were to watch them push and curse old Negro women and young Negro girls; if you were to see

---

[15]The Greek word for the early Christian church. [Eds.]

them slap and kick old Negro men and young boys; if you were to observe them, as they did on two occasions, refuse to give us food because we wanted to sing our grace together. I cannot join you in your praise of the Birmingham police department.

It is true that the police have exercised a degree of discipline in handling the demonstrators. In this sense they have conducted themselves rather "nonviolently" in public. But for what purpose? To preserve the evil system of segregation. Over the past few years I have consistently preached that nonviolence demands that the means we use must be as pure as the ends we seek. I have tried to make clear that it is wrong to use immoral means to attain moral ends. But now I must affirm that it is just as wrong, or perhaps even more so, to use moral means to preserve immoral ends. Perhaps Mr. Connor and his policemen have been rather nonviolent in public, as was Chief Pritchett in Albany, Georgia, but they have used the moral means of nonviolence to maintain the immoral end of racial injustice. As T. S. Eliot[16] has said, "The last temptation is the greatest treason: To do the right deed for the wrong reason."

I wish you had commended the Negro sit-inners and demonstrators of Birmingham for their sublime courage, their willingness to suffer, and their amazing discipline in the midst of great provocation. One day the South will recognize its real heroes. They will be the James Merediths,[17] with the noble sense of purpose that enables them to face jeering and hostile mobs, and with the agonizing loneliness that characterizes the life of the pioneer. They will be old, oppressed, battered Negro women, symbolized in a seventy-two-year-old woman in Montgomery, Alabama, who rose up with a sense of dignity and with her people decided not to ride segregated buses, and who responded with ungrammatical profundity to one who inquired about her weariness: "My feets is tired, but my soul is at rest." They will be the young high school and college students, the young ministers of the gospel and a host of their elders, courageously and nonviolently sitting in at lunch counters and willingly going to jail for conscience' sake. One day the South will know that when these disinherited children of God sat down at lunch counters, they were in reality standing up for what is best in the American dream and for the most sacred values in our Judaeo-Christian heritage, thereby bringing our nation back to those great wells of democracy which were dug deep by the founding fathers in their formulation of the Constitution and the Declaration of Independence.

---

[16]American-born British poet (1888–1965), winner of the 1948 Nobel Prize in Literature. [Eds.]

[17]First African American to enroll at the University of Mississippi, after federal troops were brought in to control demonstrators protesting his enrollment. [Eds.]

Never before have I written so long a letter. I'm afraid it is much too long to take your precious time. I can assure you that it would have been much shorter if I had been writing from a comfortable desk, but what else can one do when he is alone in a narrow jail cell, other than write long letters, think long thoughts, and pray long prayers?

If I have said anything in this letter that overstates the truth and indicates an unreasonable impatience, I beg you to forgive me. If I have said anything that understates the truth and indicates my having a patience that allows me to settle for anything less than brotherhood, I beg God to forgive me.

50   I hope this letter finds you strong in the faith. I also hope that circumstances will soon make it possible for me to meet each of you, not as an integrationist or a civil-rights leader but as a fellow clergyman and a Christian brother. Let us all hope that the dark clouds of racial prejudice will soon pass away and the deep fog of misunderstanding will be lifted from our fear-drenched communities, and in some not too distant tomorrow the radiant stars of love and brotherhood will shine over our great nation with all their scintillating beauty.

Yours for the cause of Peace and Brotherhood,

MARTIN LUTHER KING, JR.

Responding to Reading

1. What decision do the clergy members King addresses believe he should rethink? Do you believe King would have been justified in arguing that he had no alternative other than protest? Would you accept this argument?
2. In paragraph 30, King says, "Oppressed people cannot remain oppressed forever." Do you think world events of the last few years confirm or contradict this statement? Explain.
3. Throughout this letter, King uses elaborate diction and a variety of rhetorical devices: he addresses his audience directly; makes frequent use of balance and parallelism, understatement, and metaphor; and makes many historical and religious allusions. What effect do you think King intended these rhetorical devices to have on the letter's original audience of clergymen? Does King's elaborate style enhance his argument, or does it just get in the way? Explain.

Responding in Writing

Write a short manifesto advocating civil disobedience for a cause you strongly believe in. To inspire others to follow the course of action you propose, explain the goal you are seeking, and identify the opposing forces that you believe make civil disobedience necessary. Then, outline the form you expect your peaceful protest to take.

LIFEBOAT ETHICS: THE CASE AGAINST "AID" THAT HARMS

Garrett Hardin

1915–

Garrett Hardin is a biologist who writes on moral and ethical issues in his field. Hardin, who earned an ScB degree from the University of Chicago (1936) and a PhD from Stanford University (1941), taught at the University of California at Santa Barbara from 1946 until 1978. His many books include Filters against Folly: How to Survive Despite Economists, Ecologists, and the Merely Eloquent *(1985);* Living within Limits: How Global Population Growth Threatens Widespread Social Disorder *(1992);* The Immigration Dilemma: Avoiding the Tragedy of the Commons *(1994); and* Ostrich Factor: Our Population Myopia *(1999). In the following classic essay, which originally appeared in* Psychology Today *in 1974, Hardin uses the metaphor of the wealthy nations of the world as lifeboats to illustrate the dilemma facing wealthy nations as they attempt to distribute food to the world's poor.*

Environmentalists use the metaphor of the earth as a "spaceship" in trying to persuade countries, industries and people to stop wasting and polluting our natural resources. Since we all share life on this planet, they argue, no single person or institution has the right to destroy, waste, or use more than a fair share of its resources.

But does everyone on earth have an equal right to an equal share of its resources? The spaceship metaphor can be dangerous when used by misguided idealists to justify suicidal policies for sharing our resources through uncontrolled immigration and foreign aid. In their enthusiastic but unrealistic generosity, they confuse the ethics of a spaceship with those of a lifeboat.

A true spaceship would have to be under the control of a captain, since no ship could possibly survive if its course were determined by committee. Spaceship Earth certainly has no captain; the United Nations is merely a toothless tiger, with little power to enforce any policy upon its bickering members.

If we divide the world crudely into rich nations and poor nations, two thirds of them are desperately poor, and only one third comparatively rich, with the United States the wealthiest of all. Metaphorically each rich nation can be seen as a lifeboat full of comparatively rich people. In the ocean outside each lifeboat swim the poor of the world, who would like to get in, or at least to share some of the wealth. What should the lifeboat passengers do?

First, we must recognize the limited capacity of any lifeboat. 5 For example, a nation's land has a limited capacity to support a population and as the (current energy crisis) has shown us, in some ways we have already exceeded the carrying capacity of our land.

So here we sit, say 50 people in our lifeboat. To be generous let us assume it has room for 10 more, making a total capacity of 60. Suppose the 50 of us in the lifeboat see 100 others swimming in the water outside, begging for admission to our boat or for handouts. We have several options: we may be tempted to try to live by the Christian ideal of being "our brother's keeper," or by the Marxist ideal of "to each according to his needs." Since the needs of all in the water are the same, and since they can all be seen as "our brothers," we could take them all into our boat, making a total of 150 in a boat designed for 60. The boat swamps, everyone drowns. Complete justice, complete catastrophe.

Since the boat has an unused excess capacity of 10 more passengers, we could admit just 10 more to it. But which 10 do we let in? How do we choose? Do we pick the best 10, the neediest 10, "first come, first served"? And what do we say to the 90 we exclude? If we do let an extra 10 into our lifeboat, we will have lost our "safety factor," an engineering principle of critical importance. For example, if we don't leave room for excess capacity as a safety factor in our country's agriculture, a new plant disease or a bad change in the weather could have disastrous consequences.

Suppose we decide to preserve our small safety factor and admit no more to the lifeboat. Our survival is then possible although we shall have to be constantly on guard against boarding parties.

While this last solution clearly offers the only means of our survival, it is morally abhorrent to many people. Some say they feel guilty about their good luck. My reply is simple: "Get out and yield your place to others." This may solve the problem of the guilt-ridden person's conscience, but it does not change the ethics of the lifeboat. The needy person to whom the guilt-ridden person yields his place will not himself feel guilty about his good luck. If he did, he would not climb aboard. The net result of conscience-stricken people giving up their unjustly held seats is the elimination of that sort of conscience from the lifeboat.

10   This is the basic metaphor within which we must work out our solutions. Let us now enrich the image, step by step, with substantive additions from the real world, a world that must solve real and pressing problems of overpopulation and hunger.

The harsh ethics of the lifeboat become even harsher when we consider the reproductive differences between the rich nations and the poor nations. The people inside the lifeboats are doubling in numbers every 87 years: those swimming around outside are doubling on the average, every 35 years, more than twice as fast as the rich. And since the world's resources are dwindling, the difference in prosperity between the rich and the poor can only increase.

As of 1973, the U.S. had a population of 210 million people, who were increasing by 0.8 percent per year. Outside our lifeboat, let us imagine another 210 million people (say the combined populations of Colombia, Ecuador, Venezuela, Morocco, Pakistan, Thailand and the Philippines), who are increasing at a rate of 3.3 percent per year. Put differently, the doubling time for this aggregate population is 21 years, compared to 87 years for the U.S.

Now suppose the U.S. agreed to pool its resources with those seven countries, with everyone receiving an equal share. Initially the ratio of Americans to non-Americans in this model would be one-to-one but consider what the ratio would be after 87 years, by which time the Americans would have doubled to a population of 420 million. By then, doubling every 21 years, the other group would have swollen to 354 billion. Each American would have to share the available resources with more than eight people.

But, one could argue, this discussion assumes that current population trends will continue, and they may not. Quite so. Most likely the rate of population increase will decline much faster in the U.S. than it will in the other countries, and there does not seem to be much we can do about it. In sharing with "each according to his needs," we must recognize that needs are determined by population size, which is determined by the rate of reproduction, which at present is regarded as a sovereign right of every nation, poor or not. This being so, the philanthropic load created by the sharing ethic of the spaceship can only increase.

The fundamental error of spaceship ethics, and the sharing it re- 15 quires, is that it leads to what I call "the tragedy of the commons." Under a system of private property, the men who own property recognize their responsibility to care for it, for if they don't they will eventually suffer. A farmer, for instance, will allow no more cattle in a pasture than its carrying capacity justifies. If he overloads it, erosion sets in, weeds take over, and he loses the use of the pasture.

If a pasture becomes a commons open to all, the right of each to use it may not be matched by a corresponding responsibility to protect it. Asking everyone to use it with discretion will hardly do, for the considerate herdsman who refrains from overloading the commons suffers more than a selfish one who says his needs are greater. If everyone would restrain himself all would be well; but it takes only one less than everyone to ruin a system of voluntary restraint. In a crowded world of less than perfect human beings, mutual ruin is inevitable if there are no controls. This is the tragedy of the commons.

One of the major tasks of education today should be the creation of such an acute awareness of the dangers of the commons that people will recognize its many varieties. For example, the air and water have become polluted because they are treated as commons. Further growth in the population or per-capita conversion of natural resources into pollutants will only make the problem worse. The same holds true for the fish of the oceans. Fishing fleets have nearly disappeared in many parts of the world; technological improvements in the art of fishing are hastening the day of complete ruin. Only the replacement of the system of the commons with a responsible system of control will save the land, air, water and oceanic fisheries.

In recent years there has been a push to create a new commons called a World Food Bank, an international depository of food reserves to which nations would contribute according to their abilities and from which they would draw according to their needs. This humanitarian proposal has received support from many liberal international groups, and from such prominent citizens as Margaret Mead, U.N. Secretary General Kurt Waldheim, and Senators Edward Kennedy and George McGovern.

A world food bank appeals powerfully to our humanitarian impulses. But before we rush ahead with such a plan, let us recognize where the greatest political push comes from, lest we be disillusioned later. Our experience with the "Food for Peace program," or Public Law 480, gives us the answer. This program moved billions of dollars worth of U.S. surplus grain to food-short, population-long countries during the past two decades. But when P.L. 480 first became law, a headline in the business magazine *Forbes* revealed the real power behind it: "Feeding the World's Hungry Millions: How It Will Mean Billions for U.S. Business."

20 And indeed it did. In the years 1960 to 1970, U.S. taxpayers spent a total of $7.9 billion on the Food for Peace program. Between 1948 and 1970, they also paid an additional $50 billion for other economic-aid programs, some of which went for food and food-producing machinery and technology. Though all U.S. taxpayers were forced to contribute to the cost of P.L. 480, certain special interest groups gained handsomely under the program. Farmers did not have to contribute the grain; the Government, or rather the taxpayers, bought it from them at full market prices. The increased demand raised prices of farm products generally. The manufacturers of farm machinery, fertilizers and pesticides benefited by the farmers' extra efforts to grow more food. Grain elevators profited from storing the surplus until it could be shipped. Railroads made money hauling it to ports, and shipping lines profited from carrying it overseas. The implementation of P.L. 480 required the creation of a vast Government bureaucracy, which then acquired its own vested interest in continuing the program regardless of its merits.

Those who proposed and defended the Food for Peace program in public rarely mentioned its importance to any of these special interests. The public emphasis was always on its humanitarian effects. The combination of silent selfish interests and highly vocal humanitarian apologists made a powerful and successful lobby for extracting money from taxpayers. We can expect the same lobby to push now for the creation of a World Food Bank.

However great the potential benefit to selfish interests, it should not be a decisive argument against a truly humanitarian program. We must ask if such a program would actually do more good than harm, not only momentarily but also in the long run. Those who propose the food bank usually refer to a current "emergency" or "crisis" in terms of world food supply. But what is an emergency? Although they may be infrequent and sudden, everyone knows that emergencies will occur from time to time. A well-run family, company, organization or country prepares for the likelihood of accidents and emergencies. It expects them, it budgets for them, it saves for them.

What happens if some organizations or countries budget for accidents and others do not? If each country is solely responsible for its own well-being, poorly managed ones will suffer. But they can learn from experience. They may mend their ways, and learn to budget for infrequent but certain emergencies. For example, the weather varies from year to year, and periodic crop failures are certain. A wise and competent government saves out of the production of the good years in anticipation of bad years to come. Joseph taught this policy to Pharoah in Egypt more than 2,000 years ago. Yet the great majority of the governments in the world today do not follow such a policy. They lack either the wisdom or the competence, or both. Should those nations that do manage to put something aside be forced to come to the rescue each time an emergency occurs among the poor nations?

"But it isn't their fault!" Some kind-hearted liberals argue, "How can we blame the poor people who are caught in an emergency? Why must they suffer for the sins of their governments?" The concept of blame is simply not relevant here. The real question is, what are the operational consequences of establishing a world food bank? If it is open to every country every time a need develops, slovenly rulers will not be motivated to take Joseph's advice. Someone will always come to their aid. Some countries will deposit food in the world food bank, and others will withdraw it. There will be almost no overlap. As a result of such solutions to food shortage emergencies, the poor countries will not learn to mend their ways, and will suffer progressively greater emergencies as their populations grow.

On the average, poor countries undergo a 2.5 percent increase in 25 population each year; rich countries, about 0.8 percent. Only rich countries have anything in the way of food reserves set aside, and even they do not have as much as they should. Poor countries have none. If poor countries received no food from the outside, the rate of their population growth would be periodically checked by crop failures and famines. But if they can always draw on a world food bank in time of need, their population can continue to grow unchecked, and so will their "need" for aid. In the short run, a world food bank may diminish that need, but in the long run it actually increases the need without limit.

Without some system of worldwide food sharing, the proportion of people in the rich and poor nations might eventually stabilize. The over-populated poor countries would decrease in numbers, while the rich countries that had room for more people would increase. But with a well-meaning system of sharing, such as a world food bank, the growth differential between the rich and the poor countries will not only persist, it will increase. Because of the higher rate of population growth in the poor countries of the world, 88 percent of today's children are born poor, and only 12 percent rich. Year by year the ratio becomes worse, as the fast-reproducing poor outnumber the slow-reproducing rich.

A world food bank is thus a commons in disguise. People will have more motivation to draw from it than to add to any common store. The less provident and less able will multiply at the expense of the abler and more provident, bringing eventual ruin upon all who share in the commons. Besides, any system of "sharing" that amounts to foreign aid from the rich nations to the poor nations will carry the taint of charity, which will contribute little to the world peace so devoutly desired by those who support the idea of a world food bank.

As past U.S. foreign-aid programs have amply and depressingly demonstrated, international charity frequently inspires mistrust and antagonism rather than gratitude on the part of the recipient nation.

The modern approach to foreign aid stresses the export of technology and advice, rather than money and food. As an ancient Chinese proverb goes: "Give a man a fish and he will eat for a day; teach him how to fish and he will eat for the rest of his days." Acting on this advice, the Rockefeller and Ford Foundations have financed a number of programs for improving agriculture in the hungry nations. Known as the "Green Revolution," these programs have led to the development of "miracle rice" and "miracle wheat," new strains that offer bigger harvests and greater resistance to crop damage. Norman Borlaug, the Nobel Prize winning agronomist who, supported by the Rockefeller Foundation, developed "miracle wheat," is one of the most prominent advocates of a world food bank.

30   Whether or not the Green Revolution can increase food production as much as its champions claim is a debatable but possibly irrelevant point. Those who support this well-intended humanitarian effort should first consider some of the fundamentals of human ecology. Ironically, one man who did was the late Alan Gregg, a vice president of the Rockefeller Foundation. Two decades ago he expressed strong doubts about the wisdom of such attempts to increase food produc-

tion. He likened the growth and spread of humanity over the surface of the earth to the spread of cancer in the human body, remarking that "cancerous growths demand food, but, as far as I know, they have never been cured by getting it."

Every human born constitutes a draft on all aspects of the environment: food, air, water, forests, beaches, wildlife, scenery and solitude. Food can, perhaps, be significantly increased to meet a growing demand. But what about clean beaches, unspoiled forests, and solitude? If we satisfy a growing population's need for food, we necessarily decrease its per capita supply of the other resources needed by men.

India, for example, now has a population of 600 million, which increases by 15 million each year. This population already puts a huge load on a relatively impoverished environment. The country's forests are now only a small fraction of what they were three centuries ago, and floods and erosion continually destroy the insufficient farmland that remains. Every one of the 15 million new lives added to India's population puts an additional burden on the environment, and increases the economic and social costs of crowding. However humanitarian our intent, every Indian life saved through medical or nutritional assistance from abroad diminishes the quality of life for those who remain, and for subsequent generations. If rich countries make it possible, through foreign aid, for 600 million Indians to swell to 1.2 billion in a mere 28 years, as their current growth rate threatens, will future generations of Indians thank us for hastening the destruction of their environment? Will our good intentions be sufficient excuse for the consequences of our actions?

My final example of a commons in action is one for which the public has the least desire for rational discussion—immigration. Anyone who publicly questions the wisdom of current U.S. immigration policy is promptly charged with bigotry, prejudice, ethnocentrism, chauvinism, isolationism or selfishness. Rather than encounter such accusations, one would rather talk about other matters, leaving immigration policy to wallow in the crosscurrents of special interests that take no account of the good of the whole, or the interests of posterity.

Perhaps we still feel guilty about things we said in the past. Two generations ago the popular press frequently referred to Dagos, Wops, Polacks, Chinks and Krauts, in articles about how America was being "overrun" by foreigners of supposedly inferior genetic stock. But because the implied inferiority of foreigners was used then as justification for keeping them out, people now assume that restrictive policies could only be based on such misguided notions. There are other grounds.

Just consider the numbers involved. Our Government acknowledges a net inflow of 400,000 immigrants a year. While we have no 35 hard data on the extent of illegal entries, educated guesses put the figure at about 600,000 a year. Since the natural increase (excess of births over deaths) of the resident population now runs about 1.7 million per year, the yearly gain from immigration amounts to at least 19 percent of the total annual increase, and may be as much as 37 percent if we include the estimate for illegal immigrants. Considering the growing use of birth-control devices, the potential effect of educational campaigns by such organizations as Planned Parenthood Federation of America and Zero Population Growth, and the influence of inflation and the housing shortage, the fertility rate of American women may decline so much that immigration could account for all the yearly increase in population. Should we not at least ask if that is what we want?

For the sake of those who worry about whether the "quality" of the average immigrant compares favorably with the quality of the average resident, let us assume that immigrants and nativeborn citizens are of exactly equal quality, however one defines that term. We will focus here only on quantity; and since our conclusions will depend on nothing else, all charges of bigotry and chauvinism become irrelevant.

World food banks *move food to the people,* hastening the exhaustion of the environment of the poor countries. Unrestricted immigration, on the other hand, *moves people to the food,* thus speeding up the destruction of the environment of the rich countries. We can easily understand why poor people should want to make this latter transfer, but why should rich hosts encourage it?

As is the case of foreign-aid programs, immigration receives support from selfish interests and humanitarian impulses. The primary selfish interest in unimpeded immigration is the desire of employers for cheap labor, particularly in industries and trades that offer degrading work. In the past, one wave of foreigners after another was brought into the U.S. to work at wretched jobs for wretched wages. In recent years the Cubans, Puerto Ricans and Mexicans have had this dubious honor. The interests of the employers of cheap labor mesh well with the guilty silence of the country's liberal intelligentsia. White Anglo-Saxon Protestants are particularly reluctant to call for a closing of the doors to immigration for fear of being called bigots.

But not all countries have such reluctant leadership. Most educated Hawaiians, for example, are keenly aware of the limits of their environment, particularly in terms of population growth. There is only so much room on the islands, and the islanders know it. To Hawaiians, immigrants from the other 49 states present as great a threat as those from other nations. At a recent meeting of Hawaiian government officials in Honolulu, I had the ironic delight of hearing a speaker, who like most of his audience was of Japanese ancestry, ask how the country might practically and constitutionally close its door to further immigration. One member of the audience countered: "How can we shut the doors now? We have many friends and relatives in Japan that we'd like to bring here some day so that they can enjoy Hawaii too." The Japanese-American speaker smiled sympathetically and answered: "Yes, but we have children now, and someday we'll have grandchildren too. We can bring more people here from Japan only by giving away some of the land that we hope to pass on to our grandchildren some day. What right do we have to do that?"

At this point, I can hear U.S. liberals asking: "How can you justify 40 slamming the door once you're inside? You say that immigrants should be kept out. But aren't we all immigrants, or the descendants of immigrants? If we insist on staying, must we not admit all others?" Our craving for intellectual order leads us to seek and prefer symmetrical rules and morals: a single rule for me and everybody else; the same rule yesterday, today and tomorrow. Justice, we feel, should not change with time and place.

We Americans of non-Indian ancestry can look upon ourselves as the descendants of thieves who are guilty morally, if not legally, of stealing this land from its Indian owners. Should we then give back the land to the now living American descendants of those Indians? However morally or logically sound this proposal may be, I, for one, am unwilling to live by it and I know no one else who is. Besides, the logical consequence would be absurd. Suppose that, intoxicated with a sense of pure justice, we should decide to turn our land over to the Indians. Since all our other wealth has also been derived from the land, wouldn't we be morally obliged to give that back to the Indians too?

Clearly, the concept of pure justice produces an infinite regression to absurdity. Centuries ago, wise men invented statutes of limitations to justify the rejection of such pure justice, in the interest of preventing continual disorder. The law zealously defends property rights. Drawing a line after an arbitrary time has elapsed may be unjust, but the alternatives are worse.

We are all the descendants of thieves, and the world's resources are inequitably distributed. But we must begin the journey to tomorrow from the point where we are today. We cannot remake the past. We cannot safely divide the wealth equitably among all peoples so long as people reproduce at different rates. To do so would guarantee that our grandchildren, and everyone else's grandchildren, would have only a ruined world to inhabit.

To be generous with one's own possessions is quite different from being generous with those of posterity. We should call this point to the attention of those who, from a commendable love of justice and equality, would institute a system of the commons, either in the form of a world food bank, or of unrestricted immigration. We must convince them if we wish to save at least some parts of the world from environmental ruin.

Responding to Reading

1. Hardin presents his problem as one that has no comfortable solution. One alternative, welcoming all who wish to come into the lifeboat, is "complete justice, complete catastrophe" (6); the other, retaining the crucial "safety factor," is both "the only means of our survival" and "morally abhorrent to many people" (8–9). Does Hardin see these two alternatives as ethically and practically unacceptable? Do you? Is it really an either/or situation, or are there some solutions he ignores?
2. Does Hardin's use of the lifeboat metaphor clarify his arguments and present the problem he describes in vivid terms? Or do you find it simplistic, distracting, or irrelevant?
3. In paragraph 2, Hardin asks, "But does everyone on earth have an equal right to an equal share of its resources?" That is, are some people more—or less—deserving than others? How would you answer this question?

Responding in Writing

Imagine you can take only one additional person into your lifeboat. Which of the following would you choose: a baby, an elderly man who has won the Nobel Peace Prize, a single mother of three young children, a decorated soldier, or a doctor who does life-saving surgery? Explain your choice.

DOG LAB

Claire McCarthy

1963–

A graduate of Princeton University and Harvard Medical School, Claire McCarthy did her residency at Boston's Children's Hospital and is now a pediatrician at the Martha Eliot Health Center in the Jamaica Plains neighborhood of Boston. During her medical training, she kept detailed journals, which provided the basis for her books Learning How the Heart Beats: The Making of a Pediatrician *(1995) and* Everyone's Children: A Pediatrician's Story of an Inner-City Practice *(1998). McCarthy has also written for the* Boston Globe Magazine. *In the following essay, a chapter from* Learning How the Heart Beats, *McCarthy recalls her reluctance to attend an optional lab lesson in which students studied the cardiovascular system of a sedated living dog, which was then euthanized.*

When I finished college and started medical school, the learning changed fundamentally. Whereas in college I had been learning mostly for learning's sake, learning in order to know something, in medical school I was learning in order to *do* something, do the thing I wanted to do with my life. It was exhilarating and at the same time a little scary. My study now carried responsibility.

The most important course in the first year besides Anatomy was Physiology, the study of the functions and processes of the human body. It was the most fascinating subject I had ever studied. I found the intricacies of the way the body works endlessly intriguing and in-genious: the way the nervous system is designed to differentiate a sharp touch from a soft one; the way muscles move and work to-gether to throw a ball; the wisdom of the kidneys, which filter the blood and let pass out only waste products and extra fluid, keeping everything else carefully within. It was magical to me that each organ and system worked so beautifully and in perfect concert with the rest of the body.

The importance of Physiology didn't lie just in the fact that it was fascinating, however. The other courses I was taking that semester, like Histology and Biochemistry, were fascinating, too. But because Physiology was the study of how the body actually works, it seemed the most pertinent to becoming a physician. The other courses were more abstract. Physiology was practical, and I felt that my ability to master Physiology would be a measure of my ability to be a doctor.

When the second-year students talked about Physiology, they al-ways mentioned "dog lab." They mentioned it briefly but signifi-cantly, sharing knowing looks. I gathered that it involved cutting dogs open and that it was controversial, but that was all I knew. I didn't pursue it, I didn't ask questions. That fall I was living day to day, lecture to lecture, test to test. My life was organized around putting as much information into my brain as possible, and I didn't pay much attention to anything else.

I would get up around six, make coffee, and eat my bowl of cereal   5 while I sat at my desk. There was nowhere else to sit in my dormitory room, and if I was going to sit at my desk, I figured I might as well study, so I always studied as I ate. I had a small refrigerator and a hot plate so that I could fix myself meals. After breakfast it was off to a morning of lectures, back to the room at lunchtime for a yogurt or soup and more studying, then afternoon lectures and labs. Before din-ner I usually went for a run or a swim; although it was necessary for my sanity and my health, I always felt guilty that I wasn't studying instead. I ate dinner at my desk or with other medical students at the cafeteria in Beth Israel Hospital. We sat among the doctors, staff, and patients, eating our food quickly. Although we would try to talk about movies, current affairs, or other "nonmedical" topics, sooner or later we usually ended up talking about medicine; it was fast

becoming our whole life. After dinner it was off to the eerie quiet of
the library, where I sat surrounded by my textbooks and notes until I
got tired or frustrated, which was usually around ten-thirty. Then I'd
go back to the dorm, maybe chat with the other students on my floor,
maybe watch television, probably study some more, and then fall
asleep so that I could start the routine all over again the next morning.

My life had never been so consuming. Sometimes I felt like a true
student in the best sense of the word, wonderfully absorbed in learning; other times I felt like an automation. I was probably a combination of the two. It bothered me sometimes that this process of teaching
me to take care of people was making me live a very study-centered,
self-centered life. However, it didn't seem as though I had a choice.

One day at the beginning of a physiology lecture the instructor
announced that we would be having a laboratory exercise to study
the cardiovascular system, and that dogs would be used. The room
was quickly quiet; this was the infamous "dog lab." The point of the
exercise, he explained, was to study the heart and blood vessels in
vivo[1] to learn the effects of different conditions and chemicals by seeing them rather than just by reading about them. The dogs would be
sedated and the changes in their heart rates, respiratory rates, and
blood pressure would be monitored with each experiment. As the last
part of the exercise the sleeping dogs' chests would be cut open so we
could actually watch the hearts and lungs in action, and then the dogs
would be killed, humanely. We would be divided up into teams of
four, and each team would work with a teaching assistant. Because so
many teaching assistants were required, the class would be divided in
half, and the lab would be held on two days.

The amphitheater buzzed.

The lab was optional, the instructor told us. We would not be
marked off in any way if we chose not to attend. He leaned against
the side of the podium and said that the way he saw it there was a
spectrum of morality when it came to animal experimentation. The
spectrum, he said, went from mice or rats to species like horses or
apes, and we had to decide at which species we would draw our
lines. He hoped, though, that we would choose to attend. It was an
excellent learning opportunity, and he thought we ought to take advantage of it. Then he walked behind the podium and started the
day's lecture.

10   It was all anyone could talk about: should we do dog lab or
shouldn't we? We discussed it endlessly.

There were two main camps. One was the "excellent learning opportunity" camp, which insisted that dog lab was the kind of science

---

[1]Latin phrase for "in the living being." [Eds.]

we came to medical school to do and that learning about the cardio-vascular system on a living animal would make it more understand-able and would therefore make us better doctors.

Countering them was the "importance of a life" camp. The ex-treme members of this camp insisted that it was always wrong to murder an animal for experimentation. The more moderate members argued that perhaps animal experimentation was useful in certain kinds of medical research, but that dog lab was purely an exercise for our education and didn't warrant the killing of a dog. We could learn the material in other ways, they said.

On and on the arguments went, with people saying the same things over and over again in every conceivable way. There was something very important about this decision. Maybe it was because we were just beginning to figure out how to define ourselves as physicians—were we scientists, eager for knowledge, or were we de-fenders of life? The dog lab seemed to pit one against the other. Maybe it was because we thought that our lives as physicians were going to be filled with ethical decisions, and this was our first since entering medical school. It was very important that we do the right thing, but the right thing seemed variable and unclear.

I was quiet during these discussions. I didn't want to kill a dog, but I certainly wanted to take advantage of every learning opportu-nity offered me. And despite the fact that the course instructor had said our grades wouldn't be affected if we didn't attend the lab, I wasn't sure I believed him, and I didn't want to take any chances. Even if he didn't incorporate the lab report into our grades, I was worried that there would be some reference to it in the final exam, some sneaky way that he would bring it up. Doing well had become so important that I was afraid to trust anyone; doing well had become more important than anything.

I found myself waiting to see what other people would decide. I 15 was ashamed not to be taking a stand, but I was stuck in a way I'd never been before. I didn't like the idea of doing the lab; it felt wrong. Yet for some reason I was embarrassed that I felt that way, and the lab seemed so important. The more I thought about it, the more confused I became.

Although initially the students had appeared divided more or less evenly between the camps, as the lab day drew nearer the major-ity chose to participate. The discussions didn't stop, but they were fewer and quieter. The issue seemed to become more private.

I was assigned to the second lab day. My indecision was becom-ing a decision since I hadn't crossed my name off the list. I can still change my mind, I told myself. I'm not on a team yet, nobody's counting on me to show up. One of my classmates asked me to join his group. I hedged.

The day before group lists had to be handed in, the course in
structor made an announcement. It was brief and almost offhand: he
said that if any of us wished to help anesthetize the dogs for the lab,
we were welcome to do so. He told us where to go and when to be
there for each lab day. I wrote the information down.

Somehow, this was what I needed. I made my decision. I would
do the lab, but I would go help anesthetize the dogs first.

20   Helping with the anesthesia, I thought, would be taking full responsibility for what I was doing, something that was very important
to me. I was going to *face* what I was doing, see the dogs awake with
their tails wagging instead of meeting them asleep and sort of pretending they weren't real. I also thought it might make me feel better
to know that the dogs were treated well as they were anesthetized
and to be there, helping to do it gently. Maybe in part I thought of it
as my penance.

The day of the first lab came. Around five o'clock I went down to
the Friday afternoon "happy hour" in the dormitory living room to
talk to the students as they came back. They came back singly or in
pairs, quiet, looking dazed. They threw down their coats and backpacks and made their way to the beer and soda without talking to
anyone. Some, once they had a cup in their hands, seemed to relax
and join in conversations; others took their cups and sat alone on the
couches. They all looked tired, worn out.

"Well?" I asked several of them. "What was it like?"

Most shrugged and said little. A few said that it was interesting
and that they'd learned a lot, but they said it without any enthusiasm.
Every one of them said it was hard. I thought I heard someone say
that their dog had turned out to be pregnant. Nobody seemed happy.

The morning of my lab was gray and dreary. I overslept, which I
hardly ever do. I got dressed quickly and went across the street to the
back entrance of the lab building. It was quiet and still and a little
dark. The streets were empty except for an occasional cab. I found the
open door and went in.

25   There was only one other student waiting there, a blond-haired
woman named Elise. I didn't know her well. We had friends in common, but we'd never really talked. She was sweet and soft-spoken;
she wore old jeans and plaid flannel shirts and hung out with the activist crowd. She had always intimidated me. I felt as though I
weren't political enough when I was around her. I was actually a little
surprised that she was doing the lab at all, as many of her friends had
chosen not to.

We greeted each other awkwardly, nodding hello and taking our
places leaning against the wall. Within a few minutes one of the

teaching assistants came in, said good morning, pulled out some keys, and let us into a room down the hall. Two more teaching assistants followed shortly.

The teaching assistants let the dogs out of cages, and they ran around the room. They were small dogs; I think they were beagles. They seemed happy to be out of their cages, and one of them, white with brown spots, came over to me with his tail wagging. I leaned over to pet him, and he licked my hand, looking up at me eagerly. I stood up again quickly.

The teaching assistant who had let us in, a short man with tousled brown hair and thick glasses, explained that the dogs were to be given intramuscular injections of a sedative that would put them to sleep. During the lab they would be given additional doses intravenously as well as other medications to stop them from feeling pain. We could help, he said, by holding the dogs while they got their injections. Elise and I nodded.

So we held the dogs, and they got their injections. After a few minutes they started to stumble, and we helped them to the floor. I remember that Elise petted one of the dogs as he fell asleep and that she cried. I didn't cry, but I wanted to.

When we were finished, I went back to my room. I sat at my desk, 30 drank my coffee, and read over the lab instructions again. I kept thinking about the dogs running around, about the little white one with the brown spots, and I felt sick. I stared at the instructions without really reading them, looking at my watch every couple of minutes. At five minutes before eight I picked up the papers, put them in my backpack with my books, and left.

The lab was held in a big open room with white walls and lots of windows. The dogs were laid out on separate tables lined up across the room; they were on their backs, tied down. They were all asleep, but some of them moved slightly, and it chilled me.

We walked in slowly and solemnly, putting our coats and backpacks on the rack along the wall and going over to our assigned tables. I started to look for the dog who had licked my hand, but I stopped myself. I didn't want to know where he was.

Our dog was brown and black, with soft floppy ears. His eyes were shut. He looked familiar. We took our places, two on each side of the table, laid out our lab manuals, and began.

The lab took all day. We cut through the dog's skin to find an artery and vein, into which we placed catheters. We injected different drugs and chemicals and watched what happened to the dog's heart rate and blood pressure, carefully recording the results. At the end of the day, when we were done with the experiments, we cut open the dog's chest. We cut through his sternum and pulled open his rib cage. His heart and lungs lay in front of us. The heart was a fist-size muscle that squeezed itself as it beat, pushing blood out. The lungs were white and solid and glistening under the pleura that covered them. The instructor pointed out different blood vessels, like the aorta and the superior vena cava. He showed us the stellate ganglion, which really did look like a star. I think we used the electrical paddles of a defibrillator and shocked the dog's heart into ventricular fibrillation, watching it shiver like Jell-O in front of us. I think that's how we killed them—or maybe it was with a lethal dose of one of the drugs. I'm not sure. It's something I guess I don't want to remember.

35   Dan was the anesthesiologist, the person assigned to making sure that the dog stayed asleep throughout the entire procedure. Every once in a while Dan would get caught up in the experiment and the dog would start to stir. I would nudge Dan, and he would quickly give more medication. The dog never actually woke up, but every time he moved even the slightest bit, every time I had to think about him being a real dog who was never going to wag his tail or lick anyone's hand again because of us, I got so upset that I couldn't concentrate. In fact, I had trouble concentrating on the lab in general. I kept staring at the dog.

As soon as we were finished, or maybe a couple of minutes before, I left. I grabbed my coat and backpack and ran down the stairs out into the dusk of the late afternoon. It was drizzling, and the medical school looked brown and gray. I walked quickly toward the street.

I was disappointed in the lab and disappointed in myself for doing it. I knew now that doing the lab was wrong. Maybe not wrong for everyone—it was clearly a complicated and individual choice—but wrong for me. The knowledge I had gained wasn't worth the life of a dog to me. I felt very sad.

The drizzle was becoming rain. I slowed down; even though it was cold, the rain felt good. A couple of people walking past me put up their umbrellas. I let the rain fall on me. I wanted to get wet.

From the moment you enter the field of medicine as a medical student, you have an awareness that you have entered something bigger and more important than you are. Doctors are different from other people, we are told implicitly, if not explicitly. Medicine is a way of life, with its own values and guidelines for daily living. They aren't bad values; they include things like the importance of hard work, the pursuit of knowledge, and the preservation of life—at least human life. There's room for individuality and variation, but that's something I realized later, much later. When I started medical school I felt that not only did I have to learn information and skills, I had to become a certain kind of person, too. It was very important to me to learn to do the thing that a doctor would do in a given situation. Since the course instructor, who represented Harvard Medical School to me, had recommended that we do the lab, I figured that a doctor would do it. That wasn't the only reason I went ahead with the lab, but it was a big reason.

The rain started to come down harder and felt less pleasant. I 40 walked more quickly, across Longwood Avenue into Vanderbilt Hall. I could hear familiar voices coming from the living room, but I didn't feel like talking to anyone. I ducked into the stairwell.

I got to my room, locked the door behind me, took off my coat, and lay down on my bed. The rain beat against my window. It was the time I usually went running, but the thought of going back out in the rain didn't appeal to me at all. I was suddenly very tired.

As I lay there I thought about the course instructor's discussion of the spectrum of morality and drawing lines. Maybe it's not a matter of deciding which animals I feel comfortable killing, I thought. Maybe it's about drawing different kinds of lines: drawing the lines to define how much of myself I will allow to change. I was proud of being a true student, even if it did mean becoming a little like an automaton. But I still needed to be the person I was before; I needed to be able to make some decisions without worrying about what a doctor would do.

I got up off the bed, opened a can of soup, and put it in a pan on the hot plate to warm. I got some bread and cheese out of the refrigerator, sat down at my desk, and opened my Biochemistry text.

Suddenly I stopped. I closed the text, reached over, and turned on the television, which sat on a little plastic table near the desk. There would be time to study later. I was going to watch television, read a newspaper, and call some friends I hadn't called since starting medical school. It was time to make some changes, some changes back.

Responding to Reading

1. Summarize the two main schools of thought about whether or not to participate in "dog lab." Do the students really have a choice? Explain.
2. Why did McCarthy decide to help anesthesize the dogs? Does her decision make sense to you?
3. Did McCarthy believe that the knowledge she gained was worth the sacrifice of the dog? Do you agree with her? Do you think her experience in "dog lab" changed her? Do you think it made her a better doctor? Explain.

Responding in Writing

Do you see a difference in the relative value of the lives of a laboratory animal, an animal in the wild, and a pet? Or do you think the lives of all three kinds of animals have equal value? Explain your beliefs.

The Perils of Obedience

Stanley Milgram

1932–1984

Social psychologist Stanley Milgram is best known for his experiments that study aggression and human conformity, especially obedience. Born in New York City, Milgram earned an AB in political science from Queens College (1954) and a PhD in social psychology from Harvard University (1960) and went on to teach and conduct research at Yale, Harvard, and the City University of New York. He has said that "it is only the person dwelling in isolation who is not forced to respond, with defiance or submission, to the commands of others." Milgram used Nazi Germany as a tragic example of submission to obedience. In the following selection, from his book Obedience to Authority *(1974), Milgram's descriptions of some of his experiments on obedience raise perplexing and moral questions. To read more about Milgram, visit http://www.stanleymilgram.com/, a Web site hosted by social psychologist Thomas Blass, PhD.*

Obedience is as basic an element in the structure of social life as one can point to. Some system of authority is a requirement of all communal living, and it is only the person dwelling in isolation who is not forced to respond, with defiance or submission, to the commands of others. For many people, obedience is a deeply ingrained behavior tendency, indeed a potent impulse overriding training in ethics, sympathy, and moral conduct.

The dilemma inherent in submission to authority is ancient, as old as the story of Abraham,[1] and the question of whether one should obey when commands conflict with conscience has been argued by Plato, dramatized in *Antigone*,[2] and treated to philosophic analysis in almost every historical epoch. Conservative philosophers argue that the very fabric of society is threatened by disobedience, while humanists stress the primacy of the individual conscience.

The legal and philosophic aspects of obedience are of enormous import, but they say very little about how most people behave in concrete situations. I set up a simple experiment at Yale University to test how much pain an ordinary citizen would inflict on another person simply because he was ordered to by an experimental scientist. Stark authority was pitted against the subjects' strongest moral imperatives against hurting others, and, with the subjects' ears ringing with the

---

[1]Abraham, commanded by God to sacrifice his son Isaac, is ready to do so until an angel stops him. [Eds.]

[2]In Plato's *Apology,* the philosopher Socrates provokes and accepts the sentence of death rather than act against his conscience; the heroine of Sophocles' *Antigone* risks a death sentence in order to give her brother a proper burial. [Eds.]

screams of the victims, authority won more often than not. The extreme willingness of adults to go to almost any lengths on the command of an authority constitutes the chief finding of the study and the fact most urgently demanding explanation.

In the basic experimental design, two people come to a psychology laboratory to take part in a study of memory and learning. One of them is designated as a "teacher" and the other a "learner." The experimenter explains that the study is concerned with the effects of punishment on learning. The learner is conducted into a room, seated in a kind of miniature electric chair; his arms are strapped to prevent excessive movement, and an electrode is attached to his wrist. He is told that he will be read lists of simple word pairs, and that he will then be tested on his ability to remember the second word of a pair when he hears the first one again. Whenever he makes an error, he will receive electric shocks of increasing intensity.

The real focus of the experiment is the teacher. After watching the 5
learner being strapped into place, he is seated before an impressive shock generator. The instrument panel consists of thirty lever switches set in a horizontal line. Each switch is clearly labeled with a voltage designation ranging from 15 to 450 volts. The following designations are clearly indicated for groups of four switches, going from left to right: Slight Shock, Moderate Shock, Strong Shock, Very Strong Shock, Intense Shock, Extreme Intensity Shock, Danger: Severe Shock. (Two switches after this last designation are simply marked XXX.)

When a switch is depressed, a pilot light corresponding to each switch is illuminated in bright red; an electric buzzing is heard; a blue light, labeled "voltage energizer," flashes; the dial on the voltage meter swings to the right; and various relay clicks sound off.

The upper left-hand corner of the generator is labeled SHOCK GENERATOR, TYPE ZLB, DYSON INSTRUMENT COMPANY, WALTHAM, MASS. OUTPUT 15 VOLTS–450 VOLTS.

Each subject is given a sample 45-volt shock from the generator before his run as teacher, and the jolt strengthens his belief in the authenticity of the machine.

The teacher is a genuinely naïve subject who has come to the laboratory for the experiment. The learner, or victim, is actually an actor who receives no shock at all. The point of the experiment is to see how far a person will proceed in a concrete and measurable situation in which he is ordered to inflict increasing pain on a protesting victim.

Conflict arises when the man receiving the shock begins to show 10
that he is experiencing discomfort. At 75 volts, he grunts; at 120 volts, he complains loudly; at 150, he demands to be released from the experiment. As the voltage increases, his protests become more vehement and emotional. At 285 volts, his response can be described only as an agonized scream. Soon thereafter, he makes no sound at all.

For the teacher, the situation quickly becomes one of gripping tension. It is not a game for him; conflict is intense and obvious. The manifest suffering of the learner presses him to quit; but each time he hesitates to administer a shock, the experimenter orders him to continue. To extricate himself from this plight, the subject must make a clear break with authority.[3]

The subject, Gretchen Brandt,[4] is an attractive thirty-one-year-old medical technician who works at the Yale Medical School. She had emigrated from Germany five years before.

On several occasions when the learner complains, she turns to the experimenter coolly and inquires, "Shall I continue"? She promptly returns to her task when the experimenter asks her to do so. At the administration of 210 volts, she turns to the experimenter, remarking firmly, "Well, I'm sorry, I don't think we should continue."

> EXPERIMENTER: The experiment requires that you go on until he has learned all the word pairs correctly.
> BRANDT: He has a heart condition, I'm sorry. He told you that before.
> EXPERIMENTER: The shocks may be painful but they are not dangerous.
> BRANDT: Well, I'm sorry, I think when shocks continue like this, they are dangerous. You ask him if he wants to get out. It's his free will.
> EXPERIMENTER: It is absolutely essential that we continue . . .
> BRANDT: I'd like you to ask him. We came here of our free will. If he wants to continue I'll go ahead. He told you he had a heart condition. I'm sorry. I don't want to be responsible for anything happening to him. I wouldn't like it for me either.
> EXPERIMENTER: You have no other choice.
> BRANDT: I think we are here on our own free will. I don't want to be responsible if anything happens to him. Please understand that.

She refuses to go further and the experiment is terminated.

15   The woman is firm and resolute throughout. She indicates in the interview that she was in no way tense or nervous, and this corresponds to her controlled appearance during the experiment. She feels that the last shock she administered to the learner was extremely painful and reiterates that she "did not want to be responsible for any harm to him."

---

[3]The ethical problems of carrying out an experiment of this sort are too complex to be dealt with here, but they receive extended treatment in the book from which this article is adapted. [The book is *Obedience to Authority* (New York: Harper & Row, 1974)—Eds.]
[4]Names of subjects described in this piece have been changed.

The woman's straightforward, courteous behavior in the experiment, lack of tension, and total control of her own action seem to make disobedience a simple and rational deed. Her behavior is the very embodiment of what I envisioned would be true for almost all subjects.

Before the experiments, I sought predictions about the outcome from various kinds of people—psychiatrists, college sophomores, middle-class adults, graduate students and faculty in the behavioral sciences. With remarkable similarity, they predicted that virtually all subjects would refuse to obey the experimenter. The psychiatrists specifically predicted that most subjects would not go beyond 150 volts, when the victim makes his first explicit demand to be freed. They expected that only 4 percent would reach 300 volts, and that only a pathological fringe of about one in a thousand would administer the highest shock on the board.

These predictions were unequivocally wrong. Of the forty subjects in the first experiment, twenty-five obeyed the orders of the experimenter to the end, punishing the victim until they reached the most potent shock available on the generator. After 450 volts were administered three times, the experimenter called a halt to the sessions. Many obedient subjects then heaved sighs of relief, mopped their brows, rubbed their fingers over their eyes, or nervously fumbled cigarettes. Others displayed only minimal signs of tension from beginning to end.

When the very first experiments were carried out, Yale undergraduates were used as subjects, and about 60 percent of them were fully obedient. A colleague of mine immediately dismissed these findings as having no relevance to "ordinary" people, asserting that Yale undergraduates are a highly aggressive, competitive bunch who step on each other's necks on the slightest provocation. He assured me that when "ordinary" people were tested, the results would be quite different. As we moved from the pilot studies to the regular experimental series, people drawn from every stratum of New Haven life came to be employed in the experiment: professionals, white-collar workers, unemployed persons, and industrial workers. *The experimental outcome was the same as we had observed among the students.*

Moreover, when the experiments were repeated in Princeton, Munich, Rome, South Africa, and Australia, the level of obedience was invariably somewhat *higher* than found in the investigation reported in this article. Thus one scientist in Munich found 85 percent of his subjects obedient.

Fred Prozi's reactions, if more dramatic than most, illuminate the conflicts experienced by others in less visible form. About fifty years old and unemployed at the time of the experiment, he has a good-natured, if slightly dissolute, appearance, and he strikes people as a rather ordinary fellow. He begins the session calmly but becomes tense as it proceeds. After delivering the 180-volt shock, he pivots around in his chair and, shaking his head, addresses the experimenter in agitated tones:

PROZI: I can't stand it. I'm not going to kill that man in there. You hear him hollering?

EXPERIMENTER: As I told you before, the shocks may be painful, but . . .

PROZI: But he's hollering. He can't stand it. What's going to happen to him?

EXPERIMENTER (his voice is patient, matter-of-fact): The experiment requires that you continue, Teacher.

PROZI: Aaah, but, unh, I'm not going to get that man sick in there—know what I mean?

EXPERIMENTER: Whether the learner likes it or not, we must go on, through all the word pairs.

PROZI: I refuse to take the responsibility. He's in there hollering!

EXPERIMENTER: It's absolutely essential that you continue, Prozi.

PROZI (indicating the unused questions): There's too many left here, I mean, Jeez, if he gets them wrong, there's too many of them left. I mean, who's going to take the responsibility if anything happens to that gentleman?

EXPERIMENTER: I'm responsible for anything that happens to him. Continue, please.

PROZI: All right. (Consults list of words.) The next one's "Slow—walk, truck, dance, music." Answer, please. (A buzzing sound indicates the learner has signaled his answer.) Wrong. A hundred and ninety-five volts. "Dance." (Zzumph!)

learner (yelling): Let me out of here! My heart's bothering me! (Teacher looks at experimenter.)

EXPERIMENTER: Continue, please.

LEARNER (screaming): Let me out of here! You have no right to keep me here! Let me out of here, my heart's bothering me, let me out!

PROZI (shakes head, pats the table nervously): You see, he's hollering. Hear that? Gee, I don't know.

EXPERIMENTER: The experiment requires . . .

PROZI (interrupting): I know it does, sir, but I mean—hunh! He don't know what he's getting in for. He's up to 195 volts! (Experiment continues, through 210 volts, 225 volts, 240 volts, 255 volts, 270 volts, at which point Prozi, with evident relief, runs out of word-pair questions.)

EXPERIMENTER: You'll have to go back to the beginning of that page and go through them again until he's learned them all correctly.

PROZI: Aw, no. I'm not going to kill that man. You mean I've got to keep going up with the scale? No sir. He's hollering in there. I'm not going to give him 450 volts.

EXPERIMENTER: The experiment requires that you go on.

LEARNER: Ohhh. I absolutely refuse to answer anymore. (Shouting urgently now.) Let me out of here! You can't hold me here! Get me out. Get-me-out-of-here!

EXPERIMENTER: Continue. The next word is "Green," please.

PROZI: "Green—grass, hat, ink, apple." (Nothing happens. No answering buzz. Just gloomy silence.)

PROZI: I don't think he is going to answer.

EXPERIMENTER: If the learner doesn't answer in a reasonable time, about four or five seconds, consider the answer wrong. And follow the same procedures you have been doing for wrong answers. Say, "Wrong," tell him the number of volts, give him the punishment, read him the correct answer. Continue, please.

PROZI: "Green—grass, hat, ink, apple." Answer, please. (More silence. Subject just sits there.)

EXPERIMENTER: Go on with the procedure, please.

PROZI: Three hundred and fifteen volts. The answer is "ink." (Zzumph!)

LEARNER: Ohh. Oooohh.

PROZI (relieved to hear response): Next one . . .

LEARNER: I absolutely refuse to answer.

PROZI: You got to. You get a shock if you don't answer. (Experiment continues with learner refusing to answer, and, finally, failing even to grunt or groan. At 375 volts, the subject stands up.)

PROZI: I think something's happening to that fellow in there. I don't get no answer. He was hollering at less voltage. Can't you check in and see if he's all right, please?

EXPERIMENTER (with same detached calm): Not once we've started. Please continue, Teacher.

PROZI (sits down, sighs deeply): "Cool—day, shade, water, paint." Answer, please. Are you all right in there? Are you all right?

EXPERIMENTER: Please continue, Teacher. Continue, please. (Subject pushes lever. Zzumph!)

PROZI (swiveling around in his chair): Something's happened to that man in there. (Swiveling back.) Next one. "Low—dollar, necklace, moon, paint." (Turning around again.) Something's happened to that man in there. You better check in on him, sir. He won't answer or nothing.

EXPERIMENTER: Continue. Go on, please.

PROZI: You accept all responsibility?

EXPERIMENTER: The responsibility is mine. Correct. Please go on. (Subject returns to his list, starts running through words as rapidly as he can read them, works through to 450 volts.)
PROZI: That's that.
EXPERIMENTER: Continue using the 450 switch for each wrong answer. Continue, please.
PROZI: But I don't get anything!
EXPERIMENTER: Please continue. The next word is "white."
PROZI: Don't you think you should look in on him, please?
EXPERIMENTER: Not once we've started the experiment.
PROZI: What if he's dead in there? (Gestures toward the room with the electric chair.) I mean, he told me he can't stand the shock, sir. I don't mean to be rude, but I think you should look in on him. All you have to do is look in on him. All you have to do is look in the door. I don't get no answer, no noise. Something might have happened to the gentleman in there, sir.
EXPERIMENTER: We must continue. Go on, please.
PROZI: You mean keep giving him what? Four-hundred-fifty volts, what he's got now?
EXPERIMENTER: That's correct. Continue. The next word is "white."
PROZI (now at a furious pace): "White—cloud, horse, rock, house." Answer, please. The answer is "horse." Four hundred and fifty volts. (Zzumph!) Next word, "Bag—paint, music, clown, girl." The answer is "paint." Four hundred and fifty volts. (Zzumph!) Next word is "Short—sentence, movie . . ."
EXPERIMENTER: Excuse me, Teacher. We'll have to discontinue the experiment.

Morris Braverman, another subject, is a thirty-nine-year-old social worker. He looks older than his years because of his bald head and serious demeanor. His brow is furrowed, as if all the world's burdens were carried on his face. He appears intelligent and concerned.

When the learner refuses to answer and the experimenter instructs Braverman to treat the absence of an answer as equivalent to a wrong answer, he takes his instruction to heart. Before administering 300 volts he asserts officiously to the victim, "Mr. Wallace, your silence has to be considered as a wrong answer." Then he administers the shock. He offers halfheartedly to change places with the learner, then asks the experimenter. "Do I have to follow these instructions literally?" He is satisfied with the experimenter's answer that he does. His very refined and authoritative manner of speaking is increasingly broken up by wheezing laughter.

The experimenter's notes on Mr. Braverman at the last few shocks are:

Almost breaking up now each time gives shock. Rubbing face to hide 25
laughter.

Squinting, trying to hide face with hand, still laughing.

Cannot control his laughter at this point no matter what he does.

Clenching fist, pushing it onto table.

In an interview after the session, Mr. Braverman summarizes the experiment with impressive fluency and intelligence. He feels the experiment may have been designed also to "test the effects on the teacher of being in an essentially sadistic role, as well as the reactions of a student to a learning situation that was authoritative and punitive." When asked how painful the last few shocks administered to the learner were, he indicates that the most extreme category on the scale is not adequate (it read EXTREMELY PAINFUL) and places his mark at the edge of the scale with an arrow carrying it beyond the scale.

It is almost impossible to convey the greatly relaxed, sedate qual- 30
ity of his conversation in the interview. In the most relaxed terms, he speaks about his severe inner tension.

EXPERIMENTER: At what point were you most tense or nervous?
MR. BRAVERMAN: Well, when he first began to cry out in pain, and I realized this was hurting him. This got worse when he just blocked and refused to answer. There was I. I'm a nice person, I think, hurting somebody, and caught up in what seemed a mad situation . . . and in the interest of science, one goes through with it.

When the interviewer pursues the general question of tension, Mr. Braverman spontaneously mentions his laughter.

"My reactions were awfully peculiar. I don't know if you were watching me, but my reactions were giggly, and trying to stifle laughter. This isn't the way I usually am. This was a sheer reaction to a totally impossible situation. And my reaction was to the situation of having to hurt somebody. And being totally helpless and caught up in a set of circumstances where I just couldn't deviate and I couldn't try to help. This is what got me."

Mr. Braverman, like all subjects, was told the actual nature and purpose of the experiment, and a year later he affirmed in a questionnaire that he had learned something of personal importance: "What appalled me was that I could possess this capacity for obedience and compliance to a central idea, i.e., the value of a memory experiment, even after it became clear that continued adherence to this value was at the expense of violation of another value, i.e., don't hurt someone who is helpless and not hurting you. As my wife said, 'You can call yourself Eichmann.[5] I hope I deal more effectively with any future conflicts of values encounter."

One theoretical interpretation of this behavior holds that all people harbor deeply aggressive instincts continually pressing for expression, and that the experiment provides institutional justification for the release of these impulses. According to this view, if a person is placed in a situation in which he has complete power over another individual, whom he may punish as much as he likes, all that is sadistic and bestial in man comes to the fore. The impulse to shock the victim is seen to flow from the potent aggressive tendencies, which are part of the motivational life of the individual, and the experiment, because it provides social legitimacy, simply opens the door to their expression.

35   It becomes vital, therefore, to compare the subject's performance when he is under orders and when he is allowed to choose the shock level.

The procedure was identical to our standard experiment, except that the teacher was told that he was free to select any shock level on any of the trials. (The experimenter took pains to point out that the teacher could use the highest levels on the generator, the lowest, any in between, or any combination of levels.) Each subject proceeded for thirty critical trials. The learner's protests were coordinated to standard shock levels, his first grunt coming at 75 volts, his first vehement protest at 150 volts.

The average shock used during the thirty critical trials was less than 60 volts—lower than the point at which the victim showed the first signs of discomfort. Three of the forty subjects did not go beyond the very lowest level on the board, twenty-eight went no higher than 75 volts, and thirty-eight did not go beyond the first loud protest at 150 volts. Two subjects provided the exception, administering up to 325 and 450 volts, but the overall result was that the great majority of people delivered very low, usually painless, shocks when the choice was explicitly up to them.

This condition of the experiment undermines another commonly offered explanation of the subjects' behavior—that those who shocked the victim at the most severe levels came only from the sadistic fringe of society. If one considers that almost two-thirds of the participants fall into the category of "obedient" subjects, and that they represented ordinary people drawn from working, managerial, and professional classes, the argument becomes very shaky. Indeed, it is highly reminiscent of the issue that arose in connection with Hannah

---

[5]Nazi officer, executed in 1962, who engineered the mass extermination of Jews. Many concentration camp officials defended themselves afterward by saying they were "just following orders." [Eds.]

Arendt's 1963 book, *Eichmann in Jerusalem*. Arendt contended that the prosecution's effort to depict Eichmann as a sadistic monster was fundamentally wrong, that he came closer to being an uninspired bureaucrat who simply sat at his desk and did his job. For asserting her views, Arendt became the object of considerable scorn, even calumny. Somehow, it was felt that the monstrous deeds carried out by Eichmann required a brutal, twisted personality, evil incarnate. After witnessing hundreds of ordinary persons submit to the authority in our own experiments, I must conclude that Arendt's conception of the banality of evil comes closer to the truth than one might dare imagine. The ordinary person who shocked the victim did so out of a sense of obligation—an impression of his duties as a subject—and not from any peculiarly aggressive tendencies.

This is, perhaps, the most fundamental lesson of our study: ordinary people, simply doing their jobs, and without any particular hostility on their part, can become agents in a terrible destructive process. Moreover, even when the destructive effects of their work become patently clear, and they are asked to carry out actions incompatible with fundamental standards of morality, relatively few people have the resources needed to resist authority.

Many of the people were in some sense against what they did to 40 the learner, and many protested even while they obeyed. Some were totally convinced of the wrongness of their actions but could not bring themselves to make an open break with authority. They often derived satisfaction from their thoughts and felt that—within themselves, at least—they had been on the side of the angels. They tried to reduce strain by obeying the experimenter but "only slightly" encouraging the learner, touching the generator switches gingerly. When interviewed, such a subject would stress that he had "asserted my humanity" by administering the briefest shock possible. Handling the conflict in this manner was easier than defiance.

The situation is constructed so that there is no way the subject can stop shocking the learner without violating the experimenter's definitions of his own competence. The subject fears that he will appear arrogant, untoward, and rude if he breaks off. Although these inhibiting emotions appear small in scope alongside the violence being done to the learner, they suffuse the mind and feelings of the subject, who is miserable at the prospect of having to repudiate the authority to his face. (When the experiment was altered so that the experimenter gave his instructions by telephone instead of in person, only a third as many people were fully obedient through 450 volts.) It is a curious thing that a measure of compassion on the part of the subject—an unwillingness to "hurt" the experimenter's feelings—is part of those binding forces inhibiting his disobedience. The withdrawal of such deference may be as painful to the subject as to the authority he defies.

The subjects do not derive satisfaction from inflicting pain, but they often like the feeling they get from pleasing the experimenter. They are proud of doing a good job, obeying the experimenter under difficult circumstances. While the subjects administered only mild shocks on their own initiative, one experimental variation showed that, under orders, 30 percent of them were willing to deliver 450 volts even when they had to forcibly push the learner's hand down on the electrode.

Bruno Batta is a thirty-seven-year-old welder who took part in the variation requiring the use of force. He was born in New Haven, his parents in Italy. He has a rough-hewn face that conveys a conspicuous lack of alertness. He has some difficulty in mastering the experimental procedure and needs to be corrected by the experimenter several times. He shows appreciation for the help and willingness to do what is required. After the 150-volt level, Batta has to force the learner's hand down on the shock plate, since the learner himself refuses to touch it.

When the learner first complains, Mr. Batta pays no attention to him. His face remains impassive, as if to dissociate himself from the learner's disruptive behavior. When the experimenter instructs him to force the learner's hand down, he adopts a rigid, mechanical procedure. He tests the generator switch. When it fails to function he immediately forces the learner's hand onto the shock plate. All the while he maintains the same rigid mask. The learner, seated alongside him, begs him to stop, but with robotic impassivity he continues the procedure.

45   What is extraordinary is his apparent total indifference to the learner; he hardly takes cognizance of him as a human being. Meanwhile, he relates to the experimenter in a submissive and courteous fashion.

At the 330-volt level, the learner refuses not only to touch the shock plate but also to provide any answers. Annoyed, Batta turns to him, and chastises him: "You better answer and get it over with. We can't stay here all night." These are the only words he directs to the learner in the course of an hour. Never again does he speak to him. The scene is brutal and depressing, his hard, impassive face showing total indifference as he subdues the screaming learner and gives him shocks. He seems to derive no pleasure from the act itself, only quiet satisfaction at doing his job properly.

When he administers 450 volts, he turns to the experimenter and asks, "Where do we go from here, Professor?" His tone is deferential and expresses his willingness to be a cooperative subject, in contrast to the learner's obstinacy.

At the end of the session he tells the experimenter how honored he has been to help him, and in a moment of contrition, remarks, "Sir, sorry it couldn't have been a full experiment."

He has done his honest best. It is only the deficient behavior of the learner that has denied the experimenter full satisfaction.

The essence of obedience is that a person comes to view himself ⁵⁰ as the instrument for carrying out another person's wishes, and he therefore no longer regards himself as responsible for his actions. Once this critical shift of viewpoint has occurred, all of the essential features of obedience follow. The most far-reaching consequence is that the person feels responsible to the authority directing him but feels no responsibility *for* the content of the actions that the authority prescribes. Morality does not disappear—it acquires a radically different focus: the subordinate person feels shame or pride depending on how adequately he has performed the actions called for by authority.

Language provides numerous terms to pinpoint this type of morality: *loyalty, duty, discipline* all are terms heavily saturated with moral meaning and refer to the degree to which a person fulfills his obligations to authority. They refer not to the "goodness" of the person per se but to the adequacy with which a subordinate fulfills his socially defined role. The most frequent defense of the individual who has performed a heinous act under command of authority is that he has simply done his duty. In asserting this defense, the individual is not introducing an alibi concocted for the moment but is reporting honestly on the psychological attitude induced by submission to authority.

For a person to feel responsible for his actions, he must sense that the behavior has flowed from "the self." In the situation we have studied, subjects have precisely the opposite view of their actions— namely, they see them as originating in the motives of some other person. Subjects in the experiment frequently said, "If it were up to me, I would not have administered shocks to the learner."

Once authority has been isolated as the cause of the subject's behavior, it is legitimate to inquire into the necessary elements of authority and how it must be perceived in order to gain his compliance. We conducted some investigations into the kinds of changes that would cause the experimenter to lose his power and to be disobeyed by the subject. Some of the variations revealed that:

> *The experimenter's physical presence has a marked impact on his authority.* As cited earlier, obedience dropped off sharply when orders were given by telephone. The experimenter could often induce a disobedient subject to go on by returning to the laboratory.

> *Conflicting authority severely paralyzes action.* When two experimenters of equal status, both seated at the command desk, gave incompatible orders, no shocks were delivered past the point of their disagreement.

> *The rebellious action of others severely undermines authority.* In one variation, three teachers (two actors and a real subject) administered a test

and shocks. When the two actors disobeyed the experimenter and refused to go beyond a certain shock level, thirty-six of forty subjects joined their disobedient peers and refused as well.

Although the experimenter's authority was fragile in some respects, it is also true that he had almost none of the tools used in ordinary command structures. For example, the experimenter did not threaten the subjects with punishment—such as loss of income, community ostracism, or jail—for failure to obey. Neither could he offer incentives. Indeed, we should expect the experimenter's authority to be much less than that of someone like a general, since the experimenter has no power to enforce his imperatives, and since participation in a psychological experiment scarcely evokes the sense of urgency and dedication found in warfare. Despite these limitations, he still managed to command a dismaying degree of obedience.

55   I will cite one final variation of the experiment that depicts a dilemma that is more common in everyday life. The subject was not ordered to pull the lever that shocked the victim, but merely to perform a subsidiary task (administering the word-pair test) while another person administered the shock. In this situation, thirty-seven of forty adults continued to the highest level of the shock generator. Predictably, they excused their behavior by saying that the responsibility belonged to the man who actually pulled the switch. This may illustrate a dangerously typical arrangement in a complex society: it is easy to ignore responsibility when one is only an intermediate link in a chain of action.

The problem of obedience is not wholly psychological. The form and shape of society and the way it is developing have much to do with it. There was a time, perhaps, when people were able to give a fully human response to any situation because they were fully absorbed in it as human beings. But as soon as there was a division of labor things changed. Beyond a certain point, the breaking up of society into people carrying out narrow and very special jobs takes away from the human quality of work and life. A person does not get to see the whole situation but only a small part of it, and is thus unable to act without some kind of overall direction. He yields to authority but in doing so is alienated from his own actions.

Even Eichmann was sickened when he toured the concentration camps, but he had only to sit at a desk and shuffle papers. At the same time the man in the camp who actually dropped Cyclon-b into the gas chambers was able to justify *his* behavior on the ground that he was only following orders from above. Thus there is a fragmentation of the total human act; no one is confronted with the consequences of his decision to carry out the evil act. The person who assumes responsibility has evaporated. Perhaps this is the most common characteristic of socially organized evil in modern society.

Responding to Reading

1. What is the "dilemma inherent in submission to authority" (2)? How do Milgram's experiments illustrate this dilemma? Why do you suppose virtually no one predicted that the subjects would continue to obey the orders of the experimenter?
2. Do you see the subjects as ordinary people—cooperative, obedient, and eager to please—or as weak individuals, too timid to defy authority? Explain.
3. In paragraph 51, Milgram says, "The most frequent defense of the individual who has performed a heinous act under command of authority is that he has simply done his duty." In your opinion, can such a defense ever excuse a "heinous act"? If so, under what circumstances?

Responding in Writing

List all the individuals whom you see as having authority over you. What gives them this authority? Under what circumstances would you feel it was necessary to defy each of these people?

WHAT'S SO BAD ABOUT HATE

Andrew Sullivan

1963–

Born in Godstone, Surrey, England, Andrew Sullivan attended Magdalen College at Oxford and then received an MA degree in public administration (1986) and a PhD in political science (1990) from Harvard University. He joined the staff of the New Republic, *where he is now a senior editor, in 1986. Sullivan is also a contributor to the* New York Times Magazine *and the American columnist for the* Sunday Times *of London. His books include* Virtually Normal: An Argument about Homosexuality *(1995);* Same-Sex Marriage, Pro and Con: A Reader *(1997); and* Love Undetectable: Notes on Friendship, Sex, and Survival *(1998). In this essay, published in the* New York Times Magazine, *Sullivan discusses hate crimes. To read more about this author, visit his Web site, http://andrewsullivan.com.*

I.

I wonder what was going on in John William King's head two years ago when he tied James Byrd Jr.'s feet to the back of a pickup truck and dragged him three miles down a road in rural Texas.[1] King and two friends had picked up Byrd, who was black, when he was

---

[1] This event occurred in 1998. [Eds.]

walking home, half-drunk, from a party. As part of a bonding ritual in their fledgling white supremacist group, the three men took Byrd to a remote part of town, beat him and chained his legs together before attaching them to the truck. Pathologists at King's trial testified that Byrd was probably alive and conscious until his body finally hit a culvert and split in two. When King was offered a chance to say something to Byrd's family at the trial, he smirked and uttered an obscenity.

We know all these details now, many months later. We know quite a large amount about what happened before and after. But I am still drawn, again and again, to the flash of ignition, the moment when fear and loathing became hate, the instant of transformation when King became hunter and Byrd became prey.

What was that? And what was it when Buford Furrow Jr., long-time member of the Aryan Nations, calmly walked up to a Filipino-American mailman he happened to spot, asked him to mail a letter and then shot him at point-blank range? Or when Russell Henderson beat Matthew Shepard, a young gay man, to a pulp, removed his shoes and then, with the help of a friend, tied him to a post, like a dead coyote, to warn off others?

For all our documentation of these crimes and others, our political and moral disgust at them, our morbid fascination with them, our sensitivity to their social meaning, we seem at times to have no better idea now than we ever had of what exactly they were about. About what that moment means when, for some reason or other, one human being asserts absolute, immutable superiority over another. About not the violence, but what the violence expresses. About what—exactly—hate is. And what our own part in it may be.

5   I find myself wondering what hate actually is in part because we have created an entirely new offense in American criminal law—a "hate crime"—to combat it. And barely a day goes by without someone somewhere declaring war against it. Last month President Clinton called for an expansion of hate-crime laws as "what America needs in our battle against hate." A couple of weeks later, Senator John McCain used a campaign speech to denounce the "hate" he said poisoned the land. New York's Mayor, Rudolph Giuliani, recently tried to stop the Million Youth March in Harlem on the grounds that the event was organized by people "involved in hate marches and hate rhetoric."

The media concurs in its emphasis. In 1985, there were 11 mentions of "hate crimes" in the national media database Nexis. By 1990, there were more than a thousand. In the first six months of 1999, there were 7,000. "Sexy fun is one thing," wrote a *New York Times* reporter about sexual assaults in Woodstock '99's mosh pit. "But this was an orgy of lewdness tinged with hate." And when Benjamin Smith marked the Fourth of July this year by targeting blacks, Asians and Jews for murder in Indiana and Illinois, the story wasn't merely about a twisted young man who had emerged on the scene. As *The Times* put it, "Hate arrived in the neighborhoods of Indiana University, in Bloomington, in the early-morning darkness."

But what exactly was this thing that arrived in the early-morning darkness? For all our zeal to attack hate, we still have a remarkably vague idea of what it actually is. A single word, after all, tells us less, not more. For all its emotional punch, "hate" is far less nuanced an idea than prejudice, or bigotry, or bias, or anger, or even mere aversion to others. Is it to stand in for all these varieties of human experience—and everything in between? If so, then the war against it will be so vast as to be quixotic. Or is "hate" to stand for a very specific idea or belief, or set of beliefs, with a very specific object or group of objects? Then waging war against it is almost certainly unconstitutional. Perhaps these kinds of questions are of no concern to those waging war on hate. Perhaps it is enough for them that they share a sentiment that there is too much hate and never enough vigilance in combating it. But sentiment is a poor basis for law, and a dangerous tool in politics. It is better to leave some unwinnable wars unfought.

II.

Hate is everywhere. Human beings generalize all the time, ahead of time, about everyone and everything. A large part of it may even be hard-wired. At some point in our evolution, being able to know beforehand who was friend or foe was not merely a matter of philosophical reflection. It was a matter of survival. And even today it seems impossible to feel a loyalty without also feeling a disloyalty, a sense of belonging without an equal sense of unbelonging. We're social beings. We associate. Therefore we disassociate. And although it would be comforting to think that the one could happen without the other, we know in reality that it doesn't. How many patriots are there who have never felt a twinge of xenophobia?

Of course by hate, we mean something graver and darker than this kind of lazy prejudice. But the closer you look at this distinction, the fuzzier it gets. Much of the time, we harbor little or no malice toward people of other backgrounds or places or ethnicities or ways of life. But then a car cuts you off at an intersection and you find yourself noticing immediately that the driver is a woman, or black, or old, or fat, or white, or male. Or you are walking down a city street at night and hear footsteps quickening behind you. You look around and see that it is a white woman and not a black man, and you are instantly relieved. These impulses are so spontaneous they are almost involuntary. But where did they come from? The mindless need to be mad at someone—anyone—or the unconscious eruption of a darker prejudice festering within?

10   In 1993, in San Jose, Calif., two neighbors—one heterosexual, one homosexual—were engaged in a protracted squabble over grass clippings. (The full case is recounted in *"Hate Crimes,"* by James B. Jacobs and Kimberly Potter.) The gay man regularly mowed his lawn without a grass catcher, which prompted his neighbor to complain on many occasions that grass clippings spilled over onto his driveway. Tensions grew until one day, the gay man mowed his front yard, spilling clippings onto his neighbor's driveway, prompting the straight man to yell an obscene and common anti-gay insult. The wrangling escalated. At one point, the gay man agreed to collect the clippings from his neighbor's driveway but then later found them dumped on his own porch. A fracas ensued with the gay man spraying the straight man's son with a garden hose, and the son hitting and kicking the gay man several times, yelling anti-gay slurs. The police were called, and the son was eventually convicted of a hate-motivated assault, a felony. But what was the nature of the hate: anti-gay bias, or suburban property-owner madness?

Or take the Labor Day parade last year in Broad Channel, a small island in Jamaica Bay, Queens. Almost everyone there is white, and in recent years a group of local volunteer firefighters has taken to decorating a pickup truck for the parade in order to win the prize for "funniest float." Their themes have tended toward the outrageously provocative. Beginning in 1995, they won prizes for floats depicting "Hasidic Park," "Gooks of Hazzard" and "Happy Gays." Last year, they called their float "Black to the Future, Broad Channel 2098." They imagined their community a century hence as a largely black enclave, with every stereotype imaginable: watermelons, basketballs and so on. At one point during the parade, one of them mimicked the dragging death of James Byrd. It was caught on videotape, and before long the entire community was depicted as a caldron of hate.

It's an interesting case, because the float was indisputably in bad taste and the improvisation on the Byrd killing was grotesque. But was it hate? The men on the float were local heroes for their volunteer work; they had no record of bigoted activity, and were not members of any racist organizations. In previous years, they had made fun of many other groups and saw themselves more as provocateurs than bigots. When they were described as racists, it came as a shock to them. They apologized for poor taste but refused to confess to bigotry. "The people involved aren't horrible people," protested a local woman. "Was it a racist act? I don't know. Are they racists? I don't think so."

If hate is a self-conscious activity, she has a point. The men were primarily motivated by the desire to shock and to reflect what they thought was their community's culture. Their display was not aimed at any particular black people, or at any blacks who lived in Broad Channel—almost none do. But if hate is primarily an unconscious activity, then the matter is obviously murkier. And by taking the horrific lynching of a black man as a spontaneous object of humor, the men were clearly advocating indifference to it. Was this an aberrant excess? Or the real truth about the men's feelings toward African-Americans? Hate or tastelessness? And how on earth is anyone, even perhaps the firefighters themselves, going to know for sure?

Or recall H. L. Mencken. He shared in the anti-Semitism of his time with more alacrity than most and was an indefatigable racist. "It is impossible," he wrote in his diary, "to talk anything resembling discretion or judgment into a colored woman. They are all essentially childlike, and even hard experience does not teach them anything." He wrote at another time of the "psychological stigmata" of the "Afro-American race." But it is also true that, during much of his life, day to day, Mencken conducted himself with no regard to race, and supported a politics that was clearly integrationist. As the editor of his diary has pointed out, Mencken published many black authors in his magazine, The Mercury, and lobbied on their behalf with his publisher, Alfred A. Knopf. The last thing Mencken ever wrote was a diatribe against racial segregation in Baltimore's public parks. He was good friends with leading black writers and journalists, including James Weldon Johnson, Walter White and George S. Schuyler, and played an underappreciated role in promoting the Harlem Renaissance.

What would our modern view of hate do with Mencken? Proba- 15
bly ignore him, or change the subject. But, with regard to hate, I know lots of people like Mencken. He reminds me of conservative friends who oppose almost every measure for homosexual equality yet genuinely delight in the company of their gay friends. It would be easier for me to think of them as haters, and on paper, perhaps, there is a good case that they are. But in real life, I know they are not. Some of them clearly harbor no real malice toward me or other homosexuals whatsoever.

They are as hard to figure out as those liberal friends who support every gay rights measure they have ever heard of but do anything to avoid going into a gay bar with me. I have to ask myself in the same, frustrating kind of way: are they liberal bigots or bigoted liberals? Or are they neither bigots nor liberals, but merely people?

III.

Hate used to be easier to understand. When Sartre described anti-Semitism in his 1946 essay "Anti-Semite and Jew," he meant a very specific array of firmly held prejudices, with a history, an ideology and even a pseudoscience to back them up. He meant a systematic attempt to demonize and eradicate an entire race. If you go to the Web site of the World Church of the Creator, the organization that inspired young Benjamin Smith to murder in Illinois earlier this year, you will find a similarly bizarre, pseudorational ideology. The kind of literature read by Buford Furrow before he rained terror on a Jewish kindergarten last month and then killed a mailman because of his color is full of the same paranoid loopiness. And when we talk about hate, we often mean this kind of phenomenon.

But this brand of hatred is mercifully rare in the United States. These professional maniacs are to hate what serial killers are to murder. They should certainly not be ignored; but they represent what Harold Meyerson, writing in Salon, called "niche haters": cold-blooded, somewhat deranged, often poorly socialized psychopaths. In a free society with relatively easy access to guns, they will always pose a menace.

But their menace is a limited one, and their hatred is hardly typical of anything very widespread. Take Buford Furrow. He famously issued a "wake-up call" to "kill Jews" in Los Angeles, before he peppered a Jewish community center with gunfire. He did this in a state with two Jewish female Senators, in a city with a large, prosperous Jewish population, in a country where out of several million Jewish Americans, a total of 66 were reported by the F.B.I. as the targets of hate-crime assaults in 1997. However despicable Furrow's actions were, it would require a very large stretch to describe them as representative of anything but the deranged fringe of an American subculture.

20   Most hate is more common and more complicated, with as many varieties as there are varieties of love. Just as there is possessive love and needy love; family love and friendship; romantic love and unrequited love; passion and respect, affection and obsession, so hatred has its shadings. There is hate that fears, and hate that merely feels contempt; there is hate that expresses power, and hate that comes from powerlessness; there is revenge, and there is hate that comes from envy. There is hate that was love, and hate that is a curious expression of love. There is hate of the other, and hate of something that reminds us too much of ourselves. There is the oppressor's hate, and the victim's hate. There is hate that burns slowly, and hate that fades. And there is hate that explodes, and hate that never catches fire.

The modern words that we have created to describe the varieties of hate—sexism," "racism," "anti-Semitism, "homophobia"—tell us very little about any of this. They tell us merely the identities of the victims; they don't reveal the identities of the perpetrators, or what they think, or how they feel. They don't even tell us how the victims feel. And this simplicity is no accident. Coming from the theories of Marxist and post-Marxist academics, these "isms" are far better at alleging structures of power than at delineating the workings of the individual heart or mind. In fact, these "isms" can exist without mentioning individuals at all.

We speak of institutional racism, for example, as if an institution can feel anything. We talk of "hate" as an impersonal noun, with no hater specified. But when these abstractions are actually incarnated, when someone feels something as a result of them, when a hater actually interacts with a victim, the picture changes. We find that hates are often very different phenomena one from another, that they have very different psychological dynamics, that they might even be better understood by not seeing them as varieties of the same thing at all.

There is, for example, the now unfashionable distinction between reasonable hate and unreasonable hate. In recent years, we have become accustomed to talking about hates as if they were all equally indefensible, as if it could never be the case that some hates might be legitimate, even necessary. But when some 800,000 Tutsis are murdered under the auspices of a Hutu regime in Rwanda, and when a few thousand Hutus are killed in revenge, the hates are not commensurate. Genocide is not an event like a hurricane, in which damage is random and universal; it is a planned and often merciless attack of one group upon another. The hate of the perpetrators is a monstrosity. The hate of the victims, and their survivors, is justified. What else, one wonders, were surviving Jews supposed to feel toward Germans after the Holocaust? Or, to a different degree, South African blacks after apartheid? If the victims overcome this hate, it is a supreme moral achievement. But if they don't, the victims are not as culpable as the perpetrators. So the hatred of Serbs for Kosovars today can never be equated with the hatred of Kosovars for Serbs.

Hate, like much of human feeling, is not rational, but it usually has its reasons. And it cannot be understood, let alone condemned, without knowing them. Similarly, the hate that comes from knowledge is always different from the hate that comes from ignorance. It is one of the most foolish cliches of our time that prejudice is always rooted in ignorance, and can usually be overcome by familiarity with the objects of our loathing. The racism of many Southern whites under segregation was not appeased by familiarity with Southern blacks; the virulent loathing of Tutsis by many Hutus was not undermined by living next door to them for centuries. Theirs was a hatred that sprang, for whatever reasons, from experience. It cannot easily be compared with, for example, the resilience of anti-Semitism in Japan, or hostility to immigration in areas where immigrants are unknown, or fear of homosexuals by people who have never knowingly met one.

The same familiarity is an integral part of what has become 25 known as "sexism." Sexism isn't, properly speaking, a prejudice at all. Few men live without knowledge or constant awareness of women.

Every single sexist man was born of a woman, and is likely to be sexually attracted to women. His hostility is going to be very different than that of, say, a reclusive member of the Aryan Nations toward Jews he has never met.

In her book "The Anatomy of Prejudices," the psychotherapist Elisabeth Young-Bruehl proposes a typology of three distinct kinds of hate: obsessive, hysterical and narcissistic. It's not an exhaustive analysis, but it's a beginning in any serious attempt to understand hate rather than merely declaring war on it. The obsessives, for Young-Bruehl, are those, like the Nazis or Hutus, who fantasize a threat from a minority, and obsessively try to rid themselves of it. For them, the very existence of the hated group is threatening. They often describe their loathing in almost physical terms: they experience what Patrick Buchanan, in reference to homosexuals, once described as a "visceral recoil" from the objects of their detestation. They often describe those they hate as diseased or sick, in need of a cure. Or they talk of "cleansing" them, as the Hutus talked of the Tutsis, or call them "cockroaches," as Yitzhak Shamir called the Palestinians. If you read material from the Family Research Council, it is clear that the group regards homosexuals as similar contaminants. A recent posting on its Web site about syphilis among gay men was headlined, "Unclean."

Hysterical haters have a more complicated relationship with the objects of their aversion. In Young-Bruehl's words, hysterical prejudice is a prejudice that "a person uses unconsciously to appoint a group to act out in the world forbidden sexual and sexually aggressive desires that the person has repressed." Certain kinds of racists fit this pattern. White loathing of blacks is, for some people, at least partly about sexual and physical envy. A certain kind of white racist sees in black America all those impulses he wishes most to express himself but cannot. He idealizes in "blackness" a sexual freedom, a physical power, a Dionysian release that he detests but also longs for. His fantasy may not have any basis in reality, but it is powerful nonetheless. It is a form of love-hate, and it is impossible to understand the nuances of racism in, say, the American South, or in British Imperial India, without it.

Unlike the obsessives, the hysterical haters do not want to eradicate the objects of their loathing; rather they want to keep them in some kind of permanent and safe subjugation in order to indulge the attraction of their repulsion. A recent study, for example, found that the men most likely to be opposed to equal rights for homosexuals were those most likely to be aroused by homoerotic imagery. This makes little rational sense, but it has a certain psychological plausibility. If homosexuals were granted equality, then the hysterical gay-hater might panic that his repressed passions would run out of control, overwhelming him and the world he inhabits.

A narcissistic hate, according to Young-Bruehl's definition, is sexism. In its most common form, it is rooted in many men's inability even to imagine what it is to be a woman, a failing rarely challenged by men's control of our most powerful public social institutions. Women are not so much hated by most men as simply ignored in nonsexual contexts, or never conceived of as true equals. The implicit condescension is mixed, in many cases, with repressed and sublimated erotic desire. So the unawareness of women is sometimes commingled with a deep longing or contempt for them.

Each hate, of course, is more complicated than this, and in any 30 one person hate can assume a uniquely configured combination of these types. So there are hysterical sexists who hate women because they need them so much, and narcissistic sexists who hardly notice that women exist, and sexists who oscillate between one of these positions and another. And there are gay-bashers who are threatened by masculine gay men and gay-haters who feel repulsed by effeminate ones. The soldier who beat his fellow soldier Barry Winchell to death with a baseball bat in July had earlier lost a fight to him. It was the image of a macho gay man—and the shame of being bested by him—that the vengeful soldier had to obliterate, even if he needed a gang of accomplices and a weapon to do so. But the murderers of Matthew Shepard seem to have had a different impulse: a visceral disgust at the thought of any sexual contact with an effeminate homosexual. Their anger was mixed with mockery, as the cruel spectacle at the side of the road suggested.

In the same way, the pathological anti-Semitism of Nazi Germany was obsessive, inasmuch as it tried to cleanse the world of Jews; but also, as Daniel Jonah Goldhagen shows in his book, "Hitler's Willing Executioners," hysterical. The Germans were mysteriously compelled as well as repelled by Jews, devising elaborate ways, like death camps and death marches, to keep them alive even as they killed them. And the early Nazi phobia of interracial sex suggests as well a lingering erotic quality to the relationship, partaking of exactly the kind of sexual panic that persists among some homosexual-haters and anti-miscegenation racists. So the concept of "homophobia," like that of "sexism" and "racism," is often a crude one. All three are essentially cookie-cutter formulas that try to understand human impulses merely through the one-dimensional identity of the victims, rather than through the thoughts and feelings of the haters and hated.

This is deliberate. The theorists behind these "isms" want to ascribe all blame to one group in society—the "oppressors"—and render specific others—the "victims"—completely blameless. And they want to do this in order in part to side unequivocally with the underdog. But it doesn't take a genius to see how this approach, too, can generate its own form of bias. It can justify blanket condemnations of whole groups of people—white straight males for example—purely

because of the color of their skin or the nature of their sexual orientation. And it can condescendingly ascribe innocence to whole groups
of others. It does exactly what hate does: it hammers the uniqueness
of each individual into the anvil of group identity. And it postures
morally over the result.

In reality, human beings and human acts are far more complex,
which is why these isms and the laws they have fomented are continually coming under strain and challenge. Once again, hate wriggles
free of its definers. It knows no monolithic groups of haters and
hated. Like a river, it has many eddies, backwaters and rapids. So
there are anti-Semites who actually admire what they think of as Jewish power, and there are gay-haters who look up to homosexuals and
some who want to sleep with them. And there are black racists, racist
Jews, sexist women and anti-Semitic homosexuals. Of course there
are.

IV.

Once you start thinking of these phenomena less as the "isms" of sexism, racism and "homophobia," once you think of them as independent psychological responses, it's also possible to see how they can
work in a bewildering variety of ways in a bewildering number of
people. To take one obvious and sad oddity: people who are de-
meaned and objectified in society may develop an aversion to their
tormentors that is more hateful in its expression than the prejudice
they have been subjected to. The F.B.I. statistics on hate crimes throws
up an interesting point. In America in the 1990's, blacks were up to
three times as likely as whites to commit a hate crime, to express their
hate by physically attacking their targets or their property. Just as sexual abusers have often been victims of sexual abuse, and wife-beaters
often grew up in violent households, so hate criminals may often be
members of hated groups.

35   Even the Columbine murderers were in some sense victims of
hate before they were purveyors of it. Their classmates later admitted
that Dylan Klebold and Eric Harris were regularly called "faggots" in
the corridors and classrooms of Columbine High and that nothing
was done to prevent or stop the harassment. This climate of hostility
doesn't excuse the actions of Klebold and Harris, but it does provide a
more plausible context. If they had been black, had routinely been
called "nigger" in the school and had then exploded into a shooting
spree against white students, the response to the matter might well
have been different. But the hate would have been the same. In other
words, hate-victims are often hate-victimizers as well. This doesn't
mean that all hates are equivalent, or that some are not more justified
than others. It means merely that hate goes both ways; and if you try

to regulate it among some, you will find yourself forced to regulate it among others.

It is no secret, for example, that some of the most vicious anti-Semites in America are black, and that some of the most virulent anti-Catholic bigots in America are gay. At what point, we are increasingly forced to ask, do these phenomena become as indefensible as white racism or religious toleration of anti-gay bigotry? That question becomes all the more difficult when we notice that it is often minorities who commit some of the most hate-filled offenses against what they see as their oppressors. It was the mainly gay AIDS activist group Act Up that perpetrated the hateful act of desecrating Communion hosts at a Mass at St Patrick's Cathedral in New York. And here is the playwright Tony Kushner, who is gay, responding to the Matthew Shepard beating in *The Nation* magazine: "Pope John Paul II endorses murder. He, too, knows the price of discrimination, having declared anti-Semitism a sin. . . . He knows that discrimination kills. But when the Pope heard the news about Matthew Shepard, he, too, worried about spin. And so, on the subject of gay-bashing, the Pope and his cardinals and his bishops and priests maintain their cynical political silence. . . . To remain silent is to endorse murder." Kushner went on to describe the Pope as a "homicidal liar."

Maybe the passion behind these words is justified. But it seems clear enough to me that Kushner is expressing hate toward the institution of the Catholic Church, and all those who perpetuate its doctrines. How else to interpret the way in which he accuses the Pope of cynicism, lying and murder? And how else either to understand the brutal parody of religious vocations expressed by the Sisters of Perpetual Indulgence, a group of gay men who dress in drag as nuns and engage in sexually explicit performances in public? Or T-shirts with the words "Recovering Catholic" on them, hot items among some gay and lesbian activists? The implication that someone's religious faith is a mental illness is clearly an expression of contempt. If that isn't covered under the definition of hate speech, what is?

Or take the following sentence: "The act male homosexuals commit is ugly and repugnant and afterwards they are disgusted with themselves. They drink and take drugs to palliate this, but they are disgusted with the act and they are always changing partners and cannot be really happy." The thoughts of Pat Robertson or Patrick Buchanan? Actually that sentence was written by Gertrude Stein, one of the century's most notable lesbians. Or take the following, about how beating up "black boys like that made us feel good inside. . . . Every time I drove my foot into his [expletive], I felt better." It was written to describe the brutal assault of an innocent bystander for the sole reason of his race. By the end of the attack, the victim had blood gushing from his mouth as his attackers stomped on his genitals. Are we less appalled when we learn that the actual sentence was how beating up "white boys like that made us feel good inside. . . . Every time I drove my foot into his [expletive], I felt better?" It was written by Nathan McCall, an African-American who later in life became a successful journalist at *The Washington Post* and published his memoir of this "hate crime" to much acclaim.

In fact, one of the stranger aspects of hate is that the prejudice expressed by a group in power may often be milder in expression than the prejudice felt by the marginalized. After all, if you already enjoy privilege, you may not feel the anger that turns bias into hate. You may not need to. For this reason, most white racism may be more influential in society than most black racism—but also more calmly expressed.

40   So may other forms of minority loathing—especially hatred within minorities. I'm sure that black conservatives like Clarence Thomas or Thomas Sowell have experienced their fair share of white racism. But I wonder whether it has ever reached the level of intensity of the hatred directed toward them by other blacks? In several years of being an openly gay writer and editor, I have experienced the gamut of responses to my sexual orientation. But I have only directly experienced articulated. passionate hate from other homosexuals. I have been accused over the years by other homosexuals of being a sellout, a hypocrite, a traitor, a sexist, a racist, a narcissist, a snob. I've been called selfish, callous, hateful, self-hating and malevolent. At a reading, a group of lesbian activists portrayed my face on a poster within the crossfires of a gun. Nothing from the religious right has come close to such vehemence.

I am not complaining. No harm has ever come to me or my property, and much of the criticism is rooted in the legitimate expression of political differences. But the visceral tone and style of the gay criticism can only be described as hateful. It is designed to wound personally, and it often does. But its intensity comes in part, one senses, from the pain of being excluded for so long, of anger long restrained bubbling up and directing itself more aggressively toward an alleged traitor than an alleged enemy. It is the hate of the hated. And it can be the most hateful hate of all. For this reason, hate-crime laws may themselves be an oddly biased category—biased against the victims of hate. Racism is everywhere, but the already victimized might be more desperate, more willing to express it violently. And so more prone to come under the suspicious eye of the law.

V.

And why is hate for a group worse than hate for a person? In Laramie, Wyo., the now-famous epicenter of "homophobia," where Matthew Shepard was brutally beaten to death, vicious murders are not unknown. In the previous 12 months, a 15-year-old pregnant girl was found east of the town with 17 stab wounds. Her 38-year-old boyfriend was apparently angry that she had refused an abortion and left her in the Wyoming foothills to bleed to death. In the summer of 1998, an 8-year-old Laramie girl was abducted, raped and murdered by a pedophile, who disposed of her young body in a garbage dump. Neither of these killings was deemed a hate crime, and neither would be designated as such under any existing hate-crime law. Perhaps because of this, one crime is an international legend; the other two are virtually unheard of.

But which crime was more filled with hate? Once you ask the question, you realize how difficult it is to answer. Is it more hateful to kill a stranger or a lover? Is it more hateful to kill a child than an adult? Is it more hateful to kill your own child than another's? Under the law before the invention of hate crimes, these decisions didn't have to be taken. But under the law after hate crimes, a decision is essential. A decade ago, a murder was a murder. Now, in the era when group hate has emerged as our cardinal social sin, it all depends.

The supporters of laws against hate crimes argue that such crimes should be disproportionately punished because they victimize more than the victim. Such crimes, these advocates argue, spread fear, hatred and panic among whole populations, and therefore merit more concern. But, of course, all crimes victimize more than the victim, and spread alarm in the society at large. Just think of the terrifying church shooting in Texas only two weeks ago. In fact, a purely random murder may be even more terrifying than a targeted one, since the entire community, and not just a part of it, feels threatened. High rates of murder, robbery, assault and burglary victimize everyone, by spreading fear, suspicion and distress everywhere. Which crime was more frightening to more people this summer: the mentally ill Buford Furrow's crazed attacks in Los Angeles, killing one, or Mark Barton's murder of his own family and several random day-traders in Atlanta, killing 12? Almost certainly the latter. But only Furrow was guilty of "hate."

One response to this objection is that certain groups feel fear more 45 intensely than others because of a history of persecution or intimidation. But doesn't this smack of a certain condescension toward minorities? Why, after all, should it be assumed that gay men or black women or Jews, for example, are as a group more easily intimidated than others? Surely in any of these communities there will be a vast range of responses, from panic to concern to complete indifference. The assumption otherwise is the kind of crude generalization the law is supposed to uproot in the first place. And among these groups, there are also likely to be vast differences. To equate a population once subjected to slavery with a population of Mexican immigrants or third-generation Holocaust survivors is to equate the unequatable. In fact, it is to set up a contest of vulnerability in which one group vies with another to establish its particular variety of suffering, a contest that can have no dignified solution.

Rape, for example, is not classified as a "hate crime" under most existing laws, pitting feminists against ethnic groups in a battle for recognition. If, as a solution to this problem, everyone, except the white straight able-bodied male, is regarded as a possible victim of a hate crime, then we have simply created a two-tier system of justice in which racial profiling is reversed, and white straight men are presumed guilty before being proven innocent, and members of minorities are free to hate them as gleefully as they like. But if we include the white straight male in the litany of potential victims, then we have effectively abolished the notion of a hate crime altogether. For if every crime is possibly a hate crime, then it is simply another name for crime. All we will have done is widened the search for possible bigotry, ratcheted up the sentences for everyone and filled the jails up even further.

Hate-crime-law advocates counter that extra penalties should be imposed on hate crimes because our society is experiencing an "epidemic" of such crimes. Mercifully, there is no hard evidence to support this notion. The Federal Government has only been recording the incidence of hate crimes in this decade, and the statistics tell a simple story. In 1992, there were 6,623 hate-crime incidents reported to the F.B.I. by a total of 6,181 agencies, covering 51 percent of the population. In 1996, there were 8,734 incidents reported by 11,355 agencies, covering 84 percent of the population. That number dropped to 8,049 in 1997. These numbers are, of course, hazardous. They probably underreport the incidence of such crimes, but they are the only reliable figures we have. Yet even if they are faulty as an absolute number, they do not show an epidemic of "hate crimes" in the 1990's.

Is there evidence that the crimes themselves are becoming more vicious? None. More than 60 percent of recorded hate crimes in America involve no violent, physical assault against another human being at all, and, again, according to the F.B.I., that proportion has not budged much in the 1990's. These impersonal attacks are crimes against property or crimes of "intimidation." Murder, which dominates media coverage of hate crimes, is a tiny proportion of the total. Of the 8,049 hate crimes reported to the F.B.I. in 1997, a total of eight were murders. Eight. The number of hate crimes that were aggravated assaults (generally involving a weapon) in 1997 is less than 15 percent of the total. That's 1,237 assaults too many, of course, but to put it in perspective, compare it with a reported 1,022,492 "equal opportunity" aggravated assaults in America in the same year. The number of hate crimes that were physical assaults is half the total.

That's 4,000 assaults too many, of course, but to put it in perspective, it compares with around 3.8 million "equal opportunity" assaults in America annually.

The truth is, the distinction between a crime filled with personal hate and a crime filled with group hate is an essentially arbitrary one. It tells us nothing interesting about the psychological contours of the specific actor or his specific victim. It is a function primarily of politics, of special interest groups carving out particular protections for themselves, rather than a serious response to a serious criminal concern. In such an endeavor, hate-crime-law advocates cram an entire world of human motivations into an immutable, tiny box called hate, and hope to have solved a problem. But nothing has been solved; and some harm may even have been done.

In an attempt to repudiate a past that treated people differently 50 because of the color of their skin, or their sex, or religion or sexual orientation, we may merely create a future that permanently treats people differently because of the color of their skin, or their sex, religion or sexual orientation. This notion of a hate crime, and the concept of hate that lies behind it, takes a psychological mystery and turns it into a facile political artifact. Rather than compounding this error and extending even further, we should seriously consider repealing the concept altogether.

To put it another way: violence can and should be stopped by the government. In a free society, hate can't and shouldn't be. The boundaries between hate and prejudice and between prejudice and opinion and between opinion and truth are so complicated and blurred that any attempt to construct legal and political fire walls is a doomed and illiberal venture. We know by now that hate will never disappear from human consciousness; in fact, it is probably, at some level, definitive of it. We know after decades of education measures that hate is not caused merely by ignorance; and after decades of legislation, that it isn't caused entirely by law.

To be sure, we have made much progress. Anyone who argues that America is as inhospitable to minorities and to women today as it has been in the past has not read much history. And we should, of course, be vigilant that our most powerful institutions, most notably the government, do not actively or formally propagate hatred; and insure that the violent expression of hate is curtailed by the same rules that punish all violent expression.

But after that, in an increasingly diverse culture, it is crazy to expect that hate, in all its variety, can be eradicated. A free country will always mean a hateful country. This may not be fair, or perfect, or admirable, but it is reality, and while we need not endorse it, we should not delude ourselves into thinking we can prevent it. That is surely the distinction between toleration and tolerance. Tolerance is the eradication of hate; toleration is co-existence despite it. We might do better as a culture and as a polity if we concentrated more on achieving the latter rather than the former. We would certainly be less frustrated.

And by aiming lower, we might actually reach higher. In some ways, some expression of prejudice serves a useful social purpose. It lets off steam; it allows natural tensions to express themselves incrementally; it can siphon off conflict through words, rather than actions. Anyone who has lived in the ethnic shouting match that is New York City knows exactly what I mean. If New Yorkers disliked each other less, they wouldn't be able to get on so well. We may not all be able to pull off a Mencken—bigoted in words, egalitarian in action—but we might achieve a lesser form of virtue: a human acceptance of our need for differentiation, without a total capitulation to it.

55   Do we not owe something more to the victims of hate? Perhaps we do. But it is also true that there is nothing that government can do for the hated that the hated cannot better do for themselves. After all, most bigots are not foiled when they are punished specifically for their beliefs. In fact, many of the worst haters crave such attention and find vindication in such rebukes. Indeed, our media's obsession with "hate," our elevation of it above other social misdemeanors and crimes, may even play into the hands of the pathetic and the evil, may breathe air into the smoldering embers of their paranoid loathing. Sure, we can help create a climate in which such hate is disapproved of—and we should. But there is a danger that if we go too far, if we punish it too much, if we try to abolish it altogether, we may merely increase its mystique, and entrench the very categories of human difference that we are trying to erase.

For hate is only foiled not when the haters are punished but when the hated are immune to the bigot's power. A hater cannot psychologically wound if a victim cannot psychologically be wounded. And that immunity to hurt can never be given; it can merely be achieved. The racial epithet only strikes at someone's core if he lets it, if he allows the bigot's definition of him to be the final description of his life and his person—if somewhere in his heart of hearts, he believes the hateful slur to be true. The only final answer to this form of racism, then, is not majority persecution of it, but minority indifference to it. The only permanent rebuke to homophobia is not the enforcement of tolerance, but gay equanimity in the face of prejudice. The only effective answer to sexism is not a morass of legal proscriptions, but the simple fact of female success. In this, as in so many other things, there is no solution to the problem. There is only a transcendence of it. For all our rhetoric, hate will never be destroyed. Hate, as our predecessors knew better, can merely be overcome.

Responding to Reading

1. In paragraphs 20–33 and elsewhere, Sullivan attempts to define and illustrate different kinds of hate and different kinds of haters. What is his purpose in establishing these different categories? How successful is he?
2. In general terms, why is Sullivan opposed to designating certain crimes as "hate crimes"? List as many of his objections—legal, semantic, and emotional—as you can. Do his arguments convince you, or do you believe hate crimes should be prosecuted differently from other crimes?
3. Sullivan is a gay man, and he mentions this in his essay. Why? Does this personal information make his conclusion more or less credible? Do you think he should have made his sexual orientation more prominent—for example, by stating it in his introduction? Do you think he should not have mentioned it at all?

Responding in Writing

In paragraph 7, Sullivan says that "sentiment is a poor basis for law, and a dangerous tool in politics. It is better to leave some unwinnable wars unfought." What is the war to which he refers? Do you agree that this war is unwinnable? Do you agree that an unwinnable war should remain unfought?

THE ONES WHO WALK AWAY FROM OMELAS

Ursula K. Le Guin

1929–

Ursula K. Le Guin has written science fiction and fantasy, fiction, screenplays, poetry, and essays, some of which reflect her interests in Eastern philosophy and Jungian psychology. Her novels include The Left Hand of Darkness *(1969),* The Lathe of Heaven *(1971),* The Dispossessed *(1974),* A Fisherman of the Inland Sea *(1994), and* The Telling *(2000); she has also written a book of poetry,* Hard Words *(1981). In her book of essays* The Language of the Night *(1979), she says, "the use of imaginative fiction is to deepen your understanding of your world, and your fellow men, and your own feelings, and your destiny." In the 1975 story that follows, Le Guin creates a scenario that offers a test of conscience.*

With a clamor of bells that set the swallows soaring, the Festival of Summer came to the city Omelas, bright-towered by the sea. The rigging of the boats in harbor sparkled with flags. In the streets between houses with red roofs and painted walls, between old moss-grown gardens and under avenues of trees, past great parks and public buildings, processions moved. Some were decorous: old people in long stiff robes of mauve and grey, grave master workmen, quiet, merry women carrying their babies and chatting as they walked. In other streets the music beat faster, a shimmering of gong and tambourine, and the people went dancing, the procession was a dance. Children dodged in and out, their high calls rising like the swallows' crossing flights over the music and the singing. All the processions wound towards the north side of the city, where on the great water-meadow called the Green Fields boys and girls, naked in the bright air, with mud-stained feet and ankles and long lithe arms, exercised their restive horses before the race. The horses wore no gear at all but a halter without bit. Their manes were braided with streamers of silver, gold, and green. They flared their nostrils and pranced and boasted to one another; they were vastly excited, the horse being the only animal who had adopted our ceremonies as its own. Far off to the north and west the mountains stood up half encircling Omelas on her bay. The air of morning was so clear that the snow still crowning the Eighteen Peaks burned with white-gold fire across the miles of sunlit air, under the dark, blue of the sky. There was just enough wind to make the banners that marked the racecourse snap and flutter now and then. In the silence of the broad green meadows one could hear the music winding through the city streets, farther and nearer and ever approaching, a cheerful faint sweetness of the air that from time to time trembled and gathered together and broke out into the great joyous clanging of the bells.

Joyous! How is one to tell about joy! How describe the citizens of Omelas?

They were not simple folk, you see, though they were happy. But we do not say the words of cheer much any more. All smiles have become archaic. Given a description such as this one tends to make certain assumptions. Given a description such as this one tends to look next for the King, mounted on a splendid stallion and surrounded by his noble knights, or perhaps in a golden litter borne by great-muscled slaves. But there was no king. They did not use swords or keep slaves. They were not barbarians. I do not know the rules and laws of their society, but I suspect that they were singularly few. As they did without monarchy and slavery, so they also got on without the stock exchange, the advertisement, the secret police, and the bomb. Yet I repeat that these were not simple folk, not dulcet shepherds, noble savages, bland utopians. They were not less complex than us. The trouble is that we have a bad habit, encouraged by pedants and sophisticates, of considering happiness as something rather stupid. Only pain is intellectual, only evil interesting. This is the treason of the artist: a refusal to admit the banality of evil and the terrible boredom of pain. If you can't lick 'em, join 'em. If it hurts, repeat it. But to praise despair is to condemn delight, to embrace violence is to lose hold of everything else. We have almost lost hold; we can no longer describe a happy man, nor make any celebration of joy. How can I tell you about the people of Omelas? They were not naïve and happy children— though their children were, in fact, happy. They were mature, intelligent, passionate adults whose lives were not wretched. O miracle! but I wish I could describe it better. I wish I could convince you. Omelas sounds in my words like a city, in a fairy tale, long ago and far away, once upon a time. Perhaps it would be best if you imagined it as your own fancy bids, assuming it will rise to the occasion, for certainly I cannot suit you all. For instance, how about technology? I think that there would be no cars or helicopters in and above the streets; this follows from the fact that the people of Omelas are happy people. Happiness is based on a just discrimination of what is necessary, what is neither necessary nor destructive, and what is destructive. In the middle category, however—that of the unnecessary but undestructive, that of comfort, luxury, exuberance, etc.—they could perfectly well have central heating, subway trains, washing machines, and all kinds of marvelous devices not yet invented here, floating light-sources, fuelless power, a cure for the common cold. Or they could have none of that: It doesn't matter. As you like it. I incline to think that people from towns up and down the coast have been coming in to Omelas during the last days before the Festival on very fast little trains and double-decked trams, and that the train station of Omelas is actually the handsomest building in town, though plainer than the magnificent Farmers' Market. But even granted trains, I fear that Omelas so far strikes some of you as goody-goody. Smiles, bells, parades, horses, bleh. If so, please add an orgy. If an orgy would help, don't hesitate. Let us not, however, have temples from which issue beautiful nude priests and priestesses already half in ecstasy and ready to copulate with any man or woman, lover or stranger, who desires union with the deep godhead of the blood, although that was my first idea. But really it would be better not to have any temples in Omelas—at least not manned temples. Religion yes, clergy no. Surely the beautiful nudes can just wander about, offering themselves like divine soufflés to the hunger of the needy and the rapture of the flesh. Let them join the processions. Let tambourines be struck above the copulations, and the glory of desire be proclaimed upon the gongs, and (a not unimportant) let the offspring of these delightful rituals be beloved and looked after by all. One thing I know there is none of in Omelas is guilt. But what else should there be? I thought at first there were no drugs, but that is puritanical. For those who like it, the faint insistent sweetness of *drooz* may perfume the ways of the city, *drooz* which first brings a great lightness and brilliance to the mind and limbs, and then after some hours a dreamy languor, and wonderful visions at last of the very arcana and inmost secrets of the Universe, as well as exciting the pleasure of sex beyond all belief; and it is not habit-forming. For moie modest tastes I think there ought to be beer. What else, what else belongs in the joyous city? The sense of victory, surely, the celebration of courage. But as we did without clergy, let us do without soldiers. The joy built upon successful slaughter is not the right kind of joy; it will not do; it is fearful and it is trivial. A boundless and generous contentment, a magnanimous triumph felt not against some outer enemy but in communion with the finest and fairest in the souls of all men everywhere and the splendor of the world's summer: This is what swells the hearts of the people of Omelas, and the victory they celebrate is that of life. I really don't think many of them need to take *drooz*.

Most of the processions have reached the Green Fields by now. A marvelous smell of cooking goes forth from the red and blue tents of the provisioners. The faces of small children are amiably sticky; in the benign grey beard of a man a couple of crumbs of rich pastry are entangled. The youths and girls have mounted their horses and are beginning to group around the starting line of the course. An old woman, small, fat, and laughing, is passing out flowers from a basket, and tall young men wear her flowers in their shining hair. A child of nine or ten sits at the edge of the crowd, alone, playing on a wooden flute. People pause to listen, and they smile, but they do not speak to him, for he never ceases playing and never sees them, his dark eyes wholly rapt in the sweet, thin magic of the tune.

5   He finishes, and slowly lowers his hands holding the wooden flute.

As if that little private silence were the signal, all at once a trumpet sounds from the pavilion near the starting line: imperious, melancholy, piercing. The horses rear on their slender legs, and some of them neigh in answer. Sober-faced, the young riders stroke the horses' necks and soothe them, whispering, "Quiet, quiet, there my beauty, my hope. . . ." They begin to form in rank along the starting line. The crowds along the racecourse are like a field of grass and flowers in the wind. The Festival of Summer has begun.

Do you believe? Do you accept the festival, the city, the joy? No? Then let me describe one more thing.

In a basement under one of the beautiful public buildings of Omelas, or perhaps in the cellar of one of its spacious private homes, there is a room. It has one locked door, and no window. A little light seeps in dustily between cracks in the boards, secondhand from a cobwebbed window somewhere across the cellar. In one corner of the little room a couple of mops, with stiff, clotted, foul-smelling heads, stand near a rusty bucket. The floor is dirt, a little damp to the touch, as cellar dirt usually is. The room is about three paces long and two wide: a mere broom closet or disused tool room. In the room a child is sitting. It could be a boy or a girl. It looks about six, but actually is nearly ten. It is feeble-minded. Perhaps it was born defective, or perhaps it has become imbecile through fear, malnutrition, and neglect. It picks its nose and occasionally fumbles vaguely with its toes or genitals, as it sits hunched in the corner farthest from the bucket and the two mops. It is afraid of the mops. It finds them horrible. It shuts its eyes, but it knows the mops are still standing there; and the door is locked; and nobody ever comes, except that sometimes—the child has no understanding of time or interval—sometimes the door rattles terribly and opens, and a person, or several people, are there. One of them may come in and kick the child to make it stand up. The others never come close, but peer in at it with frightened, disgusted eyes. The food bowl and the water jug are hastily filled, the door is locked, the eyes disappear. The people at the door never say anything, but the child, who has not always lived in the tool room, and can remember sunlight and its mother's voice, sometimes speaks. "I will be good," it says. "Please let me out. I will be good!" They never answer. The child used to scream for help at night, and cry a good deal, but now it only makes a kind of whining, "eh-haa-, ch-haa," and it speaks less and less often. It is so thin there are no calves to its legs; its belly protrudes; it lives on a half-bowl of corn meal and grease a day. It is naked. Its buttocks and thighs are a mass of festered sores, as it sits in its own excrement continually.

They all know it is there, all the people of Omelas. Some of them have come to see it; others are content merely to know it is there. They all know that it has to be there. Some of them understand why, and some do not, but they all understand that their happiness, the beauty of their city, the tenderness of their friendships, the health of their children, the wisdom of their scholars, the skill of their makers, even the abundance of their harvest and the kindly weathers of their skies, depend wholly on this child's abominable misery.

This is usually explained to children when they are between eight 10 and twelve, whenever they seem capable of understanding; and most of those who come to see the child are young people, though often enough an adult comes, or comes back, to see the child. No matter how well the matter has been explained to them, these young spectators are always shocked and sickened at the sight. They feel disgust, which they had thought themselves superior to. They feel anger, outrage, impotence, despite all the explanations. They would like to do something for the child. But there is nothing they can do. If the child were brought up into and sunlight out of that vile place, if it were cleaned and fed and comforted, that would be a good thing, indeed; but if it were done, in that day and hour all the prosperity and beauty and delight of Omelas would wither and be destroyed. Those are the terms. To exchange all the goodness and grace of every life in Omelas for that single, small improvement: to throw away the happiness of thousands for the chance of the happiness of one: that would be to let guilt within the walls indeed.

The terms are strict and absolute; there may not even be a kind word spoken to the child.

Often the young people go home in tears, or in a tearless rage, when they have seen the child and faced this terrible paradox. They may brood over it for weeks or years. But as time goes on they begin to realize that even if the child could be released, it would not get much good of its freedom: a little vague pleasure of warmth and food, no doubt, but little more. It is too degraded and imbecile to know any real joy. It has been afraid too long ever to be free of fear. Its habits are too uncouth for it to respond to humane treatment. Indeed, after so long it would probably be wretched without walls about it to protect it, and darkness for its eyes, and its own excrement to sit in. Their tears at the bitter injustice dry when they begin to perceive the terrible justice of reality, and to accept it. Yet it is their tears and anger, the trying of their generosity and the acceptance of their helplessness, which are perhaps the true source of the splendor of their lives. Theirs is no vapid, irresponsible happiness. They know that they, like the child, are not free. They know compassion. It is the existence of the child, and their knowledge of its existence, that makes possible the nobility of their architecture, the poignancy of their music, the profundity of their science. It is because of the child that they are so gentle with children. They know that if the wretched one were not there snivelling in the dark, the other one, the flute-player, could make no joyful music as the young riders line up in their beauty for the race in the sunlight of the first morning of summer.

Now do you believe in them? Are they not more credible? But there is one more thing to tell, and this is quite incredible.

At times one of the adolescent girls or boys who go to see the child does not go home to weep or rage, does not, in fact, go home at all. Sometimes also a man or woman much older falls silent for a day or two, and then leaves home. These people go out into the street, and walk down the street alone. They keep walking, and walk straight out of the city of Omelas, through the beautiful gates. They keep walking across the farmlands of Omelas. Each one goes alone, youth or girl, man or woman. Night falls; the traveler must pass down village streets, between the houses with yellow-lit windows, and on out into the darkness of the fields. Each alone, they go west or north, towards the mountains. They go on. They leave Omelas, they walk ahead into the darkness, and they do not come back. The place the they go towards is a place even less imaginable to most of us than the city of happiness. I cannot describe it at all. It is possible that it does not exist. But they seem to know where they are going, the ones who walk away from Omelas.

Responding to Reading

1. Why do you think Le Guin's narrator keeps asking readers whether or not they "believe," whether they accept what she is saying as the truth? Do *you* "believe"? Which elements of this story do you find most unbelievable? Which do you find most believable?
2. Are the ones who walk away from Omelas any less morally responsible for the child's welfare than those who keep the child imprisoned? In other words, do you believe there is a difference between actively doing something "wrong" and passively allowing it to happen?
3. Why does the logic of the story require that the child be present? Why must the child suffer?

Responding in Writing

Might it be argued that our society has its own equivalent of the child locked in the closet and that we are guilty of failing to act to save this child? Explain.

--- **FOCUS** ---

Can We Be Both Free and Safe?

Boy going through metal detector before boarding first ferry to Liberty Island in New York Harbor after September 11, 2001, attacks.

Responding to the Image

1. What do you see in this photograph? What do you think the officer sees? What do the people in line see? What do you think the photographer wanted you to see?
2. Do you believe it is necessary to subject every visitor to important historic sites and government buildings to x-ray machines and other kinds of scrutiny? Should any group—for example, babies, the elderly, pregnant women, uniformed police officers and military personnel—be exempt? Should any individuals or groups receive extra scrutiny? Explain your reasoning.

SECURITY VERSUS CIVIL LIBERTIES

Richard A. Posner

1939–

Born in New York City, Richard A. Posner graduated from Yale University (1959) and received a law degree from Harvard University (1962). He worked as a law clerk to Supreme Court Justice William J. Brennan, Jr., taught at Stanford University and the University of Chicago, and was appointed to the US Court of Appeals for the Seventh Circuit, Chicago, in 1981. He has authored and coauthored nineteen books, most recently Frontiers of Legal Theory *(2001) and* Breaking the Deadlock *(2001). In the following essay, which appeared in the* Atlantic *in December 2001, Posner discusses how civil liberties have been interpreted during different periods of US history.*

In the wake of the September 11 terrorist attacks have come many proposals for tightening security; some measures to that end have already been taken. Civil libertarians are troubled. They fear that concerns about national security will lead to an erosion of civil liberties. They offer historical examples of supposed overreactions to threats to national security. They treat our existing civil liberties—freedom of the press, protections of privacy and of the rights of criminal suspects, and the rest—as sacrosanct, insisting that the battle against international terrorism accommodate itself to them.

I consider this a profoundly mistaken approach to the question of balancing liberty and security. The basic mistake is the prioritizing of liberty. It is a mistake about law and a mistake about history. Let me begin with law. What we take to be our civil liberties—for example, immunity from arrest except upon probable cause to believe we've committed a crime, and from prosecution for violating a criminal statute enacted after we committed the act that violates it—were made legal rights by the Constitution and other enactments. The other enactments can be changed relatively easily, by amendatory legislation. Amending the Constitution is much more difficult. In recognition of this the Framers left most of the constitutional provisions that confer rights pretty vague. The courts have made them definite.

Concretely, the scope of these rights has been determined, through an interaction of constitutional text and subsequent judicial interpretation, by a weighing of competing interests. I'll call them the public-safety interest and the liberty interest. Neither, in my view, has priority. They are both important, and their relative importance changes from time to time and from situation to situation. The safer the nation feels, the more weight judges will be willing to give to the liberty interest. The greater the threat that an activity poses to the nation's safety, the stronger will the grounds seem for seeking to repress that activity, even at some cost to liberty. This fluid approach is only common sense. Supreme Court Justice Robert Jackson gave it vivid expression many years ago when he said, in dissenting from a free-speech decision he thought doctrinaire, that the Bill of Rights should not be made into a suicide pact. It was not intended to be such, and the present contours of the rights that it confers, having been shaped far more by judicial interpretation than by the literal text (which doesn't define such critical terms as "due process of law" and "unreasonable" arrests and searches), are alterable in response to changing threats to national security.

If it is true, therefore, as it appears to be at this writing, that the events of September 11 have revealed the United States to be in much greater jeopardy from international terrorism than had previously been believed—have revealed it to be threatened by a diffuse, shadowy enemy that must be fought with police measures as well as military force—it stands to reason that our civil liberties will be curtailed. They should be curtailed, to the extent that the benefits in greater security outweigh the costs in reduced liberty. All that can reasonably be asked of the responsible legislative and judicial officials is that they weigh the costs as carefully as the benefits.

5   It will be argued that the lesson of history is that officials habitually exaggerate dangers to the nation's security. But the lesson of history is the opposite. It is because officials have repeatedly and disastrously underestimated these dangers that our history is as violent as it is. Consider such underestimated dangers as that of secession, which led to the Civil War; of a Japanese attack on the United States, which led to the disaster at Pearl Harbor; of Soviet espionage in the 1940s, which accelerated the Soviet Union's acquisition of nuclear weapons and emboldened Stalin to encourage North Korea's invasion of South Korea; of the installation of Soviet missiles in Cuba, which precipitated the Cuban missile crisis; of political assassinations and outbreaks of urban violence in the 1960s; of the Tet Offensive of 1968; of the Iranian revolution of 1979 and the subsequent taking of American diplomats as hostages; and, for that matter, of the events of September 11.

It is true that when we are surprised and hurt, we tend to overreact—but only with the benefit of hindsight can a reaction be separated into its proper and excess layers. In hindsight we know that interning Japanese-Americans did not shorten World War II. But was this known at the time? If not, shouldn't the Army have erred on the side of caution, as it did? Even today we cannot say with any assurance that Abraham Lincoln was wrong to suspend habeas corpus during the Civil War, as he did on several occasions, even though the Constitution is clear that only Congress can suspend this right. (Another of Lincoln's wartime measures, the Emancipation Proclamation, may also have been unconstitutional.) But Lincoln would have been wrong to cancel the 1864 presidential election, as some urged: by November of 1864 the North was close to victory, and canceling the election would have created a more dangerous precedent than the wartime suspension of habeas corpus. This last example shows that civil liberties remain part of the balance even in the most dangerous of times, and even though their relative weight must then be less.

Lincoln's unconstitutional acts during the Civil War show that even legality must sometimes be sacrificed for other values. We are a nation under law, but first we are a nation. I want to emphasize something else, however: the malleability of law, its pragmatic rather than dogmatic character. The law is not absolute, and the slogan "Fiat iustitia ruat caelum" ("Let justice be done though the heavens fall") is dangerous nonsense. The law is a human creation rather than a divine gift, a tool of government rather than a mandarin mystery. It is an instrument for promoting social welfare, and as the conditions essential to that welfare change, so must it change.

Civil libertarians today are missing something else—the opportunity to challenge other public-safety concerns that impair civil liberties. I have particularly in mind the war on drugs. The sale of illegal drugs is a "victimless" crime in the special but important sense that it is a consensual activity. Usually there is no complaining witness, so in order to bring the criminals to justice the police have to rely heavily on paid informants (often highly paid and often highly unsavory), undercover agents, wiretaps and other forms of electronic surveillance, elaborate sting operations, the infiltration of suspect organizations, random searches, the monitoring of airports and highways, the "profiling" of likely suspects on the basis of ethnic or racial identity or national origin, compulsory drug tests, and other intrusive methods that put pressure on civil liberties. The war on drugs has been a big flop; moreover, in light of what September 11 has taught us about the gravity of the terrorist threat to the United States, it becomes hard to take entirely seriously the threat to the nation that drug use is said to pose. Perhaps it is time to redirect law-enforcement resources from the investigation and apprehension of drug dealers to the investigation and apprehension of international terrorists. By doing so we may be able to minimize the net decrease in our civil liberties that the events of September 11 have made inevitable.

Responding to Reading

1. Posner begins his essay by explaining his view that the basic mistake made by those who treat civil liberties as "sacrosanct" (1) is "the prioritizing of liberty" (2). What does he mean? Why does he see this as "a mistake about law and a mistake about history" (2)?

2. In paragraph 3, Posner says of public safety and liberty, "They are both important, and their relative importance changes from time to time and from situation to situation"; he also paraphrases a Supreme Court justice's remark that "the Bill of Rights should not be made into a suicide pact." How would Eric Foner (below) respond to these comments? How would Declan McCullagh (p. 775) respond?

3. In paragraphs 5–7, Posner presents "the lesson of history." What is his purpose in summarizing these events? According to Posner, exactly what is the lesson of history?

Responding in Writing

After presenting his argument that increased security does not threaten Americans' fundamental civil liberties, Posner moves in his concluding paragraph to a discussion of the war on drugs. In your own words, write a brief summary of the argument Posner makes in this paragraph. Do you think he makes a logical connection between the war on drugs and the rest of his essay? Do you agree with his last two sentences? Rewrite your summary as a one-paragraph response statement in which you critique Posner's argument about the war on drugs.

THE MOST PATRIOTIC ACT

Eric Foner

1943–

Eric Foner received a bachelor's degree and a PhD from Columbia University (1963, 1969). A historian who specializes in the Civil War and Reconstruction, slavery, and nineteenth-century America, Foner has taught history at Columbia University and the City University of New York and has written more than fourteen books, including The Story of American Freedom *(1998) and* Who Owns History? Rethinking the Past in a Changing World *(2002). The following selection was published in the* Nation *in 2001.*

The drumbeat now begins, as it always does in time of war: We must accept limitations on our liberties. The FBI and CIA should be "unleashed" in the name of national security. Patriotism means uncritical support of whatever actions the President deems appropriate. Arab-Americans, followers of Islam, people with Middle Eastern names or ancestors, should be subject to special scrutiny by the government and their fellow citizens. With liberal members of Congress silent and the Administration promising a war on terrorism lasting "years, not days," such sentiments are likely to be with us for some time to come.

Of the many lessons of American history, this is among the most basic. Our civil rights and civil liberties—freedom of expression, the right to criticize the government, equality before the law, restraints on the exercise of police powers—are not gifts from the state that can be rescinded when it desires. They are the inheritance of a long history of struggles: by abolitionists for the ability to hold meetings and publish their views in the face of mob violence; by labor leaders for the power to organize unions, picket and distribute literature without fear of arrest; by feminists for the right to disseminate birth-control information without being charged with violating the obscenity laws; and by all those who braved jail and worse to challenge entrenched systems of racial inequality.

The history of freedom in this country is not, as is often thought, the logical working out of ideas immanent in our founding documents or a straight-line trajectory of continual progress. It is a story of countless disagreements and battles in which victories sometimes prove temporary and retrogression often follows progress.

When critics of the original Constitution complained about the absence of a Bill of Rights, the Constitution's "father," James Madison, replied that no list of liberties could ever anticipate the ways government might act in the future. "Parchment barriers" to the abuse of authority, he wrote, would be least effective when most needed. Thankfully, the Bill of Rights was eventually adopted. But Madison's observation was amply borne out at moments of popular hysteria when freedom of expression was trampled in the name of patriotism and national unity.

Americans have notoriously short historical memories. But it is worth recalling some of those moments to understand how liberty has been endangered in the past. During the "quasi war" with France in 1798, the Alien and Sedition Acts allowed deportation of immigrants deemed dangerous by federal authorities and made it illegal to criticize the federal government. During the Civil War, both sides jailed critics and suppressed opposition newspapers.

In World War I German-Americans, socialists, labor leaders and critics of US involvement were subjected to severe government repression and assault by private vigilante groups. Publications critical of the war were banned from the mails, individuals were jailed for antiwar statements and in the Red Scare that followed the war thousands of radicals were arrested and numerous aliens deported. During World War II, tens of thousands of Japanese-Americans, most of them US citizens, were removed to internment camps. Sanctioned by the Supreme Court, this was the greatest violation of Americans' civil liberties, apart from slavery, in our history.

No one objects to more stringent security at airports. But current restrictions on the FBI and CIA limiting surveillance, wiretapping, infiltration of political groups at home and assassinations abroad do not arise from an irrational desire for liberty at the expense of security.

They arc the response to real abuses of authority, which should not be forgotten in the zeal to sweep them aside as "handcuffs" on law enforcement.

Before unleashing these agencies, let us recall the FBI's persistent harassment of individuals like Martin Luther King Jr. and its efforts to disrupt the civil rights and antiwar movements, and the CIA's history of cooperation with some of the world's most egregious violators of human rights. The principle that no group of Americans should be stigmatized as disloyal or criminal because of race or national origin is too recent and too fragile an achievement to be abandoned now.

Every war in American history, from the Revolution to the Gulf War, with the exception of World War II, inspired vigorous internal dissent. Self-imposed silence is as debilitating to a democracy as censorship. If questioning an ill-defined, open-ended "war on terrorism" is to be deemed unpatriotic, the same label will have to be applied to Abraham Lincoln at the time of the Mexican War, Jane Addams and Eugene V. Debs during World War I, and Wayne Morse and Ernest Gruening, who had the courage and foresight to vote against the Gulf of Tonkin resolution in 1964.

10   All of us today share a feeling of grief and outrage over the events of September 11 and a desire that those responsible for mass murder be brought to justice. But at times of crisis the most patriotic act of all is the unyielding defense of civil liberties, the right to dissent and equality before the law for all Americans.

Responding to Reading

1. What is "the most patriotic act" to which Foner refers in his title?
2. Writing less than a month after September 11, 2001, Foner predicts that sentiments that call for limitations on civil liberties "are likely to be with us for some time to come" (1). Do you believe that Foner's prediction has come true?
3. In paragraphs 3–6 and paragraph 9, Foner presents examples from history to support his position. How are his examples different from those presented by Richard Posner (p. 769) in paragraphs 5–7 of his essay? Do the two writers cover any common ground? Do they interpret any historical events differently?

Responding in Writing

In the years since September 11, 2001, what kinds of increased security have you noticed on your campus and workplace and in your community? Do you think this increased security is necessary? Do you think it is effective? Do you believe any of these new security regulations violate your civil liberties?

WHY LIBERTY SUFFERS IN WARTIME
Declan McCullagh
1971–

Journalist and photographer Declan McCullagh writes and speaks frequently about technology, law, and politics. Currently chief political correspondent for CNET's News.com, *he was formerly the Washington bureau chief for* Wired News; *a reporter for* Time Digital Daily, Time's The Netly News, *and* Time *Magazine; and a correspondent for* HotWired. *McCullagh's articles have appeared in* George *magazine, the* New Republic, *the* Wall Street Journal, *and* Playboy *magazine. A native of Pennsylvania, McCullagh attended Carnegie Mellon University and teaches at Case Western Reserve University's law school. To read more about this writer, visit his Web site, http://www.mccullagh.org/.*

Anyone worried about the fate of civil liberties during the U.S. government's growing war on terrorism might want to consider this Latin maxim: *Inter arma silent leges.*

It means, "In time of war the laws are silent," and it encapsulates the supremacy of security over liberty that typically accompanies national emergencies.

Consider this: During all of America's major wars—the Civil War, World War I and World War II—the government restricted Americans' civil liberties in the name of quelling dissent, silencing criticism of political decisions and preserving national security.

It's far too soon to predict what additional powers the government will assume after the catastrophic attacks on the World Trade Center and the Pentagon. To their credit, many politicians have already stressed that sacrificing liberty for security, even temporarily, is an unacceptable trade.

"We will not violate people's basic rights as we make this nation 5 more secure," said House Majority Leader Dick Armey (R-Texas). Sen. Max Baucus (D-Montana) said: "This does not mean that we can allow terrorists to alter the fundamental openness of U.S. society or the government's respect for civil liberties. If we do so, they will have won."

These statements come as Congress is deliberating a sweeping set of proposals from the Bush administration that would increase wiretapping of phones and the Internet, boost police authority to detain suspected terrorists, and rewrite immigration laws. In response, a coalition of over 100 groups from across the political spectrum asked Congress to tread carefully in this area last week.

Yet history has shown that during moments of national crisis, real or perceived, politicians have been quick to seize new authority, and courts have been impotent or reluctant to interfere.

1798:   In July 1798, Congress enacted the Alien and Sedition Acts, ostensibly to respond to the possible threat posed by the French Revolution, but also in an attempt to punish Thomas Jefferson's Republican party. The laws made it a crime to "write, print, utter or publish" any "false, scandalous and malicious writing or writings against the government of the United States, or either house of the Congress of the United States or the president of the United States."

That enraged Kentucky and Virginia. Kentucky's legislature approved a statement saying, "This commonwealth does upon the most deliberate reconsideration declare, that the said alien and sedition laws, are in their opinion, palpable violations of the Constitution." (An earlier draft, relying on libertarian principles, went so far as to say such laws were "void and of no force.")

10   *Civil War:*   President Lincoln interfered with freedom of speech and of the press and ordered that suspected political criminals be tried before military tribunals. Much as President Bush now is concerned with protecting airplane safety, Lincoln wanted to preserve the railroads: Rebels were destroying railroad bridges near Baltimore in 1861.

Probably Lincoln's most controversial act was suspending the writ of *habeas corpus,* a safeguard of liberty that dates back to English common law and England's Habeas Corpus Act of 1671. A vital check on the government's power, *habeas corpus* says that authorities must bring a person they arrest before a judge who orders it.

The U.S. Constitution says: "The privilege of the writ of *habeas corpus* shall not be suspended, unless when in cases of rebellion or invasion the public safety may require it." But Lincoln suspended *habeas corpus* without waiting for Congress to authorize it.

Lincoln's decision led to a showdown between the military and United States Chief Justice Roger Taney. After the U.S. Army arrested John Merryman on charges of destroying railroad bridges and imprisoned him in Fort McHenry, Merryman's lawyer drew up a *habeas corpus* petition that Taney quickly signed.

When the Army refused to bring Merryman before the high court, Taney said the U.S. marshals had the authority to haul Army General George Cadwalader into the courtroom on contempt charges—but Taney would not order it since the marshals would likely be outgunned. Instead, Taney protested and called on Lincoln "to perform his constitutional duty to enforce the laws" and the "process of this court."

15   This was a controversial decision: the *New York Times* described Taney's decision the next day as one that "can only be regarded as at once officious and improper."

World War I: Soon after declaring war on Germany and its allies in 1917, Congress banned using the U.S. mail from sending any material urging "treason, insurrection or forcible resistance to any law."

It punished offenders with a fine of up to $5,000 and a five-year prison term, and the government used this new authority to ban magazines such as *The Nation* from the mail.

President Wilson asked Congress to go even further: His draft of the Espionage Act included a $10,000 fine and 10 years imprisonment for anyone publishing information that could be useful to the enemy. The House of Representatives narrowly defeated it by a vote of 184–144.

Even without Wilson's proposals, the Espionage Act gave birth to a famous civil liberties case: *U.S. v. Charles Schenck.* The Supreme Court unanimously upheld his conviction for printing leaflets that urged Americans to resist the draft.

The justices ruled: "When a nation is at war, many things that 20 might be said in time of peace are such a hindrance to its effort that their utterance will not be endured so long as men fight and that no court could regard them as protected by any constitutional right."

While there were no trials before military tribunals, the Justice Department unsuccessfully asked Congress to enact a law—punishable by death—that would have authorized such trials for anyone "interfering with the war effort."

World War II: Civil liberties groups recently have repeatedly offered reminders of the internment of Japanese immigrants and their children in walled camps in the aftermath of Pearl Harbor.

In Executive Order 9066, President Roosevelt authorized the military to remove Japanese-Americans from America's west coast, home to many military bases and manufacturing plants—and viewed at the time as vulnerable to Japanese attack. In a remarkable silence, the American Civil Liberties Union did not object to the internment camps until years later.

A collection of challenges to the internment camps found their way to the U.S. Supreme Court. In a brief supporting the camps, the states of Washington, Oregon and California noted that Japanese submarines had attacked oil platforms at Santa Barbara, California, the town of Brookings. Oregon, and a gun installation at Astoria, Oregon. On June 7, 1942, the brief said, the Japanese had invaded North America by occupying some Aleutian islands.

In its response, drafted by Chief Justice Harlan Stone in 1943, the 25 court ducked the constitutionality of internment camps, ruling only on a related curfew requirement.

The justices upheld the action: "Whatever views we may entertain regarding the loyalty to this country of the citizens of Japanese ancestry, we cannot reject as unfounded the judgment of the military authorities and of Congress that there were disloyal members of that population."

Some of America's most respected legal thinkers, while saying that the government went too far in World War II, say that some erosion of freedom in wartime is necessary.

"There is no reason to think that future wartime presidents will act differently from Lincoln, Wilson or Roosevelt, or that future justices of the Supreme Court will decide questions differently from their predecessors," William Rehnquist, chief justice of the United States, wrote in a book published in 1998.

"It is neither desirable nor is it remotely likely that civil liberty will occupy as favored a position in wartime as it does in peacetime," Rehnquist wrote in *All the Laws But One.*

30   The 100-plus groups whose representatives gathered at the National Press Club on Thursday aren't quite so certain. In a statement posted on a new website, In Defense of Freedom, they say: "We need to ensure that actions by our government uphold the principles of a democratic society, accountable government and international law, and that all decisions are taken in a manner consistent with the Constitution."

Responding to Reading

1. What is McCullagh's position on the balance between liberty and security? In what respects would he be likely to agree with Richard Posner (p. 769)? In what respects would he be likely to agree with Eric Foner (p. 772)?
2. In paragraph 7, McCullagh says, "history has shown that during moments of national crisis, real or perceived, politicians have been quick to seize new authority, and courts have been impotent or reluctant to interfere." Does he see this tendency as a bad thing? Do you?
3. The title of McCullagh's essay is "Why Liberty Suffers in Wartime," and in his introduction he quotes the saying, "In time of war the laws are silent" (2). How does he define *war* in this essay? How would you define it? For example, do you consider the war on terrorism to be a war? Do you think all the historical examples McCullagh cites qualify as "wars"? Explain.

Responding in Writing

This essay was written less than two weeks after the tragic events of September 11. Write a short narrative that traces your own experiences on that day: what you saw and heard, and what you did. On that day, were you willing to sacrifice some freedoms for increased security? Do you still feel the way you did then?

———————— WIDENING THE FOCUS ————————

The following readings can suggest additional perspectives for thinking and writing about the conflict between liberty and security. You may also want to do further research about this subject on the Internet.

- Tim Robbins, "A Chill Wind Is Blowing in This Nation" (p. 245)

- George Gerbner, "Global Media Mayhem" (p. 319)

- Edward J. Blakely and Mary Gail Snyder, "Putting Up the Gates" (p. 346)

- Thomas Jefferson, The Declaration of Independence (p. 524)

For Internet Research: Conflicts between individual freedoms and the security of communities, states, and the nation have been debated throughout US history. During both world wars, the phrase *national security* was used to justify actions that limited (or even revoked) the civil rights of many individuals. Since the passage of the USA Patriot Act following the September 11, 2001, terrorist attacks, the debate over individual liberties and national security has intensified. The US Justice Department has created a Web site to promote the benefits of the USA Patriot Act, http://www.lifeandliberty.gov/. The American Civil Liberties Union (ACLU), an organization, criticizes the provisions of the law on its Web site, http://www.aclu.org/SafeandFree/. Visit both Web sites, and analyze how each organization presents its position. Then, write an essay in which you evaluate some of the arguments presented on each Web site. Which site do you think is more persuasive, and why?

--- **WRITING** ---

Making Choices

1. What moral and ethical rules govern your behavior? Considering the ethical guidelines set forth by several writers in this chapter, define and explain your own personal moral code.

2. The question of whether or not to act to end another's suffering—possibly at one's own expense—is explored, implicitly or explicitly, in "The Deer at Providencia" by Annie Dillard (p. 669), "Shooting an Elephant" by George Orwell (p. 673), and "The Ones Who Walk Away from Omelas" by Ursula K. Le Guin (p. 761). What are your own feelings about this issue?

3. Henry David Thoreau (p. 680) says, "Unjust laws exist: shall we be content to obey them, or shall we endeavor to amend them, and obey them until we have succeeded, or shall we transgress them at once?" (17). Choose a law or practice that you consider unjust, and write an essay in which you tell why you believe it should be disobeyed. Use ideas from Thoreau's essay to support your points.

4. Is all life equally valuable? Explain your position on this issue, considering the ideas raised by Garrett Hardin (p. 715) as well as the position of Anna Mae Halgrim Seaver (p. 624).

5. Stanley Milgram (p. 732) believes that his study illustrates philosopher Hannah Arendt's controversial theory, showing that "ordinary people, simply doing their jobs, and without any particular hostility on their part, can become agents in a terrible destructive process" (39). Cite examples from recent news events or from your own experience to support his conclusion.

6. Martin Luther King, Jr. (p. 699), Milgram (p. 732), and Thoreau (p. 680) all consider the difficulties of resisting majority rule, standing up to authority, and protesting against established rules and laws. Did you ever submit to authority even though you thought you should not have? Write an essay in which you describe your experience. What were the consequences of your act? (Or, describe a time when you stood up to authority. What motivated you? Was your resistance successful? Would you do the same thing again?) Be sure you draw a conclusion from your experience, and state this conclusion as your thesis.

7. What do you believe we gain and lose by using animals in scientific research? Do you believe this practice should be continued? If so, with which animals? Under what circumstances? If not, why not? What alternative do you propose? Reread Claire McCarthy's "Dog Lab" (p. 724) and Annie Dillard's "The Deer at Providencia" (p. 669) before you begin your essay.

8. Which of the two roads identified in Robert Frost's "The Road Not Taken" (p. 666) have you chosen? In what sense has that choice "made all the difference"?

9. Do you believe it is possible both to do good (that is, to help others) and to do well (that is, to be financially successful), or do you believe these two goals are mutually exclusive? Answer this question in relation to your own personal goals, citing examples from public figures who have (or have not) managed both to do good and to do well.

10. Read the essays in the Focus section of this chapter. Then, write an argumentative essay in which you answer the question "Can we be both free and safe?" taking a stand on which you believe is more important, freedom or security. Be sure to discuss the possible dangers and sacrifices your position will entail, and support your position with specific examples from your own reading, observations, and experience as well as from the essays by Eric Foner ("The Most Patriotic Act," p. 772), Declan McCullagh ("Why Liberty Suffers in Wartime," p. 775), and Richard Posner ("Security versus Civil Liberties," p. 769).

Credits

Alexie, Sherman, "The Unauthorized Autobiography of Me." Reprinted from *One Stick Song* © 2000 by Sherman Alexie, by permission of Hanging Loose Press.

Angelou, Maya. "Graduation," copyright © 1969 and renewed 1997 by Maya Angelou, from *I Know Why the Caged Bird Sings* by Maya Angelou. Used by permission of Random House, Inc.

Barry, Lynda, "The Sanctuary of School" from *The New York Times*, January 5, 1992. Copyright © 1992 The New York Times. Reprinted by permission.

Bartlett, Bruce. "The Employment Effects of Living Wage Laws" from *The National Center for Policy Analysis*, 3/20/02. Reprinted by permission.

Blakely, Edward J. and Mary Gail Snyder, "Putting Up the Gates" published on *Shelterforce Online*, May/June 1997, a publication of the National Housing Institute. Reprinted by permission of National Housing Institute.

Blumner, Robyn, "Title IX Has Made a Mockery of Gender Equality in College Sports" from *Salt Lake Tribune*, 1/17/03. Reprinted by permission of Tribune Media Services.

Bradley, David, "Birth of a Nation" from *The Movie That Changed My Life*, edited by David Rosenberg, Viking. © 1991 by David Bradley. Reprinted by permission.

Brady, Judy, "Why I Want a Wife" from *Ms.*, 1970. Copyright © 1970 by Judy Brady. Reprinted by permission of the author.

Brown, Leslie S. P., "Who Cares about the Renaissance?" from *Newsweek*, 4/11/83.

Brownlee, Shannon, "The Overtreated American" from *The Atlantic Monthly*, January/February 2003. © 2003 by Shannon Brownlee. Reprinted by permission of the author.

Bunn, Austin, "The Bittersweet Science" from *The New York Times Magazine*, March 16, 2003. Copyright © 2003 The New York Times. Reprinted by permission.

Carver, Raymond, "My Father's Life" from *Fires: Essays, Poems Stories*, originally appeared in *Esquire* (September 1984). Copyright © 1984 by Tess Gallagher. Reprinted by permission of International Creative Management, Inc. and Tess Gallagher.

Charen, Mona, "Malpractice: By Lawyers" published on *TownHall.com*, January 31, 2003. Reprinted by permission of Creators Syndicate.

Chavez, Linda, "Remembering the Negative Side of Affirmative Action" in *The Chronicle of Higher Education*, September 27, 2002. Reprinted by permission of Creators Syndicate.

Coben, Harlan. "The Key to My Father" by Harlan Coben from *The New York Times*, June 15, 2003. Copyright © 2003 The New York Times. Reprinted by permission.

Cofer, Judith Ortiz, "The Myth of the Latin Woman: I Just Met a Girl Named Maria" from *The Latin Deli: Prose & Poetry* by Judith Ortiz Cofer. Reprinted by permission of The University of Georgia Press.

Tannen, Deborah, "Wears Jump Suit. Sensible Shoes. Uses Husband's Last Name." by Deborah Tannen, *The New York Times Magazine,* June 20, 1993. Reprinted by permission of the author. This article was originally titled "Marked Women, Unmarked Men" by the author.

Taylor, Stuart, Jr., "It's Time to Junk the Double Standard on Free Speech" from *The Atlantic Monthly,* 1/25/02. Reprinted with permission of National Journal.

Thomas, Dylan, "Do Not Go Gentle Into That Good Night" by Dylan Thomas, from *The Poems of Dylan Thomas,* copyright © 1952 by Dylan Thomas. Reprinted by permission of New Directions Publishing Corp.

Twitchell, James B., from *Lead Us Into Temptation* by James B. Twitchell. Copyright © 1999 James B. Twitchell. Reprinted by permission of Columbia University Press.

Verghese, Abraham, "The Metaphor of Blight" from *The Wall Street Journal,* 5/13/03. Copyright 2003 by Dow Jones & Co., Inc. Reprinted with permission of Dow Jones & Co., Inc. in the format Other Book, via Copyright Clearance Center.

Walker, Alice, "Beauty: When the Other Dancer is the Self" from *In Search of Our Mothers' Gardens: Womanist Prose,* copyright © 1983 by Alice Walker, reprinted by permission of Harcourt, Inc.

Wallerstein, Judith, from *The Unexpected Legacy of Divorce* by Judith Wallerstein. Copyright © 2000 Judith Wallerstein. Reprinted by permission of Hyperion.

Wenner, Jann S., "Why the Record Industry Is in Trouble" from *Rolling Stone,* September 19, 2002. © Rolling Stone LLC 2002. All Rights Reserved. Reprinted by Permission.

White, E. B. "Once More to the Lake" from *One Man's Meat,* text copyright © by E. B. White. Copyright renewed. Reprinted by permission of Tilbury House, Publishers, Gardiner, Maine.

Whitehead, Barbara Dafoe, "The Girls of Gen X" from *The American Enterprise.* Reprinted with permission of The American Enterprise, a magazine of Politics, Business, and Culture. On the web at www.TAEmag.com.

Winn, Marie, "Family Life," from *The Plug-In Drug,* Revised and Updated—25th Anniversary Edition by Marie Winn, copyright © 1977, 1985, 2002 by Marie Winn Miller. Used by permission of Viking Penguin, a division of Penguin Group (USA) Inc.

Woolf, Virginia, "Professions for Women" from *The Death of the Moth and Other Essays* by Virginia Woolf, copyright 1942 by Harcourt, Inc. and renewed 1970 by Marjorie T. Parsons, Executrix, reprinted by permission of the publisher.

Wright, Richard, Chapter XIII (titled "Library Card") from *Black Boy* by Richard Wright. Copyright, 1937, 1942, 1944, 1945 by Richard Wright; renewed © 1973 by Ellen Wright. Reprinted by permission of HarperCollins Publishers Inc.

Photo Credits

Chapter 1, page 10: Hulton | Archive by Getty Images Inc.
Chapter 1, page 11: © Bill Bachmann/PhotoEdit. All Rights Reserved.
Chapter 1, page 68: Novastock/PhotoEdit.

Chapter 2, page 100: Erlanson-Messens, Britt J./ Getty Images Inc.—Image Bank
Chapter 2, page 101: Rogelio Solis/AP/Wide World Photos
Chapter 2, page 157: Getty Images Inc.—Hulton Archive Photos

Chapter 3, page 176: © Peter Blakely/CORBIS SABA
Chapter 3, page 177: Greg Gibson/AP/Wide World Photos
Chapter 3, page 239: Robert Ginn/PhotoEdit

Chapter 4, page 258: Geoff Dann/Dorling Kindersley Media Library
Chapter 4, page 259: © 2000 Nike, Inc. All rights reserved. Reproduced by permission.
Chapter 4, page 305: AP/Wide World Photos
Chapter 4, page 319: © 1998 SCi (Sales Curve Interactive) Limited. All Rights Reserved.

Chapter 5, page 334: © Bettmann/CORBIS
Chapter 5, page 335: Spencer Grant/PhotoEdit
Chapter 5, color insert page 1, top: Fred Hultstrand History in Pictures Collection, NDIRS-NDSU, Fargo. Institute for Regional Studies, NDSU Libraries, Fargo
Chapter 5, color insert page 1, bottom: Joshua Ets-Hokin/Getty Images, Inc.—Photodisc.
Chapter 5, color insert page 2, top: Petrified Collection/Getty Images Inc.—Image Bank
Chapter 5, color insert page 2, bottom: Hince, Peter/Getty Images Inc.—Image Bank
Chapter 5, color insert page 3, top: PHOTOMONDO/Getty Images, Inc.—Taxi
Chapter 5, color insert page 3, bottom: Frank A. Cezus/Hulton Archive/Getty Images
Chapter 5, color insert page 4, top: © Nik Wheeler/CORBIS
Chapter 5, color insert page 4, bottom: Amos Morgan/Getty Images, Inc.—Photodisc.

Chapter 6, page 402: HULK™ © 2003 Marvel Characters, Inc.
Chapter 6, page 403: © Tatiana Markow/Sygma/CORBIS
Chapter 6, page 444: Romanelli, Marc/Getty Images Inc.—Image Bank

Chapter 7, page 468: Hulton | Archive by Getty Images, Inc.
Chapter 7, page 469: © David Young-Wolff/PhotoEdit Inc
Chapter 7, page 523: Archive Holdings, Inc. Levick 03RLEI, Edwin/Getty Images Inc.—Image Bank

Chapter 8, page 540: Hulton | Archive by Getty Images, Inc.
Chapter 8, page 541: AP/Wide World Photos
Chapter 8, page 594: Michael Newman/PhotoEdit

Chapter 9, page 606: National Library of Medicine
Chapter 9, page 607: © Reuters NewMedia Inc./CORBIS
Chapter 9, page 649: Printed by permission of the Norman Rockwell Family Agency. Copyright © 1929 the Norman Rockwell Family Entities. Courtesy of The Curtis Publishing Company.

Chapter 10, page 664: Sreve Maines/Stock Boston
Chapter 10, page 665: © Jose Luis Pelaez, Inc./CORBIS
Chapter 10, page 768: © Copyright 2003 CORBIS

Index of Authors and Titles